SHAKESPEARE SURVEY

ADVISORY BOARD

1. Shakespeare and his Stage
2. Shakespearian Production
3. The Man and the Writer
4. Interpretation
5. Textual Criticism
6. The Histories
7. Style and Language
8. The Comedies
9. *Hamlet*
10. The Roman Plays
11. The Last Plays (with an index to *Surveys 1–10*)
12. The Elizabethan Theatre
13. *King Lear*
14. Shakespeare and his Contemporaries
15. The Poems and Music
16. Shakespeare in the Modern World
17. Shakespeare in His Own Age
18. Shakespeare Then Till Now
19. *Macbeth*
20. Shakespearian and Other Tragedy
21. *Othello* (with an index to *Surveys 11–20*)
22. Aspects of Shakespearian Comedy
23. Shakespeare's Language
24. Shakespeare: Theatre Poet
25. Shakespeare's Problem Plays
26. Shakespeare's Jacobean Tragedies
27. Shakespeare's Early Tragedies
28. Shakespeare and the Ideas of his Time
29. Shakespeare's Last Plays
30. *Henry IV* to *Hamlet*
31. Shakespeare and the Classical World (with an index to *Surveys 21–30*)

SHAKESPEARE SURVEY

AN ANNUAL SURVEY OF
SHAKESPEARIAN STUDY AND PRODUCTION

31

EDITED BY
KENNETH MUIR

CAMBRIDGE UNIVERSITY PRESS

CAMBRIDGE

LONDON · NEW YORK · MELBOURNE

Published by the Syndics of the Cambridge University Press
The Pitt Building, Trumpington Street, Cambridge CB2 1RP
Bentley House, 200 Euston Road, London NW1 2DB
32 East 57th Street, New York, NY 10022, USA
296 Beaconsfield Parade, Middle Park, Melbourne 3206, Australia

First published 1978

Shakespeare Survey was first published in 1948. For the first
eighteen volumes it was edited by Allardyce Nicoll under the
sponsorship of the University of Birmingham, the University
of Manchester, the Royal Shakespeare Theatre and the
Shakespeare Birthplace Trust

Printed in Great Britain at the
University Press, Cambridge

The Library of Congress originally catalogued Vol. I of this serial as follows:
Shakespeare Survey; an annual survey of Shakespearian study & production. 1–
Cambridge [Eng.] University Press, 1948–
v. illus., facsims. 26 cm.

Editor: v. 1–   Allardyce Nicoll.
'Issued under the sponsorship of the University of Birmingham, the Shakespeare Memorial
Theatre, the Shakespeare Birthplace Trust.'

   1. Shakespeare, William – Societies, periodicals, etc. 2. Shakespeare, William – Criticism and
interpretation. 3. Shakespeare, William – Stage history. 1. Nicoll, Allardyce, 1894– ed.
         PR2888.C3   822.33   49–1639

ISBN 0 521 22011 4

EDITOR'S NOTE

The central theme of *Shakespeare Survey 32*, as already announced, will be the three comedies *Much Ado about Nothing*, *As You Like It* and *Twelfth Night*. It will include a retrospect by Professor M. M. Mahood. The theme of Number 33 will be *King Lear*. Contributions on that play or on other topics should reach the Editor (University of Liverpool, P.O. Box 147, Liverpool L69 3BX) by 1 September 1979. Contributors should leave generous margins, use double spacing, and follow the style and lay-out of articles in the current issue. A style-sheet is available on request. Contributions should not normally exceed 5,000 words. Books for review should be sent to the Editor at the above address, not to the publisher.

K. M.

CONTRIBUTORS

MICHAEL J. B. ALLEN, *Associate Professor of English, University of California at Los Angeles*

A. F. BELLETTE, *Lecturer in English and Art History, Victoria University of Wellington*

JOHN COATES, *Lecturer in Literature and Drama, Adult Education Department, University of Hull*

J. S. CUNNINGHAM, *Professor of English, University of Leicester*

PHILIP EDWARDS, *King Alfred Professor of English Literature, University of Liverpool*

BRUCE ERLICH, *Associate Professor of English and Modern Languages, University of Nebraska at Lincoln*

HARRIETT HAWKINS, *Professor of English, Vassar College*

G. R. HIBBARD, *Professor of English, University of Waterloo, Ontario*

R. F. HILL, *Senior Lecturer in English, King's College, University of London*

S. CLARK HULSE, *Assistant Professor of English, University of Illinois at Chicago Circle*

G. P. JONES, *Associate Professor of English, Memorial University of Newfoundland*

GRAHAM PARRY, *Lecturer in English, University of York*

E. D. PENDRY, *Lecturer in English, University of Bristol*

G. M. PINCISS, *Associate Professor of English, Hunter College, City University of New York*

ANN THOMPSON, *Lecturer in English Literature, University of Liverpool*

JOHN J. M. TOBIN, *Associate Professor of English, Boston State College*

JOHN W. VELZ, *Professor of English, University of Texas at Austin*

ROGER WARREN, *Lecturer in English, University of Leicester*

GEORGE WALTON WILLIAMS, *Professor of English, Duke University*

CONTENTS

List of Plates   *page* viii

The Ancient World in Shakespeare: Authenticity or Anachronism? A Retrospect
  by JOHN W. VELZ   1

'A Piece of Skilful Painting' in Shakespeare's *Lucrece*   *by* S. CLARK HULSE   13

Philomel in *Titus Andronicus* and *Cymbeline*   *by* ANN THOMPSON   23

Apuleius and the Bradleian Tragedies   *by* JOHN J. M. TOBIN   33

'The Choice of Hercules' in *Antony and Cleopatra*   *by* JOHN COATES   45

Structure, Inversion, and Game in Shakespeare's Classical World   *by* BRUCE
  ERLICH   53

Truth and Utterance in *The Winter's Tale*   *by* A. F. BELLETTE   65

Adumbrations of *The Tempest* in *A Midsummer Night's Dream*   *by* G. R.
  HIBBARD   77

The Old Honor and the New Courtesy: *1 Henry IV*   *by* G. M. PINCISS   85

Henry V: The Chorus and the Audience   *by* G. P. JONES   93

'The Devil's Party': Virtues and Vices in *Measure for Measure*   *by* HARRIETT
  HAWKINS   105

Shakespeare and the Healing Power of Deceit   *by* PHILIP EDWARDS   115

Shakespeare's Man Descending a Staircase: Sonnets 126 to 154   *by* MICHAEL
  J. B. ALLEN   127

A New View of Bankside   *by* GRAHAM PARRY   139

Comedies and Histories at Two Stratfords, 1977   *by* ROGER WARREN   141

Tamburlaine the Great Re-discovered   *by* J. S. CUNNINGHAM and ROGER
  WARREN   155

The Year's Contributions to Shakespearian Study:
  1   Critical Studies   *reviewed by* R. F. HILL   163

  2   Shakespeare's Life, Times and Stage   *reviewed by* E. D. PENDRY   177

  3   Textual Studies   *reviewed by* GEORGE WALTON WILLIAMS   191

Index   199

General Index to Surveys 21–30   205

PLATES

BETWEEN PAGES 112 AND 113

I A   A sketch of Bankside by Wenceslaus Hollar, from a notebook in the John Rylands Library at Manchester (English MS 883)
[*Reproduced by permission of the John Rylands Library, Manchester*]

B   Detail of Bankside from Hollar's 'Long View of London'
[*Reproduced by permission of the British Museum*]

II   *A Midsummer Night's Dream*, Stratford, Ontario, 1977. Directed by Robin Phillips. Maggie Smith as Hippolyta/Titania
[*Photo: Dominic*]

III   *A Midsummer Night's Dream*, Stratford, Ontario, 1977. Directed by Robin Phillips. Barry MacGregor as Oberon and Maggie Smith as Titania
[*Photo: Dominic*]

IV   *A Midsummer Night's Dream*, Royal Shakespeare Theatre, 1977. Directed by John Barton, designed by John Napier. Marjorie Bland as Titania and Patrick Stewart as Oberon
[*Photo: Joe Cocks*]

V   *All's Well That Ends Well*, Stratford, Ontario, 1977. Directed by David Jones. Nicholas Pennell as Bertram and Martha Henry as Helena
[*Photo: Robert Ragsdale*]

VI   *1 Henry VI*, Royal Shakespeare Theatre, 1977. Directed by Terry Hands, designed by Farrah. The Dauphin (James Laurenson) with his army
[*Photo: Joe Cocks*]

VII   *2 Henry VI*, Royal Shakespeare Theatre, 1977. Directed by Terry Hands, designed by Farrah. Henry (Alan Howard) and Margaret (Helen Mirren) after Duke Humphrey's death
[*Photo: Joe Cocks*]

VIII A   *Tamburlaine the Great*, National Theatre, 1976. Directed by Peter Hall. The arrival of Bajazeth (Denis Quilley)
[*Photo: Nobby Clark*]

B   *Tamburlaine the Great*, National Theatre, 1976. Directed by Peter Hall. Tamburlaine (Albert Finney) in his chariot
[*Photo: Nobby Clark*]

THE ANCIENT WORLD IN SHAKESPEARE: AUTHENTICITY OR ANACHRONISM? A RETROSPECT

JOHN W. VELZ

In 1680 Nahum Tate was quite positive about verisimilitude in Shakespeare: 'I am sure he never touches on a Roman Story, but the Persons, the Passages, the Manners, the Circumstances, the Ceremonies, all are Roman'. This was a substantial (though not necessarily substantiated) claim, because Tate had just asserted that 'Nature will not do [a poet's] Business, he must have the Addition of Arts and Learning': acquaintance with 'the Customs and Constitutions of Nations', and with much else, 'the Histories of all Ages', even 'the meanest Mysteries and Trades', 'because 'tis uncertain [whither] his subject will lead him'.[1] Had Ben Jonson been alive to read Tate's opinion of Shakespeare's portraits of the Roman world, he would doubtless have said something memorably contemptuous. His own scholarly pretensions to exact local and temporal verisimilitude in *Sejanus* and 'well-laboured' *Catiline* are a commonplace of literary history; everyone knows also that Jonson once described Shakespeare's portrayal of Gaius Julius Caesar in the moments before his assassination as 'ridiculous'. The Tate school of thought has had some notable adherents, Dryden, Pope, and Johnson among the early ones, but the opposed assertion, that Shakespeare's Romans are Elizabethans in togas, has always been with us.[2] From the time of John Dennis's *Essay on the Genius and Writings of Shakespear* (1712) it has been a scholarly parlor game to enumerate Shakespeare's blunders in the Roman plays.

It may be rewarding to consider the question yet once again, expanding the terms to take in Shakespeare's Greek world. When we observe that the ancient world is the setting for just one third of the Shakespeare canon – two of the comedies, both of the narrative poems, four of the five romances, and six of the eleven tragedies – the exercise justifies itself. And though this article cannot claim to survey the history of opinion in any way fully, it may usefully point to some representative studies. It may be instructive to begin with comments on three or four major attempts in the past century to deal with the Tate/Jonson polarity.

Edward Dowden tried to reconcile the two poles in 1875 in a statement that typifies the Romantic tradition in Shakespeare criticism:

> while Shakspere is profoundly faithful to Roman life and character, it is an ideal truth, truth spiritual rather than truth material, which he seeks to discover... Shakspere was aware that his personages must be men before they were Romans... He knew that the buttressing up of art with erudition will not give stability to that which must stand by no aid of material props and stays, but if at all, by virtue of the one living soul of which it is the body.[3]

We are a long way in such Platonism from Tate's Aristotelian insistence on the poet's

---

[1] Address prefatory to *The Loyal General: A Tragedy.*

[2] For a recent instance, see Myron Taylor, 'Shakespeare's Julius Caesar and the Irony of History', *Shakespeare Quarterly*, XXIV (1973), 301–8 (p. 301).

[3] *Shakspere: A Critical Study of His Mind and Art* (1875; 3rd edn., rpt. 1962), p. 276.

acquaintance with 'the Customs and Constitutions of Nations'. Dowden transmits in his assertion the consensus of the nineteenth-century German aesthetic critics he so greatly admired, and he acknowledges his debt to the English Romantic tradition (Charles Knight in particular) as well. The legacy of *Shakspere* has been as long as its ancestry – my copy of the book (1962) is from the twenty-fifth printing, and I can clearly remember being told of *Julius Caesar* in school thirty years ago very much what Dowden says here of the spirit of Rome in Shakespeare. Dowden's stance may seem to us an evasion, rather more lofty than logical, but there is no doubt of its importance in cultural history.

M. W. MacCallum, writing in 1910, perceived the relation between 'truth material', and 'truth spiritual' in the Roman plays quite differently from Dowden. Pointing out (as Paul Stapfer had done before him[1]) that Shakespeare is a very purist by comparison with those earlier Elizabethans (Thomas Lodge above all) who had dramatized Roman subjects, MacCallum declared:

No dramatist had been able at once to rise to the grandeur of the theme [of Roman history] and keep a foothold on solid earth, to reconcile the claims of the ideal and the real, the past and the present. That was left for Shakespeare to do.[2]

There is in Shakespeare more of Rome, MacCallum argued, than of Scotland or of pre-Christian Britain. Poetic license is restrained in the Roman plays (sometimes even to the detriment of dramatic impact) because Shakespeare knew that events in those Roman stories had future consequences of immediate interest to his audience; hence his invented characters in the Roman plays are lesser figures (Lucius in *Julius Caesar*, Nicanor in *Coriolanus*, Silius in *Antony and Cleopatra*) who do not figure in the main action the way invented characters in Schiller's historical plays do.

Shakespeare on the one hand loyally accepted his authorities [in the English history plays and the Roman plays alike – and for the same reasons] and never deviated from them on their main route, but on the other he treated them unquestioningly from his own point of view, and probably never even suspected that their own might be different. This is the double characteristic of his attitude to his documents, and it combines pious regard for the assumed facts of History with complete indifference to critical research. (p. 86)

But Shakespeare's loyalty to his sources

does not mean that in the Roman any more than in the English plays he attempts an accurate reconstruction of the past. It may even be doubted whether such an attempt would have been intelligible to him or to any save one or two of his contemporaries.[3] To the average Elizabethan (and in this respect Shakespeare was an average Elizabethan, with infinitely clearer vision certainly, but with the same outlook and horizon) the past differed from the present chiefly by its distance and dimness; and distinctive contrasts in manners and customs were but scantily recognised. A generation later French audiences could view the perruques and patches of Corneille's Romans without any sense of incongruity, and the assimilation of the ancient to the modern was in some respects much more thorough-going in Shakespeare's England. (p. 81)

Waving aside such anachronisms as striking clocks, Galenic medicine, and sweaty nightcaps as 'trifles that [do not] interfere with fidelity

---

[1] *Shakespeare and Classical Antiquity: Greek and Latin Antiquity as Presented in Shakespeare's Plays.* A partial translation by Emily J. Carey of *Shakespeare et l'Antiquité* (1880). See especially ch. 5, 'Shakespeare's Anachronisms'. Stapfer's is the earliest full study of Shakespeare's portrait of the ancient world; it remains one of the two or three best treatments of the subject. T. J. B. Spencer is correct in pointing out (in his introduction to the 1967 rpt. of MacCallum – see note 2, this page) that MacCallum owes a large and unacknowledged debt to Stapfer, but I do not agree that MacCallum entirely supersedes Stapfer and the other Continental writers who influenced MacCallum.

[2] *Shakespeare's Roman Plays and Their Background* (1910; rpt. New York, 1967), pp. 71–2.

[3] This idea is traceable ultimately to Goethe.

to antiquity' (p. 82), MacCallum shrewdly observed that Shakespeare stressed just those elements in Roman society and culture (e.g., soldiers of fortune and the orgies of aristocratic decadence in *Antony and Cleopatra*) which appeared also in Renaissance society and culture.

There was a good deal of such correspondence between Elizabethan life and Roman life, so the Roman Tragedies have a breath of historic verisimilitude and even a faint suggestion of local colour. There was much less between Elizabethan life and Greek life, so *Timon* and *Troilus and Cressida*, though true as human documents, have almost nothing Hellenic about them.[1]

Even in the Roman plays, he points out, Shakespeare is less at home when he portrays something (life in a republic, for example) which he had not experienced in his own culture.

MacCallum's book remains a landmark after nearly seventy years. In 1954 Madeleine Doran was to reason in more general terms and with equal persuasiveness that the Renaissance habit of mind was to perceive and fuse analogues between the native and classical traditions. In such an eclectic frame, anachronism and anatopism become aesthetic merits, not naif oversights; and a proper critical stance, one that takes art in its own terms, will rather approve than condemn.[2] In 1960 she went so far as to declare in a public lecture that the amalgam of Chaucer and Plutarch in the character of Theseus in *A Midsummer Night's Dream* is entirely harmonious and that in general the Greek and English worlds of the play belong together more naturally than has been thought; in Shakespeare 'the present assumes the past'.[3] Here, of course, is an implicit challenge to MacCallum's view of Shakespeare's Hellenism; other challenges will be discussed later in the paper.

As these accounts of the postures of Mac-Callum and Doran may suggest, the ground of argument has shifted in the twentieth century.

From MacCallum's time, scholarship has gradually abandoned the question whether 'the Persons, the Passages, the Manners, the Circumstances, the Ceremonies' in Shakespeare are authentically Roman to ask instead whether Shakespeare and his audience thought them so. And the trend of commentary since the mid-nineteen-fifties has been with increasing frequency to answer, 'Yes'. The most impressive manifestation of the new scholarly stance came early and has been exemplary. In 1957 in a volume of *Shakespeare Survey* devoted to the Roman plays, T. J. B. Spencer showed that Shakespeare's portrait of Rome as a world of tumult and flux, of shouting crowds and violent events, is congruent with his generation's view of Roman history as a succession of 'garboyles'.[4] If a Restoration critic like Tate thought Shakespeare's Rome authentic while his contemporaries Rymer and Dennis thought Shakespeare's Romans unpleasantly lacking in dignity, both had some reason. Yet Shakespeare is unlike his contemporaries, Spencer goes on, in emphasizing Plutarch's Republican vision of Rome: 'in spite of literary admiration for Cicero, the Romans in the imagination of the sixteenth century were Suetonian and Tacitan rather than Plutarchan'. It was the Empire, not the Republic, that provided moral *exempla* to the Renaissance. It can, in fact, be said that *Titus Andronicus* is a more representative 'Noble Roman Historye' by Renaissance

[1] Georg Gottfried Gervinus had asserted that Shakespeare's ostensible preference for Rome over Greece was an *English* preference, as opposed to German (read Romantic) taste; see *Shakespeare Commentaries* (1849–50) (3rd edn. trans. F. E. Bunnètt (1862) 1892), p. 680.

[2] Madeleine Doran, *Endeavors of Art: A Study of Form in Elizabethan Drama* (Madison, Wisconsin, 1954), ch. 1 *et passim*.

[3] '*A Midsummer Night's Dream*: A Metamorphosis', published in *Rice Institute Pamphlets*, XLVI, 4 (January 1960), 113–35.

[4] 'Shakespeare and the Elizabethan Romans', *Shakespeare Survey 10* (Cambridge, 1957), pp. 27–38.

standards than the other three of Shakespeare's Roman plays – it certainly has more garboyles. With some effort of the historical imagination, we must realize that it required individuality for Shakespeare to focus on the heroes and the moral environment of the Republic, especially to write *Coriolanus*, very nearly the first play ever written on the legendary Gnaeus Marcius. *Coriolanus* is, Spencer points out, the most authentic, least anachronistic, of the Roman plays, perhaps on the model of *Sejanus* – or perhaps because Shakespeare, aware of himself as an innovator, is on his mettle. Spencer's summary verdict on *Romanitas* in Shakespeare would have irritated Ben Jonson, but it is a fair one:

Setting aside poetical and theatrical considerations, and merely referring to the artist's ability to 'create a world' (as the saying is), we may ask if there was anything in prose or verse, in Elizabethan or Jacobean literature, which bears the same marks of careful and thoughtful consideration of the ancient world, a deliberate effort of a critical intelligence to give a consistent picture of it, as there is in Shakespeare's plays. (p. 35)

Before turning to the question, 'What *was* Rome to Shakespeare?' it is appropriate to consider Greece, a world that appears in the Shakespeare canon as often as Rome does. Though R. R. Bolgar echoed MacCallum in 1954 on the difference between Rome and Greece in Shakespeare,[1] not all scholars are now so ready to dismiss Shakespeare's Hellenism as insignificant.

Shakespeare is at pains to bring 'weeds of Athens' into *A Midsummer Night's Dream* whether or not he had a real sense of what they looked like historically.[2] In the same play and with the same dubious authenticity he introduces 'the ancient privilege of Athens' (I, i, 41), a father's appalling authority over his daughter's freedom and even over her life. When we remember that the rigors of 'the sharp Athenian law' (I, i, 162) are closely paralleled in the hyperbolic harshness of the Ephesian law under which Egeon is condemned to death in *The Comedy of Errors*, we may ask whether Shakespeare had a notion that ancient Greek culture was rigid and cruel. The irrational arbitrariness of Leontes in *The Winter's Tale* and the whimsical nature of Theseus's arbitration in *The Two Noble Kinsmen* (III, vi) come to mind as analogues. Of course there are other arbitrary laws in Shakespeare (one thinks of the capital penalty for fornication in *Measure for Measure*)[3] which have nothing to do with Hellenic or Hellenistic culture, and some of Shakespeare's Greek justice derives from Chaucer's *Knight's Tale*, so one must tread tentatively; but it is possibly significant that Shakespeare, setting two of his early comedies in the Greek world, arranged them so that love, familial or romantic, triumphs over rigid traditionary law which is insisted on early in each play only to be flatly overruled later.

Such a view of rigorous but vulnerable law in the Greek world might have resulted from a mistaken impression of the large number of references in Acts and the Epistles to the brutality and legalism the Apostle Paul encountered in his travels through the Hellenistic world. Paul's encounters are almost all with Jews of the Diaspora, not with Greek civil

[1] *The Classical Heritage and its Beneficiaries* (Cambridge, 1954), p. 327.

[2] II, ii, 71 *et passim*. (The Riverside Shakespeare is my authority for citations.) Shakespeare may have thought weeds of Athens exactly like weeds of Rome; see W. M. Merchant, 'Classical Costume in Shakespearian Productions', *Shakespeare Survey 10* (Cambridge, 1957), pp. 71–6 (p. 71). D'Orsay W. Pearson believes, however, that the allusion to buskins (II, i, 71) makes it clear that Shakespeare had a more accurate knowledge; see '"Unkinde" Theseus: A Study in Renaissance Mythography', *English Literary Renaissance*, IV (1974), 276–98 (pp. 279–80).

[3] See Ralph Berry, 'Shakespearean Comedy and Northrop Frye', *Essays in Criticism*, XXII (1972), 33–40, for the opinion that harsh laws in Shakespeare are not so harsh, *pace* Frye.

authorities, who normally appear rather as indifferent than arbitrary. But the number of times Paul is physically threatened after having been accused of preaching doctrine counter to 'our law' in Greek synagogues might easily give a reader of Paul the image of embattled Greek-speaking Christians in a harsh and legalistic environment. The great theme of the Pauline Epistles is, of course, the triumph of love over rigid law, of a new dispensation over an older one.[1] T. W. Baldwin showed in 1963 that the shipwreck and the geography in *Errors* owe something significant to the Acts of the Apostles, though Baldwin apparently missed the relevance of the Epistle to the Ephesians for the play.[2] He also neglected the possible importance of Paul to *Pericles*, where, as in *Errors*, shipwreck and fracture of the family lead to eventual reunion in a religious hospice at Ephesus.[3] It seems likely enough that a thoughtful study of the Pauline Epistles would show that Shakespeare's conception of the Mediterranean world comes in part from Scripture.[4]

It is not cruelty or the preeminence of law over love but dissoluteness, deception, and perfidy that T. J. B. Spencer finds in the ancient Greeks as seen through Renaissance (and Shakespeare's) eyes. In an essay complementary to his earlier paper on 'the Elizabethan Romans', Spencer documents a pejorative view of the Greek national character in Roman literature, especially in the *Aeneid* and in stage comedy, whence it found its way easily to the Renaissance.[5] There can be no doubt from Spencer's massed evidence that Greeks were pejorated in Shakespeare's time exactly as the French are in some English-speaking circles today. And there seems little room for disagreement when Spencer concludes that the right way to read *Timon* and *Troilus* is to strip away our inheritance of nineteenth-century philhellenism and recognize in them Shakespeare's participation in the traditional prejudice. Clifford Leech challenged Spencer by pointing out (quite rightly) that some Athenians are decent-minded in *Timon* and that some characters in *Troilus*, notably Cressida and Achilles, are, however tainted, more

[1] Hugh M. Richmond has reasoned that *Cym.* portrays Roman Britain's urgent need for what the Christian era will provide. See 'Shakespeare's Roman Trilogy: The Climax in *Cymbeline*', *Studies in the Literary Imagination*, v, 1 (April 1972), 129–39 – this is the best of the several articles that have recently focused on the fact that Cunobelinus was king of Britain at the time of Christ's birth.

[2] *On the Compositional Genetics of The Comedy of Errors* (Urbana, Illinois, 1963). Aemilia's lecture to Adriana in v, i on the evil of fractiousness in wives is doubtless inspired by Ephesians – and so, by extension, is Kate's lecture to the rebellious wives in v, ii of *Shrew*, a play that in other ways (including use of the same scene from *Amphitruo*) is a companion to *Com. Errors*.

[3] Though Paul Wislicenus sketched it a century ago (*Shakespeare-Jahrbuch*, XIV (1879), 87–96), the relationship of *Com. Errors* to *Per.* has until quite recently been much neglected: F. D. Hoeniger touched only in passing on the similar circumstances of the two fifth acts in his learned and very full introduction to the Arden *Pericles* (1963). The affinity lies deeper, in for example the emphasis in both plays on patience as the sane man's response to an absurd world (see James L. Sanderson, 'Patience in *The Comedy of Errors*', *Texas Studies in Literature and Language*, XVI (1975), 603–18). It seems legitimate to suppose that when he worked on *Per.* Shakespeare reassembled in his creative imagination the elements that had been important to him in *Com. Errors* – including St Paul. Roger Carson Price's doctoral dissertation, 'Pauline Perils: A Religious Reading of *Pericles*' (see *Dissertation Abstracts International*, XXXV (1975), 7266A–7A) is a nearly occult symbolic reading, but occasionally it looks in the desired direction.

[4] R. Chris Hassel (*Thought*, XLVI (1971), 371–88) and Robert C. Foy (see *Dissertation Abstracts International*, XXXIV (1973), 724A–5A) have dealt with Paul as an influence on Shakespearian comedy, but not from the proposed perspective.

[5] '"Greeks" and "Merrygreeks": A Background to *Timon of Athens* and *Troilus and Cressida*', *Essays on Shakespeare and Elizabethan Drama in Honor of Hardin Craig*, ed. Richard Hosley (Columbia, Missouri, 1962), pp. 223–33.

than satiric stereotypes, while Trojans share in the immorality ostensibly Greek;[1] but there is no denying that both plays portray sullied Greeks and a corrupt Hellas. We must agree with Spencer that the two plays are best read as orthodox Renaissance portraits of the Greek world. There is certainly no need to see in them the evidence scholarship has so often strained to find: of Shakespearian world-weariness, or of a wholehearted commitment to medieval classicism (*Troilus*), or of malice toward George Chapman (*Troilus*), or even of rebellion against 'the schoolmasters' worship of antiquity', J. A. K. Thomson's interpretation, as Spencer quotes it.

Yet this view will not answer all our questions about Shakespeare's Greeks; convincingly as Spencer explains the moral tone of two plays, he must leave five more (*The Comedy of Errors*, *A Midsummer Night's Dream*, *Pericles*, *The Winter's Tale*, *The Two Noble Kinsmen*) and, as we wish, *Venus and Adonis* unaccounted for. Even when we have granted that these six works are less studiedly Greek in setting than *Troilus* and *Timon*, we must allow that there is more to Shakespeare's Greece than the Renaissance bias. James Emerson Phillips argued nearly forty years ago that Shakespeare's conception of ancient Greece was political, as his conceptions of ancient Rome and of medieval England were, even though politics is not the center of dramatic interest in any of the Greek and Roman plays.[2] He prefigured Spencer's 'Elizabethan Romans' essay by applying Renaissance assumptions about monarchy and the state to *Caesar*, *Antony*, *Coriolanus*, *Troilus*, and *Timon*. It remained for Howard B. White to extend a political interpretation to *Dream* and *Pericles* (and to *Cymbeline* and *The Tempest*, also) and to argue that the political questions are 'Greek' in Shakespeare's Greek plays in something like the way they are English in the histories.[3] So he sees *Timon* as portraying

the decay of Athenian democracy and *Dream* as portraying the foundation of that democracy. (We might prefer to see the corruption of an entrenched oligarchy in *Timon* and a sketch for a philosopher-king in *Dream*,[4] and then to add that *The Winter's Tale* offers a vivid portrait of a tyrant in action.[5]) White's book is deeply flawed by mistaken interpretation and casual error, but it is sometimes attractively suggestive: on the psychology and ethics of ostracism in *Cymbeline*, for example, and (too briefly) on St Paul in *Pericles*.

A fuller, more tightly reasoned book remains to be written on Shakespeare's response to Greek political philosophy; such a book ought to stress his sense of the *polis* as the core of civilization. One sees it best in *Timon*, where the failure of the *polis* to manifest its ontological essence, the reciprocities of human intercourse, leads to an atavistic collapse into a barbarism conveyed by imagery of bestiality and cannibalism; only Alcibiades's eschatological purge of the city can restore the civility (both senses) of Athens. The best commentary on Timon's personal sins against reciprocity is *The Odyssey* with its insistence on hospitality as a reciprocal ethic and its portrayal of the Cyclopes in Book IX as archetypally pre-civilized, living each in isolation in his cave;

[1] 'Shakespeare's Greeks', *Stratford Papers on Shakespeare* ed. B. W. Jackson (Toronto, 1964), pp. 1–20.

[2] *The State in Shakespeare's Greek and Roman Plays* (Columbia Univ. Stud. in Engl. and Comp. Lit. 149; New York, 1940).

[3] *Copp'd Hills Towards Heaven: Shakespeare and the Classical Polity* (International Archives of the History of Ideas 32; The Hague, 1970).

[4] D'Orsay Pearson (see above, p. 4, note 2) argues that the Theseus of *MND* is no philosopher-king but the carnal and perfidious Theseus of one mythographic tradition; his first note cites some scholars who have seen in Theseus the ideal governor of another tradition. Pearson's case would be weakened by introduction of the Theseus of *TNK*, I believe.

[5] See Paul N. Siegel, 'Leontes a Jealous Tyrant', *Review of English Studies*, n.s. I (1950), 302–7.

the best commentary on the *polis* as a whole in *Timon* is the *Nicomachean Ethics* where Aristotle constantly emphasizes the centrality of reciprocity in civilized moral life.[1] Knowing Shakespeare's intellectual habits, we might expect to find similar emphases in *Coriolanus*, written at about the same time as *Timon* and based on a source in Plutarch parallel to a major source of *Timon*; and it is there, the reciprocity emblematized in Menenius's fable of the organic body politic in I, i and pervading the play as one of its great moral issues. It will be necessary to return to *Coriolanus* and the ideal of the *polis* at the end of this essay.

The political ethic of reciprocity was available to Shakespeare in places other than Aristotle's *Ethics*; it was in fact so widespread in antiquity that there is not much point in trying to establish a *locus classicus* for Shakespeare's sense of the classical polity.[2] He may have known Plato's *Republic*,[3] but he would in any case learn something of the Greek ideal of the city state in Cicero and a great deal more, both about the ideal and about the imperfect reality, in Plutarch's *Lives*, especially in 'Pericles', 'Dion' (parallel to 'Marcus Brutus'), and 'Alcibiades', which contributed something more to *Timon* than the quarrel Alcibiades has with Athens. It has sometimes been said (by Bolgar, e.g., see above, p. 4, note 1) that Plutarch taught Shakespeare little about Greece; it is time to qualify that judgment. Examination of the Greek lives in Plutarch which are parallel to Roman lives Shakespeare used shows that Shakespeare may have read more widely than his critics: Sidney Homan's article on 'Dion', 'Alexander' and 'Demetrius' is suggestive.[4]

If Shakespeare's Greece offers us as yet only partially answered questions, his Rome does so no less. What, finally, *was* Rome to Shakespeare? Was it anything more than an analogue to medieval England, or Denmark, or Scotland, or any of the other worlds Shakespeare

evoked? Twentieth-century scholarship has in two ways implicitly denied that it was anything more. First, the nearly universal failure to find a generic link among the Roman plays has implicitly suggested that they belong together less inherently than some other groups of plays in Shakespeare; it is still common to exclude *Titus* from the group, as MacCallum did.[5] Second, scholarship has conventionally studied the classical tradition and then applied it broadcast across the Shakespeare canon, as if Shakespeare had not seen the ancient world in which he set one-third of his works as in any real sense a world apart. To illustrate this second implicit challenge to the identity of Shakespeare's Roman world, two instances can stand proxy for many others. In *Hero and Saint*, Reuben Brower 'explore[s] probable analogies between the Shakespearian heroic and the Graeco-Roman heroic' (p. vii); the ancient heroic is to be found in a combination of Homer, Virgil, Ovid, Seneca, and Plutarch –

[1] The author advanced this view of *Timon* in '"According to my Bond": Reciprocity and Alienation in Shakespeare's Jacobean Plays' read at the Sixteenth International Shakespeare Conference, Stratford-upon-Avon, 1974.

[2] See Clifford Chalmers Huffman, '*Coriolanus*' in *Context* (Lewisburg, Pennsylvania, 1971), chs. 1–5 *passim* for classical, medieval, and Renaissance thought about 'the mixed state'; see also Andrew Gurr (who oddly does not mention Huffman), '*Coriolanus* and the Body Politic', *Shakespeare Survey 28* (Cambridge, 1975), pp. 63–9.

[3] Scholarship has characteristically been tentative about this; see, for example, Paul Shorey, *Platonism Ancient and Modern* (Berkeley, California, 1938), pp. 179–82.

[4] *Shakespeare Studies*, VIII (1975), 195–210; cf. E. A. J. Honigmann's excellent article on Shakespeare's eclectic reading in Plutarch, *Shakespeare Quarterly*, X (1959), 25–33. For the probable relationship of 'Pericles' to *Per.* (first in W. C. Hazlitt's 1875 edn. of J. P. Collier's *Shakespeare's Library*) and to *Timon* see J. M. S. Tompkins, *Review of English Studies*, n.s. III (1952), 315–24.

[5] See the opening pages of J. L. Simmons's book discussed below, for an account of this failure of generic criticism in the twentieth century.

the analogues in Shakespeare are Othello, Hamlet, and Lear no less than Shakespeare's Greek and Roman heroes.[1] In Milton Boone Kennedy's study of deliberative, forensic, and epideictic oratory in the Shakespeare canon no distinction at all is made between plays in which the world of classical eloquence is actually portrayed and Shakespeare's other plays.[2] No one will deny that a Brower or a Kennedy is entirely justified in seeing classical character or classical rhetoric in non-classical plays. But the effect of their method, a method applied almost universally by historical scholarship in this century, has been to encourage a fallacious inference about the ancient world in Shakespeare, Rome especially.

It can, on the contrary, be argued that Rome is a place apart to Shakespeare, a world whose mystique he attempts quite deliberately to depict. Such an argument appears in J. L. Simmons's *Shakespeare's Pagan World: The Roman Tragedies*.[3] Simmons proposes that the distinguishing characteristic of Shakespeare's Rome is its secularity; the *civitas Dei* is not yet available as a transcendent absolute, and Shakespeare's Roman heroes grope in a relative world for a moral certainty that can never be accorded them in the same sense that such certainty is available to a protagonist in Christian drama. Perhaps because Augustine contrasted his heavenly city very directly and specifically with the temporal city, *Roma*, it seems not to have occurred to Simmons to ask whether his thesis might be applied to Shakespeare's Greek characters; they too, after all, operate *sub specie temporis*. Much greater limitations than the omission of Greeks from the pagan world are the casual dismissal of *Titus* as under the umbrella of the thesis but not worth discussing, the scanty treatment of *Cymbeline*, and the total neglect of *Lucrece*. What Simmons does do, however, is well done: his vantage offers a clear view of three Roman plays, individually and collectively.

A second major attempt to see Shakespeare's Rome as a world apart has recently been made in Paul A. Cantor's *Shakespeare's Rome: Republic and Empire*.[4] Focusing closely on *Coriolanus* and *Antony and Cleopatra*, Cantor finds Shakespeare's portrayal of the Republic dominated by *thumos* (idealistic commitment, public spiritedness) while in Shakespeare's Empire *eros* (self-indulgence and the dissolution of moral boundaries) is in the ascendant. Freud would have labeled the polarity 'super ego' and 'id', though Cantor does not do so. Indeed, in a quite unfreudian way he implies repeatedly that *thumos* is preferable to *eros* and that it is somehow closer to the true spirit of Rome. Any view that Augustan opulence and hegemony are a *casus* from the virtues of the Republic runs across the grain of Virgil's insistence that those virtues survive in the Augustan world and that *Romanitas* in the *Pax Augusta* is the *telos* toward which all Roman history has tended. Yet Virgil does not appear in Cantor's index. There are other limitations: the lack of any coherent treatment of *Caesar* and the total neglect (as in Simmons) of *Lucrece* and *Titus*; the entirely mistaken argument that Rome needs a political leader in *Coriolanus* and that Caius Marcius could have been the man to lead. Yet there is much impressive criticism of both plays in this book. Two examples must suffice: Cantor demonstrates convincingly that the traditional opposition in criticism between Roman *thumos* and Egyptian *eros* is artificial, as self-indulgence dominates Roman politics and daily life in the play; he observes perceptively that the focus in *Coriolanus* is on the *urbs* while in *Antony* 'Rome' means something less defined, as the City diffuses into the Empire.

[1] *Hero and Saint: Shakespeare and the Graeco-Roman Heroic Tradition* (Oxford, 1971).
[2] *The Oration in Shakespeare* (Chapel Hill, North Carolina, 1942).
[3] Charlottesville, Virginia, 1973.
[4] Ithaca, N.Y. and London, 1976.

There are other ways in which Shakespeare might be seen to have defined Rome; the space that remains will be devoted to some of them. First is the likelihood that Shakespeare thought of *Romanitas* as *eloquentia* and that he made a deliberate effort to forge answerable styles for his Roman plays. Given Shakespeare's grammar-school education in rhetoric it is probable enough that he should have drawn the inference that *Romanitas* was a mode of utterance. I say here *styles*, not *style*, because the four Roman plays differ widely in style, a fact which may account for the neglect of this designation of Roman life in Shakespeare. Yet in all four plays style is prominent – and 'Roman', or so Shakespeare would have thought. *Titus Andronicus* and *Antony and Cleopatra* are both florid, though in quite different ways, *Titus* relying on *copia* as Ovid does to attain an aesthetic distance from the horrors it depicts,[1] and *Antony* relying on the 'Brobdingnagian' language of all the characters to elevate the love affair and its tragic consequences to the status of 'high events'.[2] The self-conscious overstatement of the play may remind us of the stylistic self-indulgence of Empire writers like Lucan or Apuleius, though *Antony* never seems merely artificial. In *Coriolanus* hyperbole serves a more complex purpose, suggesting the protagonist's loss of control as well as his colossal stature: if rhetoric is the controlled language of civilized discourse in the *urbs*, the pre-civilized hero designates himself an outsider by this failure in him of *urbanitas*. He would rather pile up the bodies of his opponents like cordwood (I, i, 197–200) than negotiate with those opponents in rational argument.[3]

The most striking of the Roman plays for its style is *Julius Caesar*, though criticism has never done it full justice. Samuel Johnson detected a Roman style, austere and unaffecting, in the play,[4] and for nearly two centuries criticism echoed him by calling the play sparse;

not until Wilson Knight's time was the play seen to have any texture to speak of. What is most 'Roman' about *Caesar*, however, is not its linguistic leanness, but its oratorical mode. Any number of commentators have observed that Plutarch offered Shakespeare the distinction between Antony's Asiatic oratorical style and Brutus's Laconic style but that Shakespeare had to devise the two orations himself with help perhaps from Appian. Few, however, have seen how much of the rest of *Caesar* is oratorical.[5] From Marullus's twenty-four-line harangue of the Plebeians in I, i (a prefiguration of Brutus's oration in its merely temporary effectiveness) to Antony's brief *laudatio funebris* of Brutus in v, v, the play is filled with the solemnity and the intensity of public utterance. Indeed, it can be said with some justice that Portia delivers an oration to her husband in the orchard (while Lady Macbeth, by contrast, communicates with hers at a less formal level) and that the impact of IV, iii in *Caesar* is a result of the descent of Brutus and Cassius from the pedestal of formal discourse to the intimacies of bickering.

Another 'Roman' element of style in *Julius Caesar* is illeism, which Shakespeare would

---

[1] Eugene M. Waith, 'The Metamorphosis of Violence in *Titus Andronicus*', *Shakespeare Survey 10* (Cambridge, 1957), pp. 39–49.

[2] This is S. L. Bethell's interpretation (and his adjective) in *Shakespeare and the Popular Dramatic Tradition* (Durham, North Carolina, 1944), pp. 144–7; an extension of Bethell's approach is 'The Protean Language of the Man-Made World', ch. 6 of Julian Markels's *The Pillar of the World: Antony and Cleopatra in Shakespeare's Development* (Columbus, Ohio, 1968).

[3] See Leonard F. Dean, 'Voice and Deed in *Coriolanus*', *University of Kansas City Review*, XXI (1955), 177–84, for a related interpretation of the meaning of rhetoric in the play.

[4] End note to *JC* in his Shakespeare ed'n., 1765. Clifford Leech uses the adjective 'marmoreal' for the style of all the Roman plays (see above, p. 6, note 1).

[5] Kennedy, for example, confines himself to the two orations in III, ii.

have found in Caesar's *Commentaries*[1] and which he may have thought characteristically Roman – at least at the time he wrote *Caesar*. A great many characters in the play (not just Caesar, as is sometimes said) refer to themselves or others by name in the third person. Shakespeare made use of this device in *Hamlet*, which abounds in Roman allusions, and in *Troilus*, which like *Hamlet* was written shortly after *Caesar*, but after that it appears much less often;[2] perhaps by the time he wrote *Antony*, *Coriolanus*, and *Cymbeline* he found illeism too artificial a rhetorical stance for drama, however classical it might sound. Such magniloquence is appropriate enough in *Troilus*, but in less satiric contexts it may jar – indeed critics who have caught Caesar and Othello employing the device have labeled both pompous.

The fact that illeism appears in *Troilus* after Shakespeare introduced it in *Caesar* makes it plain that he could readily transfer to a Greek setting something he thought of as characteristically Roman. *Timon* and *Troilus* both evoke as the Roman plays do the relation between personal decorum and verbal eloquence that Cicero and Quintilian thought of as the essence of civility and civilization. In Timon's curses the complete disjunction of eloquence from magnanimity is a living metaphor for the descent from civil conversation to barbarism in the play; when we hear magniloquence used as a cloak for bad logic by both Greeks and Trojans in *Troilus* we may recall Socrates's belief that rhetoric and moral earnestness do not always keep company. T. McAlindon's often very astute book on *Shakespeare and Decorum* does not make these points;[3] indeed, like Kennedy and Brower, he fails entirely to segregate Shakespeare's classical plays.

It was decorum in its technical sense that Samuel Johnson was referring to in his comments on the style of *Julius Caesar*, for he juxtaposed Roman style and 'Roman manners'. We may safely guess that he was

alluding to the Stoic temperament that we see in several characters, in Cicero (I, iii), for example, and in Portia (II, i), and in Brutus (IV, iii). The contrast between this phlegmatic manner and Cassius's choleric energy and overtness is one of the effective dramatic devices in the play.[4] There are other common traits of character in *Julius Caesar* that Shakespeare obviously thought distinctively Roman, notably anti-feminism (I, iii, 82–4; II, i, 119–22; II, i, 292–7 etc.); in *Antony and Cleopatra*, where a woman takes on the role of opponent and alternative to all that is Roman, such sentiments occur even more emphatically (cf. Canidius's embittered 'our leader's [led], / And we are women's men' – III, vii, 69–70). In *Coriolanus* the contrast is not so much between man and woman as between man and boy, surely because Plutarch put so much emphasis in 'Coriolanus' on valor as the Roman measure of mature masculinity[5] (we recall that for young Marcius the puberty rite was to flesh his sword against the Tarquins). There are still those who will argue that Volumnia is an Elizabethan huswife rather than a Roman matron,[6] but most scholars no longer doubt

[1] Norman N. Holland, *The Shakespearean Imagination* (New York, 1964), p. 138.

[2] S. Viswanathan ('"Illeism with a Difference" in Certain Middle Plays of Shakespeare', *Shakespeare Quarterly*, XX (1969), 407–15) sees that illeism separates the speaker from his role, the persona of a mythic figure like Caesar or Hector from the reality, but he fails to recognize its origin in the *Commentaries*.

[3] 1973.

[4] John Anson (*Shakespeare Studies*, II (1966), 11–33) and Marvin Vawter (*ibid.*, VII (1974), 173–95) are two among a number of scholars who have argued in recent years that Shakespeare was deeply critical of the Stoicism he so often portrayed in his Romans.

[5] E. M. Waith, 'Manhood and Valor in Two Shakespearean Tragedies', *English Literary History*, XVII (1950), 262–73; cf. Kenneth Muir, 'Shakespeare's Roman World', *The Literary Half-Yearly* (Mysore), XV (1974), 45–63 (p. 63).

[6] Margaret B. Bryan, *Renaissance Papers, 1972*, 43–58.

that Shakespeare was consciously striving in all his Roman works for Roman character and style of life, however he may have succeeded.

Rome to Shakespeare was not just language and national character, but institutions also. T. J. B. Spencer once said of *Titus* that Shakespeare crowded the play with all the Roman political institutions he knew, regardless of their appropriateness to the historical setting in the late Empire. 'The Author seems anxious, not to get it all right, but to get it all in' (see above, p. 3, note 4). The later Roman plays are much more careful to fit the politics to the time. There is more to Roman institutions than politics, of course; two stimulating articles in recent years have shown that Shakespeare was aware of the importance of family in Rome, even in his earliest Roman ventures. G. K. Hunter in comparing *Romeo* and *Titus* in several ways has occasion to interpret the moral structure of *Titus* as in part familial: the ordered closeness of the Andronici is the measure in the play of Saturninus's amorphous family with its step-children, its adulterous foreign *materfamilias*, its illegitimate offspring, its Moorish intruder.[1] A second essay is Coppélia Kahn's learned and intelligent analysis of the rape in Shakespeare's *Lucrece* in relation to Roman traditions of family honor and patrilineal succession as Shakespeare would have understood them; Lucrece kills herself not to protect *her* honor but to vindicate the honor of the Collatines: there must be no possibility of a genetic taint on the lineage of the dynastic family.[2]

Rome, of course, is also a place to Shakespeare. It used to be said that he had little sense of Rome as a physical entity, that he dropped allusions to the Tiber and the Capitol into early scenes to suggest locus and let it go at that.[3] Whatever the limitations of his detailed knowledge of buildings, Shakespeare thought of Rome in architectural terms: Menenius points out 'yond coign a' th' Capitol, yond

cornerstone' when he wants a symbol of steadfastness; the Triumvirate are 'pillar[s] of the world'; the Empire itself is a 'wide arch'. When the Tribunes and Plebeians shout 'What is the city but the people?', Cominius replies in a telling architectural metaphor; faction

is the way to lay the city flat,
To bring the roof to the foundation,
And bury all, which yet distinctly ranges,
In heaps and piles of ruin.   (*Cor.* III, i, 203–6)

The city is also to Shakespeare a set of psychologically significant, virtually symbolic, loci often placed in contrast with one another – the Forum, the battlefield, the Senate house, the street, the domicile. Each is a manifestation of *Romanitas*, the domicile not less than public buildings, for it is in the Roman plays that Shakespeare most powerfully contrasts public and private life, portraying them sometimes as mutually inimical.[4]

The most important edifice in Shakespeare's Rome, its wall, is seldom spoken of by scholars. To Shakespeare Rome is above all *urbs* in its etymological sense, the enclave of civilization ringed round with a protective wall, outside of which the dark forces of barbarism lurk. Coriolanus, a lonely dragon advancing on the gates of Rome or an eagle preying inside the

[1] *Shakespeare Survey 27* (Cambridge, 1974), pp. 1–9.

[2] *Shakespeare Studies*, IX (1976), 45–72. Cf. Michael Platt, '*The Rape of Lucrece* and the Republic for Which it Stands', *Centennial Review*, XIX (1975), 59–79, a strongly political interpretation with some emphasis on Roman social traditions.

[3] Carl Meinck, *Über das örtliche und zeitliche Kolorit in Shakespeares Römerdramen und Ben Jonsons 'Catiline'* (Studien zur englischen Philologie hrsg. Lorenz Morsbach, XXXVIII, 1910). Cf. Lizette Andrews Fisher, 'Shakespeare and the Capitol', *Modern Language Notes*, XXII (1907), 177–82, for Shakespeare's inaccuracy about the Capitol.

[4] Julian Markels treats *Ant.* as the epitome of this motif in the Shakespeare canon; see above, p. 9, note 2.

walls of Corioles, is Shakespeare's most compelling embodiment of the terror that threatens the *urbs* from outside its wall; this 'Mycenean' hero, more at home in battle than in the *polis*,[1] is reminiscent at Corioles of awesome Turnus in Book IX of the *Aeneid*, slaughtering inside the palisade like a wild beast. Walls, gates, and locks exist to keep the lust represented by a Tarquin outside, but tragically they cannot (*Lucrece* 302–43). The savage rape and mutilation of Lavinia in *Titus* takes place in the forest outside the wall of Rome; remembering the symbolic importance of Lavinia in the *Aeneid* we can readily think of Chiron and Demetrius as assaulting *Romanitas* itself.[2]

The wall of Rome encloses a *polis* which in its political and social decorum embodies civilization; it is the everlasting wall that Virgil spoke of at the opening of his poem, but it is eminently fragile, as both Virgil and Shakespeare knew. Shakespeare's Romans, like the Trojans in *Aeneid* II, may breach their own wall to admit barbarism and death; the preying tigers (*Titus* III, i, 55) and the monstrous horse pregnant with death both enter from without. But there is worse: one may imitate barbarism by oneself negating the values of the *polis*; it is here that Rome is most vulnerable, as the actions of both *Titus*[3] and *Coriolanus*[4] make manifest. Shakespeare is obsessed enough with this horror to transfer it from Rome to Athens: 'The commonwealth of Athens is become a forest of beasts' (*Timon* IV, iii, 347–8) no less than 'Rome is . . . a wilderness of tigers' (*Titus* III, i, 54).

When the full study we need of Shakespeare's Virgil is written,[5] it ought to deal fully with Virgilian symbolism as it appears in the Roman plays: the walls of Rome are only part of the legacy. Virgil's vision of Rome as Fate's protégé, the source of the coherence of the *Aeneid*, survives muted in Shakespeare's vision of Roman history as teleological and inexorable, larger than any man who may oppose its

momentum. It is this grand view of the history of Rome that Menenius Agrippa voices when he says in the first scene of *Coriolanus*:

> you may as well
> Strike at the heaven with your staves as lift them
> Against the Roman state, whose course will on
> The way it takes, cracking ten thousand curbs
> Of more strong link asunder than can ever
> Appear in your impediment.   (ll. 67–72)

He is addressing the riotous Plebeians, but his words apply as much to Coriolanus, who will atavistically seek to repeal the newly created institution of the *tribuni plebis*.

Virgil's mythic vision of Rome as driven (or called) by Fate toward the *Pax Augusta* was 'true' in his generation in just the same way the equally vulnerable Tudor myth was in Shakespeare's generation – that is, it was more true in its piety of invention than literalists are likely to understand. Who is to say that in basing his conception of Rome in five plays and a long poem upon Virgil's view of history Shakespeare was not portraying *Romanitas* authentically?

[1] See Brower's fine chapter, 'The Deeds of Coriolanus', in *Hero and Saint* (see above, p. 8, note 1); cf. Richard C. Crowley, '*Coriolanus* and the Epic Genre', *Shakespeare's Last Plays: Essays in Honor of Charles Crow*, ed. Richard C. Tobias and Paul G. Zolbrod (Athens, Ohio, 1974).

[2] Alan Sommers, '"Wilderness of Tigers": Structure and Symbolism in *Titus Andronicus*', *Essays in Criticism*, X (1960), 275–89.

[3] Andrew V. Ettin, 'Shakespeare's First Roman Tragedy', *English Literary History*, XXXVII (1970), 325–41.

[4] See John Arthos, 'Shakespeare and the Ancient World', *Michigan Quarterly Review*, X (1971), 149–63 (p. 158) for a fine comment on the extent of Coriolanus's self-alienation.

[5] To indicate the neglect of Virgil as an influence on Shakespeare's Rome one need only observe that in 1943 Robert A. Law regarded himself (rightly, I believe) as pointing out for the first time that the *Aeneid* is repeatedly referred to in *Titus* (*Studies in Philology*, 40, 145–53). Some have since written on Virgil in *Titus* or *Lucrece*, Ettin (note 3, this page) and Platt (above, p. 11, note 2), e.g., but there is much untouched ground.

'A PIECE OF SKILFUL PAINTING'
IN SHAKESPEARE'S 'LUCRECE'

S. CLARK HULSE

In 1593, Shakespeare promised Southampton 'some graver labour' to follow *Venus and Adonis*. Indeed, Muriel Bradbrook has persuasively argued that *Venus* itself was an attempt by Shakespeare to silence the slanders uttered by Greene in 1592 and establish himself as a respectable poet.[1] In the elaborate description of a tapestry or painting of Troy which takes up over two hundred lines in *Lucrece*, Shakespeare draws on Virgil and Classical art theorists to create for his poem a proper epic *ecphrasis*, comparable to the shield of Achilles, to the bronze doors at Carthage where Aeneas sees written the fate of his people, or to the 'clothes of *Arras* and of *Toure*' which decorate Malacasta's castle in the *Faerie Queene*. When he describes the painter's wondrous skill, Shakespeare invokes the ancient *paragone* of poet and painter, asserting his own mastery of his craft and equality to the ancient masters of the arts. When he describes the response of Lucrece to the 'well-painted piece', Shakespeare defines her stature as a woman and as the hero of his poem.

Shakespeare's *Lucrece* may be called a 'minor' epic in the sense that Ariosto or Spenser are epic, concerned with 'Knights and Ladies gentle deeds, . . . Fierce warres and faithfull loves'.[2] In the progress from *Venus and Adonis* to *Lucrece*, Shakespeare travels the Virgilian path, beginning in a middle style akin to sonnet, pastoral and comedy, and ending in the regions of epic and tragedy. The erotic and the heroic are mingled in Tarquin's siege of the fort of Lucrece's chastity, until the moment when he is able 'To make the breach and enter this sweet city'.[3] When Lucrece calls to mind the 'well-painted piece', the extended comparison between bedroom and battlefield is completed in images of the fall of Troy:

> 'For even as subtle Sinon here is painted,
>   So sober sad, so weary and so mild, –
>   As if with grief or travail he had fainted, —
>   To me came Tarquin armed to beguild
> With outward honesty, but yet defil'd
>   With inward vice. As Priam him did cherish,
>   So did I Tarquin, – so my Troy did perish.'

(ll. 1541–7)

The Troy passage is set into the poem as an extended simile or *icon*. Originally the term *icon* meant 'statue' or 'image', before becoming a technical term of rhetoric.[4] The *Rhetorica ad*

[1] 'Beasts and Gods: Greene's *Groats-Worth of Witte* and the Social Purpose of *Venus and Adonis*', *Shakespeare Survey 15* (Cambridge, 1962), pp. 62–72.

[2] *Faerie Queene*, I, prologue, i. Hallett Smith considers the poem as an historical complaint in *Elizabethan Poetry* (1952; rpt. Ann Arbor, 1968), pp. 113–17. For the relationship of historical complaint to the epyllion and epic, see my 'Elizabethan Minor Epic: Toward a Definition of Genre', *Studies in Philology*, LXXIII (1976), 302–19. The links of the poem to tragedy are examined by Harold R. Walley, '*The Rape of Lucrece* and Shakespearean Tragedy', *PMLA*, LXXVI (1961), 480–7; by Roy Battenhouse, *Shakespearean Tragedy: Its Art and Its Christian Premises* (Bloomington, 1969), pp. 3–41; and by Rolf Soellner in a forthcoming article.

[3] Line 469. Quotations are from F. T. Prince's New Arden edition (1960).

[4] Marsh H. McCall, Jr, *Ancient Rhetorical Theories of Simile and Comparison* (Cambridge, Mass., 1969), p. ix.

Herennium defines it as a comparison between two things, used either for praise or blame.[1] Aristotle notes that *icon* is best suited to poetry, and Erasmus praises it for vividness.[2] Some confusion may arise here from the different terminology used by Jean Hagstrum in *The Sister Arts*. He calls *iconic* any poetry which describes a work of the visual arts, and reserves *ecphrasis* for the rhetorical figure in which the work of art is made to speak (like Keats's urn).[3] I shall stay with the broader usage of Classical and Renaissance rhetoricians, who call any vivid, sensuous image *iconic*; define *ecphrasis* as an extended description of something, such as a person, place, battle or work of art; and use *prosopopoeia* for the lending of voice to an inanimate object.[4] This usage has the advantage of emphasizing the comparative nature of iconic imagery, and defining more closely for us the function of such imagery in a long poem. Once we have established how the Troy passage fits into the poem, we can examine it in detail to see just what kind of artifact it describes, and what it reveals about the poet and his heroine.

Shakespeare's *icon* sums up a comparison which has been carefully developed from the opening line of the poem. 'From the besieged Ardea all in post' comes Tarquin, from battle to bed, and, one may wonder, from Ardea to ardor. In a system of 'moral heraldry', as Bradbrook calls it, Shakespeare transforms the faces of both protagonists into the shields of opposing warriors.[5] In Tarquin's face and coat of arms are written the signs of his dishonor:

> 'Then my digression is so vile, so base,
> That it will live engraven in my face.
>
> 'Yea, though I die the scandal will survive
> And be an eye-sore in my golden coat;
> Some loathsome dash the herald will contrive,
> To cipher me how fondly I did dote.'
>
> (ll. 202–7)

While the foul intent of Tarquin is immediately visible to Shakespeare, to the reader and to Tarquin himself, it is hidden from Lucrece, who

> Could pick no meaning from their parling looks,
> Nor read the subtle shining secrecies
> Writ in the glassy margents of such books.
>
> (ll. 100–2)

For all her simplicity, the face of Lucrece is painted with equal subtlety:

> When beauty boasted blushes, in despite
> Virtue would stain that o'er with silver white.
>
> But beauty in that white entituled
> From Venus' doves, doth challenge that fair field;
> Then virtue claims from beauty beauty's red,
> Which virtue gave the golden age to gild
> Their silver cheeks, and call'd it then their shield;
> Teaching them thus to use it in the fight,
> When shame assail'd, the red should fence the white.
>
> This heraldry in Lucrece' face was seen,
> Argu'd by beauty's red and virtue's white;
> Of either's colour was the other queen.
>
> (ll. 55–66)

First virtue is white and beauty blushing red; then beauty is white, like Venus's doves, and virtue red by association with the golden age. The very slipperiness of the image suggests there is an ambiguity about moral heraldry. It is hard to tell from the crest just what is under the visor. If Lucrece had trouble reading Tarquin's face, her own features, however clear and honest, are no less a puzzle for the poet, and in that puzzle is something of an ambivalence toward the epic tradition. Tarquin is decidedly villainous, a perfect anti-hero, whose own soul is desecrated by his crime.[6] But

---

[1] *Rhetorica ad Herennium*, IV, xlix, 62.

[2] Aristotle, *Rhetoric*, III, iv, 1; Erasmus, *De Utraque Verborum ac Rerum Copia* (Cologne, 1566), p. 366.

[3] *The Sister Arts* (Chicago, 1958), p. 18n.

[4] Cf. *Ad Herennium*, IV, liii, 66; Quintilian, *Institutio Oratoria*, VIII, iii, 61–71; Erasmus, pp. 288–94.

[5] *Shakespeare and Elizabethan Poetry* (1951), pp. 110–16.

[6] Sam Hynes, 'The Rape of Tarquin', *Shakespeare Quarterly*, X (1959), 451–3.

Lucrece, as his opponent, is not at first clearly heroic, either in understanding or in action.

Is she, after all, sufficiently noble to be the heroine of a little epic? As Saint Augustine asked, if she was chaste, why did she kill herself, and if guilty, why worthy of praise?[1] The question has been repeated at some length by two modern Augustinians, Don Cameron Allen and Roy Battenhouse.[2] We might – should – be tempted to dismiss this out of hand as shallow misogyny, confusing the victim with the criminal, except that Lucrece repeatedly asks the same question of herself. In her first words after the rape she speaks of her 'offences', 'disgrace', 'unseen sin', 'guilt', and 'shame' (ll. 747–56). The misogyny is enough part of the poem that we must deal with it.

Livy and Ovid clearly say that Lucrece consented to her rape under duress. Chaucer is evasive. He takes Ovid's verb 'succubuit', 'she yielded', to mean that she sank away or fainted, eliminating the nagging question of her state of mind:

> She loste bothe at ones wit and breth,
> And in a swogh she lay, and wex so ded,
> Men myghte smyten of hire arm or hed;
> She feleth no thyng, neyther foul ne fayr.[3]

Shakespeare takes a third way, having Tarquin use force throughout. Even so, Lucrece spends the night examining herself and the other potential culprits, Night, Opportunity, Time, and, incidentally, Tarquin. So the unstable identity of the opening lines is still unfixed as she comes to the 'well-painted piece'. Its function as *comparatio* is all the more important for this reason. In viewing the work, Lucrece may be able to view herself, to successfully 'read' it and her own character, as neither she nor Shakespeare could do at the outset.

In seeing how Lucrece 'reads' the Troy-piece, we may first ask just what it is she is looking at. Shakespeare describes at least six different scenes: the Greek army arrayed before the walls; Nestor addressing the troops; Hector issuing forth from the gates; the battle on 'Simois' reedy banks'; the final sack of the citadel; and (out of chronological order) Sinon deluding Priam. He praises the painter's realism and his 'art of physiognomy', which is not the description of features, but the rendering of the emotions in each face. What could depict so many scenes, with such a technique? Is it a tapestry or a painting? Even to think about Elizabethan painting is to encounter next to nothing which could evoke such a description. Sidney Colvin, convinced by the detail of the passage that Shakespeare had an actual work in mind, suggested a tapestry of fifteenth-century France.[4] Margaret Thorp in 1931 thought it was a panel painting.[5] A. H. R. Fairchild suggested that Shakespeare was combining the composition of fifteenth-century French tapestries with the 'physiognomy' of sixteenth-century works.[6]

Personally, I vote for a tapestry. The only real objection to a tapestry is the term 'painted', which, as Fairchild points out, Elizabethans, and Shakespeare, used with great looseness as a synonym for 'colored' or 'portrayed'.[7] Indeed, for humanist painters, 'pinxit' is regularly interchanged with 'finxit'.[8] But there

[1] *City of God*, I, 19.
[2] Don Cameron Allen, 'Some Observations on *The Rape of Lucrece*', *Shakespeare Survey 15* (Cambridge, 1962), pp. 89–98; Battenhouse, pp. 14–17.
[3] *The Legend of Good Women*, ll. 1815–18, in *The Works of Geoffrey Chaucer*, ed. F. N. Robinson, 2nd edn. (Boston, 1957), p. 509.
[4] 'The Sack of Troy in Shakespeare's "Lucrece" and in Some Fifteenth-Century Drawings and Tapestries', in *A Book of Homage to Shakespeare*, ed. Israel Gollancz (Oxford, 1916), pp. 88–99.
[5] 'Shakespeare and the Fine Arts', *PMLA*, XLVI (1931), 687–8.
[6] *Shakespeare and the Arts of Design*, Univ. of Missouri Studies, vol. 12, no. 1 (Columbia, Mo., 1937), pp. 139–43.
[7] *Ibid.*, pp. 110, 144.
[8] Anne-Marie Lecoq, '"Finxit". Le Peintre comme "Fictor" au XVIe Siècle', *Bibliothèque d'Humanisme et Renaissance*, XXXVII (1975), 225–43.

seems little point to all this argument, since we have no evidence of what Shakespeare might have actually seen. The only painter he mentions by name is the notorious Giulio Romano, waxworker, of *The Winter's Tale*. Richard Burbage was a painter, but the two works attributed to him (at Dulwich College) are small portrait heads, hardly helpful with the vast historical piece Shakespeare describes.[1] W. S. Heckscher, having recently surveyed Shakespeare's few references to art, concludes that he is never so vague as when he is describing what he has actually seen, and never so detailed as when constructing from the imagination.[2] The passage really tells us less about the actual object than about the illusion it creates. It is sufficiently incomplete that we may see what we please as long as we see *something*.

The incompleteness of the description on such a crucial point is a sign that it is essentially a verbal, not a visual formulation. The opening of the passage stresses the painter's skill in imitation: 'In scorn of nature, art gave lifeless life' (l. 1374). The conceit is a tired one, which Shakespeare repeats in various guises in *Timon*, *Pericles*, *Venus and Adonis* and *The Winter's Tale*.[3] Fairchild has protested that Shakespeare was too refined aesthetically to be interested in mere imitation of nature and *trompe l'œil*, but a fair look at his words suggests that he, like most of his contemporaries, demands it.[4] The expressiveness for which Vasari praises painters is achieved through some particularly vivid physical detail, and Carel van Mander, the 'Vasari of the North', hails Pieter Aertsen for deceiving the eye and making the dead seem alive.[5]

Shakespeare's *ecphrasis* begins with praise for the perfect imitation of the visible (ll. 1366–86), then praise for the perfect rendering of expression (ll. 1387–407), and finally praise for the artists's ability to suggest the parts of the figure invisible to the eye (ll. 1408–28). These are the criteria by which Pliny measures the perfection of painting. First Zeuxis was able to render exactly what the eye could see. Then Parrhasios 'added vivacity to the features', and learned 'to give assurance of the parts behind, thus clearly suggesting even what it conceals'. At last Apelles excels all others, not in any particular technique, but through a certain grace which combines the excellences of others.[6] If Shakespeare had any intention of constructing a proper Roman decoration for Lucrece's house, Pliny would have been the likely place to start.

The adherence of Shakespeare's *ecphrasis* to Classical aesthetics is underscored by a parallel, first noted by E. H. Gombrich, between Shakespeare's description of Nestor haranguing the troops with the account by Philostratus of a painting of the siege of Thebes.[7] It is worth quoting in full. 'Some are seen in full figure, others with the legs hidden, others from the waist up, then only the busts of some, heads only, helmets only, and finally just spear-points. This, my boy, is perspective; since the problem is to deceive the eyes as they travel back along

---

[1] Sir Edward Cook, ed., *A Descriptive and Historical Catalogue of the Pictures in the Gallery of Alleyn's College of God's Gift at Dulwich* (1914), nos. 380, 395.

[2] 'Shakespeare in His Relationship to the Visual Arts: A Study in Paradox', *Research Opportunities in Renaissance Drama*, XIII–XIV (1970–71), 57–8.

[3] *Timon*, I, i, 35–8; *Pericles*, v, Chorus, 5–7; *Venus*, l. 291; *Winter's Tale*, IV, iv, 86–8, v, iii, 19–20, 67–8.

[4] Fairchild, p. 137. W. Moelwyn Merchant points out Shakespeare's concern and sophistication with the visual arts in *Shakespeare and the Artist* (1959), pp. 9–12.

[5] Svetlana Leontief Alpers, '*Ekphrasis* and Aesthetic Attitudes in Vasari's *Lives*', *Journal of the Warburg and Courtauld Institutes*, XXIII (1960), 193; Carel van Mander, *Grondt der Schilder-Const*, VII, 55, in *Northern Renaissance Art*, *1400–1600*, ed. Wolfgang Stechow (Englewood Cliffs, N.J., 1966), p. 63.

[6] *Historia Naturalis*, XXXV, 61–96, in *The Elder Pliny's Chapters on the History of Art*, tr. K. Jex-Blake (1896), pp. 107–33.

[7] *Art and Illusion*, rev. ed. (New York, 1961), p. 211.

with the proper receding planes of the picture.'[1]

> For much imaginary work was there, –
> Conceit deceitful, so compact, so kind,
> That for Achilles' image stood his spear
> Gripp'd in an armed hand; himself behind
> Was left unseen, save to the eye of mind:
> A hand, a foot, a face, a leg, a head
> Stood for the whole to be imagined.
>
> (ll. 1422–8)

Even in translation, the parallel strikes me as sufficiently full and detailed to be an actual borrowing. Both stress the painter's cheating skill, and linger over the spear. If Shakespeare's 'lesse Greeke' were inadequate to the task, he could have read Philostratus in any of the five Latin editions between 1517 and 1550, or in the 1578 French translation of Blaise de Vigenere.

Whether we accept Philostratus as a source or not, his *ecphrasis* establishes a rhetorical pattern for describing a visual artifact which was so widely diffused that it would have been virtually impossible for any serious poet to be ignorant of it. Philostratus does not so much describe as suggest, concentrating not on the object itself, but on how it would appear to a viewer. In a sense he practises, as does Shakespeare, exactly the kind of rhetoric and the kind of art to which Plato objected.[2] The representation, either in word, paint or marble, is not true to life, much less to an objective ideal. It is distorted to accommodate the process of perception, and those very distortions are Shakespeare's main interest.

The remainder of the passage, describing the fall of Troy, is largely modeled on two *ecphrases* in the *Aeneid*: the description of the bronze doors of the temple of Venus at Carthage in Book I, and Aeneas's account of the battle in Book II.[3] Virgil departs from the bronze doors to describe the original event itself, which his viewer, Aeneas, of course witnessed:

> ter circum Iliacos raptaverat Hectora muros
> exanimumque auro corpus vendebat Achilles.

> tum vero ingentem gemitum dat pectore ab imo,
> ut spolia, ut currus, utque ipsum corpus amici
> tendentemque manus Priamum conspexit inermis.[4]

The striking thing is Virgil's simultaneous use of telescopic and microscopic vision, picking out small details amid a scene crowded with events and passions, violating the supposed temporal boundaries of the visual arts. Quintilian had this or similar style in mind in his discussion of the ornate, which Erasmus would quote in the *Copia*:

So, too, we may move our hearers to tears by the picture of a captured town. For the mere statement that the town was stormed . . . fails to penetrate to the emotions of the hearer. But if we expand all that the one word 'stormed' includes, we shall see the flames pouring from house and temple, and hear the crash of falling roofs and one confused clamour blent of many cries.[5]

The pattern Shakespeare is following, established by Virgil, Philostratus, Quintilian, and of course Homer, was codified in the *Progymnasmata* of Hermogenes, the rhetorician of the second sophistic. *Ecphrasis* he defines as:

an account in detail, visible, as they say, bringing before one's eyes what is to be shown . . . Ecphrasis of

[1] *Eikones*, I, 4, tr. Arthur Fairbanks, Loeb ed. (1931), p. 17. While Fairbanks notes that the phrase translated as 'perspective' means literally 'the principle of proportion', Blaise de Vigenere's widely read French translation of 1578 also renders it as 'perspective' (Paris, 1615, p. 26).

[2] Gombrich, pp. 126–7.

[3] Sources for the poem are examined by Hyder E. Rollins in the New Variorum edition (Philadelphia, 1938), pp. 416–26; and by Geoffrey Bullough, *Narrative and Dramatic Sources of Shakespeare*, Vol. I (1957), 179–83.

[4] 'Thrice had Achilles dragged Hector round the walls of Troy and was selling the lifeless body for gold. Then indeed from the bottom of his heart he heaves a deep groan, as the spoils, as the chariot, as the very corpse of his friend met his gaze, and Priam outstretching weaponless hands', *Aeneid*, I, 483–7, tr. H. Rushton Fairclough, Loeb ed. (1932).

[5] *Institutio Oratoria*, VIII, iii, 67–8, tr. H. E. Butler, Loeb ed. (1921). Cf. Erasmus, pp. 288–9.

actions will proceed from what went before, from what happened at that time, and from what followed. Thus if we make an ecphrasis on war, first we shall tell what happened before the war, the levy, the expenditures, the fears; then the engagements, the slaughter, the deaths; then the monument of victory; then the paeans of the victors and, of the others, the tears, the slavery.[1]

The poet, departing from the literal limits of the scene to what came before and after, strives to make it as vivid as possible for the audience by rendering the emotions of the participants. To Quintilian this was the highest of all oratorical achievement, though not the most difficult to attain.[2]

The achievement of this vividness is a common goal for both poetry and painting in the ecphrastic tradition. Plutarch, after quoting the aphorism of Simonides that painting is silent poetry and poetry is a speaking picture, observes that the two arts differ only in the materials by which they seek the same end.[3] As the humanist theorists of each art dwelt on that material difference, they defined the limits of each art by the capacities of the other. Castelvetro, for example, says that painting can only show bodies, not the soul, while poetry can never equal the visual immediacy of painting.[4] So Shakespeare concludes in Sonnet 24 that his eyes, like painters, 'draw but what they see, know not the heart'.

The highest form of skill, then, is to surpass the limits of your material and achieve the perfection of the rival art. Pliny sums up Apelles's gift, which made him the paragon of artists, in that he could paint the unpaintable.[5] Likewise Ortelius lauds Brueghel, and Erasmus praises Dürer:

Nay, he even depicts that which cannot be depicted: fire, rays of light, thunder, sheet lightning, lightning, or, as they say, the 'clouds on a wall':...in fine, the whole mind of man as it reflects itself in the behavior of the body, and almost the voice itself.[6]

The topos appears in an entertainment for the Queen at Mitcham in 1598 attributed to John Lyly, and Shakespeare knows it when he writes act I of *Timon*.[7]

The *paragone* of the arts could be developed into a comparison of artists. Pliny likens Apelles to Homer, and Titian, the modern Apelles, was rival to Ariosto, the modern Homer.[8] The painter may take his themes from literature, as did Titian in the mythological canvases he called 'poesie', while the poet may decorate his verse with *ecphrases*. Shakespeare perfectly fulfills the goal of the *paragone* in his Troy-piece, with the variety of its action and vividness of emotion. He stresses how the painter has shown the things impossible to depict – the concealed parts of the body, the sounds of the scenes, the feelings of the participants. Since this impossible painting is so perfect, he may well praise the artist for rivalling nature. Since it is possible only in the medium of poetry, and is measured by the standard of Virgil, he is also subtly praising himself.

The Virgilian model defines not just the task of the artist, but also the response of the audience to the artist's skill. Virgil lingers over Aeneas's reaction to the scene of Troy:

constitit et lacrimans, 'quis iam locus,' inquit,
  'Achate,

[1] C. S. Baldwin, *Medieval Rhetoric and Poetic* (1928; rpt. Gloucester, Mass., 1959), pp. 35–6.
[2] *Institutio Oratoria*, VIII, iii, 70–1.
[3] *Moralia*, 346–7, tr. Frank Cole Babbitt, Loeb ed. (1936), IV, 501.
[4] H. B. Charlton, *Castelvetro's Theory of Poetry* (Manchester, 1913), p. 63.
[5] *Historia Naturalis*, XXXV, 96.
[6] *De recta Latini Graecique sermonis pronuntiatione*, in Stechow, p. 123.
[7] *Queen Elizabeth's Entertainment at Mitcham: Poet, Painter, and Musician*, ed. Leslie Hotson (New Haven, 1953), p. 20; *Timon*, I, i, 30–94. Cf. Anthony Blunt, 'An Echo of the "Paragone" in Shakespeare', *Journal of the Warburg and Courtauld Institutes*, II (1938–9), 260–2; Merchant, pp. 171–4.
[8] David Rosand, '*Ut Pictor Poeta*: Meaning in Titian's *Poesie*', *New Literary History*, III (1972), 529–32.

quae regio in terris nostri non plena laboris?
en Priamus! sunt hic etiam sua praemia laudi,
sunt lacrimae rerum et mentem mortalia tangunt.'[1]

His close identification with the emotions portrayed move Aeneas to a fresh lament over his own fate. Lucrece, too, overcome with the sorrow of Hecuba, laments that the painter gave her 'so much grief, and not a tongue':

'Poor instrument,' quoth she, 'without a sound,
I'll tune thy woes with my lamenting tongue,
And drop sweet balm in Priam's painted wound,
And rail on Pyrrhus that hath done him wrong,
And with my tears quench Troy that burns so long,
And with my knife scratch out the angry eyes
Of all the Greeks that are thine enemies.'

(ll. 1464–70)

As she moves through the tapestry, naming and sorrowing with each figure, she comes finally to Sinon, whose smooth face conceals his inner treachery. Confronting him, she must finally penetrate surfaces, and in doing so, recognize just how similar her own story is:

'It cannot be,' quoth she, 'that so much guile,' –
She would have said, – 'can lurk in such a look.'
But Tarquin's shape came in her mind the while,
And from her tongue 'can lurk' from 'cannot' took.

(ll. 1534–7)

Shakespeare's one violation of chronological order, leaving Sinon for last, is thus dictated by his rhetorical order, moving from the tapestry itself, to Lucrece's vocal response, to her recognition of the similarity to her own fate: from *ecphrasis* to *prosopopoeia* to *icon*.

We may think of Shakespeare as recapitulating the instructions for looking at a painting which Philostratus gave in sections 1–4 of the *Eikones* (concluding with the siege of Thebes). First, he tells us, the mere physical illusion of the paint creates wonder, but to interpret it properly, we must look away from the painting to the events which are depicted. As we enter the illusion, we expand the scene with our own imagination, hearing its sounds, seeing what is only suggested, until our identification with it is so close that we are actors in it: 'Let us catch the blood, my boy, holding under it a fold of our garments.'[2] This expressive view of aesthetic experience was shared as well by Renaissance art theorists. Dependent on Philostratus, Pliny and the poets for their knowledge of Classical painting, they were influenced by *ecphrasis* perhaps as deeply as their literary colleagues.[3] Alberti echoes Horace to explain how we look at paintings: 'We weep with the weeping, laugh with the laughing, and grieve with the grieving.'[4] Lucrece's response is exactly to seek out the 'face where all distress is stell'd' (l. 1444) as the analogue to her own grief.

This is not an act of simple empathy, but of judgment. As Lomazzo explains in his *Tract of Painting* (translated in 1598 by Richard Haydocke),

The picture mooveth the eye, and that committeth the species and formes of the things seene to the memory, all which it representeth to the understanding, which considereth of the truth and falshood of those things, which being perfectly understood it representeth them to the will, which if the thing be evill, it abandoneth and forsaketh, if good, it loveth, and naturally embraceth the same.[5]

Lucrece does not empathize equally with all the figures in the painting. She must penetrate

---

[1] 'He stopped and weeping cried: "What land, Achates, what tract on earth is now not full of our sorrow? Lo, Priam! Here, too, virtue has its due rewards; here, too, are tears for misfortune and mortal sorrows touch the heart".' *Aeneid* 1, 459–62.

[2] *Eikones*, 1, 4.

[3] Cf. Alpers, and Michael Baxandall, *Giotto and the Orators: Humanist Observers of Painting in Italy and the Discovery of Pictorial Composition, 1350–1450* (Oxford, 1971), pp. 85–96.

[4] *On Painting*, tr. John R. Spencer (New Haven, 1956), p. 77 and note. Cf. Horace, *Ars Poetica*, 101–3, and Cicero, *De Amicitia*, xiv, 50. Lomazzo, arguing the same point, quotes Horace in *A Tracte Containing the Artes of Curious Paintinge Caruinge & Buildinge*, tr. Richard Haydocke (1598), sig. Aa1^{r-v}.

[5] Lomazzo, sig. A2^v

the appearance of each to weigh properly the gullibility of Priam with the duplicity of Sinon. It is in looking at the painting, in examining by comparison the woes of Hecuba, that Lucrece is finally able to face the full diabolism of Tarquin and her own lack of responsibility for what has occurred. This is no easy lesson, for Hamlet needed supernatural prompting to discover that 'one may smile, and smile, and be a villain' (I, v, 108). In that moment of recognition, Lucrece reaches her fullest heroic stature.

I have claimed at this point that Lucrece bears no responsibility for what has happened. Why, then, does she kill herself? The reasoning for the final act returns us to Shakespeare's misogyny, for while Lucrece is not to blame, she is clearly guilty.[1] As Shakespeare says in l. 80, and Collatine and Lucretius in ll. 1709–10, her mind is pure though her body is soiled. Lucrece is dwelling with the most severe mind–body split conceivable, and only by suicide can she make this fully clear, so that others can read her as she has read the Troy tapestry, and revenge her, as she has sought to revenge Hecuba by tearing at Sinon with her nails.

For Lucrece has herself become an emblem, and she fears the interpretations which others may make of her. Immediately after her apostrophe to Night, she laments:

> 'Yea, the illiterate that know not how
> To cipher what is writ in learned books,
> Will quote my loathsome trespass in my looks.'
> (ll. 810–12)

She fears that she and Collatine have become an example of cuckoldry, 'And Tarquin's eye may read the mot afar' (l. 830), she adds in the technical language of devices. Yet the inability of others to interpret this way suggests that Lucrece at first misunderstands her own symbolism. When Lucrece's maid enters, she weeps at the sight of the face of her mistress

without knowing the reason. She has empathy without judgment. When the groom enters to receive the message to Collatine, he blushes from sheer nervousness, which Lucrece takes to mean that he has seen her shame.

The blushing servants, who are the first audience of the ravished Lucrece, are imperfect prototypes for her own response to Hecuba. Indeed, the maid's response, like that of Lucrece to the tapestry, is one of like to like. As Lucrece will be 'impressed' by the emotions of the tapestry, so the maid is 'impressed' by the countenance of her mistress:

> For men have marble, women waxen, minds,
> And therefore are they form'd as marble will;
> The weak oppress'd, th'impression of strange kinds
> Is form'd in them by force, by fraud, or skill.
> Then call them not the authors of their ill,
> No more than wax shall be accounted evil,
> Wherein is stamp'd the semblance of a devil.
> (ll. 1240–6)

'By force, by fraud, or skill': Tarquin, Sinon and the painter. The metaphor of wax has undergone an interesting displacement, beginning as an explanation of the behavior of the maid, but ending with what men do to women. Is it too much to speculate that the process of 'impressing' which is worked out in Lucrece's initial reaction to the Troy-piece can be a model for the rape itself: that is, that Tarquin, who is elsewhere called a devil, stamps his evil in the wax that is Lucrece?

Though Lucrece will desperately claim that 'I am the mistress of my fate' (l. 1069), she is

[1] Several of Shakespeare's heroines, especially in the comedies, are of course remarkable women, especially by comparison with those in the works of his contemporaries. I use the term 'misogyny' not to make a relative judgment about Shakespeare, but simply to refer to the portrayal of women as inferior to men in mental capacity and range of activity. For a fine analysis of the significance Shakespeare gives to the rape of a married woman in a patriarchal society, see Coppélia Kahn, 'The Rape in Shakespeare's *Lucrece*', *Shakespeare Studies*, IX (1976), 45–72.

at the outset pliant and without anything that might be called a free will. Isabella will say to Angelo in *Measure for Measure*:

> For we are soft as our complexions are,
> And credulous to false prints. (II, iv, 129–30)

Shakespeare indeed stresses the point in *Lucrece* by likening the moral condition of women to the beautiful but passive flower:

> No man inveigh against the withered flower,
> But chide rough winter that the flower hath kill'd;
> Not that devour'd, but that which doth devour
> Is worthy blame; O let it not be hild
> Poor women's faults, that they are so fulfill'd
>   With men's abuses! those proud lords to blame
> Make weak-made women tenants to their shame.
>   (ll. 1254–60)

Her inability to control her own body limits the actions of the heroic self which Lucrece defines while standing before the Troy-piece. Only at the end of the passage does she rise beyond external impressions to judge, define and act. And even then she is, paradoxically, Hecuba the sufferer, not Aeneas the rebuilder. In Hecuba,

>   the painter had anatomiz'd
> Time's ruin, beauty's wrack, and grim care's reign.
>   (ll. 1450–1)

Lucrece bears

> The face, that map which deep impression bears
> Of hard misfortune, carv'd in it with tears.
>   (ll. 1712–13)

The world crowds in on her, shaping her body and mind, while she has little scope to push back and control events. If she were a man, she could of course avenge herself. 'O God, that I were a man!' cries Beatrice in *Much Ado*, 'I would eat his heart in the market-place' (IV, i, 306–7). But they are women, and must employ men to wield their swords. The only women in Shakespeare's plays who successfully use weapons on stage are the villains: La Pucelle, Queen Margaret and Regan. There are no Jaels and no Judiths.

The only power left to Lucrece is in the realm of art. As audience, she can enter into the epic action of Troy. As artist, she can move her own audience by the vivid portrayal of the significance of her figures. Immediately after the rape, Lucrece was plagued with misreadings, seeing herself as Adultery, an image which her servants found unintelligible. After her confrontation with the Troy-piece, she is prepared to present herself as the image of woe and suffering, and to demand from Collatine and Lucretius the revenge she offered to Hecuba. Her suicide is nothing more or less than the *energeia*, or forcibleness, which gives the tableau its impact. It releases her blood, which separates into two rivers, one of pure red, the other black and foul. She shows what could not be seen, the inner self which signifies visually what all have insisted verbally:

> 'Though my gross blood be stain'd with this abuse,
> Immaculate and spotless is my mind.'
>   (ll. 1655–6)

The *ecphrasis* or detailed description of the blood is followed by *apostrophe*, in which Lucretius and Collatine each address Lucrece, pour out their sorrows, and proclaim their own impending deaths. Only Brutus seems fully to understand her meaning, and chides the others:

> 'Why Collatine, is woe the cure for woe?
> Do wounds help wounds, or grief help grievous
>   deeds?
> Is it revenge to give thyself a blow
> For his foul act by whom thy fair wife bleeds?
> Such childish humour from weak minds proceeds;
>   Thy wretched wife mistook the matter so,
>   To slay herself that should have slain her foe.'
>   (ll. 1821–7)

Is this really a condemnation of her suicide? I do not think so. What Brutus scorns is the mere empathy of answering woe with woe; he is calling for the men to perform the same vengeance on Tarquin which Lucrece herself sought to inflict on Sinon. He reprimands the men for considering suicide, calls them childish, and speaks of 'weak minds', much like the phrases Shakespeare has earlier used for all women. Her mistake, then, is that she is a woman, blocked from full heroic action in the public realm, condemned instead to constantly proving her sexual honor.

Brutus stands as a marker for the ultimate failure of Lucrece in heroic terms, but her success in artistic terms. We may compare him to that figure which Alberti recommended that the artist place at the margin of the picture:

In an *istoria* I like to see someone who admonishes and points out to us what is happening there; or beckons with his hand to see; or menaces with an angry face and with flashing eyes, so that no one should come near; or shows some danger or marvellous thing there; or invites us to weep or to laugh together with them.[1]

It is Brutus who directs the response of the audience to the story of Lucrece, pointing out to the Romans their proper course of action, and pointing out to Southampton the artistry of his servant Shakespeare.

[1] Alberti, p. 78.

PHILOMEL IN 'TITUS ANDRONICUS' AND 'CYMBELINE'

ANN THOMPSON

The dream's here still. Even when I wake it is
Without me, as within me; not imagin'd, felt.
A headless man? The garments of Posthumus?
I know the shape of's leg; this is his hand,
His foot Mercurial, his Martial thigh,
The brawns of Hercules; but his Jovial face –
Murder in heaven? How? 'Tis gone.

(IV, ii, 307–13)[1]

Thus Imogen, half way through what must be one of the most difficult speeches for an actress to deliver in the entire Shakespearian canon, described by Shaw as 'that nice Elizabethan morsel of the woman waking up in the arms of a headless corpse'.[2] The horror of the situation might be sufficient in itself to provide a challenge for most dramatists, but Shakespeare has chosen to complicate it further by giving Imogen a long and detailed speech, reminiscent not only of Hamlet's eulogy on his father but also of Thisbe's comic lamentations on discovering the body of Pyramus. This speech can have the effect of diminishing our sympathy for her, especially as her identification of the body by such precise details is in fact mistaken. Granville-Barker goes so far as to say that what Shakespeare is doing here is 'dramatically inexcusable';[3] certainly it must seem perverse and strange to most people bold enough to produce the play.

Yet the kind of awkwardness or even ineptitude we have here is strongly reminiscent of another 'impossible' moment in a much earlier Shakespearian play. The presence on stage of a sensationally mutilated human form, and the response to this in a long and seemingly overwritten speech, bringing the actor and audience close to embarrassment if not to downright laughter, is also a feature of act II, scene iv of *Titus Andronicus*, the scene in which Marcus discovers Lavinia, 'her hands cut off, and her tongue cut out and ravish'd' (stage direction). Although she is not dead, Lavinia can no more reply than Cloten can, which leaves Marcus to deliver a forty-seven-line monologue in which he describes the horrific details of her appearance and guesses at their cause. This link between a very early play and a very late one is at first surprising, and might be dismissed as coincidental, especially since *Cymbeline* is notoriously a ragbag of plot-fragments from many sources, including Shakespeare's own previous work, but there are other factors which tempt one to follow it up.

It is significant that both plays make specific reference to the story of Philomel, one of the most famous classical rape narratives. In the *Titus* scene under consideration Marcus recalls the literary precedent almost at once:

But sure, some Tereus hath deflowered thee,
And, lest thou should'st detect him, cut thy
    tongue . . .

[1] All Shakespeare quotations are from Peter Alexander ed., *William Shakespeare, The Complete Works* (1951).
[2] Edwin Wilson ed., *Shaw on Shakespeare* (Harmondsworth, 1969), p. 65.
[3] *Prefaces to Shakespeare, Second Series* (1930), p. 340.

He points out the difference between the two cases:

> Fair Philomel, why she but lost her tongue,
> And in a tedious sampler sew'd her mind;
> But lovely niece, that mean is cut from thee.
> A craftier Tereus, cousin, hast thou met,
> And he hath cut those pretty fingers off
> That could have better sew'd than Philomel.
>
> (II, iv, 26–7, 38–43)

As the Arden editor remarks in a footnote to this scene, 'The story of Tereus is constantly in Shakespeare's mind in *Titus*', and indeed the 'craftier Tereus' is ultimately Shakespeare himself who is outdoing Ovid in both the horror and the ingenuity of his narrative.[1] Even the moronic rapists, Chiron and Demetrius, point out how clever they are being when they taunt Lavinia after the deed:

> *Demetrius.*
> So, now go tell, and if thy tongue can speak,
> Who 'twas that cut thy tongue and ravish'd thee.
> *Chiron.*
> Write down thy mind, bewray thy meaning so,
> And if thy stumps will let thee play the scribe.
>
> (IV, iv, 1–4)

And when Titus later says to his daughter

> Had I but seen thy picture in this plight
> It would have madded me   (III, i, 103–4)

he is again recalling the comparatively better fortune of Philomel who was at least able to picture her plight in a tapestry. Finally, of course, Lavinia reveals the truth by pointing out the appropriate story in Ovid and confirms it by writing in the sand with a staff held in her mouth and guided by the stumps of her hands. *Cymbeline* does not contain such a closely derived plot, or such insistent reference to its source, but in the bedroom scene, at the moment of stealing Imogen's bracelet as 'simular proof' of the violation of her chastity, Iachimo goes to the trouble of telling us

> She hath been reading late
> The tale of Tereus; here the leaf's turned down
> Where Philomel gave up.   (II, ii, 44–6)

This scene then is a symbolic rape of Imogen's honour rather than a real one. She is not mutilated by the 'rapist'; rather it is her husband who later wishes 'O that I had her here to tear her limb-meal!' (II, ii, 147). And she echoes the theme herself when Pisanio tells her he has been ordered to kill her:

> Poor I am stale, a garment out of fashion,
> And for I am richer than to hang by th' walls
> I must be ripp'd. To pieces with me!
>
> (III, iv, 49–51)

'The lamb entreats the butcher', she exclaims (III, iv, 95), her willingness to die echoing that of Ovid's heroine:

> When Philomela sawe the sworde, she hoapt she should have dide,
> And for the same hir naked throte she gladly did provide.
>
> (*Metamorphoses* VI, 705–6, Golding's translation[2])

In the event, however, it is a man who finally suffers mutilation in this play, and that man is the second and more sinister rapist figure, Cloten.

Both *Titus Andronicus* and *Cymbeline* have a tendency to harp on the theme of mutilation once it has been raised. *Titus* does this very self-consciously and to an almost ridiculous extent, as when Titus makes the grimly literal pun to Aaron 'Lend me thy hand, and I will give thee mine' (III, i, 188) or when he later implores his brother

> O, handle not the theme, to talk of hands,
> Lest we remember still that we have none.
>
> (III, ii, 29–30)

The references in *Cymbeline* are less obtrusive, but act IV scene ii contains far more references to beheading than are strictly required by the plot (culminating in the line 'I have sent

---

[1] For a discussion of the wittiness and ingenuity of the play, see Albert H. Tricomi, 'The Aesthetics of Mutilation in *Titus Andronicus*', *Shakespeare Survey 27* (Cambridge, 1974), pp. 11–19.

[2] Edited by John Frederick Nims (New York, 1965).

Cloten's clotpoll down the stream' which directly recalls the heavy punning of *Titus*) and there are at least a dozen other references to the mutilation of the human body scattered through the rest of the play. Beheading as a form of mutilation is particularly important in the second sensational climax in the original Philomel story, where the heroine and her sister take their revenge upon Tereus by killing and dismembering his son Itys, cooking the pieces and serving them up to his father in a banquet. It is not until he asks for Itys (having eaten him) that the plot is revealed:

> To put him out of dout,
> As he was yet demaunding where, and calling for
>   him: out
> Lept Philomele with scattred haire aflaight like
>   one that fled
> Had from some fray where slaughter was, and
>   threw the bloudy head
> Of Itys in his fathers face.   (Ovid, VI, 830–4)

This episode is clearly more directly relevant to *Titus* than it is to *Cymbeline*, but the combination of rape with mutilation (and in particular beheading) is what makes the Philomel story appropriate to both plays, rather than the story of Lucrece which is the other famous rape narrative in the classical repertoire.[1] In that story the assault on the heroine's integrity through rape is defied or nullified, symbolically at least, by her suicide: she asserts her integrity by a complete and willed destruction of her violated body. But the story of Lucrece, as Shakespeare would have noticed when writing his poem on the subject, is a singularly claustrophobic one, with little scope for interest outside the central character and her horrific experience. The mutilation theme of the Philomel story, however unpleasant in itself, gave Shakespeare the opportunity to bring in other areas of experience, especially in *Cymbeline*, where it is not just individuals who are threatened with dismemberment but families, countries, and even the Roman empire. This

wider application of the theme seems more important for both plays than the obvious interpretation along Freudian lines which would assume that a stress on mutilation indicates at some level a fear of castration.

Shakespeare's use of the Philomel-influenced rape plot is remarkably consistent in the two plays. In *Titus Andronicus* he is depending largely on an elaboration of Ovid with some help from Seneca.[2] In *Cymbeline* he seems to be relying fairly directly on his own earlier work in *Titus*, for the relevant part of the plot is worked through in a very similar pattern. In both plays we have the same 'family' grouping: (1) a powerful mother-figure who is presented as a wicked schemer, having married the ruler for power rather than love, (2) her son (two of him in *Titus*), oafish and ludicrous, but frightening because of his powerful position in the state, and (3) the victim, a woman who has gained the hostility of the mother, even though the latter has been successful in ousting her from a position of favour with the ruler.[3] The rape plot itself is closely comparable. Both victims are married (unlike the original Philomel) and the plan is to kill the husband in the woman's sight before raping her. Chiron and Demetrius duly kill Bassianus and declare their intention to

> Drag hence her husband to some secret hole,
> And make his dead trunk pillow to our lust.
>   (II, iii, 129–30)

The mutilation of Lavinia is not mentioned at this point, though Aaron has already said of Bassianus 'His Philomel must lose her tongue to-day' (II, iii, 43), and it follows very quickly. Cloten plans a similar deed:

[1] Lucrece is however mentioned in both plays: *Titus*, II, i, 108, IV, i, 65 and 92; *Cymbeline*, II, ii, 12.

[2] See the Introduction to J. C. Maxwell's New Arden edition (1953), pp. xxxi–xxxii.

[3] It is worth noticing that this *precise* pattern does not occur in any of the usual sources given for *Cymbeline*, such as Holinshed, Boccaccio, *Frederyke of Jennen* and *The Rare Triumphs of Love and Fortune*.

With that suit upon my back will I ravish her; first kill
him, and in her eyes . . . He on the ground, my speech
of insultment ended on his dead body, and when my
lust hath dined – which, as I say, to vex her I will
execute in the clothes that she so prais'd – to the court
I'll knock her back, foot her home again.

(III, v, 140–5)

He plans a violent mutilation against the
husband ('Posthumus, thy head, which is now
growing upon thy shoulders, shall within this
hour be off' (IV, i, 19)), but his 'rough usage'
of Imogen can hardly extend so far since he
cannot expect Cymbeline to overlook the
murder of his own daughter.

In *Titus Andronicus*, the rape and mutilation
of Lavinia comprises an extremely forceful
episode in the piling up of woes for the
Andronici, but when Eugene M. Waith
describes it as 'the central symbol of disorder,
both moral and political',[1] I think he must
mean a symbol which is powerful and representative in itself rather than one which Shakespeare has deliberately turned into the linguistic
or thematic centre of the play. One might say
that justice has been raped in the play, or even
that the Roman political system has been raped,
but Shakespeare does not actually make these
metaphoric connections. Compared with the
English History plays or the other Roman plays,
Titus is much more of a family drama, less of a
political one. There are really remarkably few
images of Rome as a 'body politic' given the
obsession with parts of the body elsewhere in
the play. Right at the beginning Marcus asks
Titus to 'help to set a head on headless Rome'
(I, i, 186), and he comes back to this theme at
the end when he says to the people

> O, let me teach you how to knit again
> This scattered corn into one mutual sheaf,
> These broken limbs again into one body.

(V, iii, 70–2)

He also speaks of Rome's 'civil wound' in the
same speech, and Lucius speaks of his intention

to 'heal Rome's harms', but these few metaphors could hardly be said to add up to a
powerful pattern linking the political situation
to the rape of Lavinia. Through the middle part
of the play the image of Rome as 'a wilderness
of tigers' seems more important; this is still an
image of disorder, but a rather different one,
implying the overthrow of civilisation by
barbarity rather than a more intimate threat to
the body of the state.

Titus is of course a very early play, and it
may be argued that the linking of different
plots, themes and areas of interest in a play
through the use of figurative language is a skill
Shakespeare develops later. There are many
examples of this, but one could take as representative the way the language of commerce
and evaluation links the two 'worlds' of
Venice and Belmont in *The Merchant of
Venice*. I believe that the use of the theme of
rape and mutilation associated with the
Philomel story is in fact much more pervasive
and central in *Cymbeline* than it is in *Titus*, that
here Shakespeare uses metaphoric language in
such a way as to relate the threat to Imogen's
integrity through rape to the various threats
to those larger 'wholes', the family and the
state.

He had often in earlier plays used metaphors
from the human body to express the condition
of family or state. There are countless examples
in the History plays, and in *Hamlet* and *Troilus
and Cressida*, of the state being described as
diseased or sick – a metaphor so common one
almost forgets that it is one. More directly
relevant to the present discussion are metaphors
in which the state (or royal family) is seen as a
body wounded, dislocated or in some way

[1] 'The Metamorphosis of Violence in *Titus
Andronicus*', *Shakespeare Survey 10* (Cambridge,
1957), p. 44. Waith goes on to claim a connection
between political and moral disorder through the
play's references to Tarquin, once as ravisher (IV, i, 64)
and once as exiled king (III, i, 299).

mutilated. Such images occur in *King John* and in *Julius Caesar*, where the hacked and bleeding body of Caesar is more than once identified with that of the state.[1] Another important play in this context is *Coriolanus*, where we find Shakespeare's most explicit statement of the 'body politic' theme in Menenius's fable of the belly, which might seem to be the positive side of the case, but in context is so simplistic as to provoke considerable scepticism.[2] Alongside this implied criticism of an oversimplified view of unity in the state, Shakespeare appropriately sets the tragedy of Caius Marcius, the man whose oversimplified view of integrity in the individual leads him to inevitable disaster.

The threat to the integrity of the individual and the state is often reinforced, particularly in the History plays, with images drawn from the natural world, particularly images of trees and plants. Caroline Spurgeon has described the image of the 'deterioration, decay and destruction' of a garden or orchard as 'the most constant running metaphor or picture' in the History plays from *1 Henry VI* to *Richard II*.[3] The picture is a complex one, but the point I would like to focus on is the cutting or lopping of trees. In *3 Henry VI* Richard says that Clifford was

> not contented that he lopp'd the branch
> In hewing Rutland when his leaves put forth,
> But set his murd'ring knife unto the root
> From whence that tender spray did sweetly spring.
> (II, vi, 47–50)

And Warwick describes his own death, 'Thus yields the cedar to the axe's edge' (v, ii, 11). These images continue through *Richard III* and *Richard II* with the rival royal houses constantly seen as trees which are planted, grafted, lopped or felled.

Returning to *Titus Andronicus* and *Cymbeline*, we find that both plays use the image of the human body as a tree, but that in *Cymbeline*

it is more fully integrated into the play's wider thematic concerns. In *Titus* it occurs when Marcus asks the mutilated Lavinia

> what stern ungentle hands
> Hath lopp'd and hew'd and made thy body bare
> Of her two branches? (II, iv, 16)

But the image is related specifically neither to the destruction of the family of the Andronici as it proceeds nor to the threat to the state itself. The nearest we come to it later in the play is Marcus's desire 'to knit again / This scattered corn into one mutual sheaf' (v, iii, 70–1) which is not very close.

In *Cymbeline*, on the other hand, the tree-imagery is much more pervasive, and has indeed been used by G. Wilson Knight to prove the authenticity of the vision,[4] during which appears the tablet saying

> when from a stately cedar shall be lopp'd branches which, being dead many years, shall after revive, be jointed to the old stock, and freshly grow; then shall Posthumus end his miseries, Britain be fortunate and flourish in peace and plenty. (v, iv, 141–3)

As the soothsayer later explains, these 'lopp'd branches' are (as anyone who knew the *Henry VI* plays might have guessed) the King's sons, joyfully restored to him at the end of the play. Moreover, the tree image is also used to express the reunion of Imogen and Posthumus:

> Hang there like fruit, my soul,
> Till the tree die. (v, v, 263–4)

These images of the living and miraculously whole tree contrast with earlier moments in the play when the human body has been seen as a

---

[1] *King John*, v, ii, 152, v, vii, 112; *Julius Caesar*, particularly II, ii, 76ff. (Calphurnia's dream).

[2] See Andrew Gurr, '*Coriolanus* and the Body Politic', *Shakespeare Survey 28* (Cambridge, 1975), pp. 63–9, for an interesting discussion of this theme.

[3] *Shakespeare's Imagery* (Cambridge, 1935), p. 216.

[4] *The Crown of Life* (Oxford, 1947), p. 197.

tree threatened with destruction, as in Belarius's description of himself in earlier days:

> Then was I as a tree
> Whose boughs did bend with fruit; but in one
>   night
> A storm, or robbery, call it what you will,
> Shook down my mellow hangings, nay, my leaves,
> And left me bare to weather.
>
> (III, iii, 60–4)

Or Imogen's description of how her parting with Posthumus was interrupted:

> . . . comes in my father,
> And like the tyrannous breathing of the north,
> Shakes all our buds from growing.   (I, iii, 35–7)

Twice when heads are threatened they are described as 'growing' out of bodies (IV, i, 19; IV, ii, 123), a metaphor which is more fully realised when Lucius, seeing the headless body of Cloten, asks Imogen 'what trunk is here / Without his top?' (IV, ii, 354–5).

The direct 'body politic' metaphor also occurs towards the end of the play. Before Cymbeline knows that Guiderius and Arviragus are his sons he has described them, with their supposed father Belarius, as 'the liver, heart and brain of Britain, / By whom I grant she lives' (v, v, 14–15), confirming that they are as crucial to the restoration of integrity to the state as they are to that of the family. Pursuing this line further, the play finally re-establishes the harmonious relationship between Britain and Rome which has also been mutilated in the course of the action. This ending seems surprising in the light of the nationalistic speeches in act III, scene i, but it is the appropriate climax to the theme of integrity threatened and restored.

An important image at the end of the play is that of birth. Cymbeline reacts to the many reunions by crying

> O what am I?
> A mother to the birth of three? Ne'er mother
> Rejoic'd deliverance more.   (v, v, 368–70)

And shortly before this we have been reminded of the peculiar birth of Posthumus: in the vision his mother says

> Lucina lent me not her aid,
> But took me in my throes,
> That from me was Posthumus ripp'd
> Came crying 'mongst his foes,
> A thing of pity.   (v, iv, 43–7)

Birth can be seen as precisely the comic conclusion to some of these themes – a 'rape' which has a happy outcome and a threat to the integrity of the mother's body involving a kind of mutilation of its wholeness which results in the miraculous creation of a new being, whole in itself and adding richness and complexity to the wholeness of its parents. The rebirth theme is common in Shakespeare's final plays, as for example in Pericles's line to Marina 'Thou that begett'st him that did thee beget' (v, i, 194), but it is especially satisfying and appropriate as the climax of this particular set of themes and images.

Thus we have in Shakespeare's use of the Philomel myth a good example of the way his dramatic skills developed over time. The symbolic power of the raped and mutilated heroine as a political image as well as a moral one is present in *Titus Andronicus* but only in a latent form, whereas by the time Shakespeare came to rework the same narrative episode in *Cymbeline*, he was able to use it in combination with a wide range of associated images – not just the body politic but the natural world of the cedar tree and the miraculous world of rebirth – to provide a coherent centre for more than one strand of this unusually complicated play.

Having considered the influence of the Philomel theme in a very general sense, I shall now return to the level of specific detail by examining further the two 'impossible' speeches from which I began, paying particular attention to the influence of Ovidian narrative on their composition. Both plays are remarkable for the sheer number and range of their classical allusions: Douglas Bush has recorded that '*Titus Andronicus* carries as heavy a weight of mythology as of horrors',[1] and G. Wilson Knight has said '*Cymbeline* . . . probably exceeds any other Shakespearian play in its fecundity of classical, and especially mythological reference'.[2] The plays are alike too in that their method of using classical allusions seems to be of a narrative rather than a dramatic cast: both have strong links with Shakespeare's narrative poems,[3] and even the more melodramatic parts of the plot of *Titus Andronicus* are closer to Ovid than to Seneca. What this means in terms of the individual speeches cannot be demonstrated without quoting them in full.

On meeting the raped and mutilated Lavinia, her uncle Marcus says:

> Who is this? – my niece, that flies away so fast?
> Cousin, a word: where is your husband?
> If I do dream, would all my wealth would wake me!
> If I do wake, some planet strike me down,
> That I may slumber an eternal sleep!
> Speak, gentle niece. What stern ungentle hands
> Hath lopp'd, and hew'd, and made thy body bare
> Of her two branches – those sweet ornaments
> Whose circling shadows kings have sought to sleep in,
> And might not gain so great a happiness
> As half thy love? Why dost not speak to me?
> Alas, a crimson river of warm blood,
> Like to a bubbling fountain stirr'd with wind,
> Doth rise and fall between thy rosed lips,
> Coming and going with thy honey breath.
> But sure some Tereus hath deflowered thee,
> And, lest thou shouldst detect him, cut thy tongue.
> Ah, now thou turn'st away thy face for shame!
> And notwithstanding all this loss of blood –
> As from a conduit with three issuing spouts –
> Yet do thy cheeks look red as Titan's face
> Blushing to be encount'red with a cloud.
> Shall I speak for thee? Shall I say 'tis so?
> O, that I knew thy heart, and knew the beast,
> That I might rail at him to ease my mind!
> Sorrow concealed, like an oven stopp'd,

> Doth burn the heart to cinders where it is.
> Fair Philomel, why she but lost her tongue,
> And in a tedious sampler sew'd her mind;
> But, lovely niece, that mean is cut from thee.
> A craftier Tereus, cousin, hast thou met,
> And he hath cut those pretty fingers off
> That could have better sew'd than Philomel.
> O, had the monster seen those lily hands
> Tremble like aspen leaves upon a lute
> And make the silken strings delight to kiss them,
> He would not then have touch'd them for his life!
> Or had he heard the heavenly harmony
> Which that sweet tongue hath made,
> He would have dropp'd his knife, and fell asleep,
> As Cerebus at the Thracian poet's feet.
> Come, let us go, and make thy father blind,
> For such a sight will blind a father's eye;
> One hour's storm will drown the fragrant meads,
> What will whole months of tears thy father's eyes?
> Do not draw back, for we will mourn with thee;
> O, could our mourning ease thy misery!
>
> (II, iv, 11–57)

It is some years since Eugene M. Waith said that this 'has proved to be the most unpalatable passage in the play' in terms of naturalism or psychological appropriateness. He pinpointed the oddity of the fanciful images: 'They oblige us to see clearly a suffering body, yet as they do so they temporarily remove its individuality, even its humanity, by abstracting and generalizing.'[4] The whole passage seems more suitable to narrative than to drama, a point

[1] 'Classical Myth in Shakespeare's Plays' in H. Davis and H. Gardner eds., *Elizabethan and Jacobean Studies Presented to F. P. Wilson* (Oxford, 1959), pp. 65–85 (p. 71).

[2] *The Crown of Life* (Oxford, 1947), p. 183. By my own count there are around fifty mythological references in *Titus Andronicus* and around thirty-five in *Cymbeline*, excluding purely historical references (such as those to Caesar) in both cases.

[3] For *Titus*, see M. C. Bradbrook, *Shakespeare and Elizabethan Poetry* (1951), pp. 96–101. For *Cymbeline*, see the Introduction to James Nosworthy's New Arden edition (1955), pp. lxvii–lxxi.

[4] 'The Metamorphosis of Violence in *Titus Andronicus*', *Shakespeare Survey 10* (Cambridge, 1957), p. 47.

also made by M. C. Bradbrook, who found that the formal quality of the writing in this and other speeches had the effect of distancing the atrocities described.[1] Building on such views, Albert H. Tricomi has more recently claimed that Shakespeare is here deliberately exploring the relationship between metaphor and actuality, 'the manner in which figurative speech can diminish and even transform the actual horror of events'. For him, the effect is not always to distance the horror: 'the play deliberately "exposes" the euphemisms of metaphor by measuring their falseness against the irrefutable realities of dramatized events'.[2]

I agree that the manner of writing in a speech like the one in II, iv has a heightening effect rather than a reductive one: just because it is not naturalistic it need not reduce the rape to what Bradbrook calls 'mere moral heraldry'. I find an important clue in Marcus's words near the beginning, 'If I do dream, would all my wealth would wake me!' The effect is indeed dream-like, both in the sense that the experience itself is nightmarish (Titus is later to say 'When will this fearful slumber have an end?' (III, i, 252)), and in the frightening sense that Marcus (representing the family of the Andronici in general) is at the moment quite impotent in the face of events: he can do nothing except observe the appalling narrative which is happening around him. In this respect narrative can be more horrific than drama. The use of dramatic time here also serves to emphasise the dream-like effect. The long speech represents a strange slowing down of event and response so that we are forced to concentrate on the horror of what has happened at greater length and in more detail than if Marcus had reacted 'naturally' with a brief cry of horror and a rush offstage for help.[3] This dramatic device is one Shakespeare often uses when he wants to slow the action down to concentrate on a particular moment longer than anyone would in real life. An obvious, though very different,

example might be the passage in *Twelfth Night*, v, i, where the prolonged exchange between the reunited Viola and Sebastian is quite unnecessary in terms of the action, but vital for conveying the sense of wonder and joy at proper length.

Imogen's speech in *Cymbeline*, IV, ii also has the effect of slowing down a natural re-action so that the full meaning of the situation is allowed to filter through gradually. Awakening from her drug-induced sleep beside the headless body of Cloten dressed in her husband's clothes, she says

Yes sir, to Milford Haven. Which is the way?
I thank you. By yond bush? Pray, how far thither?
'Ods pittikins! can it be six mile yet?
I have gone all night. Faith, I'll lie down and sleep.
But, soft! no bedfellow. O gods and goddesses!
These flow'rs are like the pleasures of the world;
This bloody man, the care on't. I hope I dream;
For so I thought I was a cave-keeper,
And cook to honest creatures. But 'tis not so;
'Twas but a bolt of nothing, shot at nothing,
Which the brain makes of fumes. Our very eyes
Are sometimes, like our judgments, blind. Good faith,
I tremble still with fear; but if there be
Yet left in heaven as small a drop of pity
As a wren's eye, fear'd gods, a part of it!
The dream's here still. Even when I wake it is
Without me, as within me; not imagin'd, felt.
A headless man? The garments of Posthumus?
I know the shape of's leg; this is his hand,
His foot Mercurial, his Martial thigh,
The brawns of Hercules; but his Jovial face –
Murder in heaven! How! 'Tis gone. Pisanio,
All curses madded Hecuba gave the Greeks,
And mine to boot, be darted on thee! Thou,
Conspir'd with that irregulous devil, Cloten,

[1] See above, p. 29, note 3.
[2] 'The Aesthetics of Mutilation in *Titus Andronicus*', *Shakespeare Survey 27* (Cambridge, 1974), p. 13.
[3] Curiously, a recent Japanese film, *Pandemonium* by Toshio Matsumoto, achieves a similar effect by presenting all its savage death scenes in slow motion, thus intensifying the horror to an almost unbearable degree although the movements of the swordsmen are seen as balletic and beautiful.

Hath here cut off my lord. To write and read
Be henceforth treacherous! Damn'd Pisanio
Hath with his forged letters – damn'd Pisanio –
From this most bravest vessel of the world
Struck the main-top. O Posthumus! alas,
Where is thy head? Where's that? Ay me! where's that?
Pisanio might have kill'd thee at the heart,
And left this head on. How should this be? Pisanio?
'Tis he and Cloten; malice and lucre in them
Have laid this woe here. O, 'tis pregnant, pregnant!
The drug he gave me, which he said was precious
And cordial to me, have I not found it
Murd'rous to th' senses? That confirms it home.
This is Pisanio's deed, and Cloten. O!
Give colour to my pale cheek with thy blood,
That we the horrider may seem to those
Which chance to find us. O, my lord, my lord!

(IV, ii, 292–333)

Again there is the suggestion of dreaming but it is more paradoxical since Imogen dismisses her recent encounter with the cave-dwellers as a dream but accepts the body of 'Posthumus' as a reality with the words 'The dream's here still'. Shakespeare is evidently playing a more complex game with perceptions of reality in this play.[1] The speech itself is much more fragmented than the one in *Titus*, which is quite a 'finished' piece of writing, almost a 'purple passage' suitable for anthologising. Imogen's speech cannot be separated from the play. It is more exclamatory and confused (and to that extent more naturalistic) but the elements of which it is composed are equally strange. Instead of the high-flown formal lyricism of the *Titus* speech we find a sort of preciousness from the opening 'Od's pittikins' (not an oath Hotspur could have approved) to the over-elaborate description of the decapitated body. Imogen sees her own experiences in fairy-tale terms ('For so I thought I was a cave-keeper, / And cook to honest creatures'), and evokes a pretty pathos –

> but if there be
> Yet left in heaven as small a drop of pity
> As a wren's eye, fear'd gods, a part of it!
>
> (ll. 305–7)

Again we might feel that the language is overwrought, though in this case our knowledge that the body is *not* that of Imogen's husband helps us to accept what might otherwise seem a strange response.[2] Instead of going into arabesques of lyrical description like Marcus, Imogen flounders amongst a set of misconceived accusations and explanations taking her ever further from the audience's knowledge of the true situation. The influence of Ovidian narrative is again apparent in the leisurely pace and elaborate, even decorative detail of the speech, reminding us within the play of the 'irrelevant' lyrical beauty of Iachimo's speech in Imogen's bed-chamber (II, ii, 11–51) and his subsequent description of that room to Posthumus in II, iv.

The detailed recognition of the body by 'foot Mercurial and Martial thigh', etc., is not however a mere redundant piling up of mythological references but is important thematically, since Imogen is here repeating the experience of many people in the play of mistaking the outer for the inner man, the part for the whole. She herself has been the victim of this sort of literal synecdoche (another kind of dismemberment) in so far as Posthumus has mistaken significant 'parts' of his wife (her bracelet, the mole under her breast) for the whole. In this context the traditional use of the mole and the 'curious mantle' to identify Arviragus and Guiderius at the end of the play is another precise comic reversal.

Also the speech reveals more about Imogen's character and situation than anything Shake-

---

[1] The complications of this game are precisely and enthusiastically described by Bertrand Evans in *Shakespeare's Comedies* (Oxford, 1960), pp. 245–89. He finds this particular sequence the most ambitious in the whole canon in its exploitation of discrepant awarenesses.

[2] Not everyone would agree with this view; James Nosworthy argues that this speech is 'the finest thing in the play' in his Introduction to the New Arden edition (1955), p. lxv.

speare attempts in the *Titus* speech. After being presented as a spirited and independent woman both in words (her defiance of Iachimo and Cloten) and deeds (her clandestine marriage and her flight from the court), Imogen collapses surprisingly in the second half of the play. Her male disguise has reduced rather than increased her courage, and this speech seems to express her general confusion and inadequacy in her present situation. It is only by an heroic effort that she can invent an explanation for Lucius. She has of course suffered a considerable shock. In terms of Shakespeare's previous heroines, she has begun as Rosalind, fleeing from court to find her lover in the wilderness, turned into Desdemona, the innocent victim of a jealous husband, and has just woken as Juliet beside her husband's corpse. Her collapse may well be excusable. One significant effect of the collapse is that it makes Imogen very like Posthumus, who is also confused and aimless in this part of the play. While Imogen invents her role as the page of Sir Richard du Champ on the spur of the moment to carry her through the next stage, Posthumus changes sides (and clothes) in his attempt to find death in the final battle. What seems to be implied is that each suffers an inner collapse and loss of identity without the other – an effect which Shakespeare does not attempt elsewhere and which makes the reunion at the end more important and moving.

Thus we again find significant differences between *Titus* and *Cymbeline*. While the speeches are alike in self-consciously exploiting the bizarre effects of using narrative techniques in a dramatic context, the *Cymbeline* speech is more closely related to the rest of the play: its fragmented and confused nature takes us back to the general concern with dislocation and dismemberment. It seems less of an embarrassing set-piece, more a daring but appropriate climax. The fact that the two plays are conceived in different genres seems an important factor in the contrasts I have pointed out between them. Shakespeare must have felt, or come to feel, that the story of Philomel was intrinsically narrative rather than dramatic material: if staged it would not work as straight tragedy but only as the rather peculiar kind of melodrama we find in *Titus Andronicus*, or better still, especially as it fitted in with his growing interest in a kind of romantic pathos, as tragi-comedy. Its main drawback as dramatic tragedy is of course the passive and inevitably silent role of the heroine, which made it necessary for the Lavinia story in *Titus* to be only one thread in a complicated plot. The extent to which Shakespeare modified the story in *Cymbeline* made it possible for him to overcome this difficulty while retaining the symbolic power of the myth.

© ANN THOMPSON 1978

APULEIUS AND THE BRADLEIAN TRAGEDIES

JOHN J. M. TOBIN

Apuleius of Madaura, the rhetorician and neo-Platonic philosopher of the second century A.D., had a reputation in the Renaissance sufficiently great to have the Humanists, Vives and Erasmus, urge the study of his works for their logic and matter.[1] Many poets and dramatists of the Elizabethan period, including Chapman, Dekker, Thomas Heywood, Jonson, Marlowe, and Spenser,[2] did read the one work of Apuleius which we still enjoy today, the *Metamorphoses*, a comic novel of bestial transformation ending in a religious conversion. The work was translated as *The Golden Asse* by William Adlington in 1566 and proved so popular that it went through four more editions before the end of the sixteenth century.[3] In 1582 Gosson included the novel among those works which the dramatists were ransacking 'to furnish the Playe houses in London'.[4]

Shakespeare himself knew *The Golden Asse* and drew upon it for turns of plot and elements of characterization. It has been suggested many times that Shakespeare in *A Midsummer Night's Dream* derived the asinine transformation of Bottom from Lucius's predicament in *The Golden Asse*,[5] and Michael Lloyd has demonstrated Shakespeare's use of the novel in *Antony and Cleopatra*, particularly in terms of Cleopatra as Isis.[6]

There are several quite understandable reasons for Shakespeare's using the work beyond the fact of its popularity among his contemporaries and rivals. The work is part romance and part Milesian Tale, that is, 'a mannered story of bizarre adventure or sexual encounter'.[7] Apuleius varied his narrative

[1] See T. W. Baldwin, *William Shakspere's Small Latine and Lesse Greeke* (Urbana, 1944), I, 190; II, 26, 185, 247.

[2] See Joel H. Kaplan, 'Apuleius as a Chapman Source', *Notes & Queries*, CCXX (1975), 252; W. L. Halstead, 'Dekker's *Cupid and Psyche* and Thomas Heywood', *English Literary History*, XI (1944), 182–91; D. T. Starnes, 'Shakespeare and Apuleius', *PMLA*, LX (1945), 1,021; L. C. Martin, *Marlowe's Poems* (1931), pp. 34–5.

[3] 1566, 1571, 1582, 1596, 1600.

[4] Quoted in the very appropriate epigraph with which Professor Geoffrey Bullough begins his most valuable *Narrative and Dramatic Sources of Shakespeare* (1957), I, v.

[5] The connection between *A Midsummer Night's Dream* and Apuleius has been developed at length by Sister M. Generosa, 'Apuleius and *A Midsummer Night's Dream*: Analogue or Source, Which?', *Studies in Philology*, XLII (1945), 198–204, by D. T. Starnes in his valuable pioneering article cited above, and by James A. S. McPeek, 'The Psyche Myth and *A Midsummer Night's Dream*', *Shakespeare Quarterly*, XXIII (1972), 69–79. Starnes also argues with differing degrees of cogency for Apuleian influence upon *Venus and Adonis*, *The Comedy of Errors*, *The Two Gentlemen of Verona*, *Macbeth* (picking up a suggestion of Douce regarding the witches), *Antony and Cleopatra*, *Cymbeline*, *The Winter's Tale*, and *The Tempest*. See the appraisal of Starnes's article by John W. Velz in his excellent *Shakespeare and the Classical Tradition* (Minneapolis, 1968), p. 107.

[6] Michael Lloyd, 'Cleopatra as Isis', *Shakespeare Survey 12* (Cambridge, 1959), pp. 88–94.

[7] P. G. Walsh, *The Roman Novel* (Cambridge, 1970), p. 15. This is the best book I have seen for an understanding of the themes and structure of the *Metamorphoses*.

with a number of anecdotes and episodes dealing with witches, unfaithful wives, murder, revenge, frustrated lust, and magical practices, all within a fable whose central theme is the punishment, suffering and ultimate reformation of a man too curious for his own good. And as if these narrative treasures were not enough to capture the eye of a dramatist who was habitually moved to make use of narrative sources, there is within the novel the beautiful fairy-tale of Cupid and Psyche. I suggest that *The Golden Asse* was a favorite text of Shakespeare, one of those works like Plutarch's *Lives* and Holinshed's *Chronicles* to which he continually returned, and that his familiarity with it is evident not only in *A Midsummer Night's Dream*, *Antony and Cleopatra*, and *Much Ado About Nothing*,[1] but also from elements of theme, plot, and diction present in the four central or Bradleian tragedies.

That Shakespeare should have recalled *The Golden Asse* when he was composing *Hamlet* is not surprising when one considers the number of episodes in the novel which parallel events in the tragedy: the murder of a husband by poison in the interest of adultery (Book 2), a widow warned by the ghost of her husband to abstain from sexual intercourse with his murderous would-be successor and that widow's calculated concern with the unseemliness of too hasty a remarriage (Book 8), and parricide, adultery, and sexual tension between a stepson and stepmother in a bedchamber interview together with the attempted murder of the stepson by a poisoned drink mistakenly quaffed by another (Book 10). The near certainty that Shakespeare had Apuleius in mind during the writing of *Hamlet* is evidenced by the presence of words and phrases in this tragedy which are unique in the canon, but which occur in Adlington, often in contexts analogous to those of the play. Among these terms are 'fishmonger' (II, ii, 174, 189), 'fardels' (III, i, 75), and 'baker's daughter' (IV, v, 43).[2]

The usual gloss on 'fishmonger' is 'bawd' or 'pimp', but to quote the most recent edition of the works: 'no evidence has been produced for such a usage in Shakespeare's day'.[3] I suggest that the term is used by Shakespeare not in any sense of sexual corruption, though by extension that can be read into the term, but rather in the sense of absolute dishonesty, dishonesty which Shakespeare would have recalled from the example of the corrupt fishmonger of Book 1 of *The Golden Asse*, the seventh chapter: 'How Apuleius, going to buy fish, met with his companion Pythias':

But Pithias when hee espied my basket wherein my fish was, tooke it and shaked it, and demanded of me what I payd for all my Sprots. In faith (quoth I) I could scarse inforce the *fishmonger* to sell them for twenty pence. Which when he heard, he brought me backe again into the market, and enquired of me of whom I bought them, I shewed him the old man which sate in a corner, whome by and by, by reason of his office hee did greatly blame, and sayd, Is it thus that you serve and handle strangers, and specially our friends? Wherefore sell you this fish so *deare, which is not worth a halfepenny?* Now perceive I well, that you are an occasion to make this place, which is the principall city of all Thessaly, to be forsaken of all men, and to reduce it into an unhabitable Desart, by reason of your excessive prices of victuals, but assure your selfe that you shall not escape without punishment, and you shall know what myne office is, and how I ought to punish such as offend.[4]

Like the fishmonger Polonius is an old man and like him he is dishonest. And like the fishmonger Polonius is punished for his deception. It is of supporting interest to note that just after Polonius has left the stage, Hamlet addresses Rosencrantz and Guildenstern with

[1] For *Much Ado*, see my 'On the Asininity of Dogberry', *English Studies*, XLIX (1978), 199–201.

[2] All quotations are from *The Riverside Shakespeare*, ed. G. Blakemore Evans *et al.* (Boston, 1974).

[3] *Riverside Shakespeare*, p. 1,154.

[4] Throughout I have used Adlington's translation as it appears in *The Tudor Translations*, ed. W. E. Henley (1893), vol. IV.

'dear friends, my thanks are too *dear a half-penny*' (II, ii, 273–4), partially echoing Pythias's indictment of the old fish seller.

'Fardels' occurs in the midst of Hamlet's most celebrated soliloquy and nowhere else in Shakespeare's works:[1]

> The insolence of office, and the spurns
> That patient merit of the unworthy takes
> When he himself might his quietus make
> With a bare bodkin; who would *fardels* bear.
>   (III, i, 72–5)

The dramatist seems to have recalled the tribulations of Lucius, the ass, in Book 7 of the novel and had allowed the prince to identify himself in his frustration as an 'ass' (II, ii, 582). Lucius was mistaken in the hope that he would be freed of his burdens:

> then he that had in charge to keepe the horse, was called for, and I was delivered unto him with great care, insomuch that I was right pleasant and joyous, because I hoped that I should carry no more *fardels* nor burthens.   (p. 146)

The likelihood that Shakespeare had the prince recalling the unfair burdens of Lucius is increased when one notices that 'the insolence of office', another abuse cited by Hamlet three lines earlier, is paralleled in Book 2 of *The Golden Asse*:

> To whom he answered, Madam you in the *office* of your bounty shall prevaile heerin, but *the insolencie* of some is not to be supported.   (pp. 53–4)

Hamlet concludes his most famous soliloquy when he sees Ophelia:

> Soft you now,
> The fair Ophelia. *Nymph*, in thy *orisons*
> Be all my sins rememb'red.   (III, i, 87–9)

In *The Golden Asse* Venus is offered an 'orison' by Psyche (p. 121) who is thought to be one of the 'Nymphs' (p. 116). Ophelia's general passivity and vulnerability, her social inequality in comparison with Hamlet, her possible future pregnancy as feared by her father, and her suicide by drowning seem to be modelled on the passive Psyche's mortality in the face of Cupid's immortality, her actual pregnancy, and her attempted drowning.[2]

In her later distraction Ophelia speaks some quite puzzling lines. One of her most puzzling occurs in her exchange with the king:

King. How do you pretty lady?
Ophelia. Well, God dild you! They say the owl was a baker's daughter. Lord, we know what we are, but know not what we may be. God be at your table!
King. Conceit upon her father.   (IV, v, 41–5)

The usual gloss on the baker's daughter turned owl is to the Gloucestershire legend of Christ's having punished an ungenerous girl who objected to the amount of bread given Him. Ophelia in her confusion may say whatever comes into her head yet I suggest there is a method in madness even for Ophelia. Shakespeare stresses through Claudius here and again thirty lines later that the madness stems from her grief over her father's death. It is unclear why she should be put in mind of this legend unless it were that her creator remembered another distraught baker's daughter, one whose father had been murdered. In Book 9 of *The Golden Asse* the adulterous baker's wife,

---

[1] In a private communication Dr Harold Jenkins has pointed out that my claim that 'fardels' is unique in the canon has to stand comparison with 'farthel' of *The Winter's Tale* (IV, iv, 754, 756). I should, perhaps, emend my description of the term to 'as appearing for the first time in the canon in *Hamlet*'. I do wish to remark that Autolycus's use of the term 'farthel' to the Shepherd occurs only thirty lines before the rogue's threat against the Shepherd's son, a threat which Starnes argued as derivative from the anecdote of the burial alive of a servant in *The Golden Asse*. See Bullough, VIII, 16.

[2] Polonius's crude punning on 'tender' (I, iii, 107–9) may have been stimulated by Venus's social anxiety over the effects of Cupid's passion 'For beeing of *tender* and unripe yeares, thou hast with too licentious appetite embraced my most mortall Foe, to whome I shall bee made a mother, and shee a Daughter' (p. 117).

frustrated by the constraints and hostility of her husband, hires an enchantress to bring about either a reconciliation or the death of her husband. The enchantress, unable to change the husband's heart and fearful of losing her salary, kills him. His servants discover the body of the baker hanging from a rafter, take it down, lament, and bury it – all before the daughter learns of the death of her father:

This woman tooke the Baker by the hand, and faining that she had some secret matter to tell him, went into a chamber, where they remained a good space, till all the corne was ground, when as the servants were compelled to call their master to give them more corne, but when they had called very often, and no person gave answer, they began to mistrust, insomuch that they brake open the doore: when they were come in, they could not find the woman, but onely their master hanging dead upon a rafter of the chamber, whereupon they cryed and lamented greatly, and according to the custome, when they had washed themselves, they tooke the body and buried it. The next day morrow, the daughter of the Baker, which was married but a little before to one of the next Village, came crying and beating her breast, not because she heard of the death of her father by any man, but because his lamentable spirit, with a halter about his necke appeared to her in the night, declaring the whole circumstance of his death, and how by inchantment he was descended into hell, which caused her to thinke that her father was dead. (p. 195)

Here we have a true baker's daughter in circumstances analogous to those of Ophelia with a murdered father buried hugger-mugger. But why 'owl'? It was an enchantress who killed the baker and it was an enchantress, Pamphile, who in Book 3 transformed herself into a bird, specifically, 'she became an Owle' (p. 75). Lucius also wants to become an owl, but meets resistance from the chambermaid, Fotis, who can obtain the necessary potions. She is fearful that he will fly away and desert her:

Then said Fotis, Wil you go about to deceive me now, and inforce me to work my own sorrow? Are you in

the mind that you wil not tarry in Thessaly? if you be a bird, where shal I seek you, and when shal I see you? Then answered I, God forbid that I should commit such a crime, for though I could fly in the aire as an Eagle, or though I were the messenger of Jupiter, yet would I have recourse to nest with thee: and I swear by the knot of thy amiable hair, that since the time I first loved thee, I never fancied any other person: moreover, this commeth to my minde, that if by vertue of the oyntment I shall become an Owle, I will take heed that I come nigh no mans house: for I am not to learn, how these matrons would handle their lovers, if they knew that they were transformed into Owles. (pp. 75–6)

I suggest that the idea of desertion – the central theme of Ophelia's Saint Valentine's day song which follows immediately upon her 'baker's daughter' reference – coupled with enchantresses' turning bakers into dead men and lovers into owls, led to the allusion to the legend of the owl who was a baker's daughter.

The verbal echoes and the parallels of circumstance and theme are so numerous as to suggest that *The Golden Asse* is a narrative source of considerable influence upon the text of *Hamlet*.

Othello perhaps more than any other of the tragedies parallels the theme of *The Golden Asse* with its transformation of a man into an ass as punishment for his excessive curiosity about sexual appetite and magical practices.[1] In the tragedy there is a pattern of 'ass' puns and references which is most clearly manifested in Iago's two statements that Othello can 'as tenderly be led by th' nose/As asses are' (I, iii, 401–2) and that he will reward Iago 'for making him egregiously an ass' (II, i, 309).[2]

[1] See Walsh's (pp. 141–89) particularly interesting commentary on the pervasiveness of these themes in the *Metamorphoses*.

[2] Not all of the following words may be conscious puns and some may be simply coincidental sounds, given the limitations of vocabulary in the English language of the day, but the frequency of such terms with their punning potential suggests that at least

Within the drama there are terms both unique or occurring for the first time in the canon and also present in *The Golden Asse*. Among these are 'mandragora', 'poppy', 'castigation', 'circumstanced', and 'incontinently'. Further, the two statements of Iago about Othello's asininity are themselves strikingly close to phrases in the Latin original of *The Golden Asse*.

First, in some of his most memorable lines Shakespeare has Iago, Othello's ancient, analyze the effect of having implanted jealousy in the mind of the Moor:

> The Moor already changes with my poison:
> Dangerous conceits are in their nature poisons,
> . . . Not poppy, nor mandragora,
> Nor all the drowsy syrups of the world
> Shall ever medicine thee to that sweet sleep
> Which thou ow'dst yesterday.
>
> (III, iii, 325–6, 330–3)

L. P. Wilkinson has offered the sensitive comment that 'poppy' and 'drowsy' were inspired by *Georgics* I, 78: 'Lethaeo perfusa papavere somno'.[1] I suggest that the lines owe still more to *The Golden Asse*, Book 10, where there is the familiar episode of murder by poison in which a physician is called upon to defend himself, 'But there arose a sage and *ancient* [my emphasis] Physitian' (p. 210). He refutes his accusers by pointing out that he had suspected a crime and therefore had substituted a sleeping potion for poison. Some of the diction in the physician's apologia is strikingly parallel to the words of Iago:

for I will give you an evident proofe and argument of this present crime. You shall understand, that when this caytiffe demanded of me a present and strong *poyson*, considering that it was not my part to give occasion of any others death, but rather to cure and save sicke persons by meane of *medicines*: and on the other side, fearing least if I should deny his request, I might minister a further cause of his mischiefe, either that he would but *poyson* of some other, or else returne and worke his wicked intent, with a sword or some dangerous weapon, I gave him no *poyson*, but a doling drinke of *Mandragora*, which is of such force that it will cause any man to *sleepe*, as though he were dead. Neither is it any marvaile if this most desperate man, who is certainly assured to be put to death, ordained by an ancient custome, can suffer and abide those facill and easy torments, but if it be so that the child hath received the drinke as I tempered it with mine owne hands, he is yet alive and doth but *sleepe*, and after his *sleepe* he shall returne to life againe, but if he be dead indeed, then may you further enquire of the causes of his death. The opinion of this *ancient* Physitian was found good . . . the father of the child . . . soporiferous sleepe. (pp. 211–12)

Perhaps the 'evident proofe' the physician offers inspired Othello's request for 'ocular proofe' at III, iii, 360. What is clear is that, although Shakespeare may well have recalled Virgil for his 'poppy' (but recall that 'poppy' is one of the seeds culled by Psyche in *The Golden Asse*, p. 122), nevertheless, for his 'mandragora', 'poison', 'medicine', 'sleep', 'drowsy' ('soporiferous') he went to Apuleius in translation where he could take from an '*ancient*', just physician words which Othello's unjust 'ancient' immortally rephrased.

Second, 'incontinently' of I, iii, 305, 'I will incontinently drown myself', is unusual in that Shakespeare everywhere else uses the adjective 'incontinent' adverbially as 'he says he will return incontinent' (IV, iii, 12). The form of the adverb used to describe the directness with which Roderigo seeks to drown himself may have been suggested by the pervasive use of the adverb, 'incontinently', by Adlington in *The Golden Asse*.

Third, that Shakespeare had a knowledge

some were to be activated by the attentive listener: the terms 'ass', 'assails', 'assault', 'assay', 'assays', 'assign', 'assist', 'assur'd', 'assure', appear some fourteen times in *Othello* at I, i, 47; II, iii, 204; V, ii, 258; I, iii, 18; II, i, 120; II, iii, 207; I, iii, 285; I, iii, 246; I, ii, 11; III, iii, 1; III, iii, 11; IV, i, 30; III, iii, 20; IV, ii, 199.

[1] L. P. Wilkinson, *The Georgics of Virgil* (Cambridge, 1969), p. 295.

of Apuleius's Latin as well as of Adlington's English translation is highly probable.[1] The word 'castigation' in English is as old as Chaucer, but Shakespeare had never used it before 'a sequester from liberty: fasting and prayer,/Much castigation, exercise devout' (III, iv, 40–1). I suggest that Shakespeare was prompted to increase his active vocabulary with this term because he recalled the number of times that 'castigare' and its forms occurred in the *Metamorphoses*. The probability of such a derivation is increased when we note that the unique 'sequester' of the previous line (III, iv, 40), resulting in two unusual terms in absolute propinquity, in a context of mendacity, has a parallel in 'sequestro' (admittedly not a verb form) at *Met.* 6. 31. 18 following a 'castiget' at *Met.* 5. 30. 16 and a 'castigans' at *Met.* 7. 15. 14, 'nunc etiam mendaci fictae debilitatis et virginalis fugae *sequestro* ministroque'.[2]

Fourth, 'circumstanc'd' in Bianca's "Tis very good; I must be circumstanc'd' (III, iv, 201), is not used as a verb elsewhere in Shakespeare, but the Latin verb, 'circumsto' is used by Apuleius in the *Metamorphoses* at both 1. 12. 9 and 9. 11. 22.

Fifth, Iago's two phrases describing Othello's asininity at I, iii, 401–2 and II, i, 309 may owe something to Apuleius's Latin. An ass is a metaphor for a fool. In a context of trickery during the Cupid and Psyche episode (*Met.* 6. 19. 12) there occurs the phrase 'hunc *offrenatum* unius offulae praeda' which refers to Cerberus who is associated with a lame ass. I suggest that the image of Othello as an ass led by the nose involves a humiliating bridling, an image inspired by the concrete meaning of 'offrenatum'. The second phrase where Iago gloats over the prospect of having the Moor reward him 'for making him egregiously an ass', recalls the similar collocation of words, if not grammar, in the Latin text of the *Metamorphoses* where Haemus is the savior of the

girl and Lucius, the ass, 'et *asini* sospitator egregius' (*Met.* 7. 10. 2).

Finally, the conclusion of the play may also echo elements of *The Golden Asse*. I have elsewhere argued that Othello's flaming minister speech was inspired in part by Psyche's address to the lamp at *Met.* 5. 22. 23.[3] It may well be that Iago's Spartan taciturnity in the face of torture owes much to the behavior of the guilty servant exposed by the ancient physician who prescribed the mandragora (see p. 211).

The parallels of theme, situation, and diction between *The Golden Asse* and *Othello* seem too numerous to be coincidental. It appears that in his reading of this story of bestial transformation Shakespeare looked chiefly at the Adlington text but sometimes to the original Latin, even as he had in the case of Golding and the Ovidian original. Shakespeare has taken aspects of Apuleius's loose and episodic narrative to enhance the force of his most claustrophobically intense tragedy.

The majesty alone of *King Lear* would seem proof that this tragedy at least is free of any influence from the sportive and grotesque Apuleian novel. Yet upon closer consideration one notes that there are obvious elements common to the two works, sufficiently common for Shakespeare to have consciously or subconsciously recalled diction from *The Golden Asse* as he wrote the most moving of passages, Lear's expression of belief that the dead Cordelia still lives.

The central episode of *The Golden Asse* is the fairy-tale of Cupid and Psyche, a type of the Cinderella *Märchen* in which there are three sisters, one of whom, the youngest and

[1] See especially McPeek, p. 69.

[2] The book, section, and line references to the *Metamorphoses* are from the Loeb edition of *The Golden Ass*, Adlington's translation, revised by S. Gaselee (1915).

[3] *Notes & Queries*, n.s. 24 (1977), 112.

the best, is tormented by her less well-favored elders. It is well known that this motif is present in *King Lear* and its sources, with Goneril and Regan as the evil sisters, and Cordelia as the Cinderella figure.

Shakespeare's recognition of the parallel between the family structures of Cordelia and Psyche was likely to have extended to that of the martial hostility of each pair of elder sisters against the youngest girl. In *Lear* Goneril and Regan prepare to take the field against Cordelia while in *The Golden Asse* Cupid warns his bride:

Behold the last day, the extreme case, and the enemies of thy blood, hath armed themselves against us, pitched their campe, set their host in array, and are marching towards us, for now thy two sisters have drawn their swords, and are ready to slay thee. O with what force are we assailed this day! (p. 108)

In addition to the identical Cinderella motif in the tale of Cupid and Psyche there is a passage in the following book (7) which describes a disguised man looking like a beggar as does Edgar in his guise of Tom o'Bedlam. Indeed, 'hee was poorely apparelled, insomuch that you might see all his belly naked' (p. 140). In the known sources for Tom there is no mention of nakedness, yet Shakespeare describes Edgar's deciding

> To take the basest and most poorest shape
> That ever penury, in contempt of man,
> Brought near to beast. My face I'll grime with filth,
> Blanket my loins, elf all my hairs in knots,
> And with presented *nakedness* outface
> The winds and persecutions of the sky.
> (II, iii, 7–12)

As the story continues, the disguised man in beggar's garb adds the interesting fact, 'I am inheritour and follower of all my father's virtues, yet I lost in a short time all my company and all my riches, by one assault' (p. 140). Admittedly, there are many elements in the story of this disguised man which are not operative in the Edgar plot of *King Lear*, yet the nakedness of the beggar and his filial loyalty are striking parallels as is the curious collocation of the two words 'pomp' and 'delicacy' which occur some ninety words later in the story told by the disguised protagonist of this episode: 'despised all worldly *Pompe* and *delicacy*' (p. 141). The contiguity of the two terms seems to have led Shakespeare to recall them both in some of Lear's most celebrated lines:

> Thou'dst meet the bear i' th' mouth. When the
>   mind's free,
> The body's *delicate*; this tempest in my mind
> Doth from my senses take all feeling else,
> Save what beats there - filial ingratitude! . . .
> Prithee go in thyself, seek thine own ease.
> This tempest will not give me leave to *ponder*
> On things would hurt me more. But I'll go in.
>   . . . O, I have ta'en
> Too little care of this! Take physic, *pomp*,
> Expose thyself to feel what wretches feel,
> That thou mayst shake the superflux to them,
> And show the heavens more just.
> (III, iv, 11–14, 24–6, 33–6)

To reinforce the likelihood that Shakespeare had recalled this passage, it is important to note that the entire story is told by Lucius, the ass, who presents the narrative, 'while I *pondered* with my selfe all these things, a great care came to my remembrance' (p. 139). 'Ponder' is unique in Shakespeare. As I have above argued, Shakespeare relied primarily upon Adlington's translation yet he sometimes checked the Latin text as well. Adlington translated his work with the aid of a French version[1] and consequently missed the vividness of Apuleius's Latin: 'Talibus cogitationibus fluctuantem subit me illa cura potior' (*Met.* 7. 4. 1, 2). The effect of 'fluctuantem' is preserved in the Loeb translation: 'While I pondered *tempestuously*'.

[1] See Charles Whibley's analysis of Adlington's use of an intermediary French text in the Introduction to *The Tudor Translations*, IV, xxv–xxviii.

Shakespeare's familiarity with *The Golden Asse* was so intimate that his vocabulary was replete with echoes of the diction of the Apuleian novel, echoes which reverberated when elements of plot and circumstances were parallel in both the text he was creating and *The Golden Asse.*

If it be granted that elements of plot and diction from *The Golden Asse* are at least parallel to certain features of *King Lear*, then the conclusion of the drama and an aspect of the novel may be more easily seen as having an intimate relationship. In Book 7 just prior to the story of the beggar-like, half-naked Lepolemus, Lucius reflects upon both the blindness and the injustice of Fortune. He then describes his imperfect defense of his innocence in words which closely parallel those of Lear in his last lines:

Furthermore I, who by her great cruelty, was turned into a foure footed Asse, in most vile and abject manner: yea, and whose estate seemed worthily to be lamented and pittied of the most hard and stonie hearts, was accused of theft and robbing of my deare host, Milo, which villany might rather be called parricide than theft, yet might not I defend mine owne cause or denie the fact any way, by reason I could not speake; howbeit least my conscience should seeme to accuse me by reason of silence, and againe being enforced by impatience I endeavored to speake, and faine would have said, *Never* did I that fact, and verely the first word, *never*, I cried out once or twise, somewhat handsome, but the residue I could in no wise pronounce, but still remaining in one voice, cried, *Never, never, never.* Howbeit I settled my *hanging lips* as round as I could to speake the residue: but *why should* I further complaine of the crueltie of my fortune, since as I was not much ashamed, by reason that my servant and my *horse*, was likewise accused with me of the robbery. (pp. 138–9)

At the conclusion of the tragedy the tormented Lear speaks his moving lines:

And my poor fool is hang'd! No, no, no life!
Why should a dog, a horse, a rat, have life,
And thou no breath at all? Thou'lt come no more,

Never, never, never, never, never.
Pray you undo this button. Thank you, sir.
Do you see this? Look on her! Look her lips,
Look there, look there!   (v, iii, 306–12)

The repetition of the word 'never', the rhetorical question 'why should', the 'horse', the 'lips', 'hanging', all together suggest that Shakespeare had this passage from *The Golden Asse* in mind. Further, the theme of the passage, silence in the face of unjust accusation, recalls the origin of the problem between Cordelia and Lear. Indeed, the Cupid and Psyche episode revolved around Psyche's responsibility to keep a seal upon her lips. The themes of silence broken and inarticulateness may have led Shakespeare to be particularly attentive to those passages of *The Golden Asse* which he held in his memory as he wrote *King Lear*, a tale of an impatient father and his laconic daughter.

Buchanan in his *Rerum Scoticarum Historia* was a scholar skeptical of much received material. In describing Macbeth's defeat by Malcolm he wrote:

Mackbeth being terrified at the Confidence of his enemy, immediately fled; and his Soldiers, forsaken by their Leader, surrendered themselves up to Malcolm; Some of our writers do here Record many Fables, which are like Milesian Tales, and fitter for the Stage, than an History.[1]

Now whether or not Shakespeare took the hint from this probable source of *Macbeth*, the dramatist in writing for his stage rather than for a history text, did indeed have in mind at this moment in the play, the defeat of Macbeth, the celebrated Milesian Tale of Apuleius. Specifically, he recalled the episode in Book 4 of *The Golden Asse* in which the cornered thief, Thrasileon, is disguised as a bear.

Simple elements common to Macbeth and

[1] Quoted in Bullough, VII (1973), 516–17. Shakespeare would have had to use the original Latin.

Thrasileon include the epithet for their courage, their title, and their moral nature. They are both called 'valiant', Macbeth at I, ii, 40, and again at I, iii, 47 (and his fury is thought by some to be 'valiant', v, ii, 14); in *The Golden Asse* Thrasileon is 'that one of us being more *valiant* than the rest' (p. 91). They are both captains, Macbeth at I, ii, 34 and 'our good Captain Thrasileon...our Captain Thrasileon' (p. 94).[1] They are both thieves. Macbeth is a 'dwarfish thief' (v, ii, 22), while Thrasileon belongs to a group of 'Theeves... who...came to their den' (p. 85). There is no theme of thievery attached to the murder of Duncan in the Scottish sources, yet the imagery of the murder scene (II, iii) includes that of theft in lines spoken by both Macduff and Malcolm:

> Most sacrilegious murther hath broke ope
> The Lord's anointed temple, and *stole* thence
> The life o' th' building   (ll. 72–4)

and

>   There's warrant in that *theft*
> Which steals itself, when there's no mercy left.
>   (ll. 151–2)

Macbeth is called a 'hell-hound' to his face by Macduff (v, viii, 3), an epithet usually accepted as an echo of that other and earlier villain protagonist, Richard III, who is described by Queen Margaret in his absence as a 'hell-hound' (IV, iv, 48). Yet notice also Thrasileon's fight:

> And although I might perceive that he was well-nigh dead, yet remembered he his own faithfulness and ours, and valiantly resisted the gaping and ravenous mouths of the *hell-hounds*. (p. 93)

Both Macbeth and Thrasileon are 'bear-like'. Thrasileon is covered with a bear skin and to the last pretends to be a bear. Macbeth identifies himself in a simile as bear-like, but significantly falls short of Gloucester's more metaphoric identification in *King Lear*, 'I am

tied to th' stake, and I must stand the course' (III, vii, 54). The simile, 'They have tied me to a stake; I cannot fly, / But bear-like I must fight the course' (v, vii, 1–2), suggests that there is still distance between person and beast. Just as Thrasileon is only disguised as a bear, so Macbeth, however bestial he has become, is still a human being.[2]

There is in addition to these parallels a number of words in this episode of *The Golden Asse* whose resonance seems to have echoed in the mind of Shakespeare as he wrote *Macbeth*. Among these are 'seam', 'porter', 'compassed with', and 'butcher'.

First, in *The Golden Asse* there is a description of the taxidermy necessary to cloak Thrasileon in the guise of a bear:

> Then we put him into the Beares skin, which fitted him finely in every point, wee buckled it fast under his belly, and covered the seam with haire, that it might not be seen. (p. 91)

It is well known that tailoring images are frequent in *Macbeth*, including 'buckle' (v, ii, 15), but the first such image in the play belongs to Macbeth's killing of Macdonwald, a figure whose career anticipates Macbeth's own:

>   nor bade farewell to him,
> Till he *unseam'd* him from nave to th' chops,
> And fix'd his head upon our battlements.
>   (I, ii, 21–3)

'Unseamed' is unique in Shakespeare and there is as well no use of 'seam' in the sense of a garment working in the canon. Shakespeare may well have had in mind the seamed Thrasileon who, when killed, was 'slit' open.

[1] It must be admitted that Holinshed described Macbeth as both 'a valiant gentleman' and 'an excellent capteine'.

[2] In this play, particularly flattering to King James, Shakespeare may have looked deliberately for a reference to hunting and the chase, James's well-known enthusiasms. Accordingly, he found the cornered Thrasileon in the episode of Demochares who 'greatly delighted in hunting and chasing' (p. 90). See also the further bear image at v, viii, 29.

Second, the celebrated Porter scene (II, iii) is not accounted for by any of the known Scottish sources, though it does have a probable origin in the Mystery plays.[1] There is no Porter scene in the Thrasileon episode, but there is a concatenation of sleep, a porter, and murder:

> when we thought that every one was asleepe, we went with our weapons and besieged the house of Demochares round about. Then Thrasileon was ready at hand, and leaped out of the caverne, and went to kill all such as he found asleepe: but when he came to the Porter, he opened the gates and let us all in. (p. 92)

If Shakespeare was first impressed by Macbeth as bear-like, working back through the career of Thrasileon, he may well have noted this gate-opening episode. Particularly, he would have seen that the thieves, just before their arrival at the gates, opened 'a great sepulchre ... covered with the corruption of man' (p. 92). Such phrases might have led him to recall Mystery plays with their comic gate-keepers.

Third, 'compass'd with' is unique in Shakespeare.[2] Macduff, returning with the severed head of Macbeth, addresses Malcolm as king with the added observation, 'I see thee compass'd with thy kingdom's pearl' (v, ix, 22). Thirty lines earlier Macbeth had said to Macduff:

> I will not yield,
> To kiss the ground before young Malcolm's feet,
> And to be baited with the rabble's curse.
> (v, viii, 27–9)

The Thrasileon episode seems to have provided both 'rabble' and 'compass'd with':

> but when he was at liberty abroad yet could he not save himselfe, for all the dogs on the Streete [= rabble, cf. *O.E.D.* A.1] joyned themselves to the greyhounds and mastifes of the house, and came upon him.
> Alas what a pitiful sight it was to see our poore Thrasileon thus environed and *compassed with* so many dogs that tare and rent him miserably. (p. 93)

Fourth, Malcolm thirteen lines after Macduff's observation calls Macbeth 'this dead butcher' (v, ix, 35). 'Butcher', though frequent enough in the canon, is used only this once in this play. Following closely upon the instance of the street dogs who tore Thrasileon when he was compassed as well with mastiffs is the passage:

> no person was so hardy untill it was day, as to touch him, though hee were starke *dead*: but at last there came a *Butcher* more valiant than the rest, who opening the panch of the beast, slit out an hardy and ventrous theefe. (p. 94)

Macbeth is both bear and butcher, victim and knife, since Shakespeare has the tyrant refer to himself as bear and Malcolm call him butcher.

Finally, there is the element of play-acting common to both texts. Macbeth informs us of the nihilistic nature of life with the poor player who struts and frets and Thrasileon is praised for playing his part to the very end: 'so tooke hee in gree the pagiant which willingly he tooke in hand himselfe' (p. 93).

Shakespeare's habit of amalgamating disparate source materials has partly obscured the origin of bear-like Macbeth. But an examination of diction and theme suggests that Shakespeare did take Buchanan's unintentional hint about a Milesian Tale and turned for the conclusion of his drama of witches to the great novel about a man bewitched.[3]

All four of the central Bradleian tragedies show significant aspects of theme, plot, and diction derived from *The Golden Asse*. Indeed, many of these aspects from Apuleius occur at extremely important moments within the plays, including Hamlet's most famous solilo-

[1] Bullough, VII, 461.
[2] There are several instances of 'compass'd' in the canon but no immediately contiguous 'compass'd' and 'with' appears but for this example.
[3] For Francis Douce's argument that the witches imitate the greasy practices of Milo's wife in *The Golden Asse*, see his 1839 *Illustrations of Shakespeare* in the Burt Franklin reprint (New York, 1968), p. 245.

quy, the madness of Ophelia, Iago's haunting prophecy of the Moor's anxiety, Othello's flaming minister speech, Lear's terrible final question, and Macbeth's bestial defiance and death.

I suspect that *The Golden Asse* was one of Shakespeare's early reading experiences for the imprint of it upon his memory was so deep that at times he evoked its diction and cadences with seemingly little surface provocation from plot or character. In those instances where he recalled obviously parallel elements he was often careful to suppress Apuleius's comic conclusions of otherwise tragic episodes. Further, perhaps helped by Adlington's own lack of perception about the nature of his original, Shakespeare omits the constant and sophisticated play of wit and humor which Apuleius provides the reader in the midst of his grotesque and violent stories. Shakespeare doubtless enjoyed the novel for its own com-

pelling vivacity, but as a craftsman about his business, he saw it as a mine of short narratives, each one of which was of potential thematic or situational interest.

There are other plays of Shakespeare both early and late which are influenced by *The Golden Asse*, but it is noteworthy that Shakespeare at the time of what is arguably the height of his powers recalled a fundamentally comedic story whose episodes of magic, adultery, and bestial metamorphoses were transmuted by his creative imagination into the pure gold of the central tragedies.

I have had the encouragement and benefit of strictures from Professors Geoffrey Bullough, Kenneth Muir and John Velz, each of whom generously commented on early versions of parts of this essay and no one of whom is responsible for its final form and argument.

'THE CHOICE OF HERCULES' IN 'ANTONY AND CLEOPATRA'

JOHN COATES

The importance of the 'Choice of Hercules' in the art of the Renaissance has been made clear by the work of Erwin Panofsky[1] and its role in the culture of the sixteenth and seventeenth centuries has been illustrated by Edgar Wind.[2] From a simple story in Xenophon's *Memorabilia*, which coalesced with Scipio's dream in the *Punica* of Silius Italicus, neo-Platonist philosophy fashioned a richly-textured, highly sophisticated allegory. This allegory touched on the most vital moral question of the time: the attainment of human wholeness, perhaps the central concern of the Renaissance. My object is to explore the connection of the 'Choice of Hercules' with *Antony and Cleopatra* and to define the effect which this well-known allegory may have on the meaning of the play.

Familiar as the 'Choice of Hercules' is, it is worth briefly recalling it for the sake of my argument. In Xenophon's *Memorabilia*, the sophist Prodicus is reported to have told a story of Hercules's meeting in youth with two women; the one sober, modest-eyed and dressed in white, the other with face made-up, 'dressed so as to disclose all her charms'[3] and glancing about to see whether any noticed her. They are, of course, Virtue and Vice, and the scene which follows achieved a great familiarity in Renaissance iconography. The well-known Rubens painting is only one of scores of instances of Hercules hesitating between Vice and Virtue. Vice is made to offer every kind of sensual pleasure. Rather than wars and worries,

Hercules shall consider his choice of food, drink, sound, touch or perfume; 'what tender love can give you most joy and how to come by all these pleasures with the least trouble'.[4] Virtue reminds Hercules that if he desires success and glory he must work for them. The gods give nothing good or great without effort.[5] She attacks Vice for continually seeking artificially to stimulate human appetites, 'eating before thou art hungry, drinking before thou art thirsty, getting thee cooks to give zest to eating',[6] even searching for snow in summer to give zest to drinking.

The image of the 'Choice of Hercules' was reinforced by an imitation in Silius Italicus's boring but much read epic on the Second Punic War. The appearance of Virtue and Vice to Scipio the Elder in a dream provided a Latin source for the picture of the hero hesitating between Vice and Virtue, which undoubtedly secured its even wider dissemination. In Silius's account the enemy of Roman military virtue takes on a distinctly oriental colour: 'Pleasure's head breathed Persian odours, and her ambrosial tresses flowed free: in her shining robe Tyrian purple was embroidered with ruddy

[1] Erwin Panofsky, *Hercules am Scheidewege* (Berlin, 1930).

[2] Edgar Wind, *Pagan Mysteries in the Renaissance* (Bungay, Suffolk, 1967).

[3] Xenophon, *Memorabilia and Oeconomicus* trans. E. C. Marchant (1923), p. 95.

[4] *Ibid.*, p. 97.

[5] *Ibid.*, p. 99.

[6] *Ibid.*, p. 101.

gold'.[1] As in Xenophon she is a wanton and her beauty is studied and artificial.

In Xenophon's account *earthly* glory and fame are the reward of virtue. Silius's 'dream of Scipio' adds two other important elements; the raising of man to the divine and the rendering of him superior to Fortune. If the hero exerts himself and ignores what Fortune can give or take away he will gain the height and look down upon mankind.[2] Persistence in such a course earns immortality. Heaven is open to those who have preserved the divine element born with them.[3]

In the Renaissance the 'Choice of Hercules' was far from esoteric or eccentric; in fact it was a visual, moral and philosophical truism as Panofsky's many examples abundantly prove. This is certainly true of its simpler form, in which the hero, confronted by Vice and Virtue, chooses Virtue with its pains and rewards. (Thomas Bradshaw's *The Shepherds Star*, 1591, contains a popular version of this simpler form of the 'Choice of Hercules'.)[4]

The image of Hercules is so emphatically linked with Antony in *Antony and Cleopatra*, that it is natural to suggest a connection between the choice of the play and the 'Choice of Hercules'. Frank Kermode has, in fact, touched on the connection in a footnote in *Renaissance Essays* but has not, I feel, pursued the subject:

Shakespeare stresses the Herculean side of Antony (I, iii, 84; I, v, 23 where 'demi-Atlas' means 'the substitute of Atlas'; IV, xii, 43–7) to the degree that he converts the god who deserts Hercules (IV, iii, 12–17) from Plutarch's Bacchus into Hercules, and makes no mention of Bacchus, though to Plutarch's Antony he was at least as important as Hercules. Octavius makes it clear that Antony was familiar with the hard Prodician road to glory (I, iv, 55–64); but he prefers to Roman *gravitas* that Egypt which is represented throughout as gluttonous feasting and sensual indulgence.[5]

Kermode here summarises much of the evidence linking the 'Choice of Hercules' with *Antony*

and Cleopatra; some of the many explicit references to Hercules in the play, the clash between Vice and Virtue in eastern and western guise, above all the alteration from Bacchus, in a source which Shakespeare otherwise follows closely, to Hercules. However, the connection with the 'Choice of Hercules' only becomes really interesting when the simpler connotations of the myth are left behind. If Shakespeare did refer to it at all, he would be referring to a far richer complex of meanings than 'the temptation of the "new Hercules" of Renaissance epic . . . a conflict taken over from Plutarch between heroic virtue and sensuality'.[6] Edgar Wind has described the humanists' interest in the esoteric meanings of the 'Choice of Hercules', above all in the ideal of the reconciliation of pleasure to virtue, in the highest type of man: 'Although the humanists used it profusely in their exoteric instruction, they left no doubt that for a Platonic initiate it was but the crust and not the marrow.'[7] The theme appealed to many others besides Platonic initiates. Both Wind[8] and Harry Levin draw attention to Ben Jonson's *Pleasure Reconciled to Virtue* (1619). Jonson's masque illustrates the popularity of the subject which is indeed central to the whole culture of the Renaissance. As Levin remarks: 'The ethos of the Renaissance did not rest content with conjoining the *vita contemplativa* and the *vita activa*. Ficino also complimented Lorenzo de' Medici on his achievements within a third realm of being, the *vita voluptuosa*.'[9] It is the esoteric 'Choice of Hercules' which is most

[1] Silius Italicus, *Punica*, trans. J. O. Duff (1934), p. 327.

[2] *Ibid.*, p. 333.   [3] *Ibid.*, p. 331.

[4] Douglas Bush, *Mythology and the Renaissance Tradition in English Poetry* (1932), p. 278.

[5] Frank Kermode, *Renaissance Essays* (1973), pp. 98–9.   [6] *Ibid.*, p. 98.

[7] Wind, *Pagan Mysteries in the Renaissance*, p. 205.

[8] *Ibid.*, p. 206.

[9] Harry Levin, *The Myth of the Golden Age in the Renaissance* (New York, 1972), p. 134.

interesting in *Antony and Cleopatra*. *Pleasure Reconciled to Virtue* is worth noting as a useful introduction to some of the refinements involved in this moral choice and is, I believe, illuminating when one comes to examine the Renaissance Hercules in *Antony and Cleopatra*.

In a setting which is, significantly, 'in the mountains of Atlas' near the garden of the Hesperides, Hercules is made to reject the crude animal pleasure of the god Comus. It drowns the human personality.[1] However, what follows is not a simple moral choice between Pleasure and Virtue. The complete man can and should live in both elements. The clash between the two is over now. Virtue controls Pleasure,[2] which adds a grace and charm to the moral character. She encourages her children to pass through the element of pleasure and trusts them, giving them entrance to the Hesperides. It is fitting that they should pass through a refined pleasure and return to the hill of virtue carrying traces of its moral effect, 'for what is noble should be sweet'.[3] Having returned they are above fate and may look down 'Upon triumphed chance'.[4] *Pleasure Reconciled to Virtue* supplies the sense of the complete man living both in Pleasure and in Virtue, the linking of this higher moral state with the garden of the Hesperides, the promise that such a state is above chance.

The work of such writers as Cartari and Conti supplies other elements of the Renaissance Hercules, interesting in connection with the Herculean Antony. They emphasise his role as, in some sense, the complete man. According to Cartari's *Imagines Deorum* (1581) Hercules's courage was moral rather than physical.[5] Natale Conti in his *Mythologiae* remarks that Hercules's education by Chiron in both arms and law was a model for any prince.[6] Cartari emphasises the somewhat unfamiliar role of Hercules as a god of eloquence: 'Itaque in Arcadia templum commune cum Mercurio eloquentiae Deo habuisse fertur.

Athenienses etiam in Academia aras non solum musis, Minervae et Mercurio, verum etiam Herculi posuerunt.'[7] One of the most interesting illustrations in the *Imagines Deorum* shows Hercules in his lion-skin, with lines, presumably representing his eloquence, drawn from his mouth to the ears of young and old people of both sexes. Antony's eloquence in *Antony and Cleopatra* may well have identified him especially, for Shakespeare's first audiences, with the Hercules of contemporary mythography.

The role of complete man assigned to Hercules is made to rest by the mythographers on a moral victory. Piero Valeriano's *Hieroglyphics* (1556) connects the three apples of the Hesperides, won by Hercules, with the three most important heroic virtues, the control of anger, the curbing of avarice and a noble indifference to pleasure.[8] Panofsky suggests the strong connection of the 'Choice of Hercules' with the apples of the Hesperides and it seems clear from *Pleasure Reconciled to Virtue* that the Hesperides signify the highest ideal, the linking of the *vita activa* with the *vita voluptuosa*.

More important for *Antony and Cleopatra* is the moral interpretation of the descent of Hercules into Hades. Cartari links this descent and the carrying-off of the triple-headed dog Cerberus with man's descent into his own nature to bridle its impulses.[9] It is perhaps needless to recall that Hercules's descent into Hades gained additional currency through the

[1] *Ben Jonson*, ed. C. H. Herford and P. and E. Simpson, 11 vols (Oxford, 1925–52), VII, 483.

[2] *Ibid.*, p. 486.

[3] *Ibid.*, p. 490, line 311.

[4] *Ibid.*, p. 491, lines 337–8.

[5] Vincentio Cartari, *Imagines Deorum* (Lyons, 1581), p. 234.

[6] Natale Conti, *Natalis Comitatis Mythologiae sive Explicationis Fabularum* (Lyons, 1605), p. 697.

[7] Cartari, *Imagines Deorum*, pp. 227–8.

[8] Panofsky, *Hercules am Scheidewege*, p. 148.

[9] Cartari, *Imagines Deorum*, p. 190.

parallel drawn with Christ's Harrowing of Hell. Ralegh in his *History of the World* declares that 'the prophecies that Christ should break the serpent's head, and conquer the power of hell, occasioned the fable of Hercules killing the serpent of the Hesperides, and descending into Hell, and captivating Cerberus'.[1] As well as probably making the myth better known such an analogy would reinforce its meaning, that of a moral victory.

It is entirely proper to ask what acquaintance Shakespeare could be presumed to have with the Hercules of the Renaissance mythographers. Douglas Bush has borne testimony to the general popularity of contemporary mythological compilations: 'The mythographers, as we have seen, were not merely convenient for reference. Their allegorical interpretations were highly attractive.'[2] In Seznec's view 'there are certain indications pointing to Shakespeare having known the *Imagini* of Cartari'.[3] While it is impossible to be dogmatic, Berowne's well-known lines in *Love's Labour's Lost* in praise of love strongly suggest Shakespeare's knowledge of the mythographer's allegorical Hercules. Love

> gives to every power a double power,
> Above their functions and their offices
>
> (IV, iii, 327–8)[4]
>
> For valour, is not Love a Hercules
> Still climbing trees in the Hesperides?
>
> (iii, 336–7)

The context suggests 'the Hesperides' possess a moral significance symbolising a type of excellence, and their mention evokes ideas of mental agility and eloquence.

If Antony is seen as tinged with a reminiscence of the Renaissance Hercules, certain difficulties in the play are partially solved. Critics have frequently disputed the moral meaning of *Antony and Cleopatra* and there is no consensus. The view of Bradley[5] that the triumphant death of Antony means an endorsement of the ideal of 'the world well lost for

love' seems simplistic and sentimental. The moralist's view of L. C. Knights that the play shows a self-indulgent man conducted to 'the very heart of loss'[6] is simplistic in the opposite direction. Both views leave out too much. More sophisticated accounts see *Antony and Cleopatra* as a kind of golden chaos, or picture of the dissolving pagan world, 'moments, opinions, moods, speeches, characters, fragments of situation, forked mountains and blue promontories, imposed upon us with all the force of a "giant power"'.[7] Quite possibly this last may seem an adequate view to many readers.

If, however, we wish to attach a more precise significance to the dramatic events leading up to Antony's death, then the figure of the Renaissance Hercules is essential. One might note the figure of Antony between Octavia and Cleopatra as closely parallel to the classical accounts of Hercules between Virtue and Pleasure. It is most interesting, however, to observe what Shakespeare has done with the fall of Antony. In Plutarch's account the god departs in the night before Antony's final defeat at Alexandria and the desertion of his remaining forces. In Shakespeare there is a vital interlude, which seems to me to be best explained by reference to a sophisticated variant of the 'Choice of Hercules'.

The god Hercules leaves Antony in IV, iii,

---

[1] Bush, *Mythology and the Renaissance Tradition in English Poetry*, p. 278.

[2] *Ibid.*, p. 91.

[3] Jean Seznec, *The Survival of the Pagan Gods* (New York, 1961), p. 315.

[4] Quotations from Shakespeare are from *The Complete Works of William Shakespeare*, ed. W. J. Craig (1963).

[5] William Shakespeare, *The Tragedy of Antony and Cleopatra*, ed. Barbara Everett (New York, 1964), pp. 234–5.

[6] *The Pelican Guide to English Literature*, ed. Boris Ford, 7 vols (Harmondsworth, 1971), II, 247.

[7] John Danby, *Elizabethan and Jacobean Poets* (1965), p. 148.

by passing under the stage to the sound of hautboys. ('Musicke of the Hoboyes is under the Stage.')[1]

Second Soldier. Hark!
First Soldier.   Music i th'air
Third Soldier.   Under the earth.   (IV, iii, 13)

The text, at this point, seems to be emphasising just where the music is coming from and where Hercules is going. It may seem far-fetched to suggest that Hercules is going into Hades at this point, but such a suggestion receives support from the well-known stage convention associating the 'cellarage' with Hell. The figure of Hercules bearing the earth, which was the sign of the Globe Theatre,[2] might imply a special familiarity with the myth on the part of Shakespeare and his audience, a familiarity which might allow him to use a stage short-hand at this point.

Antony's continued display of Herculean characteristics after the god departs fits within the mythographer's philosophical scheme. As Wind remarks, Neoplatonist ideas permitted the simultaneous presence of a spiritual force in Hades and in Heaven. In fact Plotinus illustrated this 'difficult doctrine which was essential to his concept of emanation',[3] by the descent of Hercules into Hades. Far more significant, however, is the dramatic value of the descent at this particular moment in the play. On Cartari's showing it implies a descent into one's own nature to control it, perhaps through increase of self-knowledge, perhaps through grasping and purifying one's instincts. It is an ordeal and a form of purificatory suffer-ing, as the parallel with Christ's Harrowing of Hell implies. Its significance at this point in *Antony and Cleopatra* is that Antony is shown as beginning just such a self-purification, a progress in self-control. The progress involves a series of 'tests' of the virtues of the Renais-sance Hercules. Antony must demonstrate courage, rejection of avarice, mastery of

pleasure. Finally he must undergo a cleansing agony parallel to that endured by Hercules. The god leaves Antony after he has rallied from utter despair and humiliation but before he has again proved himself. Hercules departs as the prelude to a kind of spiritual ascent, a liberation of his nature from its baser elements.

The second soldier's certainty that the god is *leaving* Antony is perhaps not such a problem in this reading as it at first sight appears. There is a suggestion elsewhere in the play that the observers see events but miss their true signifi-cance. Enobarbus dismisses the return of Antony's courage as a loss of his reason. The practical Dolabella cannot share Cleopatra's sense of Antony's glory. Cleopatra's death scene is introduced by her dialogue with the clown, who jokes with her but cannot under-stand what she is about. The splendour of her dying utterance is followed by the somewhat matter-of-fact questions and comments of Caesar. Perhaps the guard's question to the dying Charmian and her reply presents in condensed form this sense of two levels of awareness. The second soldier's comment is not alien to this double level of apprehension, or indeed to the method of allegory. In one sense the god's departure has the simple mean-ing which he sees, the loss of Antony's pro-tective spirit. The greater nobility, rather than straightforward defeat, which follows, suggests a meaning to which he is blind. Dramatically the soldier's comment raises a question. It should sharpen our attention, our sense of mystery, perhaps allegory, when what follows the god's departure is *not* what we perhaps expect.

The hypothesis that this is the 'descent of

[1] *The First Folio of Shakespeare*, The Norton Facsimile, ed. Charlton Hinman (New York, 1968), p. 867.
[2] Robert K. Root, *Classical Mythology in Shake-speare* (New York, 1965), pp. 72–3.
[3] Wind, *Pagan Mysteries in the Renaissance*, p. 266.

Hercules' seems to be confirmed by what follows. Cleopatra (IV, iv) arms Antony, recalling the many Renaissance paintings of Venus arming Mars, love aiding courage. He leaves her asserting the unity in himself of lover and soldier.

> Fare thee well, dame, whate'er becomes of me;
> This is a soldier's kiss.   (IV, iv, 29–30)

On hearing of the desertion of Enobarbus, he sends his treasure after him, displaying one of Piero's heroic virtues, the curbing of avarice. The god's leaving Antony is not, as in Plutarch, the prelude to his disgrace but to the appearance of a nobler and more integrated figure:

> Your emperor
> Continues still a Jove.   (IV, vi, 28–9)

The nobility Antony shows is so striking that it overwhelms the hard-bitten Enobarbus and drives him to die of a broken heart. Antony's feasting no longer seems a continuous self-indulgence but the reward of valour (IV, viii, 32–5), and for the first time he shows a gratitude to those who serve him (IV, iii, 22–6) unlike his earlier jealousy (III, i, 17–27).

The interlude between the god's desertion and the final loss of his fleet and army, assert emphatically his possession of courage, generosity and of a noble capacity to enjoy pleasure without being possessed by it. There remains the ultimate agony of supposed betrayal by Cleopatra. At the moment of desertion by the Egyptian fleet an explicit parallel is drawn with the final agony of Hercules:

> The shirt of Nessus is upon me; teach me,
> Alcides, thou mine ancestor, thy rage;
> Let me lodge Lichas in the horns o' the moon.
>
>   (IV, xii, 43–5)

The agony of Hercules, falsely believing himself betrayed by Deianeira, runs exactly parallel to Antony's suffering believing himself betrayed by Cleopatra. ('Hercules's one

thought had been to punish her before he died, but when Hyllus assured him she was innocent as her suicide proved, he signed forgivingly.')[1]

> *Antony.*   O thy vile lady
> She has robbed me of my sword.
> *Mardian.*   No, Antony;
> My mistress lov'd thee, and her fortunes
> mingled
> With thine entirely.   (IV, xiv, 21–4)

The final suffering of Hercules had for the Greeks a purificatory significance: 'It is a reasonable as well as a common conclusion that the mortal parts of Hercules were consumed by fire that the immortal part might be free to ascend to heaven.'[2] Antony's terrible rage is followed by acceptance and a final touch of kindliness to Eros (IV, xiv, 21–2). The images of dissolving, of being unable to hold his visible shape, are reinforced by Antony's declaration that 'the torch is out' (IV, xiv, 46), a well-known Renaissance emblem of the soul being freed from the body, later repeated by Cleopatra (IV, xv, 85).[3]

The immortality which Antony promises himself and Cleopatra is one in which

> Dido and her Aeneas shall want troops
> And all the haunt be ours.   (IV, xiv, 53–4)

In its context the re-uniting of Dido and Aeneas in Hades, against Virgil's authority, surely means more than the evocation of another pair of famous lovers. Dido and Aeneas are evoked and united because like Cleopatra and Antony they suggest east and west, an identification obvious enough to all familiar with Virgil's account. Jackson Knight commenting on the ingredients in the love story of Dido and Aeneas remarks, 'there was the lure and danger of eastern luxury which Vergil had

[1] Robert Graves, *The Greek Myths*, 2 vols (Edinburgh, 1960), II, 202.
[2] G. S. Kirk, *The Nature of the Greek Myths* (1974), p. 201.
[3] Henry Green, *Shakespeare and the Emblem Writers* (1870), pp. 455–6.

contemplated in the *Georgics* and contrasted with the simple Italian life. The conflicts between love and duty, the moment and the future, are familiar; they have become familiar through Vergil'.[1] Antony as Hercules is able to reconcile these contradictions. It is highly significant that as Antony is raised to her arms Cleopatra declares,

> Had I great Juno's power
> The strong-winged Mercury should fetch thee up
> And set thee by Jove's side.   (IV, xv, 34–6)

When Hercules was received into Olympus it was by the agency of his old enemy Hera (Juno) who had forgiven him after his purificatory death.[2] Antony–Hercules has undergone his final ordeal and the reconciliation of opposed elements is complete. When he dies in Cleopatra's arms it is as a lover laying the last of many thousand kisses on her lips and as

> a Roman, by a Roman
> Valiantly vanquished   (IV, xv, 57–8)

What seems to strengthen the connection of Antony with the Renaissance Hercules and his choice, is Cleopatra's description of him after his death. There are too many points of similarity to the Hercules who blends pleasure with virtue to be dismissed as coincidence. Antony is seen as possessing the eloquence of Cartari's Hercules. He was the perfection of generosity and ripeness. Above all, he was dolphin-like, greater than the element of pleasure through which he moved. This last perhaps evokes the well-known Renaissance image of wholeness, the Aldine dolphin; '[This] and innumerable other emblematic combinations were adopted to signify the rule of life that ripeness is achieved by a growth of strength in which quickness and steadiness are equally developed'.[3]

Cleopatra's lines are packed with allegorical reference.

> His legs bestrid the ocean; his reared arm
> Crested the world; his voice was propertied

As all the tuned spheres, and that to friends;
But when he meant to quail and shake the orb,
He was as rattling thunder. For his bounty
There was no winter in't, an autumn 'twas
That grew the more by reaping; his delights
Were dolphin-like, they showed his back above
The element they liv'd in.   (V, ii, 82–90)

This conception, Cleopatra states, is the ultimate reality, far beyond the scope of imagination or dream. Pleasure reconciled to Virtue makes Antony superior to fate:

> I hear him mock
> The luck of Caesar, which the gods give men
> To excuse their after wrath.   (V, ii, 283–5)

It would be profitless to attempt to impose on *Antony and Cleopatra* a reading based on a little out of the way information, external to the text; a reading at variance with the sense of the play as derived from its entire effect. However, the Renaissance Hercules is not extraneous but very much present in the play. There is, too, much less agreement about what *Antony and Cleopatra* actually does mean, about its moral texture, than about most of Shakespeare's plays. There is, therefore, much less risk of affronting the commonly held 'sensible' view of the play; such a view does not exist. In the continuing controversy concerning the play (outlined by J. L. Simmons in *Shakespeare's Pagan World*)[4] the 'Choice of Hercules' is a suggestive piece of evidence. It tends to make against the view that Shakespeare's intentions are mainly ironical, that he is debunking the lovers. The linking of the 'Choice of Hercules' with *Antony and Cleopatra* gives a fuller value to Enobarbus's death, strengthens the case for accepting

[1] W. F. Jackson Knight, *Roman Vergil* (Harmondsworth, 1966), p. 125.
[2] Graves, *The Greek Myths*, II, 203.
[3] Wind, *Pagan Mysteries in the Renaissance*, pp. 98–9.
[4] J. L. Simmons, *Shakespeare's Pagan World* (1974), pp. 110–13.

Antony's courage at the end as genuine, and above all, allows us to accept the poetry of acts IV and V as what it surely is, the real expression of something real: nothing so callow as 'the world well lost' but a statement of Pleasure reconciled to Virtue.

© JOHN COATES 1978

STRUCTURE, INVERSION, AND GAME IN SHAKESPEARE'S CLASSICAL WORLD

BRUCE ERLICH

Troilus and Cressida exemplifies the palimpsest of conflicting and incompatible texts possible to Shakespeare through remembrance, allusion, and revision of earlier sources. On every level, the play undercuts itself. As contemporary history, it recalls the endless, brutal war in the Netherlands pursued by England even as the Greeks waged for a decade their 'just' crusade against Troy. Shakespeare assumes the audience's knowledge of traditional authorities on that ancient war – Homer, Euripides, Caxton, Chaucer – even as he takes for granted acquaintance with Tudor policies of support for Continental allies. But when Hector proves less valorous than naive, and Achilles a thug; when Pandarus inverts the stately Greek chorus into a provoker of Winchester geese; when Ulysses's banalities on 'degree, priority, and place' (mimicking the principles of Elizabethan hierarchy that social change was already reducing to nostalgia) demonstrate how any sophistry will do if it can move a listener; and when a betrayed lover cannot even (like conventional Romeo) die of his passion, but abandons soft Venus for bellowing Mars – then it is a struggle of simultaneous texts (some held in the spectator's memory, another being enacted on stage) that is occurring before the audience and which establishes the drama's singular effect, the clash of literary conventions with their ironic reversals.

While this might seem a definition of parody, a technique far more radical is actually involved. For what *Troilus* sets forth is the *loss* of texts – contemporary no less than mythic – which would justify the experiences either of love or war, either ancient or modern. Scholars wonder who was the audience for such a work that offends everyone in an Elizabethan playhouse – classical Humanists, admirers of the 'unities' in drama, respecters of martial virtue, seekers after a tale of young love, even groundlings who dislike being cursed. Art seeks acceptance by representing a world which its receivers desire to enter through imagination; even tragedy invites this complicity. But with malice aforethought, *Troilus* alienates possible audiences through corollary acts of destruction: it demolishes the old tale by declaring through Shakespeare's version that neither love nor ideals nor even the dramatic form of tragedy can any longer be meaningful; and then, in a technique of words neutralizing earlier words only then to be neutralized themselves, Shakespeare debunks his own play by rendering it so squalid in contrast to the distinguished literary norms and antecedents which it invokes that an audience will reject it after first having been led to reject the original object of its satire. The work is a supreme example of literary self-nullification.[1]

[1] Cf. Rosalie L. Colie on *Troilus* as 'a play which expresses systems undone and orders overthrown, which shows how easily, under the conditions of wartime, any system can be undone, any order overthrown', *Shakespeare's Living Art* (Princeton, 1974), p. 351; also her valuable chapter 8 on the play.

A number of studies in recent years employ aspects of linguistic theory to analyze processes in Shakespearian drama; some examples include: essays by Stephen Booth (pp. 87–103) and Jan Kott (pp. 9–36)

I begin a discussion of Shakespeare and the Ancients with *Troilus* viewed as a study of self-demolishing language in order to raise a structural and thematic issue important for the entire canon. What is the 'plot' of a Shakespearian drama – and especially of those dense and allusive plays set in the Classical world? Is it the summary of discrete, chronologically ordered events recounted by Chute or the Lambs? Or do we not, in both reading and performance, experience dimensions of the tale (like *Troilus*'s revoked sources) which are – and yet, paradoxically, are not – 'in' the text? While linked structurally to poetry and enactment, these ulterior significations depend upon audience response, upon resonance in the spectator's mind, if not exactly for their existence then certainly for their realization and import. Claudio Guillén's observations about poetry might be applied to Shakespeare:

Successful poetic form presupposes . . . a basic connection between the latent or tacit parts of the *significans* and the words actually uttered or written. The first task of stylistic research should consist in observing the adequacy of the written words to the absent words. The theoretical model would be: $A + X = B$. That is to say: a series of written components (A) plus a series of unwritten ones (X) make possible the total impact of the poem. The efficiency of A is proved by its ability to move in the direction of X, and *then*, together with X, to disclose B.[1]

Poetic form is thus a 'sign' in Ferdinand de Saussure's meaning: the union of a 'signifier' with the mental concept aroused, with the 'signified', and Shakespeare's 'infinite variety' is the potential of his drama through an open-ended reference to evoke a multiplicity of signifieds – presumably, for the Renaissance audience, and certainly for later centuries of readers.[2]

A different example of such multiplicity – and of the arbitrariness which often necessarily accompanies it — is the play's dimension as theatre. Never intended as 'great literature',

the Renaissance dramatic text remains only latent until realized in performances which differ between productions, within single productions from one day to another, and through the course of stage history. Certainly, the verbal text remains 'dominant', the backbone of any production: yet it is also but one structure among a variety of them, a skeleton until fleshed-out by others which are often intangible and irrecoverable, but which establish the specific ontology of drama as opposed to art experienced through print. I refer to time and audience mood, players' temperaments, the conditions of London when the drama first reached the boards; to Shakespeare's original use of stage space, to gesture, pronunciation and verbal music, the cadence of an unfolding action. Insofar as scholars can reconstruct it, the text is a signifier, one of whose signifieds – its theatrical setting-forth – is radically indeterminate because of its very existence as scenario for an *agon* which melts 'into thin air'. Multi-dimensional from its inception, the dramatic text is always unfinished, perpetually awaiting a new *mise-en-scène*.[3]

in Ralph Berry ed., 'Shakespeare Today', *Mosaic*, (1977); Lawrence Danson, *Tragic Alphabet: Shakespeare's Drama of Language* (New Haven, 1974); C. T. Neely, '*The Winter's Tale*: The Triumph of Speech', *Studies in English Literature*, xv (1975), 321–38; and, remembering the social functions of language, Robert Weimann, 'Shakespeare and the Study of Metaphor', *New Literary History*, vi (1974), 149–67.

[1] Claudio Guillén, *Literature as System: Essays Toward the Theory of Literary History* (Princeton, 1971), p. 266; all of his chapter 'The Stylistics of Silence' is useful on the problem of 'reference'.

[2] Roman Jakobson, 'Linguistics and Poetics', in R. and F. DeGeorge eds., *The Structuralists from Marx to Lévi-Strauss* (New York, 1972), pp. 85–122; Ferdinand de Saussure, *Course in General Linguistics*, tr. Wade Baskin (New York, 1966).

[3] Max Bluestone, *From Story to Stage* (The Hague, 1974); Roman Jakobson, 'The Dominant', in L. Matejka and K. Pomorska eds., *Readings in Russian Poetics: Formalist and Structuralist Views* (Cambridge, Mass., 1971), pp. 82–97; Jiří Veltruský,

So one 'meaning' of a play is any possible stage representation of it. Other references beyond the immediate signifiers of the text are familiar subjects for Shakespearian research: between characters, episodes, and imagery we have the analogue, cross-reference, and similitude which bind any individual play together. Beyond the single drama, we detect the recurring patterns of Shakespeare's imagination and, so, the clue for taking any single play as the implicit context for all others (certain of these relationships are discussed in a moment); there are the many existing texts which Shakespeare rifles for sources, including historians and the philosophers of political order and religious belief; finally, crucial to the Marxian–structuralist viewpoint which I shall be arguing, there are the references to events outside texts and literature, of which the nods toward theatrical controversy (Hamlet's 'little eyases'), politics (*Henry V*'s Chorus invoking Essex in Ireland), and economics (allusions to the 1607 enclosure riots in *Coriolanus*) are only the most direct and immediate. How such references occur through dramatic language – within a play, between plays, and between plays and the world – defines the poetic semantics of Shakespeare, how history is 'reflected' in his work. I return at the conclusion to the latter point, and it is implicitly the main topic of this study.

Frequently in the Classical dramas, Shakespeare tests new possibilities of his art, and sets forth his responses to changing English affairs: in particular, the evolution of his political awareness as the Tudor age becomes the Stuart is implied through a fabric of multiple (sometimes complementary, often contradictory) significations. To illustrate what is distinctive in Shakespeare's referential methods, I concentrate on two kinds of structural transformation (again, within texts, between them, and between texts and history) which are central to these plays, and the terms for which I borrow from Freudian dream symbolism – 'inversion' and 'displacement'.

Inversion is one of Shakespeare's most familiar techniques. Simply, Hamlet is flanked on one side by Horatio and on the other by Rosencrantz and Guildenstern; under the rubric of 'friendship', we have both A and its opposite, not-A. 'Husbands' may be similarly contrasted at an important moment in *Julius Caesar*: Brutus forbids his wife to kneel when she would influence his action (II, i, 261–80),[1] even as Caesar behaves so as to encourage that gesture from Calphurnia (II, ii, 7–56); the familial scene thus distinguishes political temperaments. An elaborate inversion links Viola in *Twelfth Night* and the Friend addressed in the Sonnets. She and her father are not identified by title, and so presumably are not aristocrats (e.g. v, i, 223–5); she is in disguise against a hostile world; in love; and would marry, but cannot. He is her symmetrical inversion: a male of noble birth; 'disguised' as a woman, for he is beautiful as one (and the 'master–mistress' of the sonneteer's passion); in favor with fortune; who could marry, but will not. Both are threatened with the fate of the hermaphrodite – sterility – against which Viola enjoins Olivia (I, v, 227–9) while the Friend seems to ignore the poet's pleas. He is the end of his familial line, while Viola (and here a comedic movement overcomes the stasis of the lyric poem) only believes herself to be so (II, iv, 119–20); she escapes 'a green and yellow melancholy' when Sebastian's entrance annuls the quarrels bred from mistakes over her identity (Orsino and Viola, Olivia and Viola, Andrew and Viola, Antonio and Viola), shattering the false alignments that have frozen into antagonisms and allowing the true alignments of harmony to prevail. The

'Dramatic Text as a Component of Theater', in L. Matejka ed., *Semiotics of Art: Prague School Contributions* (Cambridge, Mass., 1976), pp. 94–117.

[1] References are to *The Complete Pelican Shakespeare*, ed. Alfred Harbage (Baltimore, 1969).

regal appearances of Queen Elizabeth (to whom Sebastian is dramatic analogue) among squabbling Court factions, or in Parliament, or on 'progress' among the nation, performed just that mediatory function in resolving false divisions and healing popular discord.

Such inversions (upon which Shakespeare constructs elaborate and sustained oppositions) and their dramatic consequences might even be charted: for each '+' beside a quality of Viola, a '−' would be placed beside that of the Friend, as Claude Lévi-Strauss (following the linguists) has done in seeking the inner structure of myth. In the later tragedies, Shakespeare often inverts situations and themes from *Henry V*, perhaps because that was the last drama in which a struggle for political power was treated sympathetically; against 'gentle Harry' we have only to oppose Claudius, Macbeth, Octavius, Sicinius/Brutus, and Aufidius (not to mention Alonso and Sebastian from *The Tempest*) to discern the change. I contrast here act II of *Henry V*, on the eve of departure for France, with act III of *King Lear*, set on the wilderness of the heath. The history-play presents a 'set' (i.e. a conjunction of specific and invariant properties) which is symmetrically reversed (each '+' becoming its own '−') by *Lear* into its counter-set:[1]

Henry V (act II)	*King Lear* (act III)
Power = Right (joined in figure of the King);	Power ≠ Right (disjoined through victory of Goneril/Regan);
Traitors (Scroop, Grey, Cambridge) known in advance and crushed;	Traitors deceive the monarch and prevail over him;
Nation united behind royal authority;	King uncrowned, nation divided into contradictory factions;
England bustling, with all occupations joining in great common endeavor;	England a desert, with all bonds broken and civil war impending;
The flower of the regime and country gather for self-assertion through war;	On the heath gather beggars, madmen, the wronged, outcasts; the passive 'dregs' of the nation;
They undertake directed travel to France; the medium for this is −	They undertake directionless wandering; the medium for this is −
Water: here, sea-water upon which they cast their fortunes.	Water: here, rain, storm, chaos in which fortune acts upon them.

How does the set in the left-hand column become the counter-set on the right? There is an 'operational term' whose disappearance (especially marked in the later Roman plays) in the late 1590s first brings about this inversion: I refer to Viola's brother with a crown, to the King-as-mediator who appears in *Henry V* bridging all factions of the country (from alehouse to Court), a role that is parodied in *Lear* as the self-deluded old man. Typically in Shakespeare, the King is like Elizabeth: he maintains a compromise between contending social forces and is thus the figure through whom national unity is achieved. With such a leader removed, all rights become wrongs, all power is inverted, and chaos is come again. The transition from the Elizabethan to the Jacobean reigns may well be signaled in Shakespeare not only by the shift into tragedy, but

[1] The concepts of 'structure' (including both architecture and process) used in this essay are indebted to: Claude Lévi-Strauss, *The Raw and the Cooked*, tr. J. and D. Weightman (New York, 1969) and *Structural Anthropology*, tr. C. Jacobson and B. G. Schoepf (New York, 1963); Karl Marx, 'Introduction' (1857) to *Grundrisse*, tr. Martin Nicolaus (New York, 1973); Juri Tynjanov and Roman Jakobson, 'Problems in the Study of Literature and Language', in DeGeorge, pp. 81–3.

also through the disappearance of this ruler and his replacement by sophisticated versions of the Machiavel figure always abhorrent to the dramatist.[1] This new turn in Shakespeare's thinking about the relationship of the monarch (and, by implication, the State) to society at large may be further explained by looking at 'displacement' as a structural technique. I then return to the various more complex forms of inversion in *Antony and Cleopatra* and *Coriolanus*.

Displacement operates between plays, when the same thematic units are re-aligned so as to modify existing patterns. A very significant displacement occurs between *1* and *2 Henry IV* and *Henry V* on the one hand, and *Hamlet* on the other, with *Julius Caesar* as the mediating drama which establishes a bridge between the later histories and those mature tragedies which occupied both the most significant period of Shakespeare's career and the early years of Jacobean rule.

It is well known that *1 Henry IV* centers on the struggle between Hal and Hotspur over who is the King's 'true' son, in spirit rather than blood, and over who is Hal's 'true' father, the King or Falstaff. This struggle is paralleled by the competition of Brutus (the abstract idealist) with Antony (his inversion, the cunning manipulator) over 'sonhood' to Julius Caesar: Brutus is heir to Caesar's dream of Roman greatness, while Antony inherits his machinations with the populace for personal ends. The analogy is strengthened when we recall that Bolingbroke, too, was a 'Caesar': that is, he abolished normal political authority by usurping law and power. From roughly 1597 to 1601, Shakespeare seems to have held two ideals of sons: the 'son as vindicator' of his father, and the 'son as avenger' of his father; Prince Hal embodies the first, and Hamlet the second. The son as vindicator must (1) affirm what his father has achieved by proving the latter's decisions and actions correct;

and (2) he must succeed to his father's authority and fill that place justly. The son as avenger, however, inverts these responsibilities. He must (1) revenge what was done to the father (here, the sire is passively a victim, not actively the protagonist); and (2) he must overthrow the usurper and empty the throne which is illegally occupied (i.e. instead of triumphantly assuming the sire's place, he must annul a false authority). Antony in *Julius Caesar* is the mediating figure between the relationship of Bolingbroke and Prince Hal on the one side and of Hamlet father-and-son on the other: for Antony performs the duties of 'vindicator 1' in act III during the funeral speech, and of 'vindicator 2' in acts IV–V when he assumes co-rulership of Rome; but he also performs as 'avenger' (both 1 and 2) in defeating Brutus and Cassius. He thus stands in the middle of a definitive shift in the role of the 'son' between the histories and the later tragedies. Malcolm and Donalbain will be the later sons-as-avengers, while much of the tribulation besetting Caius Marcius Coriolanus derives from his inability to do the same for – his mother.

When, in *Hamlet*, the son becomes an avenger, he also passes out of the direct line of political succession: he becomes a *nephew* to the usurper. The latter is always childless: Caesar, Claudius, Macbeth, Lear's daughters, even Sicinius and Brutus. In *Julius Caesar* (the mediatory drama) a symbolic son (Brutus) struggles with a blood nephew (Octavius) for the mantle of Caesar, each contender armed with his own wily assistant – Cassius and Antony.[2] The shift from son to nephew in

[1] The importance of 'mediation' in Shakespeare was argued in a different way by Richard Fly, *Shakespeare's Mediated Vision: Essays on Medium and Mediators in Shakespearean Drama* (Amherst, 1976); also, J. J. Lynd, *The Mediating Figure in Shakespeare*, Diss., University of California, Davis, 1973.

[2] On Brutus's symbolic sonhood, cf. North's Plutarch: 'For Caesar did not onely save his life, . . .

Hamlet marks the first time in Shakespearian *tragedy* that the nation is without an effective mediator, a rightful leader of the commonwealth. While Hamlet chats with gravediggers and players (a sophisticated Hal in the tavern), Claudius privately disposes of war and peace and broods alone in his chamber over adultery and fratricide. The succession gone wrong will thereafter haunt Shakespeare's work, for the man who, like Elizabeth and Henry V, straddled the entire nation has been dispossessed. It is as if the State – for the first time in Shakespeare's (and perhaps England's) experience – were becoming independent in its apparatus and its monarchial person from society as a whole, a movement represented dramatically through re-alignments within the family, that basic unit of social order; with effective power disjoined from traditional right, a triumphant Machiavel takes government on a course unable to satisfy the realm he nominally leads.[1] Vengeance may arrive against the usurper (Claudius, Macbeth), but he may also achieve an ambivalent political stability (Octavius). Dramas of the final decade of Elizabeth's reign, when she had in good part withdrawn from common view and had yet definitely to name a successor, and when social change within England brought what Lyly called the 'Gallimaufrey of the age' and what Hamlet mocked as 'the toe of the peasant comes so near the heel of the courtier he galls his kibe', the second tetralogy, *Julius Caesar*, and *Hamlet* ask with extreme misgivings whether succession in time of political hiatus can be achieved without sundering the head of rulership from the body of the nation. In the final – and Roman – tragedies, politics is only power and no longer right; indeed, after *Macbeth* there are no longer even any sons who can inherit, or fathers to bestow. Implicit here may be a far more skeptical Shakespearian view of the transition between dynasties than is often admitted of this most

faithful and successful servant of the Crown, a vision that intuits the shift from Renaissance to Baroque.

Antony and Cleopatra and *Coriolanus* climax Shakespeare's meditations on politics and offer the most structurally challenging examples of inversion. We have already discussed this technique in terms of a single axis upon which A is juxtaposed to not-A, with Horatio at one extreme and Rosencrantz and Guildenstern at the other. The *Henry V–King Lear* set and counter-set also functioned as a simple reversal. But while Falstaff and Hotspur may appear to be A and not-A, this is true on but one axis, that of 'honor'; if we were to introduce a new and contrasting axis – such as 'sound government' – they suddenly find themselves together and pitted (as Falstaff discovered to his cost) against the King, the Chief Justice, and established authority. For one answer to what we mean when we say that Shakespeare 'matures' as a dramatist, that *Antony and Cleopatra* is more 'complex' in poetry, organization, and view of life than *Romeo and Juliet* (or *Twelfth Night*) is that Shakespeare increasingly constructs dramas upon internal tensions between multiple and conflicting axes which allow no mediation between their antithetic terms: what is signified is permanent, irredeemable opposition. In the comedies, Viola's resolution was possible

but furthermore, he put a marvelous confidence in him. For he had already preferred him to the Praetorshippe for that yeare, and furthermore was appointed to be Consul, ... having through Caesars frendshippe, obtained it before Cassius ... Caesar ... told them, Brutus will looke for this skinne: meaning thereby, that Brutus for his vertue, deserved to rule after him ...' (Geoffrey Bullough ed., *Narrative and Dramatic Sources of Shakespeare* (London and New York, 1957–75), v, 82.

[1] On the separation of State from society in prerevolutionary England, see H. R. Trevor-Roper, 'The General Crisis of the Seventeenth Century', in *The Crisis of the Seventeenth Century: Religion, the Reformation, and Social Change* (New York, 1968).

because Sebastian lived and entered: but in the tragedies after *Hamlet*, the option of an arriving mediator disappears. Only in the final romances – and then by force of artificial magic – can something of the old harmony be dreamed once more.

Even as an undergraduate I was fascinated but confused by *Antony and Cleopatra*, a response I have never lost; then, I formulated my problem through the objection that poetry and plot somehow did not fit together, and, subsequently, my own students have voiced the same discomfort. On the level of language, Shakespeare's most sublime verse justifies and extols a passion for which the world in all its abundance is too mean. But on the level of action, a pair of aging sensualists squabble and make up, ignore public duties, desert their armies, and disappear to make way for stable and universal peace. It is as if Shakespeare (in a quite Metaphysical technique) were 'yoking' together contradictions of A and not-A on the inclusive planes of rhetoric and enactment: poetic self-celebration wedded incongruously to farcical self-debunking.

If we assume this primary contradiction is real and deliberate, then we are alerted to a number of subsidiary conflicts which establish the tensions structuring the drama. The indicator of such contradictions is paradox, in which the play abounds: as a prominent example, unlike Brutus and Cassius, traitors whom he once defeated, the greatest Roman warrior cannot fall on his sword properly, while Cleopatra outwits the world's emperor to die (easily) on her own terms. Paradox depends upon a conflict between various axes; the extremes of each axis are 'binary oppositions' – that is, original dualisms (like the mythic contrasts of raw/cooked, honey/ashes, nature/culture charted by ethnology) experienced as irreconcilable but which characters and their creator attempt to mediate. Paradox expresses the failure of such mediation,

indicating that only a tragic outcome (and not the entrance of Sebastian) is possible. Every significant axis in the drama is crossed by others which contradict it, thus complicating the protagonists' choices and the audience's response.[1]

For example, *Antony and Cleopatra* is structured upon a primary geographic contradiction between Rome and Egypt – a meridional axis stretching between the opposites of a rising western world power and a declining eastern one. Indeed, 'power' functions as itself an axis, with Rome at its peak and Asia (a dependent colony) at its nadir; the axis of 'pleasure', however, directly contradicts it, and is, in fact, its inversion. Thus, characters high (and rising) on the axis of power – for example, Octavius – will be low on its opposite, that of pleasure; Antony, of course, is just the reverse. But power admits of many crossings and complications: Enobarbus is a male Roman officer and thus a figure of might, while Charmian and Iris are not only females but slaves too; however, when the axis of strength is crossed by that of 'fidelity', the original situation is reversed – the warrior deserts, perishing in despair, while the slave-girls stand fast and participate (also by suicide) in their mistress's triumph. These paradoxes, however (which only illustrate the conventional view of the play), hint at deeper contradictions.[2] The opposition of Rome and Egypt is not inherently moral or antagonistic, for both societies show intricate standards of

[1] How Shakespeare 'pulls' the audience 'in this way or that' is addressed in the valuable E. A. J. Honigmann, *Shakespeare: Seven Tragedies* (1976); see especially chapter 9 on *Antony*. Also, Alan C. Dessen, *Elizabethan Drama and the Viewer's Eye* (Chapel Hill, 1977) on staging and response.
[2] Image-criticism, for example, has developed on the play as the *juxtaposition* of Rome and Egypt; see G. Wilson Knight, *The Imperial Theme*, 3rd edn (1951), chapters 7–8. But it is the *meeting* of these societies, their mutual reflection through one another, that is important to Shakespeare.

behavior; each places specific values on the extremes of a tension (which both recognize) between duty and love, politics and pleasure, Mars and Venus. Within either Rome or Egypt, all is consistent and plain. What the general and his Queen attempt and fail to mediate is the *encounter* of two value-systems, each of which represents an *already* formed civilization and each of which is the inversion of the other. There is Roman love (the arranged marriage with Octavia), and there is Egyptian duty (no messenger dare bring the Queen bad news); but to the Roman, Egyptian love is 'dotage' and to the Egyptian, Roman duty is bondage. On the Egyptian axis of 'legal legitimacy', Cleopatra is Queen beyond dispute; on the same axis in Rome, she is Antony's whore and a political threat. On the Roman axis of 'love', Fulvia and then Octavia stand high, for they are wives; on the same axis in Egypt, they are burdens or mere conveniences, while Cleopatra is the goddess of Antony's heart. The problem, in brief, is Empire: the old descendants of Aeneas have entered a relationship of power with a culture which is the negative mirror of themselves, even – perhaps – as the new descendants (the English) have in the Americas. I return to this analogy in a moment.

Taken as a system and as a whole, these conflicting axes between opposing world-centers locked in a mutual inverted reflection form the 'deep structure' of the play, intuited by reader or viewer as a subliminal logic to events, but rarely articulated explicitly. This constant Shakespearian running against the grain, this crossing of every thrust of the drama by a complicating counter-thrust, is not unlike the deliberate technique of anticlimax prominent in *King Lear*: the monarch elaborates a ceremony of abdication, only to be frustrated by Cordelia; Gloucester prepares his suicide over the Dover cliffs, only to fall flat on the plains he never left; the victory of Cordelia's forces promises new life for the King, only to end, 'Thou'lt come no more, / Never, never, never, never, never'. This preparation of an outcome which Shakespeare then ruthlessly aborts is greatly responsible for the play's sense of black farce which so impressed Jan Kott.

If, in *Troilus*, language shattered both its models and itself under the reflection of war, then in *Antony* language which is prism to 'the wide arch / Of the ranged empire' deflects aside the full burden of the tragic conflict. Between plot and verse, politics and love, there is a stalemate:

> . . . and their story is
> No less in pity than his glory which
> Brought them to be lamented.
>
> (v, ii, 359–61)

The referential range of *Coriolanus* is deliberately more narrow, and the impossibility of mediation thereby emerges more starkly. Now two spatial axes dominate the play: the first stretches from the Tiber outward to Corioli and Antium, while the second (as if Egypt had become internal to Rome itself) runs between patricians and plebeians, social war echoing the battle on the frontiers. How can Rome command others when it cannot command itself, when class struggle overrides national coherence? The call to Roman unity in act I (another parody of *Henry V*) sounds hollow the moment battle is past. The Senate claims old authority, while the crowd claims present need: both are right and wrong. Menenius's belly-speech defends ancient principles of order, but does so through platitudes transparently self-serving to patrician advantage; the masses are in fact starving ('I speak this in hunger for bread, not in thirst for revenge', I, i, 20–1), but are led by cunning opportunists who trick a noble war veteran into exile. The problem of whether Caius Marcius is hero or antihero misses the point, for when the ethic of Octavius – power – no longer has the excuse that it prepares 'the time of universal peace', then all political roads are compromised from the beginning. On the axis of 'tradition', Marcius deserves to rule, but on its contradictory axis (the most persistent crossing in late Shakespearian tragedy), that of 'competence', he does not: a victor in battle (his a 'nature, never known before / But to be rough, unswayable, and free', v, vi, 24–5), yet in civil affairs 'There's no man in the world / More bound to 's mother' (v, iii, 158–9); Aufidius is not unjust that, given the mutual exclusion of warring sides –

> At a few drops of women's rheum, which are
> As cheap as lies, he sold the blood and labor
> Of our great action.   (v, vi, 45–7)

With a woman the most eloquent defender of patriarchy (Volumnia in I, iii); with Marcius upholding patrician honor by means of treason; and with Aufidius so 'struck with sorrow' that he lauds the enemy he has just conspired to assassinate, Shakespeare ends his experiments in tragedy. The monarch who united all national interests within her person is gone: when the country has become a paradox (at war internally and externally), then any political choice is but inversion of every other, equally unsatisfactory, choice. Since *Julius Caesar*, it is politics itself which has become the impossible option.

Troilus, *Antony*, and *Coriolanus* are all dramas of a people gone beyond the seas, there to encounter its own inversion as a temptation. Pursuing Helen to re-assert marital order, the Greeks only fall into disorder, giving reign to their viler princes; if Troilus escapes over the Trojan wall, fleeing war for love, the fate of love amid war returns him to battle which he then embraces with lover's passion. Even as Antony is bound to Cleopatra in the measure that she was originally his opposite, so Coriolanus is tempted by the Volscians to war on

Rome to the same degree that he once wanted to be honored by her. These are dramas of Empire, or, more specifically, of Empire succeeding upon a period of national self-consolidation – upon the Greeks assembling for a common enterprise, the Romans emerging from civil war on the brink of the Christian era, or the early Roman city expelling kings and attempting self-rule. What is the cost of transcending old boundaries, traditions, authority – and dynasties? Once an insular outpost, then a world power confronting undreamt of peoples in America, the England of 1608 might find in the early Rome of *Coriolanus* the anachronistic mirror of itself: even as, in *King Lear*, the struggle of values based upon traditional order and those rooted in self-interest evokes the moral crises of Stuart times, so the ancient class divisions found their contemporary echo in the dissolution of Tudor political alignments. Elizabeth's rule guided an effective balance among social forces no one of which was powerful enough to establish hegemony over the nation as a whole: this 'compromise' (as it has been described) of nobility, bourgeoisie, and artisan and plebeian strata was yielding by the early seventeenth century to the pull of antagonistic initiatives from aristocrats (with whom the monarchy soon aligned itself) and gentry, and it would climax in civil war.[1] How can England rule itself and America when the 'Elizabethan compromise' and 'Tudor absolutism by consent' had run their course, when national unity was a memory? And how should the new descendants of Aeneas react to that temptation latent in all 'otherness', the encounter with those dark-skinned peoples – those 'gipsy' peoples – of the New World?

[1] Karl Marx, 'The English Revolution' (1850), in *Selected Essays*, tr. H. J. Stenning (New York, 1926), pp. 196–208; A. L. Morton, *A People's History of England* (1971), chapters 7–8; Paul Siegel, *Shakespearean Tragedy and the Elizabethan Compromise* (New York, 1957); Robert Weimann, *Drama und Wirklichkeit in der Shakespearezeit* (Halle, 1958).

This essay began with the question of referentiality (within single plays, between them, and between the play and contemporary history) in Shakespeare's Classical world: with how the immanent evolution of the playwright's works, through the use of Classical subjects, and spanning the shift in political dynasties and the social transformations ending the sixteenth century, carried the times as a dimension of the texts themselves. Distinguished scholars have written about 'unity in multiplicity' as a structural principle in drama, even as Coleridge found the dissonance of Shakespearian materials to be only apparent.[1] And yet, without challenging 'unity' as a final objective of Renaissance aesthetics, I would carefully distinguish it from notions of 'organic form' that have received so much critical attention in the wake of the nineteenth-century novel. Shakespearian tragedy carries its times within the texts in a most complex and segmented way: hardly the transparent referentiality in which an older Marxian criticism sought the author's social sympathies or direct allusions to topical events, and hardly the Coleridgean reconciliation of opposites. The Classical plays present a deliberate and open multiplicity of reference – to contemporary history, to the past, to Shakespeare's other work, to themselves, to other dramatic and philosophic texts, and to sources – which can be arranged by 'sets', studied as inversion, displacement, and contradiction, and which mediates the experience of history by writer and audience through the internal structure of the dramatic artifice.[2] Obviously, such an achievement involves the closest trust and communication with its spectators: through such techniques, the larger world of Renaissance culture (and I use the word in its most inclusive sense) entered the theatre, just as the theatre situated itself as an active element in national history by offering its beholders such resonant *exempla* from the Classics.

This multi-faceted, allusive dialogue with the public over the moral and social dilemmas of the time indicates that theatre was quite unlike the church where all truths were final and the order of service invariable. If my earlier discussions (for example, of inversion) perhaps seemed 'mechanical', it is because they showed the regularity and functional ease of rules for a game. 'Drama was mixed up in the public mind with the athletics of fencing, with bear-baiting, dancing on the ropes and other activities . . . The theatre of the Elizabethans, in its social atmosphere, was less like the modern theatre than it was like a funfair.' Gamehouses were separated from playhouses by statute only after 1597, and 'game' and 'play' were often synonymous in late Tudor usage.[3] When part of holiday, theatre becomes a privileged aesthetic space – the realm of inquiry, testing, and the formation of new perspectives, a condoned popular fantasy; drama creates a new audience, which it then serves the entertainment it has induced them to want; throngs merge into a public, and the latter asks for no

[1] For example, Madeleine Doran, *Endeavors of Art* (Madison, 1954); Leo Salingar, *Shakespeare and the Traditions of Comedy* (Cambridge, 1974). On Coleridge, see M. H. Abrams, *The Mirror and the Lamp* (New York, 1958), pp. 218–25. On 'organic form' as a critical principle, see Henry James, 'Preface' to *The Tragic Muse* (1908); Terry Eagleton, 'Ideology and Literary Form', *New Left Review*, 90 (1975), 81–109.

[2] On an open literary text, with multiple significations, see Pierre Macherey, *Pour une théorie de la production littéraire* (Paris, 1966), especially pp. 101–22; also, Terry Eagleton, *Criticism and Ideology* (1976). Of course, the mainstream of Shakespearian criticism has long recognized a deliberate linking of contraries and of 'multi-consciousness' in the dramas: for example, S. L. Bethell, *Shakespeare and the Popular Dramatic Tradition* (Durham, 1944); A. P. Rossiter, *Angel with Horns* (1961).

[3] M. C. Bradbrook, *The Rise of the Common Player* (Cambridge, Mass., 1962), pp. 96–7; Glynne Wickham, *Early English Stages 1300 to 1660* (London and New York, 1972), vol. 2, Part II, pp. 30–45.

'organic form', because it seeks a mirror of conflicts which the age itself has yet to reconcile.[1] In this unique and perhaps unrecoverable spirit of testing and exploration – when Shakespeare, the audience, and the times expressed the 'form and pressure' of each other – drama is 'displaced' from emphasis upon its existence as verbal text, turning 'outward' towards the cultural abundance and opacity of national life. As Brecht understood, a theatrical act of communicative inquiry leaves the observer to impose significant form on the possibilities offered:

With Shakespeare, the spectator does the constructing. ...In the lack of connection between his acts we recognize the lack of connection in a human destiny, when it is recounted by someone with no interest in tidying it up so as to provide an idea (which can only be a prejudice) with an argument not taken from life. There's nothing more stupid than to perform Shakespeare so that he's clear. He's by his very nature unclear. He's pure material.[2]

It is perhaps in such a concept of the signifier as a 'game' perpetually open to history – Shakespeare's and our own – that the most valuable secrets of literary 'realism' are to be discovered.

[1] Bradbrook, pp. 107–10 has remarkable insights on the growth of the audience; also, Alfred Harbage, *Shakespeare's Audience* (New York, 1940), and the reconstruction of Martin Holmes, *Shakespeare's Public* (1960).
[2] Quoted in Margot Heinemann, 'Shakespearean Contradictions and Social Change', *Science and Society*, XLI (1977), 7.

TRUTH AND UTTERANCE IN
'THE WINTER'S TALE'

A. F. BELLETTE

With so much attention paid in recent criticism to the larger mythic patterns of the late romances, it is nevertheless true that it is Shakespeare's actual words, heard from the stage or read in the text, that provide our first access to these plays, and furnish us with their final meanings. So complex and finely tuned is the language of the late Shakespeare, and yet so subtly simple, that it might be likened to a natural element in which we live and breathe for the duration of the play, essential yet unheeded in itself. This is not to ignore such justly famous set pieces as Perdita's flower speech in *The Winter's Tale* or Prospero's valedictory in *The Tempest*, but to see these isolated from the verbal context of the play as a whole is to lessen our awareness of both the speech and the play. The same might be said of any literary work which makes serious intellectual and aesthetic claims upon us, yet it is an aspect of the romances which has been somewhat neglected. References to 'the late style' have usually drawn attention to its variety, its lack of any *single* style. It is recognised that in his last plays Shakespeare drew upon all his accumulated poetic resources, but it is also commonly felt that the resultant style is in many places too prolix and diffuse, even given the looser dramatic mode in which he is working. Yet it is of the essence of the late plays that there is no dominant or consistent style. Each person speaks in the way which is most directly expressive of his or her nature. Language never draws attention to itself: at

its most densely involute and at its most rustically plain it has the same function, to embody a specific perception of the world which to the speaker is truth.

A similar principle could be deduced from the earlier plays of course, particularly the histories and comedies. But it is in the last plays, from *Antony and Cleopatra* on, that the full significance of the principle is made clear, and it is *The Winter's Tale* in particular which offers the most satisfying example. First, though other plays equal it in this respect, none contains a wider range of character types drawn from all social levels. All characters are made fully articulate, and all contribute information and attitudes vital to the play's outcome and meaning. Second, and more important, there is no play which draws so much attention to the verbal act itself, not just as the expression but as the necessary endorsement of certain ways of looking at the world. From the opening scene of the play in which the courtly Archidamus says 'Verily I speak it in the freedom of my knowledge' (I, i, 11)[1] and refers to 'an unspeakable comfort of your young prince Mamillius' (I, i, 34–5), to the closing scene in which Camillo, after the descent of Hermione, says 'If she pertain to life, let her speak too!' (v, iii, 113), Shakespeare refers directly and repeatedly to the importance of speaking, and, at times, of remaining silent. The catastrophe of the first part of the play arises as inevitably

[1] Quotations and references are from the new Arden edition by J. H. P. Pafford (1963).

from a failure to recognise what should govern these functions as does the harmonious conclusion from a true perception of it.

On the face of it a mere courtly exchange, the opening conversation between Archidamus and Camillo nevertheless establishes a principle which operates throughout the play. Archidamus's words, spoken 'in the freedom of my knowledge' (I, i, 11), are words by definition true. 'Believe me, I speak as my understanding instructs me, and as mine honesty puts it to utterance' (I, i, 19–20) – it is the least, and the most, that a creature gifted with speech can do; it is a statement, too, of great poetic propriety, and in its tenor is opposed to the mere empty flourish so often mocked in the earlier plays and so carefully avoided in the Sonnets. But it does not follow that highly figured speech is in itself proof of vacuity or dishonesty, any more than rustic speech is an infallible sign of stupidity. It is possible to smile at either, and still recognise that in late Shakespeare particularly, responsibility for meaning is evenly distributed. In *The Winter's Tale* courtiers and rustics alike, with their highly distinctive speech patterns, are given that 'freedom of knowledge' which enables them to convey to audience and reader their own share of truth. Anonymous 'gentlemen', like Herbert's shepherds (and the shepherds of the play), are 'honest people', and if the understanding which instructs them is limited by their necessary exclusion from much of the play's action, it should also be remembered that no character has complete knowledge until the final scene, and even then, the 'how, is to be question'd' (V, iii, 139).

All that has been said so far might be seen as applying to any romantic tale with a complicated plot involving many people. In addition, the romance emphasis on banishment, disguise, and submission to the vagaries of fortune makes inevitable a kind of 'farming out', as it were, of the total action. But in romance generally, as its early detractors so often pointed out, such things as credibility and truth of utterance are of minor importance. Romance resists what *The Winter's Tale*, on the other hand, most insists on: fidelity of words to the observable truth of human experience. What underlies this insistence is man's need to understand the nature of his relationships with others, and his relationship with himself, and to be able to articulate that understanding in the common medium of words. It is within this context that I wish to examine the disastrous series of actions perpetrated by Leontes in the first half of the play.

Faced with the apparent suddenness of the onset of Leontes's jealousy, students of the play have been tempted to read backwards and find the germs of this jealousy in the brevity of his initial response to Polixenes's announced departure. Yet there is no need to suspect here anything more than a certain embarrassment when faced with the customary formalities of leave-taking. Leontes is not at any point in the play revealed as being skilled in the arts of polite discourse. This does not mean that he is insincere in his request that his friend stay longer. Instead, he turns naturally to his wife, who has the skill he lacks: 'Tongue-tied our queen? Speak you' (I, ii, 27). Hermione, silent up to this point, and aware of his awkwardness, is now able, tactfully, to enter into the proceedings. Her first speech, however, is directed only to Leontes, who finds it 'well said', but is apparently still unable to frame his own appropriate words. (A significant pause before Hermione resumes her speech at l. 34, and again before she addresses Polixenes at l. 38, could well serve to establish that it is Leontes who is 'tongue-tied'.) Her own eloquent persuasiveness may now be brought to bear on Polixenes. She knows instinctively the exact tone to adopt with him – a humorous chiding designed to test the sincerity of his reasons for leaving. At the same time she is careful not to exclude Leontes, and at the end of her speech finds a way to assert her love for him. Her argument is not only skilful and vigorous, but shows in addition a remarkable sense of the emotional occasion and of the needs of others – a dual accomplishment which seems only to be found in Shakespeare's women, and which will allow her to rise to great heights later in the play. For the moment, though, her immediate goal is achieved: 'He'll stay, my lord'. Leontes's reply, 'At my request he would not' (I, ii, 87), while it may contain a hint of what is to come, nevertheless must not be separated from what immediately follows: 'Hermione, my dearest, thou never spok'st / To better purpose' – words which show a proper recognition of and deference to her greater articulateness. It is significant, however, that Leontes *does* remember an earlier occasion: her simple 'I am yours for ever', spoken after three months of silence (or at least reticence) before they married. It is possible that recollection may be an oblique warning not to overstep the mark now, a response to what might be seen as a certain archness in Hermione's preceding speech. If that is so (and here tone is everything), it still obliges us to recognise that a declaration of love on Hermione's part is not something lightly undertaken. Hermione is in any case perceptive enough of any such implication to respond to it and accommodate it in her rejoinder:

> Why lo you now; I have spoke to th' purpose twice:
> The one, for ever earn'd a royal husband;
> Th' other, for some while a friend.   (I, ii, 105–7)

It is worth while to pause at this point, immediately before the offering of her hand to Polixenes, to consider briefly the weight of Hermione's words.

Like Cordelia before her, whose honesty was likewise, and with no less appalling results, put to utterance, Hermione distinguishes carefully between kinds of love –

love of a husband 'for ever' and of a friend 'for some while'. As if sensing the sudden delicacy of the situation she adopts a tone of greater seriousness in which one line balances the other in almost augustan symmetry, a brief foreshadowing of the form and content of her speeches in the trial scene. Behind the lines lies a recognition of a complex world of relationships and of the need to act and speak in such a way as to embody in careful utterance the distinctions necessary if potentially disruptive feelings are to be rationally controlled. The point is lost on Leontes. His first long speech, delivered as an aside and thus essentially isolated from the social situation, shows a man unable to respond to carefully articulated distinctions. Unable to understand her words (he has only recognised they are 'well said'), Leontes interprets her ensuing gesture as a sign of her determination 'To mingle friendship far' (I, ii, 109), thus completely missing the point of the words leading up to the gesture. His own utterances which follow are as chronically disjointed as hers were controlled. Sudden breaks, meaningless repetitions, a syntax strained and opaque, are the verbal embodiment of a mind turned disastrously in upon itself and now revealed as incapable of functioning at those levels of necessary multiple awareness that Hermione represents. Left alone with Mamillius after Hermione and Polixenes have left for the garden, Leontes hears now no words at all, only noise. He imagines himself hissed to his grave, where 'contempt and clamour / Will be my knell' (I, ii, 189–90). Whispers and guilty sighs surround him as his imagination peoples a bawdy planet with lecherous neighbours and complaisant wives. So completely realised in his language is Leontes's jealous madness that we cease to ask why or how – indeed his madness has its own terrible eloquence that might almost persuade us that his vision of this planet is a true one, so effectively is it conveyed by Shakespeare's dislocations of syntax and metre through all of Leontes's speeches in the rest of the first act.

We are reminded, however, of the persistence of the world of social order, as opposed to Leontes's distortion of it, by Camillo, whose speech beginning at I, ii, 249 is an heroic attempt to re-establish true judgement and necessary distinction. 'Among the infinite doings of the world' (I, ii, 253) Camillo sees order and pattern, and the speech itself, with its balanced articulation and its periodic and highly subordinated structures, is heard proof not only of Camillo's sanity but of the King's madness. Camillo ends with the adjuration to Leontes to 'Be plainer with me' (l. 265), but the rejoinder is a parody of the preceding speech, substituting awkward parenthesis and breathless enjambement for Camillo's lucid periods. Leontes also speaks, quite simply, logical nonsense: cogitation indeed 'Resides not in that man that does not think' (l. 272). Camillo gives up: 'You never spoke what did become you less / Than this' (ll. 282–3). It is significant that he recognises in Leontes's actual utterance the sign of the man he has become. It is not possible to reach Leontes through rational discourse, as is shown most vividly in the following exchange:

Camillo.   Good my lord, be cur'd
Of this diseas'd opinion, and betimes,
For 'tis most dangerous.
Leontes.   Say it be, 'tis true.
Camillo. No, no, my lord.
Leontes.   It is: you lie, you lie:
I say thou liest, Camillo, and I hate thee,
Pronounce thee a gross lout, a mindless
slave . . .   (I, ii, 296–301)

Nothing in the play so conveys the dual debasement of personality and utterance as this kind of confrontation. Another occurs shortly after, at the beginning of act II, when Leontes 'confronts' Hermione. After an interlude of the utmost verbal delicacy between mother and child, his outburst is doubly shocking. It is important, and in keeping with the preoccupation with utterance in this play, that Hermione should respond to Leontes's 'for 'tis Polixenes / Has made thee swell thus' (II, i, 61–2) not with a direct denial but with something on the face of it more circumspect:

          But I'd say he had not;
And I'll be sworn you would believe my saying,
How e'er you lean to th'nay-ward.   (ll. 62–4)

She stresses, in fact, the importance of the saying, the word for her being the transparent sign of the reality, and the acceptance of the word, or utterance, the guarantee that truth will prevail, through a common trust, over any individual failure of comprehension. Her point this time is not entirely lost on Leontes: in the response that follows, he makes much of the difficulties of utterance now that deception rules the world, of the hum's and ha's that 'come between, / Ere you can say "she's honest"' (ll. 75–6) – in what might be a direct comment on his own thick and broken lines. One might note the 'coming between' at the end of his speech:

          but be 't known,
From him that has most cause to grieve it should be,
She's an adultress!   (ll. 76–8)

Ironically, it seems almost as hard for Leontes to say directly that she is dishonest as it is, in his view, for others to say she's honest, and for the very reason he adduces: it is not true.

A third for whom truth of utterance is of greatest importance is Paulina. In many ways she is the counterpart of Camillo – a subject forced into 'disloyalty' yet guardian of the truth and loyal to what the King himself has destroyed. It is true, she is often injudicious, in the traditional manner of the outspoken servant. But for all her impassioned eloquence, she knows that 'The silence often of pure innocence / Persuades, when speaking fails' (II, ii, 41–2). She also knows that for the moment utterance must not be abandoned: 'I'll use that tongue I have' (l. 52). However, it is not as another rational Camillo that she comes to Leontes, but as a physician, 'with words as medicinal as true' (II, iii, 37). As if by repetition or incantation the world of order can be rebuilt, Paulina states the truth in its simplest terms: 'Good queen, my lord, good queen: I say good queen' (l. 59). It is a waste of time, since Leontes has set up stronger barriers between himself and the truth than such words can surmount: words whose power lies in the shared faith which Paulina herself will bring about at the end. Yet Leontes, beyond words, craves the Word. He turns instinctively to the divine pronouncement of Apollo as the guarantee against the terrifying possibility that, as he said earlier to Camillo, in a speech designed to deny the possibility, 'the world, and all that's in't, is nothing' (I, ii, 293). It is not so much justification Leontes seeks, or the semblance of legality, but the Word which endorses a felt truth and extends beyond itself the validity of a private vision.

If Leontes wishes to be justified, it is, from the evidence of his own despairing speeches, not so much because he needs to convince others, but because he realises that a self-created world, without reason or sanction beyond itself, is simply intolerable to live in, if for no other reason than that one cannot converse with others. Leontes cannot express this to us directly. *The Winter's Tale* is a romance, not a tragedy, and Shakespeare does not allow the King the kind of lucid self-awareness appropriate to the heroes of tragedy. Truth is not found here by proceeding deeply into the self. Indeed it might be said that in *The Winter's Tale*, as in romance generally, truth is never learned out of the *individual* experience, but only out of the communal experience. Yet Shakespeare conveys the intensity of Leontes's longing for the Word personally spoken. The power of the Oracle to relieve him of the threat of nullity and of the

burden of himself (a need perceived by Paulina, who cannot at present satisfy it); the power which will drown the vile hisses and whispers of the world he has created around him by giving them at last full voice – this power is expressed with great simplicity by Cleomenes in the interlude at the beginning of the third act:

> But of all, the burst
> And the ear-deaf'ning voice o' th'oracle,
> Kin to Jove's thunder, so surpris'd my sense,
> That I was nothing. (III, i, 8–11)

The speech prefigures Leontes's collapse in the trial scene and the reduction of that self to nothing which would have destroyed the world.

The trial scene is the turning point of the play, the moment of suspense after which we do not need to concern ourselves with what will happen, but only wonder how. Yet the scene is central, not only as a pivot but as the climax and clearest example of those themes of speech and utterance which have been outlined so far. The weight of the scene is carried by Hermione, whose three long speeches are not only a skilful self-defence but also convincing testimony to a world of order, value and relatedness created by man and expressive of his best nature. It is not one of those defences of order based on a traditional figure and rendered suspect by the circumstances of its delivery, such as we hear elsewhere in Shakespeare from such compromised authorities as Ulysses and Menenius. There is in all of Hermione's defence not the least hint of casuistry, sleight of tongue or special pleading. While her presentation of her case shows her awareness of the specific legal situation in which she finds herself, and while she responds carefully, point by point, to the charges made against her, leading up only gradually to her more impassioned oration – while, in short, both her sense of occasion and her timing are impeccable, Hermione's 'performance' at all times serves to confirm what was first made explicit by her in act I scene ii. Her 'case' rests upon such plain and unadorned words as 'honour', 'love', 'free', 'friend' – slippery words and in Shakespeare often cynically debated and abused by equivocation. But they are ultimately all we have, and their corruption is a measure of our own. On their own they can do little enough, yet within the rhetorical structure of Hermione's speech they take on great power and authority:

> For Polixenes,
> With whom I am accus'd, I do confess
> I lov'd him as in honour he requir'd,
> With such a kind of love as might become
> A lady like me; with a love, even such,
> So, and no other, as yourself commanded:
> Which, not to have done, I think had been in me
> Both disobedience and ingratitude
> To you, and toward your friend, whose love
>   had spoke,
> Even since it could speak, from an infant, freely,
> That it was yours.   (III, ii, 61–71)

The verse might appear to some rather flat. There are no colours or flourishes. The most important word, 'love', is nowhere defined or modified adjectivally. Rather, it is placed in a series of different defining contexts in which it remains constant, gaining in depth and meaning as the advancing lines with highly subordinated syntax build up their fine distinctions of meaning. The eloquence is that of simple grammatical forms linked to each other in a complex sequence of thought which never loses sight of its single, serious theme. The word 'love' is, as it were, vindicated by its careful deployment. It is revealed as being fully expressive of a variety of human situations (love of a lady for her guest, love of mature friends, love of a child) while losing none of its central meaning – a meaning not defined, or 'given', but simply demonstrated, in the course of the speech, and the play, by its varying embodiments.

That words like 'love' and 'honour' can be cynically deployed and robbed of all meaning by a similar process of 'instancing' is a simple fact known by all the clowns in Shakespeare, and the reason why all are laughed at but none trusted. What is involved in Hermione's case, and others like hers, is an act of faith – faith in the shared experience which produces the word and to which the individual experience, no matter how compelling, must return if it is to be understood within a larger frame. Ultimately it is an act of faith in language itself as at once the embodiment and the guarantee of the idea of community. Since Leontes has retreated from community, has created a world where 'love' has no meaning, there is no way he can understand Hermione's words, nor she his. After the distressingly thick and muddy outburst: 'You knew of his departure, as you know / What you have underta'en to do in 's absence' (ll. 77–8), Hermione can only state helplessly, 'Sir, / You speak a language that I understand not' (ll. 79–80). Leontes's ensuing speech reads and sounds like a parody of Hermione's (as before it had seemed a parody of Camillo's), its syntactic awkwardness once again a sign of the inner solitude and confusion.

After Hermione's defence the Oracle's verdict is in a sense anticlimactic. Admirably brief and unequivocal as it is, it is in no way allowed to overshadow Hermione, nor does it have much effect on Leontes, who says immediately there is no truth in it. This should not surprise us – for all his longing for the Word, he will still only hear it if it comes as the embodiment of what he 'knows', the bawdy planet rather than the world of nothing. But it is the latter which declares itself real in the reported death of Mamillius. The action of the play turns on the word 'dead'. It signifies the irruption into the closed consciousness, the inner world of shadow and suspicion, of an external reality as undeniable as the words of Apollo, which for all their directness could not pierce as this does. Yet this word is destructive only of the illusory world which has reduced the real world to nothing. The walls of that world once breached collapse with a swiftness equal only to that with which they were constructed. Yet Shakespeare in an admirably judged sequence conveys every necessary stage of the transition so that we are aware of no suddenness. Even as Hermione is taken away to death the world for which she stands re-enters the play in the form of Leontes's slow recognition of it, in words which now become a true echo, not a travesty, of Hermione's. The speech 'Apollo, pardon / My great profaneness . . .' (ll. 153–72) shows a mind, if not a soul, already healed, and its echoes of Hermione's speech (ll. 61–71) quoted above are only a further example of the verbal correspondences with which *The Winter's Tale* is filled:

I'll reconcile me to Polixenes,
New woo my queen, recall the good Camillo,
Whom I proclaim a man of truth, of mercy:
For being transported by my jealousies
To bloody thoughts and to revenge, I chose
Camillo for the minister to poison
My friend Polixenes: which had been done,
But that the good mind of Camillo tardied
My swift command; though I with death, and with
Reward, did threaten and encourage him,
Not doing it, and being done.   (ll. 155–65)

The lines represent the reconstruction in Leontes's consciousness of the truth about Polixenes which Hermione had already expressed in a language he did not understand. Now her language is his. Her 'Which, not to have done . . .' becomes Leontes's 'which had been done / But that . . .' The style is simple yet the constituent clauses are carefully arranged and subordinated after the initial governing statement (Hermione's 'I lov'd him as in honour he requir'd'; Leontes's 'I'll reconcile me to Polixenes'). All suggests an order now recreated, an order based on an exact awareness of others, and of the need to distinguish and

defer to the infinite number of ways in which social and emotional responsibilities are imposed and discharged in a harmonious society. Yet the words which govern here are, as in Hermione's speeches, simple ones: 'truth', 'good', 'friend', 'honour' – words accepted now in faith, and heightened, in the conclusion of the speech, to a degree of impassioned eloquence that is the necessary counterbalance, as in Hermione, to any possible dryness:

He (most humane
And fill'd with honour) to my kingly guest
Unclasp'd my practice, quit his fortunes here
(Which you knew great) and to the certain hazard
Of all incertainties, himself commended,
No richer than his honour: how he glisters
Thorough my rust! and how his piety
Does my deeds make the blacker!   (ll. 165–72)

The conclusion of the first half of the play thus stresses, in diverse ways, the power of speech to reflect truth, seen as at once both simple and complex. Like the truth it seeks to express, the word is simple in itself, complex in the contexts in which it is necessarily placed. Since no general truth is without its embodiment in a specific human situation, Leontes's denial of the Oracle is a denial of the divine word, of a source of truth outside himself; it is also a denial both of a specific fact (Hermione's honesty) and of the complex social framework within which that fact is recognised by others. These denials are manifested at every level by a collapse of language. Leontes's speech degenerates as he denies God, individual and community, and it is not regenerated, in the pattern of Hermione's, until his denial is met by the greater denial of his son's death. And now, as his 'recreation' begins its slow process, truth cannot be too often spoken: 'Go on, go on: / Thou canst not speak too much' (ll. 214–15). Paulina might wish to retract her words, soften them somewhat out of a not always remembered deference to nobility, but Leontes reminds her of what he himself has so painfully discovered: 'Thou didst speak but well / When most the truth' (ll. 232–3).

In act IV our attention is turned to other things, 'To th'freshest things now reigning' (IV, i, 13). The vivacity, variety and grace of language found throughout the Bohemian interlude speaks for itself, but the theme of truthful utterance is not further developed here. Nor should it be, for it is essentially 'placed' in Hermione and Leontes. Only when the specific situation of Sicilia shows signs of re-curring in Bohemia, that is, when innocence is threatened by violence and Camillo must once again intervene, do we begin to hear again, in Polixenes's and Camillo's lines, the same Sicilian opposition of fantasy and truth, chaos and order. But the theme I have been tracing remains implicit here, and not directly stated. In act V, however, it returns, along with the original protagonists, for its completion.

That something more than recognition and expression of truth is required to bring about the by now much anticipated regeneration of Sicilia is made apparent when Paulina refers to 'she you kill'd' (V, i, 15). Leontes turns the word over. It is a truth fully accepted but one which must now be superseded, and Paulina's words at this moment are true but no longer medicinal:

> Kill'd!
> She I kill'd! I did so: but thou strik'st me
> Sorely, to say I did: it is as bitter
> Upon thy tongue as in my thought.
>
> (ll. 16–19)

Evidently, Paulina *can* speak too much, as Cleomenes says:

> You might have spoken a thousand things that would
> Have done the time more benefit and grac'd
> Your kindness better. (ll. 21–3)

For the moment, though, Paulina stays within the pronouncements of the old law of Apollo and the 'tenor of his Oracle' (l. 38), which she repeats, while at the same time making it clear that she is to be the instrument of a new law, a new pronouncement, one that we might well suspect will be 'monstrous to our human reason' (l. 41). As Leontes goes on to remind us, 'Thou speak'st truth' (l. 55), and immedi-ately there comes to him a vision of Hermione, risen from her grave, her corpse reanimated, 'soul-vex'd', speaking words of rebuke: 'Why to me?' (l. 59). It is a kind of foreshadowing, as was Antigonus's vision of her in act III scene iii where she also spoke, but these two visions are an 'after-image' of the past rather than an anticipation of the future. Hermione's reappearance, 'again in breath' (l. 83), will be of a different nature and purpose. At the end of Leontes's speech 'The blessed gods / Purge all infection...' (ll. 167–77) a line is drawn, the past is complete. This speech, similar in tone, structure and diction to Hermione's 'For Polixenes, / With whom I am accus'd...' and his own 'I'll reconcile me to Polixenes...' (III, ii, 61–71 and III, ii, 155–65; see above), first stresses what was, then what might have been, had not the orderly sequence of things been so disastrously interrupted:

> The blessed gods
> Purge all infection from our air whilst you
> Do climate here! You have a holy father,
> A graceful gentleman; against whose person
> (So sacred as it is) I have done sin,
> For which, the heavens (taking angry note)
> Have left me issueless: and your father's blest
> (As he from heaven merits it) with you,
> Worthy his goodness. What might I have been,
> Might I a son and daughter now have look'd on,
> Such goodly things as you! (ll. 167–77)

The accents are Hermione's. As far as language may recreate her, she is already present in Leontes's words. But her actual 're-embodi-ment' will occur in a context significantly different.

The entrance of a Lord immediately after Leontes's speech, with the words 'That which I shall report will bear no credit / Were not the proof so nigh' (ll. 178–9), sets in motion the sequence of events which brings the play to its end. The rapid succession of meetings and discoveries might seem excessive were it not for the fact that Shakespeare, aware of the dangers of too much marvellous incident at this stage, causes much of the action to be reported to us at second hand. Nevertheless, we might ask why any dramatist, having allowed one character to establish that that which is merely reported bears no credit, would then proceed to allow his most important and theatrical occasion so far to be merely reported. Many explanations of a psychological or dramaturgic nature might be advanced, but I shall insist only on the fact that, far from setting the events at a 'credible' distance, Shakespeare almost perversely ensures that we are struck by their *in*credibility. It is not the first time that he has deflected fire by drawing it, emphasised those very elements in a genre which because of their potential for absurdity less bold writers will attempt to tone down. Nor is it simply because the major climax must be led up to gradually that the minor ones occur offstage. Rather, Shakespeare's handling of the last act of the play shows a consistent development of the theme I have been tracing, the word as vehicle for truth. It now seems, somewhat to our surprise, that the word is weak and the most eloquent utterance unable to do justice to truths now glimpsed.

The unnamed Gentleman of act v scene ii, confronted with wonders, can make only 'a broken delivery of the business' (l. 9). In this he fares better, even so, than the King and Camillo: 'there was speech in their dumbness, language in their very gesture' (ll. 13–14). We may recall here the 'unspeakable comfort' mentioned by Archidamus in the first scene of the play, as opposed to that which he was able to speak 'in the freedom of my knowledge'. Knowledge now, freed from sequence and

precedent, 'broken out' upon the world as if through revelation, seems to defy articulation and silence tongues. Faced with the task of describing 'a sight which was to be seen, cannot be spoken of' (ll. 43–4), the Third Gentleman relates only gestures, in which, as we know, there is language. It is in some ways a comic recital, a display of excited inadequacy, a tale of handkerchiefs and rings and bears and clowns and kings, the very stuff to arouse Sidneyan misgivings, 'an old tale still, which will have matter to rehearse, though credit be asleep and not an ear open' (ll. 62–4). It is the gesture, not the word, that matters here. This principle is consistently applied, in the 'wonders' that are reported and in the report itself, and it is carried on into the last scene of the play, where to truth in utterance is now added what is necessary to bring the play to its conclusion, truth in gesture.

The final scene, surely Shakespeare's most daring outside the tragedies, and the cause of as much critical misgiving as scholarly explanation, will be examined here solely from the point of view of utterance and gesture. With all characters on stage, and with the rest of the play in the mind's ear, it is possible to discover here a perfect resolution to the problem which has been emerging: how to find words to match the miracle of Hermione's return to the world. For it is seen, correctly, as a miracle, an extension of grace, and its origins and context are different from those pertaining to other facts and events in the play. Neither words nor gestures alone will suffice, but together they bear more than sufficient witness to a truth which transcends and unites both.

It is significant that in this final scene the verbal units are for the most part short, and consist largely of commands and exclamations. There is no return to the complex and highly structured speech patterns of act III, where both Hermione and Leontes attested to a complex and highly structured social truth. The world of social interaction, of vertical hierarchy and horizontal extension each with its own complex pattern of responsibility and obligation and so often depicted by Shakespeare as a City or a Court, is perfectly expressed by the long, periodic style. Its antithesis, the self-enclosed, self-defining world represented by Leontes in the first half of the play, is expressed by a parody of that style. But the third style of this play, the plain and simple style, points to the change in language which must occur when the truth to be conveyed transcends the individual and the social, when human complexity gives way to divine simplicity and the order of grace. Here words, joined with gesture, reflect that order by their brevity and simplicity, and sometimes even by their absence.

The final scene begins on a note of solemn, courteous formality as Paulina, in her role as thaumaturge, prepares both stage and theatre audience for a spectacle outdoing all those so far reported, yet in essence far simpler: not so much a new 'wonder', or another 'singularity' like those in the gallery passed through before entering the chapel, but a restoration of the old order of grace referred to in the play's opening by Camillo when, speaking of Leontes and Polixenes, he exclaimed, 'The heavens continue their loves' (I, i, 31). Before the drawing of the curtain Paulina's only instruction is, in contrast with the difficulties experienced by others with lesser marvels to describe, simple in the extreme: 'behold, and say 'tis well' (v, iii, 20). It is to be expected that Paulina should insist on both beholding and saying. When mere seeing is believing, truth falls victim to misinterpretation and credulity, as we have seen. Paulina is insistent that no suspicion of witchcraft or magic should attend what she is about to do, and her simple commands to both statue and onlookers reinforce the naturalness and legitimacy of the

occasion. To this end she is far more concerned with the words and gestures of her audience than she is with those of the statue itself. Leontes's silence at the drawing of the curtain is remarked on approvingly by Paulina: 'it the more shows off / Your wonder' (l. 21). But though natural, and dramatically perfect, it is not sufficient: 'but yet speak'. And when Leontes does speak, in some of Shakespeare's most exquisitely judged lines, it is to beg Hermione to speak, to validate by *her* word the truth glimpsed in 'her natural posture': 'Chide me, dear stone, that I may say indeed / Thou art Hermione' (ll. 24–5). Leontes has done much more than give his assent to the lifelikeness of the statue (though this in itself is much): he now turns to Hermione as if for the first time, and asks *her* to speak that *he* might. It is the reverse in every way of the trial scene and represents the final, accurate location of truth, not in plots, trials or even divine pronouncements, but in a natural posture and a figure now aged and wrinkled. It is a miracle of entirely human nature, not a suspension of natural law, but a fulfilment of it.

Shakespeare freezes the action here, allowing time for the 'image' of Hermione to become 'fixed', and for the other persons on stage to establish their own relationships with her, to speak each in his turn. When Leontes finally says

> What you can make her do,
> I am content to look on: what to speak,
> I am content to hear; (ll. 91–3)

he speaks in effect for everyone in the stage and theatre audience. It is noteworthy, too, that although Paulina has indicated only that she will make the statue move, Leontes assumes that it will also speak. It is inconceivable that gesture and language will not now combine in single testimony. It requires now only Leontes's gesture, the presenting of his hand (the counterpart to Hermione's earlier gesture to Polixenes) to complete the play's cycle of severance and reunion, not only of parents and children, husband and wife, but of word and act. Hermione's descent and Leontes's embrace of her are the most eloquent gestures in the play. Utterance is at last transcended and they do not speak to each other after this. Hermione speaks to the Gods and to her daughter, Leontes to Paulina, Camillo and Polixenes. Hermione's speech, so long anticipated, may disappoint if we remember her vivacity at the beginning of the play, her sustained eloquence in the trial scene. Yet it serves further to underline the perfect naturalness of the occasion which Paulina has taken such pains to establish, that it should not 'be hooted at / Like an old tale' (ll. 116–17). Yet the repeated references to 'old tales' throughout the fifth act remind us that earlier in the play such a tale was cruelly stopped, the tale of Mamillius, the winter's tale itself. In a sense it is this tale which is now resumed, this quiet dialogue between mother and child:

> You gods, look down,
> And from your sacred vials pour your graces
> Upon my daughter's head! Tell me, mine own,
> Where hast thou been preserv'd? where liv'd?
>   how found
> Thy father's court? for thou shalt hear that I,
> Knowing by Paulina that the Oracle
> Gave hope thou wast in being, have preserv'd
> Myself to see the issue.   (ll. 121–8)

The social order is re-established, fittingly, by Leontes, who first destroyed it. His final speech, and the final speech of the play, is a measured expression of communal harmony within the fruitful process of time, and is thus fully within the traditions of romance and comedy.

The last act of *The Winter's Tale* lends itself to much fruitful discussion of the reconciliation of art and nature within the human and the divine orders which Shakespeare explored throughout his dramatic works. But it is this play above all in which language and gesture, the basic elements of his art, are most fully exploited in terms of their function as signals of truth. The extraordinary harmonies of *The Winter's Tale* are not, I think, produced by any overall concept of Nature, or Time, or Providence, though these are the undeniable agencies by which the action of the play complicates and resolves itself. The play's unity of conception, and its diversity within that unity, is the reflection of its nature as a scrupulously constructed verbal artifact. Its integrity as drama lies in Shakespeare's (and Paulina's) recognition that word and action must finally fuse if we are not to be 'mock'd with art'.

ADUMBRATIONS OF 'THE TEMPEST' IN 'A MIDSUMMER NIGHT'S DREAM'

G. R. HIBBARD

As long ago as 1747, William Warburton, in his edition of Shakespeare, began his first note on *The Tempest* with the following words:

These two first plays, *The Tempest* and the *Midsummer-night's Dream*, are the noblest Efforts of that sublime and amazing Imagination, peculiar to *Shakespear*, which soars above the Bounds of Nature without forsaking Sense: or, more properly, carries Nature along with him beyond her established Limits. (Vol. 1, p. 3)

Yet even at the time when Warburton was writing the similarity between the two plays in this respect was already a commonplace of criticism, going back at least as far as Nicholas Rowe's 'Some Account of the Life, &c. of Mr. William Shakespear' (1709), where one reads:

But certainly the greatness of this Author's genius do's no where so much appear, as where he gives his imagination an entire loose, and raises his fancy to a flight above mankind and the limits of the visible world. Such are his attempts in *The Tempest, Midsummer-Night's Dream, Mackbeth*, and *Hamlet*. (*Ibid.*, p. lviii)

And behind this comment, in its turn, there lies Dryden's praise of the imagination that shaped Caliban and furnished him 'with a person, a language, and a character, which will suit him, both by the father's and mother's side'.[1] Nor, if Rowe is to be believed, was this praise original with Dryden, for he tells us:

The Observation, which I have been inform'd three very great men concurr'd in making upon this part, was extremely just; *That* Shakespear *had not only*

found out a new Character in his Caliban, *but had also devis'd and adapted a new manner of Language for that Character.*

The 'three very great men' were, he says in a note, '*Lord* Falkland, *Lord C. J.* Vaughan, *and Mr.* Selden' (Warburton, Vol. 1, p. lix). So the broad tradition within which Warburton's comment falls was, it would seem, more than a hundred years old when he made it.

That tradition has not lost its hold in the two hundred and thirty years that lie between Warburton and us. Editors and critics of the one play continue to find themselves impelled to refer to the other; and lines of approach about which Warburton knew nothing, since they did not exist in his day, lead to comparisons between them. Wolfgang Clemen, for example, writing about *The Tempest*, remarks:

We are all of us aware of the strong earth atmosphere pervading the play. Except for *A Midsummer Night's Dream* and *King Lear* there is no other play of Shakespeare's in which so many plants, fruits and animals appear. Compared to the nature-world of *A Midsummer Night's Dream*, however, the world of flora and fauna in *The Tempest* is less lovely, less 'Elizabethan', less poetic and aesthetic ... There are fewer flowers, more weeds, roots and fruits of the country.[2]

This observation is a far cry indeed from praise of the imagination 'which soars above the Bounds of Nature', yet it too links the plays

[1] *Essays of John Dryden*, ed. W. P. Ker (Oxford, 1901), I, 219.
[2] W. H. Clemen, *The Development of Shakespeare's Imagery* (1951), p. 187.

firmly together. The testimony of time and instinctive response is plain enough: *A Midsummer Night's Dream* does adumbrate *The Tempest* in many ways; so much so, in fact, that we might do well to think of these works as a distinct sub-species of Shakespearian comedy, magical comedy – magical not only in its use of magic but in the magical effect it has on audiences and readers alike.

The most obvious and immediately recognisable point of contact is the similarity, in nature as well as function, of Ariel to Puck. Both are spirits who delight in rapid uninhibited movement. Commanded by Oberon to fetch the flower Love-in-idleness, Puck replies:

> I'll put a girdle round about the earth
> In forty minutes.   (II, i, 175–6)[1]

Later, in response to another order, he tells the Fairy King:

> I go, I go; look how I go,
> Swifter than arrow from the Tartar's bow.
>   (III, ii, 100–1)

Ariel's references to his speed in flight are even more numerous and more vivid than Puck's, rising in a kind of crescendo to culminate in his eager reply to Prospero's requirement that he bring the master and the boatswain of the ship to the magician's cell:

> I drink the air before me, and return
> Or ere your pulse twice beat.   (V, i, 102–3)

Moreover, Ariel, like Puck, can make himself invisible at will and also control the weather, or at least give the appearance of doing so.

Yet swift in movement and versatile in action though they are, each of these spirits serves a master, Puck willingly but carelessly and mischievously, Ariel under a degree of compulsion but with unerring efficiency. Exercising great power and influence over many of the human characters, they still remain agents. It is their masters, not they, who con-

trol events and, in doing so, profoundly affect the structure of the plays, which is, in both cases, an extremely intricate one. The scenes in the wood outside Athens are, in effect, a play-within-the-play, written by Oberon and directed by Puck, who also functions as a highly appreciative audience much taken with the topsy-turvy situations that his own bungling has led to. There is even a point, immediately after Bottom has been given the ass's head, when we see for a brief moment a play-within-the-play-within-the-play. And this piece of gratuitous improvisation by Puck also has the good fortune to slot perfectly into Oberon's plan to win the Indian boy from his queen. There is nothing quite so complicated as this in *The Tempest*, but the play-within-the-play is even more in evidence, since everything that happens to the passengers on the ship, from the moment they set foot on the enchanted island until 'The charm dissolves apace', is part of a drama written by Prospero and executed by Ariel. Furthermore, in each play the spirit agent, acting on his own volition, affects his master's plan for the good. Puck does it, appropriately enough, by accident, since he does not know, when he turns Bottom into an ass, that the monster he has created will be the first object that Titania sees on waking. Ariel, however, a spirit of a rarer sort, makes a positive appeal to Prospero's better nature by concluding his description of the state to which Alonso and the rest, and especially Gonzalo, have been reduced by their experiences on the island with the words:

> Your charm so strongly works 'em
> That if you now beheld them your affections
> Would become tender.   (V, i, 17–19)

The dominant feature of both plays, the characteristic quality they share, a quality

---

[1] The text used for all quotations from and references to Shakespeare's writings is that of *The Complete Works*, ed. Peter Alexander (London and Glasgow, 1951).

which sets them off from the rest of the *œuvre*, is, of course, their use of magic for ends that are good, though the magic they draw on is not the same. The fairies of *A Midsummer Night's Dream*, and Puck in particular, are of native origin, part of that legacy from the Middle Ages which was so much alive still in Shakespeare's England. Springing out of a reverence for and a fear of unintelligible and uncontrollable natural forces, which had to be propitiated if they were to work for man and not against him, this fairy-lore was beginning to feel the cold breath of rationalism and was ready, at that touch from his wand which the poet gave it in *A Midsummer Night's Dream*, to shed its more malevolent and frightening aspects. Prospero's magic, on the other hand, is learned magic. He is the magus of the Hermeticists, a devout student of the universe and its operations who can command the elemental daemons of the neo-Platonic cosmology by virtue of his mastery of the holy art to the study of which he has dedicated his life. And, precisely as Shakespeare had done with the magic of the earlier play, so in *The Tempest* he caught, as it were, this other kind of magic while it still had a hold over the minds of men, just before it began to fade away under the impact of the new 'natural philosophy' which Bacon made it his business in life to propagate.

The way in which the magic works is fundamentally the same in both plays: it effects transformations. The idea is most inescapably and hilariously evident in Puck's setting of the ass's head on Bottom's shoulders, an action which draws from the astonished Snout the exclamation, 'O Bottom, thou art chang'd!', and from the no less astonished Quince the parallel exclamation, 'Bless thee, Bottom, bless thee! Thou art translated!' (III, i, 104–9). The words 'changed', 'transfigured', 'transposed' and, above all, 'translated' echo and re-echo through the comedy, which reaches

its climax in the burlesque translation into dramatic terms of Golding's sublimely bad translation into English of Ovid's narrative of Pyramus and Thisbe, which itself ends in a metamorphosis. But Bottom's translation is only one of the many translations, most of them ironical, that take place in the play. As Demetrius enters the wood, with Helena in pursuit of him, Ovidian myth is turned upside-down: 'Apollo flies, and Daphne holds the chase' (II, i, 231). Earlier still Helena tells Hermia that she would like to catch her favour, and then goes on to say:

Were the world mine, Demetrius being bated,
The rest I'd give to be to you translated.
(I, i, 190–1)

However, when the desired change has taken place and she finds herself the object of the attentions of both Demetrius and Lysander, exactly as Hermia was in I, i, she discovers that she does not like it at all. Her former friendship for Hermia is converted into hostility; and the two women come close to fighting over the two men. All this, however, is merely a consequence of Puck's mistaking. Ultimately the love-juice does what Oberon intended it to do in transferring Demetrius's affections back to his first love Helena.

But, while all comes right in the end, there is, so far as I can see, no suggestion that the transformation he has undergone in the night has in any way affected or altered either of the lovers. When they awake, Demetrius and Lysander are glad that their difficulties and differences are over, but they are quite ready to dismiss the events of the night as an idle dream. They have simply become once again what they were before Demetrius shifted his love from Helena to Hermia. Similarly, Titania, having been 'enamour'd of an ass' and having given up the Indian boy to Oberon, reverts completely to her former self as she was before she fell out with her consort. The case of Bottom, however, is, as many critics have observed, rather different. He no more understands what has happened to him during the night than does any of the others; like them, he takes it for a dream. But his dream has had no 'fierce vexation' in it. On the contrary, it has provided him with the opportunity to play both the role of the lover and of the ass. Looking back on it, while still only half awake, he accepts it as a wonderful inexplicable vision that has been vouchsafed him. Dimly aware that for a brief time he has indeed been 'translated', he cannot forbear from telling his fellows that something quite extraordinary has happened to him, but he treasures it too much to share it with them or describe it to them.

It is the experience of Bottom that comes closest to prefiguring the effect that Prospero's magic has on Alonso, for, like *A Midsummer Night's Dream*, *The Tempest* too is a play of transformations. On his initial entry, Ariel gives a vivid description of his ability to transform himself as he tells of his role in the storm:

I boarded the King's ship; now on the beak,
Now in the waist, the deck, in every cabin,
I flam'd amazement. Sometime I'd divide,
And burn in many places; on the topmast,
The yards, and bowsprit, would I flame distinctly,
Then meet and join. Jove's lightning, the precursors
O' th' dreadful thunder-claps, more momentary
And sight-outrunning were not; the fire and cracks
Of sulphurous roaring the most mighty Neptune
Seem to besiege, and make his bold waves tremble,
Yes, his trident shake. (I, ii, 196–206)

But Ariel's capacity for metamorphosing himself is part of his nature; and that nature remains the same throughout the play. He may regard Prospero as his dear master and even come to feel pity for the victims of that master's activities, but from first to last he is impelled by one over-riding motive: the desire for freedom. The more profound transformation that the play deals with is the one announced by Ariel in the song he sings to Ferdinand:

Full fathom five thy father lies;
 Of his bones are coral made;
Those are pearls that were his eyes;
 Nothing of him that doth fade
But doth suffer a sea-change
Into something rich and strange.

(I, ii, 396–401)

By seemingly depriving Alonso of his son and heir, Prospero makes him know grief, and then, through the agency of Ariel, forcibly reminds him of his past wickedness. Nor is it Ariel alone who works on the strangers to the island, for the island itself is enchanted. It appears differently to different characters. Adrian and Gonzalo are much taken with its temperate climate, its fertility and its greenness; but Antonio and Sebastian see it as a tawny desert. Under its influence men reveal themselves for what they are. Antonio and Sebastian are soon busy planning a political assassination, because power is the only thing to which their imaginations respond. As he begins his temptation of Sebastian, Antonio actually says:

My strong imagination sees a crown
Dropping upon thy head. (II, i, 199–200)

And, because these two are so limited in imagination, Prospero, for all his magic, can bring about no real change in them. All he can do is to disarm them, as it were, by holding his knowledge of their plans as a threat over them. Alonso, on the other hand, has a less limited imagination; and, by working on it, Prospero causes him to realise his guilt, to repent, and, as proof of that repentance, willingly to resign the dukedom of Milan to its true ruler. Moreover, a radical change also takes place in Caliban, who responds instinctively to the natural wealth and beauty of the island and who seems to pass his life in a twilight of consciousness where dream and waking merge imperceptibly into one another. Prospero may call him

A devil, a born devil, on whose nature
Nurture can never stick;   (IV, i, 188–9)

but by the end of the play Caliban, unlike the two savages of civilisation, Stephano and Trinculo, who have no imagination at all, has learnt something. His last words in the drama are:

> I'll be wise hereafter,
> And seek for grace. What a thrice-double ass
> Was I to take this drunkard for a god,
> And worship this dull fool!   (IV, i, 294–7)

What is the relationship between dream and waking consciousness? Both plays, to a far greater extent than any other plays in the canon, explore this question. In *A Midsummer Night's Dream* it is explicitly discussed by Theseus and Hippolyta at the opening of act V. Fascinated by the account of their experiences which she has heard from the lovers, Hippolyta begins the discussion with a statement that asks for a response:

'Tis strange, my Theseus, that these lovers speak of.

The answer she receives is the rationalist's: the imagination is a lawless faculty, a kind of madness, that provides illusory satisfactions for human hopes and desires. But Hippolyta, not content with this reply, retorts:

> But all the story of the night told over,
> And all their minds transfigur'd so together,
> More witnesseth than fancy's images,
> And grows to something of great constancy,
> But howsoever strange and admirable.
>   (IV, i, 23–7)

Her deliberate substitution of 'fancy' for Theseus's 'imagination' almost suggests that Shakespeare was on the point of making Coleridge's distinction between the two. But, however this may be, the question is not allowed to drop. As the play-within-the-play proceeds, Hippolyta becomes increasingly weary of it, and eventually says outright:

This is the silliest stuff that ever I heard.

To this Theseus gives an answer which, in the light of his previous remarks, comes as something of a surprise:

The best in this kind are but shadows; and the worst are no worse, if imagination amend them.
                                (V, i, 208–11)

So whatever function and status the imagination may have in life outside the theatre, in the theatre it is indispensable. Unless it is exercised, both play and actors will remain mere shadows. The question about the relationship between dream and waking consciousness has led on to a discussion of the nature of dramatic illusion.

Once again *A Midsummer Night's Dream* looks forward, in a way that none of the other plays does, to *The Tempest*, where issues of this kind are raised from the outset. As Anne Barton (Righter) points out,[1] the opening scene is extremely realistic. No audience witnessing it for the first time has any doubt that what is being staged is a shipwreck. Moreover, within the play itself, Miranda is quite sure that there has been a disaster. Yet no sooner has she given utterance to the pity she feels for the victims of the wreck than Prospero assures her 'There's no harm done . . . No harm'. To this assurance he adds, shortly afterwards:

> The direful spectacle of the wreck, which touch'd
> The very virtue of compassion in thee,
> I have with such provision in mine art
> So safely ordered that there is no soul –
> No, not so much perdition as an hair
> Betid to any creature in the vessel
> Which thou heard'st cry, which thou saw'st sink.
>   (I, ii, 26–32)

Like Miranda, the audience is being told that it cannot rely on the evidence of its own eyes and ears. It is at this point that Prospero begins his story by asking Miranda whether she can remember anything at all of her life before she came to the island. She replies that she can, and then elaborates:

[1] *The Tempest*, ed. Anne Righter (Harmondsworth, 1968), pp. 7–9.

'Tis far off,
And rather like a dream than an assurance
That my remembrance warrants. Had I not
Four, or five, women once, that tended me?

(I, ii, 44–7)

From this moment onwards the word 'dream' recurs time after time. Called on to face one strange event after another, the characters find it increasingly difficult to decide whether they are dreaming or not. Eventually, as in *A Midsummer Night's Dream*, the presentation of a theatrical show, the masque that Prospero puts on for Ferdinand and Miranda, brings the issue to a head. Having brought the show to an abrupt conclusion, in order to attend to the pressing matter of the conspiracy of Caliban and his confederates, Prospero turns to Ferdinand and says:

You do look, my son, in a mov'd sort,
As if you were dismay'd; be cheerful, sir.
Our revels now are ended. These our actors,
As I foretold you, were all spirits, and
Are melted into air, into thin air;
And, like the baseless fabric of this vision,
The cloud-capp'd towers, the gorgeous palaces,
The solemn temples, the great globe itself,
Yea, all which it inherit, shall dissolve,
And, like this insubstantial pageant faded,
Leave not a rack behind. We are such stuff
As dreams are made on; and our little life
Is rounded with a sleep.   (IV, i, 146–58)

I do not pretend fully to understand all that is being said here. The lines reverberate with suggestions and intuitions so closely packed together that the import of the whole is not readily grasped. As Keats wrote of the Grecian Urn, the words 'tease us out of thought / As doth eternity', which is, indeed, one of the things they are about. Present in them, however, is surely the idea that life itself has some of the qualities of dream, and, this being so, the illusion of it that the theatre can give is likely to be as true a presentation of it as it is possible to make. Seen in this light, the lines may well be Shakespeare's final word on

an issue which he had first raised, at least in any extended fashion, in the second scene of *A Midsummer Night's Dream*, the scene in which the mechanicals get themselves into such a glorious tangle about the effect that a play may have on its audience. What, they ask, is the true nature of the illusion of life that the theatre offers? Assuming that it is one of complete verisimilitude, and therefore may, with disastrous consequences, be mistaken for life itself, the actors of 'Pyramus and Thisbe' go to inordinate and wholly unnecessary lengths to ensure that no such mistake can possibly be made about their production, thus positively going out of their way to invite the destructive comments which the courtly spectators would have made uninvited.

But the mechanicals do not have the last word on the matter. Quince, anxious to forestall criticism, introduces their play with the words: 'If we offend' (v, i, 108). His apology, addressed to Theseus and his court, is picked up, expanded, and directed at the audience in the theatre by Puck, who begins his epilogue by saying:

If we shadows have offended,
Think but this, and all is mended,
That you have but slumb'red here
While these visions did appear.
And this weak and idle theme,
No more yielding but a dream,
Gentles do not reprehend.   (v, i, 412–18)

The lines come close to being a first draft of Prospero's description of the masque with which he has delighted Ferdinand and Miranda, but they contain one word, 'shadows', which he does not use. His actors have been spirits not shadows. The shadows Puck refers to are, I take it, all the actors in the play; and his equation of the actor with a shadow leads one's mind immediately to *Macbeth*, where the hero tells us:

Life's but a walking shadow, a poor player,
That struts and frets his hour upon the stage,

And then is heard no more; it is a tale
Told by an idiot, full of sound and fury,
Signifying nothing.   (v, v, 24–8)

Play (tale), player (shadow), life (dream): in the Shakespearian imagination the three were indissolubly connected with each other; and the connection was, I think, neither consoling nor encouraging. After the human characters in *A Midsummer Night's Dream* have gone off to bed, Puck comes in to say:

Now it is the time of night
That the graves, all gaping wide,
Every one lets forth his sprite,
In the church-way paths to glide.
And we fairies, that do run
By the triple Hecate's team
From the presence of the sun,
Following darkness like a dream,
Now are frolic.   (v, i, 368–76)

The fairies may be frolic, but their avoidance of daylight and their association with Hecate give them an aura of darkness. They belong, after all, to an old pagan order of things; their life is a subterranean one. So it is again in *Hamlet*, where, according to Marcellus, in the period around Christmas,

no spirit dare stir abroad,
The nights are wholesome, then no planets strike,
No fairy takes, nor witch hath power to charm,
So hallowed and so gracious is the time.
                              (I, i, 161–4)

Furthermore, the sinister figure of Hecate, tri-form goddess of hell and witchcraft, also has her place in the tragedy. In the play-within-the-play Lucianus addresses the poisonous mixture he has concocted as

Thou mixture rank, of midnight weeds collected,
With Hecat's ban thrice blasted, thrice infected,
Thy natural magic and dire property
On wholesome life usurps immediately.
                              (III, ii, 251–4)

The same Hecate is referred to as 'black Hecate' by Macbeth (III, ii, 41), and is associated by him with witchcraft (II, i, 51–2) before she finally appears in person in the dubious scene, III, v. She is not mentioned by name in *The Tempest*, but it is to her that Medea, in Ovid's *Metamorphoses*, addresses the tremendous invocation which provided Shakespeare with the material for Prospero's speech, in which he describes and abjures the 'rough magic' that has served him so well.

Perhaps Nicholas Rowe was not far out when he brought *A Midsummer Night's Dream*, *Hamlet*, *Macbeth* and *The Tempest* together in the first life of Shakespeare that we have.

© G. R. HIBBARD 1978

THE OLD HONOR AND THE NEW COURTESY: '1 HENRY IV'

G. M. PINCISS

Central to any reading of *1 Henry IV* is the dramatic opposition of the Prince of Wales with his arch-rival Henry Percy: the seriousness, energy, and courage of Hotspur are held up against the frivolous, bored, and irresponsible behavior of Hal. In large measure, the two young men, whom Shakespeare has intentionally portrayed as comparable in age, behave differently because they value differing codes of conduct. For Hotspur honor is of over-riding concern; by contrast, Hal acts as chief spokesman of another virtue, one especially appropriate for a Renaissance prince: courtesy. By analyzing the actions of both men according to the two most influential Elizabethan handbooks on courtly manners, we may arrive at a more precise evaluation of these two virtues and of those qualities that, it seems, ultimately mark Hal superior to Hotspur.

The two most prominent Elizabethan guides to courtly behavior were Castiglione's *The Courtier*, especially as translated by Sir Thomas Hoby in 1561, and the English version of Italian manner books, Sir Thomas Elyot's *The Governour* (1531).[1] Something of a national character shaped the priorities of each writer: Castiglione and his countrymen, for example, stress personal perfection and aesthetic matters; Elyot and his readers place greater weight on civil usefulness and moral considerations.[2] Nevertheless, the two works have more in common between them than either shares with a medieval manual on knightly conduct and they agree on the manners that characterize a Renaissance gentleman.

Hotspur's behavior and ethics are intimately associated with the striving for honor. He is the 'king of honour'; according to the envious Bolingbroke, he is the 'son who is the theme of honour's tongue'. For him public acclaim and reputation are to be earned chiefly by performance as a soldier – if not for, then against the crown. He is first mentioned at the very opening of the play in connection with a major victory over the Scots at Holmedon and the impressive list of his prisoners is described to the king as an 'honourable spoil'. At his first appearance in scene iii Hotspur displays something of his warrior nature, for he is plain-dealing, quick-tempered, and fearless, all those traits common to the best Elizabethan soldier-stereotype: something of his nature can be found in men like Kent, or Enobarbus, or Othello. As Hal satirizes him, the young Percy 'kills me some six or seven dozen Scots at a breakfast, washes his hands, and says to his wife, "Fie upon this quiet life, I want work."' There is more than a grain of truth in this exaggeration of Hotspur's aggressive determination.

Hotspur is also concerned with the king's

[1] A general discussion of Shakespeare's indebtedness to Castiglione, Elyot, and Lyly will be found in E. M. W. Tillyard, *Shakespeare's History Plays* (1944), pp. 314–18.

[2] Ruth Kelso, *The Doctrine of the English Gentleman in the Sixteenth Century* (Urbana, 1929), pp. 50, 84ff.

treatment of his family since this, too, reflects on his honor. Bolingbroke's refusal to ransom Hotspur's brother-in-law Mortimer, to consult with his father and uncle on matters of state, and to acknowledge the assistance of the Percys in taking the throne from Richard II are cited as particular reasons for rebelling. But all of these causes should be subsumed under one heading: his desire to 'pluck bright honour from the pale faced moon'. For Hotspur this is the *summum bonum*.[1] Exasperated by Bolingbroke's tactics and encouraged to rebellion by his uncle, Hotspur in act II no longer supports the crown against the Scots but joins them and the Welsh in an effort to unseat the king. He calls this 'so honourable an action', an action by which his father and uncle 'may redeem your banished honours'.

Hotspur is not interested in material profit. And Shakespeare takes great pains to make this clear. In response to Sir Walter Blunt's hope that he will negotiate a peaceful settlement and accept an offer full of 'grace and love' from Bolingbroke, Hotspur answers, 'And maybe so we shall'. Indeed, Hotspur's motivation is so pure and his reply to Sir Walter so honest, that Worcester, Hotspur's uncle, never tells him of 'the liberal and kind offer of the king'. Worcester persuades his companion, Sir Richard Vernon, perhaps wisely, that his nephew must never learn what Bolingbroke promised. Unlike the open and rather naive and gullible Hotspur, it is Worcester who truly understands that the politic Bolingbroke knows 'at what time to promise, when to pay'. But actually, Hotspur's honesty and directness, although laudable and appealing to us, are not entirely praiseworthy traits for a Renaissance courtier. To attain the kind of reputation Hotspur is seeking, both craftiness and calculation are occasionally excusable practices.[2]

As a Renaissance courtier Hotspur is inept. Shakespeare systematically displays his failures in the many skills, talents, and graces that every sixteenth-century nobleman should exhibit. And the deficiencies in Hotspur's nature are repeatedly displayed to the audience not only by his own actions but also by pointed comment from others. In his very first speech he confesses to the court that he answered the king's messenger 'neglectingly, I know not what . . . for he made me mad'. Although his conduct might be excusable in special circumstances, it is hardly correct or controlled behavior. Hotspur then proceeds to contradict Bolingbroke flatly, using neither the Retort Courteous nor the Quip Modest, but the Counter-check Quarrelsome and the Lie Direct. Men of good sense like Touchstone or his equally argumentative opponent stop short of such an offensive reply – from which there is no retreating without an 'if'. Bolingbroke in fury orders the Percys away. Finally, unable still to control his anger, Hotspur cannot allow his uncle to hold the floor without behaving like a 'wasp-stung and impatient fool . . . Tying thine ear to no tongue but thine own!' All this in his opening scene. Surely we are watching a young man lacking patience, moderation, and prudence, those virtues Elyot thought so essential in one who looked for a place at court.[3]

Like Elyot, Castiglione, too, would have observed several deficiencies in Hotspur's behavior. His impetuous nature and quick tongue are obviously liabilities at the council table, but in the pleasures of civilized life he is equally undeveloped and uninterested. Glendower, the Welsh chieftain, boasts that he has composed English lyrics, 'a virtue that was

[1] See Curtis Brown Watson, *Shakespeare and the Renaissance Concept of Honor* (Princeton, 1960), pp. 66ff. [2] *Ibid.*, p. 67.
[3] Miss Kelso notes that Elyot and his successors 'in general cover the same ground' in their descriptions: 'The virtues that were by common consent considered the most important for the gentleman were justice, prudence, courtesy, liberality, temperance, and fortitude', p. 76.

never seen' in Hotspur. But the younger man has no shame at his deafness to the beauties of language:

> I had rather be a kitten and cry 'mew'
> Than one of these same metre ballad-mongers.
> I had rather hear a brazen canstick turn'd
> Or a dry wheel grate on the axle-tree,
> And that would set my teeth nothing on edge,
> Nothing so much as mincing poetry.
>
> (III, i, 123–8)[1]

Obstinate in his ways, he takes delight neither in verse nor music. A lady's song is a subject for teasing his wife, and a lullaby in Welsh is less pleasing to him than the howling of his Irish wolf-hound; presumably neither the music nor the language held appeal. Had he followed the advice of Castiglione, Hotspur would have known how untutored (and French!) was his insistence on knowing 'onely the nobleness of armes'. A true courtier should

> exercise him selfe in Poets, and no lesse in Oratours and Historiographers, and also in writing both rime and prose, and especially in this our vulgar tongue. For beside the contentation that hee shall receive thereby him selfe, hee shall by this means never want pleasant intertainements with women which ordinarily love such matters.[2]

And like the great warrior Achilles, taught to play the harp by Chiron, a soldier is no less heroic for his talent with music. Castiglione insists that such skill is not effeminate: 'musicke is not an ornament, but also necessarie for a Courtier'.[3]

Hotspur's weaknesses are more than implied. His peccadilloes and his faults are named by his uncle lest we overlook them. Shakespeare must have suspected that Hotspur with his candor and spirit would draw our applause so whole-heartedly, especially when we discover him surrounded by intriguers, that we would tend to ignore his serious defects. Although Worcester may not appear the ideal teacher, his experience at dealing with men is un-questionably greater than his nephew's and his admonition is worth the heeding:

> In faith, my lord, you are too wilful-blame,
> .   .   .   .
> You must needs learn, lord, to amend this fault.
> Though sometimes it show greatness, courage,
>   blood –
> And that's the dearest grace it renders you –
> Yet oftentimes it doth present harsh rage,
> Defect of manners, want of government,
> Pride, haughtiness, opinion, and disdain,
> The least of which haunting a nobleman
> Loseth men's hearts, and leaves behind a stain
> Upon the beauty of all parts besides,
> Beguiling them of commendation.
>
> (III, i, 171, 174–83)

The charges Worcester recites sum up a rather complete bill of particulars against Hotspur. But there still remains at least one fact about the young man's attitude that shows to what an extent it is uncharacteristic of his time. When he learns that his father is unable to bring his support to the confrontation with Bolingbroke, Hotspur argues that 'It lends a larger dare to our great enterprise'. When he learns that Glendower, too, will be unable to join them, Hotspur still insists on rushing into battle. His courage and enthusiasm are admirable; his eagerness to encounter an enemy who vastly outnumbers him – 'Die all, die merrily' – reveals the extent of his idealism. But rushing into battle, rejoicing to display bravery, enduring suffering and loss or even meeting death gladly as a reward for valor are the actions of a medieval knight demonstrating the code of chivalry. Such deeds, however, are not those of a Renaissance gentleman; the ideal performance of a crusader in a romance is not the same as that of a courtier in a six-teenth-century manners book and the behavior

---

[1] References are to the Arden Edition, ed. A. R. Humphreys (1960).
[2] Baldassare Castiglione, *The Book of the Courtier*, tr. Sir Thomas Hoby (1928), p. 71.
[3] *Ibid.*, p. 77.

of a hero in a tale by Malory hardly agrees with Castiglione's recommendation:

it is behovefull both for himselfe and for his friendes, that he have a foresight in the quarrels and controversies that may happen, and let hime beware of the vantages, declaring alwaies in everie point both courage and wisedom. Neither let him runne rashly to these combats...for beside the great daunger that is in the doubtful lot, he that goeth headlong to these thinges deserveth great blame.[1]

On this subject it is interesting to review the career of the Douglas, Hotspur's Scots ally. Before the battle of Shrewsbury, Hotspur praises him as the best of soldiers, 'a braver place / In my heart's love hath no man than yourself'. And, indeed, the Douglas urges a speedy confrontation with Bolingbroke, actively seeks him in battle, and systematically attempts to kill each of those dressed like the king. His fight with the real king, however, is interrupted by Prince Hal who comes to aid his failing father. Rather than meet death at Hal's hand, the Douglas flees. All of this, of course, serves to enhance Hal's reputation in his father's and his audience's eyes. None of it is unexpected until Hal's very last speech in the play. In this, he instructs his brother John to free the imprisoned Douglas without ransom, for

> His valours shown upon our crests today
> Have taught us how to cherish such high deeds
> Even in the bosom of our adversaries.
>
> (v, v, 29–31)

That Hal would commit a public act reflecting what Prince John calls 'high courtesy' is not unlikely, but that Hal would praise for his courage an enemy who ran away when he saw defeat and death approaching is a little startling if one considers what Hotspur might have said had he seen it all! By and large it seems that Hotspur's values are not the same as those of his enemies or his friends, for unlike him both Hal and the Douglas approve of that advice that teaches one to flee when one is outnumbered or outclassed.

Hotspur's chief virtue – and he is called the 'king of honour' by the Douglas – is defined by a code of manners that is obsolete; he represents an age that is past or passing. Prince Hal on the other hand embodies the new virtues: even before he inherits the kingdom from his father he is dubbed the 'king of courtesy'.[2]

Courtesy, Hal's most distinctive attribute, is considered by both English and Italian authorities a necessary quality for a nobleman's temperament; one so central to the concept that Spenser devoted a whole book of *The Faerie Queene* to it. Courtesy is exercised by knowing what is fitting for oneself and others, and for enacting this with graciousness.[3] One's conduct, then, is affected in part by awareness of class and the lines between classes and in part by the desire to draw praise and admiration for the grace of one's behavior, especially from one's equals and betters. Such a person in Elyot's terms possesses 'a gentil and familiare visage' able to procure men's love, and 'a beautie or comelynesse in his countenance, langage, and gesture apt to his dignitie, and accomodate to time, place, and company'.[4] When a leash of drawers name him the 'king of courtesy' and promise he 'shall command all the good lads of Eastcheap', the Prince of Wales has proven some-

[1] *Ibid.*, p. 40, and for further discussion of this point see Kelso, p. 93. Shakespeare is not everywhere consistent: before the battle of Agincourt Henry V argues like Hotspur that greater glory is gained by being greatly outnumbered.

[2] For Shakespeare the question of gentility or true nobility was more than a literary topos. He himself had applied to the College of Heralds at about the time he was composing this play for his family's coat of arms. Despite the fact that the College was held in poor repute by the end of the sixteenth century, Shakespeare evidently accepted the popular notion that no one was a gentleman unless he was registered there. For further remarks on the College of Heralds see Kelso, pp. 25ff.

[3] Kelso, pp. 79–80.

[4] Sir Thomas Elyot, *The Governour* (1907), pp. 131, 121.

thing of his real worth. He is both truthful and slyly ironic when he says to Poins, 'thou hast lost much honour that thou wert not with me in this action'. Drinking-deep and sounding the very bass string of humility are evidence of his princeliness, for Hal has followed Castiglione's injunction:

in companie with men and women of al degrees, in sporting, in laughing, and in jesting, he hath in him certaine sweetnes, and so comely demeanours, that who so speaketh with him, or yet beholdeth him, must needes beare him an affection for ever.[1]

In fact, Hal satisfies most of Castiglione's criteria for courtesy: he is noble by birth, witty by nature, comely in person and countenance, and attractive with 'a certaine grace, and (as they say) a hewe, that shall make him at the first sight acceptable and loving unto who so beholdeth him'.[2] These aspects of courtesy are perhaps more gifts of nature than manners consciously learned and artificially cultivated, but such gifts, as one might expect, are part of the legacy of a royal offspring.

Recognizing Hal's natural courtesy and his supremacy in this virtue allows us to reinterpret the claims of others. For example, Hotspur's threat that Hal will 'shrink under my courtesy' seems a hollow boast when one realizes Hal's true value, and his father's criticism of Hal's conduct should also be regarded with some skepticism. Bolingbroke has 'majesty', the quality that impresses his public; but this is only half of what Elyot finds necessary for courtesy. The king never gains his public's affection, lacking what Elyot would have called 'affability', the other component of courtesy. In fact, Bolingbroke is a fraud; like Macbeth in borrowed robes, he 'dressed' himself in humility to pluck allegiance from men's hearts, and 'stole all courtesy from heaven'. His rebuke to his son, a parallel to Worcester's reprimanding Hotspur, reflects Bolingbroke's own obtuseness. Even Sir Richard Vernon, who could scarcely be expected to think favorably

of Bolingbroke's heir, appreciates Hal's innate graciousness of manner and speech. He describes to Hotspur how the Prince delivered his offer of single combat:

> . . . I never in my life
> Did hear a challenge urg'd more modestly,
> Unless a brother should a brother dare
> To gentle exercise and proof of arms.
> He gave you all the duties of a man;
> Trimm'd up your praises with a princely tongue,
> Spoke your deservings like a chronicle,
> Making you ever better than his praise
> By still dispraising praise valu'd with you,
> And, which became him like a prince indeed,
> He made a blushing cital of himself,
> And chid his truant youth with such a grace
> As if he mast'red there a double spirit
> Of teaching and of learning instantly.
>
> (v, ii, 51–64)

From Vernon's account it is clear that Hal can act with modesty, ease, and charm. He seems to embody the characteristics that Castiglione found in the young Ippolito d'Este, Archbishop of Ferrara and friend of Ariosto and Leonardo:

he hath had so happie a birth, that his person, his countenance, his words, and all his gestures are so fashioned and compact with his grace . . . that a man would weene he were more meete to teach, than needfull to learne.[3]

Indeed, Hal's princely challenge to fight Hotspur alone, made before the leaders of the opposing parties, is in accordance with Castiglione's precepts for winning 'most estimation' in time of war; Hal's proposal is effective in 'separating him selfe from the multitude' and in offering to 'undertake notable and bolde feates'.[4]

> The Prince of Wales doth join with all the world
> In praise of Henry Percy: by my hopes,
> This present enterprise set off his head,
> I do not think a braver gentleman,
> More active-valiant or more valiant-young,
> More daring or more bold, is now alive

---

[1] Castiglione, p. 33. [2] *Ibid.*, p. 33.
[3] *Ibid.*, pp. 32–3. [4] *Ibid.*, pp. 95–6.

To grace this latter age with noble deeds.
For my part, I may speak it to my shame,
I have a truant been to chivalry,
And so I hear he doth account me too.
Yet this before my father's majesty –
I am content that he shall take the odds
Of his great name and estimation,
And will, to save the blood on either side,
Try fortune with him in a single fight.

(v, i, 86–100)

In addition, his language reveals what Castiglione calls

a simplicitie of such meekenesse of minde, that a man would weene nature her selfe spake to make them tender and (as it were) dronken with sweetnes; and with such conveyance of easinesse, that who so heareth him, may conceive a good opinion of him selfe and thinke that he also . . . mighte attaine to that perfection.[1]

That he is 'facile or easie to be spoken unto' by all except poor Francis, the puny drawer, who can barely speak at all, is half of Hal's attraction; the other half is his talent for speaking 'courtaisely, with a swete speche or countenance, wherwith the herers (as it were with a delicate odour) be refressed, and alured to loue hym in whom is this most delectable qualitie'.[2]

Even what appears Hal's failing must be reconsidered by the criteria for behavior that Castiglione and Elyot describe: one should not expect that all Hal's vices will metamorphose into virtues, but at least the mold of form will be defined by the expectancy of Shakespeare's times. Bolingbroke and Hotspur both criticize Hal for his friends: he has acted like a 'sword and buckler Prince of Wales' and has 'mingled his royalty with capering fools'. But both of Hal's critics are unsympathetic to the importance of public affection, and, as we have noted, both are out of touch with the advice published in the best Renaissance guides. Castiglione, for example, believes if 'the Courtier in jesting and speaking merry conceites have a respect to the time, to the

persons, to his degree, and not use it too often . . . hee may be called pleasant and' a man of humor.[3] That Hal knows something of this is clear when in the last act he scolds Falstaff for his impertinent answer to Bolingbroke's question about the reasons for the rebellion, or again when Hal on the field of battle asks his fat friend rhetorically, 'What, is it a time to jest and dally now?' Perhaps Hal is excessively given to the frivolous, but even his taste for practical jokes merits some approval: according to *The Courtier* 'a merrie prancke is nothing els, but a friendly deceite in matters that offend not at al or very little'.[4]

Indeed, Hal's worst faults can be used to display the basic goodness of his nature. Elyot illustrates the importance of 'placability' by relating the story of Hal, the madcap prince, and the chief justice who put him in prison. By obeying the court, Hal

a prince and sonne and heire of the kynge, in the middes of his furye, more considered his iuell example, and the iuges constance in iustice, than his owne astate or wylfull appetite. . . . Wherefore I conclude that nothing is more honorable, or to be desired in a prince or noble man, than placabilitie.[5]

Finally, Hal's horsemanship symbolizes his prowess as a Renaissance prince, for it offers the most hyperbolic image of the wastrel turned courtly hero in the play. On horseback he emerges completely cleansed from the stains of riot and dishonor, appearing as Bellerophon, glittering in a golden coat:

I saw young Harry with his beaver on,
His cushes on his thighs, gallantly arm'd,
Rise from the ground like feather'd Mercury,
And vaulted with such ease into his seat
As if an angel dropp'd down from the clouds
To turn and wind a fiery Pegasus,
And witch the world with noble horsemanship.

(iv, i, 104–10)

[1] *Ibid.*, p. 57. [2] Elyot, p.130.
[3] Castiglione, p. 168. [4] *Ibid.*, p. 170.
[5] Elyot, pp. 140–1.

Such skills as Hal exhibits he might have practised at the recommendation of either Elyot or Castiglione. Elyot endorses the ability 'to ryde surely and clene on a great horse and a roughe' as 'the most honorable exercise, in myne opinion, and that besemeth the astate of euery noble persone'.[1] *The Governour* also commends as 'a ryght good exercise which is also expedient to lerne, whiche is named the vauntynge of a horse: that is to lepe on him at euery side without stirroppe or other helpe, specially whiles the horse is goynge'.[2] For his part, Castiglione would have a Courtier 'a perfect horseman for euerie saddle. And beside the skill in horses ... let him set all his delight and diligence to wade in euerie thing a little farther than other men' while accompanying 'all his motion with a certaine good judgment and grace'.[3]

To sum up this argument, we discover that judged by the standards of conduct recommended in *The Courtier* and *The Governour*, the two most influential manners books in sixteenth-century England, Hal is not truly a wastrel nor Hotspur a paragon.[4] In fact, the behavior of the Prince at Shrewsbury and even his subsequent career as king are simply the further development of those character and personality traits which Castiglione and Elyot had considered essential for success. Indeed, it is not surprising that Hal, as one of England's greatest rulers, should embody the talents and skills Elizabethans looked for in the best representatives of nobility. What is surprising is that judged by these standards Hal proves a young man of more promise and Hotspur of less than we today might appreciate without such guides to courtly behavior, for without these handbooks for reference we might well overvalue Hotspur's virtues and underrate Hal's.

[1] *Ibid.*, p. 78.   [2] *Ibid.*, p. 79.

[3] Castiglione, p. 41.

[4] *The Governour* went through eight editions in its first fifty years, and *The Courtier* probably 'did more than any other one book to persuade the Elizabethan gentleman to unite learning to courtly graces' (Kelso, pp. 118–19). Bibliographies will be found in Kelso, G. E. Noyes, *A Bibliography of Courtesy and Conduct Books in Seventeenth Century England* (New Haven, 1917), and Virgil B. Heltzel, *A Check List of Courtesy Books in the Newberry Library* (Chicago, 1942).

'HENRY V': THE CHORUS AND THE AUDIENCE

G. P. JONES

Most critical readings of *Henry V* embody certain fixed and possibly erroneous assumptions about the role of the Chorus. It is usual to associate the play as a whole, and the Chorus in particular, with an exuberant, guns and drums and trumpets type of performance, such a performance as would have tickled the fancy of the groundlings and would have stimulated irresistible patriotic fervour in the breasts of all beholders. Some critics like *Henry V* for this reason, others dislike it for the same reason; but the uncomplicated heroic strain is generally recognised. There are a few dissenting voices, but the dominant note that runs through criticism of the play is that it is essentially a crude and unreflective piece, well suited to the gross appetites of the jingoistic mob, in which the Chorus, an unavoidable concomitant of the epic mode, plays the mindless part of public cheerleader.

A. P. Rossiter, for example, views *Henry V* as 'a propaganda-play on National Unity: heavily orchestrated for the brass',[1] the brass being provided in the main by the voice of the Chorus. In similar vein, M. M. Reese sees the systematic use of the Chorus as emphasising the heroic nature of the play in general and the epic dimensions of the protagonist in particular: 'the verse of the choruses, corresponding to the passages of heightened description which a narrative poet habitually employs, has the further function of establishing the epic stature of the hero'.[2] But the function of the Chorus is also, in Reese's words, to 'apologise for

the unsuitability of any stage for the breadth and sweep of epic'.[3] Is there not a contradiction here? The editor of the New Arden edition, J. H. Walter, is also untroubled by the co-existence of aggressive invocations and defensive excuses for having embarked at all on theatrical bastardisation of the epic genre: 'No wonder Shakespeare, after the magnificent epic invocation of the Prologue, becomes apologetic; no wonder he appeals most urgently to his audiences to use their imagination, for in daring to simulate the "best and most accomplished kinds of Poetry" [*Apologie*, p. 33] on the common stage he laid himself open to the scorn and censure of the learned and judicious'.[4]

This highly respected line of interpretation, which nevertheless incorporates some uncomfortable inconsistencies, is best represented by John Dover Wilson's classic essay introducing his New Cambridge edition of *Henry V*. Writing in the aftermath of the Second World War, Dover Wilson interprets the play as the communal and sacramental expression of a triumphantly patriotic impulse, with the Chorus mediating between audience and material in a way that is 'comparable in the sphere of

[1] A. P. Rossiter, *Angel with Horns* (New York, 1961), p. 57.
[2] M. M. Reese, *The Cease of Majesty* (1961), p. 320.
[3] *Ibid.*
[4] J. H. Walter, 'Introduction', *King Henry V* (1954), p. xv,

93

theatrical art to that of a priest leading his congregation in prayer or celebration'.[1]

Dover Wilson is evidently aware, however, that the very presence of the Chorus, not to mention the insistence of the excuses offered through it, raises some difficulties. To meet them he introduces the hypothesis that the Chorus may have been played by the author himself. He explains that 'the diffident and apologetic tone, which the Chorus adopts throughout, and which sounds awkward, not to say ungracious, if interpreted, with most critics, as the impatience of an author girding against the resources of his theatre and the limitations of his actors, becomes at once natural and engaging when taken as a personal apology and plea by somebody who was author, player, and producer in one'.[2] The argument may be speculative, but at least it recognises the singularity of the Chorus of *Henry V* and attempts to account for it in terms of a distinctive set of theatrical circumstances. Less sensitive critics have not always been aware that there may be a problem, discounting the diffidence of the Chorus as being merely a standard and unremarkable part of the traditional choric routine.

The structural justification of the presence of the Chorus usually complements the thematic and generic arguments rehearsed above. The Chorus of *Henry V*, so the argument runs, performs an indispensable structural function in welding spatially and temporally disparate episodes into a unified dramatic whole. 'Undoubtedly the speeches of the Chorus are epical in tone', writes the New Arden editor, 'but they have another epical function, for in the careful way they recount the omitted details of the well-known story, they secure unity of action.'[3] Similarly, R. A. Law, encapsulating a number of orthodox misconceptions, urges that 'the actual purpose of these six poems is to sound a patriotic note in exaltation of the heroic King, to link the five acts together, and

then to apologize for inadequate expression of so great a theme'.[4] As a rule this line of argument, polished smooth by years of critical and pedagogical handling, is so persuasively presented that one wonders how Shakespeare managed to dispense with the services of a Chorus in his other historical plays. Dover Wilson, appreciating the difficulty, raises this very point: 'why should the dramatist suddenly in 1599 begin apologizing for the incapacity of himself and his theatre to cope with a historical theme and battle-scenes, when such things had been one of their chief stocks-in-trade for the past half-dozen years?'[5] Why indeed? No one would deny that the Chorus of *Henry V* performs dramatically relevant and structurally appropriate functions. But are those functions sufficiently remarkable to account for the presence of a Chorus here but not elsewhere in Shakespeare's history plays? Do the orthodox explanations really account for the uniqueness of the Chorus, or do they simply shift the problem to different ground?

For example, if it is argued (as it frequently is) that the Chorus reflects a certain historical punctiliousness on Shakespeare's part, why is it reasonable to suppose that his conscience should have started troubling him with respect to the chronology of the short reign of Henry V when he expands and contracts, fuses and confuses, and generally plays fast and loose with historical sequence in his other history plays? Dover Wilson speculates that 'Shakespeare was less free than usual to manipulate or depart from his historical sources, seeing that . . . the facts he dealt with were probably better known to his hearers than those of any

[1] J. Dover Wilson, 'Introduction', *King Henry V* (Cambridge, 1947), p. xv.

[2] *Ibid.*, p. xiii.

[3] Walter, p. xv.

[4] R. A. Law, 'The Choruses in *Henry the Fifth*', *University of Texas Studies in English*, xxxv (1956), 15.

[5] Dover Wilson, p. xiv.

other of his chronicle-plays'.[1] But were they? This sounds suspiciously like an *ex post facto* argument that might just as easily have been applied to *King John* or *Richard II* or *Richard III* had they been furnished with Choruses.

Something is wrong, then, either with the Chorus of *Henry V*, or with the traditional way of looking at it. The traditional view leaves us with a Chorus who is a public braggart braying about heroic deeds while at the same time apologising for not being able to bray more eloquently. A few critics have evidently sensed this discontinuity, though the perception has generally led simply to inversion of the orthodox view, to interpretations which take the Chorus (and consequently the whole play) ironically, or at least anti-heroically. James Black, for instance, has recently opposed the dominant heroic interpretation of the play with the argument that Shakespeare presents his hero 'not as Mars, or Alexander, or Agamemnon – although others in the play dream of him so – nor as *miles gloriosus*, but as a workman'.[2] Robert Ornstein's view of the play also exhibits his disquiet with the canons of orthodoxy. He attempts to resolve the contradictions generated by the Chorus by resorting to a cautiously ironic reading:

Although the Chorus apologizes several times for the author's feeble attempts to represent the field of Agincourt with 'four or five most vile and ragged foils,' the apology is as sly as it is gratuitous because Shakespeare makes no attempt in the play to represent an epic confrontation of armies.... The abject apology of the Chorus for the failings of the author is just one clue to the artfulness that wears so naive a guise in *Henry V*. Other clues are the ironic juxtapositions which the simple linear plot innocently allows to happen.[3]

The contention advanced in the present paper is that most critical discussion of the role of the Chorus in *Henry V* is distorted because it embodies an unexamined and questionable premise: that the Chorus is the very voice of the public playhouse. It will be argued, on the contrary, that the Chorus of *Henry V* is fundamentally incompatible with the public theatre and is fully comprehensible only in terms of performance under more specialised conditions. Contrary to what has usually been believed, there are good grounds for supposing that the Chorus is the mechanism not for adapting an episodic tale to the public stage, nor even for establishing an epic tone, but for adapting the material to a court performance. Hence, the chorusless 1600 Quarto publication may be taken as approximating the public playhouse form of the play, while the Folio text relates to the court version of the play, regardless of which of the two versions is regarded as taking precedence in point of time over the other.

The relation between the Quarto and Folio texts of *Henry V* is not much disputed nowadays. The idea that the Quarto text may represent an early sketch of which the Folio text is the completed elaboration has been largely discarded. The overwhelming weight of scholarly opinion accords precedence to the Folio text as the full acting version for London audiences, while the Quarto version is generally regarded as a report of an abridgement (or an abridgement of a report) intended for provincial performance by a reduced touring company.[4] It is by no means impossible, however, that the abbreviated, vulgarised, chorusless (and perhaps pirated) Quarto text

[1] *Ibid.*, p. xii.

[2] James Black, 'Shakespeare's *Henry V* and the Dreams of History', *English Studies in Canada*, I (Spring 1975), 22.

[3] Robert Ornstein, *A Kingdom for a Stage* (Cambridge, Mass., 1972), p. 176.

[4] This view is endorsed by the editor of the New Arden edition of the play, J. H. Walter, and, among others, by H. T. Price, *The Text of Henry V* (Newcastle-under-Lyme, 1920); Gerda Okerlund, 'The Quarto Version of *Henry V* as a Stage Adaptation', *PMLA*, XLIX (1934), 810–34; W. W. Greg, *The Shakespeare First Folio* (Oxford, 1955).

is the result not of provincial 'barbering' but reflects the acting text for the public theatre in London, the fuller Folio text reflecting the dimensions of the play as presented at court.

One of the few discussions of the Chorus in *Henry V* that challenges the usual assumptions is W. D. Smith's 'The *Henry V* Choruses in the First Folio',[1] in which it is argued, as here, that the Chorus is symptomatic of court performance of the play rather than public performance. Unfortunately, Smith's thesis is presented in combination with two other heterodox views: that the celebrated reference in prologue v to 'the general of our gracious empress' alludes not to the Earl of Essex and his Irish expedition of 1599, but to his successor as General and Lord Deputy of Ireland, Lord Mountjoy; and that, in any case, some other hand than Shakespeare's is responsible for the creation of the Chorus of *Henry V*. It is clear why the paper is not better known, despite the merits of some of the theatrical arguments advanced. Smith proposes that the unprecedented obsequiousness of the Chorus must be accounted for by unusual circumstances and suggests that if interpreted literally rather than metaphorically a number of allusive terms (scaffold – a *temporary* stage structure – cockpit, gentles, sit, etc.) point to court performance in the Royal Cockpit. While Smith's arguments about the appropriateness of the Chorus to performance in the Royal Cockpit cannot always be accepted as they stand, they certainly merit further consideration and amplification.

Much of the rhetoric of the Chorus, which has generally been regarded as suggestive of public performance, is in fact more suggestive of private performance. Most obviously, there are the apologies that emphasise the spatial inadequacies of the theatre and draw attention quite deliberately to the discrepancy between the size of the real events and the size of their theatrical representation. Specific allusions to the physical limitations of the fabric of the theatre (as opposed to apologies for shortcomings in presentation or conception) cluster together in prologue i, which wishes vainly for a 'kingdom for a stage' and then goes on to deplore the theatrical simulacrum in four different figures suggesting an acute shortage of space: 'can this cockpit hold / The vasty fields of France? . . . may we cram / Within this wooden O . . . since a crooked figure may / Attest in little space a million . . . Suppose within the girdle of these walls / Are now confin'd two mighty monarchies'. And in the epilogue, the audience is again reminded of the physical restrictions of the theatre by the apologetic 'In little room confining mighty men'. It is worth remarking that the beginnings and endings of plays are particularly vulnerable to revision to fit them to particular occasions. The fact that this type of spatial allusion does not occur throughout the role of the Chorus, but is restricted to the first and last speeches, may indicate rewriting in part or in whole for some specific performance.

Why Shakespeare should thus apologise for the limitations of the public playhouse when he does not do so elsewhere has not been satisfactorily explained. But if the Chorus constitutes a response to performance in some place other than the public playhouse, under more cramped conditions than usual, then such remarks might well be regarded as fitting and, indeed, witty exploitations of the disadvantages of a particular situation. The allusions in the first speech of the Chorus not only to the size but to the shape of the theatrical area ('wooden O', 'cockpit', 'crooked figure', 'girdle of these walls') have usually been taken to indicate an octagonal public playhouse such as The Globe. These images do not correspond with the rectangular shape of the usual locations of Tudor or Stuart performances at Whitehall:

[1] W. D. Smith, 'The *Henry V* Choruses in the First Folio', *Journal of English and Germanic Philology*, LIII (1954), 38–57.

the Great Chamber, the Great Hall, and, during James's reign, the Banquet House. Nor would complaints about lack of space be either accurate or civil under normal conditions of court presentation. The images (and the complaints) would, however, be completely and literally appropriate to performance in the Royal Cockpit, which was certainly used in James's reign for occasional dramatic presentations and which was, of course, octagonal in interior design.

The question of the date and location of a specific court performance will be taken up later; but regardless of the precise occasion on which the play is supposed to have been staged, the language of the Chorus is in general terms more congruent with the notion of court performance than with performance on the public stage. The collaborative effort insistently demanded of the audience is confidential and personal in its strategy rather than collective and public. Its appeals to the individual to liberate the forces of his imagination imply an informed, intelligent and co-operative audience, as do the recurrent allusions to the problems of translating historical reality into theatrical illusion. Requiring the audience to 'Piece out our imperfections with your thoughts' (I, 23), or to 'make imaginary puissance' (I, 25), or to 'Play with your fancies' (III, 7), or to 'eke out our performance with your mind' (III, 35), or to 'Heave him away upon your winged thoughts' (v, 8), these are requests that might have met with ribald counter-suggestions in a public forum. It is at least conceivable that this loquacious choric gentleman, together with his invitations to participate in the scene-shifting of the drama and his reiterated explanations of the technical problems faced by the author, might have seemed a trifle tedious to the paying customers of the public playhouse. A more sophisticated and cultured audience, on the other hand, might have been more tolerant of appeals to

understand and help compensate for the technical difficulties encountered by the dramatist. Such an audience might, indeed, have been mildly titillated by the calculated audaciousness of such appeals.

The obsequiousness of the Chorus of *Henry V* has frequently received comment, but the antithetical tone that also characterises the part has been less frequently remarked upon. The Chorus alternates between wheedling and hectoring, between exaggerated respect and subtly insistent familiarity. On the one hand, the audience is courted with self-deprecating formulas: 'pardon, gentles all' (I, 8), 'your humble patience pray' (I, 33), 'Linger your patience on' (II, 31), 'eke out our performance' (III, 35), 'O for pity! we shall much disgrace' (IV, 49), 'I humbly pray them to admit th' excuse' (v, 3), 'with rough and all-unable pen' (epilogue, 1). On the other hand, the audience is bullied by boldly imperative injunctions: 'Suppose ... Piece out ... divide ... Think ...' (I), 'Suppose ... Hear ... behold ... do but think ... Follow, follow! ... Work, work your thoughts ... Behold ... Suppose ...' (III), 'Heave him away ... Behold ... behold ...' (v).

The apparent contradiction is explained by the fact that the rhetoric of the Chorus draws on the techniques of the adept flatterer, who mingles frankness and hypocrisy, brusqueness and courtesy, undervaluation of self and overvaluation of the auditor. Comparable tactics are employed by Shakespeare in the Sonnets, wherein insidious flattery is authenticated, as it were, by bluntness and familiarity. The technique is especially prominent in those poems in which the poet's *persona* laments his enslavement to love (e.g., 57 'Being your slave, what should I do but tend', 58 'That god forbid that made me first your slave'), or in which he professes his continuing love despite the infidelity or imperfection of the loved one (e.g., 34 'Why didst thou promise such a beauteous day', 40 'Take all my loves, my love, yea, take them all'). Wind and holy water at court is all the more effective for a cunning admixture of candour and even a suggestion of impertinence.

The effect of denigrating the powers of the presenters while inflating the contribution of the audience in the Chorus of *Henry V* is to hand all the praise for the success of the performance to the audience, all the blame for its shortcomings to the presenters. The audience is thus complimented as the perfecters of the performance, as is indicated by the we–you oppositions running through prologue 1, emphasising the primacy of the contribution made by the audience: 'And let *us*, ciphers to this great accompt, / On *your* imaginary forces work' (17–18); 'Piece out *our* imperfections with *your* thoughts' (23); 'Think, when *we* talk of horses, that *you* see them' (26); 'For 'tis *your* thoughts that now must deck *our* kings' (28). Clearly, the audience is being cajoled into self-congratulatory acceptance of the fact that its contribution is indispensable to the realisation and perfection of what is imperfectly and insubstantially represented by the stage-ciphers.

Such insistence on the participatory role of the audience is not generally characteristic of the Elizabethan public playhouse. It is, however, characteristic in a direct and literal sense of the courtly entertainment, the masque, in which noble patrons participated as a matter of course. A leading authority on the masque asserts that 'drama is properly a form of entertainment, and involves its audience vicariously', while the masque 'is a form of play, and includes its audience directly'.[1] Shakespeare would appear to be blurring that distinction in the Chorus of *Henry V*, requiring of his audience an imaginative collaboration paralleling the physical participation that characterises the court masque. It may be noted too that a relationship of some kind between

the Chorus of *Henry V* and the court masque is established from the outset, for since the court both watched and participated in masques, it would not be vain in that context to invoke 'princes to act / And monarchs to behold the swelling scene' (I, 3–4).

The insistence on the gentility of the audience in the first two prologues is also suggestive, though it must not be interpreted too narrowly. The term 'gentle' could be used by polite metaphorical extension to refer to virtually any collection of listeners.[2] Shakespeare occasionally addresses his audience as gentle elsewhere: 'Gentles, do not reprehend' (*A Midsummer Night's Dream*, V, i, 429), 'Your gentle hands lend us' (*All's Well that Ends Well*, epilogue, 6), 'Gentle spectators' (*The Winter's Tale*, IV, i, 20), 'gentle hearers' (*Henry VIII*, prologue, 17). But nowhere does he make quite such play on the gentility of the audience as he does in the first two prologues of *Henry V*, which perhaps suggests playful emphasis on something that has some foundation in fact: 'But pardon, *gentles* all' (I, 8); '*Gently* to hear, kindly to judge, our play' (I, 34); 'the scene / Is now transported, *gentles*, to Southampton' (II, 34–5); 'charming the narrow seas / To give you *gentle* pass' (II, 38–9). In combination with the apologetic stance frequently adopted by the Chorus, this hyperpoliteness should not be lightly dismissed.

Taking all this politeness at face value, it is scarcely surprising that some commentators have been repelled by the Uriah Heepishness of the Chorus. But surely the mannered exaggeration of the posture is the practised, balanced pose of the courtier, whose tools of trade are elaborate formulas of deference, but who is able to preserve his self-respect while

[1] Stephen Orgel, 'Introduction', *Ben Jonson: The Complete Masques* (New Haven, 1969), p. 1.
[2] W. D. Smith, in fact, interprets this term very narrowly. His interpretation is conclusively dismissed by R. A. Law.

simulating slavish obsequiousness by virtue of the fact that the formulas are, after all, only formulas. Shakespeare's Sonnets again provide a parallel in those poems in which praise of the auditor and dispraise of the speaker blend into a mixture that is neither quite mockery nor quite unreserved praise, but an intelligent and ironically self-aware form of flattery. It is to be noted especially in those poems in which the poet's skill is brought into question, in Sonnets 32 ('If thou survive my well-contented day'), 38 ('How can my Muse want subject to invent'), 76 ('Why is my verse so barren of new pride?'), 77 ('So oft have I invoked thee for my Muse'), 80 ('O, how I faint when I of you do write'), and so on.

Such a stance is surely inappropriate to the public stage, where a much less deferential tone might be expected. Shakespeare of the public theatre may be less acerbic than Jonson, but he is not usually as conciliatory as he is in the Chorus of *Henry V*. His prologues are sometimes neutrally functional (*Troilus and Cressida*, *Pericles*), sometimes brusque (*2 Henry IV*: 'Open your ears'), sometimes jaunty (*Henry VIII*: 'The first and happiest hearers of the town'). But nowhere in the canon is the tone of the Chorus of *Henry V* duplicated, and its special nature demands that special circumstances be found to account for it.

All this leads inevitably to the question of the occasion on which this special performance might have taken place. As is well known, *Henry V* is generally dated by means of the lines in the prologue to act v, which have been almost universally accepted as alluding to the Earl of Essex and his ill-fated military expedition to Ireland in 1599.

> The mayor and all his brethren in best sort,
> Like to the senators of th' antique Rome,
> With the plebeians swarming at their heels,
> Go forth and fetch their conqu'ring Caesar in:
> As, by a lower but by loving likelihood,
> Were now the general of our gracious empress,

> As in good time he may, from Ireland coming,
> Bringing rebellion broached on his sword,
> How many would the peaceful city quit
> To welcome him! much more, and much more
>   cause,
> Did they this Harry.   (v, 25–35)

Essex was commissioned on 12 March 1599, left London on 27 March 1599, and returned in disgrace on 28 September 1599. It is generally assumed that the lines in question could not have been written prior to Essex's departure, though they could, in fact, have been written at an earlier date in anticipation of his departure, or even in anticipation of his receiving his commission, about which there had been considerable speculation. The impending Irish expedition was the talk of London during the final months of 1598 and the opening months of 1599. In the nine letters that John Chamberlain wrote to Dudley Carleton between 8 November 1598 and 15 March 1599, he mentions the preparations for the Irish expedition and the probability of its being commanded by the Earl of Essex in every one of them.[1] As early as 8 November 1598, the approximate date of departure is widely known ('generally held that the Earl of Essex shall go thither towards the spring as lieutenant general'), though there are recurrent doubts and difficulties. On 22 November, 'his going is not so fully resolved but that once in ten days it is in question', it 'holds still in suspense' on 8 December, and it seems 'quite dashed' by 20 December. On 3 January 1599, 'the wind is come about again for Ireland', though a further delay ('now put over till March') is reported on 17 January. The final impediment was the Earl of Essex's commission, which was, according to Chamberlain, 'agreed on, though not yet signed' on 31 January, but still 'no nearer signing' on 15 February. By 1 March,

---

[1] *The Letters of John Chamberlain*, ed. N. E. McClure (Philadelphia, 1939), I, 50–73. The quotations are modernised here.

with 'new difficulties' arising daily about the commission, Essex was so dissatisfied that 'many times he makes it a question whether he go or not'. At last, on 15 March 1599, Chamberlain reports that 'this great commission for Ireland is dispatched, and the Earl hath all his demands'.

It is clear, then, that if the allusion in prologue v is to Essex, as is generally accepted, it could have been written months before his actual departure, in anticipation not only of his victorious return, but in anticipation of his commissioning and departure. Hence, the usual *terminus a quo* for this reference, the date of Essex's departure, 27 March 1599, must be moved back several months to early November 1598.

It is equally clear that in view of the excitement being generated by the impending Irish expedition, a play providing a dramatic account of another expedition to reassert English hegemony over an errant possession would have been highly topical in the months preceding Essex's departure. The Lord Chamberlain's Men were paid for three performances at court of unspecified plays during the winter season of 1598/9: 26 December 1598, 1 January 1599, 20 February 1599.[1] On any of these occasions (but especially the last, as speculation and preparation increased), *Henry V* would have been extremely timely as a celebration of a past and future victory, with the anticipatory remark about 'the general of our gracious empress' being an earnest of loyal enthusiasm on the part of the players and the community at large (though couched in sufficiently vague terms that it would apply equally to a successor if Essex were to be replaced as commander of the force at the last moment).

The single recorded court performance of *Henry V* is, however, a non-Elizabethan one. The play was performed at the Jacobean court by the King's Men on 7 January 1605,[2] a performance which raises a number of interesting questions. One would expect that the version of the play presented on that occasion would be derived from the Folio text (with the Chorus) rather than from the Quarto text (without the Chorus), an expectation which is strongly supported by the fact that the prologue to Jonson's revised version of *Every Man in His Humour*, also presented at court by the King's Men in the same season (2 February 1605),[3] lampoons Shakespeare's history plays generally and *Henry V* in particular. Glancing at Shakespeare's apologetic 'four or five most vile and ragged foils' (iv, 50), Jonson's prologue scoffs at plays which 'with three rusty swords, / And help of some few foot and half-foot words, / Fight over York and Lancaster's long jars' (9–11). And, lest the gibe be missed, Jonson pursues it with the reassurance that his is a play where no 'Chorus wafts you o'er the seas' (15).

The prologue to *Every Man in His Humour* appears in the Folio publication of Jonson's work (1616), but does not appear in the Quarto publication of the play in 1601, presumably because it had not been written by that time. Between the Quarto publication and the Folio publication, the play underwent extensive revision. The editor of the Regents Renaissance Drama edition of *Every Man in His Humour*, J. W. Lever, endorses E. K. Chambers's view that the '"natural time for a revision" would have been prior to 2 February 1605, when *Every Man in His Humour* was revived for performance at court'.[4] This being the case, can there be any real doubt that the stimulus for Jonson's satirical introductory remarks must have been a recent performance of *Henry V* with a version of the Chorus

[1] E. K. Chambers, *The Elizabethan Stage* (Oxford, 1945), iv, 166.
[2] *Ibid.*, iv, 119.　　　[3] *Ibid.*
[4] J. W. Lever, 'Introduction', *Every Man in His Humour* (Lincoln, Nebraska, 1971), p. xi.

comparable to what is preserved in the Folio text?

The only reservation one might have is that Jonson's remarks might have been expected to preface *Every Man out of His Humour*, which was played at court on 8 January 1605, the night after *Henry V*,[1] whereas *Every Man in His Humour* was played almost a month later, by which time the allusion to the Chorus of *Henry V* would be somewhat less pointed. Two possibilities present themselves, both of them speculative: that Jonson's prologue, which is very general in substance, may originally have been written to preface *Every Man out of His Humour*, being later transferred by Jonson to *Every Man in His Humour*; or that an unrecorded repeat performance of *Henry V* may have been presented at court between the dates of the two Jonson productions, a hypothesis that is taken up below.

One of the features of the Folio text of *Henry V* that does not sit well with the 1605 court performance is the allusion to Essex in prologue v. Might not such topical allusions be expected to be written out when a play was being revised for court revival? Or might certain allusions be deliberately retained for their historical flavour? This seems unlikely until one recalls that Jonson was so unwilling to have the original conclusion to *Every Man out of His Humour* lost to the world that, even after it had been replaced for Jacobean revival, he had Macilente's paean to Queen Elizabeth printed in the Folio as an appendix to the play.

An allusion to the Earl of Essex, if that is what we have in prologue v of *Henry V*, might be more likely than other allusions to be preserved in performance before the Jacobean court. Essex was regarded as something of a martyr to the cause of King James, and, on coming to the throne, James showed extraordinary favour to Essex's young son, restoring his title and inheritance, and making him the companion of Prince Henry.

The young Prince Henry and the restored Earl of Essex would presumably have been the primary targets of any allusion of this kind. Obsessed as he was with military matters, it would be surprising if Prince Henry had not admired the most famous soldier of recent times, a principal supporter of his father's cause, and the father of his closest friend. The retention of such an allusion would be even more likely, it may be supposed, if it could in whole or in part be applied anew to Prince Henry as heir to King Henry V (whom he supposedly resembled), or to his companion, son of the dashing Essex. In the presence of the Jacobean court, might 'gracious empress' stand for Queen Anne, and might the 'general' in the case be identified with Prince Henry ('*this* Harry'), or with Robin Devereux as emulator of his father's achievements? Of course, it does not quite fit. 'As, by a *lower* ... likelihood' would not seem to be an entirely suitable comparison for a crown prince, even if the comparison is with a reigning monarch; and Ireland was no longer in a state of rebellion in 1605 (though, if a compliment were to be turned, what other potentially unruly possession of the crown was to hand to create a parallel with Henry V's reclaiming his patrimony?). Nevertheless, generally appropriate resonance of this nature might have been sufficient to sway the balance in favour of retention of the allusion.

The possibility of there having been some rewriting and adapting of *Henry V* for the court performance of 1605 is supported by the presence in the Folio text of the so-called 'international' scene (III, ii, 69ff.), which does not appear in the Quarto text. Since the Quarto text is generally accepted as being an abbreviated version, the presence in Folio of material that is absent from Quarto does not necessarily indicate subsequent rewriting. But in the case of the latter part of III, ii, which assembles

[1] Chambers, IV, 119.

Captains Gower, Macmorris, Fluellen, and Jamy, the archetypal Englishman, Irishman, Welshman and Scot, the episode is so pointedly appropriate to Jacobean politics, to James's pride at having peacefully united the possessions of the crown as Elizabeth could not, that it is extremely tempting to place the episode in the Jacobean rather than the Elizabethan period, as does Fleay ('an insertion . . . to please King James').[1] Most modern authorities raise difficulties about Jacobean provenance for this episode. Price objects to Captain Jamy's name as providing 'a decisive reason for refusing to believe that the scene in which he appears was written as a compliment to King James'.[2] Greg urges that 'the episode . . . with Jamy's comic speech, must surely have been cut when the play was acted before James I in 1605, and may have been suppressed earlier'.[3] But apart from his broad accent, which parallels that of the other characters in the scene, and which is not in itself offensive, there is no guying or satirising of Captain Jamy (as there is of Fluellen and Macmorris). On the contrary, Captain Jamy is treated deferentially by Fluellen, stands by judiciously listening to the arguments of Fluellen and Macmorris rather than participating in them, and is characterised in complimentary terms by Fluellen as 'a marvellous falorous gentleman' who is 'of great expedition and knowledge in th' aunchient wars' (III, ii, 80–2). There is, in short, nothing patently offensive about the presentation of Captain Jamy in III, ii, and nothing concrete, therefore, to contradict the view that the figure might be regarded at a Jacobean court performance as an affectionate if mildly impertinent jest.

The Chorus also shows possible marks of the recorded court performance of 1605. On the day before the presentation of *Henry V*, court festivities had culminated on Twelfth Night with a magnificent and costly production of the Inigo Jones/Ben Jonson *Masque of Blackness*,

celebrating the creation of Prince Charles as Duke of York. The *Masque of Blackness* was noteworthy not only for its sumptuousness and for its daring use of lady masquers in blackface as blackamores, but for its spectacular innovations in theatrical machinery and design – for its 'artificial sea' with 'waves which seemed to move', its 'great concave shell like mother of pearl, curiously made to move on those waters and rise with the billow', and its ingeniously costumed actors and miscellaneous stage properties, including two mermaids, two sea-horses, six tritons with blue hair, and 'six huge sea-monsters, varied in their shape and dispositions, bearing on their backs the twelve torch-bearers'.[4]

On the night after such a production, how could an ordinary play, even a play by Shakespeare, be anything but an anticlimax? The lack of machinery and special effects would be painfully evident to an audience that had just had its eyes opened to a wonderful new theatrical dimension by an extravaganza which 'brought the full resources of Italian theatrical machinery into use for the first time on an English stage'.[5] Shakespeare does his best, nevertheless, by trying to turn the absence of scenic illusion and spectacle into a virtue.

In prologue 1, apologising for the shortcomings of a presentation that lacks the financial and technical resources allocated to a court masque, he defiantly emphasises the powers of the imagination as opposed to the artifices of the stage architect. Indeed, it is possible that the invocation of the opening seven and a half lines of Prologue 1 ('O for a muse of fire', etc.), which has generally been taken seriously, is nothing more than heroic bombast, intentionally punctured by the anticlimactic 'O pardon'. Its purpose may be to reject the

---

[1] F. G. Fleay, *A Chronicle History of the Life and Work of William Shakespeare* (1886), p. 206.

[2] Price, p. 54.   [3] Greg, pp. 282–3.

[4] Orgel, pp. 48–9.   [5] *Ibid.*, p. 4.

illusionism produced by the resources of the masque, to reject the premises of what had been presented at court the night before. And if these lines are taken as mocking the extravagant literalism of Jonson's *Masque of Blackness*, the guying in turn of Shakespeare's *Henry V* Chorus in the prologue to *Every Man in His Humour* becomes even more understandable as a riposte.

The whole of prologue 1 may fruitfully be read in the light of this hypothesis, with the apologies taking on an added dimension when it is assumed that they may allude tacitly to the *Masque of Blackness* and that the self-effacing 'flat, unraised spirits', 'unworthy scaffold', and so forth are 'flat' and 'unworthy' only by contrast with the splendid display made possible by the King's munificence on the previous night.

A major difficulty remains with respect to the Chorus of *Henry V* and the court performance of 1605: the precise location of the performance. Prologue 1 alludes to a cockpit, and it is argued above that there may be grounds for reading the term literally and placing the performance in question in the Royal Cockpit. This hypothesis is much more acceptable for the Jacobean period than for the Elizabethan, but it is far from conclusive as far as the 1605 performance is concerned.

There is no record of the Royal Cockpit's having been used for the presentation of plays before the winter season of 1607/8, when it was prepared for plays 'on five separate occasions, three times in December and twice in January ... A year later the building was again used for plays, twice in January and twice in February: and much the same pattern was followed over the next two years'.[1] It is unlikely that the Royal Cockpit should suddenly be in demand for dramatic performances in 1607/8 without having been used occasionally for similar purposes previously, so that performances in the Royal Cockpit before 1607/8,

while not provable, are not altogether impossible. However, even if the likelihood of the Royal Cockpit's occasionally functioning as a playhouse prior to 1607/8 is granted, the recorded performance of 7 January 1605 appears not to have been staged there. By conflating the records of the Revels, Chamber, and Works Accounts, Glynne Wickham concludes that the recorded performances of *Henry V* and *Every Man out of His Humour* were presented in the Great Hall.[2] This being the case, 'cockpit', 'wooden O', and so on, which cannot refer to a rectangular hall, must be taken as pertaining to some other performance.

While the multiplication of hypothetical, undocumented performances is undesirable, the evidence provided by prologue 1 is sufficiently suggestive to warrant it. But while there are many occasions on which an unspecified play might have been presented at court, it is not reasonable to separate *Henry V* from the context of the winter season of 1604/5, not only because a further court revival of the play seems unlikely, but because the Chorus of the play fits so neatly between Jonson's *Masque of Blackness* and the prologue to *Every Man in His Humour*. The conclusion that may be warranted is that, despite having to follow *Masque of Blackness*, *Henry V* was sufficiently popular to be repeated shortly after the recorded performance (7 January 1605) but before the presentation of *Every Man in His Humour* (2 February 1605). One cannot imagine the play's being a particular favourite with the pacific James I, but it is certainly possible that it might have appealed strongly to the military-minded Prince Henry, especially if the physical resemblance between himself and his distant forebear had as yet been remarked, as it was to be five years later by Ben Jonson in *Prince*

[1] Glynne Wickham, *Early English Stages: 1300 to 1660* (1972), vol. 2, Part II, p. 79.
[2] *Ibid.*, vol. 2, Part II, p. 156.

Henry's Barriers, performed on 6 January 1610 ('Harry the fifth, to whom in face you are / So like', ll. 278–9).

King James left court to go hunting after the Christmas festivities on 9 January 1605.[1] According to Chamberlain, he still had not returned on 26 January 1605.[2] If a performance were given at Whitehall in the King's absence before the Prince or the Queen, the audience would in all probability have been small enough that the Chamber or the Hall would not have been required, small enough to permit the Royal Cockpit to have been used. Chambers speculates that the Cockpit would have been used for dramatic performances 'only on the less public and crowded occasions when the King was not present',[3] and he also attests that King James 'was liberal in ordering additional plays for the prince and court'[4] when he was away hunting. And, for a less formal occasion of this sort, it is possible that payment might have been made directly in the form of an *ex gratia* purse rather than going through the Chamber Accounts, where it would have left a trace.

In the comparatively restricted space of the Royal Cockpit, some such ruefulness as is evidenced in prologue 1 of *Henry V* might come quite naturally and be quite in the spirit of the occasion for players and audience accustomed to the ampler facilities of the Great Hall, Great Chamber, or Banquet House. Under such conditions, allusions to 'this unworthy scaffold', 'this cockpit', and 'this wooden O' would spring to life as pointed and witty comments on facilities that might seem well nigh spartan after the lavishness of the recent Christmas festivities. Of course, the hypothesis is speculative and rather complicated, requiring the acceptance, among other things, of the presence of several strata of composition in the Chorus of *Henry V*. But the hypothesis is plausible, fits all the known facts, and explains those facts better than alternative theories.

To summarise, then, it has been argued that the orthodox view of the Chorus of *Henry V* is distorted by not allowing for internal and external evidence that connects the play with court performance rather than public performance. The allusion in prologue V, apparently to the famous second Earl of Essex, requires that we accept the existence of the Chorus in some form or other by 1599, and possibly as early as 1598, despite its absence from the Quarto publication of 1600. Otherwise, the Chorus seems well suited in its general tenor to the documented court performance of 7 January 1605, though the allusions in prologue 1 to 'this cockpit' and 'this wooden O', if they are to be taken literally, indicate another and unrecorded performance of the play in the Royal Cockpit.

[1] 'The King to the Council. During his absence for necessary recreation, they are to assemble weekly at the Queen's Court, to transact business.' *Calendar of State Papers, Domestic, James I*, XII, 13 (9 January 1605).

[2] 'The King went to Royston two days after Twelfth-tide, where and thereabout he hath continued ever since...' (*The Letters of John Chamberlain*, I, 201; 26 January 1605).

[3] Chambers, I, 216.   [4] *Ibid.*, I, 215.

'THE DEVIL'S PARTY': VIRTUES AND VICES IN 'MEASURE FOR MEASURE'

HARRIETT HAWKINS

Where God hath a temple, the Devil will have
  a chapel.
        (Burton, *The Anatomy of Melancholy*)
Utter my thoughts? Why, say they are vile
  and false;
As where's that palace whereinto foul things
Sometimes intrude not? Who has that breast
  so pure
But some uncleanly apprehensions
Keep leets and law-days and in sessions sit
With meditations lawful?   (Iago)

Writing about 'the Integrity of *Measure for Measure*' (*Shakespeare Survey 28* (1975), pp. 89–106), Arthur C. Kirsch severely reprimands Dr Johnson, Coleridge, and numerous modern critics, including myself, for our failure to 'take the play's Christian ideas seriously'. We are guilty of a 'fatal' misunderstanding of the tragicomedy, because we have been either unable or unwilling to place ourselves 'in the position of the play's first audience'. According to Professor Kirsch, we show an absolutely unforgiving and specifically un-Christian refusal to accept the ending and pardon Angelo, whose libidinousness was miraculously transformed by the bed-trick. Indeed, in the course of his essay, Kirsch goes on to conclude that most of the problems which, over the centuries, have vexed so many commentators, can now be 'explained'. All difficulties will be made comparatively 'easy' by an 'apprehension of certain fundamental Scriptural texts', and by Kirsch's own scholarly consideration of how those texts 'might have been understood and have affected Shakespeare's contemporary audience' (quotations are from pp. 89–91). Happily, however, this is simply not true. In spite of all Kirsch's arguments, the fact remains that any number of (quite rightly) unanswered questions and unsolved problems seem, whether deliberately or unconsciously, to have been built in to the text of *Measure for Measure* by Shakespeare himself, and these problems and questions are immeasurably more interesting than the solutions to them that have been propounded by modern scholars. For after all, the duty of the artist (as opposed to the scientist) is not to provide us with solutions, but, rather, to make certain that the problems under consideration are accurately posed: 'Not a single problem is solved in *Anna Karenina* and in *Eugene Onegin*,' wrote Chekhov to his publisher–critic, 'but you find these works quite satisfactory... because all the questions in them are correctly posed.'[1]

Surely no one would deny that serious questions about certain religious values are raised by the action of *Measure for Measure*, as well as its title. But underlying many discussions of its religious references is the facile assumption that the human problems posed here are, theologically at least, soluble, as well as the equally facile (and fallacious) assumption that, back in the good old days of William Shakespeare, there was general agreement about what did, or did not, constitute proper Christian conduct. There was no such agreement.

[1] See the *Letters of Anton Chekhov*, ed. Avrahm Yarmolinsky (1974), p. 86.

Different people, different denominations, held diametrically opposite views. Confusing 'benefactors' with 'malefactors' in a series of malapropisms pointed at people like Angelo, poor Elbow reflects a general state of confusion concerning good Christian behaviour:

I know not well what they are. But precise villains they are, that I am sure of, and void of all profanation in the world, that good Christians ought to have.

(II, i, 53–5)[1]

Indeed, so far as Christian doctrines are concerned, *Measure for Measure* may itself reflect a kind of dramatic, theological, social, and emotional civil war between dialectically opposed ideologies, and this possibility will get further discussion later on. But first it seems necessary to mention several historical, dramatic, and all-too-human problems in this play that cannot be solved by scholarly appeals to contemporary orthodoxies.

Here are several questions that Shakespeare chose to raise, not to answer, in this particular tragicomedy, and no formalist, thematic, or theological interpretation can answer them for him. How important is physical purity? Given a conflict between Christian virtues, like chastity and charity, which should take precedence? Should, or should not, a brother willingly die for the sake of his sister's chastity? Should, or should not, the sister yield up her chastity to save her brother's life? What if the laws set down in heaven or on earth clash with the biological and psychological laws of human nature? What *about* shot-gun weddings (Shakespeare may have had good personal reasons to feel extremely ambivalent about them)? Is not the mutual and free consent of both parties as important in marriage as it is in sex? If it is better to marry than to burn, what constitutes a true marriage? How binding is a legal certificate when there is no marriage of true minds?[2]

And do not the confrontation scenes between Angelo and Isabella establish mysterious and powerful psychological and sexual affinities between them that make incredible the incongruously banal futures assigned them by the Duke? For that matter, what help are pious guidelines from contemporary sermons in those darker realms of human sexuality and psychology so boldly ventured upon, by Shakespeare himself, in this strange course of dramatic events?

Everyone (ask anyone) who knows *Measure for Measure* will surely remember Isabella's

[1] Quotations are from the Arden text of *Measure for Measure*, ed. J. W. Lever (1966). Other citations from Shakespeare are from *The Complete Plays and Poems*, ed. William Allan Neilson and Charles Jarvis Hill (Cambridge, Mass., 1942). So far as an easy religious orthodoxy is concerned, K. V. Thomas, A. L. Morton, and Christopher Hill (among other historians) have knocked the bottom out of the idea that the common people in the sixteenth and seventeenth centuries accepted the religious orthodoxies of their betters. See (for instance) Christopher Hill, *Irreligion in the 'Puritan' Revolution* (1974), p. 25: 'When the lid is taken off, what bubbles out must have been there all the time. Was active – as opposed to passive – irreligion there all the time? English experience suggests that this was indeed the case … the formal Christianity of the established churches never had so complete a monopoly as appears.'

[2] Kirsch argues that 'Marriage always in Shakespeare has sacramental value' (p. 100). But see also A. D. Nuttall's argument that 'Elizabethan marriage held at its centre a high mystery, but at the same time it seems plain that the ease with which it could be contracted had trivialized it … on the one hand we see old Capulet … arranging a marriage for his daughter with a casual celerity which shocks us, and on the other marriage itself is so absolute' ('*Measure for Measure*: The Bed Trick', *Shakespeare Survey 28* (Cambridge, 1975), p. 56). And what about all the things that, as Shakespeare himself reminds us, could cause serious difficulties for love and marriage alike – most notably the lack of 'sympathy in choice'?

Hermia. O Cross! too high to be enthrall'd to low.
Lysander. Or else misgraffed in respect of years –
Hermia. O spite! too old to be engaged to young.
Lysander. Or else it stood upon the choice of friends, –
Hermia. O hell! to choose love by another's eyes.
Lysander. Or, if there were a sympathy in choice, War, death, or sickness did lay siege to it.

searing, shocking, provocative and disturbing refusal to lay down the treasure of her body to the Lord Angelo:

> Were I under the terms of death,
> Th' impression of keen whips I'd wear as rubies,
> And strip myself to death as to a bed
> That longing have been sick for, ere I'd yield
> My body up to shame.   (II, iv, 100–5)

In its dramatic context, this speech is peculiarly powerful. Everything in it is associated with death, yet Isabella's references to whips and rubies of blood, to stripping herself as to a bed that she had longed for, are charged with an erotic power that might well evoke a gleam in the eye of the most depraved marquis in the audience, to say nothing of a saint-turned-sensualist like Angelo. In its psychological implications, Isabella's speech is like nothing else in Elizabethan drama. Other characters (like Claudio and Antony) associate death with sex; and other threatened heroines of the time (like Whetstone's Cassandra and Jonson's Celia) would prefer torture or death to dishonour. But here and only here – or so a lurid play-bill might put it – are fused the red and black extremes of passion and pain, the whips and longings of martyrdom and desire, of repression and sensuality. Obviously, no commercially-minded producer would dream of cutting this speech.

Yet perhaps partly *because* of their provocative power, these lines of fire and ice have (so to speak) been given a critical X-rating and effectively banned from many scholarly discussions of the text. If they are cited at all, and they usually are not, they tend to be considered 'out of character' or dismissed in a sentence or two: 'Isabella expresses her readiness to die in erotic terms.' Certainly their darker overtones, to say nothing of their obviously sado-masochistic undertones, are either utterly disregarded or summarily bowdlerized in representative scholarly commentaries like these:

There is . . . the note of strenuousness, of a kind of moral athleticism which appears in this – as in so many of Isabella's utterances.

To suppose that Shakespeare gave these burning words to Isabel so that we should perceive her to be selfish and cold is to suppose that he didn't know his job.

What this speech conveys . . . is that Isabella is afraid not only of Angelo's desires, but of her own.[1]

In effect at least, these dismissive, low-key, reductively easy, or beside-the-point interpretations of Shakespeare's lines would seem ingeniously contrived to de-fuse a dramatic bombshell that, in spite of all such efforts, will explode in any theatre, in any classroom discussion of the play. They certainly would seem to disregard important evidence concerning the dramatic nature of the confrontations between Angelo and Isabella. So, for the purposes of further argument, here is a discussion emphasizing the perversely fascinating sexual and psychological issues involved.

As Shakespeare reminds us elsewhere, 'Lillies that fester smell far worse than weeds'. It is, however, when Angelo crosses it that Shakespeare most dramatically erases the fine line between virtuous and vicious forms of human psychology and sexuality that may elevate men (and women) or degrade them. As all the world well knows, Angelo, a man who never feels the 'wanton stings' of sensuality, but 'doth rebate and blunt his natural edge / With profits of the mind, study and fast' (I, iv, 60–1) is brought in by the Duke of Vienna to

[1] Quotations are from Ernest Schanzer, *The Problem Plays of Shakespeare* (1963), p. 99; R. W. Chambers, 'The Jacobean Shakespeare', *Proceedings of the British Academy*, 23 (1937), and Kirsch (cited above), p. 97. By the way, I, too, daintily skirted the sexual and psychological issues involved here in two discussions of *Measure for Measure* – see *Likenesses of Truth in Elizabethan and Restoration Drama* (Oxford, 1972), and ' "What Kind of Pre-Contract had Angelo?" A Note on some Non-problems in Elizabethan Drama', *College English*, 36 (1974), 173–9.

bring back the birch of law. He soon goes beyond all measure in punishing sexual offences, and his self-righteousness immediately begins to manifest itself in sadism: '[I hope] you'll find good cause to whip them all' (II, i, 136). '*Punish them unto your height of pleasure*', says the Duke, much later on (v, i, 239 – italics mine) when Angelo asks to have his 'way' with Isabella and Mariana, thus significantly implying that the bed-trick certainly failed to effect any miraculous transformation so far as Angelo's gratuitous sadism is concerned.

Anyway, from the beginning of the play, the punishment of vice itself turns vicious, misapplied. Furthermore, *virtue* itself enkindles vice when the purity of a young novice ignites Angelo's desire to defile it. 'Love in thousand monstrous forms doth oft appear', wrote Spenser, and this is one of them:

> Shall we desire to raze the sanctuary
> And pitch our evils there? O fie, fie fie!

> Th' impression of *keen* whips I'd wear as rubies,
> And *strip myself* . . . as to a bed
> *That longing have been sick for*, ere I'd *yield*
> *My body up* . . .

Angelo seems to be recalling, and either deliberately or unconsciously echoing, Isabella's memory-searing lines. She must fit her consent to his 'sharp appetite' (his sexual equivalent of 'keen whips'?). She must 'lay by' (strip herself of) all blushes 'That banish what they sue for'. In short, she must come to his bed as to a bed 'That longing have been sick for' (there is surely a pointed echo in the parallel phrases here). Otherwise, he will have Claudio subjected to prolonged torture before he has him killed. Angelo's lines are far more explicitly

> What doest thou, or what art thou, Angelo?
> Dost thou desire her foully for those things
> That make her good? . . .
> O cunning enemy, that, to catch a saint,
> With saints doth bait thy hook! Most dangerous
> Is that temptation that doth goad us on
> To sin in loving virtue.   (II, ii, 171–83)

There is a vicious circle here: the saintlier Isabella is, the more Angelo desires her. So perhaps any sincere refusal from her might arouse him still further. Yet her fiery lines, with images of passionate sexuality underlying a prayer for martyrdom, for torture or death, for anything but sexual violation, would seem deliberately designed by Shakespeare to arouse Angelo as saint, as sensualist, and as a sadist. And so, of course, they do. Here is Angelo's response, his answer, his ultimatum to Isabella (for obvious reasons, parallel passages from her speech, which comes less than five minutes before his, are also cited):

> *Angelo.*   I have begun
> And now I give my sensual race the rein:
> Fit thy consent to my *sharp* appetite;
> *Lay by* all nicety and prolixious blushes
> *That banish what they sue for*. Redeem thy brother
> By *yielding up thy body* to my will;
> Or else he must not only die the death,
> But thy unkindness shall his death draw out
> To ling'ring sufferance.
>
>   (II, iv, 158–66 – italics mine)

---

sexual, his threats more sadistic, than earlier propositions urging Isabella to ransom her brother with the treasure of her body. They are also far more demanding: he insists upon a completely uninhibited response.

Indeed, one might infer from this ultimatum that Angelo sees in Isabella the feminine counterpart of himself. As he was, so she is; as he is, so she might become. As 'black masks / Proclaim an enciel'd beauty', so the saintly asceticism of her life, precisely like his own, may mask a keen appetite that could indeed give full and fit consent to his desire. As he will give the 'sensual race the rein', so must she. He will allow her no modesty, no nicety, no blushes to banish what he now believes they sue for. He will have a response equivalent to his own sexual passion.

Reading or hearing these lines, one may well wonder just what might have happened to Isabella in the bed of Angelo. How would she have responded? Could he be right in attributing to her a latent sensuality equal to his own? Who wouldn't like to find that out? Does the fact that Angelo, who was once immune to sex and is now obsessed with it, suggest that Isabella might fall too? Claudio has informed us that

> Liberty,
> As surfeit, is the father of much fast;
> So every scope by the immoderate use
> Turns to restraint.　　　(I, ii, 117–20)

So might not the reverse prove true for his sister, as it already has for Angelo? Could her restraint turn to immoderate use? Does her initial desire for more severe restraints within the convent suggest that there is something to restrain? Why does Isabella embrace martyrdom in such passionately sexual terms? Why her special emphasis on woman's frailty? Everyone I've pestered for opinions on her lines says that they seem perfect, exactly in character. I agree, but why so unless the line between saint and sinner, martyr and masochist, righteous severity and sadism – in short, the borderline between angelic and demonic extremes of virtue and of vice – is indeed a very narrow one, and all too easy to cross. At this moment in the play, the psychology, the characterization, and the poetry alike raise all sorts of impious and lurid questions. Who, in an audience listening to inflammatory speeches about stripping and whips, about beds that longing had been sick for, about sharp appetites, sensual races, fit consent, and so on, has a mind so pure but some 'uncleanly apprehensions' 'might 'in sessions sit' with medita-

tions lawful?

Far from finding in it affirmations of orthodox pieties, moralists, from Plato to Gosson and Collier, have condemned the drama for inflaming passions and raising impious speculations that they thought ought to be suppressed. Twentieth-century commentators like Kirsch, who tend to presuppose an inveterate piety on the part of Elizabethan audiences, would seem to ignore the obvious fact that there are certain moments in the drama when most members of any audience – Christian or pagan, Elizabethan, modern, or, for that matter, Greek – are virtually forced to join the devil's party, perhaps without knowing it. Given the choice, 'you can watch Marlowe's Faustus go forward, or you can watch him repent', how many people would choose the latter? Do we not join forces with Lucifer and Mephistopheles in urging Faustus on towards the midnight hour, to the very heart of darkness? Sometimes, at crucial moments in many works wherein the protagonist has decided to pursue a course of action known by his audience to be dangerous, evil, or inevitably tragic in its consequences, he may be offered an opportunity to desist or turn back. He can then decide (in the words of Macbeth) to 'proceed no further in this business'. 'Ask me no more', pleads Teiresias to Oedipus: 'I mean to spare you, and myself', and later on Jocasta implores Oedipus to abandon his tragic quest. Yet who, in the *audience*, wants Oedipus to leave the terrible truth unknown? Shortly before their final encounter with the White Whale, the virtuous Starbuck begs, and momentarily almost persuades, Captain Ahab to return to Nantucket. But does any reader really want Ahab to reverse course? Having come this far, would we not feel, to say the least, let-down, if, at this point, Ahab decided to abandon all thoughts of revenge, forget Moby-Dick, and return to his dear wife and children? Similarly, had Faustus heeded the

Old Man and managed an eleventh-hour repentance, many members of the audience might well storm out of the theatre demanding refunds from the box-office, and complaining, with good cause, about 'cop-outs' on the part of Faustus and Marlowe alike.

In certain works, the author arouses a desire, on the part of his audience, for climax, not anticlimax. Thus – sometimes – for the audience, as well as for certain dramatic heroes and heroines, there can be no contentment but in going all the way. Indeed, fictional characters of various kinds may serve as surrogates for our own desires to 'try the utmost', to experience whatever it is we most desire, or fear. It is, therefore, satisfying to watch such characters proceed to the outer limits of human experience, and, finally, to watch them face the truths and consequences inherent in our own dreams and nightmares, desires and fears. These facts of dramatic experience seem true regardless of the theological assumptions of the poet's age. So far as *Measure for Measure* is concerned, one may either relish or deplore the psychological and sexual reverberations of Shakespeare's confrontation between a fiery saint and a fallen angel, yet who would not be fascinated by them? Who would not wonder what might have happened, had Isabella yielded herself to Angelo? Where's that palace whereinto 'foul things' sometimes intrude not? In the audience? On the stage? Why, incidentally, are Isabella's last lines in the play about Angelo's desire for her?

Given the subsequent course of action, there's no knowing. Shakespeare himself apparently decided, at mid-point in *Measure for Measure*, to proceed no further in this business – or, as Dryden would put it, having first prescribed a purge, he immediately orders us to take restringents. There is, clearly, a deliberate and virtually complete withdrawal from this (his and our) fascination with the sexual and psychological proclivities of his villain and his heroine. Perhaps significantly, he never again permits them a moment alone together on the stage. He abruptly and conspicuously parts company with his sources, wherein the counterpart to Isabella *always* yields up her body, for one night, to Angelo's counterpart. But, then, in none of his sources is the sexual and emotional situation anything like so highly charged. Perhaps partly to avert a conflagration, Shakespeare resorts to a series of elaborate intrigues. He drags in the tepid Mariana to play the bed-trick, thus assuring that Angelo is securely fettered to another woman by the bonds of holy wedlock, and then – ever widening the safety-zone between his incendiary pair – he has the Duke claim Isabella for his own. Thus, officially at least, Shakespeare precludes further speculation about a sexual moment-of-truth between Isabella and Angelo. In short, the subsequent action of the play, like many scholarly discussions of it, would seem designed to encourage us to efface from the memory the extraordinary psychological and sexual reverberations of the earlier scenes. Assuming (only assuming) that Shakespeare himself wants us to disregard that dramatic evidence which he himself introduced previously, is it, in the last analysis, possible to do so?

Obviously, a master-poet like Shakespeare may consciously, or unconsciously, incite powerful emotional responses from us in any number of different ways. But it is sometimes impossible for even the greatest writer to suppress strong emotional responses which he has already, either in intent or in effect, aroused in his audience. Shakespeare's leading expert on the permanent effect of provocative sexual imagery is, of course, his very own devil-in-the-flesh, Iago. Precisely like an unethical counsel-for-the-prosecution of Desdemona, Iago intrudes all sorts of inflammatory images into Othello's mind, and then tells Othello to take no further notice of them:

I do beseech you –
... that your wisdom yet,
From one that so imperfectly conceits,
Would take no notice, nor build yourself a trouble
Out of his scattering and unsure observance.

(III, iii, 148–55)

My lord, I would I might entreat your honour
To scan this thing no further; ...
Let me be thought too busy in my fears –
As worthy cause I have to fear I am –
And hold her free, I do beseech your honour.

(III, iii, 244–8)

Thus, in legal terms, Iago 'objects' to his own testimony, and instructs Othello to 'disregard the evidence'. Or, in common parlance, he advises Othello to lock the barn doors of his imagination after having already loosed the wild horses. As his own rhetoric implies (he deliberately protests too much), Iago knows the answer to that age-old court-room question: 'How can a jury disregard evidence already presented to it?' The answer is, 'It can't'. Potent evidence may finally be out-weighed by equally potent evidence, emotions can be countered by equally powerful emotions, but no one can, by taking thought, obliterate from the imagination associations implanted in it by the very command to do so: 'Try to count to ten without thinking of a rabbit.' Thus, even as he urges him to put them out of mind, Iago effectively sears his 'dangerous conceits' into Othello's imagination and memory:

Dangerous conceits are in their natures poisons,
Which at the first are scarce found to distaste,
But with a little act upon the blood,
Burn like the mines of sulphur. I did say so.

(III, iii, 325–8)

Iago spoke these lines before a court audience on 1 November 1604. It goes without saying that the creator of Iago knew – none so well as he – all about the survival power of sexually and emotionally charged 'conceits'. And he certainly knew it when Isabella first spoke her inflammatory lines to Angelo at the court of King James on 26 December 1604. Had he

wished to, surely he could have – and would have – toned down those confrontation scenes.

Yet he didn't. Why not? He certainly had reason to, if he wished to provide us with easy solutions to the problems posed. For that matter, why doesn't Angelo say that his lust for Isabella represented a perverted appetite, and that he has finally realized his true love for Mariana? Why doesn't Isabella say that she has learned what it means to be a woman from Mariana and therefore accepts the Duke's proposal of marriage? Why did Shakespeare leave it to scholars, centuries later, to provide these solutions for him? Surely an obvious problem with the text as it stands is that the subsequent intrigues do not serve to set what has gone before in a new light, nor to over-whelm us (as Emilia overwhelmed Othello) with a new blaze of truth, but perfunctorily and ineffectually to contradict the earlier characterization and action and so, perhaps, confuse and frustrate us. Coleridge, for one, found the ending too good to be true. Seeing in this play something 'horrible', seeing sadism and criminal sexuality in him, it was impossible for Coleridge to accept 'the pardon and marriage of Angelo': 'For cruelty, with lust and damnable baseness, cannot be forgiven, because we cannot conceive of them as being morally repented of.'[1] Whatever Shakespeare might wish him to do at the end of a play

[1] See *Coleridge's Shakespearean Criticism*, ed. T. M. Raysor, I (1930), 131. Kirsch castigates Dr Johnson for his 'specifically un-Christian' lack of charity towards Angelo (p. 90). Coleridge, by Kirsch's standards, is equally 'un-Christian'. But, then, so would be Dryden, who, in *An Essay of Dramatic Poesy*, refused to accept the conversion of the Usurer in *The Scornful Lady*: that he should 'so repent, we may expect to hear in a sermon, but I should never endure it in a play'. Ben Jonson, in *Volpone* and in *The Discoveries*, also deemed certain vices incorrigible: 'They would love nothing but the vices ... It was impossible to reforme these natures ... They may say, they desir'd to leave it; but doe not trust them... they are a little angry with their follies, now and then; marry they come into grace with them againe quickly.'

ostensibly concerned with forgiveness, Coleridge (who, like Dr Johnson, was a devout Christian as well as a great critic) cannot do this: cannot forgive, cannot conceive, cannot imagine. Neither could most commentators until the twentieth century.

In recent years, Shakespeare's scholarly jury has been hopelessly split between those who can, and those who cannot, those who will, and those who will not, accept the ending of *Measure for Measure*. Those who cannot (like Coleridge) tend to be concerned with the major characters, with the consistency (or inconsistency) of their psychology, their motives, and their behaviour, and with the powerful emotional responses which they elicit. Critics who approve of the ending (like Kirsch) tend to be primarily concerned with the play's tragicomic form, its themes, and its religious overtones.

This critical deadlock surely results from problems inherent in the text itself. For though he clearly sets out to explore them, here, as elsewhere, Shakespeare was not about to subordinate his apprehension of a most protean reality to any single doctrine, dogma, or dramatic form. Throughout *Measure for Measure* there is a kind of firelight flamenco dance between comedy and tragedy, piety and impiety, virtue and vice, wherein one may threaten, arouse, change places with, embrace, or repulse, the other. So far as sexual vices and virtues are concerned, Shakespeare would seem to have here developed the photo-negative reversals, the strange changes and interchanges between benefactors and malefactors that he describes in *Romeo and Juliet*:

> For nought so vile that on the earth doth live
> But to the earth some special good doth give,
> Nor ought so good, but strain'd from that fair use,
> Revolts from true birth, stumbling on abuse.
> Virtue itself turns vice, being misapplied;
> And vice [sometime's] by action dignified.
>
> (II, iii, 17–22)

The sexual act between Claudio and Julietta, the one most severely condemned throughout the play, is, paradoxically, the only one in it that is dignified by mutual love. What is commonly deemed the 'vilest' form of sex, commercial prostitution, with all the diseases it entails, seems comparatively harmless when set beside Angelo's 'sharp appetite' and 'salt imagination', that is, when set beside the diseases of the soul.

Sometimes to avoid 'all profanation in the world' is to invite disaster. As J. C. Maxwell put it, it is certainly possible, 'without manifest distortion', to see the germs of twentieth-century psychological ideas in this play: 'I have even been told of untutored playgoers who thought that it was Jonathan Miller and not Shakespeare who conceived the notion of setting it in Vienna.'[1] For that matter, the fact that sexual repression could result in neurosis, in a diseased imagination, in sexual aberrations, was as obvious to Freud's Elizabethan predecessor, Robert Burton, as it was to Shakespeare.

In *The Anatomy of Melancholy*, Burton (very like Shakespeare in *Measure for Measure*) brings together 'Great precisians' and 'fiery-spirited zealots' as well as certain types that (by the way) surely composed a substantial part of Shakespeare's audience: there are the 'good, bad, indifferent, true, false, zealous, ambidexters, neutralists, lukewarm, libertines, atheists, etc.'.[2] In Burton, as in Shakespeare,

[1] See Maxwell, '*Measure for Measure*: The Play and the Themes', *Proceedings of the British Academy*, 60 (1974), 3.

[2] See *The Anatomy of Melancholy*, ed. Holbrook Jackson (1972) – page references are cited in my text. Surely Shakespeare's audience might have contained *some* neutralists, atheists, and libertines like Lucio, or like the ale-house keeper who, charged with having said that he would rather be in bed with his girlfriend than in heaven with Jesus Christ, compounded his offence when interrogated (in 1650) by saying 'A pox on Jesus Christ' or who, like Thomas Webbe,

Continued on p. 113.

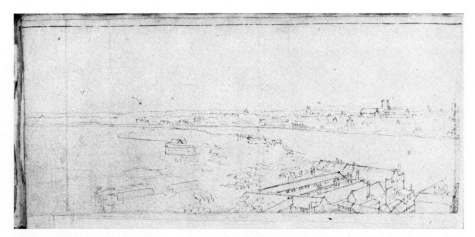

IA   A sketch of Bankside by Wenceslaus Hollar, from a notebook in the John Rylands Library
at Manchester (English MS 883)

IB   Detail of Bankside from Hollar's 'Long View of London'. British Museum

II *A Midsummer Night's Dream*, Stratford, Ontario, 1977. Directed by Robin Phillips. Maggie Smith as Hippolyta/Titania

III *A Midsummer Night's Dream*, Stratford, Ontario, 1977. Directed by Robin Phillips. Barry MacGregor as Oberon and Maggie Smith as Titania

IV *A Midsummer Night's Dream*, Royal Shakespeare Theatre, 1977. Directed by John Barton, designed by John Napier. Marjorie Bland as Titania and Patrick Stewart as Oberon

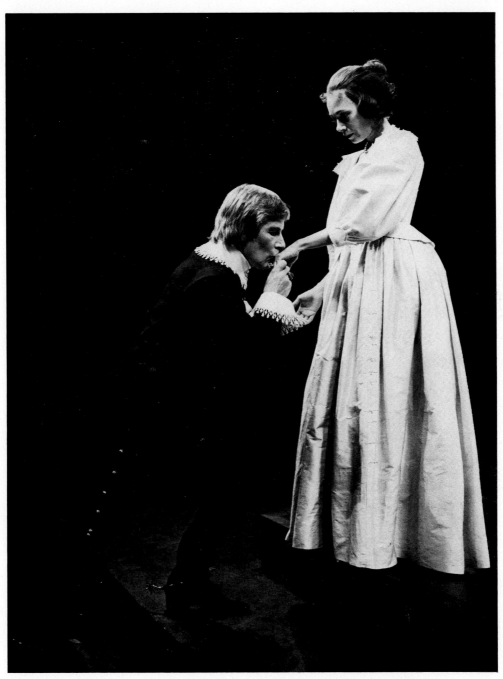

V *All's Well That Ends Well*, Stratford, Ontario, 1977. Directed by David Jones.
Nicholas Pennell as Bertram and Martha Henry as Helena

VI 1 *Henry VI*, Royal Shakespeare Theatre, 1977. Directed by Terry Hands, designed by Farrah.
The Dauphin (James Laurenson) with his army

VII 2 *Henry VI*, Royal Shakespeare Theatre, 1977. Directed by Terry Hands, designed by Farrah. Henry (Alan Howard) and Margaret (Helen Mirren) after Duke Humphrey's death

VIII A *Tamburlaine the Great*, National Theatre, 1976. Directed by Peter Hall.
The arrival of Bajazeth (Denis Quilley)

VIII B *Tamburlaine the Great*, National Theatre, 1976. Directed by Peter Hall. Tamburlaine
(Albert Finney) in his chariot

virtue itself may turn to vice: 'Howsoever they may seem to be discreet', the 'preposterous zeal' of great precisians (like Angelo) can result in forms of madness that may break out 'beyond all measure' (III, 372). In sexual matters, by seeking to avoid Scylla, one may fall into Charybdis, and 'Venus omitted' may do as much damage to the body and mind as 'Intemperate Venus': it may cause 'priapismus, satyriasis, etc.' and 'send up poisonous vapours to the brain and heart'. If the 'natural seed be over-long kept (in some parties) it turns to poison' (I, 234). For that matter, the tyranny of religious 'superstition' seemed as terrible as the tyranny of princes: 'What power of prince or penal law, be it never so strict', asks Burton, could enforce men, and women like Isabella, to do that which they will voluntarily undergo, 'As to fast from all flesh, abstain from marriage, whip themselves . . . abandon the world?' (III, 332). Zealots of this kind will endure any misery, 'suffer and do that which the sunbeams will not endure to see, *religionis acti furiis*', endure 'all extremeties', 'vow chastity', 'take any pains', 'die a thousand deaths' (III, 350).

Might not organized religion itself, rather like the Duke – or like oversimplified, 'Christian' interpretations of *Measure for Measure* – provide solutions that are false, ways out that are too easy? Discussing, and deploring, the 'general pardons' issued by Catholics (their 'easy rates and dispensations for all offences') Burton observes how 'their ghostly fathers' so 'easily apply remedies . . . cunningly string and unstring, wind and unwind their devotions, play upon their consciences with plausible speeches and terrible threats, . . . settle and remove, erect with such facility and deject, let in and out' (III, 403–4). I have never seen, anywhere, a better gloss on the dubious contrivances of Shakespeare's Duke-disguised-as-a-friar than this. Even in the end, when the organization of the play seems to encourage it,

the characterization seems to subvert an acceptance of the Duke's far too facile settlements and solutions: Angelo asks only for death, never for marriage to Mariana; Isabella's response to the Duke's proposal is silence. In the end, as in the beginning, they seem, oddly, two of a kind.

Moreover, by way of their counterparts on the stage (Claudio, Lucio, Barnardine) this play might seem quite sympathetic to the ordinary sinners in Shakespeare's audience. Markedly unlike the Duke, Shakespeare's play does not 'repel a fornicator, reject a drunkard, resist a proud fellow, turn away an idolator, but entertains all, communicates itself to all' (Burton, III, 413). It is in this spacious humanity, and, perhaps, only in this, that Shakespeare might be said to reflect the ultimate grace of God. Yet he also gives the Devil his due. In the confrontation scenes, as Coleridge observed, he confronts us with things that are 'horrible'. He crosses the boundary between the angelic and the demonic to remind us that God's temple itself may contain the Devil's chapel. Through his recalcitrant characters, he challenges the assumption that human nature can be made to perform according to a scenario of the Duke's contriving. Critical efforts to exorcize the play's demons, to disregard Shakespeare's illumination of the darker regions of the soul, in effect deny the play one of its boldest claims to truth. And to impose any external – thematic, formalist, or theological – solutions on the manifold and enduring problems posed within it is, in fact, to deny this play its rightful claim to greatness. Finally, it seems impertinent to consider it the duty of criticism to solve problems that Shakespeare himself refused to solve. What remain pertinent are the problems posed.

Continued from p. 112

might have concluded that 'There's no heaven but women, nor no hell save marriage' (see Hill, *Irreligion in the 'Puritan' Revolution*, above, p. 106, note 1).

SHAKESPEARE AND THE HEALING POWER OF DECEIT

PHILIP EDWARDS

The mark of the Shakespearian villain is deceit, rather than cruelty, ruthlessness, greed, or ambition (though he may be cruel, ruthless, greedy, ambitious). He is a man who pretends to be working for your good, and he puts on a show of loyalty, affection and honesty, while he is secretly undermining you and plotting your downfall, so that he may get your power or your possessions or your wife, or just so that he may enjoy your ruin. Deceit is the 'divinity of hell' which Iago exults in as he plans the 'honest' advice which will be the destruction of Othello, Desdemona and Cassio:

> When devils will their blackest sins put on,
> They do suggest at first with heavenly shows.
>
> (II, iii, 340–1)

The good cry out in indignation against the bad, and Lear in the storm curses the 'caitiff'

> That under covert and convenient seeming
> Has practised on man's life.   (III, ii, 56–7)

The outrage of deceit is often betokened by the smiling or impassive face:

> there's no art
> To find the mind's construction in the face.
>
> (*Macbeth*, I, iv, 11–12)

But in Sonnet 94 ('They that have power to hurt and will do none'), it *seems* to be argued that those whose faces give nothing away *can* be justified; indeed, that some people who 'do not do the thing they most do show', and are the 'lords and owners of their faces', are specially favoured of Heaven. And indeed, when one thinks about it, 'seeming', the false

presentation of the self or of events, concealing what you are and pretending to be what you are not, is a widespread activity among Shakespeare's good characters as well as among his villains. Prince Hal lets it be thought that he is an irredeemable roisterer. Portia deceives a whole court of law into thinking that she's Balthazar, a learned young he-lawyer. Hamlet pretends that he is mad. The Duke in *Measure for Measure* pretends that he has left Vienna when he is in fact very much on the spot, disguised as a Friar. The Earl of Kent, supposed banished, presents himself to King Lear as a rough honest servant called Caius. Hermione in *The Winter's Tale* deceives her husband for sixteen years by pretending she is dead.

It is not only the Shakespearian villains who are practised in deceit. Those who impose on others a fictional version of things to achieve desired ends may be heroes or heroines as well as villains. So why does Shakespeare get so worked up about deceit? It is too easy to say that you just can't compare the selfish deceit of villains with what these good characters do who are working to help other people – often, indeed, trying to save them from the malpractices of unsavoury people like Shylock or Angelo. It is worth examining the altruistic deceit of 'sympathetic' characters to measure its distance, ethically speaking, from the selfish deceit which seems to have been, for Shakespeare, the most ugly form of human behaviour.

The plays which interest me most, giving

them in the Folio order, starting with the comedies, are *The Tempest* (with Prospero as deceiver), *Measure for Measure* (the Duke), *Much Ado About Nothing* (Don Pedro), *The Merchant of Venice* (Portia), *All's Well That Ends Well* (Helena), *The Winter's Tale* (Paulina). In the histories, only *1 Henry IV* (Prince Hal). In the tragedies, *Troilus and Cressida* (Ulysses), *Romeo and Juliet* (Friar Lawrence), *Hamlet* (the Prince), *King Lear* (Edgar and Kent).

'Is our whole dissembly appeared?' as Dogberry put it? Not really, though here be 'malefactors' enough, perhaps. There are many quite important 'deceits' not in my list, like Petruchio's on Katherina in *The Taming of the Shrew*, and Rosalind's on Orlando in *As You Like It*.

In listing the plays which feature well-intentioned concealments and misrepresentations, one notices at once that they are predominantly comedies, or, if they are tragedies, that they have a well-defined tragicomic or romance structure, as in *Romeo and Juliet* and *King Lear*. Perhaps at the outset a moral investigation of the virtuous deceivers might be vetoed on the grounds that deception, especially by disguise, is a major comic convention, and is no more susceptible of ethical enquiry than a dog's use of lamp-posts. Leo Salingar's *Shakespeare and the Traditions of Comedy* (Cambridge, 1974) has a very interesting study of deceit and trickery in ancient and Renaissance comedy which reminds us that the trickster is the Atlas or Hercules on whose shoulders the world of comedy rests. Bewilderment, misunderstandings, and the defeat of expectations make up the very substance of laughter, and the proper title of almost every comedy is The Comedy of Errors. Salingar remarks that 'Renaissance critics, in spite of their unvarying preoccupation with the moral effect of literature, never seem to take notice of the ethics of comic deceivers' (p. 88). It

is interesting, however, that Salingar finds the Elizabethan dramatists 'morally cautious' about the trickster. Shakespeare, he suggests, used deceit sparingly, leaving it to his women, in whose hands illusion and disguise became the way to self-discovery, while Jonson insisted that comic deceivers were imposters and must be unmasked.

I think that Salingar's belief that in Elizabethan times we are reaching some kind of a cross-roads in moral attitudes to deceivers is well founded. On the one hand, it is indispensable to remember that in the world of comedy people may deceive, not because they have decided that for certain good ends moral imperatives may be dispensed with, but because the conventions of comedy require deceit. On the other hand there can be no question but that many of the traditional deceptions in Shakespeare's comedies are, to say the least, morally interesting. Problems of conduct in literature have got to be conveyed through conventions of one kind or another, and in this area Shakespeare (if I read him right) followed his usual practice of choosing well-established theatre conventions precisely because of the opportunities which they afforded to explore moral problems.

There would be little point in cross-examining Viola in *Twelfth Night* for disguising herself as a young man and entering Orsino's service when she is ship-wrecked in Illyria. Her disguise is needed for the plot, for the amusement which the misunderstandings arising from her disguise will cause. The adoption of disguise is not a moral matter. Nevertheless, once the disguise has been assumed, Viola (as Kierkegaard might say) is a person in concealment, and, however ridiculous the action of the play may be by the standards of our own daily life, the situations become full of moral interest. Viola, taken aback by the realisation that Olivia, believing her to be a man, has fallen in love with her, says

Disguise, I see thou art a wickedness
Wherein the pregnant enemy does much.

(II, ii, 25)

If *she* worries that dissimulation is satanic, we have some right to be a little serious about it ourselves. No doubt Shakespeare learned from Lyly's *Galathea* how to make such brilliant use of problems of sex and personality arising from quite unrealistic disguisings.

The biggest deceit-therapy in Shakespeare seems to me to lie far outside the boundary of moral discussion. I mean the conspiracy of Paulina and Hermione in *The Winter's Tale*. For sixteen years it is supposed she is dead. In fact she has been in hiding only a short distance from the royal palace. It is only fifty lines from the end of the play that both Leontes and the audience realise, as the statue comes to life, that there has been a deception. Not that it would occur to anyone to use such a word. The whole of the short period of the play remaining is taken up by the joy of the unexpected reunion not only of husband and wife but of mother and daughter. Hermione starts on an explanation to Perdita:

> Thou shalt hear that I
> Knowing by Paulina that the oracle
> Gave hope thou wast in being, have preserved
> Myself to see the issue.

But Paulina cuts her short:

> There's time enough for that,
> Lest they desire upon this push to trouble
> Your joys with like relation.

As readers, we turn the pages back to act III, scene ii, where Hermione swooned on hearing of the death of her son, immediately after the oracle had pronounced her innocent. Paulina went out with her, and then brought in the news that she had died. Perhaps she really thought she was dead, and only later found she was still alive, and decided not to let Leontes know, arranging a mock funeral? Thereafter the deceit must have been kept up by an agreement between Hermione and Paulina. But

what could possess Hermione to remain in concealment for sixteen years? At first perhaps a little residual anger against her now contrite husband for his terrible treatment of her? But for sixteen years? Her own explanation is very lame – as the oracle gave hope that Perdita was still alive she 'preserved herself' to see the issue. Why should she not have preserved herself in Leontes's company? Was there a question of refraining from cohabitation in case a male heir were born, thus defeating Perdita's chances of return? Such questioning is ridiculous. One hopes it is. A symbolic interpretation comes as a great relief. Shakespeare created a great theatrical coup with the coming alive of the statue in the last scene. The reunion of the supposedly dead wife with her husband has been totally unexpected – all the more surprising to his audience because never in twenty years of writing for them had he kept a major turn of the plot like this secret from them. The surprise and pleasure of the audience prevent them from asking questions about the mysterious interim, and the readers' worries are inappropriate to the art form of *The Winter's Tale*. Shakespeare wanted the full human emotion of a restoration undreamed of on Leontes's side. The 'preservation' which made that restoration possible is humanly non-existent. It is a device of art which cannot be discussed in moral terms. There are not many such devices in Shakespeare, and I incline to think that, where they happen, the fiction is the worse.

The most important deceit-therapists in Shakespeare are the providence figures – magi who engage in mystification in order to guide, guard, rescue, or punish. Prospero, and the Duke in *Measure for Measure* are the most important, but we should remember lesser figures like Portia in *The Merchant of Venice*, Rosalind in *As You Like It*, and Edgar in *King Lear*.

Prospero is far and away the most successful

of Shakespeare's virtuous deceivers. By his magical powers he interferes with nature and changes the course of history. He subjects his usurper-brother and the King of Naples, with their attendants, to prolonged and elaborate mystification in order to undo a wrong, regain his kingdom, and secure the marriage of Miranda to the Prince of Naples. And everything works beautifully. His magical powers make ordinary standards of moral judgement rather uncertain, and of course his doings have often been taken to represent divine rather than human activity. I like to be firm about the mortality of the Duke of Milan and see his work not as divine but as a distilment of the very human impulse to take over the reins of destiny.[1] That he succeeds so well is far from being a commendation of this impulse; it is a warning that those who indulge it ought to have Prospero's magic. Shakespeare's earlier Duke, Vincentio in *Measure for Measure*, was not so gifted. At the end of the play, it is true, the disgraced Angelo thought him like 'power divine' (v, i, 367). But the deceptions which have led to his victory have cost a great deal. The secret plan, to improve the moral condition of Vienna while testing Angelo, has brought quite extraordinary emotional distress to three people – Claudio condemned to death, Julietta punished and threatened with widowhood, Isabella faced with the nightmare choice of giving up the chastity which she is on oath to keep, or letting her brother die. By his later exertions the Duke defuses the crisis which he himself has caused, but he has made no progress at all in his initial objective of cleaning up the city of Vienna.

The Duke does most of his clandestine work disguised as a friar, and Shakespeare clearly accepted enough of the lore of Reformation drama to type-cast friars as men particularly prone to manipulation and contrivance. Chief among them is the reluctant providence-figure, Friar Lawrence, in *Romeo and Juliet*. His first

deceit-therapy is the secret marriage of Romeo to Juliet, which he agrees to perform in pure kindness to them, and with the idea that this little wrong may lead to a great right – the reconciliation of the two feuding families, the Montagues and the Capulets. The second deceit, a consequence of the first, is to give Juliet the drug which will make it seem that she is dead, and so get them all, the Friar included, out of the intolerable situation of Juliet being forced to marry Paris when she's already married to Romeo. At the point in the play when the overwrought Juliet beseeches the Friar to help her, Shakespeare, very interestingly, removed all the anxious deliberation which, in Brooke's poem which is the source of the play, the Friar went through about the morality of the device of the 'death-drug'. In the play, a resolute Juliet demands that he prevent the marriage with Paris – or she'll kill herself. Thus hemmed in as it were, he seizes on the idea of the drug on an impulse – a spontaneous and scarcely-thought-out expedient.

> Hold, Daughter! I do spy a kind of hope,
> Which craves as desperate an execution
> As that is desperate which we would prevent.
>
> (IV, i, 68–70)

The catastrophe of the play comes about through unforeseen failures of timing in the Friar's complicated plan to fetch Romeo from Mantua to rescue Juliet from the tomb when she comes to, after her death-like trance. A simulated death turns into the real deaths of Paris, Romeo and Juliet. It is of some importance to notice that the scheme fails not just because Friar Lawrence's messenger is delayed in getting through to Romeo, but because, before that messenger can get through, Romeo receives another messenger, who in good faith

---

[1] Cf. the excellent discussion of this point in Anne Barton's Introduction to the New Penguin edition of *The Tempest*, pp. 41–4 (pages which have greatly influenced this essay as a whole).

reports to him as a truth what the Friar has made a fiction – Juliet's death.

Friar Lawrence never accepts responsibility for the deaths which occur because of the failure of his schemes. To Juliet in the tomb he says

> A greater power than we can contradict
> Hath thwarted our intents.   (v, iii, 153–4)

By 'a greater power', he means God and not the Devil, for he tells the Prince that he urged Juliet to 'bear this work of heaven with patience'. At the end of his long explanation to the Prince, he says

> If ought in this
> Miscarried by my fault, let my old life
> Be sacrificed   (v, iii, 265–7)

('fault' here means 'wrong-doing'). The Friar attributes to Heaven what we see clearly to be the consequences of his two well-intentioned deceptions, the secret marriage and the simulated death. Friar Lawrence took on, as Prospero and Duke Vincentio took on, the task of managing the future by deceiving people. Not to be aware that schemes like his can go wildly wrong seems a failing in itself. Not to accept the responsibility for havoc which would never have happened but for his stratagems is worse. Actions, I take it, are not good or bad just because things turn out happily or unhappily, but in this play the results shine an accusing light on the actions. I ought to add that in the theatre there is a possible sub-text in the last scene of the play, and I think it can add to rather than detract from the power of the ending of this great play. An actor may choose to show, in the vehement disclaiming of responsibility, the Friar's own awareness of the extent of his responsibility.

The Friar's potion belongs not to the real world but to the world of folk-tale and fiction. It seems to me that it provides us with an excellent example of the way Shakespeare used the traditional contrivances of romantic narra-tive to describe that particular area of human confidence where a quiet rearrangement of things, a misrepresentation or a concealment, is undertaken, with the best motives, in order to divert the future in the interests of deserving people, and shows this confidence as an en-croachment on the prerogative of higher powers, a usurpation of Providence.

It is common justification put forward by the good deceivers that to outwit a cunning enemy it's necessary to use his weapons. 'Craft against vice I must apply', says Duke Vin-centio. Petruchio, the shrew-tamer, defeats Katherina by outplaying her at her own game. Portia is outwitting Shylock. Hamlet has to deceive the arch-deceiver Claudius – hence the antic disposition, and the mouse-trap play. In the closet scene, he looks forward to out-witting Rosencrantz and Guildenstern as well as Claudius.

> They must sweep my way
> And marshal me to knavery. Let it work;
> For 'tis the sport to have the engineer
> Hoist with his own petar; and 't shall go hard
> But I will delve one yard below their mines
> And blow them to the moon. O, 'tis most sweet
> When in one line two crafts directly meet.
> (III, iv, 204–10)

There is a grim relish in Hamlet at the thought of the contest in deception. The challenge to meet acting with acting is taken up by every 'good' deceiver *con amore*. He is fighting the good fight with weapons which every man delights to use, the skills of the theatre. And in this region of the theatre it is Prospero again who stands out. In the 'disappearing banquet' scene, Ariel in the shape of a harpy confronts and accuses the bewildering trio of bad men, and acts the part of what he calls a 'minister of Fate':

> You are three men of sin, whom Destiny
> That hath to instrument this lower world
> And what is in't, the never-surfeited sea
> Hath caused to belch up you . . .

> . . . you three
> From Milan did supplant good Prospero . . .
> . . . for which foul deed
> The powers delaying not forgetting have
> Incensed the seas and shores . . .
>
> (III, iii, 53–6; 69–70; 72–4)

It is not only the bad men in the play but literary critics who are taken in by the skill of Ariel's performance. This piece of fiction has been written for Ariel by Prospero, who congratulates him just as a playwright and director would congratulate his actors:

> Bravely the figure of this harpy hast thou
> Performed, my Ariel; a grace it had, devouring.
> Of my instruction hast thou nothing bated
> In what thou hadst to say . . .   (III, iii, 85–8)

In the next scene, arranging another show in which the gods will appear, this time not to curse but to bless, Prospero says to Ariel:

> Thou and thy meaner fellows your last service
> Did worthily perform; and I must use you
> In such another trick . . .   (IV, i, 35–7)

This other 'trick' is the masque for Ferdinand and Miranda, which he also calls 'a vanity of mine art'. The performance is broken into by Prospero's recollection of Caliban:

> I had forgot that foul conspiracy
> Of the beast Caliban and his confederates
> Against my life.   (IV, i, 139–41)

We are invited to view two worlds at once: the benign world of the therapist's fiction of Prospero's 'present fancies' (l. 122), and those less controllable areas of the real world which conflict with the world of fancy. We have something of the same feeling towards the end of *Measure for Measure*. As Duke Vincentio busies himself – keeping one step ahead of Angelo – with building up a big theatrical set-piece which will frustrate Angelo and bring him publicly and sensationally to book, the actor who takes the part of the Duke has a hard time maintaining the dignity and reverence of the role against the belittling tendency of the busy improvisations of his schemes (as when Barnardine refuses to be executed and the Duke uses the head of a dead prisoner as a token of Claudio's pretended death). It is a hard task for the actor to maintain coherence in the figure of the Duke simply because there is a doubleness that cannot be reconciled in the Duke's life. His pretensions to the position of providential guide are all the time being sabotaged by the stage-management which the theatre of providence requires.

There is one feature of his acting the part of a friar which has always jarred on me. To have the full effect of that final show-down with Angelo, it is necessary that Isabella should not know that her brother has been saved from Angelo's treacherous sentence of death. The Duke decides to elevate this necessity into the realm of spiritual education:

> But I will keep her ignorant of her good
> To make her heavenly comforts of despair
> When it is least expected.   (IV, iii, 105–7)

There is a curious incident which I found in one of Latimer's sermons of a woman, wrongly condemned to death for the murder of her child.[1] Latimer got her a pardon from the King, but hid the pardon from her up to the very time when she was to suffer. Latimer visited her in the condemned cell to 'instruct her' as he puts it. 'So we travailed with this woman till we brought her to a good trade [*way of thinking, condition of mind*]; and at the length showed her the King's pardon, and let her go.' Here is a deceit-therapy in real life. It clearly was to some extent accepted that you could falsify the truth, keep people in fear and anxiety, if the end was the improvement of the spiritual state of the victim. But the difference between Vincentio's position and that of Latimer makes all the difference. Latimer was a properly ordained clergyman; he found his prisoner languishing, and he got

[1] Ed. G. E. Corrie, Parker Society (1844), pp. 335–6.

her pardon, but he delayed telling her. Vincentio, who is acting a clerical role, actually causes Isabella's despair, which he promises to release her from with 'heavenly comforts':

Isabella. Hath yet the deputy sent my brother's pardon?
Duke. He hath released him, Isabel, from the world.
  His head is off and sent to Angelo.
Isabella. Nay, but it is not so.
Duke.   It is no other.
                                    (IV, iii, 110–13)

The basis of the despair is as false as the religious authority of the Duke.

There is another justification for some forms of deceit-therapy – that the truth is not sufficiently impressive of itself and needs the help of art.

> I have heard
> That guilty creatures, sitting at a play,
> Have by the very cunning of the scene
> Been struck so to the soul that presently
> They have proclaimed their malefactions.
>   (*Hamlet*, II, ii, 584–8)

So the play's the thing wherein to catch the conscience of the king. Who should know better than Shakespeare, who is of the trade, his nature subdued to what he works in, of the power of the fiction, the acted thing? And who would know better than Shakespeare of the dangers, when pretence is brought in to buttress reality, to shore it up – and take its place? For in the end:

> What's Hecuba to him or he to Hecuba
> That he should weep for her?

The two most remarkable examples in Shakespeare of a person being taken in by a fiction are associated with Viola in *Twelfth Night* and Edgar in *King Lear*. Though each of these is 'in concealment' as regards real identity, deliberately disguising themselves, neither of them actively imposes on the mistaking person. Olivia, vowed to seven years withdrawal from the world to mourn her brother, is attracted out of this blighting retreat

into her no doubt more proper life by falling in love with a young man called Cesario – who is in fact the girl Viola dressed up as a man. Lear with his world crashing about him in the noise of the thunder, sees a naked starving madman, poor Tom, and feels for the first time he is seeing man as he really is. 'Is man no more than this? Consider him well . . . Ha! Here's three on's are sophisticated: thou art the thing itself!' The encounter with Poor Tom is a major element in Lear's new understanding, but Poor Tom, so far from being 'the thing itself' is an earl's son on the run, disguising himself as a bedlam beggar to avoid detection. He is certainly a hard-pressed victim of man's inhumanity and injustices, but he is not what Lear takes him for any more than Viola is what Olivia takes her for. For these two people, there is a major redirection of life through mistaking a disguise for reality.

Edgar's performance as Poor Tom is magnificent. What depths he plumbs in himself to achieve the volubility of that strange accursed being is beyond guessing. In danger of his life, he has not so much entered into disguise as grown a new personality. The effect of his appearance on Lear was quite unintended. But it is as though producing that effect teaches him his mission. When the man he is escaping from, his own father, Gloucester, is brought to him blinded and ruined, he takes up mystification as though it were a profession. He becomes the great expert in the art of healing by deceit. In the guise of Poor Tom, he succours his father and then, clothed and with an altered voice, he carries out the incredible deception of trifling with his despair in order to cure it. He allows him to think that he's on the edge of the cliff at Dover, so that when Gloucester tries to end his life by falling over the cliff, he only falls flat on his face. Edgar now pretends he's yet another person at the bottom of the imaginary cliff. Picking up Gloucester, he tells him that his preservation after falling those hundreds of feet is a miracle. Much shaken by this miracle which did not take place, Gloucester vows to endure all affliction which the future may bring. Once more, a deception taken for reality brings about a major change.

In yet another role, that of a rough peasant ('Chill not let go, Zir...'), Edgar liquidates the unsavoury Oswald. Then, before the battle is fought, he comes into the British camp, 'disguised' says the stage-direction, to give Albany his challenge to his half-brother Edmund. After the battle (as we learn later), Edgar at long last reveals himself to his father, asking him for his blessing in the all-important settling of accounts with Edmund. But this revelation is too much for Gloucester, whose heart gives out. Edgar now assumes his last disguise, entering the lists as a mysterious knight in armour whose name is lost. He takes full vengeance on his half-brother, and then reveals his identity. It is during his long public explanatory speech that Kent enters, asking for King Lear, and we realise that Edgar's long-drawn-out ritual of retribution, absorbing everyone's attention, has in fact cost Cordelia her life. As Edgar and Kent watch Lear come in with the girl dead in his arms, we have a very strong feeling of the uselessness of all these secret schemes which they have been so arduously and hopefully working at. For Kent is also a deceit-therapist (the most innocent and endearing of them all, perhaps) and his schemes have gone awry. Throughout the play he has remained in disguise, in Lear's service, working to bring about the reconciliation of Lear and Cordelia – 'that full issue for which I razed my likeness' (I, iv, 3). Like Edgar, he conspicuously delays revealing himself (IV, iii, 51–4; IV, vii, 8–11). The defeat of Lear and Cordelia is too much for him, and he has some kind of seizure (V, iii, 215–16). He has come on stage a dying man, to render Lear his account. And now – 'Is this the promised end?' Kent's question has many shades of meaning; one of them reflects on the vanity of human wishes.

Edgar's extraordinary activities in *King Lear* bring together and concentrate all those qualities in the work of those who labour for the good of others by means of deceit, which make us hesitate about their good offices even as we applaud the ends they work for. He too has this tinge of arrogance in assuming the role of providence, he too seems to delight too much in acting, he too seems to believe that men are persuaded more by fiction than by the truth; and the successes which he achieves are ironic and questionable. But before drawing or trying to draw the threads of this paper together, I want to look briefly at what may be the most important play of all, with its chastening title, *Much Ado About Nothing*.

The basic structure of this play is the balancing of the 'good' deceptions of one brother, Don Pedro, with the evil deceptions of the other, Don John. Don Pedro's manipulations are not forced on him in order to counter Don John; he is, like his brother, a born schemer. When Claudio confesses that he has fallen in love with Hero, Don Pedro immediately and quite gratuitously offers to woo her for him. At the masked ball, he says,

> I will assume thy part in some disguise
> And tell fair Hero I am Claudio. (I, i, 283–4)

Shakespeare takes considerable care to relate some odd consequences of this odd wooing. Perhaps the oddest consequence is that the disguised Pedro actually wins Hero. Pedro's second deception is the device by which Benedick and Beatrice, inveterate squabblers and vowed to celibacy, are gulled into a marriage. 'If we can do this, Cupid is no longer an archer; his glory shall be ours, for we are the only love-gods' (II, i, 52–4). Each is brought to hear a little playlet in which the other is pretended to be dying of unspoken love. This double tricking of Benedick and Beatrice is a brilliantly amusing piece of theatre. And you have to be a hard-hearted critic indeed, a Don John among critics, to look at the morals of it too closely. There is no doubt that the relationship between Benedick and Beatrice before, during, and after the hoax is intensely interesting and complex, and it rightly provokes a lot of discussion. Many people feel the need to argue that the practical joke played on these two people – the false representation that the other is deeply in love – is fundamentally unimportant in creating their relationship. That is, to point out that there had previously been a relationship; that their squabbling is a form of sexual play, that Don Pedro's scheme is only the catalyst needed to end what is essentially only a superficial estrangement. I am sure that there is a measure of truth in this view of the relationship. But I think it tends to get over-stressed precisely because of the discomfort which people feel about the morality of the practical joke. They wish to play it down and diminish its role in shaping the lives of two people. We are all happy at the end of the play, but we should be wary of too cheery a view of what happens in the minds of these two people when they realise that they have been tricked.

Don Pedro himself, with Claudio, is trapped as easily and absolutely as were his victims Benedick and Beatrice by the wicked piece of theatre which Don John puts on to persuade them that Hero has been having a clandestine affair, and on the strength of the slander they brutally denounce Hero in church.

To do what he can to help the situation, Friar Francis – another Friar – puts up the elaborate scheme for pretending that Hero is dead. The news of her death, it is argued, will 'change slander to remorse' and restore Claudio's love.

> She dying, as it must be so maintained,
> Upon the instant that she was accused,

> Shall be lamented, pitied, and excused,
> Of every hearer; for it so falls out
> That what we have we prize not to the worth
> Whiles we enjoy it, but being lacked and lost,
> Why, then we rack the value, then we find
> The virtue that possession would not show us
> Whiles it was ours. So will it fare with Claudio.
> When he shall hear she died upon his words,
> Th' idea of her life shall sweetly creep
> Into his study of imagination,
> And every lovely organ of her life
> Shall come apparelled in more precious habit,
> More moving, delicate, and full of life,
> Into the eye and prospect of his soul,
> Than when she lived indeed.   (IV, i, 214–30)

This major deception, so persuasively urged by the Friar, is carried out, and it has absolutely no effect upon Claudio. He who was so easily persuaded into disbelief is not easily persuaded back into belief. It seems reasonable to argue that the big build-up of this deceit-therapy in this long speech of the Friar, and the attention given to its failure to affect Claudio, mean that there is a special importance in this part of the play. Perhaps the most distressing scenes in this multi-faceted comedy are those in which the callous self-confidence of Claudio and Pedro shows itself impervious to any appeal, and they treat the father Leonato and his brother Antonio so impertinently. When these two try to challenge the slanderers, we in the theatre find the grief of the old men very moving, in contrast with this insufferable impertinence of the younger pair.

> God knows I loved my niece,
> And she is dead, slandered to death by villains.

But in the theatre it is only seldom that at this moment we recollect that the old men, however embittered they may be about the insult to Hero, are *acting* in talking about their bereavement. If one does keep in mind the whole situation, one's feelings are completely transformed. The scene becomes even more painful. One's pity is sabotaged by one's embarrassment at the falsity of the position of the old men, and the awkwardness that the ineffectiveness of their stage-play about the dead Hero engenders. Plain-dealing and honest emotion seem hard to come by.

Hero's name is cleared without the help of the Friar's stratagem, through the stumbling endeavours of the watch, impeded by Dogberry. And now, fortunately, the stratagem of the pretended death can come in very useful; Claudio agrees to marry a new bride – who of course, when unveiled, turns out to be Hero herself. So a pleasant and playful deception brings back the bride whom the first wicked deception turned away.

Much Ado About Nothing makes no difficulties about its thesis: that people are being endlessly taken in, and are constantly making major decisions on the basis of evidence that turns out to be manufactured or illusory. Yet the people who are being taken in are often those who are busy setting up deceit-traps for others. The victor of one misrepresentation becomes the victim of the next. Hero employs Margaret to catch Beatrice. Borachio employs Margaret to catch Hero. Sometimes characters trust appearances too much; sometimes they don't trust appearances enough. The false image and the true image seem in a constant state of interchange, so much so that one wonders if people care much about the distinction. Most people find Claudio a very shallow person in his quick assent to every new thing – to Hero in the first place, to the dishonourable fiction about her in the second, and to the supposed new bride in the third. Disguise and misrepresentation often create a sense of shallowness in personal relationships – especially love relationships. The importance of the person seems depressed. I find this true of both *Twelfth Night* and *Much Ado*.

In the fear that this heavily moral attitude towards 'good' deceivers is becoming dyspeptic, I should like to go back again to the legitimacy of subjecting these Friars and Dukes

and disguised young ladies to stern enquiries whether they have been breaking universal moral laws. May it be that the importance of these theatrical tricksters is not what they do in deceiving the other characters so much as what they do in deceiving the audience? That it is *Shakespeare*'s deceit-therapy that counts most: his ability to persuade us into the unreal world which he creates by means of Prospero or Viola? No, I think the argument goes precisely the other way around. I think that the extraordinary uncertainties, embarrassments, ambiguities which I see surrounding the benevolent deceptions of his sympathetic characters tell us a very great deal about what he thought of the therapeutic power of his own fictions, his own deceits. His magic conceals from us what may have seemed tawdry enough to him. There seems to be a recurrent idea in Shakespeare that it's unwise to be on the receiving end of deceit-therapy. Those who dabble in mystification for good ends do far too much damage – even when they succeed in their plans. And he devoted a lot of attention to *lack* of success, for besides Friar Lawrence, there is also Ulysses in *Troilus and Cressida*, the man whose subtle devices are made so much of and have an entirely nil effect. And in the successful schemes, he seems careful to leave an area of equivocal silence – Antonio in *The Tempest*, Isabella in *Measure for Measure*, perhaps Bertram too, in *All's Well*, because his abrupt 'O, pardon!' doesn't really convince us that he has been spiritually recharged by Helena's elaborate stratagems to prevent him from seducing Diana and to make him her husband in full. When we think about the flimsiness of the evidence on which the subjects of the deceivers are made to act, we reflect that here at least there does seem to be a strong link between the good deceivers and the bad deceivers – a link which it would seem Shakespeare purposefully called our attention to by the parallel activities of the two brothers

SHAKESPEARE AND THE HEALING POWER OF DECEIT

in *Much Ado*, Don John and Don Pedro.

I think the evidence is that Shakespeare was deeply interested in the moral implications of well-intentioned deceit and that he used stock patterns of literary deceptions to work at them. There seems to be a real puritanism in Shakespeare. Deceit was deceit, well-meant or not. It is more an implication of this essay than a conclusion that he, as an artist, a creator of fictions, a purveyor of deceits intended to cheer people up and to help them, deceits so convincing that people mistake them for life itself, must also have questioned the honesty and the value of his own illusions. I don't press this point: I am concerned more with the characters than with their creator.

© PHILIP EDWARDS 1978

SHAKESPEARE'S MAN DESCENDING
A STAIRCASE: SONNETS 126 TO 154

MICHAEL J. B. ALLEN

Most critics still shy away from treating Shakespeare's sonnet cycle as a whole since they are in a quandary over the principle or principles of its 1609 order; they turn instead to Meres's 'sugar'd sonnets' and deal with them individually.[1] Others have indulged in what Hilton Landry calls 'the great international game' of rearranging the Quarto's order.[2] And even the few who defend it, have almost invariably done so in a spirit of resignation, *faute de mieux*.[3] I cannot agree with any of these critical positions since they derive from a failure, it seems to me, to understand the genre of both the cycle and its two constituent sequences.

I wish to take my lead from Philip Edwards, since his chapter, 'The Sonnets to the Dark Woman', is especially sensitive to the role of each poem in a coherent dramatic whole: he writes, 'Although individual poems, however brilliant, may be "failures", the cumulative effect of the [second] sequence is success of the highest order, not failure'.[4] In alluding to Patrick Cruttwell's *aperçu* that Sonnets 127 to 152 can be taken 'as a single poem', he remarks that this can only be so if they are read in the 1609 order:[5] for here we have 'a triumph of art built on a persistent demonstration of the weakness of art . . . when he is writing badly, Shakespeare does so intentionally . . . There is never a last word.'[6] My essay is intended both to complement Edwards's chapter by concentrating on the contexts of some of the weaker sonnets in the later sequence, and to push several of his intuitions further. His twin

comments that a sonnet 'gains extra depth from its position' and that 'Shakespeare sets poetry the task of describing a certain kind of hopelessness'[7] not only help to vindicate the weaker poems, but also to provide theoretical insights into the ordering principle itself.

[1] The most distinguished proponents of this approach are probably Edward Dowden ed., *The Sonnets* (1881); L. C. Knights, 'Shakespeare's Sonnets', in *Explorations* (1946), pp. 40–65; J. W. Lever, *The Elizabethan Love Sonnet* (2nd edn, 1966), pp. 162–272; and Philip Martin, *Shakespeare's Sonnets: Self, Love, and Art* (Cambridge, 1972).

[2] *Interpretations in Shakespeare's Sonnets* (Berkeley and Los Angeles, 1963), p. 3. Hyder Rollins in the New Variorum edition, *The Sonnets* (Philadelphia and London, 1944), II, 113–16, could already tabulate twenty rearrangements from Benson's in 1640 to Bray's in 1938. The most recent and the most sophisticated rearranger is Brents Stirling, *The Shakespeare Sonnet Order: Poems and Groups* (Berkeley and Los Angeles, 1968).

[3] For instance, E. K. Chambers's article, 'Shakespeare', *Encyclopaedia Britannica* (Chicago, 1957), XX, 444; R. P. Blackmur, 'A Poetics of Infatuation', in *The Riddle of Shakespeare's Sonnets*, ed. Edward Hubler (New York, 1962), pp. 131–61; Landry, *Interpretations in Shakespeare's Sonnets*; and James Winny, *The Master-Mistress* (1968).

[4] Philip Edwards, *Shakespeare and the Confines of Art* (1968), ch. 2, p. 31. Of course others like L. C. Knights have noted the dramatic nature of individual sonnets; but see particularly G. K. Hunter, 'The Dramatic Technique of Shakespeare's Sonnets', *Essays in Criticism*, 3 (1953), 152–64.

[5] Edwards, p. 19; see Patrick Cruttwell, 'Shakespeare's Sonnets and the 1950's', in *Modern Shakespearean Criticism*, ed. Alvin B. Kernan (New York, Chicago, San Francisco, Atlanta, 1970), p. 118.

[6] Edwards, pp. 17, 27, 29.   [7] *Ibid.*, pp. 27, 30.

Certain broad categories of grouping occur in the second sequence as in the cycle: some sonnets are grouped thematically, some imagistically and some rhetorically.[1] But most defy such categories, however tentative, and are simply juxtaposed. The juxtapositions are crucial though, since they force us to relate thoughts and feelings, situations and attitudes, from differing points on a narrative line. The narrative has always been easy to grasp in its essentials: it never required sequential development as its units were archetypal, and it was therefore open to constant repatterning; that is, its surface simplicity enabled Shakespeare to scramble it more than he could a tangled plot demanding chronological exposition in order to be understood.[2] The apparently chance collisions between thoughts and moods – collisions which proceed from Shakespeare's non-chronological approach – become more and more integral to the reader's experience. We begin to concentrate on the transitory, internally volatile, unpredictable mixtures themselves. Since a narrative always has other dimensions than the purely chronological, its full meaning can only emerge from juxtapositions which ignore or actively contradict the expectations we derive from the experience of linear time; and given the frames of man's perceptual apparatus, an absolutely chance encounter, or a totally gratuitous juxtaposition is well-nigh inconceivable. The Dark Lady sequence places us in the position of a maker: as we proceed, we make larger meanings from the succession of smaller ones. In R. P. Blackmur's words, 'Pygmalion is a name for sonnet after sonnet'.[3]

Let me turn to an obvious phenomenon: transference. By all accounts Sonnet 128 is a slight piece, what Winny calls 'an entirely playful address to a lady at the keyboard',[4] resulting from the working-out of one conceit:

How oft, when thou, my music, music play'st
Upon that blessèd wood whose motion sounds
With thy sweet fingers when thou gently sway'st
The wiry concord that mine ear confounds,
Do I envy those jacks that nimble leap
To kiss the tender inward of thy hand,
Whilst my poor lips, which should that harvest reap,
At the wood's boldness by thee blushing stand.
To be so tickled they would change their state
And situation with those dancing chips
O'er whom thy fingers walk with gentle gait,
Making dead wood more blest than living lips.
　　Since saucy jacks so happy are in this,
　　Give them thy fingers, me thy lips to kiss.

As Martin and many others have argued,[5] this sonnet in no way prepares us for Sonnet 129 with its pulsating rhythms and almost completely abstract landscape, bare of conceit, bare almost of image and building to its sombre climax in the couplet:

Th'expense of spirit in a waste of shame
Is lust in action; and, till action, lust
Is perjured, murd'rous, bloody, full of blame,
Savage, extreme, rude, cruel, not to trust;
Enjoyed no sooner but despisèd straight;
Past reason hunted, and no sooner had,
Past reason hated as a swallowed bait
On purpose laid to make the taker mad:
Mad in pursuit, and in possession so;
Had, having, and in quest to have, extreme;
A bliss in proof, and proved, a very woe;
Before, a joy proposed; behind, a dream.
　　All this the world well knows; yet none knows well
　　To shun the heaven that leads men to this hell.

[1] For good thematic treatments see G. Wilson Knight, *The Mutual Flame* (1955), and J. B. Leishman, *Themes and Variations in Shakespeare's Sonnets* (1961). For a treatment in terms of the imagery see Murray Krieger, *A Window to Criticism: Shakespeare's Sonnets and Modern Poetics* (Princeton, 1964). For a rhetorical approach see Stephen Booth, *An Essay on Shakespeare's Sonnets* (New Haven, 1969).

[2] Lever, pp. 163–4.

[3] Blackmur, p. 133.

[4] Winny, p. 91. Citations are to the revised Pelican edition by Douglas Bush and Alfred Harbage (Baltimore, 1970). I have adopted Kinnear's emendation, however, for 126; see below, p. 133, note 2.

[5] Martin, pp. 5–6.

Such a powerful poem attracts matter to it like a star. Read after Sonnet 128, it pulls the image of the virginal's jacks or levers that leap to kiss the tender inward of the woman's hand into its own gravitational field: the 'wiry concord' is 'enjoyed no sooner but despised straight', the 'wood's boldness' becomes 'savage, extreme, rude, cruel, not to trust'; the 'gentle gait' is 'mad in pursuit and in possession so'; the dancing fingers on the chips are now the aching of lust in action. These are not just parasitic growths that one can remove, but true symbioses. Though they throng together in bewildering variations of form and intensity and play all sorts of tricks with our memories and associations, the result is invariably dramatic. Sonnet 129 becomes the musical score for 128; the lady's response to the man's Petrarchan pose; her bait to make the taker mad; her confounding of his keys. Lever is misleading then when he refers to 129 as 'a dramatic monologue rather than a sonnet'[1] for this suggests it is free-standing. But, despite the shock of incongruity, varying quantities of 128 survive to shape our response to 129: different solutes at first, the two poems become one and the same solvent. To separate them entirely, as Brents Stirling and others have done,[2] is to ignore the drama generated by their juxtaposition.

What of the transition to 130? Lever calls both 128 and 130 'dwarf shrubs'[3] while Martin calls 130 'a clever piece of literary satire'[4] and Katharine Wilson, 'a parody' with a composite background.[5] How then do we account for Northrop Frye's opposed assessment of 130 as 'the center of gravity of the Dark Lady sonnets'?[6] Again, transference prevents us from responding to its conceits as merely witty levities: we do not retain the imagery of 129 (since it has so little) but rather its ferocity of tone, a ferocity which is itself modified by the more distant echoes of 128 – 'Yet well I know / That music hath a far more pleasing sound.' As in such scenes as the Porter's in *Macbeth* or the Nurse's in *Romeo and Juliet*, transference transforms past action into future action by establishing multiple levels of irony and expectation. Dramatically, it binds the three sonnets together as a triptych where each panel presupposes the others.

Clearly, the foregoing only touches on one of the three possible triads for each sonnet, since each sonnet can be either the first, second or third member in a triad. But whichever of the three positions a sonnet occupies at any one moment in our reading of the sequence – and eventually, of course, it occupies all three – transference is an integral and ever-present element in our response, however subtle its manifestations; as integral as in any one of Shakespeare's plays.

Often more is involved though than transference, echo and retinal image: we are compelled to switch moods, thoughts and evaluations in a vertiginous, continuously creative way; to make instantaneous adjustments that violate our needs for predictability, for causality, for various kinds of logic. Though transference may temper the violence of these adjustments, the violence is paramount. Through it even such weak sonnets as 141 and 143 enter into paradoxical relationships with stronger sonnets that qualify their apparent failures as poems. Deriving strength and additional levels of significance from their context, they react in turn on the successes. Success and failure then qualify each other, and the meaning they generate together becomes more important

[1] Lever, p. 180.
[2] Brent Stirling's theory of the printer's disarrangement of the sheets makes Sonnets 129 and 146 conclude the entire cycle and 128, 138 and 145 completely independent of the Dark Lady sequence.
[3] Lever, p. 174.   [4] Martin, p. 123.
[5] Katharine M. Wilson, *Shakespeare's Sugared Sonnets* (1974), pp. 83–8.
[6] Northrop Frye, 'How True a Twain', in Hubler, p. 51.

and more comprehensive than the meanings they generate alone. Evaluation too becomes an exceedingly complex matter. Not merely do we acknowledge the inclusion of second-rate, conventional, stereotypical experience in the sequence, since this has to be included in the 'whole' truth, we also predicate the breakdown of relationships with ascertainable values. The 'chance' encounters constitute a poetic continuum that bypasses success and failure, good and bad, *sequitur* and *non sequitur*, as distinctions that can be immediately applied: it forces us to work with an interdependence that is changing and open-ended.

Take another triad, 137, 138 and 139, a triad which is not so obviously connected by theme, recurring image or rhetorical patterning as some of the other sonnet strings and where the straightforward linear reading does not produce the obvious transference effects of 128, 129 and 130.

Of the three, Sonnet 138 is the most anthologizable:[1]

When my love swears that she is made of truth
I do believe her, though I know she lies,
That she might think me some untutored youth,
Unlearnèd in the world's false subtilties.
Thus vainly thinking that she thinks me young,
Although she knows my days are past the best,
Simply I credit her false-speaking tongue;
On both sides thus is simple truth suppressed.
But wherefore says she not she is unjust?
And wherefore say not I that I am old?
O, love's best habit is in seeming trust,
And age in love loves not to have years told.
   Therefore I lie with her and she with me,
   And in our faults by lies we flattered be.

There is remarkable lack of agreement over its tone: C. L. Barber finds it 'jaunty',[2] Martin, 'extremely elegant',[3] Winny, 'an enjoyable jeu d'esprit',[4] and Lever talks of its 'cool cynicism'.[5] Fiedler on the other hand refers to 'its Donne-like opening in which the show of brittle cynicism betrays an under-

current of profound nausea',[6] Ricks calls it a 'tragically embittered poem'[7] and Cruttwell says it is 'the most terrible and also the nakedest' of all the sonnets.[8] This range of reaction suggests we are dealing with a poem that is unrelentingly paradoxical. The pun on *lie* enunciated in the first line gathers momentum through the intervening lines until it blossoms into the final coincidences of opposites. The situation is such that truth is best served by the mutual recognition of falsehood: the lie becomes the vehicle for establishing a true, because reciprocally hypocritical, relationship. The simple truth is suppressed on both sides in the interests of a complex truth deriving from the mutual flattery of faults, the accreditation of false-speaking tongues. The rhetorical questions in lines 9 and 10 are perversely stated and they could only have complex, perverse answers: the best is in seeming trust, love does not love to have years told, and lying *to* her means that she is lying *with* me. The finale moves from two singulars to one plural; and the sense of mutuality where *she* and *I* have become the *we* of the last line and where faults and lies both flatter and comfort is an index of their love's strength and of its frailty. That simple values should end up by being so inverted is the result of frustration, compromise, hypocrisy, and self-recognition alike. But the sense that 'the levels of deception are staggering'[9] could be derived from reading

[1] We should remember that this sonnet and Sonnet 144 have a more complicated textual history than the others.

[2] C. L. Barber, 'An Essay on the Sonnets', in the Laurel Shakespeare edition of *The Sonnets* (New York, 1962), pp. 28–9.   [3] Martin, p. 50.

[4] Winny, p. 101.   [5] Lever, p. 178.

[6] Leslie A. Fiedler, 'Some Contexts of Shakespeare's Sonnets', in Hubler, p. 61.

[7] Christopher Ricks, 'Lies', *Critical Enquiry*, 2 (1975), 131.   [8] Cruttwell, p. 120.

[9] J. Bunselmeyer, 'Appearances and Verbal Paradox: Sonnets 129 and 138,' *Shakespeare Quarterly*, xxv (1974), 105.

the sonnet out of context, as most critics still read it, and as it was first read perhaps in Jaggard's collection of 1599, *The Passionate Pilgrim*.

On either side of 138 are two sonnets which are markedly inferior when taken alone but which give their triad great complexity and richness. Let me start with 139:

> O, call not me to justify the wrong
> That thy unkindness lays upon my heart;
> Wound me not with thine eye but with thy tongue;
> Use power with power, and slay me not by art.
> Tell me thou lov'st elsewhere; but in my sight,
> Dear heart, forbear to glance thine eye aside;
> What need'st thou wound with cunning when
>   thy might
> Is more than my o'erpressed defense can bide?
> Let me excuse thee: ah, my love well knows
> Her pretty looks have been mine enemies;
> And therefore from my face she turns my foes,
> That they elsewhere might dart their injuries:
>   Yet do not so; but since I am near slain,
>   Kill me outright with looks and rid my pain.

Most people do not like the sonnet: it seems unengaged psychologically and over-conceited, and it has no narrative connections with 138. What is interesting, however, is the interfacing of two levels of emotional tone: not transference so much as undermining. Sonnet 139 retreats into the stereotypes of prostrate lover and tyrannical mistress: in the Petrarchan mode it talks of her unkindness, her basilisk powers to 'kill outright with looks'; it plays with the conventional roles of eye and tongue and with the imagery of love and war, wounds and prettiness, foes and faces, not with a view to exploring real human complexities but to retreating from them. Yet its retreat gains the greater force by the juxtaposition with 138. From 138's dynamic engagement (whether the persona's or Shakespeare's is immaterial), 139 retires to static disengagement; from the former's exploration of situational puns and paradoxes, the latter withdraws into the rigidity and inflexibility of inherited love roles

and the iteration of moribund hyperboles.

It is not merely that a bad poem succeeds a good one. The human mind rarely operates on Humean lines, and succession demands some sort of relationship even when it signifies regression. Sonnet 139 dramatizes the retreat into stereotypical responses in the everyday world where growth is succeeded by decay, new successes by old failures, fulfilment by disaffection and inadequacy. But what if we reverse the reading sequence for argument's sake? Then the situation also reverses: 138 marks the inner growth, the deepening of the relationship, the metamorphosis of conceits into new strategies for engaging experience. But suppose we continue in reverse? Having witnessed the positive values of 138 succeeding the obvious limitations of 139, we still have to cross over from 138 to 137:

> Thou blind fool, Love, what dost thou to mine
>   eyes
> That they behold and see not what they see?
> They know what beauty is, see where it lies,
> Yet what the best is take the worst to be.
> If eyes, corrupt by over-partial looks,
> Be anchored in the bay where all men ride,
> Why of eyes' falsehood hast thou forgèd hooks,
> Whereto the judgment of my heart is tied?
> Why should my heart think that a several plot
> Which my heart knows the wide world's common
>   place?
> Or mine eyes seeing this, say this is not,
> To put fair truth upon so foul a face?
>   In things right true my heart and eyes have
>   erred,
>   And to this false plague are they now
>   transferred.

Though 137 has considerably more bitterness and more pungent imagery than 139, they both signal a withdrawal from the intensities and complexities of the psychological engagement that seems to underlie 138. In either case, and this is the basic factor in the experience of reading the sonnets together (regardless of our points of entrance or exit, or of direction), we are forced to confront the ceaseless process of gain and loss, loss and gain in our lives: gain from 137 to 138 and loss from 138 to 139; or gain from 139 to 138 and loss from 138 to 137. The alternations are inexorable from any angle and the extension of the series to include 136 and 140 merely underscores the pattern even as it produces further complications and modifications. It raises the possibility of incremental repetition without real growth. Whatever the direction, there is a two-way flow: because of juxtaposition, the condition of any linear sequence, any two contiguous sonnets are always in some sort of ambivalent relationship. With 138 and 139 it is paradoxical that mutuality can coexist with mistress/slave attitudes, that the acceptance of lying can be more truthful than the superficial sincerity of desire, that conceits can both illuminate and obfuscate meaning. Just as the roles we adopt in life alternate perpetually between the progressive and the regressive, so these two sonnets pass through each other's fields of force, continually influencing each other, and continually orbiting each other. Since 139 follows 138, the rigidity of the mistress/slave conceit becomes an instance of the mutual *lying*, the mutual suppression of 'simple' truth; instead of being a unidimensional poem, 139 acquires other dimensions and a layered past.

Much depends, naturally, on the speed with which we pass from one to the other in our minds, on the idiosyncrasies also of our short- and long-term memories: the quicker the transition, the greater, but not necessarily the more permanent, the transfer of power. Take Sonnet 145 as a point of departure:

> Those lips that Love's own hand did make
> Breathed forth the sound that said 'I hate'
> To me that languished for her sake;
> But when she saw my woeful state,
> Straight in her heart did mercy come,
> Chiding that tongue that ever sweet
> Was used in giving gentle doom,

And taught it thus anew to greet:
> 'I hate' she altered with an end
> That followed it as gentle day
> Doth follow night, who, like a fiend,
> From heaven to hell is flown away.
>   'I hate' from hate away she threw,
>   And saved my life, saying 'not you.'

This poem has had its authenticity questioned since it is, along with 99 and 126, a formal deviant. Critics normally consider it trivial, even namby-pamby, though Bush and Harbage's view that the diction is 'rudimentary' does not do justice to the lilting metre and to the Sucklingesque turn of the conceit.[1] Coming after Sonnet 144 with its compelling biographical conundrums and its allegorical façade, however, it certainly appears a lightweight even if we respond to an evanescent charm.

But 144 has already activated images and themes and set up reverberations that do not bypass 145 so much as flow through it like microwaves:

> Two loves I have, of comfort and despair,
> Which like two spirits do suggest me still:
> The better angel is a man right fair,
> The worser spirit a woman colored ill.
> To win me soon to hell, my female evil
> Tempteth my better angel from my side,
> And would corrupt my saint to be a devil,
> Wooing his purity with her foul pride.
> And whether that my angel be turned fiend
> Suspect I may, yet not directly tell;
> But being both from me, both to each friend,
> I guess one angel in another's hell.
>   Yet this shall I ne'er know, but live in doubt,
>   Till my bad angel fire my good one out.

The two spirits of angel and devil, saint and fiend, and the themes of temptation and suspicion, heaven and hell, purity and pride, along with that of the corrupted will – reintroduced by the couplet of 143, 'So will I pray that thou mayst have thy Will, / If thou turn back and my loud crying still', but reaching back to the triad of Will sonnets, 134, 135

[1] Bush and Harbage, p. 165n.

and 136 – all these 'place' the gallantry of 145. Rather than supplying a mere link, as Edwards suggests,[1] they supply ominous double meanings to the triple repetition of 'I hate', to the notion of the lady's 'gentle doom', and to the simile of the fiend fleeing the break of 'gentle day'. The triangulation of Sonnet 144 in fact haunts 145 to the point of possession: the lips that Love's own hands did make exhale cold comfort and despair, suggesting still.

Whatever theological interpretation we accord Sonnet 146, however, it introduces a new set of transformations:[2]

Poor soul, the centre of my sinful earth,
[Thrall to] these rebel pow'rs that thee array,
Why dost thou pine within and suffer dearth,
Painting thy outward walls so costly gay?
Why so large cost, having so short a lease,
Dost thou upon thy fading mansion spend?
Shall worms, inheritors of this excess,
Eat up thy charge? Is this thy body's end?
Then, soul, live thou upon thy servant's loss,
And let that pine to aggravate thy store;
Buy terms divine in selling hours of dross;
Within be fed, without be rich no more:
  So shalt thou feed on Death, that feeds on
    men,
  And Death once dead, there's no more dying
    then.

The lady of Sonnet 145 becomes the soul, her suitor, the body; the doom inspired by inward pity becomes surrender to the outward walls so costly gay, to the pining that cannot aggravate her store, to the fiend feeding in the mansion of physical desire. Sonnet 146 does not merely give the lie to, or in Edwards's analysis 'explode', Sonnet 145[3] in order to validate the prayer that one may hate the sinful earth and the thralled heart, it also completes the circuit, whose negative pole is 144, and thus electrifies 145 and the attitudes attending it. The tetrameters are, for a moment, live with paradox: in saving her lover's life, the lady shortens the lease of her own; instead of living on, she loses with, her servant's loss; without she is fed, within is rich no more.

The resolutive power of 146 is sufficient to work this kind of transformation on any of its predecessors and accounts for the decision of restructurers like Lever and Brents Stirling to put 146 last in the cycle as 'the one possible finale' to the 'vicious descending spiral' of earthly passion and disgust.[4] But even greater surely is the proleptic power released by the sudden, breathtaking, terrifying juxtaposition with 147:

My love is as a fever, longing still
For that which longer nurseth the disease,
Feeding on that which doth preserve the ill,
Th' uncertain sickly appetite to please.
My reason, the physician to my love,
Angry that his prescriptions are not kept,
Hath left me, and I desperate now approve
Desire is death, which physic did except.
Past cure I am, now reason is past care,
And frantic-mad with evermore unrest;
My thoughts and my discourse as madmen's are,
At random from the truth vainly expressed:
  For I have sworn thee fair, and thought
    thee bright,
  Who art as black as hell, as dark as night.

With this transition the charge established by 144 and 146 is reversed and the 'solutions' of 146 made negative, those of 145, positive: 146 becomes, as Edwards rightly notes, 'a transient insight',[5] a temporary remission in a fever that already raged in 145 and intensifies in 147. The feeding on Death which climaxed 146 turns into the feeding on that which doth preserve the ill in 147; the woeful state is

---

[1] Edwards, p. 28.
[2] See Michael West's article, 'The Internal Dialogue of Shakespeare's Sonnet 146', *Shakespeare Quarterly*, XXV (1974), 109–22, for a summary of the current debate over the sonnet's theological affiliations. His arguments on pp. 112–15 have persuaded me to adopt B. G. Kinnear's emendation for line 2, 'Thrall to'.
[3] Edwards, p. 28.
[4] Lever, p. 181; Brents Stirling, pp. 225–9.
[5] Edwards, p. 29.

reassumed as frantic mad unrest; and hell which has been an active image since 144 comes fully into its own in 147's couplet. The lover's life in the concluding line of 145 is indeed preserved, but not for the hopes implied by 146: it has been granted an eternity for random speech, for vain assays at the truth, for exile from all consolation, theological, moral or emotional, for what is past cure and past care.

But this reversion also passes and we switch back in 148 to the conventional misogynistic railing against Love's blindness that recalls 137 and anticipates 149. We could continue exploring the successive accretions and mutations here of image and theme, word and action, as we would light and darkness in *Othello*, rings and wealth in *A Merchant of Venice*, or the etymological quibbles in *Love's Labour's Lost*. But if we wish to avoid this critical mass of engagements, conflicts and disintegrating reconciliations altogether, and rest content with disparate poems, then we cannot draw on more mental energy than is needed to bring 144, 145, 146 and 147 into individual focus. Superlative concentration on the other hand with its accompanying heightening of both retention and anticipation can transform the mass into a unified drama bonded through and through by concatenations of metaphors, paradoxes and ironies. In a way the ultimate perception of each sonnet's worth – as measured by our intensity of engagement with it, not its position on our chronological scale (since we can and do suffer axiological relapses) – depends on our own poetic powers, our commitment to detecting all the figures in the ground of the enveloping juxtapositions. If we feel committed to the transition from 144 to 145 or from 145 to 146, then 145 and 146 are explorations feeding back into 144 as 144 feeds back into 143, and so on. We can either strive for the unitary experience of seeing each sonnet contributing to the tensions of an internally

consistent if complex whole, or opt for something far less, a string of fragmentary responses to unconnected, often mutually excluded, parts. The comprehensiveness of our reaction is the measure of our own creativeness in dealing with the actual juxtapositions in the sequence and with the theory of juxtaposition itself.

Expectations for definable beginnings, middles and ends and their appropriate subordination must therefore be abandoned. Such Aristotelian expectations may exist, but by refusing to satisfy them, sonnets like 145 and 146 compel us to face those fundamental aspects of experience which transcend chronological time and temporal causality and transcend the habits we derive from using them continuously as categories of explanation. By denying us the prop of narrative consistency, Shakespeare undermines our faith in time, conventionally conceived, and propels us towards non-chronological relationships, the relationships generated by what, from a chronological viewpoint, are arbitrary juxtapositions. Rather than allowing succession the task of formulating meaning, the sonnet sequence forces us to do it ourselves in a present synchronically rather than diachronically perceived.

The final consequence is a breakdown in the concepts themselves of beginning and end. Take Sonnet 126:

O thou, my lovely boy, who in thy power
Dost hold Time's fickle glass, his sickle hour;
Who hast by waning grown, and therein show'st
Thy lovers withering as thy sweet self grow'st;
If Nature, sovereign mistress over wrack,
As thou goest onwards, still will pluck thee back,
She keeps thee to this purpose, that her skill
May Time disgrace and wretched minutes kill.
Yet fear her, O thou minion of her pleasure!
She may detain, but not still keep, her treasure;
Her audit, though delayed, answered must be,
And her quietus is to render thee.

Sonnet 126 is normally considered the end of

the first rather than the beginning of the second sequence (or both or neither), and as such, a freak: Katharine Wilson is typical in suggesting that it 'could conceivably be a joke of Shakespeare's'.[1] But there are some authoritative exceptions. Blackmur observes, 'Had it become a sonnet, or even added a couplet, it must have become a curse or even an anathema';[2] and Frye refers to it as 'a masterly summary of the themes and images of the beautiful youth group . . . [and] inescapably the "envoy" of the series'.[3] Its twelve lines instead of fourteen, its six couplets instead of three quatrains and a couplet, these make it remarkable in itself; but its position does so even more. Why should Shakespeare have inserted this odd variant at a crucial point of transition – one of the few clearly signalled transitions in the entire cycle? I am tantalized by the idea that it is a poem parodying the sonnet form (in its English not Italian guise): six couplets are trying to function as a metacouplet, to summarize, to conclude a stage in the relationship of three people of which the preceding one hundred and twenty-five poems are three quatrains; ironically, though, the couplets occupy the mental space normally occupied by three quatrains while lacking their own couplet. It's as if Shakespeare were playing with the idea of being outwitted by the form itself; of being betrayed back into the quatrains' continual alternation of success and failure, even as he tried to stop the sequence by iterating the couplets that had brought earlier quatrains to a close. Shakespeare's couplets admittedly are a study in themselves: occasionally apophthegmatic and powerful, they are more frequently anticlimaxes that withdraw inadequately, pathetically or clumsily from the involvements of their quatrains and do not conclude so much as abandon them. Wilson Knight, for instance, says that many of them bring 'a drop not only in tension, since this is expected, but in quality of thought too';[4] and Martin observes ap-

positely, 'the weak couplets are generally those which seek to reverse the sonnet's previous direction of thought, while the strong ones recapitulate or extend it'[5] – and the weak couplets predominate. Sonnet 126 has six such couplets in a row and their cumulative effect is to deny the viability, even the possibility, of a couplet altogether, and therefore to surrender its ability to suggest stability, finality or resolution. Thus 126 serves paradoxically as a beginning for the second sequence rather than an end for the first. Given Shakespeare's constant play with the syntactical and rhetorical combinations of the form, such a parodic, mutilated anti-sonnet, all couplet and no quatrains from one perspective (and all quatrains and no couplet from another), is not unexpected. It could only succeed once, of course. But even so it gives the lie to the form: in its mutilation it is eloquent.

This treatment of the poem may smack of ingeniousness rather than truth; but no clear guidelines indicate the limits to ingenuity. The poem may be a silly misfit, a parodic masterpiece, neither, or both. In isolation we judge it with one set of criteria, in context, with another; and the two sets seem contradictory. Again, it is not a question of Shakespeare's intention (which we shall never know), but of the effect of repeated readings of 126. Why should the major transition in the cycle be occupied by a deviant piece; that is, what do its form and position tell us about the idea of a closed sonnet form? and about sonnet transitions? Does its apparent inferiority articulate our feelings about the earlier sonnets or prepare us for those that follow? Even after repeated analyses, we continue to worry over such problems until we move on, either intrigued or

[1] Wilson, p. 319.   [2] Blackmur, p. 154.
[3] Northrop Frye, p. 39.
[4] Wilson Knight, p. 81. We are reminded of Keats's objection that the Shakespearian couplet 'has seldom a pleasing effect'.   [5] Martin, p. 106.

irritated by the poem's irrelevant relevance. But the poem has effectively dictated its own terms as a transitional piece: functioning as beginning, middle and end but in its own unique way, it defies the usual categories both of structural analysis and of evaluation.

Sonnet 152 is usually admired. Granted straightforward narrative criteria, it would be wholly appropriate as the cycle's as well as the sequence's close, as, in Blackmur's words, 'a repudiation but also a reassertion'.[1] But what of 153 and 154? Usually, we assume with Fiedler that they are 'variant Englishings of a Greek epigram [by the Byzantine poet, Marianus, having]... little to do with what comes before'.[2] Frye dismisses them as 'mere literary' exercises;[3] Lever says that they simply 'toy with anacreontic conceits';[4] and even Edwards refers to them as 'two perfunctory sonnets'.[5] Some have been tempted to question their authenticity and detach them altogether from the cycle.[6] But the dynamics of the sequence are not directed to the kind of resolution that 152 would provide were it indeed the envoy:

> In loving thee thou know'st I am forsworn,
> But thou art twice forsworn, to me love swearing;
> In act thy bed-vow broke, and new faith torn
> In vowing new hate after new love bearing.
> But why of two oaths' breach do I accuse thee
> When I break twenty? I am perjured most,
> For all my vows are oaths but to misuse thee,
> And all my honest faith in thee is lost;
> For I have sworn deep oaths of thy deep kindness,
> Oaths of thy love, thy truth, thy constancy;
> And, to enlighten thee, gave eyes to blindness,
> Or made them swear against the thing they see;
>> For I have sworn thee fair: more perjured eye,
>> To swear against the truth so foul a lie.

One could read into this sonnet the sense of an ending; but then it would suggest the very linearity and narrative consistency which I have been arguing Shakespeare was at pains to break down: it would send us back into the

sequence with basic misconceptions about its nature revived. What Shakespeare did, therefore, was undermine our sense of an ending in much the same way as he often undermined the strength of his quatrains with a weak couplet. Given the undeniable power of 152's couplet with its triple pun on *I/aye/eye*, it has always struck me as cruelly but necessarily ironic that the Cupidian epigrams of 153 should themselves conclude in reneging on the pun by reversing the rhyme and casting it into the plural form:

> Cupid laid by his brand and fell asleep:
> A maid of Dian's this advantage found
> And his love-kindling fire did quickly steep
> In a cold valley-fountain of that ground;
> Which borrowed from this holy fire of Love
> A dateless lively heat, still to endure,
> And grew a seething bath, which yet men prove
> Against strange maladies a sovereign cure.
> But at my mistress' eye Love's brand new-fired,
> The boy for trial needs would touch my breast;
> I, sick withal, the help of bath desired
> And thither hied, a sad distempered guest,
>> But found no cure: the bath for my help lies
>> Where Cupid got new fire, my mistress' eyes.

The terrible, but veridical paradoxes of 152 emerge as the trivial oxymora of 153: the sequence reverts to the bathetic; paradox becomes bad pun; progress becomes repetition; and poetry becomes translation. Sonnet 154, in ringing the changes on 153, thwarts any sense we might entertain of closure, poetic or otherwise. It insists on being trite, on returning to

[1] Blackmur, p. 160.
[2] Fiedler, p. 58. See C. F. Williamson, 'Themes and Patterns in Shakespeare's Sonnets', *Essays in Criticism*, 26 (1976), 194.
[3] Northrop Frye, p. 49.
[4] Lever, p. 171.
[5] Edwards, p. 30.
[6] C. Knox Pooler ed., the Arden edition of *The Sonnets* (1918), pp. 142n., 144n.; Hyder Rollins, pp. 391–7; and J. Hutton, 'Analogues of Shakespeare's Sonnets CLIII–CLIV', *Modern Philology*, 38 (1941), 385–403.

the well-worn paronomasias of the tradition:

> Love's fire heats water, water cools not love.

A measure of Shakespeare's complex intentions is that he can take leave of the sonnets thus: by now the reader realizes that Ovidian trifles are as necessary to the alternations of the head and heart as fierce engagement and passionate sincerity. Arguably even, our need to detach Sonnets 153 and 154 and relegate them in some way is the ultimate irony, mirroring a deeper need to deny the declensions and anticlimaxes in ourselves. Eventually we realize that the two sonnets have to be accepted for what they are and where they stand: their unsatisfactoriness, their failure is itself an ending, since it points to other endings and other beginnings. They return us to the sequence in search of further, more fulfilling remedies for love: they make us end where we began.

I have been advocating alchemical ways, perhaps, for reading the sequence; but this is to reinforce, not undermine, the appropriateness of the Quarto's ordering. No one need blame the ordering on Thorpe or Eld and restructure it in the interests of conventional causality, or, on the other hand, continue further with the process of breakdown. The Dark Lady sequence constitutes a painting in its own right and no justification exists for making it either more naturalistic or more abstract. Clearly, Shakespeare's breakdown of narrative consistency is theoretically extendable, but we are not dealing with an abstract game plan. To cope with infinite juxtapositions (psychologically, if not strictly numerically, speaking) would, after the first excitement, fatigue the mind and heart; the ceaseless relativity and alternation would soon produce mounting frustration, alienation, the sense of hopeless inadequacy. This nexus of reactions does temporarily occur. After experiencing the poems as anthology pieces, we move into the spider's web of the sequence itself with its self-mockery, self-abasement and self-betrayal, what Blackmur calls 'the loss, the treachery, the chaos in reality'.[1] This brings on radical uncertainty and axiological breakdown; and we search for some trace of Aristotelian causality to save us from perpetually confronting the recurring lapses, delusions and lies of human failure. Hence, to read the sonnets through at a sitting may produce, as Barber observes, 'a sensation of hothouse oppression'; but I deny that such a reading 'does violence to them and to the reader'.[2] As C. S. Lewis observes, the 'naughting' never rings false.[3] Since the juxtapositions, though many and initially daunting, are finite and in a fixed sequence, they hold out the hope of ultimate comprehension and the possibility of coming to terms emotionally with them: if large, yet the circle is closed. The 'course of knowledge' is not 'a symmetrical graph', as Edwards notes,[4] but it can be plotted, and we should beware of critics who despair of responding to the sonnets as they stand together.

In concentrating on a few poems to develop my critical point, I have implied that the whole cycle could be approached similarly. Still, my contention here is that Shakespeare brought the dramatic techniques of transference, abreaction, shifts in irony, explosive juxtaposition, anticipation, and the rest, to a climax in the Dark Lady sequence, even though one may legitimately argue that this sequence is in turn affected by the whole cycle and that to isolate it is to prescind from further more intricate ironies and relationships. Notably, no other Renaissance sonnet cycle was written by a major, or even by a significant, dramatist, and the techniques Edwards and I have mentioned can all be found, and found frequently, in

---

[1] Blackmur, p. 133.
[2] Barber, p. 11.
[3] C. S. Lewis, *English Literature in the Sixteenth Century* (Oxford, 1954), p. 505.
[4] Edwards, p. 31.

Elizabethan theatre, preeminently in Shakespeare's own. Having coined his famous epithet for the sonnets, Meres went on to talk of their author as 'most passionate among us to bewaile and bemoane the perplexities of love'. It is precisely this union of passion and perplexity that accounts for the genre of the 1609's Dark Lady sequence. For not only its individual sonnets but its ordering too is the work of a supremely dramatic imagination.

A NEW VIEW OF BANKSIDE

GRAHAM PARRY

Wenceslaus Hollar's depiction of the Bankside theatres in the Long View of London, 1647, is very well known, as is his preparatory drawing; now another sketch by Hollar of Bankside has come to light (see Plate IA), and though it presents only the merest outlines of the theatres, it may help to reinforce certain notions concerning their structure. The sketch comes from a notebook of Hollar's preserved in the John Rylands Library at Manchester (English MS. 883) which contains a large number of drawings in ink and pencil from many phases of Hollar's career, beginning as early as 1626 with a view of Prague, the artist's home town. Folio 36 of this notebook bears the signature Johannes Evelynus, with the inscription, 'c'e que j'ai jay receivé / Vigilantia cum diligentia / 1641', so it appears that the book once belonged to Evelyn who probably acquired it from Hollar soon after meeting him for the first time (according to the Diary) on 28 June 1641, when he visited Arundel House to sit for his portrait to Vanderborcht. Evelyn greatly admired Hollar's work, and it may well be that, having acquired the sketchbook in 1641, he continued to paste in more drawings by Hollar over the years as he obtained them from the artist, with whom he developed an enduring friendship.

The prospect of Bankside that concerns us is pasted on the reverse of folio 24, and measures 9 in. × 4 in.; the medium is brown ink. It is one of a number of London scenes scattered through the book, including other views of Lambeth and Westminster, Scotland Yard, details of Old St Paul's, and two unusual sketches of a military encampment and earthworks in Hyde Park, dated 1644 – signs of London's readiness in the Civil War.

All of the dated drawings of London scenes are from 1643 and 1644, so we may assume a similar date for this Bankside view, which is the left-hand side of a long panoramic prospect of London, the right-hand half of which is missing. The viewpoint for the sketch is the same as for the famous Long View – the tower of St Mary's Southwark – but the general vagueness of the details shows that this sketch was not intended for an etching, but was probably made to note the salient buildings of London and their relative positions, to guide the artist in the production of a more detailed panorama, such as the Long View itself. Winchester House lies in the foreground, then the Globe on the left, which stands out as a building of considerable size, and the bear-baiting house lies by the river. The sketch helps to substantiate two or three details in the Long View etching and in the drawing for that view: the second Globe does appear to have been circular in shape, rather than polygonal, and it did have a double gable, which is a marked feature of its construction. The line midway along the outside wall suggests that the window apertures were fairly conspicuous. There is no flagpole in evidence, whereas the bear-house clearly had a very noticeable flagpole, for it can be seen here, in the Long View drawing, and in the Long View itself. Also, there is the suggestion of open space between the theatre and the bear-garden.

Naturally, we wish that Hollar had been more specific in his recording of details in this sketch, but as a glimpse of Bankside when the theatres were still standing, it has a certain value, however modest, for consolidating our knowledge of that tantalising quarter of London.

© GRAHAM PARRY 1978

COMEDIES AND HISTORIES AT TWO STRATFORDS, 1977

ROGER WARREN

In 1977 Stratford, Ontario, celebrated its twenty-fifth season: its repertoire included *Richard III* and *All's Well That Ends Well* (the two plays with which it began in 1953) and *A Midsummer Night's Dream*. Stratford-upon-Avon's repertoire also included *A Midsummer Night's Dream*, as well as the complete *Henry VI*. Both Stratfords also gave *As You Like It*, but Ontario's had not opened when I was there. The approaches, and the results, were extremely variable.

I

A Midsummer Night's Dream has always seemed to me a particularly Elizabethan play, in that its combination of courtly formality and rich, vivid evocation of the English countryside has a strong flavour of Elizabeth's own court and its progresses. This flavour was caught with particular success in Peter Hall's Elizabethan country house version, especially in the 1962/3 revival. It was totally absent from the celebrated Peter Brook version. J. L. Styan in *The Shakespeare Revolution*, reviewed below, claims that 'those who disliked [Brook's] could not see past the surface of the production'; but the meaning of a play is not to be arbitrarily separated from the style and language in which it is expressed. The wood, the wild flowers, the juxtaposed court and rural worlds are essential features of the play. They are not merely its 'surface'; they make it what it is, and to neglect them,

treating them merely as symbols for something else ('a celebration of the arts of the theatre', for instance) is to jettison not just the surface of the play but its essence as well.

In 1977 at Stratford-upon-Avon John Barton recaptured this Elizabethan combination of the courtly and the rural, while in Ontario Robin Phillips went even further and placed the figure of the Queen herself at the centre of the play. It was a great relief to find both productions taking place, not in a gymnasium, a circus tent, or on the steel staircases of a penitentiary, but in designs which bore a demonstrable relationship to the style, tone, and events of the play.

John Napier's set for Mr Barton's version beautifully reconciled court and countryside: a formally designed wooden floor with a central motif suggesting a Renaissance view of man (or even, perhaps, Oberon as he was subsequently presented). This floor was later covered by a huge, many-coloured silk cloth decorated with leaves, backed by trees, and lit by an exceptionally imaginative overhead system, a particularly useful feature of which was to isolate characters in white light at the lovers' reaction to the magic juice or Puck's confusing of the duellists or the mechanicals. The sense of a magic forest was also conveyed in mime by a group of grotesquely masked male and female fairies; these masks were perhaps too sinister for spirits who inhabit musk-rose buds and sing a charm *against* sinister creatures; there was some confusion here.

Clearly Mr Barton wanted to stress the varied ancestry of the fairies, quoting David Young in the programme: 'a curious mixture of wood spirits, . . . household gods, pagan deities'. The most striking, and much the most successful, treatment was of Oberon. 'A prince from the farthest steep of India, shadowy and exotic', says Mr Young, and Patrick Stewart was virtually naked, muscular and dark-skinned, with long curling black hair in a head-band. He began Part Two reclining on the floor playing panpipes, a pastoral god, for all the world like Nijinsky's *Après-midi d'un faune*. However surprising this may sound, the strength of the approach lay in the ease with which Mr Stewart could switch from these exotic associations to a casually humorous 'I wonder if Titania be awaked', or to a direct, compelling delivery of all the great speeches: 'I know a bank' and especially the central, crucial 'But we are spirits of another sort' had maximum impact, totally persuasive. This Oberon could range from benevolence there to fury elsewhere and to exceptional sensuous tenderness at 'wake you, my sweet queen', cradling Titania in his arms. An outstanding performance.

Against these exotic beings, the mortals were sturdily Elizabethan, court and lovers in resplendent black and white – though Helena seemed oddly scruffy, rather like Ophelia after being dragged out of the brook and left to dry. Was this self-neglect her melancholy reaction to Demetrius's desertion, or was it, perhaps, the cause of it? It wasn't hard to see why Demetrius should prefer the enchanting, musically spoken Hermia of Pippa Guard. The lovers' scenes went with boisterous gaiety, aided by a large musket with which Demetrius went in pursuit of Lysander and a lute upon which Lysander accompanied Helena's maudlin reflections about school-days with Hermia. These scenes strongly recalled Peter Hall's version, as did Richard Durden's

secure bringing out of Theseus's ironic humour at 'Saint Valentine is past' and 'No doubt they rose up early *To observe the rite of May*', which Mr Hall was the first to make plain. But whereas his Theseus was humorous throughout, a wryly pragmatic country duke, Mr Durden was otherwise young and vigorous, a striking Elizabethan gallant.

Court and wood were well balanced, contrasted yet related. In the very first court scene, the many references to the moon were emphasised, delivered up and out front, anticipating the influence of moon and moonshine in the wood later. After the return to court, some of the trees remained in half-light, as did some of the fairies, 'bodying forth / The forms of things unknown' as Theseus spoke of them, and so ironically counteracting his scepticism. The white-clad court lay down to sleep in a circle around the edge of the stage as the fairies blessed them. They later joined in with the blessing, rather oddly; and even more oddly they awoke and raised themselves into sitting positions at Puck's reference to the graves letting forth their sprites.

The mechanicals were beautifully unforced, getting laughs off the lines, not off gags. The play scene was hilarious, as almost always, but also something more: picking up Granville-Barker's query, quoted in the programme, as to 'just how bad their play was meant to be', there was a sense, almost, of near-integrity, certainly a determination on Bottom's part to get things right, whatever the obstacles. Faced with having to stab himself through a magnificent but stubbornly impenetrable breastplate, he applied himself with slow, calm logic to the problem, and took all the time in the world to get his lyre into a suitably aesthetic position before expiring grandly but slowly. Richard Griffiths conveyed Bottom's self-absorption not by boisterous rant but by solicitous advice to Quince and the others. This quiet, warm, very human performance was the chief gain of the production's declared policy of using largely untried actors; but for Titania (especially opposite *this* Oberon), more is needed. Marjorie Bland spoke with the direct clarity that characterised the production but lacked that complex sense of identification with the world around her that should make the 'progeny of evils' seem of direct concern to her.

In the Ontario version Maggie Smith's Titania certainly did have all the necessary experience and beguiling personality. Effortlessly commanding on a single word ('OUT of this wood do not desire to go' – you really did believe the summer tended upon *her* state) and exquisitely lovely in the 'humble-bees' passage, she gave the meeting with Bottom genuine enchantment in every sense, so that when the final embrace came, it seemed utterly inevitable, and so crowned the first half. Moreover, Robin Phillips's production placed quite exceptional emphasis on the role, doubled with Hippolyta: the whole play became, as it were, a dream of Queen Elizabeth I's.

Hippolyta, dressed and made-up as Elizabeth, a superb vision in Susan Benson's magnificent black and gold costume, stood spotlit at the start while a female taped voice sang Bottom's 'I have had a most rare vision'. As the lights went up, she was surrounded protectively by a bevy of ladies visually resembling her (as did Hermia and Helena) and opposed by Theseus and an enormous entourage, Elizabethan gallants all, the whole stage a dazzling vision of black and gold Elizabethan court splendour. Theseus's wry humanity was ignored in order to present a stern, humourless male threat: this, it was implied, was how the Virgin Queen saw a *husband*, whatever fantasies about *lovers* she might entertain when she took on the persona of Titania (and Theseus that of Oberon, equally stern and humourless, and Philostrate, an aged, loyal courtier – Burghley? – that of Puck).

There were constant cross-references between the two worlds: Cobweb and company were members of Theseus's entourage, exactly the kind of sensuous youths that Elizabeth might have had hot dreams about; '*enforced* chastity' seemed more ambiguous than usual, fusing fears of rape with the extra idea of Elizabeth being *compelled* to remain chaste; at Demetrius's line in the play scene, 'one lion may, when many asses do', Hippolyta's face froze in half-recollection, with a similar reaction on Theseus's 'he might yet recover, and prove an ass'. Instead of the Bergomask, 'I have had a most rare vision' was relayed over speakers, and so was Oberon and Titania's blessing of the palace, with Hippolyta and Philostrate alone on stage. Philostrate made Puck's 'from the presence of the *sun*' refer to Hippolyta/Gloriana, and as Oberon's voice referred to 'the *issue* there create', her hand moved to her childless womb.

It can be seen that this interpretation involved some forcing, and much elaborate contrivance. In order to get Oberon and Titania back into their Theseus/Hippolyta clothes, the 'Come my Queen take hands with me' passage in IV, i had to be taped, while the courtiers performed a mating dance under the giant white flowers earlier used as a canopy for Titania. Above all, in this interpretation Theseus's 'imagination' speech inevitably went to Hippolyta/Elizabeth, who also spoke Hippolyta's reply to it; there was no reason why, having gone so far, Hippolyta should not present the other side of the case, but for some reason either director or actress seemed to lose confidence, for the crucial 'transfigured so together . . . something of great constancy' phrases were gabbled, away from the audience. It was odd that the speech which should have clinched the director's concept should falter, but it emphasised that, however finely executed (as when Puck's misleading of the quarrelling lovers became an elaborate production number, with Cobweb and company misleading them like will o' the wisps, leaping in and out of pin spots), there was a basic insecurity about the interpretation, whose elaboration incurred several penalties.

The mechanicals, for instance, wholly lacked natural spontaneity. Their first scene grew out of an interpolated episode in which Quince summoned those who were thought fit to appear before the Duke out of a bustling, crowded Elizabethan market. They were self-consciously jokey, and Bottom an unbearable ham. The extra sophistication of this court cruelly exposed their inadequate characterisation: in the play scene, there was no mingling of levels: these 'funny men' merely came from another, inferior, theatrical world altogether. The funniest moment of the whole evening was Maggie Smith's irresistible throwaway delivery out into the house of 'This is the silliest stuff that ever I heard'; but its witty sophistication devastatingly exposed the ineptitude, not of the mechanicals, but of the actors.

The lovers, on the other hand, were totally successful. Here Robin Phillips's invention, and the verbal and physical agility of Domini Blythe, Stephen Russell, and Jack Weatherall seconded the text's presentation of the story, rather than confusing it: whenever they appeared, the production seemed to gain a secure confidence which the court/fairy scenes somehow missed, for all the work that had gone into them. But even here, though Martha Henry's Helena was a brilliantly funny *tour-de-force*, the massive armoury of verbal and physical effects that she brought to bear on the lines seemed to me to symbolise the whole production; though tremendously enjoyable, their elaborate contrivance ultimately lacked the unpretentious humanity of simpler versions: the RSC Helena, for instance, despite her obvious inexperience, gave an ultimately more satisfying account of the *part*.

The achievement of both productions was

to leave you marvelling at the sheer richness of the play itself, at the easy confidence of its interweaving of the various worlds, and the way in which such power of implication is thrown out with, as it seems, such inspired casualness, simply through gorgeous language and irresistible gaiety.

II

In Ontario's *All's Well*, Martha Henry's Helena again typified the strengths and weaknesses of the production. Both were clearly delivered, sombre, bitter at times, their humour wry instead of that playing for cheap laughs which sometimes afflicts productions of this play when people are afraid of it. The clarity and directness were especially rewarding in passages like the Countess's blessing of Bertram, spoken with great humanity and worldly tenderness by Margaret Tyzack. What both the production and the Helena seemed to me to lack was that final intense, impassioned commitment to the play and the part which Tyrone Guthrie achieved at Stratford-upon-Avon in 1959 (and therefore, I presume, in Ontario in 1953, which was a prototype for the Warwickshire version).

Miss Henry is an actress of great accomplishment, especially in ironic humour (with Parolles) and harsh power (when surviving humiliation). But she has mannerisms which, for me, got in the way of a complete realisation of the role: she whirls restlessly round the stage, scattering bits of the text as she goes (presumably to be fair to all the members of so wide-flung an audience; the Ontario stage is fiendishly difficult to work on; it is virtually impossible to communicate with all the audience all the time). In two crucial soliloquies ('Our remedies oft in ourselves do lie' and the central 'Nothing in France until he has no wife') this technique meant that the thread was fatally lost. She also conveys passion by constantly outstretched arms and a somewhat wailing delivery. Helena needs both single-minded concentration on her task, and also stillness while she thinks out her course of action. I remember vividly the white-hot passion Zoe Caldwell communicated by such means in 1959; but then she had Guthrie's dedication and exceptional imagination to second her at every turn, what Harold Hobson, quoted in Professor Styan's book, called a 'personal vision'.

I suspect that such a vision may be needed to give this psychologically complex, even introverted, play that extra 'lift' to seize the audience's attention, as Guthrie certainly gave the court scenes. If David Jones didn't have that inspiration, he certainly established a strong sense of a real, lived-in world: a court whose ritual indicated the King's effortless supremacy in the weary flapping gesture which was sufficient to seat a stage full of attendants; a kind of fencing-school with racks of rapiers and saddles to suggest the reality of military activity, developed in the sinister black breast-plates, helmets and plumes worn by the Duke of Florence and his army; a sundial and polished wooden garden seats for Rossillion; solid military gear and indoor furniture for Florence. Tanya Moiseiwitsch, who had so brilliantly conjured up the semi-Ruritanian world of Guthrie's *All's Well*, switched with equal ease to this Caroline one. The colours underlined the changing moods: scattered autumnal leaves and creeper for the opening Rossillion scenes, the sombre furs of a bitter winter campaign for Parolles's baiting and Bertram's growing up, touches of spring green, sunny light, and soft cream colours for the clothes of the Countess and Helena in the hopeful final scene.

Mr Jones's thoughtful care paid off in Bertram's rejection of Helena and the kiss scene. The first began with the genuine gaiety of the King leading Helena a coranto; the wards of court were sympathetic to Helena's suit, as they should be, but disastrously weren't, to cheapening effect, in another fairly recent production. On the other hand, the King seemed unable to sustain those crucial long speeches: that beginning 'Here, take her hand' (which Guthrie made an unforgettable display of autocratic power) turned more and more into uncontrolled rant so that that deadly laughter was in full swing by the time he got to 'Speak, thine answer', which indulgently sought laughs that appeared at odds with the director's careful setting up of the scene, particularly since Nicholas Pennell's Bertram retrieved the situation by offering Helena a coldly formal arm, with a lip curled in distaste, as he led her offstage to the enforced wedding.

In the kiss scene, when Helena finally blurted out her request, Bertram bent and brushed her *hand* with his lips, whereupon she seized him and held him in a prolonged kiss; his response was to break away (though not immediately) with 'I pray you, stay not, but in haste to horse', and she, a first intimacy achieved, ran lightly from the stage, the lightness only intensifying her humiliation at Bertram's 'dreadful sentence' in the next scene. It was an original interpretation. It did not sentimentalise Bertram, avoiding those intrusive 'psst's from Parolles which other directors have used to suggest that Parolles is Bertram's 'evil genius', thereby wrecking the tough, unsentimental psychological point that Bertram *needs* no tempter. On the other hand, it did not exaggerate the cruelty.

Some of Bertram's harshness elsewhere was under-done, 'Here comes my clog' thrown away, back to audience. The cutting edge of the writing was missing here and even more in the baiting of Parolles, which somehow lacked definition. With the return to Rossillion for the finale, the whole production 'lifted' with the new light, the spring colours, and some excellent groupings which underlined the progress of the scene and increased our feeling of satisfaction at the formally patterned resolution. Here William Hutt's King showed a masterful control of timing and development, so that everything built, as it should, to Helena's redemptive entry, beautifully played by Miss Henry. 'All yet *seems* well', commented Mr Hutt, and 'whate'er the course' there was a sense of genuine harmony at the close.

III

There was no such satisfying harmony at the close of Trevor Nunn's RSC *As You Like It*. His productions of the comedies become increasingly bizarre. Having turned *The Comedy of Errors* into a compromise musical, he has now turned *As You Like It* into a kind of baroque pastoral opera. One had the uneasy sensation of watching a Restoration 'improved' version, partly because of the pastiche late seventeenth-century music; and as with such settings the florid vocal elaboration had the effect of trivialising by removing attention from the meaning of the words. In fact new words began the play, a prologue for Hymen, Fortune, and Nature; however much Orlando might stress 'the something that *nature* gave me', the prologue clarified nothing in this first scene, to which it seemed totally extraneous, or in the tricky Rosalind/Celia dialogue about Fortune's work and Nature's in the second. While Wedlock, Nature, and (I suppose) Fortune are themes in the play, they arise naturally out of character and situation, not allegorised as abstract issues; when Hymen appears at the end, it is merely to emphasise that wedlock is the logical climax of the human process dramatised in the Rosalind/Orlando scenes. The play does not exist for the sake of 'ideas', as the masques were at any rate supposed to do. In fact, of course, the abstractions were usually an excuse for music, dancing, and ostentatious display; Mr Nunn appears to regard Shakespeare's play as a similar excuse.

As in *The Comedy of Errors*, if less frequently, characters had to switch off their characterisations for uneasy and quite unnecessary attempts to sing bits of text. Since 'It was a lover and his lass' was built up into a company celebration of the coming of spring to a snowy Arden, a big ritual celebration just *before* the point where Shakespeare wrote one meant that Hymen's entry in fact misfired. Descending on a baroque cloud which opened and shut, attended by cherubs with absurd wings, and drowning individual details like 'You and you are sure together / As the winter to foul weather' in an undifferentiated outpouring, sung with an enormous sheepdoggy wobble, this Hymen was rightly derided by the audience, and Mr Nunn's baroque allegorising totally backfired.

As with Wedlock, so with Nature: Mr Nunn's baroque style presented only a surface, preventing any real exploration of Shakespeare's searching analysis of the values of court and country. While a snow-bound stage suggested the reality of 'shrewd days and nights' in Arden, the music by contrast suggested an artificial idyll, and the shepherds were eighteenth-century figures with crooks. There was similar contradiction throughout: Duke Frederick's court wore Caroline silks, but the cloth behind them suggested Versailles; the cloth for Oliver's house seemed like a nineteenth-century print of an eighteenth-century chateau; the front drop and Touchstone's motley recalled Watteau's decorative panels and his image of the French and Italian comedians. These cloths, and those with painted trees, seemed even more affected, irrelevant, and old-fashioned than the mock Elizabethan stage of 1976.

Two difficult scenes, however, gained from the treatment. We regularly saw how 'men of great worth resorted to this forest' (and some of less worth, like Charles the Wrestler and Le Beau); one of these turned up during the

'Ducdame' scene so that Jaques could make 'Leaving his wealth and ease, / A stubborn will to please' apply directly to him; then Jaques dictated the parody of 'Under the greenwood tree' line by line to Amiens, who sang each line after him; and because of the florid elaboration of the vocal line, the calling of fools into a circle could be built to a genuinely humorous climax. This was the first time I have seen Mary Lascelles's suggestion that Amiens (as in the Folio, and not Jaques) should 'sing innocently this parody of his own stanzas'[1] carried out. It works well. In recent years, audiences seem to have found the formal repetitions of 'And so am I for Phebe . . . Ganymede . . . Rosalind' increasingly hard to take; here it was transformed into a sung ensemble, with the repetitions overlapping one another musically.

But other virtues owed nothing to the baroque scheme. Emrys James's Jaques and Peter McEnery's Orlando for once balanced the two characters. Jaques, in black, stood out against the snow and the white-clad foresters, isolated well downstage of the others for the satirical attacks; but Orlando's position balanced his as he spoke of his concern for Adam, thus underlining Shakespeare's point that the Orlando/Adam relationship counterbalances and softens the nihilism of Jaques's view that old age is 'sans everything'. This Orlando's intelligent, vigorous attack showed that the downbeat opening prose scene can in fact work perfectly well; it needs no officious prologue. Jeffery Dench's very human Adam was a great asset in both these scenes, and there were, indeed, several good, straightforward performances to keep the first half together: Charles Dance's Oliver, Michael Bulman's Amiens, and John Rhys-Davies's Duke Frederick, dragging his court round the stage after him in his obsession with the wrestling – the only Frederick I've seen who seemed at all interested in it.

The second half, however, was not sustained, chiefly because the big Orlando/Rosalind scenes quite lacked the vital erotic charge and ambiguity; even in the mock-wedding there was no sense of a potentially explosive situation, powerful emotion underlying the game. In other roles, Kate Nelligan has shown a warmth and tenderness which she unfortunately replaced as Rosalind with a relentlessly forceful, logical display of hard wit which became uncontrolled rant at climaxes. The harder she worked, the less moving she became. With the emotional build-up to the final scene missing, Hymen has nothing to crown; absurd, empty ritual replaced that 'concord and sexual harmony', as Anne Barton calls it in the programme, which can make the ending of *As You Like It* so satisfying.

And so, despite an elaborately inventive *tour-de-force* from Mr Nunn and Alan David's sourly witty Touchstone for the degrees of the lie, the end was most *un*satisfying – as Mr Nunn's productions will continue to be while he substitutes ear-and-eye tickling externals for an exploration of the text and its meanings. It is really very odd that a director who illuminated *Macbeth* by an imaginative probing of the text can be content with such a dimly superficial view of a masterpiece in another kind.

IV

Turning now to the histories, Ontario's *Richard III* was unremarkable, with Brian Bedford a clear, deliberate, not particularly witty or interesting Richard who built to an effective climax at Bosworth, finally impaling *himself* on Richmond's sword, prime mover to the end. Margaret Tyzack's Margaret dominated the stage at each appearance, in a performance blazing with personality and

1 'Shakespeare's Pastoral Comedy', *More Talking of Shakespeare*, ed. J. Garrett (1959), p. 81.

power, exactly what Margaret needs and what the younger Margaret didn't receive in the RSC *Henry VI*.

Directing the first unadapted *Henry VI* at Stratford-upon-Avon since 1906, Terry Hands aimed 'to show the plays simply as they are' and 'to tell the story as simply as possible'. Clearly laid out on Farrah's empty, steeply-raked stage, emblematic in grouping (as in the Roses quarrel), in colour (the French in blue leather, the English in black, with red or white accoutrements added later as appropriate) and in lighting (characters constantly picked out by follow spots), his production worked especially well for Part One, since here Shakespeare himself is 'telling the story simply', with very little complexity in the writing or in the presentation of character.

Since I had never before seen Part One un-adapted, it was of course fascinating – but disconcerting too. The drawback of the purely narrative approach is that it does nothing to clarify the text's presentation of central characters. Charlotte Cornwell's vigorous Joan carried a hint of 'inspiration' in her early recoil from a flaming torch, obviously with a pre-monition of her end; but is the inspiration divine or diabolical? Shakespeare, of course, doesn't decide; nor did the performance. Again, David Swift gave Talbot tremendous impact simply by emphasising every line to maximum effect and never letting go; but the text itself seems to rely on the popularity of a national hero ('brave Talbot, the terror of the French') rather than on any inherent interest in the man himself. Talbot's

> But if you frown upon this proffer'd peace,
> You tempt the fury of my three attendants,
> Lean famine, quartering steel and climbing fire

sounds like Tamburlaine; but the association only serves to underline Talbot's lack of real magnetism (or, indeed, personality at all). Moreover, the pathos of the Talbots' reunion

before death derived entirely from the expertise of the actors in disguising the jog-trotting ineptitude of the couplets here. I have never before felt so certain, watching a Shakespeare play, that a passage was non-Shakespearian; it is true that couplets are never Shakespeare's strongest suit, but their banality in other contexts tends to be used for plot-pushing or mockery not, as here, for a central emotional climax. 'Unadapted' presentation strongly supported those who question Shakespeare's complete responsibility for this play.

But in these two cases, for good or ill, the production reflected the text; the case of Duke Humphrey was more complicated. It is awkward enough for Humphrey to check Vernon and Bassett for 'immodest clamorous outrage' when he himself has been just as clamorous in his feud with Winchester. Here the inconsistency was emphasised by a feebly miscast, inaudible Humphrey, disastrously upsetting the balance with Winchester; and his inadequacy was the more noticeable (and the more irritating) because of the quite superlative, rock-solid accounts of the minor roles of Bedford and Mortimer by Jeffrey Dench and Clem McCallin. (It often seems, for all the fuss the RSC makes about being a 'company', that excellent service over the years brings some dusty rewards.) Mr McCallin's urgent, impassioned account of the origins of the York/Lancaster dispute was a masterpiece of dramatic story-telling by means of characterisation, that controlled mixture of humour and pathos which often indicates that an RSC actor is on top form.[1] Other small roles were particularly strongly played by James Laurenson (the Dauphin), Edwin Richfield (Exeter) and Oliver Ford-Davies (Somerset).

Mr Hands did not let his determination to tell the story simply deter him from striking effects. A slight rearrangement of scenes

[1] Clem McCallin died during the season, on 7 August.

allowed the 'bought and sold Lord Talbot' and his son to remain upstage 'ring'd about with bold adversity' while at the front Sir William Lucy upbraided first York and then Somerset for their treacherous refusal to help, Jeffery Dench again eloquently putting the case for moderation, loyalty, and unity. As Joan was dragged to her death, a slim figure emerged in soft, romantic light from behind one of the huge cannons that dominated the stage, neatly underlining Shakespeare's own juxtaposition of the arrival of Margaret, one female controller of her country's fortunes giving place to another. At the end, the French and English negotiators of peace froze upstage while Suffolk described Margaret to Henry at the front; the great bridge that had served for the walls of Orleans or Rouen descended so that Margaret could stand, spotlit, above them for the final tableau, a fittingly emblematic conclusion to the prologue, and an anticipation of things to come.

This anticipation of Margaret's dominance was not fulfilled, partly because of casting, partly because of Mr Hands's approach: in Parts Two and Three, to tell the story simply is insufficient. Shape, development, and finally meaning were absent. This, again, probably reflects the text of Part Two as it stands but not, I think, of Part Three; and it was inevitably a disappointment after *The Wars of the Roses* in 1963/4, which certainly *did* have a clear shape and a very powerful sense of purpose. Arguably it was Hall/Barton's shape, but in that it made the very most of every character and incident, I have no doubt whatever that it did Shakespeare much greater service than this one. Mr Hands hoped that his version would make the characters popular again, but most of them lacked the exceptionally vivid individuality which they had in *The Wars of the Roses*. One missed both the keen clash of sharply defined personalities and the resulting sympathy for, or at least understanding of,

each figure as he or she came to an inevitable and terrible doom.

Too often, Mr Hands merely brought people onstage and left individual actors to make the scenes work, but some were inadequate since they ranted or were inaudible or both, others were simply miscast. Richard of Gloucester was in the most excessive sub-Olivier vein, taking his cue from 'snarl and bite', ignoring the genial colloquialisms, and hammering out his lines syllable by syllable ('I / am / my / self / a / lone'); it is not Peter McEnery's fault that he lacked both 'Suffolk's imperial tongue' and the Marlovian aspiration which it expresses; ironically, James Laurenson possesses exactly those qualities of manner and delivery which both Suffolk and Richard need; but he was playing Jack Cade. Emrys James's York seemed as weirdly interpreted as his Henry IV in 1975, a little strutting man with coy, impish mannerisms, constantly sniffing his white rose; but he can certainly control both stage and audience, and his wry humour enabled him to put across his genealogy ('Edward III, my lords, had seven sons') with great clarity. But the main drawback of the production was that Helen Mirren lacked the poise, irony, rage, passion, and sheer emotional variety which Margaret demands, and which Peggy Ashcroft had supplied in such abundance. (An unfair comparison? But those were the standards which the RSC used to attain in such parts.)

In Part Two, Mr Hands appeared to be comparing and contrasting the court and the commons. From the start, the people had watched the great events, cordoned off from the court; when war finally broke out, it developed from the nobles' personal quarrels over Somerset, and was fought exclusively by the lords onstage at the time, a kind of private party for the aristocracy. On the other hand, the grotesque savagery of Cade's rebellion seemed a low-class parody of the selfishness, greed, and violence of the aristocrats: the baiting and destroying of Lord Say echoed the Court's treatment of Duke Humphrey, each victim even using similar defensive arguments. As so often with Mr Hands's productions, a 'concept' sacrifices individual details, especially humour. Fortunately James Laurenson had the personality and vocal range to carry the scenes and even to justify the odd interpretation of Cade as a zealot, a wild John the Baptist figure (suggested in some way by York's 'this *devil* here', to which Mr James gave spitting emphasis?).

Part Three was a similar mixture of the emblematic and the merely odd. Towton, like St Albans, developed straight out of the dialogue, fought only by the principals concerned, while Henry VI remained kneeling at the side of the stage throughout, so that 'This battle fares like to the morning's war' grew naturally out of it; the disputants at Tewkesbury, again, played out the battle and the brothers killed Margaret's son with ritual formality, while Margaret herself knelt front centre, her back to them; Henry VI, in white, was stabbed through the side while he hung crucified in chains. At other times, Mr Hands appeared to be stressing the grotesqueness of terrible events: 'his passions move me so' says Northumberland during Margaret's baiting of York, but it was curiously *un*moving, partly because here York's vocal mannerisms got the better of him and Margaret lacked variety and intensity, but also because of the contrived way in which it was produced: York sank slowly to his knees and Margaret knelt too, crawling to him to observe his torments closely, until he ended up with his head in her lap; they all seemed almost numbed by their excesses, but somehow missed the raw human emotions of an astounding scene.

Humanity was the quality most notably absent from the productions, with two striking exceptions. Julian Glover's Warwick grew in clarity, stature and power until he carried the second half of Part Three virtually single-handed. He physically dominated the Yorkist assemblies, both through his own size and through Mr Hands's groupings. He caught all the irony of his lines and of his own final situation, as even the great Kingmaker must acknowledge his inevitable end.

Alan Howard's Henry VI replaced David Warner's holy fool with a well-intentioned man who periodically slipped into madness, anticipated by York tapping his forehead at 'Henry put apart'. This both reflected history and helped reconcile the inconsistencies of the text, as well as coping with difficult passages. The first real attack came with Humphrey's death: for moments on end, Henry sat staring in front of him, while Margaret used that long and terribly difficult speech ('Was I for this nigh wrecked upon the sea') as a desperate attempt to bring him round and talk him out of it. Again, Henry tried to make Winchester, grovelling all round the stage in dying agony, touch the cross; it was both absurd and very moving: Mr Howard unleashed tremendous power at 'Forbear to judge!' and found a quasi-tragic quality in the role. Even he, though, ranted (in the interests of suggesting madness) Henry's moving, beautiful lament for his uncle Humphrey; and Henry appears too little for Mr Howard to carry the productions, as he did Mr Hands's *Henry V*.

Mr Hands's chief weakness as a director is that his concern for 'narrative' (or, as in Cade's case, an 'idea') seems to lead him to neglect, almost to appear uninterested in, individual characterisation and the line-by-line effectiveness of a scene. The final impression of this trilogy was of a cool, distanced outline of the story rather than an impassioned involvement in the destinies of people we had come to know, as in *The Wars of the Roses*. And the incomplete, inconclusive effect may well have had the unfortunate result of confirming those very prejudices about uninteresting 'prentice work' which it was the triumph of *The Wars of the Roses* so conclusively to banish.[1]

V

There have been several recent books on Shakespeare in the modern theatre. The argument of J. L. Styan's *The Shakespeare Revolution*[2] is that since Shakespeare's plays are essentially non-illusory, Victorian productions and criticism were fallacious in their exploration of realism, and twentieth-century directors and critics successful or not depending on how far they understood 'non-illusion': in Granville-Barker, 'Shakespeare on the stage and in the study was meteorically impelled towards the later metaphorical interpretation of Wilson Knight and Peter Brook'; and 'in its explicitly unreal mixture of supernatural, pastoral and earthy ingredients, *A Midsummer Night's Dream* provided the perfect test case'. Granville-Barker's formal fairies with gilded faces, or his Puck, emphasising stage mechanics by cuing lights and raising drop cloths, 'granted the twentieth century an insight into [Shakespeare's] mode of vision as perhaps only Peter Brook's has done since'. But neither the (sharply divided) press accounts nor the hideous visual impression suggested by the photographs make the conclusion that this was a 'beacon of a production' at all inevitable; and Professor Styan's marshalling of the evidence provided by recent *Dreams* can certainly be questioned.

For instance, he completely ignores George Devine's 1954 Stratford production which supplied a quite original image for the fairies: their costumes and make-up suggested birds, Oberon plumed like a peacock, Titania with broad white eye-streaks like a falcon. This imaginative artifice does not seem to me *essentially* different from, and most certainly not visually inferior to, Granville-Barker's; his

gilded fairies 'stood in Oriental poses and moved with a dignified, shuffling gait, making weird mechanical gestures', while each of Devine's, according to Richard David's valuably detailed review in *Shakespeare Survey 8*, had a distinct bird-like movement, gesture, and style of vocal delivery. So why should Professor Styan ignore Devine's version? Because, I suggest, it complicates his claim that only Granville-Barker and Brook really showed us Shakespeare's mode of vision in this play.

This purpose seems clearer when he plays down Peter Hall's *Dream*. He emphasises the adverse press comment on its first, tentative appearance in 1959, fleetingly acknowledging that it had improved in 1962/3 by quoting from Irving Wardle's 1963 *Times* review. But when he borrows other phrases from that review (without acknowledgement), he alters their emphasis to suit his own purposes: 'the pre-nuptial court scenes acquired a special life of their own as if the play were being presented *in non-illusory fashion* by the members of an Elizabethan wedding party' (italics mine). But Irving Wardle's point in the passage borrowed from is that the effect was the very opposite of the 'non-illusory' or the 'explicitly unreal'; far from parading artifice, each world was, Mr Wardle felt, 'anchored to reality':

The opening scene at Theseus's court, instead of being treated as a perfunctory flourish to the play proper, acquires a life of its own, exploiting to the full Theseus's pre-nuptial frustration and his embarrassment in the Egeus affair. The portrait of wry, mag-

1 It seems only fair to note here B. A. Young's diametrically opposed view in *The Financial Times* that, since the 'pure' text was 'presented in a style that Burbage himself would have recognised', 'this not only helps to justify the play, so often denigrated . . ., but sets a standard by which current Shakespearian production must now be judged' (15 July 1977). The general press reaction was represented by Bernard Levin: 'the verdict, though substantially qualified, is on balance a decidedly favourable one' (*Sunday Times*, 17 July 1977).

2 Cambridge University Press, 1977.

nanimous nobility...typifies the integrity of the production.

When a review is twisted to make the opposite point from the one the reviewer was making, suspicions inevitably arise about the handling of other evidence. It is typical of his manipulation of stage history to fit his theory that Professor Styan should casually admit that though 'the most notable collaboration of Hall and Barton' was *The Wars of the Roses*, 'attention here must shift' to other productions which better illustrate non-illusion! The absurd confusion to which the pursuit of a theory can lead is best demonstrated by his comment on Dorothy Tutin's Cressida: 'Tutin's success in realistic character-consistency pointed to the director's unwillingness to go all the way into role-playing and non-illusory theatre.' In other words, Peter Hall's and Dorothy Tutin's successful creation of a vividly convincing Cressida is, in this ideology, actually a fault. This desperate position stems from the need to play down Peter Hall's obvious achievements at the RSC in order to demonstrate that 'Peter Brook's contribution to...Stratford in the sixties was...the most far-seeing', although he only directed two and a half productions there in those years.

Given this emphasis on Brook, it is frustrating to find no extended discussion of his 1955 *Titus Andronicus* with the Oliviers, widely considered a 'revolutionary' production; it would surely have been a more valuable production to study than the *Macbeth* of the same season, whose promptbook, lavishly presented and illustrated, and edited by Michael Mullin, gives remarkably little idea of why this production was so admired, simply because Glen Byam Shaw's production seems chiefly to have been a frame for two stars whose rehearsals took place in private![1]

Ralph Berry's series of interviews with directors[2] must be faulted for failing to edit out repetitions and phrases like 'If I have understood you rightly', for indulging his own opinions at length, and for not coaxing more valuable responses from so exceptional a director as Giorgio Strehler. The most stimulating remarks come from the Polish director Konrad Swinarski on *All's Well*. He takes this play more seriously, and probes more searchingly into its characters, than directors in the West seem to manage. He responds particularly to the Court, partly because it reflects his own political world: 'in spite of being a socialistic society...the Court in our country is a kind of power which finally determines what is going on between people'. At the end, the King (whom Mr Swinarski analyses in great and convincing detail) 'knows that he has not created happiness, he has created merely a new misunderstanding in human relationships. In his Epilogue, he asks for applause – maybe you can help, when he turns to the audience – so he is deeply in doubt whether a human being can rule the country and can rule life'. His account of how he staged the King's cure and the finale make me wish I had seen his production. Even when he mistakes the sense of Lafew's phrase 'I'll make sport with thee', his determination to explore every detail of the play is striking and refreshing, seeking point and personality even in the apparently impoverished jokes between the Countess and Lavache; his comments on Lavache, whose wisdom stems from understanding 'the unfulfilled sexual relations between human beings', and on the Dumains ('in effect official spies in the diplomatic service') might well have given his production a shot in the arm at just the points where the text is most in need of it. Anyone interested in this play should consult this piece.

[1] '*Macbeth' Onstage: An Annotated Facsimile of Glen Byam Shaw's 1955 Promptbook* (University of Missouri Press, 1976).
[2] *On Directing Shakespeare* (Croom Helm, London, 1977).

The other useful articles are in the *Deutsche Shakespeare-Gesellschaft West Jahrbuch 1976.*[1] James Stedder supplements accounts of John Barton's notable RSC *Richard II* with a wealth of practical details about text, rehearsals, and the developing performances of Richard Pasco and Ian Richardson as both Richard and Bolingbroke. Best of all is R. L. Smallwood's article on John Barton's RSC *King John*. He carefully establishes, through a tangle of textual complications, why and how 'Mr Barton had to rewrite *King John* in order to make it say the things he wanted it to say', that is, to show *only* 'the corruption of power' and 'even the futility of existence'. Then with great clarity and sensitivity he *uses* the production's failure to establish the more clearly 'the heart of Shakespeare's play' which he had begun to define in his outstanding New Penguin edition of the play, 'the Bastard Faulconbridge's discovery of a personal moral integrity in the corrupt world in which he has to survive':

In Act V, as he ... 'alone upholds the day', he is the only visible candidate for the English crown. It is a splendid exploitation of the possibilities of the history play: our whole dramatic attention is focused on an unhistorical character .. . and we are momentarily lulled into thinking that history can be rewritten ... [until] Prince Henry is revealed at the end of the play, and history returns to its course.

It is in such a persuasively argued, thoughtful piece, rather than in windy deliberations about non-illusion, that the mutual interplay of theatre and study can achieve something valuable, so that even a disappointing production 'at least served the purpose ... of making one think about the structure of Shakespeare's play, and await, with even greater interest, a revival of it'.

[1] Quelle and Meyer, Heidelberg, 1976.
© ROGER WARREN 1978

'TAMBURLAINE THE GREAT' RE-DISCOVERED

J. S. CUNNINGHAM AND ROGER WARREN

JSC. The integrity of *Tamburlaine*, in virtually a full text, as a two-part play; its diversity and forcefulness as theatre; its resourcefulness as drama: Peter Hall's production at the National Theatre has put such claims as these beyond reasonable doubt. Admirers of the play need no longer suspect that they may be wishfully imposing their cherished views on a primitive original.

RW. To those who (like myself) admired its poetic power but had fears about possible monotony, it provided a shatteringly convincing answer: virtually *everything*, virtually every single scene worked. Everything in this production came straight out of the text, though executed with quite exceptional flair and imagination. Peter Hall seized, for instance, on Marlowe's visual symbolism of the white, red, and black tents and made such symbolism a basic principle of the whole production. In the first two scenes alone, the entire colour-scheme of the stage changed three times – pink for the court of the effeminate Mycetes, blue for the crowning of Cosroe, and gold for the arrival of Zenocrate and Tamburlaine. The production strikingly established how bold colour changes can reflect changes of situation, long before Tamburlaine's tents appeared, themselves vividly and uncompromisingly realised: everything (including costumes, props, and furniture) would move from white to scarlet to black, achieving Marlowe's effect with a thoroughness that his own theatre can scarcely have managed. And so with the appearance of each new dramatic group: blazing red and gold for the Turks, whether under Bajazeth or Orcanes; Crusaders' white with black crosses for Sigismund and the Christian troops; cool mauve and silver grey for the Soldan and the Men of Memphis.

JSC. Bold, but essentially simple – even, chastened – contrasts in style: echoing and enforcing the verse, not sensationally distracting from it or fussily refining upon it. In black at the sack of Babylon, as the text implicitly requires, Tamburlaine's three main followers were, consequently, in black when they uttered the three-part threnody over the onset of his fatal illness –

> For Hell and Darkness pitch their pitchy tents.

One felicitous extension of the colour-coding marked the ceremonious re-uniting of Theridamas, Techelles, and Usumcasane with Tamburlaine early in Part Two, each of them fully blazoned by one of his three symbolic colours (white, for instance, being particularly right for the cool, restrained Theridamas). And the three followers, dressed in these three colours, formed one of three groups of three during the death-scene of Zenocrate, with Tamburlaine (now white-haired) in white to speak the line

> Black is the beauty of the brightest day.

Essentially true to the text, such effects might have been expected. For me, the real surprise was the lively diversity of the human interplay among the characters between and within the bold groupings, and between them and the audience. Not that simple motives and bold impressions were capriciously embroidered: complications were themselves kept well-defined and simple. Drawn into the web of response and judgement promptly, laughing at the seemly ineptitudes of Mycetes, we were soon involved with the human material – the experience, convincingly grasped, of Cosroe, Zenocrate, Theridamas, each of them creatively conceived. Tamburlaine himself excited an expectant delight from the outset, admiration of his temerity and verve ever ready to broaden into partisan laughter. And this human involvement (as distinct from exploiting the text for mannerisms and jokes) meant that the audience was all the more painfully confronted with the cruelty, wilfulness, even 'madness' of Tamburlaine and the world he creates (or de-creates). We were partisan, to our amusement, and invigorated – to our cost.

RW. All this was acted out on a bare but strikingly designed stage. An enormous golden circular lighting grid was suspended over the whole stage, pouring down light on to another matching circle painted on the floor. On to this floor was projected, before the play began, a map of Tamburlaine's conquests. The whole stage design was perhaps a Renaissance symbol of heaven and earth; more immediately, it provided a focal point for the action of each scene without cramping it. At the back and sides, panels either reflected the current colour-scheme or slid back to reveal huge golden friezes of soldiers or horsemen to suggest armies, notably Bajazeth's two thousand horse (see Plate VIIIA), or Theridamas's thousand, whose

> plumed helms are wrought with beaten gold,
> Their swords enamell'd, and about their necks
> Hangs massy chains of gold down to the waist:
> In every part exceeding brave and rich.[1]

Within so boldly uncompromising a design scheme, the action had to be equally bold and formal, and so it was, utterly symmetrical. But this symmetry again and again reinforced the point of a scene, especially in the first encounter between Tamburlaine and Bajazeth, for me the highlight of the first play, where the staging mirrored every shift and contrast of personality and emphasis.

Marlowe's structure here is strictly symmetrical: Bajazeth is accompanied by his queen Zabina, her maid, and his three contributory kings, Tamburlaine by Zenocrate, her maid, and his three lieutenants; after the antithetical 'And dar'st thou bluntly call me Bajazeth/And dar'st thou bluntly call me Tamburlaine', the three contributory kings have speeches which are then exactly paralleled by the three lieutenants'; Bajazeth seats Zabina and gives her his crown to wear; Tamburlaine echoes the process with Zenocrate; the rivals fight off-stage, while Zabina and Zenocrate engage in balanced mutual recrimination onstage. These symmetrical antitheses were not only scrupulously observed, but *used* to sharpen the dramatic impact. Marlowe's requirement of the two thrones, for instance, suggested a nice point: Bajazeth was carried on by attendants, sitting in the elaborate throne in which he had first appeared, 'the greatest potentate of Africa'; as he was lowered to the ground, Tamburlaine hastily adjusted the positioning of his own throne so that it exactly balanced Bajazeth's, in order to lose no advantage in his 'encounter with that Bajazeth'. The others were grouped round them with severest symmetry: Zabina marking Zenocrate, the two maids behind them, the three contributory kings on one side of the stage marking the three lieutenants on the other.

JSC. This scene was a momentous and richly entertaining climax in the absorbing process

[1] All quotations are from the text prepared for the production by John Russell Brown, Rex Collings, 1976.

of Tamburlaine's discovery of his own powers, the evolving of his own style, assisted by the observant, half-parodic mimicry of imperial style, above all the style of Bajazeth. The process blended wit, opportunism, a strutting confidence, and engagingly mischievous provocations to mirth. Tamburlaine had basked in homage from his supporters after the defeat of Cosroe, defiantly front of stage, palms open, drawing audience applause – childlike partisanship on our part, surprised by sheer high spirits and risky verve. He registered a fleeting fear of being overshadowed and out-spoken by Bajazeth, but recovered to match him, his own impromptu stage-director, setting up Zenocrate's throne to counterbalance Zabina's, and evolving a verbal style more than adequate to the challenge. This sense that the early Tamburlaine is inventing his own style, trying out formal poses and gestures, learning to out-Herod Herod, can lie dormant on the page. Awaking it, Albert Finney's interpretation was totally convincing, rich in mirth, playing fluency off against formality: the reader's possible impression of monotonous and ready-made verbosity was contradicted (except, of course, for the powerful adverse criticisms that emerge, to Tamburlaine's own cost, when he, too, hardens into a ranting automaton).

RW. The effect of the Bajazeth/Tamburlaine confrontation was repeated in Part Two when Tamburlaine encounters Bajazeth's son; again symmetry emphasised, rather than freezing, point and humour, as in Almeda's desperate plea to Tamburlaine on being offered a crown by Callapine: 'Good my lord, let me take it!' But obviously the greatest effect of the symmetry was to reinforce the large-scale issues of the play, especially Tamburlaine's facing death or challenging heaven. The placing of the *three* sons, *three* lieutenants, *three* doctors in the scene of Zenocrate's death was equally emphatic; and so was the entire stage picture whenever Tamburlaine appeared in his chariot, especially during the burning of the Koran.

JSC. Stage area, lighting, tableaux groupings – these all carried a powerful symbolic charge without hardening into a code which would unduly limit the play's implications. The stage circle shaded off beyond the rim of lights, which brightened suggestively from time to time, into *terra incognita*. A stain of blood at each horrific moment of conquest obliterated the circle of the known world – which is itself, as Tamburlaine declares, mapped by those who tread over it and conquer it. These visual hyperboles matched those of the text, and had a simple validity, in experience: each atrocity, each imaginative probing of the unknown, transforms the known.

RW. The lighting from the overhead grid caught and highlit characters at crucial moments: Zenocrate in her first scene; the dead Zenocrate and Theridamas to reinforce 'for she is dead'; the three lieutenants as they emphasised, in extremely formal repetitions, both Tamburlaine's approaching death and his still surviving greatness:

Earth droops, and says that hell in heaven is plac'd.

The more detailed effects derived equally from the text: the panels at the back provided walls to be scaled; the lieutenants exchanged their scimitars of Part One for huge muskets in Part Two, mounted on elaborate stands to shoot down the Governor of Babylon, who was suspended in mid-air between the back panels; a trap in the centre of the floor lowered to form a pit either to dispose of bodies or to provide the repeatedly required flames to burn Larissa, Olympia's family, and above all the Koran, ten great bundles of it. Here, especially, none of the stage-directions were shirked, and their implications were developed. Usumcasane's grinning relish of the book-burning had viciously barbaric Hitlerian overtones.

The scene posed, in the most striking way possible, the central dilemma of the play: how far is Tamburlaine actually defeated in Part Two, how far does he in fact decline? He was placed in his chariot above Usumcasane, who sat by the smoking pit; in contrast to Usumcasane's sadistic grinning, Tamburlaine grimly challenged Mahomet to react. A pause followed, as they all looked up to heaven, waiting; then Tamburlaine quietly concluded, 'Mahomet remains in hell'. But as the chariot was swung round and moved off, Tamburlaine was 'distemper'd suddenly'; the movement after the challenging stillness raised the possibility of Mahomet's revenge, reinforced by the subsequent build-up of Callapine – only to shatter that possibility by Tamburlaine's triumphant routing of him. *Maybe* Mahomet could hear, maybe not – this exactly catches Marlowe's equivocal tone.

JSC. Tamburlaine glanced up, when struck ill, as if to acknowledge Mahomet's intervention – and yet, I agree, the production kept faith with Marlowe's own refusal to allow us the solace of such a simple allegorising of the event. What is equivocal, in this play, is borne in upon us as the collision of powerful contraries – contrary values, colours, styles – with a Titanic figure at the centre who dares to attempt, and in part contrives to sustain within his own enterprise, the stress of these oppositions. The trap at the centre of the stage circle (the round earth's imagined centre) served a range of purposes whose very diversity concentrated our awareness of these contraries that mark the extreme limits of experience. Forming a raised plinth for Zenocrate in grief, it disposed of the dead Agydas, driven to suicide by a stare of displeasure; Zenocrate's death-bed was brought on to the trap straight after the descent of the dead King of Hungary; as the chariot backed offstage at the end, Tamburlaine went down into the pit that had seen so many of his atrocities,

dead but undefeated across her coffin – futile and magnificent. The collisions and transitions were at once extravagant and rudimentary: triumph and atrocity, crownings and dyings, sharpened in the one lens. The pressure this put us under cannot be adequately represented in terms of morality's approvals and disapprovals.

RW. Marlowe's ambiguity was reinforced by pervasive humour, from the very start. When the posturing Mycetes claimed that he might command his brother to be slain for telling him home truths, 'Meander, might I not?', Meander wryly answered 'Not for so small a fault, my sovereign lord', at once making the point and, by releasing the audience's laughter, allowing them to unwind for much of the first play, before making such demands on them later on. Again, Tamburlaine's radiant 'milk-white harts' speech to Zenocrate *appeared* to be sent up by an off-hand 'women must be flattered'; but the joke was used to emphasise the contrasted conviction of the next line, 'But this is she with whom I am in love'. The magnificent golden carpet laden with blindingly glaring jewels was both a marvellously concrete embodiment of

See how [Jove] rains down heaps of gold in showers
As if he meant to give my soldiers pay;[1]

yet the lightly humorous delivery was also part of Tamburlaine's winning over of Theridamas by his magnetic personality. Humour also helped to make clear points of Marlowe's which one can miss in reading. After the killing of Bajazeth's contributory kings, Tamburlaine's

[1] It is worth emphasising that such concrete embodiment is becoming part of the Hall/Bury house style for Elizabethan/Jacobean drama at the National: in their *Volpone*, Paul Scofield's lithe, majestic Volpone rapidly reversed green-covered walls to reveal beaten gold panels and dazzling treasures within, while a treasure chest at the front of the stage split open to embody, in the most concrete terms, Volpone's fortune: the spectacle literally dazzled the eye; it might, indeed, 'put out both the eyes of our St Mark'.

three lieutenants romped onstage with their crowns, obviously thinking they were now theirs for the wearing, only to be deflated by Tamburlaine's

> Why kingly fought i' faith.
> Deliver them into my treasury,

so that he could bestow them at the subsequent banquet, dropping a crown on to each head as the captains squatted on enormous red cushions, all part of the resplendent red-and-gold-covered stage at that point.

Humour was especially used to round the characterisation of the Turks, notably well done by Marlowe himself, and also by Hall and his Bajazeth (Denis Quilley) and Orcanes (Robert Eddison). The treatment of both strongly recalled how Peter Hall in his Stratford days would mine a Shakespeare text for humorous potential, not in order to cheapen character but on the contrary to emphasise its roundness and humanity. At his first grand entry, enthroned on high, with the world at his feet (see plate VIIIA), Bajazeth didn't need over-emphasis: 'You know our army is invincible' was genially urbane; he was hard put to remember the name at 'one Tamburlaine'; he offered a truce, condescendingly, 'because I hear he bears a valiant mind'; to his contributory kings' effusive praise, he could only conclude, 'All this is true', again genially. All this served to make his fall the greater, both humorous ('O Mahomet! O *sleepy* Mahomet!') and grim also, when Tamburlaine trod on him to ascend his throne.

JSC. With 'Ah fair Zabina, we have lost the field', we experienced yet another switch of sympathy – achieved, like much else, by a quite natural call on our resources of human feeling.

RW. Orcanes was given an even more rounded, expansive portrayal by Robert Eddison, again seconded by humour throughout his dealings with the Christians, a rumpled collection with rouged cheeks, the only characters *overtly* sent up, but that matches Marlowe's own emphasis, as Sigismund breaks the truce in order to 'take the victory our God hath given'. This extended Clifford Williams's treatment of Christian duplicity in his RSC *Jew of Malta*, which culminated in Ferneze's outrageous

> let due praise be given
> Neither to fate nor fortune, but to heaven,

so similar to Sigismund's view. Against the caricature Christians was Eddison's endlessly varied delivery, infinite distaste packed into the word 'Christian', and a hovering defiance (almost like Tamburlaine to Mahomet) in his emphatic 'Thou [*pause, then challengingly emphatic*] – Christ – that art esteemed omnipotent'. His mocking reminder to Sigismund that he wasn't always King of Hungary ('thyself, then County Palatine') was angrily picked up by Sigismund, doubly provoked by the rapid, ironic smile Orcanes suddenly switched on after his speech of defiance. Orcanes and the Turks found Sigismund's 'issue of a maid' extremely amusing; similarly the Christians reacted with embarrassed distaste to Orcanes's obeisance to Mahomet. This clash of political and cultural interests in a less than central scene was exactly the kind of point which Peter Hall used to bring out so superbly in his Stratford days; but the strength of the technique is that it is vastly entertaining and at the same time brings out meaning: Orcanes's superb hedging of his bets after victory ('Christ *or Mahomet* hath been my friend' or 'Yet in my thoughts shall Christ be honoured, / Not doing Mahomet an injury') absolutely reflects Marlowe's ambivalent attitude to heavenly influences in this play.

Elsewhere, too, the bold, uncompromising style of the production encouraged strong performances, often re-valuing apparently unimpressive characters. Brian Cox's Theridamas, for instance, was consistently developed as a voice of reason counteracting Tamburlaine's sweeping dismissal of the reasonable. Though echoing Tamburlaine's praise of kingship, he could add wryly, 'Nay, though I praise it, I can live without it'; though impressed by Tamburlaine, he could be daunted by his sheer nerve: 'A jest to charge on twenty thousand men!' At the 'feeding' of Bajazeth, he could voice the doubts of an ordinary man (thus helping the production underline the barbarous cruelty here): 'Dost thou think that Mahomet will suffer this?' and 'If his highness would let them be fed it would do them more good'. Marlowe, of course, is inconsistent on such matters, for soon Theridamas is enjoying the spectacle with the rest. Still, the strength of the portrayal gave Theridamas added authority as he quietly and directly brought home to Tamburlaine the unpalatable truth of Zenocrate's death:

> Ah good my lord, be patient. She is dead
> And all this raging cannot make her live. . . .
> Nothing prevails, for she is dead, my lord.

So interesting had Theridamas become that the death of Olympia *almost* came off; but not quite, for here Marlowe's over-ingenuity and the pale echo (?parody) of Tamburlaine/Zenocrate seem irretrievably contrived. Calyphas, a powerful, bearded figure, was no stereotype of weakness. 'My wisdom shall excuse my cowardice' was taken seriously, the policy of a rational being opposed to pointless, showy slaughter:

> I know sir what it is to kill a man:
> It works remorse of conscience in me.

Perhaps the anger he expressed here conflicts somewhat with the jokes about fighting a naked lady in a net of gold but it hung together surprisingly well, and there was no attempt to underplay Tamburlaine's bestiality in his savage cutting of Calyphas's throat.

This brings us to the production's view of Tamburlaine himself. Just before the opening,

Peter Hall said in an interview in *The Times* (20 September 1976):

Tamburlaine uses a morality play structure to be totally immoral. Indeed it's the most immoral play before Genet. It sets out to prove that there is no God, no Jove, no Mohammed, no Nirvana. Man, for all his aspirations, ends up with Hitlers, Mussolinis, Tamburlaines.

And yet the production itself suggested something less clear-cut, more varied and interesting, and in the process made Marlowe's ambivalence seem genuine ambivalence, not mere fumbling or confusion. Certainly the dare-devil gaiety of Part One darkened decisively in the savage scenes of Tamburlaine's feast with Bajazeth's torment and death, and Zabina's madness. Nothing was shirked here: terrifying percussion underscored the braining against the cage; Barbara Jefford's superlative Zabina went mad with harrowing, effortless conviction; 'Is there left no Mahomet, no God?' certainly rang out on this darkened, empty stage; Susan Fleetwood's Zenocrate developed the mood with 'another bloody spectacle' at her entry.

JSC. This entry itself enforced silently the awareness that Zenocrate is herself one of the victims of Tamburlaine's career: the production was punctuated by horrific entries of the maimed after battle, from the deep recesses of centre-stage, like travesties of triumphal arrivals. We were spared none of the consequences of our impulse to admire the conqueror. Zenocrate's betrothed staggered on with one arm lopped off to say of himself:

> And let Zenocrate's fair eyes behold
> That as for her thou bear'st these wretched arms
> Even so for her thou diest in these arms,
> Leaving thy blood for witness of thy love.

Zenocrate witnesses this; and the stage bears the brained corpses of Zabina and Bajazeth and a bloody dress from the murder of the Virgins: 'such are objects fit for Tamburlaine', as he triumphantly boasted, in a climactic moment of stress on our comprehension. We speak habitually of ambiguity, sometimes al-most as a point of doctrine: it was a truly painful feature of the play for us to reflect on as we applauded Tamburlaine – not just the play, but, embarrassingly, the hero – as he left this obscene stage in triumph at the end of Part One.

RW. Zenocrate's repetitions and variations of 'the Turk and his great emperess' showed how apparent artifice can in fact reveal intense emotion when delivered with such raw, committed power; and the whole sequence demonstrated the flexibility of the production, the bare stage, and ultimately of the play itself. The stage was at its barest as Albert Finney sat on the floor in the centre, thinking his way through the 'What is beauty' speech. Far from jumping arbitrarily from one excess (killing the virgins) to another (feeding Bajazeth), as it can seem to do when merely read, the speech seemed to lead logically to the conclusion of sparing the Soldan for the sake of 'sweet Zenocrate' ('That will we chiefly see unto, Theridamas') – to the marked amazement of the captains. Their reactions (and those of Tamburlaine's sons) were constantly used to mark developments in Tamburlaine, as when he ordered them to attack the heavens at Zenocrate's death, and when, in a shrewd piece of psychological interpretation, Tamburlaine's long lesson in fortification to his sons was interpreted as a desperate attempt to keep his mind off Zenocrate after her death. They were amazed too, when he first hit on the idea of the Kings drawing the chariot; this follows the savage killing of Calyphas, and the whole sequence – the astounding treatment of the Kings, the shooting of the Governor of Baby-lon, the burning of the Koran, the daring Mahomet out of heaven – these certainly built up the maniac element with full brute force.

JSC. Albert Finney's delivery of the speech

about military techniques – 'his fourme of exhortation and discipline to his three sons' – was an astounding feat of dramatic *invention*. I had thought of it as a diversion, awkwardly stitched in from Marlowe's recent reading of a (known) military text-book. It was spoken rapidly, as if learnt by heart, up to a moment of breathlessness, as a diversion of Tamburlaine's own attention from the fact of Zenocrate's death – and to the incredulous shock of his sons and followers. This incredulity ranked with other moments in the play, giving stage embodiment for the audience's feelings. Cos-roe, dying horribly on a full description of the process of dying, was kneeling as he heard, astounded, the bragging celebration of 'the thirst of reign and sweetness of a crown'. And here again, one effect opens the way to another, adjusting our feelings and complicating our efforts to judge: Cosroe's killers knelt in their turn to witness his death, in formal recognition of a momentous human event, for all their outlandishness ('the strangest men that ever nature made'), with Cosroe's curse leading directly into Tamburlaine's seizure of the crown.

RW. But all the time the grandeur of Tambur-laine remained; he never seemed *totally* a Hitler; at one point the chariot moved off, drawn by the kings, stressing the horror; but then it stopped with them in unemphatic sideways positions and Tamburlaine head on to the audience to make the most of the splen-did speech about riding in golden armour like the sun. Callapine was set up for a Malcolm-like victory, only to be utterly routed (onstage) *despite* his prayer to Mahomet and *despite* the possiblity that Mahomet appeared to be taking revenge on Tamburlaine by afflicting him with illness in the previous scene. To the end, the ambiguous quality remained: Tamburlaine looks forward to a 'higher throne' and to living 'in all your seeds *immortally*'. Albert Finney's tremendous achievement was his sheer staying power; he not only had the vital animal vigour for the part, but the ability to *keep us interested* to the end, and especially to keep Marlowe's, and Tamburlaine's, options open. He did nothing the easy way, skimped nothing in the part, and kept to the end that essential balance between aspiration –

> Come let us march against the powers of heaven
> And set black streamers in the firmament –

and mortality:

> Ah friends, what shall I do? I cannot stand.

So whatever the intention, the final impression given by Tamburlaine was of something subtler, more enigmatic, than a mere Hitler or Mussolini, making clear once and for all that the double nature of Marlowe's vision is deliberate and effective, not, as might have been feared, merely contradictory.

JSC. I can't recall a single arbitrary or capricious effect. Even the most direct raids on audience response were wholly in tune with the way in which the production set itself to redeem from grandiloquent oblivion the diverse and pressing human sense of the play. An engaging air of teasing connivance – 'look you I should play the orator', 'shall I prove a traitor' – landed *us* with the answering of the questions, in our comfortable seats. Praised by his mother, Celebinus raised a prizefighter's arm to the audience, to coerce hero-worshipping applause. The cast continuously registered the surprises and the scope of the play they were in. A comic variant of this was (brilliantly) Mycetes declaring 'I am the King', only to be suddenly aware of the meaning of that assertion. And all of this was framed, at the National, by a kind of 'scholarly' introduction to each Part – the title-page descriptions from the octavos declaring for us the play's gist, and the Prologue giving his words a corresponding decorum of utterance.

RW. Productions of this stunning impact are the best (indeed the only real) answer to the niggardly critics of Peter Hall's direction of the National. Achievements of this kind can't happen every day, of course; but this one, richly, exhaustingly rewarding, a reinstating in the theatre of a major play, seemed to me quite simply the most remarkable event we have seen in the British theatre since Peter Hall's RSC production of *The Wars of the Roses* in 1963/4.

© J. S. CUNNINGHAM and ROGER WARREN 1978

THE YEAR'S CONTRIBUTIONS TO
SHAKESPEARIAN STUDY

1. CRITICAL STUDIES

reviewed by R. F. HILL

An appropriate book with which to begin is one concerned with Shakespeare's origins, Emrys Jones's[1] challenging study of *Titus Andronicus* and the early histories, which provides rich pickings for critical discussion. It may claim originality in several respects, proposing that the significance of the mystery cycles for Shakespeare's dramaturgy is far greater than has hitherto been acknowledged, that Shakespeare's learning, product of Erasmian humanism, is still under-estimated, in particular his knowledge, via Latin translations, of Greek tragedy, and that formative influences may exert themselves not only through specific and readily identifiable debts, but also through broad situational features and even tone. Although presumptively likely, these positions are not easily susceptible of proof. The case for the possible influence of Euripides's *Hecuba* on *Titus Andronicus* rests upon circumstantial evidence and similarity of 'fundamental structure', but the similarity is so broad as to be inconclusive. Much the same may be said of the alleged influence of deep-seated memories of the passion sequence of the mystery cycles, particularly on episodes in the *Henry VI* plays, although here the detail is more persuasive. To speak more generally, while the creative imagination draws both arcanely and manifestly upon its store of experienced art, it also draws upon direct experience. The possibility of indebtedness, especially in 'grey' areas of broad similarity, is balanced by the possibility of originality.

We may even doubt specifics; Shakespeare did not need to learn from the *Phaedo* about the physiology of dying as evidenced in Falstaff's death, nor from Quintilian that actors can be moved to tears. Nonetheless, the book certainly opens up new perspectives. It abounds with knowledge and is written with persuasive advocacy; 'sources' and 'background' lose their woodenness and fuse with the plays to produce the sense of an organic cultural process.

The most impressive essays in a collection on the Sonnets edited by Hilton Landry[2] are those by Winifred Nowottny, Paul Ramsey, and Theodore Redpath. Winifred Nowottny[3] considers some of the last thirty sonnets addressed to the Friend, in particular the relationship between sonnet 'pairs'. Comparisons yield a rich commentary on the quality and status of individual sonnets, while the fine response to detail, especially metrical, is recorded with a precision and eloquence worthy of its subject. Paul Ramsey[4] investigates the problem of the apparent extra syllables in some lines of the Sonnets. He argues that they do not, in fact, exist and that the metrical foot is always disyllabic. The case looks strong but is incomplete without supporting

[1] *The Origins of Shakespeare* (Oxford University Press, 1977).
[2] *New Essays on Shakespeare's Sonnets* (AMS Press Inc., New York, 1976).
[3] 'Some Features of Form and Style in Sonnets 97–126', *ibid*.
[4] 'The Syllables of Shakespeare's Sonnets', *ibid*.

evidence from the plays. Theodore Redpath,[1] with a varied armoury of historical and statistical evidence, argues for the traditional practice of modernising the Quarto punctuation of the Sonnets, noting among other valid objections to the original punctuation that its supposed 'fluidity' (dangerously attractive to some modern critics) is seriously open to question. Suggestions are offered for the punctuation of modern editions but, that aside, the study has meat for critic and editor to chew upon. Rodney Poisson[2] shows how Shakespeare re-deploys the classical heritage of ideas about friendship to portray a relationship in which disparities of age and social standing provide poetically sustaining tensions. Martin Seymour-Smith,[3] while doubting the existence of a physical sexual relationship with the Friend, finds evidence of Shakespeare's wrestling with homosexual feelings. W. G. Ingram[4] effectively demonstrates the unifying function of 'tonal harmony', and examines some of the formal variations achieved within the English sonnet pattern. Hilton Landry[5] does an efficient demolition job on John Crowe Ransome's and Yvor Winter's wrong-headed censuring of the Sonnets, and Anton M. Pirkhofer[6] offers some reflections on their dramatic character. Finally, Marshall Lindsay[7] finds considerable limitations in French translations of the Sonnets; a bibliography of translations is appended.

There is little else on the non-dramatic poetry. William Bowman[8] offers a close critique of Sonnet 104 and several others to demonstrate his conviction that it is the greatest of those which confront the processes of time. Three pivotal sonnets (recently described by G. Melchiori as 'dramatic meditations') are seen by C. T. Neely[9] as attempts, only partially successful, to achieve impersonality and detachment from the conflicts of the sequence. Coppélia Kahn[10] examines the question of the rape in *Lucrece*; that Lucrece regards herself

as guilty must be explained by her conception of herself as a woman in a patriarchal society in which the importance of her husband's honour is paramount, and her moral responsibility irrelevant. R. S. White[11] examines the metaphoric connection between love and hunting in *Venus and Adonis* and several of the romantic comedies, concluding that 'the hunt gives a bracing effect to the romantic tendency to idealize love'. The case seems over-stated in relation to the evidence.

Twelve months is too long for a play was the wry thought of Berowne, and he might also have thought that a book was too long for the play in which he appears, let alone the two full-length critical studies which now jostle for our attention. However, William C. Carroll's[12] study of *Love's Labour's Lost* justifies itself in the liveliness of the writing and the sharp-eyed analysis of the play's tongues and teasings, even if the excitement over detail occasionally causes the reader to lose sight of the wood for the trees. The author is fascinated by the play's organic unity, and from his unfolding of all the component and counterpointed material central preoccupations

[1] 'The Punctuation of Shakespeare's Sonnets', *ibid.*
[2] 'Unequal Friendship: Shakespeare's Sonnets 18–126', *ibid.*
[3] 'Shakespeare's Sonnets 1–42: a Psychological Reading', *ibid.*
[4] 'The Shakespearean Quality', *ibid.*
[5] 'In Defense of Shakespeare's Sonnets', *ibid.*
[6] 'The Beauty of Truth: the Dramatic Character of Shakespeare's Sonnets', *ibid.*
[7] 'French Translations of the Sonnets', *ibid.*
[8] 'A Poem Turned in Process', *English Literary History*, XLIII (1976), 444–60.
[9] 'Detachment and Engagement in Shakespeare's Sonnets: 94, 116, and 129', *Publications of the Modern Language Association of America*, XCII (1977), 83–95.
[10] 'The Rape in Shakespeare's *Lucrece*', *Shakespeare Studies*, IX (1976), 45–72.
[11] ' "Now Mercy goes to Kill": Hunting in Shakespearean Comedy', *Durham University Journal*, XXXVIII (1976), 21–32.
[12] *The Great Feast of Language in 'Love's Labour's Lost'* (Princeton University Press, 1976).

gradually emerge. He sees the play as a debate on the right uses of rhetoric, poetry, and the imagination; what is rejected is not art but bad art. The final songs, like the ladies of the play, embody 'living art', and the play's burthen is not a rejection of gay spring for the reality of a wintry life, but the acceptance of both in a decorous union. Like Carroll's book that of Louis A. Montrose[1] started life as a dissertation, but wears its erudition less lightly, especially in a style encrusted with jargon to the point of obscurity, and some high-flying concepts about the significance of form. The book does not cohere well despite the drive underlying the analysis of poetic and ethical topics – to demonstrate the play's exposure of the lords' flight from reality. The author acknowledges in passing the mirthful aspects of the play but all sense of that is lost in his solemn reading which finds no assurance that marriages will follow the year's penances. The book has some interesting things to say about the relationship of *Love's Labour's Lost* to other of Shakespeare's plays, and chapter 4, 'Politics', is fresh, but it cannot be recommended as engaging reading. (The duplication of pages 15, 16 and 201, 202, does not help.) By contrast John Wilders,[2] starting from the debate feature of earlier dramatic tradition, administers a salutary check to simplistic moral readings of *Love's Labour's Lost*, although his views on its complexity and irresolution are open to some re-adjustment.

The other romantic comedies have not attracted much attention. J. Dennis Huston[3] argues that Petruchio makes a puppet out of Katherina, paradoxically to deliver her from the bondage of a former puppet-like existence; this action is supposed to be re-iterated in the way Shakespeare awakens the audience to perception after first manipulating its responses in arbitrary ways in the Induction. It is all very puzzling. With similar ingenuity Richard Horwich[4] discusses the dilemmas of Venice

and the riddles of Belmont, arguing that the ring trick is not a practical joke but a device by which Portia may exercise her free will by accepting Bassanio as her husband, a power of choice earlier denied by the will of a dead father. Maura Slattery Kuhn[5] teases out the various thematic significances of 'if' usage in *As You Like It*, but the essay's real interest lies in its first three pages which propose that when Rosalind re-enters with Hymen in the last scene she should still be dressed as a boy. Robert B. Bennett[6] argues that Jaques begins by affecting melancholy but that nature, working from both within and without him, is continually undercutting that pose, and he ends the play in a state of genuine intellectual melancholy.

Of the few articles on the 'dark comedies' the most interesting is that by I. Donaldson[7] on *All's Well That Ends Well*; various apparent endings in the course of the play's action are prefaces to new beginnings, and if the end of the play falls short of the full happiness characteristic of the comedies yet it is one from which new life may flow. Less cheerful is the view of John M. Love[8] who

[1] *'Curious-Knotted Garden': The Form, Themes, and Contexts of Shakespeare's 'Love's Labour's Lost'*, Salzburg Studies in English Literature (Universität Salzburg, 1977).

[2] 'The Unresolved Conflicts of *Love's Labour's Lost*', *Essays in Criticism*, XXVII (1977), 20–33.

[3] ' "To Make a Puppet": Play and Play-making in *The Taming of the Shrew*', *Shakespeare Studies*, IX (1976), 73–87.

[4] 'Riddle and Dilemma in *The Merchant of Venice*', *Studies in English Literature*, XVII (1977), 191–200.

[5] 'Much Virtue in *If*', *Shakespeare Quarterly*, XXVIII (1977), 40–50.

[6] 'The Reform of a Malcontent: Jaques and the Meaning of *As You Like It*', *Shakespeare Studies*, IX (1976), 183–204.

[7] '*All's Well That Ends Well*: Shakespeare's Play of Endings', *Essays in Criticism*, XXVII (1977), 34–55.

[8] ' "Though many of the rich are damn'd": Dark Comedy and Social Class in *All's Well that Ends Well*', *Texas Studies in Language and Literature*, XVIII (1977), 517–27.

locates the darkness of the play in class barriers; undeniably class is a factor but the strain here to magnify it suggests more a moral crusade than objective criticism. Ralph Berry[1] finds the dialectic of freedom-restraint in *Measure for Measure* expressed through a cluster of words which can be construed in higher and lower (sexual) meanings; his reading of repressed sexuality in the play has important consequences for one's conception of the Duke.

F. David Hoeniger's[2] tactfully selective survey of work on the romances since 1958 is written with a degree of astringency and temperate scepticism which would be appropriate to some of the material now under review. Not, however, to Barbara A. Mowatt's[3] book on the romances which has the uncommon virtues of firm argument, lucidity, and unpretentiousness. Registering the strangeness of these plays, despite their formal and thematic links with the rest of the canon, the author explores the dramaturgy of *Cymbeline*, *The Winter's Tale*, and *The Tempest* on the assumption that oddities are not flaws but part of Shakespeare's deliberate strategy. Three features of the formal pattern of these plays are analysed – the conflation of tragedy and comedy, of presentational and representational styles, of narrative and dramatic modes – the uniqueness argument being sustained by comparison with such features in Shakespeare's other plays. The romances emerge as 'open form drama', that is to say drama in which 'cause-and-effect patterns are broken, generic conventions abandoned ... and the dramatic illusion repeatedly broken through narrative intrusion, spectacle, and other sudden disturbances of the aesthetic distance'. The experience of the audience is one of bewilderment as expectations are unfulfilled, or fulfilled in unexpected ways, as it is varyingly confronted by the plays as illusion and as representations of reality. The plays are Shakespeare's attempt to say more than he had ever said about the mystery of the human story, its contrarieties of mood, of belief and disbelief.

Caesarea Abartis,[4] in yet another American graduate dissertation published in the Salzburg Studies in English Literature Series, sets out to demonstrate the relative merits of *Cymbeline* and *The Winter's Tale* as tragicomedies. An unnecessary survey of previous criticism is followed by a flat, lengthy discussion of Guarini and Beaumont and Fletcher which, for all it contributes to the two remaining chapters on the plays, could have been dispatched in a couple of pages. The scarcely original conclusion is that *The Winter's Tale* is successful tragicomedy because unified by parallel and contrasting actions in its two parts, whereas *Cymbeline* is unsuccessful because the genre-required reconciliation does not properly resolve the several moral questions raised by its several parts.

Phyllis Gorfain[5] explores the intricacies of riddling and ritual in *Pericles* in the context of folklore and anthropology; riddling 'as an expressive model of discontinuity and integration' is central to the play's meaning. *Cymbeline's* problems have exercised several critics. The question of its unity is taken up by Marjorie Garber[6] who posits a deep structure deriving from the myths of Pandora and Prometheus, while Roger Warren[7] opposes the

---

[1] 'Language and Structure in *Measure for Measure*', *University of Toronto Quarterly*, LXVI (1976–7), 147–61.

[2] 'Shakespeare's Romances since 1958: a Retrospect', *Shakespeare Survey 29* (Cambridge University Press, 1976), pp. 1–10.

[3] *The Dramaturgy of Shakespeare's Romances* (University of Georgia Press, 1976).

[4] *The Tragicomic Construction of 'Cymbeline' and 'The Winter's Tale'* (Universität Salzburg, 1977).

[5] 'Puzzle and Artifice: the Riddle as Metapoetry in *Pericles*', *Shakespeare Survey 29* (Cambridge University Press, 1976), pp. 11–20.

[6] '*Cymbeline* and the Languages of Myth', *Mosaic*, X (1977), 105–15.

[7] 'Theatrical Virtuosity and Poetic Complexity in *Cymbeline*', *Shakespeare Survey 29* (Cambridge University Press, 1976), pp. 41–9.

idea of a deliberate distancing of emotion and argues for a pin-pointing of moments of intense emotion, achieved by a setting off of theatrical virtuosity against language both simple and dense. Harry Zuger[1] seeks psychological consistency in the actions of Posthumus; the explanation of his omitting to take Imogen into exile with him – that 'acquiescence in the separation' helps him to rationalise his sexual failure – is startling. A less colourful account of Posthumus is offered by James E. Siemon[2] who shows how structural parallels enforce likenesses within the apparent contrast between Cloten and Posthumus, although the play finally affirms the triumph of the latter's better self. In a sensitive reading of the poetry and symbolism of *The Winter's Tale* L. C. Knights[3] demonstrates Leontes's final inclusion in the 'richness of positive living' associated with Perdita.

The fruitful interplay of stage and study is illustrated by two amateur directors of the romances. Richard Proudfoot's[4] essay, arising from the experience of directing *The Winter's Tale* for the English department of King's College, London University, reinforces with much new evidence of verbal connections the recognised links by parallel and contrast between the two halves of the play; points of value to both critic and director are made concerning doubling, disguise, and stage setting, in their thematic bearings. Nick Shrimpton,[5] in directing *The Tempest* for the English Department of Liverpool University, was forced to come to terms with the play's diversity of elements and apparent lack of suspense. Thence followed a fresh view of the play: Prospero experiences a real moral crisis whose resolution requires from him an acceptance of the world's disunity and contradictions.

Shakespearians of any degree of learning should welcome Peter Saccio's[6] readable account of the periods of history covered by Shakespeare's history plays. This is not another source study in the usual sense but history written by a literary scholar with the needs of Shakespearians in mind. The narrative interweaves three perspectives: the history according to the Tudor chroniclers, Shakespeare's version of that, and as understood by modern historians. It is a useful aid to memories which understandably stumble amidst the thorns and briars of the Plantagenet thicket; particularly welcome are the genealogical charts, the chronological chart, and index of persons. From information we move to areas of speculation. One gets the impression from David L. Frey's[7] book on the first tetralogy that Divine Providence is to be doubted because the innocent suffer and God never intervenes, although how we should know when He is intervening is not clear. Refusal to make concessions to the mystery of God's ways does not in itself invalidate the book's main thesis – another assault on the view that the early histories embody the Tudor myth of a Providential design. However, a good case is not strengthened by an extended comparison between *Henry VI*, parts two and three, and *The Contention* and *The True Tragedy* to 'show a consistency of purpose in emphasizing themes and issues in the Folio, which are not to be found developed in the quartos'. Such consistency is no evidence for Shakespeare's re-working of *The Contention* and *The True*

[1] 'Shakespeare's Posthumus and the Wager', *Shakespeare Jahrbuch*, CXII (1976), 133–42.

[2] 'Noble Virtue in *Cymbeline*', *Shakespeare Survey* 29 (Cambridge University Press, 1976), pp. 51–61.

[3] ' "Integration" in *The Winter's Tale*', *Sewanee Review*, LXXXIV (1976), 595–613.

[4] 'Verbal Reminiscence and the Two-part Structure of *The Winter's Tale*', *Shakespeare Survey* 29 (Cambridge University Press, 1976), pp. 67–78.

[5] 'Directing *The Tempest*', *Shakespeare Survey* 29 (Cambridge University Press, 1976), pp. 63–7.

[6] *Shakespeare's English Kings: History, Chronicle, and Drama* (Oxford University Press, 1977).

[7] *The First Tetralogy: Shakespeare's Scrutiny of the Tudor Myth* (Mouton, The Hague, 1976).

Tragedy for the argument could be used in reverse. Among its better things is the book's consideration of the problematic relationship of Divine Providence and Machiavellian ethics in these histories. There are numerous printing errors.

Of the articles on the history plays two stand aside from the rest. James A. Riddell[1] finds that in act II, scene iii of *1 Henry VI*, Talbot displays qualities of magnanimity which are to be contrasted with the values of the schemers in the following Temple Garden scene. Stephen Booth[2] examines the relationship of syntax to character in *Richard II*, arguing, in particular, that a moderation in Richard's syntax from the perverse to the more straightforward is a factor in the audience's response to him as between the first and second halves of the play. The remaining articles focus on various kinds of complexity of feeling and motivation. Donald M. Friedman[3] argues that John of Gaunt, in his deathbed panegyric to England, is not simply a disinterested spokesman for orthodoxy, but is outraged at the passing of the land from the hands of the feudal nobility; Bolingbroke has similar mixed motivations. Edward I. Berry[4] makes what would seem to be an unanswerable case against simplistic readings of the Falstaff rejection scene, whether sentimental or moralistic, and offers a balanced view of 'its conflicting feelings, its tensions, ambiguities, and clarifications'. Writing in a similar spirit, Moody E. Prior[5] locates disturbing complexities of response to the scene in a clash between the worlds of pure comedy and political power. Gordon Ross Smith[6] presents evidence for the diversity of Renaissance opinion in various spheres of thought, thence arguing that *Henry V* embodies contradictory and unresolved attitudes towards the King and his war. Many details of the play are shown to undercut the surface heroism and rectitude; the patriotism is genuine in the sense that patriotism is a smoke-screen to obscure self-serving purposes. To this may be related Karl P. Wentersdorf's[7] probing of the silence maintained by the King and the conspirators as to the true motive of the plot upon his life, the Earl of Cambridge's bid for the throne; Henry covers up with pious rhetoric while the conspirators avoid the question in the hope of mitigating the hardship that befell the families of traitors.

These depressing views lead naturally to the offerings on *Troilus and Cressida*. Grant L. Voth[8] finds Ulysses's stratagems motivated by pride and malice, not public spirit; far from providing any kind of moral centre for the play Ulysses serves his own 'particular will' as much as any of its characters. Zdeněk Stříbrný[9] examines the techniques of double time in *Troilus and Cressida*, the 'tension between the sudden pressures of the moment and the slow processes of history, or mythology', finding that the reality of the former persistently deflates the implied values of the latter. In a study of character correspondences and parallels Leo Rockas[10] contributes usefully to an awareness of the play's unity; the original pattern of mistress–cuckold–lover is repeated in Cressida–Troilus–Diomedes, and, homosexually, in

[1] 'Talbot and the Countess of Auvergne', *Shakespeare Quarterly*, XXVIII (1977), 51–7.

[2] 'Syntax as Rhetoric in *Richard II*', *Mosaic*, X (1977), 87–103.

[3] 'John of Gaunt and the Rhetoric of Frustration', *English Literary History*, XLIII (1976), 279–99.

[4] 'The Rejection Scene in *2 Henry IV*', *Studies in English Literature*, XVII (1977), 201–18.

[5] 'Comic Theory and the Rejection of Falstaff', *Shakespeare Studies*, IX (1976), 159–71.

[6] 'Shakespeare's *Henry V*: Another Part of the Critical Forest', *Journal of the History of Ideas*, XXXVII (1976), 3–26.

[7] 'The Conspiracy of Silence in *Henry V*', *Shakespeare Quarterly*, XXVII (1976), 264–87.

[8] 'Ulysses and "particular will" in *Troilus and Cressida*', *Shakespeare Jahrbuch*, CXIII (1977), 149–57.

[9] 'Time in *Troilus and Cressida*', *Shakespeare Jahrbuch*, CXII (1976), 105–21.

[10] ' "Lechery eats itself": *Troilus and Cressida*', *Ariel*, VIII (1977), 17–32.

Patroclus–Ajax–Achilles, thus confirming Thersites's vilifications.

The tragedies have been subjected to investigations daunting in weightiness and extent. The relevance of Richard Fly's[1] book is not restricted to the tragedies but it may be conveniently considered here. He has undertaken a difficult enterprise and has not avoided perplexing the reader. His concern is with problems of mediation in two senses; the medium of poetic drama through which Shakespeare conveys his vision, and the substance of that vision, the intractable nature of that which mediates all human communication. He studies *Romeo and Juliet*, *Troilus and Cressida*, *Measure for Measure*, *King Lear*, and *Timon of Athens*, which he finds significantly embody problems of human mediation, and also chart Shakespeare's progress in mastering his mediating form. These two spheres appear to overlap, as if problems of mediation between Shakespeare's characters were also a projection of his sense of the recalcitrance of his medium. Fly's complex sense of his subject can puzzle. In particular instances of flawed mediation are we to believe that Shakespeare is in control, successfully portraying human phenomena, or are they the result of his failure to master his medium, or is Shakespeare, conscious of inadequacies in human communication, mirroring this in the way that he handles his medium? For all that, he sets problems of form in *Troilus*, *Measure*, and *Timon* in perspectives that merit attention, and the study of *Lear* finely demonstrates Shakespeare's medium to be 'fully responsive to his vision of a tragic human insufficiency'.

Harold Skulsky's[2] study (mainly a refashioning of already published materials) of *Hamlet*, *Measure for Measure*, *King Lear*, demands concentration and mental agility if one is to follow the subtle reasonings of philosopher, theologian, and lawyer that he brings to bear on the plays. He locates their power in what he calls 'speculative suspense', which challenges the moral premises on which we base our concern for a character, and our faith that other minds are ultimately accessible. With a battery of classical and contemporary authorities the author analyses the characters' contradictions, insufficiencies, and ignorance, in motive and action. Shakespeare's purpose is not to blame them, nor to leave the audience with uncertain and divided responses, but to lead it to a fuller understanding of moral questions. The theatrical dimension, the way in which the dramatic vehicle actually mediates this suspense, is largely ignored. Furthermore, it is hard to believe that Shakespeare's audience was equipped to respond to the niceties that the author distinguishes with the aid of his authorities, and even harder with respect to a modern audience.

We saw in Emrys Jones's book that the religious mines are still not exhausted, and there are two more books to prove it. Edmund Creeth[3] starts with two premises: that in studying the influence of religious drama we should not necessarily suppose evolution from recently preceding forms, and that it is the design of the hero's experience, rather than the allegorical form, which is the significant factor in English morality plays. Thus armed, he traces correspondences in design between the earliest extant English moralities, *The Castell of Perseverance*, *Wisdom Who is Christ*, *The Pride of Life*, and *Macbeth*, *Othello*, *King Lear*, respectively. Influence of intervening Tudor moralities is not excluded but, so far as concerns the 'Temptation' and 'Coming of Death' types of plot, these three Shakespearian tragedies are said to have their closest affinity with the early moralities, and in this stand

[1] *Shakespeare's Mediated World* (University of Massachusetts Press, 1976).

[2] *Spirits Finely Touched* (University of Georgia Press, 1976).

[3] *Mankynde in Shakespeare* (University of Georgia Press, 1976).

alone in the drama of Shakespeare's age, not excluding *Dr Faustus*. Interesting things are said about Shakespeare's success in adapting the temptation plot to tragedy, but it requires the author's own faith to see so much correspondence between the sets of plays considered. The thesis also requires a conjecture to be hardened into a certainty – that Shakespeare saw performances of these plays, or versions of them now lost. Robert G. Hunter,[1] having in a previous book considered religious influence on the comedies, now turns his attention to the tragedies. An important source of the power of Shakespeare's Christian tragedies, it is argued, is their various embodiment of free will and predestination in the Providential design for man – a matter of terror and mystery. The Shakespearian analysis is preceded by an examination of the French miracle play, *Robert le Dyable*, *The Conflict of Conscience*, and *Dr Faustus*, dramatisations of the central theological positions, the chapter on *Dr Faustus* forcibly locating its terror in the unresolved interplay of Augustinian and Calvinist beliefs. However, the move to Shakespeare is a move from bold outline to chiaroscuro. Not that Hunter is guilty of oversimplification in his analyses, but the very complexity through which he picks his way blurs the issues, and inclines one to question the significance for the plays' tragic power of theological issues so closely pressed, although admittedly it might have been different for a contemporary audience. Clearly the mystery of Divine dispensation is an important factor in Shakespeare's tragic pattern, but what seems doubtful is the value of giving that mystery theological habitation and name. It may well be that Richard III and Claudius are Calvinist reprobates and that Hamlet is elect, but such recognition, if it be valid, will remain on the edge of one's consciousness, brought to the plays' mysteries rather than arising insistently from them. None the less, there are good points

of detail, and the broad characterisation of each tragedy in terms of its particular religious focus makes helpful distinctions. The chapter on *King Lear* is especially impressive.

Digging deeper still, P. J. Aldus[2] rejects a literal reading of *Hamlet* in favour of the hypothesis that it should be read as a literary myth. Others have discovered mythic matter embedded in the play as something below the literal meaning, but Aldus argues that the literal surface is at all points metaphorical, so that his analysis minutely scrutinises verbal and structural detail. Hamlet, it appears, is a mythic representative of Man, and his 'character' is unfolded in multiple parallels and correspondences. Time itself is timeless, and the sequential ordering of events in the play is less important than their reiteration of deep-seated crises and impulses, which can be traced back into mythology and pre-history; characters are not separable identities but expressions of aspects of Hamlet's psyche. This mythic man is driven less by revenge than by sexual obsession which both desires and abhors; we are to believe not only that Hamlet violated Ophelia and desired his mother, but that the Ghost (as an extension of Hamlet) was stained with the sin of lust towards Gertrude. The mouse-trap is directed at Gertrude not Claudius. *Hamlet*, thus seen, becomes Protean in elusiveness like the book itself. Shakespeare is unable to avoid a pun, and his knowledge of classical mythology is, by implication, recondite. What the author says of the response of a rational age to mythic-ritual performances might be applied to his book: 'At best one may expect a mixed response, partial enigma for most experiencers, total enigma for far more, indeed "caviary to the general".'

[1] *Shakespeare and the Mystery of God's Judgements* (University of Georgia Press, 1976).
[2] *Mousetrap: Structure and Meaning in 'Hamlet'* (University of Toronto Press, 1977).

Maurice Charney[1] perceives a distinct middle movement in *Hamlet*, designed to bring out powerfully the bloodiness and unnaturalness of Hamlet the revenger, followed by a third movement in which the character of revenge changes to a matter of readiness. The endeavour to elicit the more primitive sense which would have struck the play's first audiences and to reason away ambiguities makes a refreshing change, but it ignores the first half of the play. Geoffrey Hughes[2] believes that the corruption of moral sensibility which he finds in Hamlet's response to the Player's speech, his encounter with Fortinbras, and his contrivance of the deaths of Rosencrantz and Guildenstern, stems from the Ghost (status undefined), and ends in the damnation of that Ghost's son. W. L. Godshalk[3] offers another version of *Hamlet* as the tragedy of a man who knows not 'seems', cannot penetrate the tragic mask of seeming, and finds truth only in death. With something less than novelty and critical rigour V. Chatterjee[4] would persuade us that Hamlet's tragedy is that he talks too much and exhausts his energy in the process. H. R. Coursen,[5] briefly but convincingly, refutes M. Stevens's argument (*Shakespeare Quarterly*, Summer 1975) that Hamlet had pre-arranged his meeting with the pirates.

Two more publications in the Salzburg Studies in English Literature reinforce one's doubts about this series. Jagodish Purkayastha,[6] writing on *Hamlet* and *King Lear*, makes no concessions to the reader, and almost none to the usual conventions. His book has no footnotes, no index, and refers to only one literary critic, G. Wilson Knight. It consists of two long essays, and the author's monologue is unbroken by sub-divisions or, in the *Lear* section, any observable marshalling of ideas into graspable units for the benefit of the reader. As for content, the view that Hamlet's revenge purpose is blunted by a persistent association in his mind of Claudius and Gertrude is hardly new. The *Lear* section has more to offer. The controlling idea is of the 'convulsive' nature of experience and expression that the play offers, something so strong that 'the complete release of painful emotions by the audience after the last convulsion remains an impossibility'. The ethico-psychological analysis is deeply felt, but lacking in discipline. Mathilda M. Hills[7] sees a correlation between the spiritual journey of King Lear and his physical journeyings across his kingdom. Lear's journey is a painful one, and that of the reader of this book is somewhat wearying, conducted as he is on a relentless progress of textual commentary encompassing all manner of stylistic and allusive points. Occasional interesting passages and perceptions tend to be swamped in the tide of detail, over-interpretation, and learning not convincingly relevant to the matter in hand. Of the three articles on *King Lear* that of James R. Siemon[8] is the most stimulating, although not easy to assimilate. He suggests a new direction in charting the play's depths, finding a powerful iconoclasm in the way in which the play's actions subvert the confined meanings which emblematic schemata would impose. Jacqueline

[1] 'The "Now could I drink hot blood" Soliloquy and the Middle of *Hamlet*', *Mosaic*, x (1977), 77–86.
[2] 'The Tragedy of the Revenger's Loss of Conscience: a Study of *Hamlet*', *English Studies*, LVII (1976), 395–409.
[3] 'Hamlet's Dream of Innocence', *Shakespeare Studies*, IX (1976), 221–32.
[4] 'The Meaning of *Hamlet*: an Approach through Language', *Praci-Bhasha-Vijan Indian Journal of Linguistics*, II (1975), 118–33.
[5] 'Hamlet and the Pirates Reconsidered', *English Language Notes*, XIV (1976), 20.
[6] *The Tragic Vision of Life in 'Hamlet' and 'King Lear'* (Universität Salzburg, 1977).
[7] *Time, Space, and Structure in 'King Lear'* (Universität Salzburg, 1976).
[8] '"Turn our impressed lances in our eyes": Iconoclasm in *King Lear*', *Literature and Iconoclasm: Shakespeare* (State University of New York at Buffalo, 1976), pp. 4–17.

E. M. Latham[1] analyses the function of rhetoric and wordplay in Goneril and Regan's professions of love for Lear in revealing the underlying truth of their characters and values. Duncan S. Harris[2] writes on the interweaving of four different kinds of resolution which comprise the ending of *King Lear*.

The two articles on *Othello* propound novel views. S. N. Gardner[3] draws a picture of the real Desdemona (as distinct from the idealisations of Othello and Cassio), a woman who gradually loses her energy and courage, and ends feeling in her heart that she had made a mistake in marrying Othello. Marjorie Pryse[4] would have us believe, among other interesting readings, that *the* problem of *Othello* is the need of the major characters for an admiring audience; that Othello was unable to consummate his marriage (twice interrupted by Iago); that Desdemona's dying refusal to admit Othello her murderer results from her determination not to give him credit for being a man of action.

Each of the classical tragedies has received some attention. Albert H. Tricomi[5] studies the two main image clusters in *Titus Andronicus*, animal imagery and mutilated plant imagery, and finds that their deployment to express the clash between barbarism and civilisation is evidence of the play's metaphoric and imaginative integrity. Marvin L. Vawter[6] locates the destructive force in *Julius Caesar* in Brutus's stoicism, which has 'misconstrued', or re-shaped everyone he has touched into an imitation of himself, 'clean from the purpose' for which human beings were created. Poor Brutus. Duncan S. Harris[7] points to the tension between 'telling' and 'showing' resulting in a conflict of response to Antony and Cleopatra, a conflict which is resolved in the play's last scene where both 'telling' and 'showing' affirm the value of the lovers' lives and deaths. As with many books which start life as a dissertation Leigh Holt's[8] study of *Coriolanus*

(Salzburg Studies in English) offers the obligatory initial survey of criticism and variety of viewpoint. That apart, the book is generally long-winded, and the sections on the political scene under Elizabeth and James, although effective in opening up questions of power as understood by Shakespeare and his audience, help little towards the goal of the book which is an affirmation of the tragic status of Coriolanus. That, it is said, rests not on the rightness of his viewpoint but on the intensity of his dedication to his beliefs, an idealism which excites respect even while we recognise compromise and pragmatism as the inevitable political norms. Essentially we are being offered another version of the integrity defence.

A helpful contribution to the understanding of *Timon of Athens* is provided by Lewis Walker[9] who examines the play in the light of contemporary ideas about Fortune, especially as whore and flatterer; in this context Timon is seen as decisively implicated in the guilt of his false friends. William W. E. Slights[10] explains the formal characteristics of *Timon of Athens* as a deliberate blending of masque,

[1] 'Unconscious Self-Revelation by Goneril and Regan', *Shakespeare Jahrbuch*, CXIII (1977), 164–7.

[2] 'The End of *Lear* and a Shape for Shakespearean Tragedy', *Shakespeare Studies*, IX (1976), 253–67.

[3] 'Shakespeare's Desdemona', *Shakespeare Studies*, IX (1976), 233–52.

[4] 'Lust for Audience: An Interpretation of *Othello*', *English Literary History*, XLIII (1976), 461–78.

[5] 'The Mutilated Garden in *Titus Andronicus*', *Shakespeare Studies*, IX (1976), 89–105.

[6] '"After Their Fashion": Cicero and Brutus in *Julius Caesar*', *Shakespeare Studies*, IX (1976), 205–19.

[7] '"Again for Cydnus": The Dramaturgical Resolution in *Antony and Cleopatra*', *Studies in English Literature*, XVII (1977), 219–31.

[8] *From Man to Dragon: a Study of Shakespeare's 'Coriolanus'* (Universität Salzburg, 1976).

[9] 'Fortune and Friendship in *Timon of Athens*', *Texas Studies in Language and Literature*, XVIII (1977), 577–600.

[10] '*Genera Mixta* and *Timon of Athens*', *Studies in Philology*, LXXIV (1977), 39–62.

anti-masque, satire, and tragedy, in order to widen the range of effects available to current stage satire.

G. Wilson Knight's[1] latest book provides a transition from the tragedies to Shakespeare in the modern theatre. It is an expanded account of lecture-recitals on the tragic heroes, performed over several years at many academic centres in England, Canada, and the United States. As the recitals developed, dramatic performance became more prominent, some use being made of costume, and greater emphasis was placed on *Timon of Athens*; the book includes the text of the *Timon* part of the recital. Two interrelated themes are developed: that the tragic hero's story is a rise to a triumph beyond defeat and ethical considerations, a rise registered in the quality of his poetry; that the realisation of its power by the actor demands 'poetic acting', to be understood as including the expressive power of the whole body. The accumulated wisdom of much of a long lifetime devoted to acting and production, together with the author's almost messianic conviction about his themes, give the book strength. However, he is inclined to write as one offering more novelty than is the case, although he might counter that if there is familiarity the debt is to him. Alexander Leggatt[2] reminds the reader of Shakespeare of the importance of the theatrical dimension of the plays, supporting his arguments with a judicious discussion of insights afforded by specifics of particular productions. Taking some clues and support from T. S. Eliot, Terence Hawkes[3] writes on 'the oral, non-discursive, *performed* dimensions of the play that lie beyond the words, animate, and ultimately transcend them'. In a brief and difficult essay Michael Goldman[4] insists yet more radically on the primacy of the theatre experience, specifically the primacy of the actor. Examining the different kinds of demands made on actors by some Shakespearian tragic roles he argues

that 'the very problems posed by the need to achieve the qualities demanded by the role become part of the meaning of the play'. Henning Krabbe[5] introduces an account by the nineteenth-century Danish actress, Johanne Luise Heiberg, of her conception of the role of Lady Macbeth the chief interest of which is the insistence that she should be played as youthful, fired by ambition, but not hardened in sin.

Shakespeare Quarterly, XXVIII (Spring 1977) is devoted to Shakespeare in the modern theatre. In addition to reviews of recent festivals and productions on both sides of the Atlantic there are several articles: Morris Carnovsky[6] discusses his playing of the role of Lear; John Duffy[7] writes about the music he composed for John Houseman's 1967 production of *Macbeth*; G. Harold Metz[8] surveys the fortunes of *Titus Andronicus* in the theatre and, reflecting on the brilliant productions of Peter Brook and Joseph Papp, and the play's popularity during the last twenty-five years, wryly remarks that it must have 'something to say to the contemporary world'; Homer Swander[9] traces the evolution of the Oregon Shakespeare Festival and pays tribute to its founder and presiding genius, Angus Browner. Also included is a genial discussion between

[1] *Shakespeare's Dramatic Challenge* (Croom Helm, London; Barnes and Noble Books, New York, 1977).
[2] 'The Extra Dimension: Shakespeare in Performance', *Mosaic*, x (1977), 37–49.
[3] '"That Shakespeherian Rag"', *Essays and Studies*, xxx (1977), 22–38.
[4] 'Acting Values and Shakespearean Meaning: Some Suggestions', *Mosaic*, x (1977), 51–8.
[5] 'A Danish Actress and her Conception of the Part of Lady Macbeth', *Shakespeare Survey 29* (Cambridge University Press, 1976), pp. 145–9.
[6] 'The Eye of the Storm: on Playing King Lear', pp. 144–50.
[7] 'Brakedrums and Fanfares: Music for a Modern *Macbeth*', pp. 151–3.
[8] 'Stage History of *Titus Andronicus*', pp. 154–69.
[9] 'Shakespearean Gold in the Oregon Hills', pp. 170–83.

J. C. Trewin and Robert Speaight[1] in which they reminisce informatively over the major figures and events of the Shakespeare scene during this century. Against the general confidence of the foregoing Daniel Seltzer[2] strikes a discordant note in a fairly inclusive diatribe against the state of Shakespearian production on both sides of the Atlantic; he locates the evil in the very nature of large establishment companies and festival organisations which inevitably turn art into merchandise; salvation is to be found in the true ensemble work of smaller productions and experimental workshop theatres.

There remains a large bag of assorted contributions. Chief among them is Harry Levin's[3] gathering of already published papers, impressive in range though variable in quality. He is adept at the panoramic view, magisterially surveying Shakespeare's critical fortunes down the centuries, and tracing the parabolic curve of English drama from Elizabeth's accession to the closing of the theatres. Critically more rewarding are the essays of narrower focus (although always reaching out to historical and comparative contexts), such as those on Gloucester's suicide and the magician–manipulator roles of Prospero and Jonson's Subtle. Individual plays discussed include *Romeo and Juliet*, *Twelfth Night*, *Othello*, and *Timon of Athens*, and there is an entertaining piece on Shakespeare's ways with names. Marvin Spevack[4] examines some of the critical implications of spin-off data from the tapes of his *Concordance*. He notes, for example, that Shakespeare's vocabulary shows a regular and orderly increase throughout his career, and that likewise there is a regular increase in words which occur in one work and never again, yet these phenomena cannot be explained by reference to other dramatic features. He does not expect to pierce the mystery of Shakespeare's language, but other examples provided demonstrate the importance for critical analysis of a mutually qualifying interaction of close and panoramic

scrutiny. Marjorie Garber[5] argues that in Shakespeare's plays transitions from childhood to adulthood, to the maturity of sexual relationship and marriage, necessitate the breaking of other human bonds, the refusal to do so having disastrous consequences; her neat thesis involves some questionable readings. Francis Fergusson[6] posits a kinship between Dante and Shakespeare, deriving from their shared Classical–Christian heritage, and a mode of writing which is realistic, but allegorical in the sense of including moral and religious levels of meaning. A comparison is made of analogous themes and situations from the *Divine Comedy* and Shakespeare's plays, especially stressing faith in love and faith in the right king as controlling beliefs. The tracing of supposedly shared preoccupations does not always account for the full evidence of Shakespeare's text. The book's contribution to the understanding of Shakespeare's plays may be thought to be fitful. R. Kirkpatrick[7] defines differences in the dramatic quality exhibited in the styles of Dante and Shakespeare, illustrating from *Othello* its specifically theatrical character in Shakespeare's writing.

Moving from comparison to translation brings us a number of items for comment. Olga Akhmanova and Velta Zadornova[8] consider the translating of Shakespeare into

[1] 'Talking about Shakespeareans', pp. 133–43.
[2] 'Acting Shakespeare Now', *Mosaic*, x (1977), 59–75.
[3] *Shakespeare and the Revolution of the Times* (Oxford University Press, 1976).
[4] 'Shakespeare Microscopic and Panoramic', *Mosaic*, x (1977), 117–27.
[5] 'Coming of Age in Shakespeare', *The Yale Review*, LXVI (1977), 517–33.
[6] *Trope and Allegory: Themes Common to Dante and Shakespeare* (University of Georgia Press, 1977).
[7] 'On the Treatment of Tragic Themes in Dante and Shakespeare', *Modern Language Review*, LXXVII (1977), 575–84.
[8] 'The Russian Translations of "To be or not to be" and "The quality of mercy is not strained"', *Shakespeare Jahrbuch*, CXII (1976), 150–60.

Russian, arguing that what is required is not further independent efforts by poets but translations based upon exhaustive philological research, and upon elements from past versions which will survive philological scrutiny. Whatever the merits of this ideal it seems inapplicable for translation into Estonian. Jaak Rähesoo's[1] discussion of the first complete Shakespeare edition in Estonian (published 1959–75, in seven volumes) notes the comparative paucity of earlier translations, and the complicating factor that Estonian has only in this century become a cultivated literary language. This edition is an important pioneer work, providing in translation and a very full critical apparatus a solid basis for future studies. Anna Kay France[2] discusses Boris Pasternak's translation of *Othello*, showing how modifications of the lines of Iago and Othello seem to stem from the translator-poet's own imaginative predispositions. Balz Engler's[3] edition of *Othello* is part of a dual-language series of Shakespeare's plays under the general editorship of Werner Habicht, Ernst Leisi and Rudolf Stamm. The text, equipped with a literal prose translation into German on the opposite page and generous annotation of linguistic, textual, and other difficulties, should be found extremely helpful by German university students of Shakespeare. The introduction gives a brief but useful account of sources, date, and text, as well as offering some critical comments. The translation of *Coriolanus* into modern Spanish prose by José B. Acuña[4] is, in general, accurate, sensible, and very sensitive. There are, however, some mistakes and omissions; for example, some nine lines are missing from act I, scene i, and some fourteen lines from act I, scene v. The text has not been supplied with introduction, notes or bibliography.

It would appear from the following group of items that Marxist criticism of Shakespeare is not yet toeing one line. John Scott Colley[5] offers a brief reading of *Richard II* as illustra-tive of the possibilities of the Marxist approach, the special virtue of which is said to be its union of critical and historical perspectives. Anne Paolucci[6] examines the springs and limitations of Marx's critical thinking, especially in relation to *Timon of Athens*, concluding that the best Marxist critics of recent years have tended 'to saturate their criticism with a mood of... an existential sort of social despair, that envisions no Marxist heavenly denouement on earth'. The Marxist character of a group of papers given at the Shakespeare festival held in Dresden in April 1975, and printed in *Shakespeare Jahrbuch*, CXII (1976), is all too plain. Shakespeare is seen as a conscious mediator of social change, placed in time between the German peasant revolts and the 'bourgeois English revolution', in various ways sowing doubts about the system of his age. Those interested further in Marxist approaches to Shakespeare should consult *Science & Society* (Spring 1977) which prints a number of contributions to a seminar held at the International Shakespeare Association Conference in Washington D.C., April 1976. The chairman, Robert Weimann, argues for the virtues of Marxist methodology; Margot Heinemann, Thomas Metscher, and Annette Rubinstein, examine various social and international aspects of the plays. Michael Hamburger argues that critics have under-estimated the importance of Shakespeare's proximity to popular dramatic

[1] 'The First Complete Shakespeare Edition in Estonian: Background and Perspectives', *Shakespeare Jahrbuch*, CXIII (1977), 178–84.

[2] 'Iago and Othello in Boris Pasternak's Translation', *Shakespeare Quarterly*, XXVIII (1977), 73–84.

[3] *William Shakespeare, Othello* (Francke Verlag, Munich, 1976).

[4] *La tragedia de Coriolano* (Universidad de Costa Rica, 1973).

[5] 'The Economics of *Richard II*?', *Shakespeare Jahrbuch*, CXIII (1977), 158–63.

[6] 'Marx, Money, and Shakespeare: The Hegelian Core in Marxist Shakespeare-Criticism', *Mosaic*, X (1977), 139–56.

expression – the *gestic* element in his plays, and Bruce Erlich writes on the social function of the theatre as exemplified by *The Tempest*.

There is a little miscellany of other critical approach pieces. Qualifying the traditional view that Hazlitt's Shakespeare criticism is limited by its character preoccupations, John Kinnaird[1] argues that, in Hazlitt's essays on the four major tragedies at least, he does in certain respects concern himself with design, and that his 'psychological interests may be seen as subsumed in a larger study of dramatic *imagination* – the supreme "faculty" of Shakespeare's genius, that which shapes the unity of a play'. Stanley Wells[2] sensibly lets Max Beerbohm do much of the talking in his account of the Shakespearian material contained in Max's theatre criticism for *The Saturday Review*; despite some odd prejudices about Shakespeare, and the limited horizons of his own day, he has something to teach the modern critic about honesty and directness of response. Richard Levin[3] pillories that kind of historical criticism which, by a crude imposition from without of so-called accepted ideas of the time, distorts rather than illuminates the plays. Carole McKewin[4] writes sympathetically of the value of the new feminist criticism of Shakespeare's women when free of its real or imagined air of polemic, even though its Britomart, Juliet Dusinberre, is rather more fallible than that lady.

Several aids to study complete the critical scene. Two more plays have been added to the Casebook series, *Troilus and Cressida*, edited by Priscilla Martin,[5] and *Coriolanus*, edited by B. A. Brockman.[6] Both editors bring together a representative range of viewpoints, and the omission of a detailed source essay from the *Troilus and Cressida* volume is partially covered by the introduction. The net is cast wide if one takes into account footnote references and the bibliography, although the latter is very select in both volumes. The *Coriolanus* volume is more successful in placing the play in the canon.

Although critics today may rightly see no virtue in lumping *Troilus and Cressida* with the so-called problem plays, the refusal of Priscilla Martin even to mention the term – let alone the critical tradition – in her introduction is odd; so also the omission of any general books on the problem plays from her bibliography. In her volume there are some slight discrepancies between the page numbering of the contents list and that of the text. A useful aid has been provided by David M. Zesmer;[7] it is intended to serve the needs of students, but teachers will find the extensive bibliographical footnotes to each chapter a convenient source of information. The guide comprises introductory chapters on topics such as theatre, language, text, chronology, and sources, followed by chapters on the non-dramatic poetry and the plays in appropriate groupings. The critical discussion is of a preliminary kind, outlining problems and viewpoints, and there is nothing wrong with that provided the student pursues matters further with the aid of the footnotes. Questionable generalisations and regretted omissions are inevitable with a work of this kind, but laborious sifting and condensation have produced much information and sensible guidance in a little space. Jeanne Addison Roberts,[8] Norman Sanders,[9] and

[1] 'Hazlitt and the "Design" of Shakespearean Tragedy: a "Character Critic" Revisited', *Shakespeare Quarterly*, XXVIII (1977), 22–39.

[2] 'Shakespeare in Max Beerbohm's Theatre Criticism', *Shakespeare Survey 29* (Cambridge University Press, 1976), pp. 133–44.

[3] 'Shakespeare or the Ideas of His Time', *Mosaic*, X (1977), 129–37.

[4] 'Shakespeare Liberata: Shakespeare, the Nature of Women, and the New Feminist Criticism', *Mosaic*, X (1977), 157–64.

[5] Macmillan, 1976.   [6] Macmillan, 1977.

[7] *Guide to Shakespeare* (Barnes and Noble Books, New York, 1976).

[8] 'American Criticism of Shakespeare's Comedies', *Shakespeare Studies*, IX (1976), 1–10.

[9] 'American Criticism of Shakespeare's History Plays', *Shakespeare Studies*, IX (1976), 11–23.

Kenneth Muir[1] have provided readable and useful surveys of American criticism of Shakespeare; Jeanne Roberts ends by noting territories for further exploration, Norman Sanders with a fairly cheerful acceptance of much more criticism to come, and Kenneth Muir by ruefully wishing for more 'wise passiveness' among critics of Shakespeare.

[1] 'American Criticism of Shakespeare's Tragedies', *Shakespeare Studies*, IX (1976), 25–30.

© R. F. HILL 1978

2. SHAKESPEARE'S LIFE, TIMES, AND STAGE

reviewed by E. D. PENDRY

Samuel Schoenbaum's *William Shakespeare: A Documentary Life* (Oxford, 1975) has already won high praise for its elegance and scholarship. Now, in *William Shakespeare: A Compact Documentary Life*[1] we are given the substance of the lavish parent volume in a more portable form and at a lower, if hardly popular, price. But it would be a mistake to regard it as a lesser and merely derivative work. Schoenbaum has taken the opportunity to revise and correct, and even to augment, what he has written before. As he foreshadowed in an article in *The Times Literary Supplement*,[2] he is now able, for instance, to give further details of William Bott, a former owner of New Place who was declared by his son-in-law to have murdered his own daughter with ratsbane in 1563; this makes of New Place a remarkably unsavoury locality, since the very next owner, William Underhill, was to be murdered by his son in 1597. A letter of Schoenbaum's to *The Times Literary Supplement*[3] contains corrections both to his article and to the *Compact Life* itself. Amongst the same letters Eric McLellan comments on the vexed legal question of the widow's portion. The dustjacket of the *Compact Life* carries a miniature portrait of Shakespeare by George Vertue (1684–1756); in *The Shakespeare Quarterly*[4] Schoenbaum remarks that the water-colour, though of Shakespeare in profile, is evidently after the Chandos painting.

One of Shakespeare's contemporaries, John Manningham, was a law-student when he saw *Twelfth Night* performed in the Great Hall of the Middle Temple on 2 February 1602, and when he heard gossip about Shakespeare outwitting Burbage for the favours of a city woman after a performance of *Richard III*. These titbits he jotted down in his so-called diary, which has come out in a new edition by Robert Parker Sorlien.[5] It is very handy for research to have the entire manuscript made available and furnished, as it is, with a thorough scholarly apparatus. In addition to the somewhat meagre Shakespeare material, there are allusions to well-known literary figures such as Donne, Jonson, Marston, Davies, Raleigh, etc.; and there is the celebrated account of the death of the old Queen and the accession of James.

However, it must be admitted that no new light is cast on the Shakespeare passages themselves, though Sorlien does emphatically prefer the reading 'Touse' (i.e. William Towse of the

[1] Clarendon Press, Oxford, 1977.
[2] 22 April 1977, pp. 483–4.
[3] 6 May 1977, p. 560.
[4] 'A New Vertue Shakespeare Portrait', *Shakespeare Quarterly*, XXVIII (1977), 85–6.
[5] *The Diary of John Manningham of the Middle Temple 1602–1603* (University Press of New England for the University of Rhode Island, 1976).

Inner Temple, one of Manningham's chief informants) to Schoenbaum's 'Curle' (Edward Curle of the Middle Temple, Manningham's chambermate and eventual brother-in-law) for the teller of the *Richard III* anecdote. The contexts of the passages prove not to be particularly revealing. Manningham's is a really rather commonplace mind: he is one for whom the form of the commonplace-book (which is what his diary really is) is ironically just right, since for him as for others it traces a vain and wandering search for intellectual distinction. Unfortunately, he seems to have had no great interest in the ordinary playhouses, and did not visit them. The histrionic art he most enjoyed was the sermon, which he took down in copious notes. Thus he records a preacher at St Clement's in 1602 declaring that 'every one must take upon him some calling and profession, and this calling must be allowed of God; therefore the trade of stageplayers unlawfull'.

Another, much more significant contemporary of Shakespeare's was his patron the Earl of Southampton. G. P. V. Akrigg,[1] who published a book about him in 1968, has made a couple of further discoveries in manuscripts. One, in the Bibliothèque Nationale, is a report, about 1612, of the religious loyalties of English noblemen: Southampton's name is given the unique endorsement 'o' – meaning perhaps 'atheist'.

Two books relate the composition of Shakespeare's works to his life and times. Robert Speaight[2] believes it an innovation 'to set a discussion of his art within a biographical framework'. In undertaking to do this, he sees both himself and his reader as laymen: this can hardly excuse the deficiencies of scholarship. The book is smothered in errors of assertion, date and quotation. More seriously perhaps, the literary discussion is desultory, lacks edge, and cannot be said, despite its programme, to illuminate the life with the plays or the plays with the life.

Muriel Bradbrook[3] concerns herself with the circumstances of theatre, court and nation at large in which the dramatist found himself, and to which, she argues, he constantly responded. But, for all her learning and claim to method, hers is a rambling treatment of the subject, and she is content, it seems, to leave many ideas in the shell. Thus one has many misgivings. How can one say that the Elizabethan theatre was an integrative force in the community without going into the facts of the fierce Puritan opposition to it? Are we to accept without question the old conventional view that the chronicle history plays, with their panorama of tyranny upon tyranny, treachery and bloodshed, express pride in country? Does the death of Prince Henry really colour *The Duchess of Malfi*, the Gunpowder Plot *Macbeth*, the Union *King Lear*? Actually, Muriel Bradbrook's most vivid interest does not lie in the historical background, which she exploits rather than develops, nor in theatre conditions as such, since her handling of plays is mainly literary, but rather in the aesthetic qualities of romance, pastoral, and masque, and it is a telling treatment of these, and Shakespeare's plays related to them, that is her sub-text.

Paul Delany[4] gives a Marxist reading of *King Lear*. In Shakespeare's day the 'feudal-aristocratic society of medieval England' was in process of being superseded by 'the emergent bourgeois state', of which, rather surprisingly, Edmund is the principal exponent.

It is Gustav Ungerer's theory[5] that a real

[1] 'Something More About Shakespeare's Patron', *Shakespeare Quarterly*, XXVIII (1977), 65–72.

[2] *Shakespeare: The man and his achievement* (Dent, 1977).

[3] *The Living Monument: Shakespeare and the Theatre of his Time* (Cambridge University Press, 1976).

[4] 'King Lear and the Decline of Feudalism', *PMLA*, XCII (1977), 429–40.

[5] *A Spaniard in Elizabethan England: The Correspondence of Antonio Pérez's Exile*, 2 vols (Tamesis Books Ltd, 1974, 1976).

person, Antonio Pérez, is portrayed as Armado in *Love's Labour's Lost*. Pérez was a famous or infamous defector from Spain. At one time King Philip's principal secretary, he fled to France and England where, for his political knowledge and expertise, and for his jaundiced view of royal absolutism, he commanded the fascinated and at times alarmed attention of the great, including Essex. The identification with Armado was first made in 1905 by Martin Hume in *The Spanish Influence on English Literature*. Ungerer marshals his vast scholarship in support of Hume, and in particular represents Armado's letters as parodies of the anti-Ciceronian style which was adopted and indeed promoted by the real Spaniard, and which was fashionable throughout Europe in the nineties in such circles as that of Essex and his scholar secretaries. If one remains unmoved by the argument, it is not only because it rests on such frail evidence but because, ironically, the more one learns of Pérez through the main body of Ungerer's work, the less one is prepared to see this formidable paranoid as susceptible of such parody. Indeed years ago Pérez was put forward as the original of Iago.

For Keith Brown[1] it is a foreign country, Denmark, or its Elizabethan English image, that has left its imprint on Shakespeare's work, in this instance *Hamlet* of course. Among the characters, Brown would associate Polonius with the Pomeranian Henrik Ramel, Hofmeister to Prince Christian at the Danish court; Ramel was Polonian to the extent that he had been in the service of the King of Poland and owned estates in that country.

Margaret Loftus Ranald[2] follows up Pater's famous description of the deposition scene in *Richard II* as an 'inverted rite'. From a study of ceremonial degradation from knighthood, from military rank and from ecclesiastical office, she comes to the conclusion that the traditions were still very much alive and could well have influenced Shakespeare.

Stratford archives shed some light on Falstaff's thirst. By examining the records of hospitality in the Chamberlain's Accounts, T. J. King[3] determines that Falstaff's sack cost him much less at Eastcheap than it would have done at Stratford, and that his halfpenny would have bought him half a loaf.

Archives once belonging to the English Jesuit Mission in Saint Omer yield information of a quite different kind. Having found a play of *Pericles* listed in a book catalogue compiled in the Mission in 1618 or 1619, Willem Schrickx[4] notes that some early performances of Shakespeare's play were by or to those likely to be sympathetic to Catholicism, and that the history of Antiochus IV Epiphanes and Judas Machabeus was often used allusively in religious controversy. This is solid enough. But the further suggestions that George Wilkins was a Catholic, and that he was Shakespeare's collaborator, are without foundation. Roger Prior[5] also has something to say of George Wilkins. Signatures in a Chancery suit show that the George Wilkins who was a victualler in Turnmill Street was the same man who gave evidence in the Belott-Mountjoy suit. Whether the victualler was the writer is another question.

Hard as it may be, to anyone's satisfaction but one's own, to fix Shakespeare in the material and human setting of his age, it is harder still to derive his patterns of thought from those of

1 'Polonius, and Fortinbras (and Hamlet?)', *English Studies*, LV (1974), 218-38.
2 'The Degradation of Richard II: An Inquiry into the Ritual Backgrounds', *English Literary Renaissance*, VII (1977), 170-96.
3 'Falstaff's Intolerable Deal of Sack: Notes from Stratford-upon-Avon, 1590-1597', *Notes & Queries*, n.s. XXIV (1977), 105-9.
4 '*Pericles* in a Book-List of 1619 from the English Jesuit Mission and Some of the Play's Special Problems', *Shakespeare Survey* 29 (Cambridge University Press, 1976), pp. 21-32.
5 'George Wilkins and the Young Heir', *ibid.*, pp. 33-9.

his contemporaries or educators. J. W. Lever[1] makes a lucid and penetrating survey of scholarship, mainly from this century, which has tried to do so. Lever's principal subject is the rise and fall of the school, of whom Tillyard is the most widely read, who imposed a rigid scheme of historical, political and even cosmic beliefs upon Shakespeare. He is happy to find, in the more recent tendency amongst scholars to seek out contraries, polarities and ambivalences, a return to a better sense of the rich complexity of Shakespeare and his age. This is sanguine enough. But the time may yet come when criticism dies of a surfeit of ambiguities.

George Watson[2] continues the debate about the Elizabethan Englishman's knowledge and understanding of Machiavelli's works, and makes the unorthodox proposal that even the Machiavel of the theatre may at times be taken as a telling criticism rather than as an ignorant misrepresentation: 'The widest study of machiavellianism in English renaissance drama, and its most penetrating critique, is surely *Macbeth*'.

But the play that has attracted most attention from those interested in the ideas of the time has been *The Merchant of Venice*. First, E. F. J. Tucker[3] takes to task a number of scholars who have rashly ventured to expound the judicial proceedings in the play, and to allege a conflict on principle between the common lawcourts and Chancery in Shakespeare's London. Equity, Tucker shows, was the term applied to the interpretation of statutes according to their intention, and it would have been a familiar concept to common lawyers. Portia is an entirely admirable exponent of such equity at common law. If the spirit of the old lawyers is not dead, nor is that of the old theologians. Austin C. Dobbins and Roy W. Battenhouse[4] are convinced that an Elizabethan would not condemn Jessica for theft, disobedience, lying and frivolity, since familiarity with commentary on such texts as

that of the Israelites robbing the Egyptians (Exodus 3: 21–22) or of Jacob's spoiling Laban (Genesis 31) would suggest to him traditional habits of mind in which seeming misdemeanours might be justified as serving higher and redemptive designs. A learned article by John S. Coolidge[5] is more difficult to summarise. He explores the theological connotations of actions and words in the play, bringing out the familiar confrontation there between Old and New Testament values. Ruth M. Levitsky[6] has much the same field of interest as Coolidge, though she ranges much less widely, and she is content to make the one point, on the evidence of sixteenth- and seventeenth-century books, that Shylock's lack of a religious understanding of justice is that of the unredeemed, natural man.

Some withering attention has been paid to *The Tempest*, which under such scrutiny is made out to be a rather grim and deeply disturbed play. To explain tensions within Prospero himself, three writers invoke the divinity of kings: none of them is put out by the fact that Prospero is not a king. For no very good reason that is apparent, Norman Louis Morgan[7] takes Prospero to be a contradictory portrait of King James, who is at once

[1] 'Shakespeare and the Ideas of his Time', *ibid.*, pp. 79–91.

[2] 'Machiavel and Machiavelli', *Sewanee Review*, LXXXIV (1976), 630–48.

[3] 'The Letter of the Law in *The Merchant of Venice*', *Shakespeare Survey 29* (Cambridge University Press, 1976), pp. 93–101.

[4] 'Jessica's Morals: A Theological View', *Shakespeare Studies*, IX (1976), 107–20.

[5] 'Law and Love in *The Merchant of Venice*', *Shakespeare Quarterly*, XXVII (1976), 243–63.

[6] 'Shylock as Unregenerate Man', *ibid.*, XXVIII (1977), 58–64.

[7] 'King James, Magic, the Masque, and *The Tempest*', *Literature and Iconoclasm: Shakespeare*, Occasional Papers II by Members of the Program in Literature and Philosophy, ed. Brian Caraher and Irving Massey (State University of New York at Buffalo, 1976), 18–27.

a king celebrated in masques for his super-natural powers and an unreserved antagonist of witches both white and black. The elements of conflict in Prospero are varied by Patrick Grant,[1] who finds on the one side the magus/king and on the other the sceptic and empiricist of a new scientific spirit. A reconciliation of the two is effected by Miranda, who embodies the principle of charity consistent with both. '*The Tempest* is the most bitter of Shakespeare's plays', writes Jan Kott,[2] preparing us for an interpretation that brings this fragile romance into line with the brutal chronicle histories (as interpreted by Kott). In two condensed, not to say curt, articles, which are drawn from his forthcoming book, to be called, surprisingly, *Shakespeare Not Our Contemporary*, Kott has the play express the failure of men's hopes for a brave new world, notably in America, and the allegedly inevitable pattern in political affairs by which turmoil forever repeats itself. This is not *The Tempest* most readers will recognise. Let us hope theatre directors are not looking Kott's way.

Shakespeare's plays undoubtedly have as much or more in common with the arts than with the politics of his day. But when Ernest B. Gilman[3] seizes upon the image of perspective pictures used by Bushy in a difficult passage about the false effects of grief in *Richard II*, II, ii, 14ff., it is to make the analogy of this art and that of the *memento mori* serve as a mere decoration of his own critical purposes, which are to show that the play depends for its effect upon paradox, shifting sympathies and ambiguities. A warning about iconographic criticism comes from Dieter Mehl,[4] author of *The Elizabethan Dumb Show* (1965): noting the fashion of recent years to point out the emblematic or iconographic aspects of Elizabethan staging, he calls for moderation; it cannot be assumed that anything and everything can bear an emblematic interpretation such as has been arrived at in the study. The

test must be what would be comprehensible to an Elizabethan audience in actual performance. It is questionable perhaps whether such an audience would readily associate Ophelia with the nymph Flora, as Bridget Gellert Lyons[5] would have us believe, in an iconographic study of *Hamlet*, that they would. But even so she writes interestingly of the complex impression conveyed by Ophelia, who even puzzles other characters in the play. Especially in her madness, she is said to embody both the contradictory figures of Flora known to the Renaissance: the pastoral goddess and the urban harlot. Robert C. Fulton[6] studies the iconographical background of the masque in *Timon of Athens* and likewise finds that both Cupid and the Amazons are highly ambivalent figures, so that what might within the play appear to be a celebration of love and harmony covertly presages malevolence, death and destruction, and rampant whoredom. The traditions of art may be resisted rather than adopted; such is the assumption underlying Jill L. Levenson's article[7] on *Troilus and Cressida*. She surveys some of the medieval and Renaissance tapestries that depict the Trojan legend, mainly along the literary lines laid down by Benoît de Sainte-Maure, as splendid and opulent, though also intellectually demanding and even somewhat ironical. In contrast, Shakespeare's play is highly

[1] 'The Magic of Charity: a Background to Prospero', *Review of English Studies*, XXVII (1976), 1–16.
[2] '*The Tempest*, or Repetition', *Mosaic*, X (1977), 9–36.
[3] '*Richard II* and the Perspectives of History', *Renaissance Drama*, n.s. VII (1976), 85–115.
[4] 'Emblematic Theatre', *Anglia*, XCV (1977), 130–8.
[5] 'The Iconography of Ophelia', *Journal of English Literary History*, XLIV (1977), 60–73.
[6] 'Timon, Cupid, and the Amazons', *Shakespeare Studies*, IX (1976), 283–99.
[7] 'Shakespeare's *Troilus and Cressida* and the Monumental Tradition in Tapestries and Literature', *Renaissance Drama*, n.s. VII (1976), 43–84.

reductive of both love and war, and indeed of all endeavour.

A good deal has been written about the specific and general sources in literature of Shakespeare's plays. James C. Bulman[1] continues his work on the MS *Timon*, and would like to have this comedy installed as a collateral source of *Timon of Athens*. Lucian's *Misanthropos*, at present considered the main source, is not to be ruled right out; but much that has been attributed to it may derive from or through the comedy, and in some cases there are parallels to Shakespeare's play in the comedy alone. William W. E. Slights[2] accounts for the complications of *Timon of Athens* by representing Shakespeare as deliberately working up distinct genres such as masque, morality, satirical comedy and tragedy into a new amalgam designed to give 'multiple perspectives' to the themes of authority and social order.

Andrew S. Cairncross[3] claims that the original Italian *Orlando Furioso*, cantos iv–vi, was Shakespeare's source for the Hero–Claudio story in *Much Ado*, for Edmund's trial by combat in *King Lear*, and Othello's demand for ocular proof. R. S. White[4] examines allusions to hunting in a number of plays, and shows how expressively it is used as a metaphor for love.

Judy Z. Kronenfeld[5] compares Jaques, as a pastoral melancholic, with other such figures in Petrarch, Sannazaro and Sidney. Renaissance writers are commonly aware of the idleness and self-indulgence into which the ostensibly contemplative life, now secularised but with pretensions to sensitivity, can degenerate. Thus Jaques takes his place in the pastoralism of the play as an object-lesson; and one is to see his distress over the weeping deer, for instance, as a parody of his self-pity over his own lot. In seeking out the former usurping Duke, however, he bids fair at last to adopt a removed way of life in which true self-examination will bear fruit.

Two contributions to source-study actually refer to works which are no longer extant, and indeed may never have existed. On the basis of internal evidence in *The Merchant of Venice* S. J. Schönfeld[6] postulates and reconstructs lost Jewish sources for the play. The author's arguments are in the circumstances unverifiable, though this does not detract from their fascination. It is not claimed that Shakespeare had any knowledge of Hebrew. The volume represents a life-time of research, and it is regrettable that its publication in German and Hebrew will inhibit a wider circulation. G. Stacy's conjecture[7] is a very much smaller one. He argues that Arthur Brooke's reference in *Romeus and Juliet* to 'the same argument lately set foorth on stage' does not mean that he knew a play which was specifically about Romeo and Juliet, but that, rather more generally, one about 'the shamefull and wretched endes of such, as have yelded their libertie thrall to fowle desires' – in other words, a morality play for the edification of the young.

The most varied and extensive work on sources has to do with Shakespeare's dependence on the classics. In his note on *Troilus and*

[1] 'Shakespeare's Use of the *Timon* Comedy', *Shakespeare Survey* 29 (Cambridge University Press, 1976), pp. 103–16.

[2] '*Genera mixta* and *Timon of Athens*', *Studies in Philology*, LXXIV (1977), 39–62.

[3] 'Shakespeare and Ariosto: *Much Ado About Nothing*, *King Lear*, and *Othello*', *Renaissance Quarterly*, XXIX (1976), 178–82.

[4] ' "Now Mercy goes to Kill": Hunting in Shakespearean Comedy', *Durham University Journal*, LXIX (1976), 21–32.

[5] 'Shakespeare's Jaques and the Pastoral Cult of Solitude', *Texas Studies in Literature and Language*, XVIII (1976), 451–73.

[6] *Eine Jüdische Quelle im 'Kaufmann von Venedig'* (Shikmona Publishing Co. Ltd, Jerusalem, 1976). J am grateful to Dr James Simpson of Liverpool University for his comments on this book.

[7] 'Arthur Brooke and the Lost Play of *Romeo and Juliet*', *English Studies*, LVIII (1977), 110–13.

Cressida, III, i, 122–8, J. L. Simmons[1] shows that the phrase 'generation of Vipers' might be connected not only with Scripture but also (with a pun) with Pliny's *Natural History*, in which the sexual habits of vipers are described. Uniquely apt to this play, for instance, is Pliny's assertion that in the very act of generation the female bites off the head of the male; in this, love and death are inseparable. Moreover, the chapter following the passage on vipers deals more widely with the sexual behaviour of land animals, and emphasises most strikingly the absurdity and tragedy of man's own. Simmons concludes that Shakespeare may have been reading Philemon Holland's translation of Pliny printed in 1601. Elizabeth S. Sklar[2] finds the likening (indirect, it must be said) of Bassanio to Jason a confirmation of the moral ambiguity that hangs about Portia's suitor in *The Merchant of Venice*. Jason appears in Gower's *Confessio Amantis* Book V, which contains analogues of the casket motif, and which takes as its theme covetousness in love, such as marrying for money; Jason's betrayal of Medea exemplifies the perjury that results from such insincerity. Marvin L. Vawter[3] argues that Caesar and Brutus in *Julius Caesar* both demonstrate such characteristic weaknesses of Stoicism as the Sceptic Cicero scorned: they misconstrue sense impressions and abuse reasoning to suit themselves and their conception of destiny. J. J. M. Tobin[4] finds common features in Othello's killing of Desdemona and Psyche's attempt on Cupid in *The Golden Ass* Book V, chapters xxii and xxiii. Herbert B. Rothschild[5] promises to consider afresh the relation of *Antony and Cleopatra* to its source in Plutarch by keeping in mind the critical debate in the Renaissance about the significantly different functions of history and poetry: accordingly Shakespeare's conception of the story is to be seen as not merely adapting but as being actually played off against Plutarch's. In the event Roths-

child's exposition of the play, though sensitive, is based on the familiar dialectic, and it hardly seems to matter whether the opposed terms are Rome against Egypt, love against duty, or (as here) a reductive historical interpretation against the theatrical illusion of people fully living. John Dean[6] finds resemblances in tone, structure and story-material between Herodotus's *Histories*, published in English translation in 1584, and Shakespeare's last plays. George M. Logan[7] takes some passages in *Richard II* which have points of similarity with Daniel's *Civil Wars* and shows that Daniel's work is closer than Shakespeare's to Lucan's *Pharsalia*, which was indeed Daniel's over-riding model. The conclusion, if accepted, must be that Shakespeare borrowed from Daniel, and did so in or after late 1594, when *The Civil Wars* was entered on the *Stationers' Register*.

C. Whitworth[8] objects to the careless handling of the established source for *As You Like It*, Lodge's *Rosalynde*. There is a widespread tendency amongst scholars to read into Lodge relationships of Shakespeare's own invention: thus in fact Gerismond and Torismond are two kings, not dukes, and are not

---

[1] 'Holland's Pliny and *Troilus and Cressida*', *Shakespeare Quarterly*, XXVII (1976), 329–32.

[2] 'Bassanio's Golden Fleece', *Texas Studies in Literature and Language*, XVIII (1976), 500–9.

[3] '"After Their Fashion": Cicero and Brutus in *Julius Caesar*', *Shakespeare Studies*, IX (1976), 205–19.

[4] 'Apuleius and *Othello*', *Notes & Queries*, n.s. XXIV (1977), 112.

[5] '"The Oblique Encounter": Shakespeare's Confrontation of Plutarch with Special Reference to *Antony and Cleopatra*', *English Literary Renaissance*, VI (1976), 404–29.

[6] *Shakespeare's Romances and Herodotus's Histories*, published with James T. Henke, *The Ego-King* (Universität Salzburg, 1977), pp. 95–100.

[7] 'Lucan–Daniel–Shakespeare: New Light on the Relation Between *The Civil Wars* and *Richard II*', *Shakespeare Studies*, IX (1976), 121–40.

[8] '*Rosalynde*: As You Like It and as Lodge Wrote It', *English Studies*, LVIII (1977), 114–17.

related to each other; Rosalynde and Alinda are not cousins.

Does Shakespeare borrow from himself? William H. Matchett[1] gives examples from *The Merchant of Venice*, *Othello* and *Sir Thomas More* of how passages in one play may remind us of passages in another. This goes to confirm Shakespeare's share in *Sir Thomas More*. But his further claim that a play (*Sir Thomas More*) in which 'thematic elements' are concentrated in a cluster must be later in date than one (*The Merchant of Venice*) in which they are dispersed is open to question. D. J. Lake[2] is also concerned to date *Sir Thomas More*, this time with the aid of stylistic tests applied to spellings by hands D and E. This is very thin ice indeed.

There is a kind of critical discussion which it hardly seems accurate to term 'source-study', since the derivation of one text from another is not actively claimed in it, and the comparison of texts is an almost belletrist technique to sharpen the wits. One such analogy-study comes from Douglas J. Stewart.[3] In early Greek myth, he tells us, the hero is brought up apart from his father (who may be deified or disabled) in the care of a father surrogate, a centaur. While denying that Shakespeare could have been influenced by such Greek models, Stewart would have us believe that he arrived at a similar pattern in *Henry IV*. In order to accept this, one is obliged to see King Henry as a thoroughly discredited, virtually disowned, father, and Falstaff as 'an ambassador of the rawest nature' who inculcates in his young charge a self-contained honesty of purpose. Eamon Grennan[4] likewise will not have it that he is proposing *The Shepheardes Calender* as a source of *As You Like It*, but he works almost as if he were, showing how much the two have in common as pastoral, whether in the plaintive, recreative or moral aspects (to use E.K.'s analysis). R. Kirkpatrick[5] examines some passages in Dante and *Othello*

and comes to the conclusion that, though both may be generally described as *dramatic*, there is a distinct *theatricality* in *Othello* lacking in Dante which has to do with our sense of physical presence on the stage and which overcomes our isolation from the characters.

Several essayists consider Shakespeare in relation to later writers. Marjorie Beam[6] contrasts Hamlet's malaise with that of Swift's Tale-teller in *A Tale of a Tub*. No definite or sustained case is made out that the resemblances between the two are solely owing to Swift's imitating Shakespeare; and indeed Hamlet emerges from the comparison playing the rather unfamiliar role of optimist and man of faith opposite the Tale-teller, who is in despair at the modern world. In comparing Shakespeare and Brecht, Ladislaus Löb and Laurence Lerner[7] are mainly exercised to show how Brecht has converted Shakespeare's tragedy into an 'optimistic' Marxist play where the populace, under economic stress, engage in a rational class struggle and make their way forward to a better society without such dispensable leaders as Marcius. In surveying the work of John Ford, Kenneth Muir[8] considers his

[1] 'Shylock, Iago, and *Sir Thomas More*: With Some Further Discussion of Shakespeare's Imagination', *PMLA*, XCII (1977), 217–30.

[2] 'The Date of the *Sir Thomas More* Additions by Dekker and Shakespeare', *Notes & Queries*, n.s. XXIV (1977), 114–16.

[3] 'Falstaff the Centaur', *Shakespeare Quarterly*, XXVIII (1977), 5–21.

[4] 'Telling the Trees from the Wood: Some Details of *As You Like It* Re-examined', *English Literary Renaissance*, VII (1977), 197–206.

[5] 'On the Treatment of Tragic Themes in Dante and Shakespeare', *Modern Language Review*, LXXVII (1977), 575–84.

[6] ' "The Reach and Wit of the Inventor": Swift's *Tale of a Tub* and *Hamlet*', *University of Toronto Quarterly*, XLVI (1976), 1–13.

[7] 'Views of Roman History: *Coriolanus* and *Coriolan*', *Comparative Literature*, XXIX (1977), 35–53.

[8] 'The Case of John Ford', *Sewanee Review*, LXXXIV (1976), 614–29.

dependence on and his understanding of Shakespeare.

Three bibliographies have appeared that will be of value to scholars not only of Renaissance drama in general but of Shakespeare in particular: Julia C. Dietrich[1] lists contributions to the study of folk drama, so often said nowadays to be directly or indirectly an influence on Shakespearian comedy and romance; Floriana T. Hogan[2] lists all the alleged links, some of them extraordinarily tenuous, between Spanish literature and English drama, including Shakespeare's; and Philip C. Kolin[3] lists work done since 1926 on the 'little eyases'.

This brings us to the study of the Shakespearian theatre. The Rose was the property of Philip Henslowe and the home of the company that competed most vigorously with Shakespeare's. But in the years 1592–4 two of Shakespeare's own plays, *1 Henry VI* and *Titus Andronicus*, were performed there. Ernest L. Rhodes[4] offers a detailed reconstruction of the Rose based upon a painstaking study of pictures (lavishly reproduced), documents and play texts. The pictorial evidence is not strong, and Rhodes's dependence on two tiny sketches by the map-maker Norden comes of desperation. The documentary evidence is almost embarrassingly rich, since practically the whole of Henslowe's Diary and papers, and the plays named in them, may be thought to bear on the one theatre. Even so the architectural facts hardly speak for themselves: and there is, for instance, no reason to assume from the Rose contract, as Rhodes does, that because the garden-plot on which the playhouse was erected was 94 foot square the building must have been 94 feet in diameter. But it is most to be regretted that from the start Rhodes is determined, through thick or thin, to bring the Rose into conformity with the engravings of theatres found by Frances Yates in Robert Fludd's *Ars Memoriae* (1619) and used by her to conjecture the interior of the Globe. In

consequence his reconstruction shows an Elizabethan theatre without a thrust stage, but with a playing area built round on three sides and provided with five openings, the entire audience being seated, as in a Roman theatre.

The Rose is also involved in two articles about staging. In considering how *The Spanish Tragedy*, a play at the Rose, might have been staged, Eleanor M. Tweedie[5] inevitably deals with such practical problems as the arbour, the hangings, and the placing of observers above. Mary E. Smith[6] sees every reason to accept the assignment of Marlowe's *Dido Queene of Carthage* to the Children of the Chapel rather than (with H. J. Oliver) to the Admiral's Men at the Rose; she has the stage divided down the middle by some kind of wall, with the countryside imagined on one side and the city on the other.

New information has been unearthed about the Salisbury Court Theatre, the last London theatre to be built before the Interregnum. Using two law-cases first discovered by C. W. Wallace about 1910 but not then published, G. E. Bentley[7] finds that the partners concerned in the venture seem to have spent about £600 in converting a barn into the theatre. Here for a few years they ran a boys' company which they explicitly regarded as a nursery for

---

1 'Folk Drama Scholarship: The State of the Art', *Research Opportunities in Renaissance Drama*, XIX (1976), 15–32.

2 'Elizabethan and Jacobean Dramas and Their Spanish Sources', *ibid.*, pp. 37–47.

3 'An Annotated Bibliography of Scholarship on the Children's Companies and Their Theaters', *ibid.*, pp. 57–82.

4 *Henslowe's Rose: The Stage & Staging* (The University Press of Kentucky, 1976).

5 ' "Action is Eloquence": The Staging of Thomas Kyd's *Spanish Tragedy*', *Studies in English Literature 1500–1900*, XVI (1976), 223–39.

6 'Staging Marlowe's *Dido Queene of Carthage*', *ibid.*, XVII (1977), 177–90.

7 'The Salisbury Court Theater and Its Boy Players', *Huntington Library Quarterly*, XL (1977), 129–49.

the King's Men. O. L. Brownstein[1] elicits from a parish report on new foundations in St Bride's Parish indications of the precise location of the Salisbury Court, on the east end of what was to become Fisher's Alley after the Great Fire. The building seems to have measured some 60′ × 40′ externally, and Brownstein discusses the probable position of Beeston's dwelling-house and proposed dancing-school over the stage.

John Orrell[2] is concerned to correct a current error about performances at the Paved Court Theatre in Somerset House. Documents prove that Walter Montagu's pastoral *The Shepherd's Paradise* was produced there on o January 1632/3 and perhaps subsequently; but the play on Shrove Tuesday, 5 March following, was a masque. Inigo Jones, who had designed the original theatre, considered it necessary to make alterations in the auditorium for the accommodation of the different piece. In another article, John Orrell[3] establishes that Inigo Jones was probably supplied with the Florentine prints that influenced his later masques through the good offices of the Florentine Resident in London.

Work has gone forward on theatres in the provinces. David Galloway[4] discusses the references in Great Yarmouth records to a 'game place' and 'game place house'. That there was an open space, with a house adjoining, and that plays were performed thereabouts, are incontestable facts; but there is no reason to assume that the performances took place in the house. The Chamberlain's Accounts of Aldeburgh for 1566–92, 1624–49, from which J. C. Coldewey[5] transcribes extracts, record the visit of the Queen's players and several other companies over the years, often on tours which included Ipswich. Sheffield's men are not heard of before their appearance at Aldeburgh in 1576–7. A. D. Mills[6] reprints from Churchwarden's Accounts for Sherborne, Dorset entries for the performances in 1543–9

and 1572–6 of a Corpus Christi play, with amongst other figures Lot's Wife, made up with a peck of wheaten meal, price 6d. As for the staging, truth may prove stranger than conjecture, even in the inventive scholarship of medieval drama: at St Mary's Church the actors seem to have worked in tents in the churchyard, and spectators were accommodated 'vppon the churche Leaddes'. Amongst visiting players received at Sherborne were the Queen's Men in 1598 and 1599. But the most enduring entertainment there was the whirligig. Why do editors of *Twelfth Night* prefer the gloss 'spinning-top' for Feste's word, when there is the much more festive 'round-about' (or 'swing')?

Neil Carson[7] has taken a closer look at a rough drawing in the Alleyn–Henslowe papers at Dulwich, first printed in *Shakespeare Survey 13* in 1960, and is convinced that what it depicts is a flight of stairs set in banks of seats, the *ingressus* to the first-floor gallery of (perhaps) the Globe. In two articles Leonie Star[8] objects to the assumption that Eliza-

---

[1] 'New Light on the Salisbury Court Playhouse', *Educational Theatre Journal*, XXIX (1977), 231–42.

[2] 'Productions at the Paved Court Theatre, Somerset House, 1632/3', *Notes & Queries*, n.s. XXIII (1976), 223–5.

[3] 'Inigo Jones and Amerigo Salvetti: A Note on the Later Masque Designs', *Theatre Notebook*, XXX (1976), 109–14.

[4] 'The "Game Place" and "House" at Great Yarmouth, 1493–1595', *Theatre Notebook*, XXXI (1977), 6–9.

[5] 'Playing Companies at Aldeburgh 1566–1635', *Collections IX* (Oxford University Press for the Malone Society, 1971 (1977)), pp. 16–23.

[6] 'A Corpus Christi Play and other Dramatic Activities in Sixteenth-century Sherborne, Dorset', *ibid.*, pp. 1–15.

[7] 'The Staircases of the Frame: New Light on the Structure of the Globe', *Shakespeare Survey 29* (Cambridge University Press, 1976), pp. 127–32.

[8] 'The Middle of the Yard: a Second Inner Stage?', *Theatre Notebook*, XXX (1976), 5–9; 'The Middle of the Yard, Part II: the Calculation of Stage Sizes for English Renaissance Playhouses', *ibid.*, pp. 65–9.

bethan theatres projected into 'the middle of the yarde'. Only the Fortune is certainly known to have done so; and even in this case it may be asked whether, in calculating the depth of the stage from the dimensions of the yard, allowance should not be made for the depth of the tiring-house.

On the subject of actors and acting, Robert Mullally[1] shows that the woodcut of a lady and gentleman on the title page of *Fulgens and Lucrece* derives from an earlier French block and can have little to do with the persons of the play. John C. Coldewey[2] gathers together evidence from the local records of Chelmsford, Maldon, Heybridge and elsewhere that in the first half of the sixteenth century the more elaborate amateur dramatic festivals in the home counties were supervised by a paid expert brought from London and known as the 'property player'. D. J. Lake[3] tries to settle what works to attribute to Robert Armin by vocabulary tests of an extreme finesse: *Quips upon Questions*, for instance, is Armin's because it contains one instance of *betwixt* instead of *between*. T. J. King[4] corrects an error in Bentley, according to which the King's Men visited Stratford in 1618. The date should read 1622, when a company called the 'King's players' were paid 5s 'for not playinge in the hall'. They may be distinct from the company for which Shakespeare had written. Ronald J. Palumbo[5] looks at instances in *The Spanish Tragedy*, *Richard II*, *Romeo and Juliet* and *Antonio and Mellida* where characters fling themselves to the ground in a self-indulgence of grief which is also expressed in patterned language.

A great deal of attention is paid nowadays to post-Elizabethan productions of Shakespeare's plays. G. Harold Metz[6] corrects the impression that *Titus Andronicus* has never been a popular play. He shows that it has enjoyed four widely-spaced periods of success: 1594–1620 in the original version, 1678–1724

and 1849–60 in adaptations; and then of course during our own time, when between 1951 and 1974 there were no fewer than twenty-three separate productions of Shakespeare's text. Dennis Kennedy[7] deplores the scorn directed at Nahum Tate's version of *Lear*, which should be regarded, like Brook's *Lear* production of 1962, as making acceptable to contemporary taste and understanding a play that in the original state is too rich for the theatre. But it is the nineteenth century that excites most interest amongst scholars. Michael R. Booth[8] tells the story of how the Victorians, beginning with Macready, devoted themselves, on what were often the highest of motives, to pictorial elaboration and archaeological accuracy in their productions of Shakespeare. Russell Jackson[9] gives an account of the career of the Hon. Lewis Strange Wingfield (1842–91), who established himself in the 1880s as an 'archeological adviser' in a number of important Shakespeare productions in London. William E. Kleb[10] scotches the often-made assertion that

[1] 'The Source of the *Fulgens* Woodcut', *ibid.*, pp. 61–5.
[2] 'That Enterprising Property Player: Semi-Professional Drama in Sixteenth-Century England', *ibid.*, XXXI (1977), 5–12.
[3] 'The Canon of Robert Armin's Works: Some Difficulties', *Notes & Queries*, n.s. XXIV (1977), 117–20.
[4] 'The King's Players at Stratford-upon-Avon, 1622', *Theatre Notebook*, XXXI (1977), 4–6.
[5] 'From Melodrama to Burlesque: A Theatrical Gesture in Kyd, Shakespeare, and Marston', *Theatre Survey*, XVII (1976), 220–3.
[6] 'Stage History of *Titus Andronicus*', *Shakespeare Quarterly*, XXVIII (1977), 154–69.
[7] '*King Lear* and the Theatre', *Educational Theatre Journal*, XXVIII (1976), 35–44.
[8] 'Shakespeare as Spectacle and History: The Victorian Period', *Theatre Research International*, I (1976), 99–113.
[9] 'The Shakespearean Productions of Lewis Wingfield, 1883–90', *Theatre Notebook*, XXXI (1977), 28–41.
[10] 'E. W. Godwin and the Bancrofts', *ibid.*, XXX (1976), 122–32.

the Victorian designer E. W. Godwin, who published his ideas for a historically accurate Shakespeare, put them into practice in the Bancrofts' *Merchant of Venice* in 1875. Some biographical details about Godwin are added by Edward Craig.[1]

Turning to actors and directors, we have C. B. Hogan[2] setting out the ramifications of the Kemble family. Carol J. Carlisle[3] tries to recapture the quality of Helen Faucit's acting in Victorian times: she was evidently cut out to make a triumph of Hermione in the statue scene. In a second article,[4] we learn that Helen Faucit was baptised Helena Faucit Savill, probably as early as 1814. Henning Krabbe[5] writes of a Danish actress, Johanne Luise Heiberg, born in 1812, who dominated the stage in Denmark for more than a generation and gave much thought to her playing of Lady Macbeth.

A. H. Saxon[6] hits upon an unusual line of enquiry about nineteenth-century actors of note, such as Kemble, Macready, Irving, etc., by investigating the exhibition of their effigies, many of them alleged to have been taken from life, in Madame Tussaud's. The original figures do not survive, but in some cases the moulds do, and it is these to which one might look for authentic impressions.

Henry Irving's Shakespeare productions come in for re-assessment. Edward M. Moore[7] concludes that the critics of Irving's day had the right of it, and Irving's acting was poor – self-centred, sentimental and melodramatic – and, like his lavish productions, showed scant regard for Shakespeare's texts. In contrast, Richard Foulkes[8] maintains that in the staging of the trial scene in *The Merchant of Venice* in 1879 Irving placed more emphasis on the acting than had Kean and the Bancrofts, who favoured scenic display. Michael Mullin[9] does his best to rescue Beerbohm Tree from some of the obloquy he has received for eccentricity and 'tricky business': in his *Macbeth* in 1911 the

elaborate sets and business gave subtle expression to the innermost psychology of the Macbeths. Granville-Barker's *Midsummer-Night's Dream* in 1914 was chiefly revolutionary for its restoration of the whole text; Trevor Griffiths[10] finds that Granville-Barker did not always break with tradition, and when he did, as in dressing the fairies in gold, the result was distracting to the audience. J. L. Styan's three stars are Poel, Granville-Barker and Tyrone Guthrie.[11] It was Poel who patiently worked towards 'a more authentically Elizabethan regard for the play', especially in his sensitivity to the musical structure and rhythmical continuity of the scenes; he believed that the realism to be aimed at was not that of illusion but 'the realism of an actual event'. Granville-Barker and Tyrone Guthrie followed in his footsteps by establishing (or

[1] 'E. W. Godwin and the Theatre', *ibid.*, XXXI (1977), 30–3.

[2] 'The Kemble Family: A Genealogical Record, 1704–1925', *ibid.*, XXX (1976), 103–9; 'Kemble Family Correction', *ibid.*, XXXI (1977), 39–40.

[3] 'Helen Faucit's Acting Style', *Theatre Survey*, XVII (1976), 38–56.

[4] 'Two Notes on Helen Faucit', *Theatre Notebook*, XXX (1976), 99–103.

[5] 'A Danish Actress and Her Conception of the Part of Lady Macbeth', *Shakespeare Survey 29* (Cambridge University Press, 1976), pp. 145–9.

[6] 'Waxworks as a Source of Theatrical Iconography: Madame Tussaud's and the Nineteenth-Century British Stage', *Theatre Notebook*, XXX (1976), 52–7.

[7] 'Henry Irving's Shakespearean Productions', *Theatre Survey*, XVII (1976), 195–216.

[8] 'The Staging of the Trial Scene in Irving's *The Merchant of Venice*', *Educational Theatre Journal*, XXVIII (1976), 312–17.

[9] 'Strange Images of Death: Sir Herbert Beerbohm Tree's *Macbeth*, 1911', *Theatre Survey*, XVII (1976), 125–42.

[10] 'Tradition and Innovation in Harley Granville Barker's *A Midsummer Night's Dream*', *Theatre Notebook*, XXX (1976), 78–87.

[11] 'Elizabethan Open Staging: William Poel to Tyrone Guthrie', *Modern Language Quarterly*, XXXVII (1976), 211–20.

restoring) an intimacy of actor and audience through the use of a built-out stage.

The continuing need to clear up difficulties of meaning in Shakespeare's text has been met by a large number of contributions. They may be conveniently reviewed in play groupings. First, in the chronicle-history plays, R. Ann Thompson[1] decides it is unlikely that the two buckets image in *Richard II* derives from *The Knight's Tale*. Paul A. Jorgensen[2] takes as his starting-point Falstaff's enigmatic 'The better part of valor is discretion' (*1 Henry IV*, v, iv, 119) and shows that, in the face of an English predilection for mindless valour, military writers of Shakespeare's age urged (not without irony) the superior claims of 'policy', or 'wit', or 'prudence', or indeed 'discretion', a word which may in such contexts signify 'strategy' rather than 'discreditable circumspection'. 'Part' may refer diversely to logic, acting, and sex. According to M. A. Shaaber,[3] Pistol's row of Latin and English tags in his exchange with Falstaff in *2 Henry IV*, v, v, 24–9 owes its origin first to a commonplace motto and then to far-off echoes of two statements by St Augustine, one about God, 'Deus . . . extra quem nihil . . . est', and the other about the soul, that it 'in toto tota est, et in qualibet ejus parte tota est'.

In the comedies, Mats Rydén[4] suggests that the 'Cuckow-budds of yellow hew' in the song at the end of *Love's Labour's Lost* is not to be identified with any particular flower but is made up by Shakespeare to serve the associations of cuckoldry in the context. Raymond B. Waddington[5] sees in Jessica's purchase of a monkey in *The Merchant of Venice*, III, i, 109, an allusion to the fable, which found its way into the emblem books, of the monkey which escaped while its miserly master was dining out and scattered his gold from an upstairs window; this might imply that Jessica's elopement was ape-like, sexually base. Maura Slattery Kuhn[6] argues that in *As You Like It*,

v, iv, 107, Rosalind appears not in her own person dressed as a girl but, just as revealingly, as Ganymede once more; Touchstone's talk of lies and ifs fits in with the constant preoccupations of the play with conditions, suppositions, and deceptions. As regards *Twelfth Night*, I, iii, 42, J. F. Killeen[7] proposes that *Castiliano* means 'the Devil' (as in 'Talk of the Devil') and *vulgo* 'in common speech'.

In the problem plays, Eliot Slater[8] has used statistical tests of vocabulary to establish that *All's Well* has most in common with *Troilus and Cressida*, *Measure for Measure* and later plays; this makes against any theory that the play is the revision of an earlier *Love's Labour's Won*. In two opaque notes on *Measure for Measure*, Klaus Bartenschlager[9] comments on III, i, 33–9 to little effect, and then shows that at lines 108–11 *force* the law may mean to *violate* it rather than (or should one say 'as well as'?) *enforce* it. Two sixteenth-century readings that may throw light on *Measure for Measure*, III, i, 93, 96, and its seeming nonceword *prenzie* are reported by Anthony S. G. Edwards and Anthony W. Jenkins.[10] George

---

[1] 'The "two buckets" image in *Richard II* and *The Isle of Gulls*', *Archiv*, CCXIII (1976), 108.
[2] 'Valor's Better Parts: Backgrounds and Meanings of Shakespeare's Most Difficult Proverb', *Shakespeare Studies*, IX (1976), 141–58.
[3] 'Pistol Quotes St Augustine?', *English Language Notes*, XIV (1976), 90–2.
[4] 'Shakespeare's Cuckoo-buds', *Studia Neophilologica*, XLIX (1977), 25–7.
[5] '*The Merchant of Venice* III.i.108–13: Transforming an Emblem', *English Language Notes*, XIV (1976), 92–8.
[6] 'Much Virtue in *If*', *Shakespeare Quarterly*, XXVIII (1977), 40–50.
[7] '*Twelfth Night*, I.iii.42; "*Castiliano vulgo*"', *ibid.*, pp. 92–3.
[8] 'Word Links with *All's Well That Ends Well*', *Notes & Queries*, n.s. XXIV (1977), 109–12.
[9] 'Two Notes on *Measure for Measure*', *Deutsche Shakespeare-Gesellschaft West Jahrbuch 1976*, pp. 160–3.
[10] '"*Prenzie*": *Measure for Measure*, III.i', *Shakespeare Quarterly*, XXVII (1976), 333–4.

Cavendish has *prensell, c.* 1554/5, and William Nevill *pryncy porte*, 1518. The meaning indicated is 'princely'.

The nonceword *ribaudred* may be the product of a compositor's carelessness with space quads; Robert H. Ray[1] declares that *ribaud red* (ribald red) fits the context as two separate words both because of Cleopatra's wantonness and because the colour continues the plague imagery.

In the tragedies, William E. Miller[2] looks at authorities on falconry and determines that eyases (as in *Hamlet*, II, ii, 342) were disliked by falconers – though apparently for different reasons. The mildew referred to in *King Lear*, III, iv, 120–4, may be ergot, writes Mario L. D'Avanzo:[3] this is a poisonous blight on grain which induces insanity, gangrene, convulsions and death; it may contribute to the imagery of eating filth. Dennis R. Klinck[4] draws attention to a seeming proverb in Simon Robson, *The Choise of Change* (1585), that we may hope for no goodness of a tamed wolf – a parallel to the Fool's warning in *King Lear*, III, vi, 18–19. Rodney Poisson[5] thinks *Othello*, III, iii, 394–6, refers not to the contemplation of suicide or torture, but rather to that of murder (of Desdemona), Othello being actuated by a sense of his dishonour rather than by uncertainty; the sixteenth-century Italian code was for a husband to execute his guilty wife himself. In 'As Liberal as the North' (*Othello*, V, ii, 221) James F. Forrest[6] suggests that the reading 'North' is justifiable as indicating the traditional abode of Satan.

Nicolas K. Kiessling[7] would have us believe that in *The Winter's Tale*, II, iii, 103–7, Paulina fears that Perdita, if she inherits her father's proclivity to jealousy, may suspect that her own children have been fathered or replaced by an incubus.

In conclusion, there are a number of articles which offer sidelights on Shakespearian critics and editors. Francis Hayman prepared thirty-one drawings which were engraved for Sir Thomas Hanmer's edition of Shakespeare in 1744. Marcia Allentuck,[8] besides reproducing twenty-seven of these drawings, transcribes Hanmer's directions to Hayman about them which she has herself discovered. Hanmer is insistent on fidelity to the text, but it is noteworthy that, despite all the draperies, doorways and perspectives in the illustrations, there was evidently no intention to observe or preserve stage practice. John Kinnaird[9] reconstructs Hazlitt's theorising about Shakespearian tragedy. It emerges that, far from being a simple character critic, Hazlitt constantly paid regard to the integrated design of a work, which he saw as subject to dynamic change actuated by 'power', the release of conflicting emotions from sources both good and evil, but mainly evil. John W. Velz[10] writes an account of Joseph Crosby, an Englishman settled in Zanesville, Ohio, in the 1840s, who built up a major Shakespearian library and

[1] 'The "Ribaudred Nagge" of *Antony and Cleopatra*, III.x.10: A Suggested Emendation', *English Language Notes*, XIV (1976), 21–5.

[2] ' "Little Eyases" ', *Shakespeare Quarterly*, XXVIII (1977), 86–8.

[3] ' "He Mildews the White Wheat": *King Lear*, III.iv.120–4', *ibid.*, pp. 88–9.

[4] 'Shakespeare's "Tameness of a Wolf" ', *Notes & Queries*, n.s. XXIV (1977), 113–14.

[5] 'Death for Adultery: A Note on *Othello*, III.iii.394–96', *Shakespeare Quarterly*, XXVIII (1977), 89–92.

[6] ' "As Liberal as the North": *Othello*, V, ii, 221', *Notes & Queries*, n.s. XXIV (1977), 112–13.

[7] 'The Winter's Tale', II.iii.103–7: An Allusion to the Hag-Incubus', *Shakespeare Quarterly*, XXVIII (1977), 93–5.

[8] 'Sir Thomas Hanmer Instructs Francis Hayman: An Editor's Notes to his Illustrator (1744)', *ibid.*, XXVII (1976), 288–315.

[9] 'Hazlitt and the "Design" of Shakespearean Tragedy; A "Character" Critic Revisited', *ibid.*, XXVIII (1977), 22–39.

[10] 'Joseph Crosby and the Shakespeare Scholarship of the Nineteenth Century', *ibid.*, XXVII (1976), 316–28.

corresponded on textual matters with leading scholars of similar interests. Tennyson's comments on Shakespeare, recorded by his son and now transcribed by James O. Hoge,[1] include a few passing references to prominent actors, but will not set the Thames on fire. So, too, Stanley Wells's account[2] of Max Beerbohm's theatre criticism sheds much more light on Beerbohm than on Shakespeare.

[1] 'Tennyson on Shakespeare: His Talk about the Plays', *Texas Studies in Literature and Language*, XVIII (1976), 147–70.
[2] 'Shakespeare in Max Beerbohm's Theatre Criticism', *Shakespeare Survey 29* (Cambridge University Press, 1976), pp. 133–44.

© E. D. PENDRY 1978

3. TEXTUAL STUDIES

reviewed by GEORGE WALTON WILLIAMS

Last year this review took unaccustomed note of the deaths of three eminent Shakespearian editors, and it is with regret that it must add to its Necrology this year the names of Alfred Harbage and Charlton Hinman, the former the general editor of the Pelican Shakespeare in America, the latter the author of the monumental study of the printing of the First Folio.

Perhaps the most important item of bibliographical interest in 1976–7 was the publication of Volume 2 (I–Z) of the revised *Short Title Catalogue*, edited by W. A. Jackson and F. S. Ferguson, completed and seen through the press by the generous and capable Katharine F. Pantzer. Yet, important as it surely is, the new *STC* adds little to Shakespearian bibliography: two late issues of the Second Folio published after 1640 and one edition of *The Passionate Pilgrim* earlier than the 'first' edition in the unrevised *STC* (unique copy, fragmentary, at the Folger Library). The fact that the revision offers so few new entries – one new edition in a series of 93 numbers – is a mark of the thoroughness of the study of Shakespeare's text; for Edmund Spenser, on the other hand, the new *STC* provides in a series of 19 numbers eight new issues and editions. The revision includes up to five location symbols for each

side of the Atlantic, the identifying number for the plays from Greg's *Bibliography*, and occasional bibliographical notes.

An extremely useful volume is Anthony G. Petti's *English literary hands from Chaucer to Dryden*.[1] The monograph illustrates handsomely in sixty-seven plates 'the hands of the leading authors of the period' (p. v). Plates 36/37 contain Shakespeare's signatures and the upper portion of folio 9 of *The Booke of Sir Thomas More* (see also below); plates 38/39 contain – surprisingly – examples of forgeries by Ireland and Collier. The great virtue of the volume, however, is the introduction which discusses in understandable terms the substance and forms of manuscripts, the various English hands and their development, and techniques of editing. The notes and bibliography are invaluable for much more than Shakespearian study.

Following his *Orthography in Shakespeare and Elizabethan Drama*, A. C. Partridge has published *A Substantive Grammar of Shakespeare's Nondramatic Texts* in which he analyses the first editions of the poems and their preliminaries in terms of accidence, syntax, prosody, contractions, rare words and innova-

[1] *English Literary Hands from Chaucer to Dryden* (Edward Arnold, 1977).

tions, spelling, typography, and punctuation.[1] Examining the printed texts in great detail, he has accumulated a mound of information. Yet some disquiet remains. In spite of a long section on 'Compositor and Other Problems', Partridge does not seem to have studied closely the compositorial habits of the printers of the poems. One does not sense a firm base on which the grammar might have been constructed, and the notion that the 'inconsistent' printing of verso running titles in the Sonnets is a typographical anomaly (p. 142) is not one that inspires confidence. Such 'inconsistencies' might have contributed to an analysis of those titles which would have given Partridge's work a surer footing.

The Bibliographical Society of Northern Illinois has introduced a new periodical, *AEB* (*Analytical and Enumerative Bibliography*), a quarterly, the first issue bearing date of January 1977, to publish 'articles and notes on any bibliographical subject'. The fourth issue of each volume will include an 'Index to Reviews of Bibliographical Publications'. The lead article in the new journal is John Velz's report on the Joseph Crosby Letters at the Folger Shakespeare Library, 260 manuscript letters (over 2,000 pages) written by Joseph Crosby, of Zanesville, Ohio, 'a bibliophile and a learned annotator of the text of Shakespeare' (p. 7).[2] The second issue (April) offers Peter Davison's sobering cautions on the selection and presentation of bibliographical evidence and on the degree of credulity we should advance in accepting what our colleagues present as evidence.[3] Davison reminds us that the bibliographical method is not 'scientific', that its findings may (in our ignorance) be based on the exceptional rather than the normal, that human behaviour is illogical. Admitting his own propensities to be selective and partial, he illustrates his argument from the work of Hinman and Alan Craven on the compositors in Simmes's shop. He finds in their studies so

much selectivity as seriously to affect the validity of their conclusions, even where the evidence on the practice of using or not using stops after unabbreviated names in prefixes was, as we have supposed, clear. He presents a dozen rules of thumb on these matters; they emphasise the need for completeness in presenting each kind of evidence, for awareness of all kinds of evidence in a single book and in other books from the same shop, and for acceptance of the probability of lost information (uncorrected formes which have not survived), and he makes the interesting suggestion that one compositor might have corrected in proof what his fellow had set. The new journal is off to a good start.

Matters of authorship in two plays have occupied critics during the year: *Pericles* and *Sir Thomas More*. The importance of George Wilkins's interests in the preparation of *Pericles*, noted in this review last year, is developed by Willem Schrickx on the basis of a 1619 book-list.[4] George Wilkins had through

---

[1] *A Substantive Grammar of Shakespeare's Non-dramatic Texts* (Charlottesville, Va.: Bibliographical Society, 1976). Studies of contractions continue elsewhere: D. Nicholas Ranson reports on the findings of E. B. Everitt that the incidence of contractions (fourteen forms) provides a set of statistics that corresponds to the traditional dating of the plays, always moving towards a 'flexible speech-like versification' ('Shakespearian Contractions: The Text & Order of Shakespeare's Plays', *Shakespeare Newsletter*, XXVII (April 1977), 14). John Hazel Smith explains the policy of the Old Cambridge editors in handling 'the -ed/-'d suffix for past tenses of weak verbs' ('Verbal Suffixes in Several Shakespeare Editions', *ibid.*, p. 15).

[2] 'The Joseph Crosby Letters: A New Resource for Bibliographers', *AEB*, 1 (1977), 7–25; this article continues the report made by Velz in *Shakespeare Quarterly*, XXVII (1976), 316–28.

[3] 'The Selection and Presentation of Bibliographic Evidence', *AEB*, 1 (1977), 101–36.

[4] '*Pericles* in a Book-list of 1619 from the English Jesuit Mission and Some of the Play's Special Problems', *Shakespeare Survey 29* (Cambridge University Press, 1976), pp. 21–32.

other work developed an interest in the figure of Antiochus whom he came to regard as 'the embodiment of sinfulness . . . not only because of his sexual dissipation but also because of his sacrilegious attitude towards . . . the true religion' (p. 26). The triumph of Judas Machabeus over Antiochus was a topic popular in continental dramas, one of which Wilkins may well have seen (thus influencing II, iv, 6–12). The fact that the Antiochus theme 'has no integral connexion' (p. 31) with the later episodes of *Pericles* adds weight to the thesis that Wilkins may have been Shakespeare's collaborator for the first part of the play.

Another of the continuing riddles of Shakespearian textual studies is the attribution of Hand D in *Sir Thomas More*. The score for 1976–7 is, we may say, in favor of Shakespeare. A. G. Petti's comments in the volume cited above and Giles Dawson's observations in *TLS* (cited below) clearly support the attribution. D. J. Lake, working from the same assumption, sees the date of the Hand D additions as contemporary with *Hamlet* and *Measure for Measure*, though he recognises that other critics, notably P. W. M. Blayney, date the manuscript about 1592–3. He argues on the basis of linguistic preference that the Hand E additions by Dekker (an attribution generally accepted) are post 1600.[1] This review last year noted also the article by Michael L. Hays questioning the attribution,[2] and the present year's work has produced an article by Paul Ramsey which restates the uncertainty of it.[3] Ramsey surveys the arguments from paleography ('slightly negative'), orthography ('slightly for the identification'), literary evidence ('somewhat against'), meter ('inconclusive'), rhythm ('against') and, leaning on his 'first and continuing literary and sonal impression', he decides that 'D is not Shakespeare' (pp. 345–6). Ramsey is a poet (a Professor of English as well) and his 'impression' based on his own poetic sensitivity

is the determining element in his conclusion, just as Maunde Thompson's impression as a paleographer led him in the opposite direction. Hays and Ramsey have both cited the work of Sgt. C. A. Huber of the R.C.M.P. The paleographer, the poet, and the police sergeant – specialists all – have reached conclusions which must indicate that the case is neither proved nor disproved beyond all doubt; but Petti summarises: 'the case is generally held sufficiently proved with the support of linguistic, orthographic and stylistic evidence' (p. 87).

Another kind of revisionist problem is examined by Balz Engler whose concern is the 160 lines of *Othello* that appear in the Folio version only.[4] Since these lines do not derive from the source in Cinthio and since they 'move the play farther away from its source' and 'strengthen the theatrical features of the text' (pp. 518, 517), he concludes that they are an addition to the version found in the Quarto, made perhaps at the request of individual actors during rehearsals for the first performance.

James G. McManaway invites studies of the printing history of the Third Folio, pointing out that critics have paid little attention to this volume.[5] He cites Greg's *Bibliography* as giving

---

[1] 'The Date of the "Sir Thomas More" Additions by Dekker and Shakespeare', *Notes & Queries*, 24 (April 1977), 114–16.

[2] 'Shakespeare's Hand in *Sir Thomas More*: Some Aspects of the Paleographic Argument', *Shakespeare Studies*, VIII (1975), 241–53.

[3] 'Shakespeare and *Sir Thomas More* Revisited: or, A Mounty on the Trail', *Papers of the Bibliographical Society of America*, LXX (1976), 333–46. Ramsey had evidently not been able to see Hays's study before publishing his own. Ramsey cites the awkwardness of 'momtanish', yet, though 'mountainish' is not found elsewhere in Shakespeare, 'mountainous' appears in *Coriolanus*, II, iii, 117, where it is elided.

[4] 'How Shakespeare Revised *Othello*', *English Studies* (Amsterdam), 57 (1976), 515–21.

[5] 'New Discoveries in the Third Folio of Shakespeare', *Papers of the Bibliographical Society of America*, 70 (1976), 469–80.

'the best description', but he lists errors and corrections in the printing that he has discovered by examining multiple copies in the Folger Library (more than one can play at that game, it would seem). He argues that six sheets of the Folio had to be reprinted (in *Merry Wives*, *Love's Labour's Lost* [two sheets], *Pericles*, *Cromwell*, *Oldcastle*) because the runs on those sheets were short. 'It would ... seem probable that after Daniel completed his job in F3 (1664), he was instructed to reprint enough extra sheets and copies to complete the binding of the Folio' (p. 473). He presents many of the variant readings between the first and second settings of these F3 sheets.

Sailendra Kumar Sen informs us that Malone was dissatisfied with his 1790 edition of Shakespeare and continually revised his thinking in preparation for a second edition.[1] He was, however, by death departed from that right, and Boswell edited the 1821 edition from Malone's papers. Sen believes that the 1821 edition is set up variously from uncorrected pages of 1790, from pages annotated by Malone, and from autograph notes of Malone – the whole subjected to Boswell's idiosyncrasies and carelessness in proof-reading.

Compositorial analyses and analyses of those analyses sometimes generate more heat than light. Peter W. M. Blayney takes issue with S. W. Reid, defining his position on the Pavier Quartos in *The Library* of June 1976; Reid replies in the December issue with further refinements and explanations.[2] What is manifest from this *contretemps* is that evidence on the Pavier compositor(s) is not yet adequate to draw final conclusions on that set of Quartos. Reid's conclusions that we shall 'in the not too distant future' (p. 394) solve that problem and that we should in the meanwhile 'get on with the study of F1' (p. 393) seem reasonable, hopeful and judicious.

An example of that getting on is John S. O'Connor's study of Compositors C and D,

two compositors 'not so important as ... B ... [but] more manageable' (p. 58).[3] O'Connor analyses the work of the two men when setting from Quarto copy: 42 pages for C, 25.5 pages for D – a fair sample from which to draw conclusions. O'Connor finds that C transposed words frequently, D seldom; that C substituted words through memorial error, D through misreading (though he did not misread the word order); that C omitted words frequently through carelessness and in order to save space, D less frequently though more likely than C to skip an entire line; C interpolated words in prose and kept regular meter in verse, D interpolated words in verse and so spoiled the meter. Having drawn up these standards on the basis of observed characteristics, O'Connor then applies them to the textual cruces in the plays set by these two men from MS. Though he advances in this study no new emendations of his own, he gives solid and demonstrable reasons why an editor should look for particular kinds of corruption. The essay is a model of methodology.

In a study not quite in that league, Jonathan H. Spinner analyses the bad Quarto of *Henry V*, arguing that two compositors were at work.[4] The thesis may, indeed, be correct, but the evidence brought forward is not such as will support it and is often irrelevant to it. We are told, for example, that the existence of a single anomalous running title and the presence of three different stocks of paper in the Quarto suggest two-compositor work; no attempt is made, however, to explain how these two pieces of evidence support the thesis or relate

[1] 'Malone's Two Shakespeare Editions', *Library*, XXXI (1976), 390–1.
[2] 'The Compositors of the Pavier Quartos', *Library*, XXXI (1976), 143–5; 392–4.
[3] 'A Qualitative Analysis of Compositors C and D in the Shakespeare First Folio', *Studies in Bibliography*, XXX (1977), 57–74.
[4] 'The Composition and Presswork of *Henry V*, Q1', *Library*, XXXII (1977), 37–44.

to a division of labor between two compositors. Furthermore, Spinner has imagined a scenario in which the text of the full play, 'staied' on 4 August 1600 was abridged by the actors hastily so as to secure its printing before the copyright was transferred to Pavier on 14 August. The actors' haste contributed to the compositors' confusion. This re-construction seems inventive.

After a close study of recurring types, Frank E. Haggard demonstrates that sheets A–D of *Romeo and Juliet* (Q1), printed by Danter, were set by formes, and by the same technique he confirms an earlier analysis (based on type shortage) that sheets E–K, printed by Allde, were also set by formes.[1] Though evidence from the recurrence of types is as nearly irrefutable as bibliographical evidence can be, it cannot answer all the questions and, like other techniques, it is subject to human fallibility (see his footnote 5).

E. A. J. Honigmann summons editors to an examination of stage directions and speech prefixes as careful as that they give to dialogue.[2] He notes the inexact or inconsistent location of entry directions in early and in modern editions, and he recommends that certain directions be relocated so as to increase the dramatic effectiveness of the scene: after Volumnia's final appeal to Coriolanus (v, iii, 182), we have in the Folio:

I am husht untill our City be afire, & then Ile speak
a litle
        Holds her by the hand silent.
Corio. O Mother, Mother!
What have you done? Behold! the Heavens do ope,

Honigmann suggests that the silence will more appropriately follow than precede the initial response from Coriolanus; as the text stands (and modern editors follow), 'the actor has the very difficult task of conveying an overwhelming emotion without the help of words' (p. 119). Metrical considerations give some support to this suggestion, for Coriolanus's response completes his mother's half-line; to interrupt a metrical unit with a long pause is to render it no metrical unit. Honigmann also rejects the designation 'Aside' for speeches that he thinks other characters on stage should hear. So Hamlet's contemptuous remarks about Osric (v, ii, 83–90) marked 'Aside' to Horatio should be heard by Osric – to his own benefit, we may suppose. In the same fashion, 'A little more than kin, and less than kind' (i, ii, 65), may not inappropriately be heard by Claudius – a 'semi-aside'; to follow Theobald's 'Aside' here is to deprive the line of its 'nervy edge'. Honigmann also discusses the delivery of speeches prefixed 'All' or 'Both' and the proper reading of 'O!', which he considers no particular sound but an indication to the actor to make the sound proper to the context ('*A long sigh.*', '*Othello cries out in pain.*'). Editors of texts will be well advised to take these comments to heart and to head.

Theobald's celebrated emendation at *Henry V*, II, iii, 18–19 still challenges editors and critics. In support of the Folio 'a Table of greene fields', Robert F. Fleissner calls attention to Ophelia's songs (*Ham.*, IV, v, 21–43) in which also a woman laments the death of a man, 'He is dead and gone ... / At his head a grasse-*greene Turfe*, at his heeles a *stone*', and 'God be at your *Table*!'(italics indicate significant echoes). He suggests that in *Hamlet*, 'the playwright was echoing his own words and ideas [from *Henry V*]..., unconsciously...' (p. 148). He recalls the

[1] 'Type-Recurrence Evidence and the Printing of *Romeo and Juliet* Q1 (1597)', *Papers of the Bibliographical Society of America*, 71 (1977), 66–73.

[2] 'Re-enter the Stage Direction: Shakespeare and some Contemporaries', *Shakespeare Survey* 29 (Cambridge University Press, 1976), pp. 117–25. It is to be regretted that Honigmann did not comment on C. B. Lower's interesting suggestion of simultaneous speech at *Romeo and Juliet*, IV, v, described in *Shakespeare Studies*, VIII (1975), 177–94. Maurice Charney also has considered 'Hamlet's O-groans', *Shakespeare Newsletter*, XXVII (April 1977), 16.

traditional association between death and the color green (a pallor that may lurk, it might be added, under the freshness of Claudius's green memory of his dear brother's death [i, ii, 21]), especially as it appears in the ballad of 'Captain Wedderburn's Courtship': 'Death is greener than the grass' (p. 149). Fleissner would understand the line to mean that 'Falstaff, nose and all, was a veritable picture of green death' (p. 148).[1]

In support of Theobald's 'a babbled of green fields', J. M. Maguin, endorsing the psalmodic interpretation of the passage, suggests that the coldness of Falstaff at the moment of death recalls the death of King David and the efforts made to revive him (1 Kings 1: 1-4) by the stimulation of the virgin Abishag. Maguin suggests further that the psalm records the moment of death: the staff of the Good Shepherd comforts; the fat knight offers only a 'false staff'.[2] Giles Dawson approaches the problem paleographically, examining the forms and spellings of Hand D in *Sir Thomas More* to explain how 'babbled' came to be misread 'Table'.[3] The acceptance of the misreading 'Table' for 'babbled' requires the acceptance of three troublesome propositions: '(a) that Shakespeare spelt the key word *babld*; (b) that ... he so formed the initial *b* that the compositor took it for a *t*; (c) that the compositor read the terminal *d* as an *e*'. The last proposition can be easily accepted, for this type of error is a commonplace to editors of Shakespeare. The first cannot be accepted at all. 'The hand [D] that wrote [charterd, clothd, pleasd, ruld, willd, etc.] could certainly write *babld*'; could possibly, but evidently did not. Unhappily there is no other example of 'babbled' in Shakespeare; but, though that word does not appear, there are over thirty examples of dabbled, doubled, scribbled, tabled, trembled, troubled in various First Quartos and First Folio: none is spelled *-bld*. No preterite in print of these parallel verbs omits both the *-e-* and the apostrophe. Dawson's argument for

'babld' as a Shakespearian spelling will not hold up. The second proposition seems at first unlikely; none of the modern editors of *Sir Thomas More* has been guilty of this misreading. Yet an examination of the manuscript forms with this possibility in mind reveals that such a misreading might have occurred. Kellner observes that 'Elizabethan ... *to* and *be* can hardly be told from one another', yet he gives no convincing examples.[4] Dawson's recognition that in at least one hand of the period (Hand D) initial *b* could be misread as *t* removes a major impediment to the acceptance of Theobald's emendation. In that recognition, the problem of the preterite vanishes. Once the compositor had made his initial *t*:*b* misreading, he had placed himself in a situation that was hopeless. Perhaps the MS read 'babeld'; misreading the initial *b* as *t* and the terminal *d* as *e*, the compositor would produce 'tabele', which he would normalize to 'table'. (Dawson does not mention the fact that Folio reads *T*, not *t*; in this context, this distinction is one without a difference.) Theobald's emendation may never be proved right, but it has never been proved wrong; Dawson's argument is strong support for it.[5]

Three emendations, not immediately con-

[1] ' "A Table of Greene fields", Grasse-greene/ Table, and Balladry', *Shakespeare Jahrbuch* (Weimar), 112 (1976), 143–9.
[2] 'A Note on a Further Biblical Parallel with the Death of Falstaff', *Cahiers élizabéthains*, No. 10, pp. 65–6.
[3] 'Theobald, *table/babbled*, and *Sir Thomas More*', *Times Literary Supplement*, 22 April 1977, p. 484.
[4] Leon Kellner, *Restoring Shakespeare* (Leipzig, 1925), p. 105.
[5] If Theobald's emendation is accepted, Shakespeare uses the word 'babble' twice in the play, once in the description of the speech of Falstaff, once in Fluellen's description of the speech of those who disregard the disciplines of the wars. Shakespeare thus balances his characters in the use of the word; for just as Fluellen's care and valor supersede Falstaff's cant and vanity, so Fluellen's repudiation of those who babble repudiates Falstaff's undisciplined

vincing, deserve consideration by future editors. Robert H. Ray suggests that 'Yon ribaudred Nagge of Egypt' in *Antony and Cleopatra* results from the compositor's failure to insert a space between 'ribaud' (i.e., 'ribald') and 'red'.[1] (The presence of the adjective 'red' has been suggested already in the emendation 'riband-red'.) The term 'red' describes the spots (tokens) on the skin of a victim of the plague ('Nagge' recalls Plutarch's and Plato's 'horse of the minde ... the unreyned lust of concupiscence'.). Though this is not implausible, one wonders why Scarus should wish for leprosy to overtake a carrier of the plague. Mary J. H. Gross proposes for *Richard III* a reassignment of the speeches of Richard and Hastings at I, i, 134–44.[2] The present assignment, as she rightly indicates, presents an awkwardness, but that awkwardness is not so insuperable as she supposes. It is probably easier to accept the present assignment, since she does not offer any bibliographical argument for the division and reassignment of speeches in her proposal. She raises two questions, hard to answer: (Q) Why does Richard ask for news about his own brother? (A) Because, as always, he wishes to appear ignorant of court affairs and far removed from them. (Q) How does Hastings know the answers? (A) Shakespeare gives them to him so that he can demonstrate the answer to the first question. Gilian West thinks that 'estridges that with the wind / Bated, like eagles ...' in *1 Henry IV*, IV, i, 98–9, should be 'estridges that withe the wind, / Baited like eagles ...', i.e., hawks that master the wind.[3] (One thinks of Hopkins.) Though the verb 'withe' is uncommon, its use here makes possible the continuation of a typically Shakespearian parallelism; 'Baited' then takes the meaning 'refreshed or revived'. The interpretations of the two verbs make for a clearer and more forceful reading than those of the 'received text', but they are both strained out of their normal contexts – probably too much so.

Various efforts to gloss difficult passages in the text have met with varying success. William E. Miller finds a second significance for the term 'eyases' (nestlings) (*Ham.*, II, ii, 336) – foolish and disagreeable.[4] Though this interpretation is apt enough for *Hamlet*, it will scarcely serve for Shakespeare's other use of the word where Romeo calls Juliet by this name (II, ii, 168). J. F. Killeen would read the difficult phrase, '*Castiliano vulgo*' (*Twelfth Night*, I, iii, 39), to mean 'talk of the devil and he'll appear'.[5] The word '*vulgo*' was common in introducing proverbs, or, as here, a translation of a proverb into the vulgar speech; '*Castiliano*' Killeen sees as equivalent to 'Spaniard' and hence from an Italian (i.e., Illyrian) point of view equivalent to the devil. This gloss is perhaps too elliptical. Anthony S. G. Edwards and Anthony W. Jenkins support the authenticity of Folio 'prenzie' (*M. for M.*, III, i, 95, 98) having found the word 'pryncy' (= 'princely') in *The Castell of Pleasure* (1518) and having discovered a comparable word 'prenselles' (= 'princesses') in a MS of 1554/5.[6] (They admit that another

method of speaking. It is not to strain too far to suggest that this 'rejection' of Falstaff indicates that Falstaff's entire discourse has been no more than babbling and thus comparable to the 'eloquence' of Francis in II, iv, and of Hotspur in II, iii, of Part One.

[1] 'The "Ribaudred Nagge" of *Antony and Cleopatra*, III.x.10: A Suggested Emendation', *English Language Notes*, XIV (1976), 21–5.

[2] 'Some Puzzling Speech Prefixes in *Richard III*', *Papers of the Bibliographical Society of America*, 71 (1977), 73–5.

[3] '"Estridges that with the wind": A Note on *1 Henry IV*, IV.i.97–100', *English Studies* (Amsterdam), 58 (1977), 20–2.

[4] 'Little Eyases', *Shakespeare Quarterly*, XXVIII (1977), 86–8.

[5] '*Twelfth Night*, I.iii.42; "*Castiliano vulgo*"', *ibid.*, pp. 92–3.

[6] '"Prenzie": *Measure for Measure*, III.i', *ibid.*, XXVII (1976), 333–4.

editor of the text has read the word differently.) Stanley Wells suggests that when Lysander threatens to kill Demetrius and terms his name 'vile' (*MND*, II, ii, 107) Shakespeare is re-calling not the Demetrius from North's *Plutarch* but rather the Demetrius of *Titus Andronicus*, a figure frequently seen on the Elizabethan stage.[1] The most successful of these glosses is that of Lucy Brashear for *Othello*.[2] Since critics now date the writing of Lady Cary's tragedy of *Mariam* before *Othello* (though not published until 1613), this tragedy of the death of an innocent wife by the actions of her jealous husband may have been available to Shakespeare before he wrote *Othello*. The most interesting aspect of this thesis is that it defines 'the base Judean' (Folio, v, ii, 350) as Herod. This interpretation of the word was standard in eighteenth-century editions of the play – Theobald cites *Mariam* as a 'later' parallel to *Othello* – but the story is no longer familiar to readers (and critics), and Shakespeare's allusion has been lost; it may now be reclaimed.

In a paper delivered before the Shakespeare Association of America, the present reviewer discusses facts and problems in the text of *2 Henry IV*.[3] Most of his paper rehearses the considered opinions of other critics, but in the concluding section he advances the hypothesis that the manuscript used as copy for the Folio text of the play was one prepared specifically for the Cobham family to prove to Oldcastle's descendants that the fat knight was 'not the man', a suggestion which, though not demonstrable, is not necessarily unlikely.

[1] 'A Note on Demetrius's *Vile Name*', *Cahiers élizabéthains*, No. 10, pp. 67–8.

[2] 'A Case for the Influence of Lady Cary's Tragedy of *Mariam* on Shakespeare's *Othello*', *Shakespeare Newsletter*, XXVI (Sept. 1976), 31.

[3] 'The Text of *2 Henry IV*: Facts and Problems', *Shakespeare Studies*, IX (1976), 173–82.

INDEX

Abartis, Caesarea, 166
Abrams, M. H., 62n
Acuña, José B., 175
Adlington, William, 33, 38, 39, 43
Akhmanova, Olga, 174–5
Akrigg, G. P. V., 178
Alberti, L. B., 19, 22
Aldus, P. T., 170
Alexander, Peter, 23n, 78n
Allen, Don Cameron, 15
Allentuck, Marcia, 190
Alpers, Svetlana Leontief, 16n, 19n
Anson, John, 10n
Apelles, 18
Appian, 9
Apuleius of Madaura, 33–43
Ariosto, 18
Aristotle, 7, 14
Armin, Robert, 187
Arthos, John, 12n
Ashcroft, Peggy, 149
Augustine, St, 8, 15, 189

Baldwin, C. S., 18n
Baldwin, T. W., 5, 33n
Bancrofts, the, 188
Barber, C. L., 130
Bartenschlager, Klaus, 189
Barton, Anne (Righter), 81n, 118n, 147
Barton, John, 141–2, 149, 152, 153
Battenhouse, Roy, 13n, 15, 180
Baxandall, Michael, 19n
Beam, Marjorie, 184
Bedford, Brian, 147
Beerbohm, Max, 176, 191
Bennett, Robert B., 165
Benson, Susan, 143
Bentley, G. E., 185
Berry, Edward I., 168
Berry, Ralph, 4n, 54, 152, 166
Bethell, S. L., 9n, 62n
Black, James, 95
Blackmur, R. P., 127n, 128, 135, 136, 137
Bland, Marjorie, 143
Blayney, Peter W. M., 193, 194
Bluestone, Max, 54n
Blunt, Anthony, 18n
Blythe, Domini, 144
Boccaccio, 25n
Bolgar, R. R., 4, 7
Booth, Michael R., 187
Booth, Stephen, 53n, 128n, 168

Bott, William, 177
Bowman, William, 164
Bradbrook, Muriel C., 13, 14, 29n, 30, 62n, 63n, 178
Bradley, A. C,. 48
Bradshaw, Thomas, 46
Brashear, Lucy, 198
Brecht, Bertolt, 63, 184
Brockman, B. A., 176
Brook, Peter, 141, 151, 152, 173, 187
Brooke, Arthur, 182
Brower, Reuben, 7, 10, 12n
Brown, John Russell, 156n
Brown, Keith, 179
Browner, Angus, 173
Brownstein, O. L., 186
Bryan, Margaret B., 10n
Buchanan, George, 40, 42
Bullough, Geoffrey, 33n, 35n, 40n, 42n, 58n
Bulman, James C., 182
Bulman, Michael, 147
Bunselmeyer, J., 130n
Burbage, Richard, 16, 177
Burton, Robert, 105, 112–13
Bury, John, 158n
Bush, Douglas, 29, 46n, 48, 128n, 132

Cairncross, Andrew S., 182
Caldwell, Zoe, 145
Cantor, Paul A., 8
Carnovsky, Morris, 173
Carroll, William C., 164
Carson, Neil, 186
Cartari, Vincentio, 47, 48, 49, 51
Cary, Lady, 198
Castelvetro, 18
Castiglione, B., 85, 86, 87, 89, 90, 91
Cavendish, George, 189–90
Chamberlain, John, 99–100, 104n
Chambers, E. K., 100, 104n, 127n
Chambers, R. W., 107n
Chapman, George, 6, 33
Charles, Prince (Charles I), 102
Charlton, H. B., 18n
Charney, Maurice, 171
Chatterjee, V., 171
Chaucer, Geoffrey, 3, 4, 15
Chekhov, Anton, 105
Cicero, 3, 7, 19n
Clemen, Wolfgang, 77
Coldewey, John C., 186, 187

Coleridge, S. T., 62, 105, 111–12
Colie, Rosalie L., 53n
Colley, John Scott, 175
Collier, J. P., 7n
Colvin, Sidney, 15
Conti, Natalie, 47
Cook, Edward, 16n
Coolidge, John S., 180
Corneille, P., 2
Cornwell, Charlotte, 148
Coursen, H. R., 171
Cox, Brian, 159–60
Craig, Edward, 188
Craig, W. J., 48n
Craven, Alan, 192
Creeth, Edmund, 169
Crosby, Joseph, 190–1, 192
Crowley, Richard C., 12n
Cruttwell, Patrick, 127, 130

Danby, John, 48n
Dance, Charles, 147
Daniel, Samuel, 183
Danson, Lawrence, 54n
Dante, 174, 184
D'Avanzo, Mario L., 190
David, Alan, 147
David, Richard, 151
Davis, H., 29n
Davison, Peter, 192
Dawson, Giles, 193, 196
Dean, John, 183
Dean, Leonard F., 9n
DeGeorge, R and F., 54n
Dekker, Thomas, 33, 193
Delany, Paul, 178
Dench, Jeffery, 147, 148, 149
Dennis, John, 1, 3
Dessen, Alan C., 59n
Devine, George, 151
Dietrich, Julia C., 185
Dobbins, Austin C., 180
Donaldson, I., 165
Doran, Madeleine, 3, 62n
Douce, Francis, 42n
Dowden, Edward, 1–2, 127n
Dryden, John, 1, 77, 110, 111n
Duffy, John, 173
Durden, Richard, 142

Eagleton, Terry, 62n
Eddison, Robert, 159
Edwards, Anthony S. G., 189, 197

INDEX

Edwards, Philip, 127, 133, 136, 137
Eliot, T. S., 173
Elizabeth, Queen, 56, 58, 143
Elyot, Thomas, 85, 86, 88n, 89, 90, 91
Engler, Balz, 175, 193
Erasmus, 14, 17, 18, 33
Erlich, Bruce, 176
Essex, Robert Devereux, Earl of, 99, 100, 104; his son Robin, 101
Etlin, Andrew V., 12n
Euripides, 163
Evans, Bertrand, 31n
Evans, J. Blakemore, 4n, 34n
Evelyn, John, 139

Fairbanks, Arthur, 17n
Fairchild, A. H. R., 15, 16
Faucit, Helen, 188
Ferguson, F. S., 191
Fergusson, Francis, 174
Ficino, Marsilio, 46
Fiedler, Leslie A., 130, 136
Finney, Albert, 157, 161–2
Fisher, Lizette Andrews, 11n
Fleay, F. G., 102
Fleetwood, Susan, 160
Fleissner, Robert F., 195–6
Fludd, Robert, 185
Fly, Richard, 57n, 169
Ford, Boris, 48n
Ford, John, 184
Ford-Davies, Oliver, 148
Forrest, James F., 190
Foulkes, Richard, 188
Foy, Robert C., 5n
France, Anna Kay, 175
Frederyke of Jennen, 25n
Freud, S., 4
Frey, David L., 167
Friedman, Donald M., 168
Frye, Northrop, 129, 135, 136

Galloway, David, 186
Garber, Marjorie, 166, 174
Gardner, H., 29n
Gardner, S. N., 172
Generosa, Sister M., 33n
Gervinus, Georg Gottfried, 3n
Gilman, Ernest B., 181
Glover, Julian, 150
Godshalk, W. L., 171
Godwin, E. W., 188
Goethe, J. W. von, 2n
Goldman, Michael, 173
Gollancz, Israel, 15n
Gombrich, E. H., 16
Gorfain, Phyllis, 166
Gower, John, 183
Grant, Patrick, 181
Granville-Barker, H., 142, 151, 188
Graves, Robert, 50n

Green, Henry, 50n
Greene, Robert, 13
Greg, W. W., 95n, 102n, 191, 193
Grennan, Eamon, 184
Griffiths, Richard, 142
Griffiths, Trevor, 188
Gross, Mary J. H., 197
Guard, Pippa, 142
Guillén, Claudio, 54
Gurr, Andrew, 7n, 27n
Guthrie, Tyrone, 144, 145, 188

Habicht, Werner, 175
Haggard, Frank E., 195
Hagstrum, Jean, 14
Hall, Peter, 141, 142, 149, 151, 152, 155, 158n, 159, 160, 162
Halstead, W. L., 33n
Hamburger, Michael, 175
Hands, Terry, 148–51
Hanmer, Thomas, 190
Harbage, Alfred, 63n, 128n, 132, 191
Harris, Duncan J., 172
Hassel, R. Chris, 5n
Hawkes, Terence, 173
Hawkins, Harriett, 107n
Hayman, Francis, 190
Hays, Michael L., 193
Hazlitt, William, 176, 190
Hecksher, W. S., 16
Heiberg, Johanne Luise, 173, 188
Heinemann, Margot, 63n, 175
Heltzel, Virgil B., 91n
Henley, W. E., 34n
Henry, Martha, 144–5
Henry Frederick, Prince of Wales (son of James I), 101, 103
Henslowe, Philip, 185
Hermogenes, 17
Herodotus, 183
Heywood, Thomas, 33
Hill, Charles Jarvis, 106n
Hill, Christopher, 106n, 113n
Hills, Mathilda M., 171
Hinman, Charlton, 49n, 191, 192
Hobson, Harold, 145
Hoby, Thomas, 85, 87n
Hoeniger, F. David, 5n, 166
Hogan, C. B., 188
Hogan, Floriana T., 185
Hoge, James O., 191
Holinshed, R., 25n, 34, 41n
Holland, Norman N., 10n
Holland, Philemon, 183
Hollar, Wenceslaus, 139
Holmes, Martin, 63n
Holt, Leigh, 172
Homer, 6, 7, 17
Honigmann, E. A. J., 7n, 59n, 195
Horace, 19
Horwich, Richard, 165

Hosley, Richard, 5n
Hotson, Leslie, 18n
Houseman, John, 173
Howard, Alan, 150
Huber, C. A., 193
Hubler, Edward, 127n
Huffman, Clifford Chalmers, 7n
Hughes, Geoffrey, 171
Hulse, S. Clark, 13n
Hume, Martin, 179
Humphreys, A. R., 87n
Hunter, G. K., 11, 127n
Hunter, Robert G., 170
Huston, J. Dennis, 165
Hutt, William, 146
Hutton, J., 136n
Hynes, Samuel, 14n

Ingram, W. G., 164
Irving, Henry, 188

Jackson, B. W., 6n
Jackson, Russell, 187
Jackson, W. A., 191
Jakobson, Roman, 54n, 56n
James I, King, 41, 101, 102, 103, 104
James, Emrys, 147, 149, 150
James, Henry, 62n
Jefford, Barbara, 160
Jenkins, Anthony W., 189, 197
Jenkins, Harold, 35
Johnson, Samuel, 1, 5, 9, 10, 105, 111n, 112
Jones, David, 145
Jones, Emrys, 163, 169
Jones, Inigo, 102, 186
Jonson, Ben, 1, 4, 33, 46–7, 100–1, 102, 103, 111n, 158n
Jorgensen, Paul A., 189
Julius Caesar, 10

Kahn, Coppélia, 11, 20n, 164
Kaplan, Joel H., 33n
Keats, John, 135n
Kellner, Leon, 196
Kelso, Ruth, 85n, 86n, 88n, 91n
Kembles, the, 188
Kennedy, Dennis, 187
Kennedy, Milton Boone, 8, 9n, 10
Ker, W. P., 77n
Kermode, Frank, 46
Kiessling, Nicolas K., 190
Killeen, J. F., 189, 197
King, T. J., 179, 187
Kinnaird, John, 176, 190
Kinnear, B. G., 128n, 133n
Kirk, G. S., 50n
Kirkpatrick, R., 174, 184
Kirsch, Arthur C., 105, 106n, 107n, 109, 111, 112
Kleb, William E., 187–8

Klinck, Dennis R., 190
Knight, Charles, 2
Knight, G. Wilson, 9, 27, 29, 59n, 128n, 135, 151, 171, 173
Knight, W. F. Jackson, 50
Knights, L. C., 48, 127n, 167
Kolin, Philip C., 185
Kott, Jan, 53n, 181
Krabbe, Henning, 173, 188
Krieger, Murray, 128n
Kronenfeld, Judy Z., 182
Kuhn, Maura Slattery, 165, 189

Lake, D. J., 184, 187, 193
Landry, Hilton, 127, 163, 164
Lascelles, Mary, 147
Latham, Jacqueline E. M., 171-2
Latimer, Hugh, 120
Laurenson, James, 148, 149, 150
Law, Robert A., 12n, 94, 98n
Lecoq, Anne-Marie, 15n
Leech, Clifford, 5
Leggatt, Alexander, 173
Leishman, J. B., 128n
Leisi, Ernst, 175
Lerner, Laurence, 184
Levenson, Jill L., 181
Lever, J. W., 100, 106n, 127n, 128n, 129, 130, 133, 136, 180
Lévi-Strauss, Claude, 56
Levin, Bernard, 151n
Levin, Harry, 46, 174
Levin, Richard, 176
Levitsky, Ruth M., 180
Lewis, C. S., 137
Lindsay, Marshall, 164
Livy, 15
Lloyd, Michael, 33
Löb, Ladislaus, 184
Lodge, Thomas, 2, 183
Logan, George M., 183
Lomazzo, 19
Love, John M., 165-6
Lucan, 183
Lucian, 182
Lyly, John, 18, 85n, 117
Lynd, J. J., 57n

McAlindon, T., 10
McCall, Marsh H., 13n
McCallin, Clem, 148
MacCallum, M. W., 2-3, 7
McClure, N. E., 99n
McEnery, Peter, 147, 149
Macherey, Pierre, 62n
Machiavelli, 180
McKewin, Carole, 176
McLellan, Eric, 177
McManaway, James G., 193
McPeek, James A. S., 33n, 38n
Maguin, J. M., 196

Malone, Edmund, 194
Mander, Carel van, 16
Manningham, John, 177-8
Markels, Julian, 9n, 11n
Marlowe, Christopher, 33, 109, 155-62, 170
Martin, L. C., 33n
Martin, Philip, 127n, 128, 129, 130, 135n
Martin, Priscilla, 176
Marx, Karl, 56n, 61n, 175
Matchett, William H., 184
Matejka, L., 54n, 55n
Matsumoto, Toshio, 30n
Maxwell, J. C., 25n, 112
Medici, Lorenzo de', 46
Mehl, Dieter, 181
Meinck, Carl, 11n
Melchiori, G., 164
Merchant, W. Moelwyn, 4n, 16n
Meres, Francis, 127, 138
Metscher, Thomas, 175
Metz, G. Harold, 173, 187
Miller, William E., 190, 197
Mills, A. D., 186
Mirren, Helen, 149
Moiseiwitsch, Tanya, 145
Montagu, Walter, 186
Montrose, Louis A., 165
Moore, Edward M., 188
Morgan, Norman Louis, 180
Morton, A. L., 61n, 106n
Mowatt, Barbara A., 166
Muir, Kenneth, 10n, 177, 184
Mullaly, Robert, 187
Mullin, Michael, 188

Napier, John, 141
Neely, C. T., 54n, 164
Neilson, William Allan, 106n
Nelligan, Kate, 147
Nevill, William, 190
Nosworthy, James, 31n
Nowottny, Winifred, 163
Noyes, G. E., 91n
Nunn, Trevor, 146-7
Nuttall, A. D., 106n

O'Connor, John S., 194
Okerlund, G., 95n
Oliver, H. J., 185
Oliviers, the, 152
Orgel, Stephen, 98n, 102n
Ornstein, Robert, 95
Orrell, John, 186
Ortelius, 18
Ovid, 7, 15, 24, 25, 29, 31, 79, 83

Pafford, J. H. P., 65n
Palumbo, Ronald J., 187
Panofsky, Erwin, 45, 46, 47

Pantzer, Katherine F. 191
Paolucci, Anne, 175
Papp, Joseph, 173
Partridge, A. C., 191-2
Pasco, Richard, 153
Pasternak, Boris, 175
Paul, St, 4-5
Pearson, D'Orsay W., 4n, 6n
Peel, William, 188
Pennell, Nicholas, 145
Pérez, Antonio, 179
Petti, Anthony G., 191, 193
Phillips, James Emerson, 6
Phillips, Robin, 141, 143, 144
Philostratus, 16, 17, 19
Pirkhofer, Anton M., 164
Platt, Michael, 11n
Plato, 7, 17, 197
Pliny, 16, 18, 19, 183
Plotinus, 49
Plutarch, 3, 7, 9, 10, 18, 34, 46, 48, 57n, 183, 197, 198
Poisson, Rodney, 164, 190
Pomorska, K., 54n
Pooler, C. Knox, 136n
Pope, Alexander, 1
Price, H. T., 95n, 102n
Price, Roger Carson, 5n
Prince, F. T., 13n
Prior, Moody E., 168
Proudfoot, Richard, 167
Pryse, Marjorie, 172
Purkayastha, Jagodish, 171

Quilley, Denis, 159
Quintilian, 14n, 17, 18

Rähesoo, Jaak, 175
Ralegh, Walter, 48
Ramsey, Paul, 163, 193
Ranald, Margaret Loftus, 179
Ransome, John Crowe, 164
Rare Triumphs of Love and Fortune, The, 25n
Ray, Robert H., 190, 197
Redpath, Theodore, 164
Reese, M. M., 93
Reid, S. W., 194
Rhodes, Ernest L., 185
Rhys-Davies, John, 147
Richardson, Ian, 153
Richfield, Edwin, 148
Richmond, Hugh M., 5n
Ricks, Christopher, 130
Riddell, James A., 168
Righter, Anne, see Barton, Anne
Roberts, Jeanne Addison, 176, 177
Robson, Simon, 190
Rockas, Leo, 168
Rollins, Hyder, 127n, 136n
Romano, Giulio, 10

Root, Robert K., 49n
Rosand, David, 18n
Rossiter, A. P., 62n, 93
Rothschild, Herbert B., 183
Rowe, Nicholas, 77, 83
Rubens, P. P., 45
Rubinstein, Annette, 175
Rulton, Robert C., 181
Russell, Stephen, 144
Rydén, Mats, 189
Rymer, Thomas, 3

Saccio, Peter, 167
Sainte-Meuve, Benoît de, 181
Salingar, Leo, 62n, 116
Sanders, Norman, 176, 177
Sanderson, James L., 5n
Saussure, Ferdinand de, 54
Saxon, A. H., 188
Schanzer, Ernest, 107n
Schiller, J. C. F. von, 2
Schoenbaum, Samuel, 177
Schönfeld, S. J., 182
Schrickx, Willem, 179, 192
Scofield, Paul, 158n
Seltzer, Daniel, 174
Sen, Sailendra Kumar, 194
Seneca, 7
Seymour-Smith, Martin, 164
Seznec, Jean, 48n
Shaaber, M. A., 189
Shakespeare, William
    editions
        Alexander, Peter, 23n, 78n
        Arden, 136n
        Casebook, 176
        Complete Pelican, 55n, 191; revised
            Pelican, 128n
        Craig, W. J., 48n
        Folio, 95, 100, 101
        Folio 1, facsimile, 49n, 191
        Folio 2, 191
        Folio 3, 193-4
        Neilson, William Allan, and Char-
            les Jarvis Hill, 106n
        New Arden, 13n, 25n, 29n, 65n,
            87n, 93, 94
        New Cambridge, 93
        New Penguin, 118n, 153
        New Variorum, 17n, 127n
        Quarto: 'bad', 194; Henry V,
            95-6, 100, 101; Sonnets, 137
        Quarto, Pavier, 194
        Riverside, 4n, 34n
    plays
        All's Well That Ends Well, 98,
            116, 124, 144-6, 152, 165-6,
            189
        Antony and Cleopatra, 2, 3, 6, 8, 9,
            10, 33, 34, 45-52, 57, 58, 59-61,
            65, 172, 183, 190, 197

As You Like It, 116, 117, 146-7, 165,
    182, 184, 189
Comedy of Errors, The, 4, 5, 6, 33n
Coriolanus, 2, 4, 6, 7, 8, 9, 10, 11
    12, 27, 55, 57, 58, 60, 61, 172,
    175, 176, 195
Cymbeline, 5n, 6, 8, 10, 23-32, 33n,
    166
Hamlet, 10, 20, 26, 34-6, 55, 57,
    58, 77, 83, 115, 116, 119, 121,
    169, 170, 171, 179, 181, 184, 190,
    193, 195-6, 197
Henry IV, 184
1 Henry IV, 57, 85-91, 115, 116,
    189, 197
2 Henry IV, 57, 99, 189, 198
Henry V, 55, 56, 57, 58, 60, 88n,
    93-104, 168, 194
Henry VI, 148-51, 163
1 Henry VI, 168, 185
2 and 3 Henry VI, 167
3 Henry VI, 27
Henry VIII, 98, 99
Julius Caesar, 1, 2, 6, 8, 9, 10,
    27, 55, 57, 58, 172, 183
King John, 27, 153, 182
King Lear, 38-40, 56, 58, 60, 77,
    115, 116, 117, 121-2, 169, 170,
    171-2, 178, 187, 190
Love's Labour's Lost, 164-5, 179,
    189, 194
Macbeth, 9, 33n, 40-2, 58, 77, 82,
    83, 115, 152, 169, 173, 180, 188
Measure for Measure, 4, 21, 105-
    13, 115, 116, 117, 118, 119, 120,
    121, 124, 166, 169, 189, 193, 197
Merchant of Venice, The, 9, 26, 115,
    116, 117, 119, 165, 180, 182, 183,
    184, 188
Merry Wives of Windsor, The, 194
Midsummer Night's Dream, A, 3,
    4, 6, 33, 34, 77-83, 98, 141-4,
    188, 198
Much Ado About Nothing, 21, 34,
    116, 122-4, 182
Othello, 10, 36-8, 110-11, 115, 169,
    172, 174, 175, 182, 183, 184, 190,
    193, 198
Pericles, 5, 6, 7n, 16, 28, 99, 166,
    179, 192-3, 194
Richard II, 27, 153, 168, 175, 179,
    181, 183, 187, 189
Richard III, 27, 41, 147-8, 177,
    178, 197
Romeo and Juliet, 11, 58, 112, 116,
    118-19, 169, 174, 187, 195
Taming of the Shrew, The, 5n, 116,
    119, 165
Tempest, The, 6, 33n, 56, 65, 77-83,
    116, 117-18, 119-20, 124, 166,
    167, 176, 180-1

Timon of Athens, 3, 5, 6, 7, 10, 12,
    16, 169, 172-3, 174, 181, 182
Titus Andronicus, 3, 7, 8, 9, 11, 12,
    23-32, 152, 163, 172, 173, 185,
    187, 198
Troilus and Cressida, 3, 5, 6, 10, 26,
    53-4, 60, 61, 99, 116, 124, 168,
    169, 176, 181, 182-3, 189
Twelfth Night, 30, 55, 56, 58, 116-
    17, 121, 124, 174, 177, 186, 189,
    197
Two Gentlemen of Verona, The, 33n
Two Noble Kinsmen, The, 4, 6
Wars of the Roses, The, 149, 150,
    152, 162
Winter's Tale, The, 4, 6, 16, 33n,
    35n, 65-75, 98, 115, 116, 117, 166,
    167, 190
poems
    Rape of Lucrece, The, 8, 11, 12, 13-
        22, 25, 164
    Sonnets, 99, 127-40, 163-4, 191
    Venus and Adonis, 6, 13, 16, 33n,
        164
Shaw, Glen Byam, 152
Shorey, Paul, 7n
Shrimpton, Nick, 167
Siegel, Paul N., 6n, 61n
Siemon, James E., 167,
Siemon, James R., 171
Silius Italicus, 45
Simmons, J. L., 4, 7n, 8, 51, 183
Sir Thomas More, 184, 192, 193, 196
Sklar, Elizabeth S., 183
Skulsky, Harold, 169
Slater, Eliot, 189
Slights, William W. E., 172, 182
Smallwood, R. L., 153
Smith, Gordon Ross, 168
Smith, Hallett, 13n
Smith, Maggie, 143, 144
Smith, Mary E., 185
Smith, W. D., 96, 98n
Soellner, Rolf, 13n
Sommers, Alan, 12n
Sorlien, Robert Parker, 177
Southampton, Henry Wriothesley, 3rd
    Earl of, 178
Speaight, Robert, 174, 178
Spencer, T. J. B., 2n, 3-4, 5, 6, 11
Spenser, Edmund, 13, 33, 108, 184, 191
Spevack, Marvin, 174
Spinner, Jonathan H., 194-5
Spurgeon, Caroline, 27
Stacy, G., 182
Stamm, Rudolf, 175
Stapfer, Paul, 2
Star, Leonie, 186-7
Starnes, D. T., 33n
Stedder, James, 153
Stevens, M., 171

INDEX

Stewart, Douglas J., 184
Stewart, Patrick, 142
Stirling, Brents, 127n, 129, 133
Strehler, Giorgio, 152
Stříbrný, Zdeněk, 168
Styan, J. L., 141, 151, 152, 188
Swander, Homer, 173
Swift, David, 148
Swift, Jonathan, 184
Swinarski, Konrad, 152

Tate, Nahum, 1, 3, 187
Taylor, Myron, 1n
Tennyson, Alfred, 191
Theobald, Lewis, 195, 196, 198
Thomas, K. V., 106n
Thompson, E. Maunde, 193
Thompson, R. Ann, 189
Thomson, J. A. K., 6
Thorp, Margaret, 15
Tillyard, E. M. W., 85n
Titian, 18
Tobias, Richard C., 12n
Tobin, John J. M., 34n, 183
Tompkins, J. M. S., 7n
Tree, H. Beerbohm, 188
Trevor-Roper, H. R., 58n
Trewin, J. C., 174
Tricomi, Albert H., 24n, 30, 172
Tucker, E. F. J., 180
Tussaud, Madame, 188
Tutin, Dorothy, 152
Tweedie, Eleanor M., 185

Tynjanov, Juri, 56n
Tyzack, Margaret, 144, 147–8

Underhill, William, 177
Ungerer, Gustav, 178–9

Valeriano, Piero, 47
Vasari, G., 16
Vawter, Marvin L., 1on, 172, 183
Veltrusk, J., 54n
Velz, John W., 7n, 33n, 190, 192
Vertue, George, 177
Vigenere, Blaise de, 17
Virgil, 5, 7, 8, 12, 13, 17, 18, 37, 50–1
Viswanathan, S., 1on
Vives, 33
Voth, Grant L., 168

Waith, Eugene M., 9n, 1on, 26, 29
Walker, Lewis, 172
Wallace, C. W., 185
Walley, Harold R., 13n
Walsh, P. G., 33n, 36n
Walter, J. H., 93, 95n
Warburton, William, 77
Wardle, Irving, 151
Warner, David, 150
Warren, Roger, 166–7
Watson, Curtis Brown, 86n
Watson, George, 180
Weatherall, Jack, 144
Webbe, Thomas, 112n–113n
Weimann, Robert, 54n, 61n, 175

Wells, Stanley, 176, 191, 198
Wentersdorf, Karl P., 168
West, Michael, 133n
Whibley, Charles, 39n
White, Howard B., 6
White, R. S., 164, 182
Whitworth, C., 183
Wickham, Glynne, 62n, 103
Wilders, John, 165
Wilkins, George, 179, 192–3
Wilkinson, L. P., 37
Williams, Clifford, 159
Williams, George Walton, 198
Williamson, C. F., 136
Wilson, Edwin, 23n
Wilson, John Dover, 93–4, 94–5
Wilson, Katharine M., 129, 135
Wind, Edgar, 45, 46, 49, 51n
Wingfield, Lewis Strange, 187
Winny, James, 127n, 128, 130
Winter, Yvor, 164
Wislicenus, Paul, 5n

Xenophon, 45, 46

Yates, Frances, 185
Young, B. A., 151n

Zadornova, Velta, 174–5
Zesmer, David M., 176
Zolbrod, Paul G., 12n
Zuger, Harry, 167

INDEX TO VOLUMES 21–30

Bold figures indicate a volume number.

Abbott, E. A., **23**, 9n, 11n
Abercrombie, Lascelles, **22**, 148
Abrahams, Roger, **29**, 18n
Acton, J. E. E. D. (Lord Acton), **28**, 21
Acton, Richard, **21**, 98
Acuña, J. B., **28**, 160
Adamian, Petros, **24**, 169
Adams, Barry B., **24**, 162
Adams, Brooks, **24**, 97
Adams, Charles Francis, **24**, 89, 100n, 101
Adams, Henry Brooks, **24**, 87–104
Adams, J. C., **29**, 130n, 131
Adams, John Quincy, **23**, 126, 175; **24**, 88, 93, 101; **25**, 5n; **26**, 82, 86
Adams, Joseph Q., **26**, 82, 86; **27**, 93, 111n, 112, 113, 118, 121n, 129; **29**, 104; **30**, 167n
Adams, Richard, **30**, 206n
Adelman, J., **28**, 156, 157
Ades, John I., **24**, 168n; **25**, 185
Adlard, John, **30**, 195
Adler, Gerhard, **21**, 133
Adling, Wilfried, **27**, 179n
Adlington, W., **23**, 61
Admiral's Men, **27**, 130, 133, 134n, 136, 173, 178
Aeschylus, **29**, 31; **30**, 104
Aggas, E., **28**, 39n
Agnew, G. K., **23**, 143
Agrippa, Cornelius, **25**, 126; **28**, 119
Aikman, J., **28**, 64n
Aitken, A. J., **26**, 164n
Akrigg, G. P. V., **21**, 148; **23**, 159–60; **25**, 174
Albee, Edward, **22**, 4, 27, 28, 29, 32; **24**, 19
Albert, Archduke, **29**, 22, 27, 28, 30
Albert, P., **24**, 81n
Albrecht, L., **25**, 7
Albright, Evelyn May, **28**, 8, 9
Alciati, Andrea, **24**, 66
Aldrich, Putnam, **23**, 164
Alexander, Nigel, **22**, 158, 170; **23**, 152; **26**, 23n, 25, 160; **27**, 46n, 59, 54, 55, 56n; **28**, 113n; **29**, 27n; **30**, 101n, 206
  'Thomas Rymer and *Othello*', **21**, 67–77
  Studies on Shakespeare's Life, Times and Stage, *reviewed*: (1971) **25**,

186–93; (1972) **26**, 168–76; (1973) **27**, 172–9
Alexander, Peter, **21**, 4, 27n, 155, 161, 162; **23**, 27n, 49n, 99n, 143, 185; **24**, 156; **25**, 7n, 8, 30n, 200; **26**, 69n, 72n, 95n, 181; **27**, 62n, 119n, 129n, 132n, 135; **28**, 11n, 66n, 76n; **29**, 15n, 24n, 120n, 184; **30**, 1n, 35n, 61n, 86n, 135n
Alexander, Sir William, **21**, 165
Alexander the Great, **27**, 72, 75, 78, 79; **30**, 4
Alexejew, Michail Pawlowitsch, **23**, 158–9
Alger, Horatio, **24**, 92
Allde, Edward, **22**, 182; **24**, 176
Allen, Don Cameron, **23**, 187
Allen, John A., **22**, 154; **27**, 164
Allen, Ned B., **23**, 151
  'The Two Parts of *Othello*', **21**, 13–29
Allen, Percy, **30**, 110n
Alleyn, Edward, **24**, 40; **27**, 134; **29**, 127–32
Allison, A. F., **24**, 72n; **29**, 21n
Alma-Tadema, Sir Lawrence, **26**, 142; **29**, 176
Almeida, Barbara de, **22**, 175n
Alonso, Dámaso, **23**, 82n
Alston, L., **28**, 63n; **29**, 93n
Altick, Richard, **24**, 41
Altieri, J., **28**, 162
Ames, William, **27**, 90
Amiel, H. F., **28**, 44
Amiot, Jacques, **29**, 103
Amneus, D., **27**, 90
Andersen, Hans, **29**, 145, 146
Anderson, J. J., **26**, 153
  'The Morality of *Love's Labour's Lost*', **24**, 55–62
Anderson, M. D., **26**, 73n, 75n, 76n
Anderson, Ruth I., **29**, 82
Andreadis, A. Harriette, **29**, 174
Andrewes, Launcelot, **23**, 84, 167
Andrews, J. F., **27**, 185; **30**, 207
Andrews, Mark Edwin, **27**, 95, 98, 104
Andrews, Michael C., **23**, 171n; **25**, 182; **28**, 155
Androzzi, Fulvio, **29**, 21
Angus, William, **21**, 156
Anikst, A., **21**, 131; **23**, 165, 168n, 174n, 175n, 176n

Anne of Denmark, **27**, 172; **30**, 162, 165
Anne, Queen, **29**, 4
Annis, Francesca, **30**, 175, 176
Anson, John, **21**, 132
Ansorge, Peter, **24**, 122n, 132n
Antiochus IV Epiphanes, **29**, 24, 25, 26–7
Aoki, K., **28**, 159
Apollonius of Tyrus, **29**, 30; **30**, 6
Appia, Adolphe, **29**, 176
Apuleius, **22**, 5; **23**, 61, 62
Aquinas, Thomas, **23**, 86; **24**, 91n, 140; **29**, 80, 88
Arber, E., **29**, 29
Arden, Agnes, **21**, 148
Arden, John, **22**, 28; **28**, 141
Arden, Mary, **21**, 148
Arden, Robert, **21**, 148
Arens, J. C., **23**, 186
Ariosto, Ludovico, **22**, 51
Aristophanes, **22**, 1, 3, 4, 5, 8, 36
Aristotle, **21**, 67, 68, 69, 74, 130; **22**, 1, 4; **23**, 147, 148; **24**, 79, 139, 140; **26**, 167; **27**, 78, 160; **28**, 29, 57, 63; **29**, 7, 99, 134, 162; **30**, 19, 103, 135, 192
Armin, Robert, **25**, 161, 167; **27**, 163, 178; **28**, 177; **29**, 178; **30**, 194
Armstrong, E. A., **23**, 99; **29**, 180
Armstrong, W. A., **22**, 116n, 117n; **27**, 23n, 31n, 179
Armstrong, William, **26**, 40n
Arnold, Aerol, **27**, 26n
Arnold, Arthur, **26**, 176n
Arnold, Matthew, **24**, 127, 134
Aronson, Alex, **25**, 186; **27**, 171
Arpe, Verner, **29**, 176
Arthos, John, **22**, 168; **25**, 3n; **26**, 166; **27**, 163; **29**, 8
Asals, H., **28**, 163
Ascham, Roger, **22**, 169
Ashcroft, Dame Peggy, **23**, 131; **24**, 43; **26**, 147; **27**, 142; **28**, 171
Ashe, Thomas, **23**, 102; **27**, 97; **29**,
Ashwin, A. E., **28**, 119n
Asp, C., **26**, 155
Asper, Helmut G., **29**, 175
Astley, John, **26**, 173
Atkins, Eileen, **27**, 149
Atkins, Robert, **28**, 148, 171
Auberlen, Eckhardt, **23**, 121
Aubrey, John, **29**, 135

Auchincloss, Louis, **24**, 138
Auden, W. H., **21**, 3, 10n, 11n; **22**, 10, 14n, 48, 51; **25**, 153; **28**, 75; **29**, 93, 180
Audley, Hugh, **28**, 19
Auerbach, Erich, **26**, 53
Augustin, Alexander, **23**, 118
Austen, Jane, **23**, 40
Austin, John, **28**, 65
Austin, Warren B., **26**, 182, 184; **27**, 130n
Avery, Susan, **25**, 137n
Aycock, Roy E., **26**, 175
Ayer, Miles, **25**, 144
Ayrer, Jakob, **21**, 153
Ayres, Philip J., **24**, 163n

Babb, Lawrence, **25**, 189; **29**, 82
Babington, Anthony, **23**, 41
Babula, W., **29**, 166
 'Whatever Happened to Prince Hal? An Essay on *Henry V*', **30**, 47–59
Back, Guy, **25**, 178
Bacon, Sir Francis, **21**, 128; **22**, 172; **23**, 49, 58; **24**, 153, 157; **26**, 37, 44; **27**, 95; **28**, 6, 9, 13, 15, 16, 19, 20–1, 170; **29**, 87
Badenhausen, Rolf, **29**, 176
Badham, Ann, **25**, 148–9
Badham, John, **25** 148
Baer, Ann, **30**, 202
Bagchi, Jasodhara, **21**, 131; **22**, 158
Bagshaw, Christopher, **21**, 72, 73, 74, 75, 76
Bailey, Banjamin, **24**, 114
Bailey, Nathaniel, **24**, 175
Baker, D. C., **23**, 168
Baker, George, **29**, 152
Baker, Herschel, **26**, 163n; **28**, 174; **29**, 81
Baker, J. H., **29**, 94n, 96n, 97n
Baker, Sir Richard, **30**, 10n
Baker, Stewart A., **24**, 146
Bald, R. C., **21**, 146; **25**, 37n; **27**, 178
Baldi, Sergio, **22**, 165
Baldwin, Thomas W., **22**, 113; **23**, 69, 71, 73, 74, 143, 161; **25**, 9, 82, 83; **27**, 59n, 105, 106n, 127n, 129, 132n, 134n; **28**, 71n; **29**, 22n, 104n; **30**, 61n, 89
Baldwin, William, **28**, 1, 41
Bale, Bishop, **28**, 138, 141
Bale, John, **21**, 59, 61
Ball, Robert Hamilton, **23**, 174; **28**, 171n, 172
Ballard, Henry, **26**, 184
Baltazarini, **22**, 168
Bandel, Betty, **24**, 168
Bandello, Matteo, **26**, 172; **27**, 172
Banerje, Srikumar, **21**, 140
Bang, W., **26**, 4
Barber, C. L., **21**, 130; **22**, 9, 31, 35, 154;

23, 137, 147; **24**, 150; **25**, 108, 109, 110, 111, 158; **28**, 160
'"Thou that beget'st him that did thee beget": Transformation in *Pericles* and *The Winter's Tale*', **22**, 59–67
Barber, John, **24**, 126n
Barber, Lester E., **25**, 178
Barber, Richard, **28**, 76n
Barber, Samuel, **24**, 5, 8
Barbieri, Richard, E., **29**, 175
Barclay, Bishop, **24**, 60
Bardskier, Hanns, **22**, 123
Bareham, T., **25**, 178
Barish, Jonas A., **24**, 165; **25**, 193; **27**, 171; **28**, 161
Barker, Felix, **27**, 34n
Barker, Kathleen M. D., **26**, 175; **30**, 196
Barker, Robert, **26**, 37, 42n
Barnes, Barnabe, **26**, 173
Barnes, Peter, **28**, 139, 140
Barnes, Richard, **25**, 149
Barnes, W., **24**, 177n
Barnet, Sylvan, **23**, 144; **26**, 154; **27**, 16n; **29**, 89
Barnett, Howard B., **23**, 164
Barnfield, Richard, **26**, 103
Barrett, Wilson, **29**, 176
Barroll, J. Leeds, **25**, 175, 199n; **26**, 182n; **27**, 31n, 160; **28**, 152; **29**, 171, 172
Barry, J. G., **28**, 153
Bartenschlager, Klaus, **25**, 177–8; **30**, 210
Bartholomeusz, Dennis, **23**, 173; **26**, 81, 84–6
Bartlett, John, **23**, 176, 177–8; **25**, 76n, 94; **28**, 177, 178
Bartolommeo, Fra, **26**, 54
Barton (Righter, Roesen), Anne, **23**, 132; **24**, 54, 124; **26**, 165; **27**, 44, 152, 165; **28**, 156, 174; **29**, 42; **30**, 14, 125, 171
 'Shakespeare and the Limits of Language', **24**, 19–30
Barton, J. L., **29**, 93n, 97n
Barton, John, **22**, 137, 138, 140, 142–4; **23**, 132, 133, 134, 135; **24**, 117, 122, 123, 124, 125, 129, 130, 131, 177; **25**, 45n, 48, 51n, 58n, 158, 164, 167; **26**, 175; **27**, 141, 144, 151, 152, 153; **28**, 103n, 138, 139, 140, 141, 142, 143; **29**, 180; **30**, 171–2, 173, 174–6
Bartoshevich, A., **23**, 168
Basu, Kajal, **21**, 132
Bates, Paul A., **22**, 165
Batho, E. C., **28**, 120n
Batley, E. M., **26**, 167
Batman, Stephen, **26**, 111n; **28**, 121
Battenhouse, Roy W., **24**, 139–40, 143; **25**, 6, 183; **26**, 16n, 127n, 161; **28**, 158; **29**, 88n, 161; **30**, 185

'The Relation of Henry V to Tamburlaine', **27**, 71–9
Bauduin, J., **25**, 180
Bauer, Robert J., **23**, 153; **24**, 158
Bawcutt, N. W. **23**, 169–70; **24**, 158
 Studies on Shakespeare's Life, Times and Stage, *reviewed*: (1974) **28**, 164–72; (1975) **29**, 168–77; (1976) **30**, 191–203
Baxter, James, **25**, 147
Baxter, Richard, **23**, 167; **27**, 87n
Bayley, John, **21**, 4, 5, 6, 9, 10n; **29**, 162–3
Bayne, Ronald, **25**, 127n
Baynham, Sir Edmund, **24**, 157n
Beach, Elizabeth, **24**, 154, 155
Beaujour, Michael, **29**, 14n
Beaumont and Fletcher, **22**, 1, 114, 164; **23**, 46; **26**, 1, 4, 33, 55, 66, 67, 100
Beaumont, Francis, **23**, 171; **24**, 159; **28**, 180; **29**, 3, 4, 7
Beaumont, Thomas, **21**, 145
Beaurline, L. A., **23**, 170
Bebb, Richard, **24**, 2n
Beck, Ervin, **30**, 192
Beck, Rosalie, **23**, 167
Beckerman, Bernard, **22**, 35; **23**, 174n; **25**, 6, 191; **26**, 155; **30**, 17, 197
Becket, Thomas à, **26**, 75
Beckett, Samuel, **22**, 4, 5, 28; **24**, 19; **26**, 93; **30**, 188
Becon, Thomas, **28**, 92
Beechey, Gwilym, **23**, 164
Beerbohm, Max, **29**, 133–44
Beeston, Christopher, **30**, 161–3, 166, 167
Beeston, William, **30**, 167
Beethoven, L. van, **21**, 3; **22**, 2
Begg, Edleen, **29**, 84
Beith-Halahmi, Esther Yael, **29**, 174
Belasco, David, **24**, 167
Beldam, Joseph, **30**, 165n
Bell, A. H., **26**, 158; **28**, 157
Bell, Mary, **22**, 145; **23**, 50n
Belleforest, François de, **21**, 152; **27**, 172; **29**, 171
Bellenden, John, **28**, 120
Belott, Stephen, **25**, 138–9, 141, 147
Bellringer, A. W., **24**, 147
Belsey, Catherine, **27**, 159; **30**, 192
Belsye, Anna, **23**, 42
Bembo, P., **25**, 103, 104
Bennett, Josephine Waters, **21**, 52n, 134; **22**, 160, 182; **25**, 4, 7, 29; **28**, 89n
Bennytt, William, **25**, 144
Benson, Frank, **25**, 1, 114–15, 117, 118, 122; **29**, 136, 137, 143
Benson, John, **22**, 182; **23**, 158
Benson, Lady Constance, **25**, 115n
Benson, Mrs, **29**, 141
Bentley, Eric, **22**, 28; **26**, 143

Bentley, G. E., **21**, 146; **22**, 174; **23**, 126, 127, 172n; **24**, 53; **25**, 200; **26**, 5, 9, 98, 168, 169, 170; **28**, 167, 169; **29**, 2; **30**, 161n, 163n, 167

Bercovitch, Sacvan, **23**, 161n; **24**, 162n, 169; **28**, 49n

Berger, Harry, **25**, 177

Berger, Ludwig, **23**, 122

Berger, Thomas L., **29**, 180

Bergeron, David M., **23**, 172; **24**, 163; **26**, 38n, 39n, 45n, 160; **27**, 166; **29**, 177; **30**, 199

Bergman, Ingmar, **24**, 13

Bergson, Henri, **22**, 1, 9, 16, 36

Berkeley, David, **22**, 186

Berkeley, George, **24**, 97

Berkes, Randall, **29**, 33n

Berlin, Normand, **28**, 171n

Berlioz, Hector, **21**, 80

Berman, Ronald, **22**, 155, 161, 165; **26**, 163; **27**, 24n, 159; **30**, 47n

Berners, Lord, **28**, 3

Bernhardt, Sarah, **29**, 143

Bernhardt, W. W., **23**, 150; **24**, 166

Bernheimer, R., **28**, 117, 118

Bernini, **26**, 116n

Berry, Francis, **25**, 83–4; **29**, 172

Berry, Herbert, **21**, 154, 155; **23**, 128, 172; **26**, 170; **28**, 169

Berry, Ralph, **24**, 55n, 61n, 149; **25**, 180; **26**, 154, 162, 167, 174; **27**, 162; **28**, 157; **29**, 165, 176; **30**, 188

'The Words of Mercury', **22**, 69–77

'"To Say One": an Essay on *Hamlet*', **28**, 107–15

Bertram, Paul, **21**, 146

Best, John, **30**, 161, 163, 164n, 165, 166

Best, Michael R., **23**, 169

Bethell, S. L., **21**, 62; **23**, 61n, 67n; **24**, 42; **25**, 10n; **29**, 88n; **30**, 112

Betterton, Thomas, **30**, 200

Bevan, Elinor, **21**, 143

Bevington, David M., **21**, 131; **23**, 168; **26**, 100n; **27**, 72, 165; **29**, 90; **30**, 39, 47n, 198

Bharracharji, Amal, **21**, 138

Bhattarcharjee, Jyotsna, **21**, 150

Bielmann, J., **29**, 29n

Biese, Y. M., **23**, 13n

Biggs, Murray, **28**, 84n

'A Neurotic Portia', **25**, 153–9

Biller, J., **23**, 171n

Billings, W., **26**, 157

Billington, Michael, **30**, 174n

Bilton, Peter, **23**, 158; **29**, 159

Birch, T., *and* Oldys, W., **27**, 56

Bircher, Martin, **23**, 154; **28**, 172

Birje-Patil, J., **25**, 176

Birkoff, Steven, **24**, 13n

Biswas, D. C., **25**, 188

Björnson, Maria, **28**, 146

Black, J., **28**, 159, 162; **29**, 164

'The Unfolding of *Measure for Measure*', **26**, 119–28

Black, M. W., **28**, 2n

Blackmur, R. P., **30**, 137

Blake, William, **23**, 93n; **24**, 107

Blakely, Colin, **26**, 149–50

Blakeway, M. G., **24**, 157

Bland, D. S., **23**, 164n; **24**, 156; **27**, 118n

Blanpied, J. W., **29**, 160

Blayney, G. H., **25**, 149n; **29**, 35n

Blayney, P. M. W., **26**, 183; **27**, 185; **30**, 206, 207

Blench, J. W., **23**, 84

Bliss, L., **29**, 165

Blisset, William, **22**, 163; **23**, 170; **26**, 163; **29**, 7

Blistein, Elmer M., **24**, 143n

Block, K. S., **21**, 65n

Blok, Alexander, **21**, 129

Blom, Benjamin, **23**, 173

Blount, Sir Christopher, **21**, 100

Blount, Edward, **24**, 170; **26**, 181

Blow, John, **23**, 164

Blow, Suzanne, **27**, 176

Bluestone, Max, **24**, 161; **29**, 169–70

Blume, Friedrich, **23**, 164

Boas, Frederick S., **24**, 160; **25**, 2; **26**, 6

Boas, Guy, **29**, 80

Boccaccio, Giovanni, **22**, 85, 91; **25**, 3, 45, 46, 48, 51, 52, 53, 56, 59, 61; **29**, 169

Bodin, Jean, **28**, 119, 121

Bodkin, Maud, **21**, 9, 62

Bodley, Sir Thomas, **26**, 168

Bodmer, Martin, **26**, 177

Bodtke, Richard, **27**, 177

Boece, Hector, **28**, 120

Boethius, **24**, 151

Bogard, John, **29**, 28

Bogey, John, **25**, 149

Boguet, Henry, **28**, 121

Böhm, Rudolf, **22**, 166; **23**, 115

Bohr, Nils, **22**, 147

Boiardo, M. M., **29**, 104

Boito, Arrigo, **21**, 87–94

Boklund, Gunnar, **23**, 145; **24**, 164; **26**, 8

Bolen, Frances, **28**, 48n

Boleyn, Anne, **26**, 41

Bolger, Stephen G., **25**, 174

Bolte, Johannes, **22**, 119

Bolton, Joseph S. G., **27**, 191

Bolton, W. F., **27**, 191; **30**, 204

Boltum, Thomas, **22**, 121–3

Bonazza, Blaze O., **22**, 152

Bond, Edward, **25**, 182; **26**, 176; **28**, 146; **29**, 175

Bond, Richard, **23**, 44

Bond, R. Warwick, **23**, 180; **27**, 111n, 112, 113, 119; **28**, 39; **29**, 104n, 108, 111n; **30**, 125, 127

Bonheim, Jean, **22**, 155; *and* Bonheim' Helmut, **26**, 156; **27**, 24n

Bonian, Richard, **21**, 161; **25**, 7; **26**, 33n

Bonjour, A., **23**, 156

Bonnard, Georges A., **27**, 112, 113, 119; **28**, 46n; **29**, 111n

Bonner, Bathsuba, **29**, 34, 37

Bonner, John, **25**, 142, 146, 147; **29**, 34, 35, 36, 37–9

Bonner sisters, **29**, 35, 36

Bonner, Thomas, **29**, 35, 36, 37–8

Booth, Edmund, **22**, 133

Booth, Edwin, **24**, 100; **25**, 192; **27**, 34n; **30**, 199

Booth, Junius Brutus, **24**, 100

Booth, Lionel, **23**, 1n

Booth, Stephen, **23**, 157–8; **24**, 144, 161

Borew, Jurij, **22**, 36

Borgerhoff, J.-L., **21**, 86n

Borinski, Ludwig, **24**, 153, 157

Born, Hanspeter, **25**, 187; **29**, 173

Born, Lester K., **30**, 61n

Bosch, H., **22**, 141

Bose, Analendu, **22**, 153

Bose, Kalidas, **22**, 165

Böse, Peter, **23**, 118

Bose, Tirthankar, **21**, 146

Boswell, James, **21**, 10n, 68; **24**, 37; **30**, 3

Boswell-Stone, W. G., **23**, 160; **26**, 82n, 87n

Botticelli, **27**, 139

Boughner, D. C., **24**, 150

Bourgy, Victor, **26**, 171

Bourke, Major-General Sir Richard, **22**, 126

Bournonville, A. A., **29**, 146

Bouton, James, **28**, 171

Bowden, William R., **21**, 132; **25**, 177

Bowdler, Thomas, **29**, 183

Bowen, Catherine Drinker, **27**, 100n

Bowers, Frederick, **23**, 164n

Bowers, Fredson, **21**, 52n, 141, 143, 150, 155n, 160–1, 162; **23**, 148; **24**, 151, 172, 174, 176, 177; **25**, 195, 198n; **26**, 4–5, 39n, 180; **28**, 180; **30**, 207, 208

Bowers, T., **27**, 45n

Boyle, Harry H., **25**, 188

Bracey, W., **25**, 200

Brack, O. M., Jr, **24**, 177n

Bradbrook, Muriel C., **21**, 138, 139, 142, 143, 152; **22**, 7, 69, 79, 80, 85, 89, 90, 153; **23**, 49; **24**, 15, 19, 41, 45–6, 47; **25**, 3, 6, 9, 52n, 57, 64, 174; **26**, 3–4, 26n, 47; **27**, 11n, 89–90, 91n, 113–14, 115, 116–17, 118, 119, 122, 127, 130n; **28**, 86n; **29**, 109, 111n

Bradbury, M. and Palmer, D. J., **27**, 162n, 163n, 164n, 165n, 167n, 170n

Bradford, Alan Taylor, **29**, 171, 175; **30**, 195
Bradford, William C., Jr, **29**, 180
Bradley, A. C., **21**, 1, 2, 3–4, 5, 8, 9, 16, 27n, 28n, 39, 45, 61, 134, 138; **22**, 148, 157, 163; **23**, 31, 36, 37, 149, 151; **24**, 1, 37, 93, 99, 139; **25**, 2, 111, 192; **26**, 13–14, 151, 167; **27**, 72, 156, 157, 160; **28**, 89, 152; **29**, 82; **30**, 35, 98n, 189
Brady, William E., **25**, 181
Brae, Andrew, **23**, 103, 104, 105, 111; **27**, 107, 108
Braekman, W., **24**, 156
Braid, Hilda, **28**, 139
Brainerd, B., **29**, 183
Bramelo, Prudence, **23**, 44
Brandes, George, **27**, 106n
Brandl, Alois, **21**, 53, 57; **26**, 44; **28**, 39n
Brantôme, **30**, 201, 202
Bratcher, T., **21**, 152
Braun, Erich, **23**, 120
Braun, Margareta, **23**, 116
Brecht, Bertolt, **22**, 3, 175; **26**, 94
Brekle, H. E., **23**, 23n
Brereton, Geoffrey, **23**, 147–8, 149
Breton, Nicholas, **22**, 112; **23**, 165; **25**, 188
Brett-James, Norman, **30**, 161
Brett-Smith, H. F. B., **30**, 202
Breuer, Horst, **29**, 175; **30**, 188
Brewer, Derek, **23**, 85n
Breyer, Bernard, **22**, 111, 117n
Bridges, Robert, **24**, 37, 39, 46; **26**, 165; **29**, 137
Briggs, A., **29**, 183n
Briggs, W. D., **29**, 79
Bright, Timothy, **22**, 168; **24**, 71; **29**, 82
Brinkman, Karl, **23**, 174n; **26**, 176
Brisman, Leslie, **27**, 192
Brissenden, A., **27**, 172
Britten, Benjamin, **21**, 87
Broby-Johansen, R., **23**, 165n
Brockbank, J. P., **21**, 140; **26**, 163; **29**, 3, 5, 8, 87; **30**, 203–4
'*Pericles*' and the Dream of Immortality', **24**, 105–16
'Hamlet the Bonesetter', **30**, 103–15
Brome, Richard, **22**, 174
Bromley, John, **27**, 72n
Bromley, J. S., **28**, 24n
Bromly, J. C., **26**, 155–6
Bronson, Bertrand, **23**, 175
Bronstein, Herbert, **23**, 144
Bronzino, **26**, 50, 56–7
Brook, Arthur, **25**, 127
Brook, Peter, **23**, 132; **24**, 60n, 118, 119, 125, 126, 128, 131, 132–4; **25**, 27–35, 158n; **26**, 175; **27**, 143, 145, 167; **28**, 144; **29**, 151; **30**, 21
Brooke, C. F. Tucker, **22**, 180; **27**, 98n, 99n, 112n, 119; **29**, 111n, 180

Brooke, Christopher, **27**, 120
Brooke, Nicholas, **23**, 142; **27**, 1n, 31n, 34, 35, 40n; **28**, 111n; **29**, 89
'All's Well that Ends Well', **30**, 73–84
Brooke, Rupert, **26**, 2
Brooks, Harold F., **22**, 18, 26n, 40; **23**, 180; **24**, 177, 178; **25**, 84n, 87, 88; **27**, 191
Broude, R., **27**, 159; **29**, 173
Brower, Reuben, A., **26**, 159; **27**, 173; **30**, 135n
Brown, Arthur, **26**, 9
Brown, Carleton, **21**, 140
Brown, Charles, **24**, 116
Brown, H., **26**, 164
Brown, Ivor, **23**, 159
Brown, John, **30**, 200
Brown, John Russell, **21**, 118, 127n, 130, 139–40, 142, 153–4; **22**, 166, 177; **23**, 137; **24**, 145, 154, 161; **25**, 10n, 84n, 93n, 171, 185; **26**, 9, 24n, 140, 141, 176; **27**, 145, 148, 162; **28**, 82n, 150; **29**, 7, 64, 93n, 101, 153, 154; **30**, 148n
'Free Shakespeare', **24**, 127–35
Brown, Keith, **23**, 149–50; **26**, 173; **28**, 153
'"Form and Cause Conjoined": *Hamlet* and Shakespeare's Workshop', **26**, 11–20
Brown, Pamela, **24**, 3n, 8
Brown, S. J., **29**, 164
Browne, E. Martin, **24**, 39
Browne, Sir Thomas, **23**, 167
Browne, William, **21**, 145–6
Browning, Robert, **22**, 48; **24**, 39, 43
Brownlow, F. W., **23**, 165
Brownstein, O. L., **25**, 191
Bruce, Brenda, **22**, 139; **23**, 134; **24**, 122
Bruce, J., **29**, 173
Bruegel, **26**, 49, 54
Brugmann, K., **23**, 28n
Brunkhorst, Martin, **27**, 179; **28**, 172n
Brunvand, J. H., **21**, 151, 153
Bryan, George B., **22**, 121; **23**, 175
Bryan, Margaret B., **30**, 185
Bryant, J. A., Jr, **25**, 108n; **29**, 88n
Bryant, Peter, **22**, 154; **30**, 184
Bryden, Ronald, **23**, 131
Buc, George, **25**, 188
Buchanan, George, **27**, 172; **28**, 64; **30**, 68n
Buchell, Arend van, **28**, 128n
Büchler, Klaus, **30**, 197
Buchloh, Paul Gerhard, **23**, 121
Büchner, Georg, **28**, 172; **29**, 175
Buckingham, Duke of (George Villiers), **28**, 23
Buckingham, Mr, **22**, 131
Buckley, G. T., **26**, 171; **30**, 202
Bucknill, J. C., **30**, 81n

Buland, Mabel, **21**, 27n
Bull, George, **27**, 46n
Bull, Thomas, **22**, 119–23
Bullen, A. H., **25**, 149n; **30**, 202
Bullough, Geoffrey, **21**, 150; **23**, 60n; **24**, 106n; **25**, 7, 9, 41n, 45n, 51, 96n; **26**, 113n, 115; **27**, 16n, 19n, 28n, 112, 172, 173, 174; **28**, 3, 4n, 67n; **29**, 4, 5, 27, 105n, 111, 169; **30**, 69, 125n
Bulman, James C., **30**, 203
'The Date and Production of *Timon* Reconsidered', **27**, 111–27
'Shakespeare's Use of the *Timon* Comedy', **30**, 103–16
Bülow-Møller, Anne Marie, **29**, 148n
Bundy, Murray W., **29**, 81, 82
Buntrock, Dietrich, **23**, 118
Bunyan, John, **23**, 178; **27**, 91
Burbage, James, **24**, 166
Burbage, Richard, **22**, 51; **24**, 40, 43; **26**, 26n, 45; **30**, 15, 199
Burby, Cuthbert, **25**, 79n
Burckhardt, Sigurd, **21**, 148; **23**, 140; **27**, 83, 91; **30**, 93
Bürger, G. A., **23**, 122
Burghley, Lord (William Cecil), **21**, 99; **23**, 41, 44; **28**, 15n, 20, 21, 23
Burke, Kenneth, **21**, 139
Burke, Peter, **24**, 158
Burkert, Walter, **30**, 103n, 115n
Burkhart, R. E., **28**, 158; **30**, 209
Burn, Michael, **25**, 173
Burney, A. L., **28**, 151
Burrell, Sheila, **24**, 118
Burton, D. M., **29**, 184
Burton, Richard, **23**, 174; **24**, 3; **30**, 21, 23
Burton, Robert, **23**, 167
Burton, T. G., **26**, 161
Bush, Douglas, **21**, 141; **29**, 81
Bush, Geoffrey, **29**, 87, 89
Bushnell, N. S., **29**, 83
Butler, Francelia, **21**, 138; **29**, 103n
Butler, Samuel, **26**, 165
Buxton, John, **24**, 159; **26**, 174n
Byrne, Muriel St Clare, **21**, 142; **23**, 39–40, 41, 44
Byrne, Sister St Geraldine, **24**, 2n
Byron, Lord, **21**, 81
Byron, H. J., **29**, 136

Caesar, **23**, 36
Caiger-Smith, A., **26**, 73n, 74n, 75n
Cain, H. E., **30**, 35n
Cairncross, A. S., **23**, 51, 180; **25**, 194; **26**, 69–70, 166, 180–1, 183; **27**, 132n, 135, 181–2, 183, 185; **29**, 174, 181, 185; **30**, 203, 207
Calderón de la Barca, Pedro, **23**, 82, 84, 85, 86, 88; **24**, 169n; **29**, 3

Calderwood, James L., **21**, 139; **25**, 3n; **26**, 152; **27**, 27n; **30**, 135n, 136n
Caldwell, John, **24**, 158
Caldwell, Zoe, **24**, 3n
Calvert, Louis, **25**, 119
Calvete de Estrella, Juan Cristóbal, **23**, 81n, 83, 87
Calvin, John, **23**, 80, 83, 86, 87
Camden, C., **22**, 147
Camden, William, **28**, 66; **30**, 205
Cameron, Elizabeth, **24**, 99n, 102
Cameron, Mrs, **22**, 128, 131
Cammarano, **21**, 88
Campbell, K. T. S., **26**, 164
Campbell, Lily B., **22**, 148; **28**, 1n, 2, 7, 121n; **29**, 82, 83, 85, 88; **30**, 63, 65
Campbell, Mrs Patrick, **29**, 136
Campbell, Oscar James, **21**, 141, 151, 159n; **25**, 5n, 6, 9, 67; **26**, 5, 114n; **27**, 120n; **29**, 88n, 103n
Campbell, Thomas, **29**, 149n
Campion, Thomas, **21**, 145; **22**, 51
Camus, Albert, **25**, 181
Cannon, Charles Kendrick, **24**, 159; **25**, 182
Cantrell, Paul L., **25**, 73n
Canuteson, John, **24**, 164
Canzler, David G., **23**, 168
Capell, Edward, **23**, 61n, 185; **26**, 181, 182; **27**, 187; **28**, 37, 38n; **29**, 105n; **30**, 204–5
Caravaggio, **30**, 80, 83
Cardan, J., **28**, 40, 41n
Carew (Cary), Sir George, **27**, 99, 101, 103, 104
Carew, George, Earl of Totnes, **21**, 104
Carew, Thomas, **21**, 149
Carey, Robin, **26**, 176n
Carlell, Ludowick, **24**, 166
Carleton, Sir Dudley, **23**, 44
Carlisle, Carol, J., **22**, 159; **25**, 172
Carlyle, Thomas, **27**, 21
Carpenter, F. I., **25**, 138n
Carr, V. M., **27**, 161; **29**, 174
Carroll, D. Allen, **26**, 184; **28**, 180; **29**, 175
Carson, Neil, **26**, 154; **30**, 197–8
'The Staircases of the Frame: New Light on the Structure of the Globe', **29**, 127–32
Cartari, G., **29**, 109
Cartari, Vincenzo, **26**, 112n
Carteret, Sir Edward de, **30**, 163n
Cary, Sir George, **29**, 99n
Case, John, **23**, 164
Cassirer, Ernst, **29**, 91
Castelvetro, L., **28**, 57
Castiglione, Baldassare, **25**, 103; **27**, 56, 163
Castrop, Helmut, **23**, 121
Catalini, Angelica, **23**, 109
Catherine of Aragon, **26**, 41

Cauthen, I. B., **25**, 197n; **30**, 207n
Cawarden, Sir Thomas, **28**, 170
Cawelti, John G., **24**, 91
Cawley, R. R., **28**, 120n
Caxton, William, **21**, 150; **24**, 113n
Cecil, Lord David, **29**, 133, 134n
Cecil, Sir Robert, **21**, 99, 100; **27**, 94; **28**, 4, 15, 16, 19, 20, 21, 23, 24–7, 151; **30**, 199
Cecil, William (Lord Burghley), **27**, 94
Centeno, Augusto, **26**, 90n
Cercignani, Fausto, **26**, 171
Cervantes, Miguel de, **22**, 11, 166; **23**, 83; **26**, 49
Chaderton, Laurence, **27**, 83n
Chadwick, Hubert, **29**, 22n, 29n
Chakravorty, Jagannath, **21**, 143; **22**, 158; **24**, 142–3
Chakravorty-Spivak, Gayatri, **21**, 141
Chalmers, George, **25**, 7n
Chaloner, Thomas, **27**, 59, 60, 61, 62, 63, 65, 66n, 67, 68, 69
Chamberlain, John, **23**, 44; **30**, 161
Chamberlain's Men, **27**, 134n, 136, 173, 178; **30**, 208
Chambers, E. K., **21**, 31; **22**, 119; **24**, 52; **25**, 2, 8, 73n, 110, 186; **26**, 2, 3, 5, 20n, 33n, 74n, 81n, 82; **27**, 1n, 95n, 98n, 106n, 127n, 129n, 132, 134n, 135; **28**, 4, 5n, 6n; **30**, 6, 38
Chambers, R. W., **25**, 5, 64; **26**, 119n, 170; **27**, 173; **28**, 89n, 120n, 167, 170; **29**, 81, 86n, 168
Chambrun, L. de, **28**, 38
Champion, Larry S., **25**, 178; **26**, 163; **29**, 161; **30**, 187
Chan, Mary Joiner, **24**, 156
Chang, Joseph S. M. J., **21**, 144; **22**, 152; **24**, 148
Chaplin, Charlie, **22**, 4
Chapman, George, **21**, 146, 147; **22**, 52, 171, 172; **23**, 46, 97, 129, 161, 170; **24**, 156, 159, 161n, 163; **25**, 9, 189; **26**, 1, 3, 5, 6, 8, 9, 34, 55, 168, 173; **27**, 175, 176, 179, 186; **29**, 170
Chapman, Gerald W., **25**, 111n
Charles, Prince, **26**, 36, 40n, 43, 44, 45
Charles, I, King, **25**, 48, 166; **28**, 22, 23, 65, 170
Charlton, H. B., **21**, 31, 137; **22**, 14n; **27**, 25n; **29**, 80
Charney, Maurice, **21**, 154; **23**, 183; **24**, 144, 162; **26**, 23n; **28**, 113n, 150
Charron, Pierre, **22**, 111, 116n; **29**, 81, 82
Chase, Richard, **24**, 98
Chasles, Philarète, **28**, 42
Chastel, André, **24**, 158
Chatterjee, Bhabatosh, **21**, 143n; **22**, 166, 175n

Chatterjee, V., **29**, 167
Chatterton, Thomas, **24**, 108; **29**, 136
Chaucer, Geoffrey, **21**, 27, 150; **22**, 1, 52, 147, 166, 169; **25**, 9; **27**, 109n; **30**, 193–4, 196
Chaudhuri, Sujata, **21**, 141
Chekhov, Anton, **22**, 3; **23**, 176; **24**, 19, 38
Cheney, David R., **22**, 168
Chernyshevsky, Nikolay, **23**, 159
Chester, Robert, **21**, 140
Chester cycle, **21**, 55, 57
Chettle, Henry, **21**, 148; **24**, 176; **26**, 182, 183; **27**, 130n
Chetwood, W. R., **29**, 183
Chevalley, Sylvie, **24**, 85n
Chew, Samuel C., **21**, 52n
Child, Harold, **25**, 1n
Chomsky, N., **23**, 11n
Christmas family, **23**, 172
Christophersen, P., **23**, 13n
Church, Tony, **25**, 165; **27**, 148; **30**, 176
Cibber, Colley, **22**, 128, 132; **28**, 139n; **29**, 176
Cicero, **22**, 109, 110, 111; **23**, 36; **24**, 150; **25**, 99; **29**, 100n
Cinthio, Geraldi, **21**, 13–15, 16, 17, 19, 20, 24, 27n, 32, 33, 41, 50, 135; **27**, 172
Cipolla, Carlo M., **24**, 47n
Cirillo, A. R., **26**, 154
Clark, Sir Kenneth, **26**, 51
Clark, William Mark, **25**, 107
Clarke, A. W. Hughes, **25**, 144n
Clarke, Charles Cowden, **25**, 107
Clarke, George, **23**, 126
Clayton, Thomas, **21**, 134; **22**, 183; **24**, 155; **25**, 199; **28**, 161
Clemen, Wolfgang H., **21**, 7, 144; **22**, 151, 155; **23**, 113–14, 116, 141; **24**, 2n, 145; **26**, 151–2; **27**, 11n, 24n, 25n, 26n, 29n, 32n; **28**, 30, 31–2, 46n, 151n
Clements, John, **24**, 3n; **27**, 142
Clemons, W. H., **29**, 110, 111n
Cletten, Gertrud, **22**, 121–2
Cletton, Raf, **22**, 121
Clifford, Peter, **23**, 43
Clive, Lady Mary, **23**, 167
Clopton, Joyce, **21**, 104
Close, A. J., **24**, 158
Clubb, Louise George, **22**, 167
Cobham family, **25**, 110, 112
Cobham, Lord, **21**, 113; **25**, 174
Cockeram, Henry, **23**, 156
Cody, Richard, **24**, 62; **29**, 91
Coghill, Nevill, **21**, 134, 155, 161, 162; **22**, 8, 14n, 93–4, 98; **25**, 7, 40n; **26**, 127n; **27**, 82n; **28**, 86n; **29**, 7, 88n
Cohen, Eileen, **25**, 184

Cohn, Ruby, 30, 190
Cokayne, G. E., 26, 36n
Coke, Sir Edmund, 23, 43–4
Coke, Sir Edward, 27, 95n; 28, 8, 64, 68; 29, 95, 96, 98
Coldewey, John C., 30, 196
Coldwell, Joan, 29, 177
Coleridge, E. H., 24, 44
Coleridge, Mrs H. N., 21, 65n
Coleridge, S. T., 21, 3, 4, 6, 24, 61, 74, 141; 22, 151; 23, 97, 101–11, 175; 24, 6, 44, 127, 153; 25, 45, 127, 128, 185, 187; 28, 89; 29, 87; 30, 2, 88, 104
Colie, Rosalie L., 21, 145; 28, 149; 29, 52n
Collé, Charles, 24, 84n, 85
Colley, J. S., 28, 163
Collier, J., 22, 177
Collier, John Dyer, 23, 102
Collier, John Payne, 23, 101–11; 25, 185, 187, 200; 26, 81, 82, 85; 29, 136
Collinder, Björn, 24, 162n
Collinson, Patrick, 22, 169
Colman, E. A. M., 22, 163
Colman, George, 25, 192
Colman, George, the younger, 22, 128
Combe, Don Thomas, 28, 166
Combe, Thomas, 25, 188; 29, 34n
Combes, John, 27, 99
Combes, Thomas, 27, 99
Combes, William, 27, 99
Comorovski, C., 29, 166
Condell, Henry, 28, 173, 177
Congreve, William, 24, 43
Conover, James H., 24, 163
Conrad, Joseph, 26, 8
Contarini, Gaspar, 26, 172
Conybeare, F. C., 25, 100n
Cook, Ann Jennalie, 29, 172
Cook, A. M., 21, 152
Cook, D., 26, 157
Cook, Ivor R. W., 21, 155n; 23, 160
 'William Hervey and Shakespeare's Sonnets', 21, 97–106
Cooke, G. F., 28, 171
Cooke, K., 26, 167
Cooper, J. R., 25, 179
Cooper, Thomas, 26, 112n
Cooper, William, 25, 147
Copernicus, 26, 49; 29, 85
Coppedge, Wendy, 22, 158
Corder, Jim W., 21, 152n, 156n
Corderius, 22, 168
Corneille, Pierre, 24, 82
Cornelius Agrippa, 29, 159
Cornwallis, Sir Charles, 29, 23, 24n
Cornwallis, Sir William, 28, 39; 30, 63
Corrigan, Beatrice, 24, 161
Corvinus, Antonius, 28, 92
Coryate, Thomas, 30, 201

Cosimo I, 26, 56
Cotarelo y Mori, Emilio, 23, 79n
Cotes, Thomas, 22, 182
Cotton, Sir Robert, 28, 170
Council, N., 27, 160–1; 28, 159
Coursen, Herbert Randolph, 23, 149, 156, 169; 25, 179; 26, 157, 176n
Courtenay (Courtney), James, 21, 97, 100
Couson, Herbert R., Jr, 22, 162
Coverdale, Miles, 23, 30
Cowell, John, 28, 65; 29, 99n
Cox, Lee Sheridan, 23, 156; 29, 67, 69
Cox, Roger L., 21, 133; 24, 146; 30, 185
Craig, Gordon, 23, 174; 29, 141, 142, 144, 176
Craig, Hardin, 23, 141; 26, 9, 111n; 27, 96n, 106n; 28, 40, 107n; 29, 81, 82, 83n, 88; 30, 47n
Craig, W. J., 23, 15n; 24, 55n; 28, 117n
Craigie, James, 21, 48
Craik, T. W., 24, 163, 164; 27, 191; 29, 171, 177; 30, 198
Cranach, Lucius, 25, 103
Crane, Hart, 22, 55
Crane, Ralph, 22, 178; 23, 182, 183; 27, 181, 184, 185
Cranfill, T. M., 29, 167
Cranmer, Thomas, 21, 130; 23, 79, 81, 162
Craven, Alan E., 26, 183; 27, 186; 29, 182
Craven, Babette, 29, 177
Crawford, Jane, 22, 183
Creede, Thomas, 25, 79n; 30, 210
Creigh, Geoffrey, 23, 161
Creswell, Joseph, 29, 21, 23, 24n, 32
Crews, F. C., 26, 164n
Croll, Morris, W., 25, 193
Cromer, Martin, 22, 168
Crompton, R., 30, 69
Cromwell, Thomas, 28, 18, 20, 21, 26
Cronin, Peter, 23, 152; 26, 162
Cross, F. L., 26, 116n
Crouch, J. H., 24, 168; 26, 176n
Crow, John, 25, 151n; 29, 7
Crupi, Charles, 23, 165n
Cruttwell, Patrick, 24, 154
'C.T.S.', 27, 116n
Cubeta, P. M., 27, 39n
Cuffe, Henry, 30, 195
cummings, e. e., 28, 177
Cummings, R. M., 23, 164
Cunliffe, J. W., 29, 80
Cunningham, John E., 21, 143
Curry, W. C., 21, 148; 28, 117; 29, 83
'Curtesse, Flaminio', 21, 38
Curtis, J. R., 28, 154
Curtius, Ernst Robert, 21, 144
Cusack, Bridget, 25, 184
 'Shakespeare and the Tune of the Time', 23, 1–12
Cushman, Robert, 21, 53, 57; 30, 169

Cust, Lionel, 26, 74n
Custodio, Alvaro, 24, 169; 25, 183
Cutts, John P., 22, 165; 23, 155, 160; 24, 141–2; 25, 180; 29, 2, 185; 30, 148n
Cutts, Thomas, 25, 144

Daatter, Jehanne Thygis, 22, 122
Daatter, Suenndtz, 22, 122
Däbritz, Fritz, 30, 200
Dahl, Liisa, 24, 177
Daiches, David, 27, 54n; 29, 183
Dalton, Timothy, 27, 147, 150, 151
Daly, Augustin, 25, 113, 115–16
Damiani, Peter, 26, 115
Damler, Artus, 22, 119–21, 123
Danby, J. F. (John), 22, 62; 23, 66n; 24, 112, 155; 26, 7; 27, 22n, 31n; 29, 4, 51n, 86
Dancy, Richard, 29, 34, 35, 36, 37
Daneau, Lambert, 27, 190
Daniel, P. A., 21, 16, 27n; 25, 74n, 198
Daniel, Samuel, 21, 145, 151; 22, 152, 170; 23, 74, 97, 166, 167n; 24, 68; 26, 33, 35, 39, 41, 43, 45, 47, 48, 107; 27, 131; 28, 3, 4, 171, 174; 29, 4, 171, 174; 30, 8
Daniell, Richard, 25, 145
Daniels, Barry Vincent, 30, 200
Danielsson, B., 23, 11n
Danson, Lawrence N., 27, 160; 28, 155; 29, 163; 30, 85n, 93n
Dante, 21, 81, 83, 128; 22, 1, 146, 159, 162; 26, 161; 28, 31, 60; 29, 80, 86
Danter, John, 21, 148; 24, 176; 27, 135–6
Danti, Vincenzo, 26, 112n
Daphinoff, Dimiter, 30, 195
Dare, Daphne, 24, 120
D'Argens, Marquis, 23, 173
Dariell, Richard, 29, 33n
Dark, Gregory, 26, 176n
Darling, Lieut.-General Ralph, 22, 126
Darlington, W. A., 22, 144
D'Arnaud, Baculard, 24, 85
Darrel, John, 26, 72
Darwin, Charles, 22, 48
Das Gupta, Arun Kumar, 21, 134
Dash, Irene, 26, 192
Davenant (D'Avenant), Sir William, 22, 57, 130, 182; 23, 126, 173; 24, 167, 169; 25, 113; 26, 81; 30, 166, 167n, 198, 199
David, Richard, 24, 53, 55n; 25, 4, 28, 29, 30; 26, 176
 'Of an Age and for All Time: Shakespeare at Stratford', 25, 161–70
Davidson, Clifford, 23, 154; 24, 163; 26, 161
Davies, D. W., 21, 42
Davis, Jo Ann, 29, 170

Davis, Norman, **24**, 159
Davis, Walter R., **23**, 164n
Davison, P. H., **22**, 179; **25**, 191; **26**, 35n, 38n, 180; **27**, 181
Davy, Sir Humphrey, **23**, 103, 105
Daw, Carl P., Jr, **23**, 169
Dawison, Bogumil, **24**, 100
Dawson, Giles E., **25**, 200; **27**, 93, 134n
Dawson, J. P., **29**, 96n
Day, John, **25**, 138, 149; **29**, 23
Dean, Leonard F., **21**, 129n, 132, 142; **23**, 148
Dean, Winton, 'Verdi's Otello; A Shakespearian Masterpiece', **21**, 87–96
De Calleja, F. Diego, **23**, 82
De Cazalla, Augustín, **23**, 81
Dee, John, **24**, 166; **29**, 158
Defoe, Daniel, **22**, 175
Deguileville, Guillaume, **23**, 168
Deighton, K., **29**, 110
Deimling, Hermann, **21**, 65n
Dekker, Thomas, **21**, 48, 112; **22**, 52, 72; **23**, 46, 48; **24**, 40, 163; **25**, 144, 147; **26**, 4, 35, 39, 41, 43, 47, 147, 168, 172; **27**, 176, 178; **28**, 134; **29**, 170
Delacroix, Eugène, **21**, 79–86; **23**, 176
De la Fuente, Constantino, **23**, 81n
De la Primaudaye, Pierre, **27**, 45n
De L'Armessin, Nicolas, **23**, 165n
Delbrück, B., **23**, 28n
Del Carro, Emilio, **21**, 32, 38n
Del Sarto, Andrea, **26**, 54; **28**, 143
Delille, Maria Manuela, **30**, 189
Deloney, Thomas, **28**, 55n, 56n
De Loutherborg, Philippe Jacques, **29**, 176
De Luca, D. M., **28**, 154
De Luca, V. A., **30**, 188
De Luna, B. N., **21**, 145; **24**, 155; **27**, 178
De Medici, Catherine, **27**, 172
De Mendonça, Barbara Heliodora C., **23**, 152
  'Othello: a Tragedy Built on a Comic Structure', **21**, 31–8
De Molen, Richard L., **28**, 170
De Montemayor, George, **22**, 168; **23**, 141; **27**, 131; **29**, 4
De Montespan, Mme, **22**, 19
De Musset, Alfred, **21**, 81, 83–4
De Nagy, N. Christoph, **22**, 166
Dench, Jeffery, **27**, 147, 149
Dench, Judi, **23**, 132, 134; **25**, 164, 167; **27**, 137–42; **29**, 73; **30**, 169, 172, 173, 176, 177, 179
  Conversation with Gareth Lloyd Evans, **27**, 137–42
Dennis, Carl, **25**, 176; **28**, 162
Dennis, John, **21**, 67

Dent, R. W., **24**, 145, 162n
De Ronsard, Pierre, **26**, 115n
De Rougemont, Denis, **25**, 95
De Rueda y Cuebas, Juan, **23**, 82
De Sant' Agata, Francesco, **26**, 112n
De Sant' Hierónimo, Fr. Miguel, **23**, 82
De Strycker, E., **29**, 30n
De Tervarent, Guy, **26**, 112n
De Tocqueville, A., **24**, 88
De Torres Naharro, Bartholomé, **23**, 79, 80, 81
De Vega, Lope, **22**, 167; **24**, 169n
De Velasco, Juan López, **23**, 80
Devereux, E. J., **23**, 162
Devereux, James A., **23**, 162
De Quincey, Thomas, **21**, 9; **30**, 188
Derby, Earl of, **21**, 153
Derby's Men, **27**, 133n, 135, 136
Derry, T. K., **24**, 157
Descartes, René, **22**, 23; **24**, 97
Deschamps de Pas, L., **29**, 28
De Selincourt, E., **27**, 96n
De Silva, Derek, **27**, 176
Desné, R., **22**, 175n
Dessen, Alan C., **22**, 172n; **25**, 182; **28**, 159; **30**, 38, 39
Dessoir, Louis, **24**, 100
Detre, Simon, **22**, 120–1, 123
Deubel, Volker, **25**, 190
Deutsch, B., **24**, 1n
Deutschbein, Max, **28**, 39n, 40n, 42
De Vigny, Alfred, **21**, 80; **30**, 200
De Witt, J., **28**, 127, 131; **29**, 129; **30**, 166, 169
D'Heere, Lucas, **29**, 26
Dickens, Charles, **22**, 2; **24**, 45
Dickey, Franklin, **29**, 82, 83
Dickinson, Emily, **24**, 104
Dickinson, J. W., **25**, 6n; **29**, 95
Dickson, George B., **25**, 139, 140
Diderot, Denis, **22**, 175n; **24**, 85
Digby, George, **24**, 110, 111, 113
Digges, Thomas, **27**, 45n
Dignam, Mark, **26**, 143, 144
Diogenes, **26**, 94
Dionysius of Halicarnassus, **28**, 71–4; **30**, 193
Dipple, Elizabeth, **23**, 166
Dircks, P. T., **27**, 172
Di Salsa, Francisco Berio, **21**, 81, 84
Dixon, John, **29**, 34, 37
Dixon, Priscilla, **29**, 34, 37
Dixon, W. H., **23**, 101
Dobrée, Bonamy, **25**, 2; **26**, 5
Dodd, Kenneth M., **25**, 192
Dodd, Wayne, **22**, 161
Dodds (Nowottny), W. M. T., **25**, 5, 8; **28**, 48
Doe, Paul, **24**, 158
Doebler, Betty Anne, **22**, 167; **28**, 158

Doebler, John, **27**, 157; **28**, 162, 170; **29**, 159
  'Orlando: Athlete of Virtue', **26**, 111–17
Doh, Herman, **29**, 182
Dollerup, Cay, **29**, 173; **30**, 202
Dolmetsch, K., **25**, 117
Donaldson, Ian, **23**, 170n; **26**, 173
Donatello, **26**, 116
Donatus, **30**, 192
Don John of Austria, **29**, 26
Donne, John, **23**, 98, 167; **24**, 19; **25**, 190; **26**, 79, 168; **27**, 93, 94, 109, 120; **28**, 43, 44; **29**, 27, 175; **30**, 9
Donner, H. W., **24**, 146
Donohue, Joseph W., **22**, 174; **25**, 192
Donow, Herbert S., **23**, 144; **25**, 183
Doran, Madeleine, **22**, 151, 161; **24**, 146; **25**, 7; **26**, 7; **28**, 161; **29**, 83; **30**, 190
Dorsch, T. S., **22**, 114, 116n; **26**, 171n, 176n, **29**, 139
Dostoevsky, **26**, 22, 26, 30; **28**, 55
Douce, Francis, **28**, 54
Douglas, Mary, **29**, 18
Douglass, Miss, **22**, 128, 130–1
Dove, John Roland, **23**, 153; **25**, 181
Dowden, Edward, **24**, 55, 62, 139, 153; **25**, 1; **27**, 176; **29**, 79, 135
Dowland, John, **23**, 165
Dowling, Margaret, **28**, 8n
Downer, Alan S., **21**, 155; **26**, 154; **28**, 139n
Downs, Brian, **24**, 85n
Draffen, Robert A., **25**, 173
Draper, John W., **21**, 28n, 142; **22**, 154; **25**, 185; **26**, 163
Drayton, Michael, **22**, 170; **23**, 167; **24**, 22; **26**, 14, 103, 107
Dresden, S., **23**, 163n
Drew-Bear, Annette, **27**, 176
Drummond, William, **23**, 106
Dryden, John, **21**, 67; **22**, 49, 53, 57, 132; **23**, 150, 173; **24**, 53, 127, 166; **25**, 113, 189; **26**, 6, 67, 159, 175; **28**, 36, 160; **29**, 175
Du Bartas, Silvester, **21**, 48; **24**, 145
Ducis, Jean-François, **21**, 79–80; **24**, 79–86; **30**, 200
Dudley, Robert, **27**, 118n
Dudley, William, **28**, 144
Dugdale, William, **27**, 115n
Dumas, Alexandre, **21**, 80
Duncan, Joseph E., **23**, 163
Duncan-Jones, Katherine, **23**, 166n; **26**, 172
Dundes, Alan, **29**, 15n, 17n
Dunkel, Wilbur, **25**, 6n; **27**, 93n, 94n; **29**, 95
Dunn, Catharine M., **24**, 151

Dunn, Esther, **24**, 87n, 99n, 103
Durden, Richard, **30**, 172
Dürer, Albrecht, **24**, 156; **30**, 119, 123
Durrant, G., **27**, 167
Dürrenmatt, F., **25**, 174
Dusinberre, J., **29**, 159
Duthie, G. J., **21**, 137; **23**, 121; **25**, 73n, 74, 77n, 79, 80n; **26**, 184
Dutton, John, **27**, 134
Dutton, Laurence, **27**, 134
Duţescu, D., **29**, 166
Duţu, Alexandru, **22**, 175n; **24**, 150
'Dwarf Bob', **27**, 178
Dyball, **22**, 128, 131
Dyce, Alexandre, **23**, 102; **27**, 111n, 112, 115n, 116n, 117n; **29**, 105n, 124
Dyke, Daniel, **28**, 48n

Eagleson, Robert D., **29**, 174
Eagleton, Terence, **22**, 148–9; **25**, 12
Eames (Emms), Geoffrey, **25**, 141, 146, 147
Eames, Roger, **25**, 147
Eastman, Arthur M., **23**, 175
Easty, John, **22**, 133n
Ebel, Julia, G., **24**, 159
Eccles, Mark, **24**, 159; **25**, 137; **27**, 99, 102n, 129n; **29**, 33
Echerno, M. J. C., **25**, 179
Eddison, R., **24**, 3n
Eden, Richard, **29**, 5
Edinborough, Arnold, **23**, 174n; **24**, 167; **25**, 175
Edman, Irwin, **25**, 103n
Edmond, Mary, **30**, 196
Edmunds, *alias* Weston, **26**, 72
Edmunds, John, **21**, 152; **24**, 167
Edward III, King, **28**, 8, 174
Edward VI, King, **30**, 61
Edwards, Philip, **21**, 145; **22**, 62; **23**, 139–40; **24**, 60n; **25**, 5; **26**, 5, 9, 119n, 155, 167; **28**, 105n; **29**, 1, 2, 4, 9, 10; **30**, 203, 205, 206, 207
Edwards, Thomas, **24**, 171
Egan, Richard, **27**, 71, 72, 170
Egan, Robert, **22**, 173; **28**, 118
Egerton, Sir Thomas (Lord Ellesmere), **24**, 158; **27**, 94, 95, 99, 100; **29**, 93, 95, 96n, 97
Eggers, Walter F., **30**, 185
Eidson, Donald, **22**, 156
Eikhenbaum, B., **23**, 174n
Eisler, Colin, **26**, 115
'E.K.', **23**, 166
Ekeblad (Ewbank), Inga-Stina, **27**, 177
Eld, George, **26**, 184; **29**, 181–2
El Greco, **22**, 59; **26**, 49, 50, 53, 55, 63, 64, 65, 66
Eliot, George, **21**, 11n; **26**, 8; **30**, 96, 121
Eliot, T. S., **21**, 4, 6–7, 11n, 45, 67, 68, 77, 128; **22**, 5, 66, 67, 162, 166; **23**,

152; **24**, 19, 39, 41, 42, 46, 116; **25**, 10, 64; **26**, 3, 51; **27**, 11; **28**, 30, 31; **29**, 1, 80, 81, 86, 87; **30**, 4, 5–6, 102, 120
Elizabeth, Princess, **26**, 36, 40n, 41, 43, 44, 45, 46, 47, 48
Elizabeth I, Queen, **21**, 48; **23**, 79, 81, 87, 120, 147, 154, 166; **24**, 155, 157; **26**, 37, 38n, 41, 46, 99; **27**, 93, 100, 134; **28**, 3, 7, 8, 9, 15, 20, 21, 22, 23–4, 151, 165, 166; **30**, 132
Ellegard, Alvar, **23**, 11n
Ellesmere, Baron, (Sir Thomas Egerton), **29**, 95, 97
Elliott, G. R., **25**, 81, 83
Elliott, John R., Jr, **21**, 152; **23**, 146, 168; **24**, 161
Ellis, F. S., **24**, 113n
Ellis, George, **26**, 3
Ellis, J., **27**, 158
Ellis, R. L., **28**, 16n; **30**, 172
Ellis-Fermor, Una, **23**, 145; **24**, 42; **25**, 8, 11n; **26**, 3, 4, 89; **30**, 55n
Elloway, D. R., **30**, 206n
Ellrodt, Robert, **29**, 90; **30**, 193
  'Self-Consciousness in Montaigne and Shakespeare', **28**, 37–56
Else, Gerald F., **23**, 148
Elton, G. R., **28**, 64n, 65
Elton, Oliver, **27**, 106n
Elton, W. R., **21**, 134, 136; **25**, 18n; **29**, 89, 184
Elyot, Sir Thomas, **24**, 66; **28**, 80n; **29**, 85, 87; **30**, 61, 189
Emden, Cecil S., **28**, 154
  'Shakespeare and the Eye', **26**, 129–37
Emerson, Ralph Waldo, **24**, 87
Emery, J. K., **27**, 104n
Emmerová, Jarmila, **21**, 129n
Empson, William, **21**, 3, 5, 9, 140, 155n, 162; **23**, 170; **25**, 5, 8; **29**, 91, 177; **30**, 37
Emunds, Karl, **23**, 119
Ende, Richard von, **21**, 144
England, George, **21**, 65n
Engler, B., **26**, 166n; **28**, 172
Engler, James, **21**, 100
Engstrom, J. Eric, **21**, 142
Enright, D. J., **24**, 138
Epstein, Joel J., **24**, 157
Erasmus, **22**, 112; **23**, 80, 144, 161, 162; **27**, 56–69; **29**, 91, 104, 159; **30**, 61–3, 64
Ergang, Robert, **22**, 169
Erskine-Hill, H., **26**, 159
Eschenberg, J. J., **26**, 166
Essex, Earl of, **21**, 100, 103; **23**, 43, 97; **27**, 129n; **28**, 6, 7, 8, 9, 20, 23, 24; **29**, 168
Esslin, M., **21**, 38n

Ettin, Andrew V., **25**, 176
Euripides, **21**, 75; **22**, 3, 5, 109
Evans, Bertrand, **21**, 130; **22**, 25, 26n, 41, 166; **23**, 137; **25**, 3, 9, 54, 90, 110, 192
Evans, B. Ifor, **23**, 13n, 48
Evans, Dame Edith, **23**, 131; **25**, 27, 66
Evans, G. Blakemore, **21**, 162; **23**, 176; **25**, 186, 196; **26**, 181; **28**, 173–7; **29**, 184; **30**, 125n, 208
Evans, Hugh C., **24**, 153, 157
Evans, K. W., **25**, 181
Evans, M., **29**, 162
Evans, Malcolm, **24**, 52
Evans, Maurice, **21**, 65n; **23**, 131
Evelyn, Sir Thomas, **21**, 97, 100
Everett, Barbara, **21**, 10n; **24**, 172n, 173; **25**, 4; **29**, 89
  '*Hamlet*: A Time to Die', **30**, 117–23
Everitt, E. B., **27**, 129n
Ewbank (Ekeblad), Inga-Stina, **21**, 138, 146; **24**, 164; **26**, 165; **27**, 163; **29**, 6, 7; **30**, 188, 198
  '"More Pregnantly than Words": Some Uses and Limitations of Visual Symbolism', **24**, 13–18
  '*Hamlet* and the Power of Words', **30**, 85–102
Eyre, Ronald, **25**, 164, 166
Eyre, Simon, **26**, 98

Faber, M. D., **24**, 156; **25**, 180; **26**, 162
Fabian, John, **29**, 175
Faccio, Franco, **21**, 89
Fain, John Tyree, **23**, 156
Fairfax, Edward, **24**, 73n
Falk, Doris V., **21**, 134
Falk, Robert, **24**, 87n, 99n
Farmer, John S., **21**, 65n; **30**, 10n
Farmer, Norman, Jr. **24**, 158n
Farmer, Richard, **27**, 106
Farnham, Willard, **25**, 183; **26**, 89; **27**, 111n; **29**, 81, 103n, 109n
Farquhar, George, **22**, 125
Farr, Dorothy M., **22**, 172n
Farrah, **27**, 150; **29**, 156
Fauré, François, **21**, 135; **26**, 157
Fawkes, Guy, **26**, 40
Feather, John P., **27**, 178, 190; **29**, 175
Fechter, Charles, **28**, 171; **30**, 198
Fehrenbach, Robert J., **24**, 167
Feinstein, Blossom, **23**, 164n
Feis, Jacob, **28**, 41
Felheim, Marvin, **23**, 144; **25**, 115, 116
Felperin, Howard, **21**, 153; **22**, 164; **27**, 168–9
Fenner, Dudley, **26**, 154; **27**, 84
Fenton, George, **28**, 146
Ferguson, Francis, **28**, 104n; **29**, 164; **30**, 104n, 107, 109
Ferguson, W. Craig, **24**, 176; **27**, 186, 187

Fergusson of Kilkerran, Sir James, **24**, 156

Fermor, Henry, **25**, 144

Feuillerat, A., **28**, 54n

Feydeau, Georges, **22**, 52

Fiedler, Leslie A., **23**, 62; **27**, 171

Field, Richard, **28**, 38

Fielding, Henry, **22**, 2, 5; **29**, 152; **30**, 200

Figgis, J. N., **28**, 65n

Fineman, **26**, 167–8

Finkelpearl, Philip J., **24**, 159; **27**, 114n, 119, 120n

Finkelstaedt, T., **29**, 183

Finsher (ffinsher), Abigall, **29**, 34, 37

Finsher (ffinsher), Robert, **29**, 34, 37

Firth, Tazeena, **27**, 146, 151

Fisch, Harold, **21**, 142; **23**, 141; **24**, 148; **25**, 175; **26**, 160–1; **27**, 81–92; **29**, 163
    '*Antony and Cleopatra*: the Limits of Mythology', **23**, 59–67
    'Shakespeare and the Puritan Dynamic', **27**, 81–92

Fischer-Weimann, Waltrad, **27**, 179n

Fisher, John, **25**, 144; **28**, 171n

Fisher, Thomas, **26**, 74

Fishman, J. A., **23**, 11n

Fiske, Alison, **25**, 166

Fitch, Robert E., **22**, 163; **24**, 138–9, 140

Fitton, Mary, **26**, 2

Fitz, L. T., **29**, 165

Fixer, John, **21**, 99, 100

Flatter, Richard, **21**, 33, 138

Fleay, Frederick G., **21**, 16, 27n; **25**, 110; **27**, 106n, 107

Fleetwood, Susan, **23**, 133; **28**, 142, 143

Fleischer, Martha Hester, **29**, 173

Fleissner, Robert F., **22**, 168; **23**, 160; **24**, 146; **25**, 182; **27**, 105–10; **29**, 162; **30**, 201
    '"Love's Labour's Won" and the Occasion of "Much Ado"', **27**, 105–10

Fleming, William H., **25**, 115

Fletcher, Angus, **21**, 145n

Fletcher, John, **21**, 146; **22**, 157 (*see also* Beaumont and); **23**, 121; **24**, 155; **26**, 8, 34, 42, 169, 177, 184, (and Beaumont) 1, 4, 33, 55, 66, 67, 100; **27**, 176; **28**, 178, 180; **29**, 3, 4, 7, 169, 170

Florio, John, **23**, 45n; **24**, 76n; **27**, 45n, 50n, 52n, 54n; **28**, 38, 39, 41, 42, 98n, 134; **29**, 79

Flower, A. C., **29**, 165

Fluchère, Henri, **21**, 137

Fludd, Robert, **21**, 155; **23**, 172; **24**, 166

Fly, R. D., **28**, 155; **29**, 163

Flynn, John T., **25**, 182

Foakes, R. A., **21**, 145, 153; **22**, 107n, 179; **25**, 4, 9, 12n, 50, 51, 82, 185;

187, 191; **26**, 9, 99n, 153, 170, 173; **27**, 134n, 163; **28**, 153; **29**, 3, 8–9, 42, 43, 127, 128, 129; **30**, 95
    'The Text of Coleridge's 1811–12 Shakespeare Lectures', **23**, 101–11
    'The Art of Cruelty: Hamlet and Vindice', **26**, 21–31

Foley, Henry, **24**, 72n

Folger Shakespeare Library, **22**, 151; **27**, 104

Folkenflik, Robert, **30**, 200

Folland, H. F., **28**, 159

Fontane, Theodor, **23**, 122

Forbes-Robertson, Sir Johnston, **29**, 142

Ford, Gerald, **28**, 65

Ford, John, **21**, 40; **23**, 171; **24**, 5, 6, 11, 165; **26**, 1, 4, 5, 8, 66, 169; **30**, 4

Ford, Worthington Chauncey, **24**, 89n

Forker, Charles R., **23**, 171n; **24**, 165

Forman, M. Buxton, **24**, 110n, 114n 116n

Forman, Simon, **23**, 173; **26**, 81–8; **28**, 4, 5, 7; **29**, 2

Forrest, Edwin, **30**, 199

Forrest, James F., **27**, 160, 179

Forset, Edward, **28**, 65–6, 67

Fortescue, Sir John, **27**, 72; **29**, 85

Fortin, Rene E., **23**, 148; **27**, 165; **28**, 152, 154

Foster, Elizabeth Read, **28**, 25n

Foucart, Jean, **29**, 29

Foulkes, Richard, **23**, 173

Fowler, A. D. S., **23**, 164; **25**, 183; **26**, 14–15, 173; **27**, 109n

Fowler, F. G., **29**, 105n

Fowler, H. W., **29**, 105n, 106, 108, 109, 110, 112

Fowler, John, **29**, 32

Fowler, Katherine, **25**, 143; **29**, 32, 33

Fox, Levi, **24**, 157; **27**, 175

Foxe, John, **23**, 169; **28**, 22

Francis, F. C., **24**, 171n

Franz, W., **23**, 11n, 13

Fraser, John, **23**, 156

Fraser, Russell, **25**, 190; **27**, 177; **30**, 150

Frazer, J. G., **23**, 63; **25**, 108

Frazier, Harriet C., **22**, 167n; **25**, 187

Frederick II, King of Denmark, **22**, 119

Freedberg, S. J., **26**, 65n

Freehafer, John, **23**, 157, 170n, 171n, 175n; **24**, 155, 168; **26**, 166, 175

Freeman, Arthur, **22**, 167n, 173, 182; **24**, 162, 168n, 171; **27**, 178

Freeman, James A., **29**, 171

Freeman, Sir Ralph, **23**, 171

French, A. L., **21**, 134; **22**, 155; **23**, 145; **24**, 152, 163; **26**, 156; **27**, 31n

Frere, W. H., **25**, 127n

Fresneda, Bernardo de, **23**, 81n

Freud, Sigmund, **21**, 133; **22**, 15, 16, 65, 145, 146; **23**, 133; **25**, 11; **26**, 59n

Fricker, Robert, **21**, 129; **28**, 42

Fridner, Elis, **22**, 183

Fried, Erich, **23**, 122; **26**, 166

Friedberg, E., **28**, 53n

Friedman, Alan Warren, **30**, 188

Friedman, Donald M., **23**, 165

Friedman, Elizebeth, **28**, 15n

Friedman, Martin B., **24**, 183

Friedman, W. F., **28**, 15n

Friesner, Donald Neil, **23**, 141; **24**, 154, 155

Frings, Josef, **23**, 141

Fripp, E., **26**, 74

Fritzsche, Max, **24**, 145

Froissart, Jean, **28**, 3

Frost, David L., **22**, 171; **26**, 8

Frye, Dean, **21**, 139

Frye, Northrop, **22**, 31, 153, 156–7; **23**, 137; **24**, 148; **25**, 107, 108n; **26**, 167; **27**, 144n; **29**, 3, 4, 7, 8, 9–10; **30**, 147, 149n, 151, 153
    'Old and New Comedy', **22**, 1–5

Frye, R. M., **21**, 148; **22**, 149; **23**, 79, 82, 83, 85, 86–7, 88, 148, 162n, 176n; **25**, 6, 186; **29**, 51n, 64, 89

Fryer, Elizabeth, **25**, 148

Fryer, Thomas, **25**, 148

Frykman, Erik, **23**, 138; **24**, 157

Fuegi, John, **26**, 166, 176

Fujimara, Thomas H., **21**, 131

Fujita, M., **26**, 159

Fulgentius, **26**, 112n

Funston, J. Louis, **29**, 174

Furness, H. H., **21**, 22, 52n, 163; **27**, 43n, 107, 108n

Furnivall, F. J., **21**, 65n; **23**, 168; **24**, 111n, 154; **25**, 1; **27**, 132

Fussner, F. Smith, **22**, 147

Gabler, Hans Walter, **23**, 118; **25**, 193; **27**, 190
    'Shakespeare Studies in German: 1959–68', **23**, 113–23

Gager, Jean, **22**, 160

Gaines, Barry J., **25**, 200

Gair, W. R., **24**, 159 **28**, 170

Galloway, David, **23**, 125n, 128n; **24**, 53; **25**, 6n, 191; **26**, 34n, 155n, 166n, 170; **27**, 181n; **28**, 169

Gamble, Peter, **23**, 153; **25**, 181

Gang, T. M., **23**, 165

Garber, M. B., **28**, 151

Gardener, S. R., **28**, 19n

Gardner, Dame Helen, **21**, 136, 149; **23**, 87, 137, 151; **24**, 168, 171; **25**, 180; **26**, 79n
    '*Othello*: A Retrospect, 1900–67', **21**, 1–11

Gardner, William, **27**, 94

Garnet, Henry, **29**, 32

Garnier, Robert, **27**, 173

Garrett, J., **29**, 41n

Garrick, David, **21**, 117; **22**, 129, 133; **23**, 173; **24**, 14, 43, 81, 84n; **25**, 48, 113n, 192; **29**, 143, 146, 177; **30**, 189, 198, 200, 201, 206

Gascoigne, George, **21**, 52; **26**, 172

Gaskell, Charles Milnes, **24**, 88

Gassendi, Pierre, **22**, 23

Gaunt, D. M., **23**, 161

Gearin-Tosh, Michael, **25**, 177

Geckle, G. L., **25**, 176

Geddis, Peter, **25**, 165

Gelb, Hal, **25**, 176

Gelber, Norman, **23**, 169

Gellert, Bridget, **22**, 168; **24**, 145

Genet, Jean, **22**, 27, 28

Gent, C. I., **26**, 155

Gentili, S., **30**, 64, 68, 69

Gentili, Vanna, **24**, 162

Gentillet, **21**, 143–4

Genzel, H. J., **26**, 157

Geoffrey of Monmouth, **28**, 120

George, David, **25**, 188

Georges, Robert A., **29**, 15n, 17n

Gerard, Thomas, **21**, 103

Gerevini, Silvano, **26**, 183

Gerlach, John, **28**, 171n

Gervinius, **27**, 106n

Gesner, Carol, **25**, 178; **29**, 6

Ghose, Sisirkumar, **22**, 166, 176

Ghosh, Prabodh Chandra, **21**, 138

Gianakaris, C. J., **23**, 170

Gibbons, Brian, **22**, 171

Gibbs, Willard, **24**, 97

Gibson, C. A., **24**, 165; **30**, 207

Gide, André, **24**, 6, 12; **28**, 43, 107

Gidion, H., **26**, 166n

Gielgud, Sir John, **21**, 115–19, 122, 125; **23**, 131, 174; **24**, 3, 43; **25**, 29; **27**, 142, 145; **28**, 148

Gilbert, A. J., **27**, 179

Gilbert, Allan H., **25**, 110; **28**, 104

Gilbert and Sullivan, **22**, 2

Gilbert, Bridget, **22**, 156

Gilbert, Creighton, **23**, 165

Gilbert, Sir William, **22**, 5

Gilbert, Stuart, **24**, 158n

Gilbertus, **24**, 146

Gildon, Charles, **21**, 67; **24**, 168

Gill, Peter, **28**, 144

Gillet, Joseph E., **23**, 80

Gillett, Peter J., **29**, 174

Gillman, James, **23**, 101

Giovius, Paulus, **29**, 171

Girard, René, **29**, 14n

Giraudoux, Jean, **22**, 21, 28, 29, 32, 38

Gladstone, W. E., **24**, 92

Glick, Claris, **23**, 173

Gligore, Ana-Maria, **29**, 166

Glover, Brian, **27**, 148–9

Goddard, H. C., **27**, 72; **30**, 49n, 51n

Godfrey, Derek R., **25**, 166; **26**, 162

Godshalk, William Leigh, **21**, 153; **23**, 143; **26**, 174n; **27**, 92n, 167; **28**, 152, 162, 167

Godwin, E. W., **29**, 176

Goethe, J. W. von, **21**, 81, 88; **23**, 122; **24**, 145; **26**, 157, 166; **30**, 3, 201

Goffman, Erving, **29**, 20n

Goldberg, S. L., **28**, 155, 156

Golder, J. D., **26**, 161

'*Hamlet* in France 200 Years Ago', **24**, 79–86

Golding, Arthur, **21**, 150; **23**, 85, 161, 166; **24**, 156, 159, 162; **25**, 125, 137; **26**, 104; **27**, 160, 179; **30**, 153n

Golding, P., **22**, 153

Goldman, Lloyd, **23**, 167n

Goldman, Michael, **27**, 171; **28**, 105n, 111; **29**, 8; **30**, 48n, 139, 147, 190

Goldsmith, Oliver, **22**, 2

Goldsmith, Robert Hilles, **25**, 50, 51; **27**, 59n, 113n; **29**, 111n, 116

Goldstein, Leonard, **22**, 162

Goldstien, N. L., **29**, 162

Goldwyn, Sam, **29**, 64

Gondomar, Conde de, **23**, 86–7

Góngora, Luis de, **23**, 82

Goodbody, Buzz, **24**, 117, 118, 130; **27**, 148; **29**, 151, 153

Goodman, O. B., **25**, 200

Goodstein, Peter, **24**, 160

Goody, Jack, **24**, 48

Goolden, P., **29**, 13n

Gordon, D. J., **23**, 148

Gordon, George S., **22**, 7, 14n; **23**, 11n, 13n; **26**, 73

Goring, Marius, **27**, 142

Gorfain, Phyllis, 'Puzzle and Artifice: The Riddle as Metapoetry in *Pericles*', **29**, 11–20

Gorki, Maxim, **23**, 176

Gorley, Putt, S., **24**, 165

Görne, Dieter, **22**, 164

Goslicius, **22**, 168

Gossett, Suzanne, **27**, 178

Gossman, Lionel, **22**, 23

Gosson, Henry, **25**, 145

Gosson, Stephen, **29**, 174

Gostelow, Gordon, **25**, 169–70

Gottfried, R., **25**, 138n

Gottschalk, P., **27**, 157; **28**, 154

Gouch, Anthony, **25**, 147; **29**, 34

Gouge, William, **27**, 90

Gould, Jay, **24**, 94

Gourlay, P. S., **26**, 161

Gow, Gordon, **26**, 140n

Gower, John, **24**, 60, 101, 108, 109, 111, 112, 114, 115; **29**, 30

Grafton, Richard, **28**, 4

Grammaticus, Saxo, **27**, 172; **29**, 171

Grant, P., **27**, 158

Grant, Thomas Mark, **27**, 175–6

Grant, Ulysses S., **24**, 91, 92, 93, 94

Granville-Barker, Harley, **21**, 1–2, 27n, 153; **23**, 11n; **24**, 1, 167; **25**, 8, 153, 155, 172; **26**, 5; **27**, 48; **28**, 47n, 168; **29**, 48, 55, 56n, 161

Graves, Robert, **25**, 126, 132; **26**, 112n

Graves, Wallace, **28**, 166

Gray, Henry David, **27**, 106, 107, 108

Gray, James, **30**, 201–2

Graziani, René, **23**, 166n, 167n

Grebanier, Bernard, **21**, 149–50; **30**, 198–9

Greco, A., **27**, 167

Green, A. Wigfall, **27**, 114n, 115, 116n, 118n

Green, F. C., **24**, 80

Green, Henry, **25**, 99n

Green, Thomas, **27**, 99

Green, William, **25**, 109, 110

Greene, Graham, **27**, 149

Greene, G. S., **25**, 137n

Greene, John, **28**, 172

Greene, Robert, **22**, 51, 52; **23**, 88n, 160, 169; **24**, 176; **25**, 188; **26**, 46, 182; **27**, 16, 130, 132, 134; **28**, 45; **29**, 4, 6, 169; **30**, 14, 79, 196

Greene, Thomas M., **21**, 148; **26**, 153

Greeneham, Richard, **25**, 148

Greenfield, Thelma N., **22**, 164; **29**, 55n–6n

Greer, David, **26**, 173

Greg, Sir W. W., **21**, 159; **23**, 179; **24**, 172, 177; **25**, 7, 73n, 75n, 76n, 110, 197, 199, 200; **26**, 13n, 16n, 35n, 180, 183, 184; **27**, 133, 185; **28**, 175; **29**, 117, 127, 128; **30**, 202, 208, 209

Gregorye, Richard, **25**, 147

Grene, David, **22**, 163

Grenewy, Richard, **28**, 67

Greville, Fulke, **21**, 112; **23**, 166; **27**, 117n; **30**, 64, 158

Grieves, **22**, 175

Griffin, Bartholomew, **26**, 103, 107, 108–9

Griffin, John, **25**, 148, 149

Griffin, Robert P., **27**, 177

Grimald, Nicholas, **25**, 99; **26**, 112n

Grivelet, Michel, **21**, 142; **24**, 149; **25**, 173; **27**, 157; **30**, 190

'Shakespeare, Molière, and the Comedy of Ambiguity', **22**, 15–26

'Shakespeare's "War with Time": the Sonnets and *Richard II*', **23**, 69–78

Groom, B., **23**, 13n, 21n

Grosart, A. B., **21**, 140; **23**, 43n; **26**, 39n

Gros Louis, Kenneth R. R., **23**, 163

Gross, Alan Gerald, **22**, 156; **23**, 146; **24**, 78

Gross, Manfred, **23**, 120
Grotowski, Jerzy, **25**, 28
Grove, Fred, **25**, 119n
Grove, Mr, **22**, 128, 131
Grover, P. R., **22**, 158
Grudin, Robert, **30**, 184
Gruhn, Klaus, **23**, 120
Grundy, Joan, **24**, 16
Guarini, G. B., **30**, 192
Guarini, J. F., **28**, 104
Guha, P. K., **22**, 160
Guilday, Peter, **29**, 21n
Guilhamet, L., **29**, 162
Guilpin, Everard, **28**, 180
Gulick, C. B., **25**, 100n
Gunby, D. C., **22**, 172n; **24**, 165
Gundolf, F. L., **26**, 166
Gunn, J. A. W., **23**, 162
Günther, Peter, **23**, 154
Gupta, S. C. Sen, **21**, 153; **28**, 12; **29**, 88
Gurr, Andrew, **21**, 155; **25**, 188, 189;
  26, 164; **28**, 158
  'Coriolanus and the Body Politic', **28**,
  63–9
  'Henry V and the Bees' Common-
  wealth', **30**, 61–72
Gury, Jacques, **30**, 200
Guthrie, Sir Tyrone, **22**, 79; **24**, 53; **25**,
  45n, 66–7; **30**, 83
Gwilym, Mike, **30**, 175

Haaken, Ann, **22**, 174
Haas, R., **29**, 184n
Habicht, Werner, **23**, 112; **24**, 145; **28**,
  168
  'Shakespeare Studies in German,
  1959–68', **23**, 113–23
Haehlen, J., **26**, 166
Hack, Keith, **28**, 143, 146, 147
Hackett, James H., **24**, 88, 101; **28**, 139n
Hackforth, R., **24**, 51
Haeckel, Ernst, **24**, 97
Haffenreffer, Karl, **30**, 195
Hainsworth, J. D., **30**, 200
Haislund, N., **23**, 13n
Hake, Edward, **29**, 93
Hakluyt, R., **21**, 106n
Hale, David G., **23**, 163; **28**, 63n
Hale, D. C., **26**, 158
Hale, J. R., **22**, 159
Hales of Eton, **26**, 166, 175
Halio, Jay L., **22**, 157, 158, 166; **25**, 94n;
  27, 160; **28**, 171n, 179
Hall, Edward, **24**, 63; **25**, 172; **27**, 28n,
  72; **28**, 2, 3; **29**, 84
Hall, G. K., **28**, 172n
Hall, Joseph, **21**, 140; **22**, 38, 39, 182;
  23, 98; **30**, 49n
Hall, Peter, **21**, 119, 120, 121; **22**, 136,
  138; **23**, 132, 133; **24**, 117, 128,
  177; **26**, 139, 141; **28**, 121, 171

Hallam, Lewis, **30**, 199
Halle, M., **23**, 11n
Hallen, A. W. C., **25**, 139n
Hallett, Charles A., **24**, 164
Halliday, F. E., **27**, 106n
Halliwell, J. O., **23**, 102
Halliwell-Phillipps, J. O., **25**, 200; **27**,
  97n, 106n; **28**, 179–80; **29**, 168
Hallstead, R. N., **22**, 161
Hamburger, Michael P., **23**, 151
Hamer, Douglas, **23**, 161n; **24**, 155; **28**,
  49n, 166
Hamilton, A. C., **22**, 151; **26**, 174; **27**,
  11n, 17n, 18; **29**, 88
Hamilton, D. B., **28**, 157, 167
Hamilton, D. M., **27**, 167
Hamilton, Henry, **29**, 136
Hammond, Kay, **27**, 142
Handel, **21**, 96
Hands, Terry, **23**, 132, 133; **24**, 118, 119,
  120, 129, 131; **25**, 153, 155, 158,
  164; **27**, 144, 150, 151; **29**, 154,
  155
Hanmer, Thomas, **27**, 49n
Hann, T., **26**, 142
Hansen, Jørgen Wildt, **30**, 193
Hapgood, E. R., **27**, 144n
Hapgood, Robert, **22**, 155; **24**, 154, 161;
  25, 3n; **26**, 159; **27**, 144n
  'Hearing Shakespeare: Sound and
  Meaning in Antony and Cleo-
  patra', **24**, 1–12
Haponski, W. C., **26**, 176n
Harbage, Alfred, **21**, 65n, 129, 141; **24**,
  163, 172n, 173, 174; **25**, 8, 171;
  26, 7, 55n, 100, 168; **29**, 87, 167,
  170, 172; **30**, 14, 109
Harcourt, John B., **28**, 158; **29**, 170
Hardiman, Terence, **22**, 141
Harding, Davis P., **25**, 6n
Harding, D. W., **24**, 145
Hardison, O. B., **24**, 162; **26**, 174; **30**,
  194
Hardy, John, **21**, 149
Hardy, Thomas, **24**, 37, 38, 46; **30**, 3
Hardy, W. J., **25**, 139
Hargrave, Francis, **29**, 97n
Hargreaves, H. A., **25**, 181
Harington, Sir John, **27**, 136n; **28**, 21
Harker, J. C., **26**, 142
Harlow, C. G., **21**, 152; **24**, 159
Harmon, Alice, **28**, 39, 40; **29**, 81
Harrington, Lord, **26**, 41
Harris, A. J., **25**, 192
Harris, Bernard, **21**, 127n, 140; **25**, 84n;
  26, 9, 24n; **29**, 3; **30**, 148n
Harris, Frank, **29**, 133, 135, 139
Harris, John, **28**, 170; **30**, 157–8, 161
Harris, Kathryn M., **25**, 173
Harris, Thomas, **29**, 34, 35, 36, 37–9
Harrison, C. T., **26**, 167

Harrison, G. B., **21**, 138, 141, 157; **26**, 50
  27, 16n, 21n; **28**, 118n; **30**, 15;
Harrison, Stephen, **26**, 39n
Harrison, Thomas P., **23**, 11n, 141n;
  26, 172
Harrison, William, **29**, 22, 24; **30**, 8
Harsnett, Samuel, **24**, 71, 72, 77; **26**,
  71–2; **27**, 172, 173; **28**, 119; **29**,
  24; **30**, 193
Hart, Alfred, **25**, 74n, 76n; **29**, 84; **30**, 6,
  89, 90n
Hart, Clive, **24**, 165
Hart, H. C., **27**, 112, 119, 120, 121,
  122
Hart, John A., **24**, 175
Hart-Davis, R., **29**, 133n, 139n
Harting, J. E., **21**, 142
Hartley, Lodowick, **25**, 182
Hartmann, Robert, **24**, 97
Hartsock, Mildred E., **21**, 132; **22**, 114;
  24, 153
Hartwig, Joan, **25**, 177; **27**, 158; **28**, 162;
  29, 52n
Harvey, Gabriel, **21**, 48; **23**, 171n; **24**,
  77, 159; **26**, 20; **27**, 117n, 130;
  28, 45; **30**, 209
Harvey, Nancy L., **24**, 148
Harvey, Sir William, **24**, 151; **25**, 4
Hasler, Jorg, **23**, 143; **25**, 184; **29**, 161
Hassell, Chris R., **25**, 179
Hassell, R. C., Jr, **27**, 164
Hatcliffe, William, **28**, 165
Hatton, Sir Christopher, **28**, 23, 24; **29**,
  94
Hathaway, Anne, **23**, 159; **26**, 164
Hathaway, Michael, **23**, 163n
Hathway, Richard, **26**, 103
Hauger, George, **27**, 144
Hauser, Arnold, **26**, 49, 50, 54, 58, 59n,
  60n, 61n, 63, 64, 65; **28**, 152–3
Hauser, Frank, **27**, 140
Havelock, E. A., **24**, 50n
Havely, C., **27**, 157
Haviland, William, **25**, 118
Hawkes, Terence, **24**, 6n; **25**, 173; **26**,
  165; **28**, 150, 155
  'Shakespeare's Talking Animals', **24**,
  47–54
Hawkins, Harriett, **23**, 170; **27**, 162; **28**,
  89, 91, 100n
Hawkins, Sherman, **22**, 153
Hawthorne, Nathaniel, **24**, 169
Hay, John, **24**, 90, 102, 103
Hay, Sir James, **29**, 4
Haydn, Hiram, **29**, 85
Hayes, Patricia, **28**, 144, 145
Hayman, Ronald, **24**, 131n
Haynes, F. O., **29**, 94, 98, 100
Hays, Michael L., **29**, 185; **30**, 208
Hayter, A., **26**, 161
Hayward, John, **28**, 8, 9

Haywood, Charles, **23**, 175; **24**, 154, 168n, 169

Hazlitt, William, **21**, 3, 107; **22**, 8; **24**, 45; **25**, 199; **26**, 90, 140; **29**, 105n, 134, 143

Hazlitt, W. Carew, **21**, 65n; **22**, 8; **27**, 111n; **28**, 38

Heath, D. D., **28**, 16n

Heawood, Edward, **23**, 127

Hecht, Hans, **30**, 164n

Heffner, Ray L., **28**, 8n; **30**, 186

Hegel, Georg, **22**, 36, 37

Hegel, G. W. F., **24**, 97

Heiberg, Johanne Luise, **29**, 145–9

Heilman, Robert B., **21**, 8, 62, 63, 131, 137, 150–1; **27**, 27n, 28n

Heilpern, John, **24**, 131n

Helgerson, R., **26**, 165; **30**, 195

Hellenga, Robert R., **30**, 184–5

Heminge, John, **28**, 173, 177

Hemingway, Samuel B., **25**, 111n

Henderson, W. B. Drayton, **28**, 39n

Heneage, Sir Thomas, **21**, 104

Heninger, S. K., Jr, **23**, 163; **24**, 158; **28**, 161

Henke, James T., **29**, 174

Henkel, Arthur, **26**, 117n

Henn, Hans Georg, **23**, 122; **26**, 166

Henn, T. R., **26**, 165

Henning, Hans, **29**, 177

Henning, Standish, **22**, 182; **24**, 156

Henry, IV, King, **28**, 8

Henry IV, King of France, **29**, 26, 27, 28

Henry V, King, **30**, 5

Henry VI, King, **30**, 45

Henry VII, King, **26**, 44, 45n; **28**, 20

Henry VIII, King, **26**, 41; **28**, 18, 20, 21, 63, 165, 166; **30**, 63, 192

Henry, Prince, **26**, 36, 40n, 41, 43, 44, 45, 46, 47, 48; **29**, 4

Henry, William, **21**, 149

Henslowe, Philip, **23**, 173; **26**, 42, 168; **27**, 134, 135, 136, 173; **28**, 3; **29**, 34, 127–32; **30**, 202

Hentz, Louise, **21**, 134

Henze, Richard, **25**, 176, 179, 180; **27**, 170; **28**, 161; **29**, 162

Heracleitus, **30**, 119

Herbert, Sir Henry, **29**, 51n

Herbert, William, **30**, 102, 181, 182

Herford, C. H., **25**, 100n; **26**, 39n; **27**, 106n, 112n, 118, 120, 123, 124, 125, 126

Herndl, George C., **25**, 180

Herringman, John, **27**, 191

Hertford, Earl of, **25**, 188

Hervey, Elizabeth, **21**, 97, 100

Hervey, Frances, **21**, 97, 100

Hervey, Gawen and Roger, **21**, 97

Hervey, Henry, **21**, 97

Hervey, of Kidbrook, *see* Kidbrook

Hervey, William, **23**, 160

Hervey, William, 'of Chessington', **21**, 97–105; **23**, 160

Herwegh, G., **23**, 174

Hesiod, **25**, 99

Hexham, H., **23**, 34

Heylyn, Peter, **26**, 81n

Heywood, Thomas, **22**, 21, 52; **23**, 76, 171; **24**, 54, 155n; **26**, 9, 41, 103, 168, 169; **27**, 129; **29**, 104, 170, 182; **30**, 198

Hibbard, George R., **21**, 158; **22**, 171, 178; **23**, 152; **24**, 172n, 173; **25**, 185; **27**, 171; **28**, 178; **29**, 109n; **30**, 9n, 198, 210

'*Othello* and the Pattern of Shakespearian Tragedy', **21**, 39–46

'Words, Action, and Artistic Economy', **23**, 49–58

'*Henry IV* and *Hamlet*', **30**, 1–12

Critical Studies, *reviewed*: (1967), **21**, 127–41; (1968), **22**, 145–66; (1969), **23**, 49–58

Hieatt, A. Kent, **27**, 109n

Higgins, J., **27**, 172

Hill, Christopher, **29**, 90

Hill, E. G., **26**, 176n

Hill, G. Birkbeck, **21**, 10n; **24**, 37n

Hill, Geoffrey, **23**, 155

Hill, R. F., **21**, 146; **27**, 33; **30**, 183

'*The Merchant of Venice* and the Pattern of Romantic Comedy', **28**, 75–87

Critical Studies, *reviewed*: (1976), **30**, 181–90

Hill, Thomas, **24**, 68

Hillebrand, H. N., **25**, 9

Hinchcliffe, Edgar, **23**, 165n

Hinman, Charlton, **23**, 184, 185; **24**, 170, 171, 172, 174; **25**, 129; **26**, 177, 182, 183; **27**, 179, 181, 182, 183, 184, 189, 190; **30**, 206

Hirsch, Richard S. M., **29**, 170

Hirt, H., **23**, 28n

Hitchcock, Alfred, **26**, 175

Hobbes, Thomas, **23**, 145; **24**, 20; **25**, 18n; **28**, 65

Hobday, C. H., **23**, 147; **30**, 53n

'Imagery and Irony in *Henry V*', **21**, 107–13

'Shakespeare's *Venus and Adonis* Sonnets', **26**, 103–9

Hobson, Harold, **24**, 43; **27**, 34n

Hoby, Sir Edward, **28**, 4, 6; **30**, 199

Hoby, Sir Thomas, **25**, 103n; **27**, 56n

Hoccleve, Thomas, **30**, 65n

Hockey, Dorothy, **25**, 93

Hodge, Harold, (H.H.), **29**, 139

Hodgen, Margaret, **28**, 37

Hodges, C. Walter, **24**, 174; **28**, 132, 135, 167–8; **29**, 130, 131; **30**, 196

Hodges, W. C., **22**, 35, 173

Hodgson, William, **25**, 146

Hoefnagel, Joris, **26**, 112n

Hoeniger, F. D., **21**, 149; **23**, 180; **24**, 106, 110, 113n; **25**, 137n; **29**, 11n, 22

'Shakespeare's Romances since 1958: A Retrospect', **29**, 1–10

Hoffmann, Gerhard, **21**, 143; **26**, 166n

Hoffmeier, Dieter, **21**, 149; **22**, 162, 175n

Hogan, Jerome W., **29**, 175

Hogarth, William, **30**, 164, 165

Hogg, Ian, **26**, 143, 148

Hogg, James, **27**, 175; **29**, 166, 173

Hoius, Andreas, **29**, 28, 29, 30

Holaday, Alan, **23**, 144

Holbein, Hans, **24**, 158

Holden, William H., **30**, 164n

Hole, Sandra, **23**, 153

Holinshed, Raphael, **21**, 111, 132, 151; **23**, 146, 160; **24**, 63–4, 163; **25**, 172; **26**, 36n, 42, 81, 82, 83, 84, 85n, 86, 87, 113, 157; **27**, 35, 36, 131, 172; **28**, 1, 3, 12, 120; **30**, 8, 49n, 53

Holland, Henry, **28**, 119

Holland, J. F. **26**, 164

Holland, Norman N., **22**, 145–6, 166

Holland, Philemon, **23**, 61

Hollar, W., **28**, 130, 134, 167

Holloway, John, **21**, 4, 5; **23**, 66

Holly, M., **28**, 155

Holm, Ian, **30**, 22

Holmes, David W., **23**, 170

Holmes, Denis, **27**, 147

Holmes, Martin, **23**, 162n

Holmes, M. R., **22**, 175n

Holmes, R., **22**, 166

Holt, Charles Lloyd, **23**, 156

Homan, Sidney R., **24**, 163; **25**, 175, 181; **26**, 156; **27**, 170

Homer, **22**, 15, 147, 168; **22**, 21, 97; **27**, 119; **30**, 190

Honey, William, **23**, 159

Honigmann, E. A. J., **21**, 145; **22**, 179–80, 181; **24**, 77n; **25**, 145, 194n, 196; **27**, 112n, 113, 116n, 132n; **29**, 25, 104; **30**, 187–8, 206

'Re-enter the Stage Direction: Shakespeare and some Contemporaries', **29**, 117–25

Studies on Shakespeare's Life, Times and Stage, *reviewed*, **21**, 141–57

Hooker, Elizabeth R., **28**, 42n, 64, 65, 66; **29**, 79

Hooker, Richard, **23**, 106; **25**, 76n; **29**, 85, 86, 87, 88, 158

Hooper, Richard, **25**, 99n

Hope, A. D., **26**, 159

Hope, Anthony, 25, 166
Hoppe, H. R., 22, 182; 24, 176; 25, 73n, 77
Hopkins, John, 27, 141
Horace, 22, 47, 27, 62, 119, 122, 30, 192
Horalék, Karel, 21, 153
Horobetz, Lynn K., 23, 174n; 26, 176n
Horowitz, David, 28, 110n
Horsman, E. A., 27, 189
Horwich, Richard, 25, 188
Hoskyns, John, 27, 120
Hosley, Richard, 21, 145, 150, 151; 22, 35, 173, 183; 23, 127, 128, 160–1, 185; 24, 168; 25, 73n; 26, 9, 96n; 27, 77n, 135, 175, 190; 28, 133; 29, 171, 172; 30, 196
Hotson, Leslie, 21, 147; 25, 109, 110; 27, 94, 119n; 28, 125, 134; 29, 179; 30, 167n
Houghton, Alexander, 24, 155; 28, 166
Houghton, William, 23, 160
Houser, David J., 28, 168
Housman, A. E., 23, 176
Hovenden, R., 25, 143n
Howard, Alan, 22, 140; 24, 122, 130; 25, 70; 28, 139; 29, 154–5, 156
Howard, Charles, Lord Admiral, 23, 44, 45; 25, 188
Howard, James, 21, 156
Howard, L., 26, 154
Howard, Lady Frances, 26, 57
Howard, Leslie, 27, 138
Howard, Lord Thomas, 21, 103
Howard-Hill, T. H., 23, 176, 177, 178–9, 184; 24, 172n; 25, 199n, 200; 26, 179; 27, 181, 182, 183, 184, 188; 29, 181, 184; 30, 207
Howarth, R. G., 23, 171n; 30, 164
Howarth, Herbert, 29, 88
Howell, Roger, 22, 170
Howells, William Dean, 24, 104
Howlett, Robert, 30, 164
Hoy, Cyrus, 28, 2, 3, 152–3
  'Jacobean Tragedy and the Mannerist Style', 26, 49–67
Hoye, André van, see Hoius
Hoyle, J., 26, 156; 30, 185
Huarte, Juan, 29, 81
Huber, Anneliese, 23, 119n
Huber, E., 30, 208–9
Huberd, Edward, 27, 99, 101, 102
Hudson, H. N., 27, 192
Hudson, Kenneth, 24, 40; 25, 185
  'Shakespeare's Use of Colloquial Language', 23, 39–48
Huesmann, Heinrich, 23, 122
Hughes, Henry, 28, 38n
Hughes, John, 27, 191
Hughes, Paul L., 30, 161n, 163n
Hughes, Robert, 26, 78n

Hugo, Victor, 21, 80
Hulme, Hilda M., 23, 11n; 25, 181; 30, 204
Huloet, R., 23, 28
Hume, David, 24, 97
Hume, R. D., 28, 157
Humphreys, A. R., 22, 154, 179; 25, 141n, 173, 199; 26, 177; 27, 37n, 131n; 30, 29n, 35n, 37, 38, 40n, 42n, 43n
Hunt, Christopher, 27, 106n
Hunt, Hugh, 24, 167
Hunt, J. D., 27, 163
Hunt, John, 27, 101, 102, 103
Hunt, Leigh, 29, 143
Hunt, R. W., 26, 81, 82
Hunt, Sir David, 28, 134n
Hunt, W. H., 25, 139n, 27, 129n
Hunter, Edwin R., 23, 100n
Hunter, John, 22, 125
Hunter, G. K., 21, 127, 137, 158; 22, 14n, 79, 80, 83, 88, 151, 173; 23, 152, 167, 169; 24, 165; 25, 2, 4, 47n; 26, 24n, 119, 177–8; 27, 106n, 190; 29, 8, 9, 42–3, 163; 30, 35, 73, 75, 81n, 125, 127, 128, 133n, 135, 192
  'Shakespeare's Earliest Tragedies: Titus Andronicus and Romeo and Juliet', 27, 1–9
Hunter, Robert Grams, 21, 127; 25, 4, 6, 58n, 175; 28, 161; 29, 8, 59n
Hunter, S., 24, 165
Hunter, Sir Mark, 26, 97; 29, 80
Hunter, William B., 25, 180
Hurstfield, Joel, 26, 171; 29, 90; 30, 1
  'The Politics of Corruption in Shakespeare's England', 28, 15–28
Hurtgen, Charles, 23, 158, 174n
Hussey, Dyneley, 21, 96
Huston, J. D., 25, 177; 28, 161
Hutchings, Geoffrey, 25, 164
Huttar, Charles A., 23, 158
Hutton, V., 25, 182
Huxley, Aldous, 25, 185
Hyde, Nicholas, 28, 68
Hyman, L. W., 25, 179; 29, 163
Hyman, S. E., 26, 162
Hyman, William, 21, 144; 25, 179

Ibsen, Henrik, 22, 3, 35, 163; 24, 13, 14, 43; 29, 9, 136, 146; 30, 85, 86n, 189
Ingham, Barrie, 23, 134; 28, 147
Ingham, Patricia, 22, 182
Inglar, William, 21, 100
Ingleby, C. M., 23, 102, 103
Ingledew, John, 25, 94n
Ingram, R. W., 27, 172; 29, 2; 30, 198
Ingram, William, 26, 175–6; 28, 168
Institor, H., 28, 119

Ionescu, Eugene, 22, 4; 24, 19
Ireland, Samuel, 24, 168
Ireland, William Henry, 21, 149; 25, 187; 29, 136
Irvin, Eric, 24, 167n
  'Shakespeare in the Early Sydney Theatre', 22, 125–33
Irving, Sir Henry, 23, 173; 24, 14, 37; 25, 118; 28, 171; 29, 138, 142, 143, 176
Isler, Alan D., 22, 155, 171; 23, 166; 25, 174
Iwasaki, I., 26, 161
Iwasaki, S., 28, 157
Iwasari, Soji, 22, 161; 27, 179

Jackson, Andrew, 24, 88
Jackson, B. A. W., 25, 173n; 26, 176n; 27, 163n, 166n, 172
Jackson, J. R. de J., 21, 141; 23, 175
Jackson, MacD. P., 21, 146; 26, 172–3; 29, 171, 181–2
Jackson, Russell, 29, 176
Jacobs, Nicholas, 29, 175
Jacobs, Sally, 24, 125
Jacquot, J., 27, 170
Jaeger, Ronald, W., 26, 173
Jaggard, Isaac, 24, 170, 178
Jaggard, William, 21, 160, 162; 22, 181, 182; 23, 185; 25, 197; 26, 41, 103–4, 109, 181, 182; 27, 180, 181, 182, 185; 28, 180; 29, 178
Jahn, J. D., 27, 156
James, D. G., 21, 2; 22, 165; 29, 5, 87, 89
James, Emrys, 23, 132; 25, 167; 28, 139; 29, 155
James I, King, (James VI), 21, 47–9, 52, 130, 135, 140; 23, 120, 121, 151, 162; 25, 7, 180; 26, 34, 35, 36, 37, 40, 41, 42, 43, 44, 45, 46, 47, 72, 98; 27, 95, 133, 172; 28, 15, 16, 19, 20, 21, 22, 23, 24, 25, 27, 28, 64, 65, 68, 93, 117–23, 163, 170; 29, 3, 4; 30, 161, 162, 165, 195
James IV, King of Scotland, 26, 44
James VI, King, 27, 172
James, Gerald, 26, 144, 145
James, Henry, 21, 141; 22, 5; 24, 104: 30, 89, 93, 94
James, Louis, 25, 117, 118
James, Polly, 25, 168
Jameson, Thomas H., 23, 147
Jamete, Esteban, 23, 80, 81
Jamieson, Michael, 28, 89n
  'The Problem Plays, 1920–1970: a Retrospect', 25, 1–10
Janicker, Irene, 23, 170
Janson, H. W., 26, 116n
Jarrett-Kerr, Martin, 30, 63n, 65
Jayne, Sears, 21, 131

Jeaffreson, John Cordy, **25**, 139, 140n
Jeffares, A. Norman, **23**, 146
Jefferson, D. W., **23**, 141n; **30**, 11n
Jefford, Barbara, **25**, 29; **27**, 142
Jeffrey, D. L., **27**, 158
Jeffrey, L. N., **26**, 161
Jeffs, R., **25**, 149
Jenkins, Gladys, **24**, 71n, 72n
Jenkins, Harold, **25**, 196; **26**, 117n; **28**, 153; **30**, 201
Jennings, Paul, **23**, 39
Jensen, Ejner, J., **24**, 166n
Jepson, Laura, **27**, 11n
Jerrold, Douglas, **22**, 128
Jesperson, O., **23**, 13, 28; **25**, 192
Jetter, Kurt, **23**, 118
Jewel, John, **23**, 84
Jewell, Simon, **30**, 196
Jiji, Vera M., **30**, 183
Jochums, M. C., **26**, 154
Jodelle, Etienne, **24**, 157
Jofen, Jean, **26**, 172
Johnson, Charles, **26**, 114n
Johnson, James T., **27**, 90n
Johnson, Lee, **21**, 81, 84
Johnson, Mary, **29**, 34, 37
Johnson, Richard, **24**, 3n, 8; **26**,146–7
Johnson, Robert Carl, **23**, 168; **24**, 160, 161; **25**, 182
Johnson, Samuel, **21**, 3, 4, 6, 28n, 149; **22**, 12, 158; **23**, 137, 175; **24**, 18, 48, 107, 153, 177; **25**, 45, 46, 53, 57, 60, 111n; **26**, 71n, 123, 181, 182; **28**, 57, 89, 90–1, 112, 125; **30**, 3n, 58n, 96n, 110, 121, 187, 201, 202
Johnson, William, **29**, 34, 37; **30**, 196
Jolles, Frank, **23**, 122
Jones, David, **22**, 139–40; **23**, 132; **27**, 146, 148
Jones, E., **26**, 151; **27**, 159
Jones, E. L., **25**, 94n
Jones, Emrys, **23**, 162n; **29**, 3, 4, 67, 160
'Othello, Lepanto, and the Cyprus Wars' **21**, 47–52
Jones, Ernest, **21**, 133; **30**, 112, 113, 114
Jones, Mrs Harriet, **22**, 128, 130–2
Jones, Inigo, **23**, 125–9; **24**, 13; **26**, 33, 35, 41, 45, 57–8, 169; **28**, 168, 170; **29**, 2; **30**, 157–68, 191
Jones, J. H., **26**, 162
Jones, Millard T., **28**, 180; **30**, 206
Jones, Robert C., **21**, 100; **30**, 192
Jones, William, **21**, 100; **25**, 148
Jones, W. J., **22**, 169; **27**, 94n, 101, 103; **29**, 93n, 94n, 95n, 96n, 99n
Jones, Zachary, **23**, 160
Jones-Davies, Marie-Thérèse, **22**, 172n; **28**, 162
Jonns, Daniel, **22**, 121
Jonson, Ben, **21**, 48, 52n, 67, 140, 145, 161; **22**, 1, 2, 8, 35, 43–6, 47–9, 51–8, 109, 110, 111, 115, 171, 172; **23**, 33, 46, 100, 119, 141, 160, 167n, 169–70; **24**, 13, 40, 47, 48, 52, 62, 68, 107, 127, 146, 150, 164, 165; **25**, 9, 68, 78, 100, 104n, 125, 162, 190, 193; **26**, 1, 3, 4, 15, 33, 34, 35, 39, 40, 41, 45, 48, 56–7, 90, 94, 96, 168, 169, 170; **27**, 83, 112, 119, 120, 121, 122, 123, 124, 126, 127, 135, 176, 178; **28**, 57, 59, 134, 149, 164, 174; **29**, 9, 110, 170, 184; **30**, 3, 4, 89, 191, 195, 196, 201
Joppien, Rüdiger, **29**, 176
Jordan, R., **24**, 166
Jorgens, Jack J., **28**, 171n
Jorgensen, Paul A., **22**, 161; **24**, 153; **25**, 93; **29**, 160; **30**, 64n, 65n, 68
Joseph, Lois, **21**, 141
Joseph, Sister Miriam, **27**, 84n; **30**, 89
Joseph, Stephen, **26**, 140
Joubin, André, **21**, 86n
Jourdain, Sylvester, **25**, 127n
Joyce, James, **26**, 92
'J.S.', **23**, 171
Judges, A. V., **26**, 71n
Juel-Jensen, Bent, **24**, 159
Jump, John, **25**, 185; **30**, 185
Jung, C. G., **21**, 133; **22**, 146; **23**, 133; **27**, 171
Juvenal, **27**, 119

Kable, William S., **21**, 162; **22**, 181; **26**, 182; **27**, 185
Kachler, K. G., **28**, 172n
Kahn, Coppelia H., **29**, 11n, 16
Kaiser, Gerhard W., **23**, 120
Kaiser, Walter, **29**, 91
Kalson, Albert E., **29**, 176
Kane, John, **24**, 125n
Kane, R. J., **29**, 24n
Kanini, Mary, **23**, 162n
Kant, Immanuel, **24**, 97
Kantak, V. Y., **24**, 148
'An Approach to Shakespearian Comedy', **22**, 7–14
Kantorowitz, Ernst, **27**, 44; **28**, 2, 63
Kaplan, Joel H., **24**, 160, 163, 164
Katayev, Valentin, **27**, 143
Kau, Joseph, **29**, 171
Kaufmann, R. J., **22**, 160; **25**, 9, 14n, 19n; **26**, 158
Kaula, David, **21**, 135; **27**, 167; **30**, 184, 192–3
'Hamlet and the "Sparing Discoverie"', **24**, 71–7
Kay, C. M., **26**, 157
Kean, Charles, **22**, 133; **24**, 168; **25**, 113, 114, 115, 116, 119, 120, 121; **29**, 176
Kean, Edmund, **21**, 80; **23**, 122; **28**, 139; **29**, 143, 177; **30**, 198
Kean, Ellen, **22**, 133
Keating, Charles, **28**, 142
Keats, John, **21**, 129; **22**, 8, 146, 164, 166, 175; **23**, 98; **24**, 35, 44, 108, 110, 114, 115, 127
Keeling, William, **28**, 6
Keene, Laura, **22**, 133
Keeton, George W., **22**, 169–70; **29**, 96, 98
Kelliher, W. Hilton, **25**, 192; **28**, 38n
Kellison, Matthew, **29**, 21
Kelly, F. L., **28**, 158
Kelly, Henry A., **25**, 172–3
Kelly, H. H., **29**, 88
Kelly, Robert L., **23**, 147
Kelly, T., **27**, 165
Kemble, Charles, **21**, 80; **30**, 200
Kemble, Fanny, **22**, 121, 174
Kemble, John Philip, **23**, 173; **24**, 17, 168; **25**, 185; **29**, 176, 177
Kemp, William, **21**, 113; **22**, 39, 40, 121; **25**, 161, 165, 166, 167; **28**, 177
Kennedy, John F., **28**, 15, 28
Kennedy, Judith M., **22**, 168
Kennet, W., **27**, 61, 62, 63, 64, 65, 66, 67, 68
Kenny, R. W., **24**, 157
Kenny, T., **27**, 106n
Ker, W. P., **26**, 76n
Kermode, Frank, **22**, 153; **25**, 8, 125, 126; **28**, 117, 119n, 122, 174; **29**, 5, 44; **30**, 149, 151, 152
Kernan, Alvin B., **24**, 151; **28**, 150, 170; **29**, 171, 172
Kernodle, George R., **28**, 170
Kéry, Lásló, **25**, 179
Kestelman, Sara, **24**, 124
Kettle, Arnold, **21**, 141; **25**, 13n; **30**, 114
Kiasashvili, N., **29**, 167
Kidbrook, Lord Hervey of, **21**, 98–9, 100
Kierkegaard, Søren, **29**, 145, 146
Kilbey, James A., **25**, 183
Killigrew, Thomas, **23**, 126
Kimbrough, Robert, **25**, 9, 176
Kindermann, Heinz, **28**, 172n
King, Arthur H., **23**, 11n
King, Clarence, **24**, 101, 102n
King, Lucille, **29**, 84
King, T. J., **25**, 190; **28**, 169
King, Walter, N., **23**, 144
King's Men, **28**, 169, 180
Kingsford, C. L., **23**, 45n; **29**, 79
Kingsley, Ben, **24**, 125n; **29**, 152–3
Kingston, Felix, **24**, 72n
Kinkaid, A. N., **27**, 178
Kinney, Arthur F., **29**, 174
Kip, J., **30**, 164n
Kipling, Rudyard, **25**, 125
Kirchner, Walter, **22**, 124n

Kirck(mann) John (Johann), **22**, 119–20

Kirkman, Francis, **27**, 175

Kirov, Todor T., **23**, 142

Kirsch, Arthur C., **22**, 164, 175; **24**, 168; **29**, 3, 9; **30**, 184

   'The Integrity of *Measure for Measure*', **28**, 89–105

Kirsch, James, **21**, 133

Kirschbaum, Leo, **23**, 148, 160; **24**, 77n; **25**, 75n, 76n, 79n

Kissoon, Jeffrey, **28**, 148

Kistner, A. L., **28**, 155

Kistner, M. K., **28**, 155

Kitchin, Laurence, **30**, 144

Kitt, Johann Jakob, **23**, 154

Kitto, H. D. F., **23**, 154; **27**, 160

Kittredge, G. L., **24**, 2n, 4; **25**, 51; **27**, 130n; **30**, 91n

Kjellmer, Göran, **23**, 138; **24**, 157

Klein, David, **22**, 173

Klein, Joan Larson, **30**, 194

Klein, Richard, **29**, 20n

Klein, Ursula, **29**, 177; **30**, 201

Klene, J., **29**, 164

Klethen, Raf, *see* Cletten, Raf

Klose, Dietrich, **23**, 143

Klosová, Ljuba, **22**, 175n

Klotz, Gunther, **29**, 175

Kluge, F., **23**, 28n

Knafla, Louis, A., **24**, 158n

Kniazevsky, B., **23**, 165

Knight, Charles, **22**, 183; **25**, 110; **27**, 106n

Knight, Edward, **28**, 180, 181

Knight, Grant C., **24**, 98

Knight, G. Wilson, **21**, 2, 3, 7, 11n, 62, 120, 137, 142, 148; **22**, 79, 80, 81, 149, 162; **23**, 151; **25**, 2, 4, 5, 8, 11n, 16n, 29, 39n, 64; **26**, 89, 127n, 151, 162, 167; **27**, 71, 82n; **28**, 89n; **29**, 1, 8, 9, 51, 88, 89, 103n; **30**, 112n

Knight, W. Nicholas, **28**, 164–5; **29**, 95n, 96

   'Equity, *The Merchant of Venice* and William Lambarde', **27**, 93–104

Knights, L. C., **21**, 137; **22**, 147, 158, 162; **23**, 42, 66n, 69, 144, 152, 155; **25**, 5, 8, 12n, 185; **26**, 76; **27**, 54n; **28**, 21n, 89, 107; **29**, 87, 165; **30**, 44n, 112n

Knolles, Richard, **21**, 40, 48, 51, 52

Knollys, Sir Francis, **28**, 8

Knowland, A. S., **25**, 9

Knowles, Conrad, **22**, 127–8, 129–32

Knowles, Mrs, *see* Jones, Mrs Harriet

Knowles, Richard, **21**, 132, 153; **25**, 96n, 97n, 99n, 172; **26**, 112n, 114n, 115n; **27**, 172, 190

Knowlton, Jean, **23**, 172

Knox, Bernard, **22**, 49

Kodama, J. H., **26**, 153

Kohl, Norbert, **23**, 117

Kohler, Estelle, **24**, 124; **25**, 66; **27**, 147, 150, 151

Kökeritz, Helge, **23**, 11n; **25**, 93; **26**, 171; **27**, 189

Kolakowsky, L., **29**, 91

Kolin, Philip C., **26**, 172; **28**, 167; **29**, 174

Kolve, V. A., **28**, 91n

Komisarjevsky, Theodore, **25**, 81, 88; **28**, 171

Kopecký, Jan, **21**, 129

Koppenfels, W. von, **26**, 154

Kornilova, H., **23**, 175

Korninger, Siegfried, **21**, 143; **23**, 115

Koskimies, R., **25**, 183

Koss, Siegfried, **30**, 202

Kossmann, E. H., **28**, 24n

Koszul, A., **25**, 126

Koteliansky, S. S., **24**, 38n

Kott, Jan, **21**, 74, 129; **22**, 30, 159; **23**, 119; **24**, 154; **25**, 19n, 22, 23n, 28, 171, 186; **27**, 159; **28**, 156; **30**, 195

Koyro, Hans Georg, **23**, 122

Kozintsev, Grigori, **21**, 128; **27**, 179n

Krabbe, Henning, **27**, 192; **29**, 148n

   'A Danish Actress and her Conception of the Part of Lady Macbeth'. **29**, 145–9

Krafft, John, **22**, 119–20

Kramer, Joseph E., **25**, 176; **28**, 181

Krantz, Albert, **24**, 156; **29**, 171

Krapp, G. P., **25**, 3

Kristella, P., **29**, 91

Kronenberger, Louis, **24**, 98

Kross, Jaan, **23**, 159

Küchelbekker, W. K., **23**, 174

Kuckhoff, Armin-Gerd, **23**, 142, 174n; **25**, 186; **26**, 166

Kujoory, Parvin, **30**, 191

Kumar, Mihir, **22**, 166

Kuner, Mildred C., **23**, 174n; **24**, 167

Kurke, Eduard, **23**, 149

Kyd, Thomas, **21**, 25, 150; **22**, 54, 152, 159, 171; **23**, 28n, 49, 117, 160, 169; **24**, 32, 44, 142, 162, 174; **26**, 1, 41; **27**, 173, 178; **30**, 110, 119

Labov, W., **23**, 111n

La Branche, Anthony, **21**, 132; **22**, 163n

La Bruyère, **26**, 89

Lachmann, Karl, **25**, 195

Ladkins, Robert, **25**, 149

La Farge, John, **24**, 96

La Fontaine, **22**, 16, 20

Lagarde, Fernand, **23**, 171n

Laguardia, Eric, **22**, 170

Laidlaw, J. C., **23**, 141n

Lake, David, **24**, 155; **30**, 207

Lamb, Charles, **23**, 105; **24**, 1n, 168; **25**, 185; **29**, 134, 177

Lamb, Margaret, **29**, 175

Lamb, Mary, **24**, 1n

Lambarde, William, **27**, 93–104; **28**, 3, 8, 9, 131n, 164–5; **29**, 95n, 96n, 97

Lambert, Edmund, **27**, 97, 98, 102, 103, 104

Lambert, John, **27**, 98–104

Lambin, G., **21**, 162; **22**, 160, 164; **25**, 53; **30**, 201

Lambley, Kathleen, **28**, 38n

Lambrechts, Guy, **21**, 151; **23**, 74, 160

Lancashire, Ann Begor, **30**, 127, 134n

Lancashire, Anne C., **23**, 143; **24**, 148, 162n, 163

Landry, Hilton, **22**, 165

Landt, D. B., **21**, 152

Lane, Richard, **27**, 99

Langdon, Anthony, **24**, 118

Langer, Susan, **22**, 9

Langley, Francis, **28**, 168

Lanham, John, **27**, 134

Lanham, Richard A., **26**, 174n

Lansdowne, B. L., **30**, 166n

Lapotaire, Jane, **28**, 144, 148

La Primaudaye, **22**, 112; **29**, 82

La Rochefoucauld, **28**, 48n

Larkin, James F., **30**, 161n, 163n

Larra, Mrs, **22**, 131

Lascelles, Mary, **25**, 7; **26**, 120; **28**, 89, 100n, 155

   '*King Lear* and Doomsday', **26**, 69–79

Laski, Harold, **27**, 83n

Lasso, Orlando di, **26**, 173

Latham, Agnes, **29**, 177

Latham, Jacqueline E. M., **30**, 195

   '*The Tempest* and King James's *Daemonologie*', **28**, 117–23

Latham, R. E., **21**, 100

Latter, D. A., **30**, 196

   'Sight-Lines in a Conjectural Reconstruction of an Elizabethan Playhouse', **28**, 125–35

Laughton, Charles, **25**, 64

Lavater, L., **27**, 173

Laver, James, **21**, 155

Lavin, J. A., **23**, 162; **24**, 176; **25**, 191; **26**, 184; **27**, 166; **28**, 169

Law, R. A., **27**, 133n

Law, T. G., **24**, 71n

Lawes, William, **26**, 33

Lawless, Donald S., **23**, 171n

Lawlor, John, **25**, 189; **28**, 170; **29**, 4

Lawrence, D. H., **21**, 44; **24**, 31, 35; **26**, 8

Lawrence, W. W., **25**, 2, 3, 5, 6, 7, 8; **26**, 119; **29**, 51, 53

Lawry, J. S., **27**, 165

Lea, K. M., **25**, 125n

Lea, Philip, **30**, 164n
Leach, Edmund, **29**, 18n
Leason, John, **27**, 182
Leavenworth, Russell E., **29**, 174
Leavis, F. R., **21**, 4, 5, 9 10n 11n, 28n, 62; **23**, 152; **25**, 5, 7, 29; **26**, 123n; **27**, 82n
Le Blanc, L'Abbé, **24**, 79
Le Comte, Edward, **23**, 167n
Lee, Sir Sidney, **23**, 91; **26**, 107; **28**, 39n; **29**, 140–1
Lee, Virgil, **29**, 174
Leech, Clifford, **21**, 129, 131, 135; **23**, 132, 149–50, 180, 181; **24**, 11, 143, 150, 176; **25**, 3, 6, 47, 48, 60n; **26**, 166; **27**, 157n, 158n, 164n, 165n, 170n, 179n, 188; **28**, 77n, 153, 169; **29**, 1, 6, 89, 171; **30**, 9n, 11n, 37, 39
  'Studies in Shakespearian and Other Jacobean Tragedy, 1918–1972: A Retrospect', **26**, 1–9
Lees, F. N., **21**, 52n; **30**, 195
Lees, R. B., **23**, 14n
Legate, John, **27**, 190
Leggatt, Alexander, **24**, 164; **26**, 155; **28**, 82, 159–60; **29**, 171, 172
Legh, Gerard, **27**, 14n, 118n
Legouis, Pierre, **30**, 193
  '*Titus Andronicus*, III, i, 298–9', **28**, 71–4
Le Hardy, William, **25**, 139, 140n
Lehmann, Beatrix, **27**, 153
Lehmann, H. T., **28**, 53n
Lehnert, Martin, **22**, 166
Leicester, Earl of, **27**, 129; **28**, 20, 23, 24, 151
Leider, Emily W., **24**, 146
Leigh, J. H., **25**, 118
Leigh, Mike, **28**, 137
Leigh, Sir Robert, **25**, 144
Leighton, Margaret, **24**, 3n
Leigh-Hunt, Barbara, **30**, 173
Leimberg, Inge, **22**, 151–2; **23**, 117, 119; **24**, 153; **26**, 163
Leishman, J. B., **22**, 82, 90; **23**, 41n, 69–70; **29**, 47
Leisi, E., **21**, 162; **23**, 118, 185; **24**, 149; **25**, 5; **27**, 189
Lemaître, Frederick, **28**, 148
Lemon, R., **23**, 41n
Lemmon, J., **28**, 150
Lengler, **23**, 119; **26**, 161
Lennam, T. N. S., **23**, 169; **25**, 191; **27**, 163
Leno, Dan, **29**, 143
Leonardo, **23**, 163
Lerma, Duke of, **23**, 87n
Lerner, Laurence, **21**, 142; **25**, 81n
Leslie, John, **27**, 172
Leslie, Nancy T., **28**, 169n

Lesnick, Henry G., **23**, 169
Lesser, Simon O., **25**, 181
Lessing, Gotthold, **22**, 35, 166; **26**, 167
Letourneur, Pierre, **24**, 86
Levenson, J., **27**, 158
Lever, J. W., **22**, 82; **23**, 69; **25**, 7; **26**, 9, 122, 126, 127n, 177; **27**, 92n; **28**, 79n, 90n; **30**, 191
  'Shakespeare and the Ideas of his Time', **29**, 79–91
Levey, Barnett, **22**, 126–8
Levin, D., **22**, 175n
Levin, Harry, **24**, 150; **25**, 111; **27**, 61n, 63n, 65n, 67n; **28**, 40, 41, 47n, 108, 157, 174, 178; **29**, 167
  'Two Magian Comedies: *The Tempest* and *The Alchemist*', **22**, 47–58
  'Shakespeare's Misanthrope', **26**, 89–94
Levin, Richard, **22**, 172n; **24**, 162; **25**, 182, 192; **26**, 4, 173, 184; **27**, 191; **28**, 7, 151, 163; **29**, 167
Levin, Y. D., **23**, 159, 174n
Levinson, Judith, C., **28**, 173
Lévi-Strauss, Claude, **22**, 16; **29**, 11n, 12n
Levitchi, L., **29**, 166
Levitsky, R. M., **27**, 158, 159
Levy, Charles S., **24**, 159
Levy, F. J., **26**, 174n
Lewalski, B. K., **23**, 144; **24**, 156; **25**, 103n, 104n
Lewes, G. H., **29**, 134
Lewis, Anthony J., **25**, 184; **26**, 175
Lewis, C. S., **23**, 158; **24**, 40; **28**, 43; **30**, 82
Lewis, Wyndham, **21**, 5; **22**, 8
Lewkenor, Sir Lewis, **26**, 172
Leyris, P., **26**, 164
Lichtenberg, Georg Christoph, **21**, 125n; **29**, 143
Lichtenhahn, Fritz, **24**, 145
Liddell, Mark Harvey, **26**, 82n, 85
Lilburne, John, **23**, 167
Lincoln, Abraham, **24**, 99
Lind, Kenny, **29**, 146
Lindheim, B. von, **23**, 13n
Lindeheim, Nancy R., **26**, 174
Lindenbaum, P., **29**, 161–2
Lindroth, Colette, **24**, 99n
Lindroth, James, **24**, 99n
Lindsay, Barbara N., **23**, 179
Lindtberg, Leopold, **24**, 145; **28**, 172n
Ling, Nicholas, **26**, 184; **28**, 41n
Lings, Martin, **21**, 128
Lipka, L., **23**, 23n
Lipman, Maureen, **27**, 149
Lippincott, H. F., **29**, 174; **30**, 194
Littleton, Betty J., **24**, 160n
Littlewood, J. C. F., **22**, 163
Livermore, Ann, **21**, 152
Livingstone, Sid, **29**, 152

Livy, **28**, 67, 71–4; **30**, 193
Lloyd, Bernard, **27**, 151
Lloyd Evans, Gareth, **22**, 175; **23**, 174n; **24**, 117, 137, 167; **26**, 175; **27**, 137–42, 163, 169–70; **28**, 103n; **29**, 48, 91
  'Shakespeare and the Actors: Notes towards Interpretations', **21**, 115–25
  'The Reason Why: The Royal Shakespeare Season 1968' *reviewed*, **22**, 135–44
  'Interpretation or Experience? Shakespeare at Stratford', **23**, 131–7
  'Directing Problem Plays': interview with John Barton, **25**, 63–71
  Conversation with Judi Dench, **27**, 137–42
Lloyd, Michael, **23**, 61n; **30**, 195
Locke, John, **22**, 145
Locke, Philip, **24**, 118
Lockhart, Adrienne, **30**, 202
Lockhart, Calvin, **26**, 148–9
Lodge, Thomas, **23**, 88n, 98; **26**, 113, 115; **27**, 130, 173; **28**, 167 29; **29**,
Loeben, Maria-Beate von, **23**, 118
Loeffler, Peter, **29**, 176
Logan, George M., **23**, 169
Loggan, D., **30**, 163n
Lombardo, Agostino, **23**, 153–4
Lonicerus, **23**, 169
Long, E. T., **26**, 74n
Long, Michael, **30**, 186, 187
Loomie, A. J., **29**, 21n, 30n
Lord Chamberlain's Men, **28**, 6
Lord, Gisela, **24**, 153
Lothian, J. M., **21**, 140; **29**, 177, 178
Louis XIV, King, **22**, 19
Love, Harold, **27**, 188
Lovejoy, Arthur O., **27**, 44; **29**, 85
Lovell, Sir Robert, **21**, 100
Low, Anthony, **23**, 171n; **25**, 181
Low, Donald A., **24**, 178
Lowe, R., **27**, 106n
Lowell, James Russell, **24**, 87, 89, 99, 102, 103, 104
Lower, Charles B., **25**, 184
Lowes, John Livingston, **25**, 127, 128; **26**, 99n
Lucan, **23**, 169
Lucas, F. L., **26**, 4
Luccock, Halford, **24**, 88n
Luce, Morton, **26**, 72n
Lucian, **22**, 5; **27**, 111, 116n, 117, 119, 121n, 127; **29**, 103, 104, 108, 109, 110, 111, 112, 116; **30**, 195
Lucretius, **23**, 36; **25**, 128
Luis de Granada, **23**, 82, 87
Lumby, J. R., **28**, 27n
Lumbye, H. C., **29**, 145
Lunghi, Cherie, **30**, 172, 174

Lunacharsky, 21, 128
Luther, Martin, 23, 80, 86; 26, 49; 28, 53, 56n
Lüthi, Max, 21, 153; 23, 114
Lydgate, John, 21, 150; 22, 118n; 24, 60
Lyle, E. B., 24, 179; 26, 172; 27, 159, 179
Lyly, John, 21, 131; 22, 36, 69; 23, 169; 24, 44, 71, 162; 26, 153; 28, 41n, 76, 80n; 29, 174; 30, 125–34, 198
Lynche, Richard, 26, 112n
Lyons, Bridget Gellert, 25, 189
Lyons, Charles, 22, 160

McAlindon, T., 23, 150; 25, 13n, 14n, 24n, 182; 26, 155; 28, 149–50, 155
Macallum, Sir Mungo, 22, 170
Macaulay, G. C., 24, 109n
Macaulay, Thomas, 21, 68
McAvoy, William Charles, 27, 59n
McCabe, William H., 29, 23n
McCallin, Clement, 24, 118
McCanles, Michael, 22, 163
Maccoby, Hyam, 25, 179
Maccoll, Alan, 23, 167n
McCollom, William G., 22, 154
McCombie, Frank, 29, 164
  'Hamlet and the Moriae Encomium', 27, 59–69
McCown, Gary M., 30, 194
McCracken, George E., 30, 62n
McCutcheon, Elizabeth, 23, 167n
McDonnell, Robert F., 30, 150
McElroy, B., 28, 152, 155
McElroy, John F., 27, 176
McEwan, Neil, 30, 188
McFadden, Fred R., Jr, 29, 183
McFarland, T., 27, 168
McGee, Arthur R., 21, 137
McGinn, D. J., 25, 5
McGrath, Patrick, 22, 169; 24, 71n
McGugan, Ruth, 27, 190
McGuire, P. C., 28, 154
McGuire, Richard L., 22, 156
Mach, Ernst, 24, 97
Machabeus, Judas, 29, 26, 27, 28–9
Machiavelli, Niccolò, 21, 143–4; 22, 115, 148; 23, 145, 162; 24, 158; 26, 49; 27, 45, 46, 53, 72, 74–5; 28, 10; 29, 79, 80, 85, 88, 90, 164
McIlwain, C. H., 28, 64n, 68
McIntosh, Angus, 23, 11n; 26, 164n
MacIsaac, W. J., 25, 174
Mack, Maynard, 26, 9, 96; 28, 111
Mack, M., Jr, 27, 161
McKay, Maxine, 29, 94, 95–6, 98
Mackay, Mr, 22, 130–1
McKellen, Ian, 23, 131; 26, 140; 30, 169, 173, 174, 177, 178
McKenzie, D. F., 23, 184–5; 25, 191; 26, 180; 27, 180, 190; 28, 174
Mackenzie, James J., 24, 178

McKern, Leo, 27, 140
McKerrow, R. B., 23, 162n; 24, 170; 26, 45n; 28, 175
Mackie, W. S., 23, 14
Mackintosh, Iain, 30, 157, 167n, 168
McLauchlan, Juliet, 29, 164
  'The Prince of Denmark and Claudius's Court', 27, 43–57
McLay, Catherine, 22, 193
Maclean, Hugh, 21, 132
MacLure, Miller, 27, 175; 28, 19n
McLuskie, Kathleen E., 26, 163
  'Shakespeare's "Earth-treading Stars": the Image of the Masque in Romeo and Juliet', 24, 63–9
McMahon, Morgan, 22, 133n
McManaway, James G., 21, 162; 22, 167n, 183; 24, 152n, 169, 171, 172; 25, 110, 183; 28, 3n; 29, 180
McManaway, J. Q., 30, 110n
McManaway, Mary R., 25, 138n
McMaster, Juliet, 24, 165
McMillin, Scott, 30, 196
McNair, Lord, 24, 156
McNamara, P. L., 27, 157
MacNeice, Louis, 24, 44
McNeir, Waldo F., 22, 183; 23, 153; 25, 174; 26, 158, 163; 29, 55n
McPeek, J. A. S., 26, 154
McPherson, D., 27, 165, 179
Macready, Charles, 30, 199
Macready, William, 21, 62, 80; 22, 132
McVicker, 25, 113–14, 115, 116, 117, 118
Madden, Sir Frederick, 28, 38n
Maede, Hans Dieter, 21, 133
Magarshack, David, 26, 22n; 28, 55n
Magee, W. H., 26, 155
Maguin, Jean-Marie, 27, 173
Mahaney, William E., 27, 177; 29, 174
Mahood, M. M., 22, 107n, 152, 166, 178; 23, 67n, 69, 132; 24, 28; 26, 165; 28, 114; 29, 7
Maitland, F. W., 29, 94
Maitra, Sitansu, 22, 146
Makařovský, Jan, 21, 140
Malcolm, J. P., 30, 164n
Malibran, Mme, 21, 81
Malleson, Miles, 27, 142
Malone, Edmond, 21, 101–2, 149; 22, 145; 24, 107, 168, 171n, 175, 178; 25, 111, 125, 187; 26, 71, 91, 172; 27, 107, 111n, 129; 29, 168, 170, 179; 30, 191, 205
Malory, Sir Thomas, 29, 123
Mandel, J., 27, 164
Mandeville, Sir John, 30, 72
Manheim, M., 28, 157
Manley, Frank, 21, 153; 26, 157
Mann, F. O., 28, 56n
Mann, Thomas, 26, 163; 29, 9
Manning, Roger B., 24, 157

Manningham, John, 29, 173
Manocchio, T., 30, 188
Mansell, Darrell, Jr, 21, 135
Mansfield, Richard, 23, 131
Maranda, Elli Köngäs, 29, 17n
Maranda, Pierre, 29, 17n
Marcel, Gabriel, 28, 45
Marc'hadour, G., 21, 152
Marchand, H., 23, 14n, 18, 20, 23n, 28n
Marchant, E. C., 25, 100
Marder, Louis, 21, 148
Mare, M., 30, 165n
Marenco, Franco, 23, 166
Mares, F. H., 22, 172n; 25, 180
Margaret, Queen of Scotland, 26, 44
Margeson, J. M. R., 22, 172; 27, 157n, 158n, 164n, 165n, 170n, 179n; 30, 9n
Markels, Julian, 22, 175n; 24, 147
Marker, Lise-Lone, 24, 167; 25, 191
Markland, Murray F., 24, 166n
Marlorate, Augustine, 28, 101n
Marlowe, Christopher, 21, 155, 162; 22, 32, 51, 138, 139, 140–1, 147, 148, 173, 183; 23, 49, 51, 97n, 117, 121, 141, 148, 149, 154, 155, 159, 166, 169; 24, 20–1, 22, 23, 40n, 42, 44, 117, 143, 161, 162, 165; 25, 190; 26, 3, 6, 8, 9, 54, 103, 108; 27, 18, 31, 71–9, 130, 132, 135, 176, 178; 28, 45, 46, 169; 29, 170; 30, 4, 5, 11, 14, 198
Marmion, Shackerley, 28, 170
Marotti, Arthur F., 23, 167n
Marowitz, Charles, 25, 28; 27, 148; 28, 138; 29, 176
Marrian, F. J. M., 21, 147n
Marriott, J. A. R., 29, 80
Marriott, W. K., 27, 46n
Marsh, D. C. R., 30, 154
Marston, John, 22, 52, 164, 171; 23, 46, 98, 100; 25, 9, 68, 189, 191; 26, 9, 55, 57, 99, 153, 169, 173; 27, 99; 28, 38, 41; 29, 2, 3, 7, 9, 10, 170, 184; 30, 110, 191, 192
Marti, M., 24, 162n
Martial, 22, 47
Martin, Richard, 27, 120
Martin, Walther, 21, 135; 22, 166
Martinet, Marie-Madeleine, 30, 202
Martz, Leo, 29, 5
Martz, Louis, 23, 87
Mary, Princess, 26, 44n
Mary, Queen of Scots, 26, 36n, 41, 46, 48; 28, 8, 151, 166
Marx, Jenny, 23, 173
Marx, Karl, 23, 176; 26, 92
Masefield, John, 25, 45n, 46; 26, 103; 27, 106n; 30, 43
Mason, Brewster, 22, 139, 140; 23, 132; 29, 154, 155

Mason, H. A., **21**, 138; **22**, 162
Mason, William, **24**, 178
Massehian, Houhannes, **24**, 169
Massinger, Philip, **23**, 88, 171; **24**, 165; **25**, 68–9; **26**, 5, 9, 169; **28**, 180, 181; **30**, 207
Matchett, William H., **21**, 140, 151; **24**, 151; **29**, 7, 67
  'Some Dramatic Techniques in *The Winter's Tale*', **22**, 93–107
Mattauch, Hans, **23**, 150, 174n
Matteo, G. J., **29**, 166
Matthäi, Hans Rudolf, **23**, 120
Matthews, Brander, **25**, 3n; **26**, 119
Matthews, R., **29**, 165
Maugham, Somerset, **21**, 77
Mauron, Charles, **22**, 16
Maverty, S. C., **28**, 158
Maxwell, Baldwin, **26**, 9; **29**, 83n, 180
Maxwell, J. C., **21**, 146, 147, 153, 155n, 159, 162; **22**, 62, 154, 156, 168; **23**, 151, 161, 180; **24**, 164, 166; **25**, 5, 7, 181; **26**, 105, 184; **27**, 106n, 111n, 112n, 136n, 191; **28**, 181; **29**, 41, 103n, 108, 111n; **30**, 195, 203
Maxwell, W. C., **23**, 21n
May, Marcel, **28**, 39n
May, Stephen W., **27**, 178; **28**, 174
May, Thomas, **22**, 4
Meaden, Dan, **28**, 147
Meadowcroft, J. W. R., **23**, 185
Meagher, John C., **25**, 200; **27**, 179, 191
Meckier, Jerome, **25**, 185
Medici, Giulio de', **25**, 166
Medwall, Henry, **30**, 36
Mehl, Dieter, **21**, 143; **23**, 115, 116, 172; **25**, 184; **26**, 155, 161, 166, 176
Mehlin, Urs H., **25**, 182
Meillet, A., **23**, 28n
Meiss, Millard, **26**, 115n
Melanchthon, Philip, **25**, 188
Melchiori, Giorgio, **30**, 181
Mellers, Wilfrid, **21**, 144
Melville, Herman, **21**, 141; **22**, 175; **26**, 89, 91, 94
Melzi, Robert C., **21**, 152; **25**, 188
Memo, Paul E., Jr, **21**, 131
Menander, **22**, 4, 35
Mendham, William, **25**, 144
Mendilow, A. A., **23**, 138, 186
Menenius, **23**, 99n
Merbury, Francis, **23**, 169; **28**, 177
Mercer, Peter, **23**, 152
Merchant, Christina, 'Delacroix's Tragedy of Desdemona', **21**, 79–86
Merchant, Paul, **21**, 162
Merchant, W. Moelwyn, **21**, 138, 157; **24**, 15n

Meredith, George, **22**, 36
Meredith, John, **22**, 128–30
Meredith, Mrs, **22**, 128–30
Meres, Francis, **21**, 48; **25**, 110; **26**, 108; **27**, 105, 107, 108, 132; **30**, 201
Meri, George, **23**, 152, 159; **29**, 166, 167
Merrill, Thomas F., **23**, 167
Merrix, Robert P., **30**, 56n
Merriman, R. W., **23**, 42n
Meszaros, Patricia K., **30**, 186
Metz, G. Harold, **29**, 170
Meyer, Edward, **29**, 79
Meyerhold, V. E., **24**, 125; **27**, 143, 144
Meyrick, Sir Gilly, **28**, 6–7
Michelangelo, **21**, 3; **22**, 60; **26**, 60, 116; **28**, 55
Michel-Michot, P., **23**, 161
Middleton, Richard, **30**, 197
Middleton, Thomas, **21**, 24, 146; **22**, 171; **23**, 46, 132, 133, 170–1; **24**, 40, 179; **25**, 141n; **26**, 4, 5, 7, 8, 9, 39, 54, 56, 57, 66; **27**, 176; **29**, 123, 173; **30**, 161n, 192, 198, 207
Midgley, Graham, **28**, 85, 86
Mifflin, Houghton, **25**, 186
Milhous, Judith, **30**, 200
Mill, Anna J., **24**, 160, 161
Mill, John Stuart, **24**, 88
Miller, Arthur, **27**, 81
Miller, Jonathan, **24**, 129, 131; **25**, 154; **27**, 174
Miller, Perry, **27**, 83n
Miller, Ronald F., **30**, 183
Miller, Walter, **25**, 99n
Milles, Thomas, **21**, 163; **22**, 161, 168
Mills, John A., **28**, 171
Milne, A. T., **24**, 177n
Milner, Ian, **21**, 139
Milton, Ernest, **23**, 131
Milton, John, **22**, 1, 56, 170; **23**, 167; **24**, 42, 159; **26**, 114
Milward, Peter, **21**, 148; **22**, 167; **23**, 160; **26**, 162; **28**, 151, 165–6
Mincoff, Marco, **21**, 135; **22**, 157, 174; **25**, 6, 188; **26**, 13–14, 113n, 117n; **29**, 170; **30**, 125
Minto, William, **26**, 184
Mirandola, Pico della, **25**, 103; **30**, 190
Mitchell, Charles, **22**, 156
Mitchell, J. L., **29**, 183n
Mitchell, Yvonne, **27**, 142
Miyauchi, B., **26**, 159
Moffett, Robin, **29**, 3
Molière, **21**, 35, 141; **22**, 1, 2, 8, 15, 16, 17–26, 35; **24**, 38, 149; **26**, 90, 94; **29**, 123; **30**, 117–18
Monmouth, Geoffrey of, **26**, 35, 36n, 41, 42, 43; **29**, 171
Monro, C., **29**, 97n
Montagu, Mrs, **25**, 185

Montaigne, Michel de, **22**, 48; **23**, 45, 161; **25**, 125; **26**, 49; **27**, 44–5, 50, 52n, 56, 173; **28**, 37–50, 98, 167; **29**, 5, 79, 80, 81, 85, 88, 89, 90, 164; **30**, 119, 193
Monteagle, Lord, **28**, 6
Montgomery, Earl of, **21**, 141
Montgomery, Mrs, **23**, 44
Montgomery, Robert L., **23**, 146, 157
Moore, Edward, N., **26**, 175
Moore, J. R., **22**, 175n
Moore Smith, G. C., **27**, 112, 118
Moore, William H., **23**, 167
Moorthy, P. R., **27**, 159
Morality plays, **30**, 36–9, 104, 192
Moray, Thomas, **21**, 48
Morden, Robert, **30**, 164n
More, Ann, **23**, 167
More, Sir Thomas, **23**, 144; **28**, 27, 177, 178; **29**, 86, 121, 159; **30**, 203–4
Morelli, Cesare, **21**, 48
Morgan, Morris Hicky, **30**, 159
Morgan, Paul, **30**, 202
Morgan, W. W., **26**, 154
Morgann, Maurice, **24**, 178; **26**, 167–8; **30**, 3, 35
Morley, Christopher, **24**, 122; **26**, 140, 142; **27**, 149
Morozov, Mikhail, **21**, 129
Morris, Brian, **24**, 164; **25**, 9, 23n, 24n
Morris, C., **29**, 90
Morris, Harry, **22**, 162; **25**, 182; **30**, 183
Morris, Helen, **23**, 154; **24**, 156
Morris, Irene, **28**, 172
Morris, Ivor, **26**, 23, 24; **27**, 155
Morris, John, **22**, 169
Morris, Johnny, **23**, 47
Morris, Thomas, **25**, 146
Morsberger, Robert E., **29**, 174
Mortensen, Peter, **29**, 170
Moseley, C. W. R. D., **24**, 163n
Moulton, R. G., **21**, 28n
Mountjoy family, **28**, 38
Mountjoy, Christopher, **25**, 138
Mowat, Barbara Adams, **23**, 156; **25**, 184
Moxon, J., **27**, 180, 190
Mudford, Peter G., **25**, 181
Mueller, Dennis M., **25**, 145
Mueller, Janel M., **23**, 167
Mueschke, Miriam, **22**, 154
Mueschke, Paul, **22**, 154
Muir, Edwin, **26**, 76; **29**, 86
Muir, Kenneth, **21**, 130, 137, 141, 146; **22**, 62, 152, 155, 163, 180; **23**, 54n, 73n, 156; **24**, 71n, 76n, 106n, 157; **25**, 4, 7, 12n, 39n, 126n, 142n, 185, 196n; **26**, 5, 71, 72, 82, 166, 172; **27**, 18n, 24n, 34, 59n, 133, 145, 146, 154, 156, 170; **28**, 4n, 39, 48, 74, 123n; **29**, 4, 6, 9, 31, 90, 106n, 165; **30**, 15n, 99n

Kenneth Muir (*cont.*)
  'Shakespeare's Poets', 23, 91–100
  'Shakespeare the Professional', 24, 37–46
Mukherji, A. D., 21, 143; 22, 157
Mulcaster, Richard, 26, 38n, 45n; 28, 170
Mullany, Peter, 24, 165
Müllenbrock, H.-J., 29, 184n
Müller, Heiner, 25, 173
Müller, Johannes, 29, 29n
Müller-Schweife, Gerhard, 23, 115n
Mullin, Michael, 28, 171
Mulryne, J. R., 26, 9
Mumford, Lewis, 24, 87
Munday, Anthony, 23, 161, 171, 181; 26, 35, 39, 43, 45, 47, 103, 183
Munro, John, 26, 44n
Munson, William F., 24, 161
Murdock, D., 26, 161
Murphy, Arthur, 26, 175
Murphy, G. N., 21, 146–7
Murphy, J. L., 23, 168
Murray, Gilbert, 30, 103–4, 106, 107
Murray, Patrick, 23, 137; 26, 166–7
Murray, W. A., 21, 137
Murry, John Middleton, 21, 4, 9, 137; 22, 10, 14n; 23, 98n; 25, 107, 111, 155, 158n; 26, 103
Musgrove, S., 23, 172; 24, 172; 25, 179
Musk, John, 27, 167n
Mustaph, Nirmal, 22, 157
Myers, James Phares, 23, 170n
Myrick, Kenneth O., 29, 88
Mystery plays, 30, 192

Nabokov, Vladimir, 26, 89
Naef, Irene, 30, 185
Nagarajan, S., 28, 51n
Nagler, A. M., 21, 125n
Naik, M. K., 22, 167
Nameri, Dorothy, 30, 194
Nandy, Dipak, 30, 42n
Napier, John, 28, 142; 30, 172, 176
Napoleon, 28, 22
Nardi, 21, 96n
Naremore, James, 28, 171n
Nashe, Thomas, 21, 138; 23, 160, 169; 24, 52, 71, 159; 25, 188; 26, 170, 184; 27, 130, 135; 28, 45n
Nathan, Norman, 22, 164; 24, 178
Nazarjan, S., 25, 6n
Neale, J. E., 28, 17n
Neely, C. T., 29, 165
Neher, Caspar, 29, 176
Neidig, W., 27, 185
Neiiendam, Robert, 29, 145
Neill, Michael, 23, 171n
Neilson, Francis, 30, 154n
Nels, Sophia, 23, 174n
Nelson, Cathryn A., 29, 175
Nelson, Norman E., 27, 84

Nelson, Thomas, 27, 179
Nelson, Timothy G. A., 24, 162
Nelson, William, 23, 163n
Nemirovich-Danchenko, V. I., 23, 174n
Nesbitt, Frank, 22, 132
Neuhaus, H. J., 29, 183
Neville, John, 27, 34n, 141
Nevinson, J. L., 22, 167n
Nevo, Ruth, 22, 163; 23, 143; 27, 155–6
New, John F. H., 24, 157
Newcastle cycle, 21, 56, 57
Newman, Franklin B., 21, 132
Newton, J. M., 25, 5n
Nicholls, John Gough, 26, 39n, 74
Nicholls, Sutton, 30, 164n
Nicoll, Allardyce, 21, 35, 145, 146; 25, 45n; 26, 3, 4, 9
Nietzsche, F. W., 22, 156; 28, 109; 30, 186
Niklaus, Thelma, 21, 33, 38n
Nikolynkin, Alexandre, 21, 128n
Nilan, Mary M., 29, 176
  '*The Tempest* at the Turn of the Century: Cross-currents in Production', 25, 113–23
Noble, Richmond, 25, 37n, 125, 126, 127n, 130n; 28, 98n; 29, 88
Nobre, António, 30, 189
Norburie, George, 29, 97n
Norfolk, Dukes of, 28, 17–18, 19
North, Sir Thomas, 21, 14; 22, 112; 23, 184; 28, 66; 29, 103, 110, 115; 30, 97, 135, 204, 205
Northrop, Douglas A., 23, 166
Norton, F. J., 29, 16n
Norton, M. D. Herter, 23, 164n
Norton, Thomas, 30, 206
Norwich mystery cycle, 21, 57
Nosworthy, J. M., 23, 173, 182, 183; 24, 172; 25, 110; 26, 20n, 81, 82–4, 85n; 27, 111, 116, 118n, 122n, 127n, 133n; 29, 1, 45, 52, 53n
Nottingham, Charles, Earl of, 24, 157
Novak, E., 23, 173
Nowottny, Winifred (W. M. T. Dodds), 24, 25; 25, 5, 8
Nungezer, E., 22, 119
Nunn, Trevor, 22, 141; 23, 132, 133; 24, 117, 122, 128n, 130, 131; 25, 27; 26, 139, 140, 141, 148; 27, 137, 138–9; 28, 137; 29, 73; 30, 169–71, 173, 176–8
Nüssel, Heide, 23, 122
Nuttall, A. D., 22, 164; 23, 151; 25, 6, 37, 42, 90n; 27, 170; 29, 90; 30, 184
  '*Measure for Measure*: the Bed-trick', 28, 51–6

Oakley, Francis, 23, 162
Oates, J. C., 21, 134

O'Brien, Timothy, 24, 124; 27, 146, 151; 29, 176
Ochester, Edwin F., 24, 166
Ockham, William of, 24, 91
O'Connor, John J., 24, 157; 29, 181
Odell, G. C. D., 29, 141n
Odo, Geraldus a, 29, 99
O'Flaherty, Mrs, *see* Winstanley, Eliza
Ogilvy, J. D. A., 27, 162
Okes, Nicholas, 25, 197; 28, 180
Oldys, W., *and* Birch, T., 27, 56
Oliver, H. J., 21, 162; 22, 178; 23, 180; 24, 162n; 25, 198; 27, 111n, 112n, 113; 28, 178n; 29, 103n, 104, 115; 30, 207, 208
Olivier, Lord, 21, 115–19, 122, 125, 141; 22, 94; 23, 131, 173, 174; 24, 129; 25, 28; 26, 150, 176; 27, 145; 30, 144
O'Loughlin, Sean, 25, 126n
Olsson, Yngve B., 24, 156; 29, 171
O'Malley, C. D., 23, 163
Omans, Stuart, 24, 161n
Ong, W. J., 24, 47, 48n, 49n
Onions, C. T., 23, 36
Oppel, Horst, 23, 114, 121, 123; 24, 145; 26, 163
Oppenheimer, J. Robert, 22, 147
Orbison, Tucker, 23, 171
Orgel, Stephen, 24, 164; 28, 169, 170
Ormerod, David, 27, 164
  'Faith and Fashion in *Much Ado About Nothing*', 25, 93–105
Ornstein, Robert, 21, 138–9; 23, 174n; 24, 150, 168; 25, 5n; 26, 4, 6, 8; 27, 161; 28, 2, 3, 5n, 6, 10, 48n; 29, 87; 30, 58n, 65, 68
  'Shakespearian and Jonsonian Comedy', 22, 43–6
Orr, Peter, 24, 3n
Orrell, John, 'Inigo Jones at The Cockpit', 30, 157–68
Ortego, P. D., 26, 158
Ortiz, Antonio, 29, 30
Orwell, George, 23, 97
Osanai, Kaoru, 23, 174n
Ostrowski, 22, 35
O'Sullivan, Mary I., 29, 82
Otway, Thomas, 25, 189
Outhwaite, R. B., 23, 162n
Over, Alan, 22, 145; 23, 50n
Overbury, Nicholas, 27, 100
Overbury, Sir Thomas, 21, 140; 24, 165; 27, 100
Overmyer, J., 26, 162
Ovid, 22, 56, 110, 151; 23, 51, 73, 74, 85, 92, 143, 161, 166; 24, 166; 25, 125; 26, 104, 107, 108; 27, 2, 16–17, 19, 160, 192; 29, 5, 175; 30, 104, 134
Owen, L., 28, 162

Owst, G. R., **26**, 76n
Oxberry, William, **24**, 162n
Oyama, Toshikazu, **22**, 158; **23**, 154

Packard, Frederick C., Jr, **24**, 2n
Padel, J. H., **30**, 181
Padelford, F. M., **23**, 21n
Padhi, Shanti, **30**, 184
Pafford, J. H. P., **21**, 148; **24**, 177; **28**, 121n; **29**, 4, 76, 183
Painter, William, **25**, 45, 46, 48, 52, 54, 57
Palfrey, John Graham, **24**, 101n
Palitzsch, Peter, **23**, 174n
Palladio, **30**, 160
Palmer, Mr, **22**, 128–9
Palmer, D. J., **21**, 134; **24**, 149; **25**, 174, 175; **26**, 154; **27**, 149, 159, 163n, 164, 165n, 167n, 170n; **28**, 104n; **29**, 3
   Critical Studies, *reviewed*: (1973), **27**, 155–72; (1974), **28**, 149–64; (1975), **29**, 157–67
Palmer, John, **27**, 31n, 32n
Palmer, Paulina, **21**, 149
Palmer, Rupert E., **24**, 158n
Palmerston, Lord, **24**, 92
Palsson, H., **26**, 164n
Panofsky, Erwin, **23**, 49n; **25**, 102n, 103, 189; **26**, 57; **29**, 91
Pantzer, Katharine F., **23**, 162n
Paolucci, Anne, **24**, 6n
Paradin, George, **25**, 188
Paré, Ambroise, **28**, 121
Parfitt, G. A. E., **23**, 170
Parker, A. A., **23**, 84n, 88n
Parker, Barbara L., **25**, 181
Parker, David, **24**, 153
Parker, Dorothy, **28**, 91
Parker, John, **25**, 148
Parker, M. D. H., **28**, 19n
Parker, Robert W., **26**, 174n
Parks, George B., **23**, 164
Parmigianino, **26**, 50, 54
Parrott, Y. M., **26**, 4, 173
Parsons, Robert D., **23**, 161n
Parsons, William Barclay, **23**, 163
Partee, Morris H., **25**, 182
Partridge, Eric, **27**, 18, 189
Pascal, Blaise, **22**, 16; **29**, 89
Pasco, Richard, **25**, 166, 169, 170; **27**, 149, 150, 152; **28**, 140
Pasta, Mme, **21**, 81
Paster, Gail Kern, **30**, 192
Pasternak, Boris, **21**, 11n; **24**, 41
Pater, Walter, **22**, 8, 155; **25**, 1; **27**, 146; **28**, 104, 105
Paterson, John, **30**, 85n
Pätges, Christian, **29**, 145
Patrick, D. L., **23**, 179; **25**, 193; **30**, 209
Paul, Henry N., **21**, 52n; **25**, 111; **26**, 85n; **28**, 123n

Pausanias, **22**, 17; **25**, 103
Pauvert, J.-J., **21**, 86n
Pavier, Thomas, **22**, 181–2; **27**, 181, 182, 185
Payne, M., **28**, 155
Payne, Waveney, R. N., **24**, 169
Peacham, Henry, **25**, 188; **26**, 98
Pearce, F. M., **26**, 154; **28**, 162
Pearlman, E., **24**, 167
Pearson, D. W., **28**, 163, 173
Pearson, Karl, **24**, 97
Peaslee, Richard, **24**, 126
Pecheux, M. Christopher, Mother, **29**, 175
Peck, Bob, **29**, 152
Peck, Russell A., **22**, 162
Pederson, Lauritz, **22**, 124n
Pedley, Anthony, **27**, 153
Peele, George, **21**, 131; **23**, 117, 169; **24**, 162; **27**, 130, 132, 135; **28**, 4, 119n; **30**, 79, 121, 198
Peend, Thomas, **23**, 166
Pelikan, J., **28**, 53n
Pember, Ron, **28**, 144, 145, 146
Pembroke, Earl of, **21**, 141; **27**, 134; **28**, 165
Pembroke's Men, **27**, 129–36; **30**, 196
Pendry, E. D., **27**, 178
Pennington, Michael, **28**, 147, 148; **30**, 175
Pepys, Samuel, **22**, 57; **29**, 135
Percy, Sir Charles, **28**, 6
Percy, Sir Jocelyn, **28**, 6
Percy, Thomas, **26**, 40
Perez de Moya, Juan, **23**, 84, 85
Perkins, William, **27**, 83n, 84, 85–8, 90, 91; **28**, 92, 102
Perrett, Wilfred, **26**, 36n, 41n; **27**, 173
Personn (Persen), Johann, **22**, 119–21, 123
Persons, George, **29**, 29
Persons, Robert, **24**, 71, 72, 74; **28**, 166; **29**, 22, 29, 30
Perugino, **26**, 54
Petersen, D., **27**, 169
Peterson, Douglas, **29**, 11n, 16n, 53n
Petitt, W., **30**, 188
Petrarch, **23**, 69; **28**, 49
Petronella, V. F., **28**, 153, 154, 159, 160
Petry, Michael John, **27**, 177
Pettet, E. C., **26**, 98; **28**, 63n, 86n; **29**, 106n
Pettigrew, John, **25**, 174; **30**, 45n
Pettitt, Henry, **29**, 136
Pfister, M., **28**, 159
Phelps, Charles E., **29**, 94, 95, 96
Phelps, Samuel, **23**, 173n; **25**, 113, 115
Phialas, Peter G., **21**, 130; **24**, 57n, 60n
Philip II, King of Spain, **24**, 155; **29**, 22, 27
Philip III, King of Spain, **23**, 86; **29**, 30, 32n

Phillips, Augustine, **28**, 6, 7
Phillips, Hugh, **30**, 164n
Phillips, J. E., Jr, **29**, 83, 84
Phillips, O. Hood, **26**, 171
Phillips, Robin, **24**, 121, 129
Philostratus, **25**, 100n
Picasso, Pablo, **29**, 177
Picinelli, Filippo, **29**, 29
Pickeryng, John, **30**, 13, 16
Pickup, Ronald, **25**, 27
Pierce, Robert B., **25**, 180; **26**, 156; **30**, 58n
Pierret, **21**, 80
Pies, Eike, **28**, 172n
Piggott-Smith, Tim, **28**, 142
Pinciss, G. M., **30**, 196
   'Shakespeare, Her Majesty's Players, and Pembroke's Men', **27**, 129–36
Pindar, **22**, 15
Pinero, Sir Arthur Wing, **29**, 134, 137
Pinhorn, Malcolm, **21**, 148
Pinter, Harold, **21**, 37; **22**, 28, 32; **23**, 39; **24**, 19, 43
Pirandello, Luigi, **22**, 28
Pirie, D., **27**, 157
Pitcher, Seymour, **27**, 131n
Pitts, Rebecca, E., **24**, 145
Planché, J. R., **21**, 155
Plantagenet, Henry, **28**, 120
Plato, **23**, 93; **24**, 50–1, 52, 148n; **25**, 103; **28**, 29, 43, 63; **29**, 85; **30**, 189
Platt, Hugh, **30**, 201
Platt, Michael, **30**, 185
Platter, Thomas, **30**, 164
Plautus, **22**, 1, 3, 8, 15, 16, 17, 19, 21, 23; **23**, 161; **25**, 82; **27**, 2, 18, 119; **30**, 192
Plesington (Pleasington), Anne, **25**, 144
Plowden, Edmund, **29**, 99, 100
Plummer, Christopher, **24**, 3n
Plutarch, **21**, 14, 132; **22**, 112, 113, 140, 157; **23**, 60, 61, 62, 63, 95, 96, 161, 184; **24**, 8, 12, 16, 140; **25**, 127, 128, 129; **27**, 111, 112n; **28**, 10, 67; **29**, 103, 104, 105, 111, 116, 170, 171; **30**, 4, 135, 140, 143, 195, 204, 205
Poe, E. A., **21**, 17
Poel, William, **23**, 123; **25**, 1, 116, 117, 122, 123, 172; **26**, 147, 175; **29**, 140
Pogson, Beryl, **22**, 154
Poincaré, Henri, **24**, 97
Poirier, Michel, **28**, 45n
Poisson, Rodney, **21**, 163; **22**, 161; **30**, 194
Polanski, Roman, **28**, 174
Polišenský, Josef, **21**, 153
Pollard, Alfred W., **21**, 65n; **22**, 180; **23**, 92; **25**, 75n, 79; **26**, 181; **27**, 129

Pollen, J. H., **24**, 71n, 77
Polo, Gil, **22**, 168; **29**, 180
Pompeius Trogus, **29**, 25
Ponce de la Fuente, Constantino, **23**, 81
Ponsonby, W., **28**, 54n
Pontanus, Jakob, **29**, 29, 30
Pontormo, **26**, 50, 51, 54, 55
Poole, R., **27**, 129n
Pope, Alexander, **21**, 6; **22**, 16; **24**, 175, 176; **25**, 73, 85; **26**, 181, 182
Pope, Elizabeth Marie, **25**, 6; **28**, 94
Pope, Thomas, **22**, 121
Pope-Hennessy, John, **26**, 112n, 116n
Porter, Eric, **22**, 141
Potter, Lois, **28**, 11n; **29**, 160–1
'The Antic Disposition of Richard II', **27**, 33–41
Potter, Robert, **29**, 171
Powell, J., **27**, 167
Powell, L. F., **21**, 10n
Powle, Stephen, **27**, 100
Powle, Thomas, **27**, 100, 101, 102, 103
Praetorius, C., **27**, 132n
Prager, Leonard, **22**, 175n
Preuschen, Karl Adalbert, **30**, 202
Praz, Mario, **25**, 53n
Presson, Robert K., **21**, 154; **22**, 165; **23**, 170; **25**, 9
Preston, Amyas, **21**, 103
Preston, D. R., **25**, 179
Prévost, L'Abbé, **24**, 79
Price, F. W., **30**, 200
Price, George R., **24**, 163
Price, Hereward T., **24**, 152; **27**, 11n
Price, Jonathan R., **28**, 89n
Price, Joseph G., **23**, 151; **25**, 4, 45n, 48n, 50, 51, 56, 57, 60; **27**, 106n; **30**, 80
Price, J. R., **24**, 152
Price, Peter, **24**, 158n
Prince, F. T., **23**, 76n, 180
Prior, Moody E., **28**, 10n–11n
Prior, Roger, **29**, 25, 26, 31–2
'The Life of George Wilkins', **25**, 137–52
'George Wilkins and the Young Heir', **29**, 33–9
Proctor, F., **25**, 127n
Prosetler, Mary, **22**, 109
Prokoviev, **30**, 5
Proser, Matthew N., **23**, 148; **26**, 164
Prosser, Eleanor, **22**, 157–8; **26**, 23, 25n, 161; **28**, 37n; **30**, 208
Proudfoot, Richard (G. R.), **21**, 146; **22**, 167n; **28**, 181; **29**, 1
Textual Studies, reviewed: (1968) **22**, 176–83; (1969), **23**, 176–86; (1970), **24**, 170–9; (1971), **25**, 193–200; (1972), **26**, 177–84; (1973) **27**, 179–92; (1974), **28**, 173–81; (1975), **29**, 177–85; (1976) **30**, 203–10

'Verbal Reminiscence and the Two-Part Structure of The Winter's Tale, **29**, 67–78
Proudhon, P. J., **28**, 65
Proust, Marcel, **28**, 30
Prouty, Charles, T., **25**, 179
Publius Sicilius, **29**, 170
Purdon, Noel, **29**, 173
Purvis, J. S., **23**, 42n
Püschel, Ursula, **23**, 174n; **26**, 162
Pushkin, **23**, 176; **26**, 167
Puttenham, Richard, **22**, 3
Pyle, Fitzroy, **23**, 155–6; **26**, 167; **29**, 1, 2, 4, 6, 67
Pyman, Avril, **21**, 128

Quarrell, W. H., **30**, 165n
Quayle, Anthony, **24**, 3n, 8, 10; **25**, 3, 94n; **26**, 119; **27**, 106n
Queen's Men, **27**, 129–36; **30**, 196
Quiller-Couch, Sir Arthur, **24**, 52; **25**, 3, 94n
Quin, James, **21**, 117
Quiney, Thomas, **28**, 38
Quinn, D. B., **21**, 142
Quinn, Edward G., **21**, 141
Quinones, J., **29**, 16n
Quintilian, **30**, 14

Raab, Felix, **21**, 143–4; **29**, 90
Rabelais, François, **22**, 5; **29**, 91
Rabkin, Norman, **22**, 146–7, 158; **24**, 12, 145n, 161; **25**, 11–12, 16n; **26**, 163; **27**, 164; **29**, 9, 89–90
Racine, Jean, **22**, 22, 163; **24**, 38, 79, 81, 83; **27**, 157; **29**, 9, 165
Rackin, Phyllis, **24**, 146; **26**, 159
Radcliffe, Mrs, **30**, 200
Rae, T. I., **21**, 142
Raleigh (Ralegh), Sir Walter (ob. 1610), **21**, 103; **22**, 147; **23**, 43–4, 161; **26**, 103, 114n; **27**, 56; **28**, 7, 21, 24, 28; **29**, 178
Raleigh, Sir Walter (ob. 1922), **21**, 8, 28n; **25**, 1; **26**, 73; **27**, 112
Ram, Alur Janaki, **23**, 149
Ramel, Henrik, **22**, 121
Ramel, Jacques, **22**, 172n
Ramsey, Jarold W., **21**, 138; **25**, 176; **28**, 155; **29**, 173
Ramus, Peter, **27**, 83, 84
Randolph, John, **24**, 93
Rank, Otto, **22**, 15
Ranzau, Gert, **22**, 121, 123
Ranzau, Henrik, **22**, 121
Raphael, **26**, 54, 65; **27**, 55
Rastell, John, **29**, 98, 99n
Rattray, R. F., **25**, 1n
Rauber, D. F., **24**, 145
Raven, C. E., **23**, 45n
Ravn, V. C., **22**, 119, 124n

Ray, George W., **24**, 161
Raymond, Henry, **24**, 92
Raysor, T. M., **23**, 102, 103, 104n, 106, 107, 109, 110; **24**, 44; **25**, 45n
Rea, John D., **27**, 59n
Reaney, P. H., **22**, 124n
Reaske, C. R., **26**, 153; **29**, 175
Reddington, John, **28**, 171n
Redgrave, Corin, **26**, 147
Redgrave, Sir Michael, **26**, 147
Redgrave, Vanessa, **23**, 132; **28**, 142
Reed, G., **28**, 154
Reed, Henry, **21**, 52n
Reed, Isaac, **21**, 49–50, 52n
Reed, Robert Rentoul, Jr, **23**, 146
Reed, Victor, **23**, 165n
Rees, D. G., **21**, 147
Rees, Joan, **21**, 145; **23**, 166n; **26**, 34, 36, 165
'Revenge, Retribution, and Reconciliation', **24**, 31–5
Rees, Roger, **25**, 166; **30**, 176, 178
Reese, J. E., **24**, 148
Reese, M. M., **27**, 32n, 41; **29**, 85; **30**, 49n, 56n, 58n
Reeve, Henry, **24**, 88
Reichert, Günter, **23**, 116
Reid, S., **26**, 155
Reid, Stephen A., **25**, 176
Reid, S. W., **28**, 180; **29**, 181; **30**, 206, 207
Reif, Patricia, **23**, 163
Rembrandt, **24**, 99
Remy, N., **28**, 121
Renan, Ernest, **22**, 48, 119, 121, 123
Replogle, Clare, **24**, 143
Reyher, Paul, **28**, 42
Reynoldes, Edward, **25**, 148
Reynolds, G. F., **22**, 35; **25**, 9
Reynolds, William, **21**, 148
Ribeiro, Alvaro, **27**, 178
Ribner, Irving, **21**, 151; **22**, 155; **24**, 164; **26**, 7; **27**, 71; **28**, 4n, 7, 9; **29**, 83, 84, 89, 90
Ricci, Luigi, **27**, 46n
Rice, J. C., **28**, 155
Rice, John, **26**, 45
Rice, J. R., **28**, 156
Rich, Penelope, **27**, 178
Richard II, King, **25**, 188
Richards, I. A., **26**, 9; **28**, 29
Richards, Kenneth, **23**, 171n, 172
Richardson, Ian, **21**, 115, 116, 122–5; **22**, 139, 140; **23**, 131; **24**, 117, 119, 121, 124, 130; **25**, 65; **29**, 146–7, 152; **28**, 142, 143, 144, 147; **29**, 153, 154
Riche, Barnabe, **29**, 180
Richmond, H. M., **23**, 144, 157; **26**, 152, 164; **30**, 47, 52n, 53n
Richter, Bodo I. O., **21**, 154

Rickert, R. T., **27**, 134n; **29**, 127, 128, 129
Ricketts, Charles, **29**, 141
Rickey, Mary Ellen, **25**, 12n
Ricks, Christopher, **27**, 44
Ricks, Don M., **24**, 152
Ricordi, Giulio, **21**, 89
Riddell, James A., **29**, 174
Ridler, Anne, **24**, 168; **26**, 119n
Ridley, M. R., **21**, 27n; **22**, 180; **23**, 61n; **24**, 3n
Riehle, Wolfgang, **23**, 116; **26**, 158
Riemer, A. P., **22**, 162; **24**, 1n
Riewald, J. G., **29**, 134n, 135n
Rigg, Diana, **23**, 132
Riggs, David, **26**, 157; **27**, 78–9; **30**, 192
Righter (Barton, Roesen), Anne, **22**, 35, 178; **25**, 7, 107; **26**, 16; **29**, 6,7
Righter, William, **25**, 189
Rinehart, Keith, **26**, 172
Ringler, Richard N., **23**, 146n
Ringler, William A., Jr, **23**, 172; **27**, 178; **28**, 174
Rissanen, Matti, **25**, 180
Ritson, Joseph, **24**, 171n
Rivers, Anthony, **24**, 72
Robbins, R. H. A., **21**, 149; **22**, 182
Roberts, James, **24**, 72, 77; **26**, 181; **27**, 136n, 181; **28**, 176, 180
Roberts, Jeanne Addison, **25**, 200; **27**, 164; **29**, 162, 180; **30**, 210
  'The Merry Wives of Windsor as a Hallowe'en Play', **25**, 107–12
Roberts, R. J., **27**, 190
Roberts, Sydney, **26**, 123n
Roberts-Baytop, Adrianne, **29**, 173
Robertson, J. M., **26**, 3; **28**, 37n, 39n 40n, 41, 42; **29**, 115n
Robertson, Roderick, **23**, 168
Robinson, Forrest G., **24**, 159
Robinson, Henry Crabb, **23**, 154
Robinson, Ian, **23**, 154
Robinson, James E., **22**, 173
Robinson, James F., **28**, 61
Robinson, J. W., **28**, 171
Robinson, Robert, **23**, 40–1
Robinson, Thomas, **23**, 102
Robson, Flora, **25**, 64
Robson, Frederick, **21**, 134
Robson, W. W., **30**, 188
Rochett, W., **27**, 170
Rockas, L., **28**, 161; **29**, 165
Rocque, John, **30**, 164n
Roddman, Philip, **24**, 6n
Rodin, Auguste, **22**, 99
Rodway, Norman, **24**, 118, 119
Roe, F. Gordon, **22**, 167n
Roe, Sir John, **27**, 178
Roesen, (Righter, Barton), Bobbyann, **22**, 71; **24**, 57n, 58n
Rogers, D. M., **24**, 72n; **29**, 21n
Rogers, Robert, **23**, 153

Rogers, S., **28**, 154
Rohmer, Rolf, **21**, 149; **22**, 166; **25**, 186; **26**, 166
Rolfe, John C., **30**, 69n
Rollins, Hyder E., **23**, 69n; **25**, 9
Romano, Giulio, **26**, 65; **30**, 202
Romei, Annibale, **27**, 45n
Ronan, C. J., **26**, 158
Rose, Marvin, **24**, 160; **26**, 161n
Rose, Paul L., **24**, 147
Rose, Steven, **24**, 149
Rosen, Barbara, **28**, 118, 121
Rosen, William, **21**, 139
Rosenberg, Edgar, **24**, 162
Rosenberg, John D., **21**, 136
Rosenberg, Marvin, **21**, 62, 65n; **23**, 173; **26**, 155, 163; **27**, 158; **28**, 171; **29**, 176
Rosenfeld, Sybil, **21**, 146; **22**, 175; **29**, 176; **30**, 197
Rosignoli, Maria P., **23**, 162n
Rosinger, Lawrence, **23**, 153, 166n; **30**, 194
Ross, Alan S. C., **21**, 147
Ross, Lawrence J., **21**, 136; **23**, 146
Rossini, **21**, 81, 82, 83–4, 85
Rossiter, A. P., **22**, 31; **25**, 2, 63; **26**, 120; **27**, 24n, 31n; **28**, 1n, 12, 91n, 100n; **29**, 87, 89; **30**, 140
Rosso, **26**, 50, 51, 54
Roston, Murray, **21**, 142n; **22**, 172
Rostron, David, **23**, 173; **25**, 192
Rothe, Hans, **23**, 121
Rothenberg, A., **26**, 164
Rothman, J., **27**, 166
Rothschild, H. B., Jr, **27**, 161
Rothstein, Eric, **23**, 146n
Rothwell, K. S., **28**, 171n
Rotrou, Jean, **22**, 21
Rouse, W. H. D., **30**, 153n
Rousseau, J.-J., **26**, 94; **28**, 65
Rousset, Jean, **28**, 46n
Rowan, D. F., **25**, 191; **28**, 168; **30**, 157, 198
  'A Neglected Jones/Webb Theatre Project: "Barber Surgeons' Hall Writ Large"', **23**, 125–9
Rowe, Nicholas, **24**, 107, 176; **27**, 187, 191; **28**, 75; **29**, 179
Rowell, George, **30**, 200
Rowland, Beryl, **25**, 176
Rowlands, Samuel, **28**, 159
Rowlandson, Thomas, **30**, 164, 165
Rowley, Samuel, **27**, 129
Rowley, William, **22**, 171; **25**, 138; **26**, 54; **29**, 23, 182
Rowse, A. L., **21**, 97; **28**, 5
Roy, S. N., **22**, 175n
Rubel, V. L., **23**, 21n
Rubens, **29**, 29; **30**, 83
Rubinstein, E., **25**, 174

Rudenstine, Neil L., **22**, 170
Rudolf II, King, **29**, 24n
Rudolph, J., **26**, 164; **29**, 177
Rudyerd, Sir Benjamin, **27**, 114n
Rüegg, August, **23**, 150, 161
Ruggles, Eleanor, **24**, 100n
Rundle, James U., **24**, 157
Rusche, Harry, **23**, 153
Russ, J. R., **26**, 165; **29**, 175
Russell, Lord John, **24**, 92, 93
Russell, Thomas, **21**, 148
Rutherford, Mary, **28**, 145
Rutland, Earl of, **21**, 103
Ryan, Richard, **28**, 7
Ryan, Robert, **26**, 143
Ryan, Lawrence V., **22**, 169
Ryken, Leland, **24**, 159
Rylands, George, **24**, 3n
Rymer, Thomas, **21**, 16, 27n, 41, 67–77; **23**, 152

Saccio, Peter, **24**, 162n; **30**, 198
Sacharoff, M., **26**, 155; **27**, 166
Sachs, Arieh, **23**, 186n
Sackler, Howard, **24**, 3n
Sackville, Thomas, Lord Buckhurst, **24**, 157; **30**, 61
Sacrobosco, G., **23**, 167
Saha, Narayan Chandra, **21**, 141
Sahel, P., **26**, 158
St Augustine, **21**, 152; **24**, 140; **27**, 157; **28**, 43; **30**, 61, 63, 64
St Denis, Michel, **27**, 142
St Francis Borja, **23**, 82, 83
St Germain, Christopher, **27**, 95, 96, 97; **29**, 93, 94n, 99
St Paul, **27**, 83, 86; **28**, 68; **29**, 5, 170; **30**, 104
Sale, Roger, **22**, 160
Salgādo, Gāmini, **27**, 163; **29**, 176
  '"Time's Deformed Hand": Sequence, Consequence, and Inconsequence in The Comedy of Errors', **25**, 81–91
Salingar, L. G., **21**, 144; **23**, 132; **29**, 157
Salisbury, Lord, **26**, 46; **29**, 23
Salmi, Mario, **26**, 114n
Salmon, Vivian, **23**, 11n; **25**, 184
  'Some Functions of Shakespearian Word-Formation', **23**, 13–26
Salomon, Brownell, **30**, 191, 197
Salter, H. E., **30**, 163n
Salusbury, Sir John, **21**, 140
Salusbury, Sir Thomas, **24**, 159
Salvian of Marseille, **29**, 21
Salvini, T., **30**, 198
Samarin, Roman, **21**, 128n
Sames, Mawline, **25**, 146–7, 149
Sampson, George, **23**, 87n; **24**, 155
Samuels, Ernest, **24**, 92n, 93n, 98
Samwaise, Magdalen, **29**, 33–4, 35

Sanders, Gerald, **27**, 106n

Sanders, Norman, **21**, 145
Critical Studies, *reviewed*: (1970), **24**, 137–54; (1971) **25**, 171–86; (1972), **26**, 151–68
'The True Prince and the False Thief: Prince Hal and the Shift of Identity', **30**, 29–34

Sanders, Wilbur, **22**, 147–8; **26**, 8; **29**, 89

Sandys, George, **23**, 161

Saner, Reginald, **23**, 154; **24**, 168n

Sankey, Fr William, **23**, 79, 80–1, 82, 83; **25**, 6n

Sardou, Victorièn, **22**, 2

Sargent, R. M., **25**, 188; **27**, 16n

Sarrazin, G., **23**, 22n, 34n

Sartre, Jean-Paul, **22**, 5; **28**, 43, 44

Satin, J., **26**, 161

Saunders, Edward, **29**, 110n

Saunders, George, **23**, 173

Saunders, J. W., **22**, 169

Saunders, Norman, **23**, 180n, 181, 183

Savage, James E., **27**, 178

Savage, R., **26**, 74n

Saviolo, Vincentio, **24**, 144

Savoy, Duke of, **26**, 46

Sawyer, Paul, **25**, 192

Sayle, R. T. D., **26**, 39n

Saxl, Fritz, **25**, 189

Saxony, Elector of, **22**, 121

Scarfe, Gerald, **22**, 141

Schaar, Claes, **23**, 72, 74; **26**, 173

Schabert, Ina, **26**, 176

Schäfer, Jürgen, **23**, 119, 161; **24**, 176; **26**, 172; **27**, 59n; **30**, 208

Schaller, Rudolf, **23**, 122

Schamp, Dieter, **27**, 189

Schanzer, Ernest, **21**, 134; **22**, 62, 114, 118n, 153, 157; **23**, 148, 172, 182, 183; **24**, 152; **25**, 2, 5, 6n, 176; **26**, 97, 119n, 122, 126; **28**, 51n, 52–4, **29**, 6, 8, 67, 69, 77; **30**, 189
'Shakespeare and the Doctrine of the Unity of Time', **28**, 57–61

Schell, Edgar T., **23**, 168; **24**, 151; **28**, 154; **30**, 44

Scheller, B., **26**, 164

Schelp, H., **26**, 166n

Scheyer, T. E., **28**, 161

Schibsbye, K., **23**, 13n

Schlegel, A. W., **23**, 122

Schlegel, F. W., **28**, 107; **30**, 201

Schleiner, Winifried, **29**, 174

Schloesser, Anselm, **21**, 132; **22**, 153; **23**, 141, 142–3; **25**, 176; **26**, 163

Schmid, E. E., **28**, 41n, 42

Schmid, Hans, **28**, 171

Schmidt, Alexander, **23**, 22, 34; **30**, 87

Schmidt di Simoni, Karen, **23**, 117

Schmitt, Natalie Crohn, **24**, 160

Schoek, R. J. **26**, 164

Schoenbaum, S., **21**, 65n; **23**, 171; **25**, 1n, 186–7, 191, 196n; **26**, 5; **29**, 138n, 168; **30**, 15n, 185, 191
'*Richard* II and the Realities of Power', **28**, 1–13

Schondonk, Giles, **29**, 30n

Schöne, Albrecht, **26**, 117n

Schopenhauer, Arthur, **24**, 97; **30**, 186

Schrader, W., **26**, 156

Schrickx, W., **23**, 161; **27**, 157
'*Pericles* in a Book-List of 1619 from the English Jesuit Mission and Some of the Play's Special Problems', **29**, 21–32

Schröder, Rudolf Alexander, **23**, 122; **26**, 166; **28**, 172

Schuchter, J. D., **22**, 156

Schücking, Levin L., **21**, 9, 24, 25; **26**, 119; **29**, 137

Schulz, H. C., **24**, 159

Schumann, H., **26**, 157

Schwarz, Elias, **22**, 154; **25**, 181; **27**, 166

Schwarz, H., **26**, 166n

Schwertz, M. M., **26**, 164

Scofield, Paul, **21**, 115, 119–22, 125; **28**, 171; **30**, 21

Scot, Reginald, **24**, 156; **28**, 119, 122

Scott, J. W., **26**, 172

Scott, Mary Augusta, **25**, 103

Scott, Sir Walter, **26**, 70n

Scoufos, Alice Lyle, **21**, 152; **24**, 151; **25**, 174; **30**, 35n

Scouten, Arthur H., **30**, 184

Scragg, Leah, **23**, 152; **28**, 5n
'Iago, Vice or Devil?', **21**, 53–65
'Macbeth on Horseback', **26**, 81–8
'Shakespeare, Lyly and Ovid: The Influence of "Gallathea" on *A Midsummer Night's Dream*', **30**, 125–34

Studies on Shakespeare's Life, Times and Stage, *reviewed*: (1968), **22**, 167–76; (1969), **23**, 159–76; (1970), **24**, 154–69

Scribe, **22**, 2

Scrimgeour, Gary J., **22**, 165

Seaman, John E., **22**, 161; **25**, 182

Seaton, Ethel, **25**, 128, 129n

Sebonde, Raymond, **27**, 45n

Sedlak, Werner, **24**, 153

Seehase, Georg, **25**, 186; **26**, 156

Sehrt, Ernst Theodore, **21**, 143; **23**, 115, 120; **28**, 172n

Seiden, M., **25**, 177

Seiler, R. M., **26**, 161

Sell, Roger D., **24**, 159

Seller, H., **26**, 162

Seltzer, Daniel, **21**, 155; **24**, 154; **29**, 2; **30**, 13n
'Prince Hal and Tragic Style', **30**, 13–27

Semon, K. A., **28**, 163

Sen Gupta, Subodh Chandra, **21**, 129; **27**, 72n, 156

Sen, Taraknath, **21**, 129n, 138, 158

Seneca, **22**, 109, 110–13, 151; **23**, 121, 169; **24**, 156; **27**, 16, 17, 19, 165, 173, 179; **28**, 40n; **29**, 80, 81, 87; **30**, 61, 62, 104, 109, 112, 192, 193

Seng, Peter J., **22**, 177; **26**, 111n

Sérullaz, Maurice, **21**, 81, 82

Šešplaukis, Alfonsas, **21**, 153n; **23**, 159

Seward, Frederick, W., **24**, 93n

Seward, J., **29**, 164

Seward, William H., **24**, 92n

Sewell, Arthur, **21**, 10n

Seymour, Charles, **26**, 112n

Seymour, E. H., **30**, 96n

Seymour, M. C., **28**, 120n

Sexton, William, **21**, 103

Shaaber, M. A., **24**, 149; **25**, 183, 196, 199; **26**, 184

Shackford, Martha Hale, **22**, 116n

Shadoian, J., **26**, 160

Shadwell, Thomas, **24**, 167

Shaheen, Naseeb, **23**, 155; **24**, 157

Shakeshafte, William, **28**, 166

Shakespeare, Edmund, **30**, 199

Shakespeare, Hamnet, **27**, 94, 98

Shakespeare, John, **22**, 167; **27**, 94, 98–104; **28**, 165

Shakespeare, Mary, **27**, 98–104

Shakespeare, William
editions
Alexander, P., **22**, 92n; **23**, 27n, 49n; **26**, 69n, 95n, 181; **29**, 24n; **30**, 1n, 35n, 61n, 86n, 135n
Arden, **22**, 92n; **23**, 71n, 76n, 180; **24**, 55n, 58, 106n, 113n; **26**, 12, 13, 72, 82n, 113n, 119n, 122n, 126n; **27**, 34n, 38n, 92n, 133; **28**, 39, 117, 121n; **29**, 1, 5, 11n, 110, 139; **30**, 47n, 73n, 193, 203
Booth, Lionel, **23**, 1n
Cambridge, **25**, 73; **26**, 181; **27**, 132n; **28**, 38n
Clarendon, **30**, 206
Craig, W. J., **23**, 15n
Craig, Hardin, **26**, 111n; **30**, 47n
Eighteenth Century Shakespeare, **24**, 171
Folger Library, **21**, 142; **22**, 116n, 169n; **28**, 172, 179, 180
Folios: **21**, textual studies of, 157–63; **22**, 109, 114; textual studies of, 176–83; **23**, 1, 18, 102, 121, 122, 143, 156; facsimiles of, 15n, 178, 186; copies of, 79, 80, 82, 86; textual studies of, 176–85; **24**, 52, 53, 54, 74n, 106, 150; Norton facsimile of, **24**, 170, 172; textual studies of, 170–9; **25**, 5,

Shakespeares Folios (*cont.*)
6n, 7, 9, 49n–50n, 73–80, 85n;
textual studies of, 193–200 *passim*; 26, 12n, 177–84 *passim*; 27,
49n, 105n, 106n, 108, 132, 135;
editorial research on, 187–92;
textual studies of, 179–92 *passim*;
facsimiles of, 189; 28, textual
studies of, 173–81 *passim*; 29,
24, 51, 77, 105n, 117–25 *passim*;
textual studies of, 177–85 *passim*;
30, 86n, 194, 198; textual studies
of, 203–10 *passim*
Globe, 23, 1n; 25, 73n
Griggs (facsimile), 22, 181; 26, 12,
13
Humphreys, A. R., 26, 177
Hunter, G. K., 26, 177–9
Macmillan, 30, 206
Malone Society, 27, 130n
Munro, John, 26, 44n
New Arden, 21, 27n; 22, 26n, 77n;
23, 51, 180; 24, 52, 76n, 172, 177;
25, 4, 47n, 82, 84n, 85n, 87n, 126,
137n, 198; 26, 5, 69, 71n; 27, 34n,
38n, 92n, 106n, 111n, 133; 28, 55,
90; 29, 22, 43n, 45n, 51n, 76n,
93n, 105n, 177; 30, 29n, 35n, 61n,
203, 204, 205
New Cambridge, 25, 2, 5, 9; 27,
62n, 71n, 106n; 30, 48n, 86n, 203,
208
New Penguin, 21, 157–8; 22, 178–
80; 23, 181, 182; 24, 172, 176;
26, 177; 27, 188, 190; 28, 178–9;
29, 6, 67; 30, 203, 210
New Shakespeare, 21, 114n, 146n,
147n; 24, 52, 171, 172; 29, 41n
New Variorum, 22, 177; 23, 69n
Oxford, 28, 117n, 175
Pelican, 24, 172, 173–5; 26, 55n
Quartos, 21, textual studies of,
157–63 *passim*; 22, textual studies
of, 176–83 *passim*; 23, 121, 133,
textual studies of, 176–85 *passim*;
24, 52, 53, 74n, 106, textual
studies of, 170–9 *passim*; 25, 7, 8,
73–80, textual studies of, 193–200
passim; 26, 33n, textual studies of,
177–84 *passim*; 27, 45n, 113,
135; textual studies of, 179–92
passim; 28, 109, textual studies
of, 173–81 *passim*; 29, 117–24
passim; textual studies of, 177–85
passim; 30, 86n, textual studies of,
203–10 *passim*
Riverside, 28, 173–7, 178; 29, 184;
30, 125n, 208
Rowe, 27, 191
Scolar facsimiles, 22, 181
Signet Classic, 22, 67n; 27, 34n

Variorum, 21, 27n; 22, 116n; 27,
28n, 29n, 43n, 69, 106, 107, 108n;
30, 96n
Yale/Oxford, 23, 1n

plays
All's Well that Ends Well, 21, 24,
127, 162, Pl. vB; 22, 79–92, 95,
138, 149, 160, 170; 23, 71, 80,
140, 141, 151; 24, 150, 172, 173,
176, 178; 25, 1, 2, 3, 4, 45–61, 63,
66–7, 176; 26, 119, 153, 154,
155n, 172; 27, 106, 107, 108,
165n, 166; 28, 39, 49n, 53, 54–5,
56, 102, 104, 141, 176; 29, 43n,
157; 30, 73–84, 153, 184, 192
Antony and Cleopatra, 21, 14, 87,
108, 109, 128, 138, 139, 158; 22,
32, 47, 98, 151, 156, 157, 162–3;
23, 7, 10, 16, 25, 29, 35, 59–67,
118, 154, 159; 24, 1–12, 23, 43,
138, 146–7, 153, 157, 168, 169,
175, 176; 25, 2, 128–9; 174, 189;
26, 16n, 58, 62–4, 95–101, 131n,
134, 141, 142, 146–8, 151, 158,
159, 165, 179, Pls. VII, VIII; 27, 3,
65, 156, 160; 28, 16, 29–36, 149,
150, 156, 157; 29, 51n, 68, 82, 84,
115, 121, 165, 172, 185; 30, 5, 7,
144, 182, 186, 187, 195
As You Like It, 21, 131, 153, 162;
22, 2, 7, 11, 12, 13, 46, 135, 139–
40, 149, 150, 153, 177, 178,
Pls. IV, VA; 23, 2, 17, 23, 24, 80,
95, 99, 140, 144, 151, 158, 161;
24, 149; 25, 27, 50, 63, 101, 110,
171, 180; 26, 111–17, 128, 154;
27, 59, 69, 108, 130, 131, 144, 146,
148, 162, 165, 167, 168, 169,
Pl. IV; 28, 39, 75, 77, 78, 149,
160, 162; 29, 6, 117, 138, 142,
162, 174, 177, 178; 30, 5, 83,
183, 195, 199, 201
Comedy of Errors, The, 21, 130, 139;
22, 1, 15, 16, 17–18, 25, 39, 50,
127, 132, 137, 151, 152, 153, 167;
23, 4–5, 8, 10, 17, 18, 35, 143,
161, 177n; 24, 29, 142, 149;
25, 60, 64, 81–91, 179; 26, 140,
142; 27, 2, 18, 93, 95, 163, 188,
189; 28, 57–8, 76, 77, 159, 160;
29, 8, 51; 30, 6, 169, 176–7, 183
Coriolanus, 21, 139, 156, 157, 158,
Pl. vA; 22, 47, 156, 162, 163, 175;
23, 16, 26, 33, 35, 138, 139, 144,
154, 159, 173; 24, 16, 17, 27, 28,
140, 146, 148, 175; 25, 127, 189;
26, 38, 58, 60, 61–2, 92, 95–101,
141, 142–4, 146, 158, 159, 179;
27, 60, 160, 179, 192; 28, 22–3,
63–9, 157, 170; 29, 8, 68, 83, 87,
119, 121, 122, 136, 158, 163, 165,

176; 30, 5, 7, 85n, 90n, 135–46,
182, 187, 203–5
Cymbeline, 21, 25, 127, 140; 22, 99,
127, 132, 164, 174n, 177; 23, 18,
28, 29, 31, 32, 155; 24, 33, 34, 37,
105, 107, 151, 157, 172, 174; 25,
178; 26, 42, 44–5, 47, 64, 65, 66,
70, 106, 134n, 153, 156, 164, 179,
184; 27, 133n; 28, 141, 144, 148,
163, 180, Pl. II; 29, 1, 2, 3, 4, 5,
6, 7, 8, 9, 41–9, 51–61, 65, 74,
123, 158, 169, 185; 30, 7, 84,
154n, 195
Hamlet, 21, 1, 2–3, 10n, 26, 27n,
49, 87, 107, 133, 134, 146, 147,
149, 153, 154, 160, 163, Pl. IIIA;
22, 42, 125, 127, 130, 132, 133,
146, 147, 156, 158–9, 162, 165,
166, 167, 168, 175, 176, 183,
Pl. I; 23, 4, 9, 16, 17, 18, 20, 23,
31, 47, 64, 83, 97, 99n, 116, 120,
121, 122, 138–9, 140, 142, 147,
148, 149–50, 156, 161, 173, 174,
176, 179, 185; 24, 15, 32, 40–1,
44, 49–50, 71–104, 118, 122–3,
128, 130, 139, 141, 142–5, 152,
153, 161, 167, 169, 170, 171, 175,
176, 178, Pls. I, II; 25, 2, 4, 15,
63, 94, 110, 135, 172, 182, 184,
188, 189, 194, 196; 26, 1, 3, 11–20,
21–31, 54, 56, 58, 59, 67, 73, 89,
99, 122n, 134n, 135n, 137, 159,
160–1, 162, 167, 175, 176, 179,
181, 184; 27, 1n, 43–57, 59–69,
85, 90, 130, 132, 133, 136, 157,
161, 172, 173, 176, 181, 186; 28,
6, 16, 19n, 30, 31, 36, 37, 38n, 39,
40–2, 45, 47, 49, 58, 107–15,
149, 153–4, 165, 176, 180, 181;
29, 66, 82, 83, 86, 87, 88, 120, 121,
123, 137, 138–9, 140, 141–2, 143,
151–3, 156, 159, 161, 163, 164,
166, 171, 173, 174, 175, 176, 183,
Pl. III; 30, 1–12, 14–16, 21,
103–15, 117–23, 188, 190, 192,
193, 194, 200, 201, 202, 206n, 209,
210
Henry IV, 21, 26, 128, 132, 152;
22, Pl. IC; 23, 69, 70, 138, 145,
146–7; 25, 111, 173, 174, 192;
26, 105n, 156, 157, 179; 27, 64,
94; 28, 141n, 159; 30, 1–12, 21–7,
29–34, 35–45, 47, 49, 68, 192
1 Henry IV, 21, 152; 22, 54, 93, 125,
127, 131, 149, 155, 156, 173, 178,
179, 181; 23, 1, 3, 6, 10, 11, 16,
30, 69, 95; 24, 22, 23, 32, 151, 167,
178; 25, 107, 110, 111, 192; 26,
69, 99, 129, 132, 134n, 157n, 183;
27, 24, 27n, 75, 160, 161; 28, 39n,
173; 29, 122, 160; 30, 1–12,

1 Henry IV (cont.)

30–1, 35, 37, 38, 50, 62, 65, 67, 69–70, 122, 185, 195

2 Henry IV, **21**, 109, 112, 132, 160· **22**, 95, 149, 155, 156, 176, 181; **23**, 2, 3, 11, 19, 24, 69; **24**, 22, 23, 40; **25**, 63, 107, 110, 111, 192, 194, 196, 199; **26**, 131, 154n, 172, 173, 184; **27**, 132n, 135, 154, 161, 182, 191; **28**, 47, 152, 178; **29**, 155, 175, Pl. IV; **30**, 1–12, 32–4, 35–45, 63, 65

1 & 2 Henry IV, **29**, 68, 84, 171, 172, 185; **30**, 14, 18, 21–7, 36, 59, 104

Henry V, **21**, 107–14, 119, 123, 132; **22**, 155, 173, 178, 179; **23**, 2, 3–4, 5, 6, 8, 9, 11, 19, 25, 26, 120, 132, 147; **24**, 139, 167; **25**, 110, 111n, 167, 168, 169, 174, 189, 198, 199; **26**, 131, 157; **27**, 71–9, 109, 186, 189; **28**, 9, 22, 39, 47, 58, 59, 159, 178; **29**, 83, 84, 123, 136, 143, 154, 155, 161, 171, 172, 185, Pl. IV; **30**, 1, 4–5, 43, 47–59, 61–72, 121, 185, 209

Henry VI, **23**, 116, 142, 180; **26**, 108, 157n; **27**, 22, 79, 136; **28**, 46, 158, 171; **29**, 84, 87, 88, 160, 173; **30**, 182, 185

1 Henry VI, **21**, 108, 111, 131, 132; **22**, 93, 110, 138, 151, 155; **23**, 9, 10, 18, 81, 160; **24**, 29, 39, 152, 177; **27**, 1n, 182; **28**, 46; **29**, 122, 160; **30**, 7

2 Henry VI, **21**, 107, 109, 111, 152; **22**, 93, 94, 105, 138, 151, 155, 173, 182; **23**, 2, 17, 24, 49–52, 54–5, 57, 58, 81; **24**, 137, 152, 177; **26**, 69, 98; **27**, 132n, 135, 154, 161, 182, 191; **29**, 121, 122; **30**, 201, 209

3 Henry VI, **22**, 93, 96, 138, 151; **23**, 49, 50, 142; **24**, 43–4, 137, 152, 177; **25**, 37; **27**, 22, 23n, 132n, 135; **28**, 45; **29**, 118, 122; **30**, 7, 14, 209

Henry VIII, **21**, 130, 140, 153; **22**, 95, 155, 165, 177; **23**, 11, 79, 81, 83, 116, 121, 141, 144, 157; **26**, 33, 35, 47, 177, 184; **27**, 110, 170; **28**, 177, 180; **29**, 1, 6, 124, 165; **30**, 4

Julius Caesar, **21**, 13, 14, 22, 25, 132, 142, 147, 157, 158; **22**, 109–15, 127, 132, 139, 140, 155, 156, 157, 171, 174, Pl. II; **23**, 16, 17, 57–8, 65, 95–7, 122, 140, 142, 144, 148, 149, 173, 183, 186; **24**, 146, 147–8, 152, 156, 167; **25**, 2, 15, 19, 94, 127, 171, 175; **26**, 97, 99, 131,

132n, 133, 137, 141, 142, 144–6, 151, 158, 182; **27**, 1, 159, 179, 191; **28**, 22, 39, 47, 156; **29**, 84, 86, 87, 103, 122, 124, 139, 158, 170, 176; **30**, 4, 5, 11, 186, 189

King John, **21**, 132, 148, 151, 152, 153; **22**, 127, 132, 155; **23**, 10, 17, 23, 56–7, 58, 79, 140, 145; **24**, 85n, 117, 118, 130, 142, 152, 174; **25**, 174; **26**, 96, 105n, 106, 132, 158, 183; **27**, 106n, 148, 180; **28**, 45, 47, 49, 138, 139, 140, 141, 166, 172, 172, 179, 180, Pl. I; **29**, 136, 140, 144; **30**, 7

King Lear, **21**, 1, 2–3, 10n, 27n, 49, 87, 127, 128, 129, 133, 136, 145, 146, 149, 153, 160, 162, Pls. IB, II, IIIB; **22**, 46, 57, 63, 99, 127, 131, 132, 133, 136, 137, 139, 141–2, 156, 161–2, 165, 166, 168, 175, 182, 183, Pl. VB; **23**, 8, 15, 17, 18, 19, 20, 25, 26, 31, 34, 35, 36, 50, 59, 64, 65, 85n, 88, 114, 117, 118, 120, 121, 123, 140, 141, 153, 159, 174, 175–6, 179; **24**, 17–18, 24, 25, 26, 27, 34–5, 41, 72, 76n, 77, 85n, 97, 127, 138, 139, 141, 145–6, 170, 171, 174, 175, 179; **25**, 163, 172, 175, 180, 181, 184, 194, 195, 196, 197, 200; **26**, 33–48, 54, 55, 56, 58, 59, 69–79; 89, 123, 130, 134, 151, 155, 159, 161, 162, 164, 165, 167, 171, 176, 177–9; **27**, 2, 3, 18n, 43, 59, 98, 109, 112n, 113, 127, 132, 133, 156, 158, 160, 168, 169, 172, 173, 174, 179, 182, 185, 186, 190, 192; **28**, 22, 30, 31, 32, 36, 39, 51, 122, 149, 155, 156, 157, 175, 176, 179; **29**, 6, 8, 23, 24, 82, 87, 88, 89, 111n, 124, 139, 150, 163, 164, 171, 176, 185; **30**, 5, 7, 21, 26–7, 90, 100n, 148, 149, 150, 152, 182, 186, 187, 188, 190, 192, 193, 194, 200, 202, 206, 207

Love's Labour's Lost, **21**, 131, 143; **22**, 7, 11, 12, 13, 29, 39, 69–76, 82, 99, 151, 152, 153, 178, 181; **23**, 4, 5, 6, 7, 11, 12, 19, 34, 56, 90, 92, 118, 138, 140, 143, 172; **24**, 23, 24, 25, 50, 51–3, 55–62, 142, 149, 176; **25**, 64, 179, 188, 200; **26**, 16n, 90, 103, 105n, 109, 135, 136, 152, 153, 165, 179; **27**, 105, 106n, 107, 108, 131, 146, 148, 162, 163, 168, 191, Pls. I, II, III; **28**, 7, 39n, 46, 58, 75–6, 77, 78, 149, 161; **29**, 41, 45, 124, 162; **30**, 6, 7, 83, 125, 133, 201

Macbeth, **21**, 24, 26, 27n, 47, 49, 107, 119–22, 127, 128, 133, 137,

138, 157, 158, 159–60, 162, Pl. VI; **22**, 42, 99, 125, 127, 130–1, 133, 148, 156, 162, 174, 177; **23**, 15, 19, 50, 52–4, 57, 58, 64, 114, 116, 119, 120, 123, 138, 139, 147, 148, 153–4, 159, 173; **24**, 13n, 14, 32, 42, 77n, 138, 141, 145, 153, 156, 163, 167, 178, 179; **25**, 172, 180, 181n, 184, 185; **26**, 35, 40, 42, 53, 58, 60, 69, 70, 78, 81–8, 131, 132n, 133, 137, 151, 161, 172, 176, 177; **27**, 43, 47, 48n, 55, 145, 156, 158, 161, 172, 173, 179, 192; **28**, 5n, 137, 151, 155, 157, 166, 171, 174, 176, 177, 179; **29**, 8, 9, 77, 82, 83, 88, 123, 135, 136, 139, 145–9, 165, 174; **30**, 5, 6, 21, 87, 95, 169, 170, 177–9, 182, 189, 190, 192, 198, 206n, Pl. VIIIB

Measure for Measure, **21**, 3, 24, 46n, 47, 52n, 127, 128, 134–5, 143, 162; **22**, 27, 29–30, 32, 88, 150, 160, 170, 176; **23**, 16, 23, 26, 31, 34, 42, 79, 82, 83, 118, 120, 140, 151, 176, 177n, 182, 183; **24**, 43, 123, 124, 125, 129, 149, 150, 155, 167, 173, Pl. III; **25**, 1, 2, 4, 5, 6, 7, 8, 27–35, 36–44, 45, 50, 60, 61, 63, 64–5, 101, 130n, 158, 175, 176, 177, 191; **26**, 119–28, 130, 136, 153, 155, 167, 172, 175; **27**, 81, 82–3, 84–92, 108, 109n, 145, 166, 167, 176, 177, 184, 189; **28**, 7, 38n, 39, 40, 51–6, 89–105, 137, 143, 146, 147, 162, 180; Pls. V, VI; **29**, 52, 61, 67, 94, 95, 98, 123, 157, 158, 163, 166; **30**, 43, 83–4, 182, 184, 186, 187, 192, 193

Merchant of Venice, The, **21**, 130, 131, 141, 152, 157, 160, 162; **22**, 7, 11, 32, 93, 101, 113, 127, 131, 132, 133, 150, 154, 177; **23**, 17, 25, 30, 120, 138, 144; **24**, 128, 129, 131, 167, 169, 172, 176, 178, Pls. VII; **25**, 95, 109, 110, 153–9, 164, 165–6, 176, Pl. VII; **26**, 130n, 154, 179, 181, 182; **27**, 81, 82, 90, 91, 93–104, 107, 108, 131, 164, 181, 185, 186; **28**, 39n, 75–87, 89, 160, 171, 172, 176, 180; **29**, 51, 52, 93–101, 136, 139, 157, 158, 162, 178; **30**, 183, 195, 201

Merry Wives of Windsor, The, **21**, 130; **22**, 139, Pl. III; **23**, 3, 4, 6, 177n, 178; **25**, 107–12, 192, 198, 199, 200; **27**, 108, 164, 165n, 177, 184, 185, 186; **28**, 77, 160, 178; **29**, 10, 51, 135, 137, 152, 154, 172,

Merry Wives of Windsor, The
(cont.)
183, 185, Pl. VIII; **30**, 2, 4, 87n,
209, 210

Midsummer Night's Dream, A, **21,**
25, 87, 130, 157; **22,** 4, 7, 11, 12,
27, 30–1, 83, 151, 152, 153, 173;
23, 4, 5, 7, 10, 16, 23, 92–3, 94,
120, 122, 132, 138, 143, 144, 161,
172, 173; **24,** 118, 119, 125–6,
128, 132–4, 156, 168, 178, Pls.
VII, VIII; **25,** 35, 158n, 164, 178,
179, 186; **26,** 92, 106, 135, 152,
153, 156, 172, 179; **27,** 7n, 59, 95,
107, 108, 162, 163, 164, 185, 186,
187; **28,** 7, 75, 76, 78, 161, 173,
176, 178; **29,** 48, 121, 122, 124,
138, 140, 141, 142, 151, 161, 162,
170, 173, 177, 184; **30,** 87n, 125–
34, 183, 201, 206

Much Ado About Nothing, **21,** 127,
130, 162; **22,** 7, 11, 31, 44, 133,
135, 139, 144n, 149, 153, 154,
178, 179; **23,** 9, 95, 144; **24,** 128,
149, 156, 173; **25,** 27, 93–105,
110, 161, 164, 165, 166, 169, 178,
180, Pls. III, IV; **26,** 70, 129, 130,
134n, 154, 177, 179; **27,** 105–10,
162, 164, 180, 186, 191; **28,** 76, 77,
78, 160, 161; **29,** 8, 51, 52, 58,
141, 157, 162, 179, 181, 185;
30, 7, 169, 171–2, 173, 169n, 201,
Pls. VIB, VIIA

Othello, **21,** 1–12, 13–29, 31–8, 39–
46, 47–52, 53–65, 67–77, 79–86,
87–96, 115, 136, 141, 149, 159,
160, 163, Pls. IIIC, VIII; **22,** 97–8,
125, 127, 129–30, 133, 154, 156,
161, 167, 177, 178, 179, 180; **23,**
23, 25, 31, 32, 34, 35, 97–8, 116,
120, 140, 151–3, 162, 173, 176,
179; **24,** 41–2, 85n, 141, 146, 152,
153, 170, 171, 175, 178; **25,** 23,
69, 76n, 172, 181, 194, 196, 197,
Pl. v; **26,** 56, 129, 151, 159, 162,
163n, 176, 179; **27,** 43, 143, 148n,
157, 172, 179; **28,** 149, 154–5, 167,
172, 175, 176, 180, 181; **29,** 8, 52,
58, 82, 88, 89, 118, 123, 139, 142,
164, 166, 169; **30,** 16, 17, 21, 100n,
187, 189, 192, 194, 200, 206, 207

Pericles, **21,** 147, 150, 152, 162;
22, 25, 43, 59, 61–5, 67, 95, 98,
145, 163, 164, 174, 176; **23,** 1n,
5, 10, 132, 133, 180, Pl. III;
24, 28–30, 105–16, 150, 151, 155,
174; **25,** 85, 137, 145, 149, 150,
151, 158n, 177, 200; **26,** 33, 44⁶
46, 47, 64, 65, 66, 130n, 163, 179;
27, 80, 175, 186; **28,** 59, 146, 167,
181; **29,** 2, 6, 7, 8, 11–20, 21–32,

67, 74, 165, 166, 171; **30,** 6, 147,
155, 185, 203, 205–6

Richard II, **21,** 13, 26, 108, 109, 115,
132, 141, 142, 147, 151, 152,
Pl. IV; **22,** 99, 148, 155; **23,** 8, 10,
18, 24, 25, 69–78, 120, 138, 142,
145, 146, 147, 182; **24,** 15, 21–2,
27, 49, 141, 142, 153; **25,** 64, 167,
168–9, 170, 173–4, 194, 195, 197,
198, Pl. VI; **26,** 105n, 152, 155,
156, 175, 179; **27,** 1n, 21, 33–41,
144, 146, 151, 152, 161, 180, 186,
Pls. VI, VII; **28,** 1–13, 46, 138,
141, 158–9; **29,** 160, 170, 175;
30, 7, 18, 20, 65, 185, 199

Richard III, **21,** 141, 149, 159, 160;
22, 125, 127, 128–9, 130, 132,
133, 148, 151, 155, 170, 176, 179,
181; **23,** 8, 56, 114, 142, 145, 158,
173, 179; **24,** 32, 42, 76, 83n, 106,
118, 119–20, 129, 171, 177; **25,**
102, 158n, 184, 185, 193–4,
195–6, 197–8; **26,** 69, 131n, 132n,
134n, 157, 158n, 179, 183; **27,** 1n,
18, 21–32, 132, 133, 135n, 186;
28, 46, 141n, 151, 157, 158, 171;
29, 84, 86, 87, 118, 121, 136, 153,
159, 160, 174, 176; **30,** 7, 16, 18,
206n, 209

Romeo and Juliet, **21,** 25, 40, 43,
107, 109, 128, 156, 157; **22,** 125–6,
127, 130, 131, 133, 151, 152, 156,
167, 182, 183; **23,** 1, 2, 3, 6–7, 8,
9, 10, 17, 18, 25, 27, 34, 35, 47,
80, 83, 95, 108, 117, 118, 120,
122, 142, 143, 167n; **24,** 40,
63–9, 85n, 128, 137, 142, 170,
174, 176; **25,** 7, 20, 51, 64, 73–80,
98, 127, 171, 182, 200; **26,** 41,
126, 131, 134n, 135, 137, 152,
163n, 172, 179, 184n; **27,** 1–9,
131, 135n, 137, 144, 146, 150,
191, Pls. V, VIII; **28,** 56, 149, 153,
174, 177, 180, 181; **29,** 52, 82,
120, 163, 164, 174; **30,** 7, 18, 169,
170, 179n, 193, 194, 200, 206,
208, 209

Taming of the Shrew, The, **21,** 107,
130, 131, 147, 150–1; **22,** 125,
127, 129, 151, 152, 153, 178–9;
23, 4, 10, 93–4, 143, 185; **24,** 142,
156; **25,** 179; **26,** 104, 106; **27,** 2,
106, 107, 108, 109, 132, 135,
136, 142, 146; **28,** 77, 78, 160,
172, 178; **30,** 183, 209

Tempest, The, **21,** 25, 127, 128, 140,
153; **22,** 2, 29, 48–53, 56, 62, 98,
127, 164–5, 176, 178; **23,** 29, 80,
111, 149, 156, 157, 173, 175n,
177n; **24,** 30, 33, 46, 105, 106,
112, 117, 129, 130, 131, 150, 151,

167, 168, 178; **25,** 83, 91, 113–23,
125–35, 177–8, Pls. I, II; **26,** 33,
34, 42, 46, 48, 64, 66, 111n, 130,
153, 163, 168; **27,** 60, 88, 89,
108, 162, 167, 170, 172, 183, 184,
191; **28,** 36, 37, 38n, 54, 59,
117–23, 137, 159, 160, 161; **29,** 1,
2, 5, 6, 7, 9, 10, 63–7, 74, 77, 83,
138, 158, 159, 165, 169, 176, 184;
30, 7, 27, 120, 121, 147–55, 182,
190, 191, 193, 195, 197, 202, 206n

Timon of Athens, **21,** 2, 3, 25, 88,
138, 146, 147, 148, 150, 152, 158;
22, 156, 162; **23,** 4, 16, 24, 98–
100, 119, 138, 140, 141, 154–5,
159, 180; **25,** 2, 63, 198; **26,** 8, 9,
58, 59, 60, 89–94, 106, 156, 160;
27, 111–27; **28,** 157, 165; **29,** 84,
103–16, 119, 120, 122; **30,** 203,
207

Titus Andronicus, **21,** 71, 88, 107,
150; **22,** 93, 94, 151, 167; **23,** 9,
10, 35, 121, 123, 138, 142–3,
161n, 180; **24,** 148, 153, 175;
25, 176, 188; **26,** 98, 108, 141,
142, 148–50, 151, 152, 159, 160,
179; **27,** 1–9, 11–19, 135, 136,
159, 191; **28,** 71–4, 155, 180;
29, 118, 121, 163, 170, 185; **30,**
18, 103, 104, 193, 203

Troilus and Cressida, 11n, 113, 131,
134, 141, 150, 155, 160, 161; **22,**
5, 32, 137–8, 139, 142–4, 154,
156, 159–60, 164, 166, 168, 176,
Pl. VI, VII; **23,** 6, 9, 13, 15, 17, 19,
20, 23, 24, 33, 55, 60, 97, 117,
140, 150, 161, 179; **24,** 148, 150,
152, 153, 170, 174, 175; **25,** 1, 2,
6, 7, 8, 9, 10, 11–25, 63, 64,
67–8, 69, 70, 174, 175, 176, 184,
196, 197; **26,** 7, 9, 38, 90, 100,
155, 159, 179; **27,** 22, 59n, 69,
119, 127, 166, 176; **28,** 39, 48, 49,
112, 162, 168, 177; **29,** 8, 9, 82,
83, 84, 87, 121, 162–3, 181, 184,
185; **30,** 6, 7, 87n, 88, 136, 174–6,
179n, 184, 186, 192, Pl. VIIIA

Twelfth Night, **21,** 128, 130, 131,
139, 152; **22,** 7, 11, 12, 44, 150,
153, 154, 178; **23,** 7, 15, 28–9, 47,
71, 132, 133, 134–5, 140, 144,
151, Pl. v; **24,** 24, 29, 172; **25,** 50,
63, 64, 86, 109, 161, 164, 166–7,
171, 178, 179, 190; **26,** 111n, 135,
152, 154; **27,** 82, 91, 107n, 108,
110, 131, 141, 165, 166, 172, 189,
192; **28,** 77, 78, 79, 80, 137, 144,
159, 162, Pl. III, IV; **29,** 42, 43,
44, 46, 137, 141, 143–4, 161, 162,
173, 175, 177, 179, 180; **30,** 5,
122, 182, 184, 206n

plays (*cont.*)

Two Gentlemen of Verona, The, **21**, 131; **22**, 35–41, 151, 152, 153, 177; **23**, 6, 91, 138, 143, 177n, 178, 180–1; **24**, 120, 129, 149, 160n, 176; **25**, 179; **26**, 104, 106; **27**, 108, 109, 131, 142, 163, 184, 188, 189; **28**, 46, 75, 76, 77, 78–9, 80, 161, 174; **29**, 9, 162, 180; **30**, 83

Winter's Tale, The, **21**, 127, 131, 140, 141, 152, 153, 162; **22**, 25, 48, 49, 50, 59–60, 63–6, 93–107, 164, 176; **23**, 17, 19, 25, 26, 32, 35, 59, 99n, 133–4, 138, 139, 155–6, 182, 183, 186, Pl. VII; **24**, 13n, 16, 33–5, 46, 105, 108, 138, 150, 151, 172, 173; **25**, 91, 95n, 177; **26**, 33, 34, 38, 42, 45–6, 47–8, 64, 65–6, 91, 106, 111n, 132, 136, 153, 163, 164n; **27**, 57, 86, 89, 103, 108, 137, 139, 167, 168, 179, 180, 184; **28**, 59, 163, 166, 180; **29**, 1, 2, 4, 6, 7, 8, 9, 51n, 65, 67–8, 123, 165, 169; **30**, 7, 19, 27, 79, 147, 148, 150, 154, 173–4, 179n, 184, 195, 202, 205, Pl. VIIB

poems

Lover's Complaint, A, **21**, 146; **27**, 178

Passionate Pilgrim, The, **22**, 176, 182; **26**, 103–9

Phoenix and the Turtle, The, **21**, 140; **24**, 153; **26**, 164; **28**, 163

Rape of Lucrece, The, **22**, 151, 176, 181; **23**, 2, 10, 30, 54–6, 58, 71, 73, 76, 121, 157; **24**, 139, 169; **26**, 177; **27**, 2, 178; **29**, 166; **30**, 6, 185

Sonnets, **21**, 97–105, 128, 140, 147, 148, 153, 162; **22**, 79–92, 164, 165, 181, 182; **23**, 10, 69–78, 142, 157–8, 160, 176; **24**, 15, 16, 38, 138, 151, 153, 154, 157; **27**, 179; **28**, 49, 78, 80n, 149, 163; **29**, 175, 181–2; **30**, 6, 90, 100, 181–2

Venus and Adonis, **21**, 149, 153; **22**, 151, 176, 181; **23**, 10, 71, 73, 121, 157, 186; **25**, 3, 102; **26**, 103–9, 164, 172–3; **27**, 2, 130n, 156, 178; **28**, 163; **29**, 45; **30**, 189

Shalvi, Alice, **23**, 138; **27**, 176

Shand, George, **24**, 160

Shanker, Sidney, **30**, 182

Shapiro, I. A., **21**, 142, 145, 155; **23**, 172

Shapiro, Michael, **25**, 192

Shapiro, Stephen A., **21**, 138

Sharma, R. C., **29**, 164

Shattuck, Charles H., **24**, 100n, 168; **25**, 115n, 119n; **28**, 174; **30**, 199

Shaw, D. J., **23**, 163n

Shaw, George Bernard, **21**, 113; **22**, 2, 3, 4, 8, 79; **23**, 39, 175; **24**, 37, 38, 40, 42, 154, 168; **25**, 1, 11, 45, 117, 166; **26**, 3; **27**, 34n; **28**, 143; **29**, 133, 134, 137, 145; **30**, 83

Shaw, Glen Byam, **27**, 145

Shaw, John, **21**, 136, 139; **22**, 173; **28**, 157

Shaw, Sebastian, **22**, 138, 142, 143; **24**, 117, 122, 123; **25**, 65

Shearman, John, **28**, 153

Sheavyn, Phoebe, **22**, 169

Sheldon, Esther K., **22**, 174

Shelton, Thomas, **28**, 59

Sheppard, Morgan, **25**, 169

Shepperd, John, **30**, 162

Sherbo, Arthur, **23**, 175n; **25**, 45n; **28**, 90n

Sherburne, Edward, **30**, 161n

Shergold, N. D., **23**, 79n, 84n

Sheridan, Richard, **22**, 2

Sheridan, Thomas, **22**, 174

Sheriff, W. E., **26**, 158

Sherley, John, **25**, 148

Sherley, Lorraine, **21**, 156

Sherley, Robert, **29**, 24

Sherley, Sir Anthony, **29**, 23–4, 32

Sherman, S. P., **26**, 4

Sherwin, Walter K., **29**, 174

Shingler, Rebecca, **29**, 34, 37

Shingler, Thomas, **29**, 34, 37

Shirley, James, **26**, 5; **30**, 36n

Shore, Jane, **29**, 174

Short, Peter, **26**, 183

Shrimpton, Nick, 'Directing *The Tempest*', **29**, 63–7

Shuman, S., **25**, 188

Shvedov, Y., **23**, 152

Sibley, John, **21**, 143, 152

Sickermann, C. M., **27**, 160

Sider, John W., **26**, 173; **27**, 162

Siddons, Mrs Sarah, **22**, 174; **24**, 43; **29**, 135, 146, 148

Sider, John W., **26**, 173; **27**, 162

Sidgwick, Frank, **30**, 202

Sidney, Sir Philip, **21**, 48, 67; **22**, 38, 155, 170, 171; **23**, 92, 93, 99, 165–6; **24**, 24, 153, 159; **26**, 7, 174; **27**, 117n, 168, 169, 172; **28**, 49, 55, 57, 59, 66, 76; **29**, 4, 8, 170

Siegel, Paul N., **23**, 139; **27**, 81n, 91n; **28**, 159; **29**, 88n

Siegmund-Schultze, Dorothea, **23**, 150

Siemon, James Edward, **25**, 179; **27**, 162; **28**, 163; **29**, 67, 69

'Noble Virtue in *Cymbeline*', **29**, 51–61

Silverman, J. M., **27**, 166

Simmes, Valentine, **26**, 177, 184; **27**, 180, 181, 186, 187; **29**, 182

Simmons, J. L., **23**, 148; **24**, 147, 152; **26**, 165; **28**, 157, 169n

'*Antony and Cleopatra* and *Coriolanus*, Shakespeare's Heroic Tragedies: A Jacobean Adjustment', **26**, 95–101

Simmons, Joseph, **22**, 128, 129–31

Simons, Joseph, **27**, 178

Simons, R. T., **29**, 166

Simpson, Percy and Evelyn, **25**, 100n; **26**, 39n; **27**, 112n, 118, 120, 123, 124, 125, 126

Sinden, Donald, **23**, 131, 132; **30**, 169, 172

Sinfield, Alan, **30**, 188

Singer, S. W., **23**, 102

Singleton, Charles S., **27**, 56n

Sipahigil, T., **25**, 181; **26**, 162, 172; **28**, 167; **30**, 202

Sipe, Dorothy L., **22**, 150

Sisk, John P., **23**, 144; **26**, 162

Siskin, Clifford

'Freedom and Loss in *The Tempest*', **30**, 147–55

Sisson, Charles J., **25**, 2, 4, 5, 94n; **26**, 170; **28**, 38n, 117; **29**, 22–3, 81

Sjoberg, Elsa, **23**, 147

Sjögren, G., **21**, 149, 163; **22**, 168; **24**, 166n

'Thomas Bull and other "English Instrumentalists" in Denmark in the 1580s', **22**, 119–24

Skeat, W. W., **29**, 104n

Skein, Valentinn, **22**, 120, 123

Skelton, John, **23**, 165; **28**, 21

Skulsky, Harold, **21**, 136–7; **24**, 143; **28**, 154

Slater, Ann Pasternak, **27**, 170

'Variations Within a Source: from Isaiah XXIX to *The Tempest*' **25**, 125–35

Slater, Eliot, **27**, 178; **29**, 172, 185; **30**, 182

Sledd, James, **23**, 141n

Slights, C., **28**, 162

Small, R. A., **27**, 122n

Smallwood, R. L., **27**, 166; **28**, 178

'The Design of *All's Well That Ends Well*', **25**, 45–61

Smart, J. S., **25**, 187

Smidt, Kristian, **23**, 154, 179n; **24**, 163; **25**, 193–4

Smith, A. Hassell, **28**, 18n

Smith, A. J., **24**, 164

Smith, Alan, **23**, 163n

Smith, Bruce R., **30**, 192

Smith, Denzell S., **22**, 154; **26**, 158

Smith, Derek, **27**, 147, 149

Smith, G. C. Moore, **29**, 111n

Smith, Hallett, **22**, 167; **25**, 99n, 105, 26, 112n; **27**, 168; **28**, 174; **29**, 4, 5, 8, 9, 11n; **30**, 148n, 201

Smith, Henry, **28**, 166

Smith, Irwin, **22**, 173; **23**, 158; **25**, 178
Smith, J., **28**, 160
Smith, J. C., **27**, 96n
Smith, J. Oates, **22**, 159; **25**, 14n
Smith, Jonathan, **23**, 156
Smith, J. P., **27**, 163
Smith, Lucy Toulmin, **21**, 65n
Smith, Marion Bodwell, **21**, 128; **29**, 89
Smith, Peter D., **24**, 167
Smith, Sir Thomas, **28**, 63, 64, 68n; **29**, 93
Smith, Warren D., **22**, 152; **24**, 67; **25**, 5; **30**, 197
Smith, W. J., **25**, 137n
Smithers, G. V., **25**, 184
   'Guide-Lines for Interpreting the Uses of the Suffix "-ed" in Shakespeare's English', **23**, 27–37
Smithson, Harriet, **21**, 80; **30**, 200
Smyth, Richard, **27**, 102
Snowden, John, **21**, 99–100, 105
Snyder, F. E., **28**, 170
Snyder, Susan, **25**, 182
Socrates, **22**, 3
Soellner, Rolf, **23**, 141; **24**, 150
Soens, Adolph L., **22**, 170; **23**, 143, 153, 172; **24**, 166; **25**, 181
Sohm, Rudolf, **28**, 53
Somers, **21**, 103
Somers, William, **26**, 72
Somerset, Earl of, **27**, 100; **28** 23
Somerset, J. A. B., **30**, 192, 198
   'Falstaff, the Prince, and the Pattern of 2 Henry IV', **30**, 35–45
Somma, **21**, 88
Sommer, H. O., **26**, 78n
Sommers, Alan, **27**, 11n
Sonnenschein, E. A., **22**, 117n
Sonnino, Lee, A., **23**, 164
Sophocles, **21**, 75, 77; **22**, 50, 158, 163, 164; **24**, 84n; **30**, 104, 105–6, 112, 113, 115
Sorelius, Gunnar, **21**, 156; **25**, 192; **28**, 179
Sotheby, William, **24**, 44
Soulié, Frédéric, **30**, 200
Southall, Raymond, **25**, 13n, 15n
Southampton, Mary, Countess, of, **21**, 97, 100, 103, 104; **23**, 160; **24**, 154
Southampton, Third Earl of, (Henry Wriothesley), **21**, 97, 104, 141; **23**, 43, 160; **24**, 151; **26**, 108; **27**, 129n; **28**, 165
Southern, Richard, **27**, 174–5; **28**, 130, 131n; **29**, 129, 130n, 131n
Southey, Robert, **23**, 104
Southwell, Robert, **28**, 166
Spakowski, R. E., **25**, 176
Spalding, T. A., **29**, 79, 83
Spangenberg, Heidemarie, **23**, 123
Spargo, J. W., **30**, 35

Speaight, Robert W., **23**, 174n; **24**, 167; **25**, 1n, 117n; **26**, 175, 176n; **29**, 87
Spearing, A. C. and J. E., **30**, 206n
Spedding, J., **28**, 16n
Speed, John, **30**, 163n
Spencer, Christopher, **21**, 156; **24**, 167; **26**, 181
Spencer, Lois, **22**, 168
Spencer, Theodore, **25**, 8, 11n, 13n; **27**, 51n, 56n; **29**, 85, 86
Spencer, T. J. B. (Terence), **21**, 129, 150, 157; **22**, 168; **23**, 141; **24**, 53, 64n; **26**, 89, 166; **29**, 115; **30**, 97n
Spenser, Edmund, **22**, 51, 166, 170; **23**, 21, 23, 61, 98, 166; **25**, 103, 105, 138; **26**, 107, 114n; **27**, 96, 99–100, 109, 117n, 169, 172, 191; **28**, 20, 41n, 76, 78, 122; **29**, 173
Spevack, Marvin, **22**, 157, 176; **23**, 176, 177; **25**, 94, 199; **28**, 177, 178; **29**, 183, 184; **30**, 89n, 90n, 95n, 209
Spiker, S., **25**, 145n
Spillane, Mickey, **27**, 177
Spingarn, J. E., **21**, 46n
Spivack, Bernard, **21**, 3, 33, 53, 54, 57, 58, 61; **23**, 152; **26**, 7, 171; **27**, 23n; **30**, 36, 41n
Spivack, Charlotte, **22**, 171
Sprague, Arthur C., **21**, 156; **22**, 133n, 165; **24**, 120; **25**, 185; **26**, 114n; **27**, 34n; **28**, 171; **30**, 91n
Sprenger, J., **28**, 119
Spriet, Pierre, **23**, 166–7
Spriggs, Elizabeth, **22**, 139; **23**, 131; **25**, 166
Sprinchorn, Evert, **24**, 166n
Sprott, S. E., **24**, 157n
Spurgeon, Caroline, **21**, 11n, 107; **22**, 162; **24**, 26; **28**, 30, 32, 35
Spurgeon, F. E., **25**, 8
Spurling, Hilary, **30**, 173n
Stabler, A. P., **21**, 152; **29**, 171
Stadler, Edmund, **29**, 176
Staebler, W., **29**, 164
Stafford, T. J., **26**, 154, 180n, 184n
Stahl, H., **23**, 13n
Stalder, Verena, **23**, 156
Stallo, J., **24**, 97
Stamm, Rudolph, **22**, 159; **23**, 114; **25**, 12n, 14n, 23n, 24n, 174n; **26**, 166n
Stampfer, Judah, **29**, 89
Stanford, D., **26**, 165
Stanford, Henry, **28**, 174
Stanislavsky, Konstantin, **23**, 174; **24**, 167; **26**, 140; **27**, 144; **29**, 153; **30**, 13n, 16, 26
Stanton, Barry, **28**, 148
Stanyhurst, R., **23**, 164–5
Staples, Jasper, **25**, 148

Stark, James, **22**, 133
Stark, Mrs James, **22**, 133
Starnes, De Witt T., **26**, 112n
Starr, G. A., **22**, 109
States, B. O., **28**, 153
Stauffer, Donald A., **27**, 22n
Staunford, J., **29**, 100
Stavig, Mark, **23**, 171; **24**, 165
Staviski, Aron Y., **24**, 153
Stedefeld, G. F., **28**, 40, 41n
Steevens, George, **25**, 111n; **27**, 69, 111n, 112, 119; **29**, 111n
Stehlíková, Eva, **21**, 134
Stein, Arnold, **23**, 150
Steiner, George, **30**, 88
Steiner, Grundy, **21**, 142; **24**, 20
Stellmacher, Wolfgang, **21**, 149; **22**, 166
Stempel, Daniel, **23**, 152
Stendhal, **21**, 81, 82
Stensgaard, Richard K., **26**, 172
Štěpanék, Vladimír, **21**, 140
Stephanus, Robert, **24**, 53
Sterne, Richard L., **23**, 174n
Sterling, John, **28**, 40
Sternfeld, F. W., **22**, 178; **23**, 183; **24**, 112n, 156; **26**, 173; **29**, 2
Sternlicht, Sanford, **21**, 134; **27**, 177
Stetner, S. C. V., **25**, 200
Stevens, Martin, **24**, 160; **30**, 188
Stevenson, David Lloyd, **21**, 52n, 135; **25**, 7, 29; **28**, 93n
Stevenson, Robert, **26**, 71, 72
Stewart, B. T., **26**, 161
Stewart, J. I. M., **21**, 4, 9–10; **22**, 65; **27**, 45n, 159
Stewart of Bothwellhaugh, **24**, 156
Stewart, Patrick, **24**, 117, 121; **26**, 143, 145, 157
Still, Colin, **29**, 9
Stirling, Brents, **21**, 22, 25; **23**, 157–8; **24**, 12; **27**, 39n
Stockholder, Katherine S., **23**, 150; **24**, 148; **28**, 154
Stocking, F. H., **26**, 164
Stodder, Joseph H., **28**, 172
Stoll, E. E., **21**, 9, 11n, 16, 24, 137; **22**, 146, 166; **23**, 159; **29**, 137; **30**, 109, 148n
Stone, Francis, **25**, 147
Stone, Harlan F., **27**, 104
Stone, Lawrence, **24**, 47n; **29**, 90
Stoppard, Tom, **26**, 175; **30**, 97
Storey, Graham, **27**, 31n
Storozhenko, Nicolai Ilyich, **23**, 175
Storr, F., **30**, 113n
Story, Richard, **29**, 33
Stovell, J., **27**, 98
Stow, John, **23**, 45; **27**, 131; **28**, 1, 3; **30**, 69n, 164n
Stowe, J., **26**, 81n
Strachey, Lytton, **29**, 138

Strachey, William, 25, 127n, 128, 131
Strang, B. M. H., 23, 23n
Strange's Men, 27, 129, 134, 136; 30, 202
Straumann, Heinrich, 28, 172
Streete, Peter, 29, 130
Streitberger, W. R., 30, 189
Stříbrný, Zdeněk, 21, 129, 153n; 22, 166; 28, 158; 29, 90, 160
Stride, John, 27, 138
Strindberg, A., 24, 8
Strong, Roy, 24, 158n; 28, 170; 30, 157n, 167n
Stroup, T. B., 26, 17n
Strype, John, 30, 164n
Stuart, Betty Kantor, 22, 162
Studing, Richard, 25, 177
Stürzl, Erwin, 21, 144
Styan, J. L., 22, 173
Suchet, David, 27, 149, 151; 28, 140, 142
Suddard, Mary, 27, 18
Summers, Montague, 28, 119n
Suerbaum, E., 26, 157, 166n
Suerbaum, Ulrich, 30, 208
Suetonius, 22, 109; 27, 119
Summerson, John, 30, 158n
Sussex's Men, 27, 134, 135, 136
Sutcliffe, Matthew, 30, 63, 64
Sutherland, James, 29, 41, 46n
Suzman, Janet, 22, 138–9; 26, 147, 149
Swaminathan, S. R., 24, 156
Swander, Homer D., 24, 168; 29, 5, 53n, 55n–6n, 60n
Swift, Clive, 25, 48
Swift, Jonathan, 26, 92
Swigg, R., 22, 162
Swinburne, A. C., 21, 3; 23, 94, 95; 24, 154; 26, 3
Swinburne, Henry, 28, 52, 53
Swinden, Patrick, 28, 160; 29, 6
Sybant, Abraham, 28, 172
Sykes, Dugdale, 25, 137n, 138n
Symonds, J. A., 26, 3
Synge, J. M., 26, 139, 140
Szenczi, Miklos, 21, 129

Taborski, Boleslaw, 22, 159; 25, 19n
Tacitus, 28, 67
Tagore, Rabindranath, 29, 167
Takei, N., 26, 160
Talbert, Ernest William, 22, 148, 155; 26, 112n
Tallis, T., 24, 158
Talma, François Joseph, 21, 79; 24, 85, 86
Tannenbaum, Samuel A., 26, 81, 82, 83, 85n, 86; 28, 37n, 38
Tanner, Alice, 25, 143
Tanselle, G. Thomas, 24, 177; 26, 180
Tarlton, Richard, 22, 38, 39, 40, 42; 23, 114; 27, 133, 136; 28, 133n
Tate, Nahum, 22, 131; 23, 153; 26, 34; 28, 138; 30, 194

Tatlock, J. S. P., 25, 9
Tauber, Anne-Marie, 23, 115
Taubert, 25, 116
Taylerson, Marilyn, 30, 173, 174
Taylor, A. B., 23, 161n, 166; 24, 162
Taylor, G. C., 28, 37n, 38n, 40n, 41; 29, 79, 81
Taylor, John, 25, 188
Taylor, Michael, 23, 143; 24, 143; 25, 181, 182; 26, 163; 27, 164, 165; 28, 152, 156
Taylor, Mrs Maria, 22, 128–32
Taylor, Myron, 23, 149
Taylor, Neil, 25, 179; 26, 184; 27, 188
Taylor, Robert, 29, 32n
Taylor, Rupert, 27, 132n
'T.B.', 21, 48
Tchertkoff, V., 23, 39
Teliver, Harold E., 21, 144
Tennyson, Alfred Lord, 24, 39
Terence, 22, 3, 4; 24, 150; 30, 192
Terry, Ellen, 28, 143
Thaler, A., 23, 93n, 99n
Thaler, Brigitte, 23, 115
Theobald, Lewis, 24, 155, 178; 25, 187, 198; 26, 71, 72, 181, 182, 184; 27, 187, 192; 28, 177; 29, 124, 179
Thibaudet, A., 28, 44n
Thirlby, Styan, 26, 181n, 182
Thomas, Charles, 23, 131, 132
Thomas, Helen, 24, 161
Thomas, Keith, 28, 118
Thomas, M. O., 26, 157
Thomas, Sidney, 21, 148; 28, 181; 30, 208
'The Queen Mab Speech in Romeo and Juliet', 25, 73–80
Thomson, A. Landesborough, 21, 142n
Thomson, James, 24, 17
Thomson, Patricia, 21, 147; 23, 150; 25, 8
Thomson, Peter, The Royal Shakespeare Season 1970, reviewed, 24, 117–26
'No Rome of Safety': The Royal Shakespeare Season 1972, reviewed, 26, 139–50
'Shakespeare Straight and Crooked': a Review of the 1973 Season at Stratford, 27, 143–54
'The Smallest Season': The Royal Shakespeare Company at Stratford in 1974, reviewed, 28, 137–48
'Towards a Poor Shakespeare': the Royal Shakespeare Company at Stratford in 1975, reviewed, 29, 151–6
Thompson, Ann, 30, 193, 195–6
Thompson, E. Maunde, 28, 38n
Thompson, Karl F., 21, 134; 22, 160; 26, 159–60
Thoreau, Henry David, 24, 87, 88, 103, 104

Thorne, B., 26, 153
Thorne, J. P., 26, 164
Thorne, S. E., 29, 93n
Thorne, William Barry, 23, 155; 25, 177; 29, 11n
Thornton, Frank, 28, 144, 145
Thornton, R. K. R., 24, 165
Thorpe, James, 26, 180
Thorpe, Thomas, 21, 97, 102, 104; 22, 182; 23, 160
Thorvaldsen, B., 29, 145, 146
Thrale, Mrs, 26, 168
Thumboo, Edwin, 25, 181
Thynne, Francis, 24, 66n
Tide, Andreas, 22, 123
Tieck, Dorothea, 26, 166
Tieck, Ludwig, 23, 122; 29, 175
Tierney, Margaret, 26, 141n
Tilley, M. P., 27, 189
Tillotson, Kathleen, 29, 182
Tillyard, E. M. W., 21, 135; 22, 10, 14n, 72, 79, 80, 84, 148, 155, 159; 23, 145; 24, 55n. 56n; 25, 2, 3, 6; 27, 11n, 12n; 28, 2, 89; 29, 84, 85, 88; 30, 47
Tintoretto, 26, 49, 50, 51, 52, 53, 55, 64, 65
Titian, 26, 52; 27, 55
Tobias, R. C., 29, 165
Tobin, Terence, 23, 173n
Todd, D. K. C., 29, 164
Toliver, Harold E., 27, 27n
Tolkien, J. R. R., 30, 82
Tolman, Albert H., 27, 106–7, 108
Tolstoy, Leo, 21, 113; 22, 147; 28, 30, 55
Tomlinson, Philip, 24, 38n
Tomlinson, T. B., 26, 7, 8
Tompkins, Eugene, 24, 99n
Tonson, Jacob, 27, 191
Toole, William B., 22, 159; 25, 2; 26, 29, 160
'The Motif of Psychic Division in Richard III', 27, 21–32
Toppen, W. H., 21, 137
Tough, A. J., 26, 162
Tourneur, Cyril, 22, 137, 171; 26, 7, 41, 55, 57, 153; 29, 170
Townshend, Aurelian, 28, 169
Traci, P. J., 26, 158–9
Traherne, Thomas, 23, 167
Trautvetter, Christine, 24, 149; 27, 189
Traversi, Derek A., 21, 142; 22, 158; 23, 132, 133, 140–1; 25, 1n, 2; 25, 5, 8, 12n, 13n; 27, 72; 29, 59; 30, 52n
Tree, Herbert Beerbohm, 25, 113, 118–23; 26, 142; 27, 34n; 28, 172; 29, 134, 135, 139, 143; 30, 200
Tree, Viola, 25, 119
Trevelyan, C. E., 23, 44n
Trevelyan, W. C., 23, 44n

Trevor-Roper, Hugh, **29**, 90
Trewin, J. C., **23**, 131; **25**, 1n, 115n
Tricomi, Albert H., **26**, 173; **29**, 163
  'The Aesthetics of Mutilation in *Titus Andronicus*', **27**, 11–19
Tristram, E. W., **26**, 74, 75n
Tromley, F. B., **29**, 165
Trousdale, Marion, **28**, 168
Truffaut, François, **26**, 175
Tucker, E. F. J., 'The Letter of the Law in *The Merchant of Venice*', **29**, 93–101
Tucker-Brooke, C. F., **23**, 51n, 69, 72n
Türck, Susanne, **28**, 37n, 39, 40n, 41
Turner, F., **26**, 151
Turner, Godfrey, **26**, 114
Turner, Myron, **26**, 174n
Turner, R. W., **29**, 97n
Turner, R. Y., **25**, 3n; **29**, 159–60
Turner, Victor, **29**, 18n
Turner, William, **23**, 45
Tutin, Dorothy, **22**, 140; **28**, 144
Tuve, Rosemond, **21**, 145n; **23**, 87
Twain, Mark, **24**, 99
Twine, Laurence, **24**, 108, 111; **29**, 30
Tybbes, William, **23**, 144
Tynan, Kenneth, **30**, 21–2, 23, 26
Tyzack, Margaret, **26**, 144, 149

Uchigama, Takato, **22**, 155
Uffenback, Zacharias von, **30**, 165
Uhlig, Claus, **22**, 168; **23**, 119, 144, 161; **29**, 184n
Underwood, R. A., **28**, 163
Ungerer, Friedrich, **23**, 116
Upham, A. H., **28**, 39n, 40n
Uphaus, R., **26**, 163
Urban, Raymond A., **30**, 202
Ure, Peter, **21**, 134, 151; **22**, 71n; **24**, 165; **25**, 2; **26**, 5, 9; **27**, 33n, 34n, 38n; **28**, 46
Usher, Roland G., **28**, 65
Usurer, William, **29**, 33, 34
Utterback, R. V., **28**, 153; **30**, 202

Vaghan (Vaughan), Justice, **25**, 144
Valck, Gerard, **23**, 165n
Valency, Maurice, **28**, 76n
Valéry, Paul, **23**, 176
Vallone, A., **24**, 162n
Vančura, Zdeněk, **21**, 129
Van Dam, B. A. P., **25**, 77
Van den Berg, Kent Talbot, **30**, 183
Van den Branden, L., **29**, 32n
Vanderhoof, Mary, **24** 80n
Van Der Niss, I. W., **23**, 186
Vandersee, Charles, **24**, 87ff, 93n; **26**, 116
  'The Hamlet in Henry Adams', **24**, 87–104
Van Dijk, Maarten, **29**, 176

Van Doren, Mark, **23**, 148; **24**, 4n; **28**, 10; **30**, 47, 58n
Van Dyck, Sir Anthony, **24**, 158; **28**, 24
Van Dyke, Joyce, 'Making a Scene: Language and Gesture in *Coriolanus*', **30**, 135–46
Van Emden, W. G., **29**, 170
Van Eerde, Katherine S., **23**, 162
Van Gogh, Vincent, **22**, 99
Van Laan, Thomas F., **21**, 133
Van Nassau-Sarolea, Annie, **28**, 172
Van Tieghem, Ph., **24**, 85n
Varey, J. E., **23**, 79n, 84n
Varma, R. S., **27**, 190
Vawter, M., **28**, 156
Vasari, **26**, 112n
Velz, John W., **22**, 174; **23**, 149, 169, 174, 186; **24**, 156, 167, 168; **25**, 175; **26**, 181; **27**, 59n, 160, 179; **29**, 170, 176
  'Clemency, Will, and Just Cause in *Julius Caesar*', **22**, 109–18
Velz, Sarah C., **27**, 167; **28**, 91n; **29**, 170, 176
  'Man's Need and God's Plan in *Measure for Measure* and Mark IV', **25**, 37–44
Vendryes, J., **23**, 28n
Verdi, Giuseppe, **21**, 6, 87–96
Vergil, **22**, 147; **23**, 36, 65; **25**, 125, 128 172; **29**, 5; **30**, 61
Vergil, Polydore, **24**, 174; **27**, 28n
Veronese, Paolo, **21**, 52n
Verplanck, Gulian, **27**, 106n
Verrocchio, **26**, 116n
Vespucci, Amerigo, **30**, 194
Vickers, Brian, **22**, 149–50, 168; **24**, 40, 173; **27**, 83; **28**, 164; **29**, 167; **30**, 189, 200
Vida, M. G., **23**, 83
Villarejo, Oscar M., **22**, 167
Villey, Pierre, **28**, 37, 38n, 40n
Vincent, E. R. P., **27**, 46n
Viswanathan, S., **24**, 152; **30**, 201
Vitruvius, **24**, 166
Vives, **29**, 159
Vivis, Anthony, **23**, 174n
Vočadlo, O., **21**, 142
Voitl, Herbert, **24**, 153
Voltaire, **24**, 79, 81, 84; **25**, 185; **28**, 30
Vos, Jan, **24**, 156
Voskerchian, Haig, **24**, 169n
Vyvyan, John, **23**, 83; **28**, 80; **29**, 91

Waad, Armigail, **25**, 15n
Waddington, Raymond, B., **21**, 138; **23**, 59n, 170n
Wadsworth, Frank W., **21**, 156
Wain, John, **23**, 132
Waith, Eugene M., **25**, 189; **26**, 6, 99; **27**, 11n, 16, 111n

Wakefield Cycle, **21**, 55
Walcutt, Charles C., **21**, 133
Waldo, T. R., **29**, 166
Walkeley, Thomas, **26**, 181
Walker, Alice, **23**, 177; **24**, 172; **25**, 9, 13n, 67, 196, 198; **27**, 183; **29**, 118n, 181
Walker, Frank, **21**, 96n
Walker, Ralph S., **22**, 118n
Walker, Roy, **22**, 116n
Wallace, C. W., **25**, 138
Wallack, J. W., **21**, 80
Waller, D., **22**, 133
Waller, David, **22**, 142; **24**, 119, 122; **28**, 144, 145; **30**, 170, 175
Waller, Emma, **22**, 133
Waller, G. F., **25**, 177
Waller, Lewis, **29**, 136, 142
Walley, Henry, **21**, 161; **25**, 7; **26**, 33n; **29**, 184
Walsh, W., **24**, 1n
Walsingham, Lord, **23**, 41; **28**, 20, 23
Walter, J. H., **21**, 111, 113; **23**, 161n; **30**, 47n, 48n, 53n, 56n, 58n, 61n, 64n, 71
Walter, John, **25**, 147
Walton, Anne, **23**, 43
Walton, George, **25**, 147
Walton, J. K., **25**, 193, 194–8; **26**, 184
  Textual Studies, *reviewed*, (1967), **21**, 157–63
Walton, Judyth, **25**, 147
Warburton, William, **23**, 61n; **26**, 181
Warcope, Thomas, **21**, 98
Ward Howe, Julia, **24**, 100
Warde, Frederick, **25**, 117, 118
Wardroper, John, **23**, 165
Wardropper, B. W., **23**, 84n, 88n
Warner, David, **23**, 132; **24**, 43; **27**, 34n
Warner, G. F., **23**, 111; **29**, 34n
Warr, Michael, **27**, 142
Warren, Austin, **24**, 91n; **28**, 150
Warren, Michael J., **25**, 200
Warren, Roger, **23**, 143–4; **24**, 150, 151; **25**, 179; **27**, 165
  'Why Does it End Well? Helena, Bertram, and The Sonnets', **22**, 79–92
  'Theatrical Virtuosity and Poetic Complexity in *Cymbeline*', **29**, 41–9
  'Theory and Practice': Stratford 1976, **30**, 169–70
Warrin, Thomas, **22**, 120–1, 123
Washington, George, **24**, 99
Wasson, John, **24**, 150, 155; **25**, 6n
Waterhouse, Osborn, **21**, 65n; **24**, 159
Watermeier, Daniel J., **25**, 192
Waterschoot, W., **29**, 26n
Watkin, E. I., **24**, 71n
Watkins, R., **28**, 150; **30**, 185

Watkins, W. B. C., 22, 166
Watling, E. F., 30, 113n
Watson, George, 25, 192, 193
Watson, Thomas, 25, 188
Watson, William, 24, 72, 75, 76
Watt, Ian, 24, 48
Watts, Robert A., 23, 153
Webb, John, 23, 125–9; 30, 166, 167n
Webbe, Agnes, 21, 148
Webber, Joan, 23, 167n
Weber, Elizabeth, 23, 117
Webster, John, 21, 44–5; 23, 160, 171; 24, 164–5; 25, 162, 163, 164; 26, 1, 2, 4, 8, 9, 39, 57, 90, 168, 174, 175; 27, 177, 184; 28, 38; 29, 173
Wedderborn, Richard, 22, 121
Wedgwood, C. V., 22, 151
Weedin, E. K., Jr, 29, 164
Weeks, John, 30, 195
Weidhorn, Manfred, 23, 148; 24, 152
Weil, Herbert S., Jr, 24, 149, 150; 25, 6; 26, 175; 27, 167
  'Comic Structure and Tonal Manipulation in Shakesheare and some Modern Plays', 22, 27–33
  'The Options of the Audience: Theory and Practice in Peter Brook's Measure for Measure', 25, 27–35
Weimann, Robert, 21, 156; 22, 166, 172, 175; 23, 114, 143, 171, 174n; 24, 149, 160; 25, 179; 26, 158; 27, 171–2, 179; 29, 90, 167
  'Laughing with the Audience: The Two Gentlemen of Verona and the Popular Tradition of Comedy', 22, 35–42
Weinberg, Gail S., 23, 165n
Weiner, A. D., 26, 153
Weingarten, Samuel, 21, 132
Weinstein, P. M., 25, 177
Weinstock, Horst, 21, 151; 23, 117
Weiss, T., 26, 152
Weitz, Morris, 21, 134; 25, 181; 28, 41n; 30, 186
  'Literature Without Philosophy: Antony and Cleopatra', 28, 29–36
Weixlmann, Joseph, 28, 170
Weld, John, 30, 182–3
Wellek, René, 28, 150; 30, 189
Wells, Stanley, 21, 130–1, 139, 143, 145, 157; 22, 175; 23, 137, 181, 182; 25, 189–90; 26, 170; 27, 39, 162, 188; 28, 164; 29, 4, 177; 30, 148n
  'Shakespeare in Max Beerbohm's Theatre Criticism', 29, 132–44
Welsford, Enid, 27, 59n; 29, 1, 91
Welsh, James M., 29, 184
Wendel, Karl-Heinz, 23, 117
Wendell, B., 27, 106n

Wentersdorf, Karl P., 27, 129n, 179, 192; 28, 167
Wertheim, A., 27, 164
Wertheim, Ursula, 25, 186
Wertzman, W., 23, 175
West, Alick, 22, 166
West, Gillian, 30, 185
West, M., 28, 160
West, R. H., 24, 140–1; 28, 118; 29, 89, 90
West, William, 27, 95, 96, 97
Westlund, Joseph, 22, 153
Westwell, Raymond, 26, 143, 144
Weyer, John, 28, 119
W.H., Mr, 22, 165; 23, 157, 160; 28, 165
Whatley, J., 29, 165
Whateley, Thomas, 25, 185
Whetstone, George, 21, 135; 25, 31, 45; 28, 94
Whibley, Charles, 23, 61n
Whitaker, Virgil K., 22, 148; 25, 7; 28, 156; 29, 51n, 86
White, H. B., 26, 156
White, Patrick, 26, 8
White, R. G., 25, 76n, 93
Whiter, Walter, 22, 145, 163; 23, 50; 25, 39, 127
Whitfield, Christopher, 21, 147–8; 29, 34n
Whitgift, Archbishop, 27, 135
Whitney, Geoffrey, 24, 66n; 25, 99; 29, 171; 30, 194
Whythorne, Thomas, 24, 158
Wicht, Wolfgang, 21, 139
Wickham, Glynne, 21, 137, 139, 156; 22, 35; 23, 138–9; 26, 169–70; 28, 163, 169–70; 29, 3, 4, 158; 30, 157, 168, 164n
  'From Tragedy to Tragi-Comedy: King Lear as Prologue', 26, 33–48
Widmann, Ruth I., 27, 187; 29, 184
Wigfall, A., 27, 114n
Wilberg, Wolff Rainer, 29, 176
Wilbur, Richard, 24, 174
Wilde, Oscar, 22, 2, 5, 141; 23, 91; 29, 133
Wilder, Thornton, 26, 90
Wilding, Michael, 21, 148
Wildman, R. I., 24, 178
Wilds, L., 29, 166
Wilkes, G. A., 30, 64n
Wilkes, John, 24, 100
Wilkins (Wilkinson), Alice, 25, 143
Wilkins, Bartholomew, 25, 143
Wilkins, George (Wilkinson), 21, 150, 152; 23, 133; 24, 107, 113n, 155; 25, 127–52, 142–3; 26, 44; 29, 22, 23, 25, 26, 29n, 31, 32, 33–9; 30, 205
Wilkins, Katherine, 29, 33

Wilkinson, Andrew M., 21, 132
Wilkinson, C. H., 23, 125
Wilkinson, Valentine, 29, 32
Wilks, Robert, 24, 167
Willcock, Gladys D., 23, 11
Willeford, William, 24, 162n
Willey, Margaret, 24, 2n
William of Orange, 29, 26
Williams, Bishop, 29, 94
Williams, Clare, 30, 164
Williams, Clifford, 22, 137; 23, 132; 25, 163; 30, 176, 177
Williams, Edith, 28, 167
Williams, Franklin, B., Jr, 22, 180; 23, 160
Williams, G., 29, 160
Williams, George Walton, 23, 146–7; 25, 73n; 27, 179; 30, 203, 210
Williams, Gordon, 25, 188
Williams, Harcourt, 23, 132
Williams, John Antony, 21, 140
Williams, Mary C., 27, 176
Williams, Michael, 22, 137; 25, 164; 27, 139; 30, 174
Williams, Philip, 30, 37n
Williams, Raymond, 22, 148
Williams, Sarah, 23, 44n
Williams, Tennessee, 22, 3
Williams, W. P., 24, 178
Williamson, Audrey, 27, 34n
Williamson, C. F., 23, 167n; 30, 182
Williamson, Marilyn L., 23, 147, 154; 25, 175
Williamson, Nicol, 28, 137, 144, 145; 29, 153
Willichius, 30, 61n
Willoughby, John, 23, 44
Wills, W. G., 29, 136
Willson, Robert F., Jr, 23, 171n; 24, 156; 28, 161; 30, 201
Wilmanns, W., 23, 28n
Wilmeth, Don B., 28, 171
Wilmot, R., 22, 152
Wilson, Arthur, 28, 28n
Wilson, Daniel, 25, 114
Wilson, Edward M., 'Shakespeare and Christian Doctrine: Some Qualifications', 23, 79–89
Wilson, Edwin, 25, 45n, 117n; 27, 34n
Wilson, F. P., 23, 40, 47, 137–8, 143, 167–8; 24, 168, 171; 26, 70, 72; 27, 83n; 28, 4n, 38, 41n
Wilson, Gayle Edward, 23, 170
Wilson, Harold S., 21, 149; 23, 166; 24, 12; 25, 3
Wilson, J., 27, 61
Wilson, John, 21, 16, 27n; 23, 183
Wilson, John Dover, 21, 4, 23, 27n, 28n, 107, 110, 113, 147; 22, 35, 75, 180; 23, 56n, 145; 24, 2n, 52, 53, 171; 25, 3, 5, 73n, 75n, 94n; 26, 3,

Wilson John Dover (*cont.*)
81, 82, 85n, 97, 98, 137, 182;
27, 11n, 51n, 62, 71n, 106n, 132n,
135, 192; 28, 3, 4n, 38n, 58, 107;
29, 82, 83, 86, 166, 179, 180, 181;
30, 36, 38n, 42–3, 48n, 71, 86n,
91n, 96n, 98n, 112, 181, 193, 208
Wilson, Robert, 27, 130n; 29, 162; 30, 38
Wilson, Thomas, 26, 103, 112n
Wimsatt, James I., 24, 143
Wimsatt, W. K., 28, 57n
Wind, Edgar, 24, 66, 67; 25, 103n, 104n;
26, 116n; 28, 76n; 29, 91
Wine, M. L., 28, 167, 179
Wingfield, A., 27, 112
Winny, James, 23, 145, 158; 27, 45n
Winstanley, Eliza, 22, 128, 130
Winstanley, Lilian, 21, 52n
Winstanley, Mr, 22, 130
Winter, William, 21, 103; 25, 192
Winters, Yvor, 24, 91
Winterton, J. B., 24, 179
Winwood, R., 29, 23n
Wisbey, R. A., 27, 187
Wise, Andrew, 25, 194
Wittgenstein, L., 24, 105
Wittkower, Rudolf, 28, 168; 30, 158n
Wodehouse, P. G., 22, 3
Wolfe, John, 21, 148
Wolff, Cynthia Griffin, 23, 165
Wolff, T., 26, 167
Wölfflin, Heinrich, 26, 49
Wolfit, Sir Donald, 23, 131; 24, 37
Wolk, A., 26, 154

Wolsey, Thomas, Cardinal, 28, 20, 21;
29, 94
Wood, Charles, 23, 39
Wood, H. H., 28, 41n
Wood, James O., 21, 147, 163; 25, 177,
188; 27, 160, 191; 28, 167, 181
Wood, John, 26, 145, 147, 148, 149
Wood, Peter, 24, 3n
Woods, Charles P., 26, 9
Woodstock, Thomas of, 28, 1, 4, 5, 8
Woodthorpe, Peter, 25, 166, 168
Woodvine, John, 30, 171, 172, 178
Woodward, Daniel H., 23, 166n
Woodward, Fraunces, 27, 99
Woolf, Rosemary, 30, 192
Woolfe, John, 25, 148
Woolfenden, Guy, 30, 176
Wordsworth, William, 21, 68
Worth, Irene, 24, 3n, 4, 8
Wotton, Sir Henry, 23, 171; 28, 131
Wren, Robert M., 24, 166n
Wright, Ernest Hunter, 29, 107n, 111n
Wright, Louis, B., 24, 169
Wright, W., 21, 148
Wriothesley, Henry, *see* Southampton,
Third Earl of
Wyatt, Mr, 22, 132
Wyatt, R. O., 28, 167
Wyatt, Sir Thomas, 23, 165
Wylton, Tim, 29, 154

Xenophon, 25, 99, 100n

Yale, D. E. C., 29, 93n, 97n, 98n

Yamada, Akihiro, 22, 171; 24, 161, 167
Yates, Frances A., 21, 155; 23, 172; 24,
48, 166; 27, 45n; 28, 39; 29, 26n,
158, 173; 30, 166
Yeats, W. B., 21, 141; 24, 11, 46, 169; 26,
139; 28, 10; 29, 26; 30, 1, 90, 104
Yelverton, Henry, 28, 68
Yoder, R. A., 27, 158, 166; 28, 156
'"Sons and Daughters of the Game":
an Essay on Shakespeare's *Troilus
and Cressida*', 25, 11–25
Yong, Bartholomew, 22, 168
York cycle, 21, 54, 55; 23, 120
Young, A. R., 29, 164, 171
Young, C. B., 26, 85
Young, D., 27, 167, 168
Young, David P., 22, 153; 29, 6, 8, 90;
30, 128, 131n
Young, Edward, 21, 67
Young, Steven C., 23, 168

Zarian, Rouben, 24, 169
Zeeveld, W. Gordon, 26, 98; 28, 63n,
68; 29, 84, 157–8
Zeffirelli, G. Franco, 24, 65, 128
Zimansky, Curt A., 21, 27n, 67, 68, 73;
26, 9
Zimbardo, R. A., 27, 163–4
Zimmermann, Heinz, 30, 189
Zitner, S. P., 22, 156, 183; 24, 144; 27,
179
Zoega, Mathias, 22, 119–20
Zolbrod, P. G., 26, 158; 29, 165
Zucker, David Hard, 27, 176